SIXTH EDITION

Judicial Process

LAW, COURTS, AND POLITICS IN THE UNITED STATES

DAVID W. NEUBAUER

University of New Orleans

STEPHEN S. MEINHOLD

University of North Carolina Wilmington

WADSWORTH
CENGAGE Learning·

Australia • Brazil • Japan • Korea • Mexico • Singapore • Spain • United Kingdom • United States

WADSWORTH
CENGAGE Learning·

Judicial Process: Law, Courts, and Politics in the United States, Sixth Edition
David W. Neubauer and Stephen S. Meinhold

Vice President of Editorial, Business: Jack W. Calhoun

Senior Publisher: Suzanne Jeans

Executive Editor: Carolyn Merrill

Associate Developmental Editor: Katherine Hayes

Editorial Assistant: Scott Greenan

Assistant Editor: Laura Ross

Marketing Program Manager: Caitlin Green

Rights Acquisition Specialist: Jennifer Meyer Dare

Manufacturing Planner: Fola Orekoya

Art Director: Linda Helcher

Internal Designer, Production Management, and Composition: PreMediaGlobal

Cover Designer: Jenny Willingham

Cover Image: Shutterstock 61124077

For product information and technology assistance, contact us at **Cengage Learning Customer & Sales Support, 1-800-354-9706**.

For permission to use material from this text or product, submit all requests online at **www.cengage.com/permissions**. Further permissions questions can be emailed to **permissionrequest@cengage.com**.

Library of Congress Control Number: 2011933867

ISBN-13: 978-1-111-35756-6

ISBN-10: 1-111-35756-0

Wadsworth
20 Channel Center Street
Boston, MA 02210
USA

Cengage Learning is a leading provider of customized learning solutions with office locations around the globe, including Singapore, the United Kingdom, Australia, Mexico, Brazil, and Japan. Locate your local office at **international.cengage.com/region**.

Cengage Learning products are represented in Canada by Nelson Education, Ltd.

For your course and learning solutions, visit **www.cengage.com**

Purchase any of our products at your local college store or at our preferred online store **www.cengagebrain.com**.

Instructors: Please visit **login.cengage.com** and log in to access instructor-specific resources.

Printed in the United States of America
1 2 3 4 5 6 7 16 15 14 13 12

To Carole and Jennifer

Brief Contents

Contents

Part II

Interpreters of the Law

Chapter 5

Lawyers and Legal Representation   117

Chapter 6
Judges   *156*

Part III

CONSUMERS OF THE LAW

Chapter 7
Mobilizing the Law: Litigants, Interest Groups, Court Cases, and the Media   *194*

Part IV

TRIAL COURTS

Chapter 8

Trial Courts: The Preliminary Stages of Criminal Cases   221

Part V

APPELLATE REVIEW

Chapter 13
The Appellate Process   381

Chapter 14
The Supreme Court: Deciding What to Decide   414

Chapter 15

The Supreme Court: The Justices and Their Decisions   446

Preface

This book is written for undergraduate courses that deal with America's judicial system and are usually taught under some variation of the title judicial process or judicial politics; the American legal system; or law, courts, and politics. The intended readers are students majoring in political science, prelaw, or criminal justice; students interested in going to law school; or those simply needing a social science elective. That student interest in judicial process courses remains steady reflects the fact that law, courts, and politics remain important topics of discussion in American society. Indeed, as Chapter 1 discusses, it is hard to read the day's news without being confronted with some aspect of court actions or how the law influences the choices that people and institutions make.

How does this book differ from other texts on judicial process? It differs in two principal ways.

First, *Judicial Process: Law, Courts, and Politics in the United States* is designed to be a comprehensive, stand-alone text. Some judicial process texts are too short, omitting important topics and providing only cursory coverage of others. This book provides an adequate breadth of coverage and an appropriate depth of treatment.

Second, this book presents a balanced treatment of both law and politics. Other texts provide only minimal coverage of important aspects of law and the legal process while focusing too much on politics; others err in the opposite direction. This book offers a full and focused discussion of legal topics such as the adversary system, common law, precedent, and major branches of law while, at the same time, recognizing the political, social, and economic conditions that underlie and impact law and the legal process.

MAJOR THEMES

Working within the framework of law and politics, *Judicial Process: Law, Courts, and Politics in the United States* focuses on the social, political, and economic dynamics of the legal system. Toward this end, the book stresses two themes: courts as legal institutions and courts as political institutions.

Courts as Legal Institutions

This text provides readers with a working knowledge of the major structures and basic legal concepts that underlie the judiciary in the United States. Court jurisdiction, the role of the Constitution, and other legal processes and institutions are all important matters that are carefully explained. To understand the legal system, however, students need to know more than just the formal rules. Also necessary is an understanding of the assumptions underlying these rules, the history of how they evolved, and the goals they seek to achieve. Moreover, we stress that the American judiciary is not monolithic. Rather, the judicial process consists of a number of separate, and often competing, units. Conflicts over the goals that these units are expected to achieve, in turn, influence how justice is dispensed.

Courts as Political Institutions

Many books leave the false impression that an understanding of the formal law and major court structures is all that one needs to know about the judicial process. This kind of approach provides only a limited view of the dynamics of how courts administer justice. In particular, it omits the key fact that courts often must make discretionary choices. The idea that the law is not self-executing is expressed in terms of the courts as political institutions. As the newly written first chapter emphasizes, the courts are best viewed in the same way as any other branch of government. As political scientists, we are not afraid to say that courts are political and properly so. All too often, calls for removing judges and juries from politics amount to little more than attempts to capture these institutions by one set of political interests at the expense of others.

TOPICS IN THIS EDITION

The Sixth Edition covers both fundamental and up-to-date topics to emphasize the twin themes of courts as legal institutions and courts as political institutions.

New to This Edition

- Addition of Deepwater Horizon (BP) Oil Spill examples in many chapters to provide context for law, courts and politics in action
- Updated coverage of the impact of the War on Terrorism on the U.S. legal system
- Thorough updates to all tables, graphs, and charts
- Updates on controversial court decisions involving same-sex marriages and the display of religious symbols
- Expanded coverage of female judges and three female justices on the Supreme Court
- Inclusion of several new media feature boxes including *Boston Legal* and *Blood Diamond*
- Updated content on comparative legal systems around the world
- New coverage of U.S. Supreme Court and cases dealing with judicial conduct and the War on Drugs
- Continuing coverage of Supreme Court decision making and the Roberts Court

Focus on Fundamentals

Coverage of the essential structure and practices of the U.S. judiciary system remains thorough and complete and includes the following:

- Origins of U.S. law
- Institutions, consumers, and interpreters of law
- Federal and appellate court systems
- The complex structure of state courts
- Lawyers: their education and their role
- Selection and discretion of judges
- Steps in civil and criminal trials
- A close look at the Supreme Court

KEY FEATURES

To provide multiple perspectives on the complex issues of law and its administration, each chapter of *Judicial Process*, Sixth Edition, includes the following:

Case Close-Up

To highlight the importance of courts as legal institutions, each chapter contains at least one Case Close-Up. Many of the cases featured are landmark decisions of the U.S. Supreme Court; others are state or local cases chosen to illustrate key features of the impact of court decisions on American society. These discussions move beyond the dry legal prose to look at the people involved and what happened after their brief experience with the judiciary.

Debating Law, Courts, and Politics

To highlight the importance of courts as political institutions, the Debating Law, Courts, and Politics boxes engage students in a current debate about some aspect of the judicial process. (In earlier editions, this box was called Controversy.) Most of these Debating Law, Courts, and Politics boxes start with a question and end by asking for students' opinions. These boxes challenge readers to move beyond the immediate, sometimes emotional, aspect of an issue and probe more deeply into why people hold differing opinions about the question.

Law and Popular Culture

A good deal of what students "know" about the legal system is based on what they watch on television or see in the movies. Although some of what popular culture implies about law is indeed true, other aspects of it are not. Each of these Law and Popular Culture boxes discusses a movie or television show about the legal system to encourage students to think about the blurred line between fact and fiction and to contrast popular culture with what they read in this book and discuss in class.

Courts in Comparative Perspective

To highlight the relationship between the judiciary and the societies served each of the Courts in Comparative Perspective boxes focuses on some aspect of a legal system in another nation. Most students are familiar only with the way justice is dispensed in the United States and are shocked to discover that justice systems in other countries operate very differently from ours. These boxes shape such amazement into a more comparative way of thinking.

PEDAGOGICAL INNOVATIONS

Several pedagogical innovations anchor this edition to encourage active learning and deeper engagement with the text.

Critical Thinking Questions

Each chapter ends with Critical Thinking Questions, which ask students to pull material from the chapter together and apply key concepts to new material.

World Wide Web Resources

Whether students are Net savvy or Net shy, they will find a lot of helpful guides to supplement their reading with online resources. The Internet is a major source of information, and the Web makes learning and exploring easier. Facts, figures, and opinions are readily available. Some Web pages, however, are little more than thinly veiled propaganda pieces, presenting the world from the vantage point of one interest group.

To encourage active, rather than passive, learning, each chapter contains several Web resources designed not only to sharpen students' Web skills but also to further their understanding of concepts discussed in the chapter.

Glossary

Another key feature of this edition is the comprehensive Glossary. More than just a compilation of the terms highlighted in boldface throughout the text, it also defines the most commonly used legal terms.

Key Developments

To provide a better sense of how the discussions in the chapters relate to material covered in other courses—such as constitutional law—several chapters contain features labeled "Key Developments," which summarize the major legal developments concerning the topic at hand. We suggest that you use these as cross-references for other courses and also update the material when the Supreme Court hands down new decisions or Congress passes new laws.

Steps of the Process

To provide an overview of the key steps of the judicial process, appropriate chapters in the book contain features labeled "Steps of the Process," which present the chronological history of a case. We suggest that you use these as mental maps that provide an overall context for the various stages of a lawsuit.

Online Instructor Resources

An Instructor's Manual/Test Bank and book-specific PowerPoint® lectures are available for instructors on Wadsworth's SSO (Single Sign On). The revised Instructor's Manual/Test Bank offers chapter key points, suggestions for class discussions, writing assignments, and exam questions to make course preparation easier. A set of book-specific PowerPoint lectures make it easy for you to assemble, edit, publish, and present custom lectures for your course. The slides provide outlines specific to every chapter of JUDICIAL PROCESS 6E, include tables, statistical charts, graphs, and photos from the book as well as outside sources. In addition, the slides are completely customizable for a powerful and personalized presentation. The Instructor's Manual/Test Bank and PowerPoint® lectures have all been updated with new material to reflect changes in the new edition. Access these instructor resources at www.cengage.com/sso. Sign in to your existing Cengage account or register by clicking on "Create a New Faculty Account."

Companion Website

Judicial Process has an extensive website available for students and researchers interested in law, courts, and politics in the United States. For students, it includes open access to learning objectives, chapter glossaries, flashcards, and crossword puzzles, all correlated by chapter. For researchers, it provides features on law and courts research as well as links to databases and other useful places to locate information about the judicial process. Visit www.cengage.com/politicalscience/neubauer/judicialprocess6e and check out its many resources.

TO THE STUDENTS

This book is written with you in mind. Over the years, our students have helped us evaluate a variety of topics and approaches, and the best of what works is used in this book. A spiral approach—beginning from a core of information and working outward to cover a wider range of relevant perspectives—allows you to start with the people who sparked a case and expand your view to the broader issues involved.

Our major objective is to demystify law, courts, and politics in the United States. We have found that people often approach the law as an ideal system that is set apart from the rest of society. In fact, courts do not stand in silent isolation, somehow removed from the community they serve. Law and courts are at the core of how our nation governs itself.

This is not to suggest that the judicial process in the United States is perfect. Far from it. But when people begin to discuss what needs to be changed, they often disagree. And these disagreements often reflect political, social, and economic divisions in our society.

The Sixth Edition contains several special features that will help make this introduction to the judicial process more informative, more enjoyable, and more relevant for you:

- *Case Close-Up* These highlight important decisions—of the Supreme Court and of state or local courts—that illustrate the impact courts have on our everyday lives. In addition to the case history itself, each chapter looks closely at the people involved and what happened to them after their brief experience with the judicial system.
- *Debating Law, Courts, and Politics* These items analyze current debates about some aspect of the judicial process to help you look beyond the emotional aspects of an issue to the deeper reasons people disagree. They all start with a question and end by asking your opinion: What do your answers suggest about you as a person?
- *Law and Popular Culture* Although some parts of what the media show you about law are true, other aspects of it are not. Each of these boxes highlights a film or television show to help contrast popular culture with the realities of the judicial process.
- *Courts in Comparative Perspective* These presentations help you discover what is unique about the U.S. courts by comparing them with other nations' systems.

Other Helpful Features

Critical Thinking Questions   Each chapter ends with a set of critical thinking questions to integrate material from the chapter and to help you consider what you are reading and relate it to your own experiences. Contrast how the concepts presented in the book relate to recent events.

Glossary   The basic terminology of law, courts, and politics is explained throughout this book. Typically, the language of the law strikes students as both foreign and familiar. Some of our legal terms are indeed foreign because they are derived from Latin and French. But, with a little guidance, these "foreign" terms are readily understandable. Important terms are set in **boldface type**, and these terms are collected with their definitions in the Glossary.

Indexes   To help locate important topics, this book contains a detailed Subject Index, including authors and subjects, and a separate Case Index of court decisions discussed in the text. By studying the U.S. judicial process, you explore one of the most important aspects of our society—and ourselves.

Steps of the Process   To provide an overview of the key steps of the judicial process, appropriate chapters in the book contain features labeled "Steps of the Process," which present the chronological history of a case. We suggest that you use these as mental maps that provide an overall context for the various stages of a lawsuit.

Website A comprehensive website to accompany *Judicial Process* can be found at www.cengagebrain.com/shop/ISBN/1111357560. It is designed to complement your learning by making a variety of study aids available. It is also designed to give you opportunities to see how political scientists study law, courts, and politics and to provide you with the basic tools to start doing your own research on the judicial process.

ACKNOWLEDGMENTS

Writing the Sixth Edition was made easier by the assistance and encouragement of people who deserve special recognition. We would like to thank the political science team at Wadsworth/Cengage Learning—Carolyn Merrill, Rebecca Green, and Katherine Hayes.

We would like to send a special thanks to the reviewers of this edition: David Roebuck, Columbia College; Sheldon Goldman, University of Massachusetts at Amherst; Valerie Hoekstra, Arizona State University; William Wilkerson, SUNY Oneonta; Robert Bradley, Illinois State University; Jasmine Farrier, University of Louisville.

We also gratefully acknowledge the help of a number of people who provided invaluable input to previous editions, including Keith Boyum, California State University–Fullerton; Robert C. Bradley, Illinois State University; Richard A. Brisbin, Jr., West Virginia University; James Eisenstein, Pennsylvania State University; Margaret Ellis, University of Oklahoma; James C. Foster, Oregon State University; Barbara L. Graham, University of Missouri–St. Louis; Scott E. Graves, Georgia State University; Ed Heck, San Diego State University; Valerie Hoekstra, Arizona State University; Mark Iris, Northwestern University; David Jones, University of Wisconsin–Oshkosh; Mark Kaplinsky, Xavier University; William E. Kelly, Auburn University; Mark Landis, Hofstra University; Drew Lanier, University of Central Florida; William McLaughlan, Purdue University; Steven Puro, St. Louis University; Elliot Slotnick, Ohio State University; Rorie Spill Solberg, Oregon State University; Ruth Ann Strickland, Appalachian State University; Susette Talarico, University of Georgia; Neal Tate, Vanderbilt University; Jan P. Vermeer, Nebraska Wesleyan University; Russ Wheeler, Federal Judicial Center; Robert Whelan, University of New Orleans; and Alissa Pollitz Worden, State University of New York–Albany.

About the Authors

David William Neubauer was born in Chicago, Illinois, on February 25, 1944. He grew up in Aurora, graduating from West Aurora High School in 1962. After receiving an A.B. in political science in 1966 from Augustana College in Rock Island, he undertook graduate work at the University of Illinois, receiving his Ph.D. in 1971.

Neubauer has taught at the University of Florida, Washington University in St. Louis, and, most recently, at the University of New Orleans (UNO). He regularly teaches a judicial process class, a course on the criminal courts, and a graduate seminar in public law. Promoted to professor in 1981, he chaired the Department of Political Science at UNO from 1982 to 1986.

Professor Neubauer is the author of *Criminal Justice in Middle America* (General Learning Press, 1974); *America's Courts and the Criminal Justice System*, Eighth Edition (Wadsworth, 2005); and *Debating Crime: Rhetoric and Reality* (Wadsworth, 2001). Most recently, he wrote, with Stephen Meinhold, *Battle Supreme: The Confirmation of Chief Justice Roberts and the Future of the Supreme Court* (Wadsworth, 2006). He has published in *Law and Society Review*, *Judicature*, the *Justice System Journal*, and *Justice Quarterly*.

Stephen Scott Meinhold was born in St. Charles, Missouri, on August 17, 1968. He graduated from Francis Howell High School in 1986 and received a B.A. in political science from the University of Missouri at St. Louis in 1990. Meinhold received his Ph.D. from the University of New Orleans in 1995. He is currently Professor of Political Science and Associate Dean of Research at the University of North Carolina Wilmington.

His research has examined public perceptions of the litigation explosion, lawyers and their political party activity, and the relationship between the president and the solicitor general. Professor Meinhold's current research focuses on college students' use of attorneys, their plans to attend law school, and their attitudes about the legal system. He has published articles in the *Political Research Quarterly*, the *Social Science Quarterly*, the *Justice System Journal*, and *PS: Political Science and Politics*. Most recently, he wrote, with David Neubauer, *Battle Supreme: The Confirmation of Chief Justice Roberts and the Future of the Supreme Court* (Wadsworth, 2006).

LAW, COURTS, AND POLITICS

In Scott County, Kentucky (Georgetown), the courthouse is at the intersection of two major streets. Courthouses across the nation often find themselves at the intersection of law, courts, and politics.

David Neubauer

Barely a week after the Deepwater Horizon started spewing oil into the Gulf of Mexico, lawsuits began flowing into court. Acy Cooper and Ronnie Anderson, commercial fisherman living along the Louisiana coastline, alleged in federal court that the fast spreading oil slick threatened their livelihood, and demanded BP (and others) pay. Cooper and Anderson were but the first to file suit or threaten to file suit in the wake of the largest environmental catastrophe in the United States.

The Deepwater Horizon (a floating rig) was drilling for oil more than three miles beneath the ocean's surface when a sudden surge of methane gas (termed a kick by petroleum engineers) ignited a fireball on the rig, killing 11 workers and starting the largest oil spill in U.S. history. For the next 87 days crude oil (the color of brown mousse) flowed into the Gulf of Mexico despoiling vacation beaches, killing wildlife, staining the marshes, and throwing thousands of people out of work.

1

Amidst a massive clean-up effort the obvious questions arose: why did the disaster occur? How much should those responsible be forced to pay? And who should be able to collect?

In the long process of answering these questions, the law, courts, and politics will all play a role. But the course they take is not clear. Lawyers and litigants face choices about which claims to file, which courts to file them in, what legal points to argue and when is it time to settle. During this process judges and jurors will rule on legal claims, assess conflicting versions of what happened and eventually place a dollar amount on how much the defendants owe the plaintiffs.

The decisions made in the judicial process affect the political process (and vice versa). The president made several critical decisions including imposing a temporary moratorium on deep-water drilling, deciding to launch a criminal investigation and forcing BP to create a $20 billion claims fund. Similarly, Congress has held hearings and will certainly pass new legislation; some of which might retroactively increase damage amounts. The choices ahead clearly reflect partisan differences that will become issues in elections and the focus of interest group activity. In the end, how the court of public opinion assesses who is at fault will play a major role in determining how jurors award damages in a court of law.

The above examples, drawn from the Gulf of Mexico oil spill, illustrate a broader point: in the U.S. questions about law usually become questions about politics. Supreme Court decisions on matters like abortion, gun control, and display of religious items on public property often spark heated debates. But these are just a few of the issues heard by courts across the nation. Every day in courthouses across the nation judges and juries decide matters like the amount of damages after an automobile accident and how many years a convicted drug dealer must serve in prison. Collectively, decisions made in the courts determine the balance between law and politics and, ultimately, affect the way we live.

Judicial Process: Law, Courts, and Politics in the United States, sixth edition, looks at the nation's legal system through the lens of political science. **Political science** is the systematic study of government and politics, and the research it produces helps to guide our presentation of the judiciary. Toward that end, this chapter examines courts from four complementary perspectives: courts and government, courts as legal institutions, courts as political institutions, and courts and controversy.

COURTS AND GOVERNMENT

Courts are distinct from the legislative and executive branches of government in several ways: Most of the principal actors have law degrees, procedures in court are formal, and the language used differs from ordinary English. But emphasizing how distinctive courts may be also gets in the way of thinking about the broader role of courts in American politics. In sometimes controversial ways, the courts are interconnected with every aspect of American politics, including the Constitution, federalism, the president, legislatures, elections, political parties, interest groups, public opinion, and the media. Let's look at each interaction in turn.

The Constitution   The Constitution is one of the most powerful symbols of American government. Because the public associates courts, particularly the Supreme

Court, with the Constitution, the judiciary in the United States is granted considerable respect. That grant of legitimacy, however, doesn't always mean that the public likes how the Supreme Court interprets the Constitution. For example, the Supreme Court decision in *Miranda v. Arizona* (1966), which required police to warn suspects of their right to silence before interrogation, is opposed by many because it seems to unduly protect criminals. Likewise the high Court's decision in *Roe v. Wade* (1973), finding a constitutional right to privacy that includes abortion, continues to divide the nation. State supreme courts likewise interpret their own respective state constitutions, and those decisions at times also prove controversial. For example, decisions declaring legislatively passed tort reform unconstitutional produce strong condemnation from the business community. Similarly, opinions recognizing same-sex marriages provoke vehement opposition from social conservatives.

Federalism   The United States has a federal form of government; that is, power is divided between state governments and the national government. Where to draw the line between the respective powers of state and national governments has been one of the longest-running political battles in the United States. The issue clearly divided the framers of the Constitution, and some of those differences of opinion eventually were settled by a bloody civil war.

Often, the U.S. Supreme Court has been called on to decide disputes over federal versus state power, and, not surprisingly, its decisions frequently provoke profound controversy. For example, how far may cities and states go in imposing gun control. Likewise courts are faced with a series of lawsuits involving state attempts to enforce federal immigration law.

The Executive Branch   In the modern era, presidents have viewed the courts as an important part of their political agenda. When running for office, presidential candidates often denounce court decisions they dislike and pledge to appoint justices who will reshape the judiciary. After election, they use the courts and lawsuits to seek policy changes that are to their liking. Most important, they seek to influence the future decisions of courts through their nominations to the bench.

State and local executives (governors and mayors) also use the courts to advance their policy objectives. Republican governors and state attorney generals have filed lawsuits attempting to block President Obama's health care laws. Meanwhile, Democratic attorney generals have filed lawsuits to protect consumers in disputes with big business. Moreover, in some jurisdictions, executives also have a great deal of control over who becomes a judge.

The Legislature   At every level, the relationship between courts and legislatures is best viewed as a struggle for institutional balance (Geyh 2008; Campbell and Stack 2001). Legislatures sometimes find themselves unhappy with the interpretation of their laws made by courts. Sometimes, they have power over the jurisdiction or the composition of courts, but, at other times, they share that power with the voters or the executive. Responsible for passing the laws that the courts will apply, legislatures often do so without regard for the unintended consequences for the legal system. For example, in most jurisdictions, legislatures have enacted wars on drugs or strict sentencing guidelines that swell court dockets and fill already-overcrowded prisons.

Elections   Over the years, courts have been called on to decide disputed elections. The best example is *Bush v. Gore* (2000), in which, for the first time in our nation's history, the high court actually selected the president. But lawsuits contesting elections are hardly unique. In virtually every state, candidates who have lost elections by a narrow margin have turned to the courts, alleging election irregularities or even voter fraud. On occasion, courts have even declared the election-night loser to be the eventual winner. Just as important, courts across the nation routinely consider election laws, even deciding such fundamental issues as who gets on the ballot, what they get to say, and who gets to vote (Banks and Green 2001). Although *Bush v. Gore* (2000) is atypical because it selected the president of the United States, it is not atypical of judicial involvement in elections.

Not only do courts influence elections, but the opposite is also true—elections affect the judiciary. In many jurisdictions, judges are elected directly by voters. One of the questions we examine in Chapter 6 is whether popularly elected judges act differently than those selected in other ways, such as appointment.

Political Parties   Historically, political parties valued judgeships as an important source of patronage. That practice continues today in some of the nation's largest cities, but, increasingly, political parties view judgeships in symbolic terms. At the national level, in particular, officeholders view nominations to the bench as opportunities to show the party faithful that they are working on their behalf. Thus, the right wing of the Republican Party demands that Republican presidents appoint staunch conservatives. Likewise, modern-era Democrats have used nominations to vacant judgeships to publicly support important members of their governing coalition—women and racial minorities.

Increasingly, political parties use nominations not only to reward their followers but also to derail the judicial nominees of the other party. The result has been pitched political battles in the Senate, with Republicans attempting to defeat Democratic nominees who are characterized as too liberal on issues such as abortion and the death penalty, and Democrats trying to derail Republican nominees whom they portray as too conservative on affirmative action and gun control. In Chapter 6, therefore, we examine this question: Has federal judicial selection become too partisan?

At the state level, the political party that controls the governorship can influence the types of people selected to the bench. In turn, judicial reform has often focused on reducing the influence of political parties in judicial selection.

Interest Groups   America, it is said, is a nation of joiners. Not all of the resulting associations are formed with political action in mind, but, no matter their primary focus, interest groups try to influence governmental policy through a variety of methods, including cash contributions to campaigns and lobbying legislative and executive officials. On a regular basis, these interest groups also attempt to influence governmental policy by filing lawsuits either to gain victories in court that have been denied them in the legislative or executive arena or to protect victories gained in the other branches of government.

The most notable example of an interest group winning a major victory in court occurred in the area of civil rights. The National Association for the Advancement of Colored People (NAACP) sponsored *Brown v. Board of Education* (1954) and other lawsuits that led to racial desegregation. Based on that success, a broad array of liberal and conservative interest groups now appear regularly in court to advocate their views.

Public Opinion   After *Bush v. Gore* (2000), politicians and political scientists alike pondered whether the Supreme Court had wounded itself in the eyes of the public. Evidence suggests that there was no diminution of Court legitimacy, and the Supreme Court remains as respected as ever (Kritzer 2001). But the possibility that high courts might lose the public's respect because of the decisions they make highlights the importance of public opinion for the judiciary. Although courts are shielded in the short term from the vagaries of public opinion, in the long run, public support for the fairness and impartiality of the institution is important (Gibson, Caldeira, and Baird 1998). Court officials at all levels have expressed concern about public dissatisfaction with the judiciary and have sought ways to increase public trust and confidence.

The jury provides a direct link between the courts and public opinion. To some, the jury is the most democratic of institutions, allowing ordinary citizens to pass judgments on their peers. To others, it allows randomness into the decision-making process and, thus, erodes the rule of law. These are more than philosophical issues. Some people are concerned that juries are too prone to acquit the guilty. Other people are concerned that juries are all too likely to find businesses liable in civil matters and are too willing to award excessive damages to plaintiffs.

The Media   The media play an important role in what we know about the courts and how we view the actions of judges, juries, lawyers, and litigants. Through their coverage of courts at the national and local level, the Internet, television, radio, and newspapers provide information about everything from gruesome crimes to Supreme Court decisions. Not all the coverage is so serious; the media also provide a regular diet of stories about dumb crooks and greedy plaintiffs. But the role of the media goes beyond just reporting the news. Sometimes, it affects the judiciary directly. For instance, it may be difficult to find a fair and impartial jury when a case has generated considerable pretrial publicity.

Media coverage of our nation's judiciary extends beyond real cases to include fictional portrayals as well. To some, Judge Judy is the model of how judges should act. Alas, drawing the line between myth and reality is not always easy. We explore that issue in Law and Popular Culture boxes, each of which examines a major film or television program about the U.S. judiciary.

Clearly, courts and government are intricately related. In every way described previously, law, courts, and politics intersect to provide opportunities for interaction—when and how the courts decide to exercise that discretion is a focus of this book.

COURTS AS LEGAL INSTITUTIONS

Courts provide a forum for resolving disputes through the application of legal rules. Although they are only one part of the U.S. legal system, in many ways the courts are the part most familiar to citizens.

FIGURE **1.1**
The Legal System

FIGURE **1.1**
The Legal System

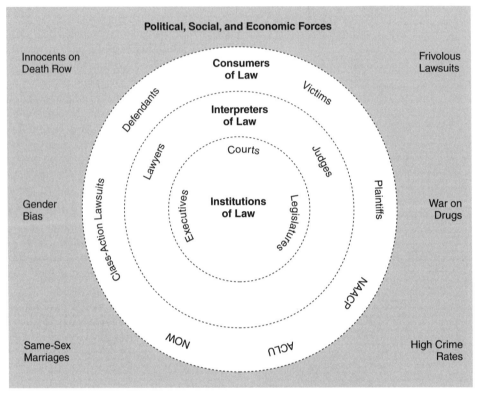

Legal system is a comprehensive term that encompasses an array of governmental institutions, a number of key actors, and a variety of other participants. As Figure 1.1 suggests, we can view the legal system as three concentric circles (Jacob 1995; Johnson and Canon 1984). At the center stand the institutions of law—law and courts primarily. They are the lawgivers. In the second ring are the interpreters of the law—lawyers and judges, predominantly. They serve as gatekeepers, largely determining which consumers of law have their cases decided by the institutions of law. Finally, the outer ring consists of consumers of justice—plaintiffs, defendants, victims, witnesses, and jurors. They bring disputes to the courts, are objects of legal activity, or are essential participants. In turn, each ring is affected by broader social, economic, and political forces.

The Inner Ring: Institutions of Law

The inner ring of the American legal system consists of the institutions of law: law and courts. **Law** is a body of rules, enacted by public officials in a legitimate manner and backed by the force of the state. **Courts** are institutions in which judges and juries resolve disputes based on law. Thus, we commonly speak of courts of law. Indeed, in modern industrialized societies it is impossible to speak sensibly of law and courts separately.

All three branches of government are active participants in deciding what the law is and how fast it changes. Today, legislatures are the principal lawgivers. They pass laws setting forth broad public policies. In implementing these general mandates, executive agencies issue detailed rules and regulations that likewise have the force of law. But these laws, whether passed by legislatures or implemented by executive agencies, may be ambiguous or contradictory. The judiciary, therefore, is the governmental institution entrusted with settling disputes on the basis of law. But the doctrine of separation of powers oversimplifies a complicated reality. Courts in the United States do not just interpret the law enacted by the other two branches of government; the courts also make law. Courts, like legislative and executive bodies, are part of the political process of fitting law to the needs of a dynamic society. Court decisions have had a major impact on how the United States is governed. Often the Court is called upon to decide how quickly (or slowly) law should change. Consider, for example, the issue of executing juveniles. One side argued that the meaning of the prohibition against cruel and unusual punishment should be limited to its eighteenth-century meaning, while others countered that interpreting this phrase should reflect contemporary understandings.

The more than 17,000 courts in the United States range from rural justice of the peace courts to the U.S. Supreme Court. Clearly, the most distinctive feature of the organization of American courts is the dual court system—one national court structure and court structures in each of the fifty states. The consequences of this system for the judicial process lead to questions such as these: Are too many lawsuits filed in federal courts? and When should federal courts limit the amount of money state juries award in punitive damages?

The Middle Ring: Interpreters of Law

The middle ring of the legal system consists of the interpreters of law, who serve as gatekeepers between the institutions of law (the inner ring) and the consumers of law (the outer ring).

A popular saying states that ours is a society of laws and not of men. That is certainly true up to a point, because it suggests that no person is above the law. No matter how rich or powerful you may be, you still must obey the law or face the consequences. At the same time, that saying is misleading, because it seems to suggest that somehow human minds play no role. But they do. Men and women perform a variety of roles of critical importance in the legal system. One of the most important functions is interpreting the law.

Lawyers are important interpreters of the law. In the privacy of their offices, they interpret the law to their clients, many of whom will never see a judge. Thus, lawyers serve as the principal gatekeepers for the legal system. Except for minor civil cases (small claims primarily), almost no one in the United States files a case in court without first hiring a lawyer. Litigation is a highly structured process that defines disputes in special and technical ways. Thus, litigation is dominated by professionals who understand the special language and esoteric techniques needed to translate general concerns into legal issues that courts recognize (Milner 1986). Two contradictory topics about lawyers, therefore, dominate public discussions: Does the United States have too many lawyers? Does the United States have too few lawyers who work for the poor?

Judges are society's authoritative interpreters of the law. People often disagree about the meaning of the law. Although their contrasting views deserve respect, ultimately judges have the final word in declaring the meaning of law. There is no agreement on how judges should be selected or what factors should be most important. Therefore, selection occurs in a variety of ways—election by the voters, appointment by the executive, or merit selection that combines the two. Which judicial selection system produces the best judges is a topic of continual political debate in the United States.

The Outer Ring: Consumers of Law

The outer ring of the American legal system is composed of the consumers of law. On a daily basis, the courts require the presence of literally thousands of citizens to perform a variety of important roles. Some consumers initiate action: By calling the police or filing a lawsuit, they provide the raw materials for the courts. Conversely, other consumers are objects of court actions. They are the defendants charged with burglarizing a house or failing to pay money owed under a contract. To resolve those disputes, judges and lawyers may summon witnesses, who may be the participants themselves or complete strangers who have been called upon to give their account of the events. A special set of consumers are jurors—ordinary citizens who are selected because they know nothing about the dispute in question. Although untrained in the law, they are still asked to render a verdict.

Some of the consumers of law are individual citizens who sue because they have been injured in an automobile accident or the like. Others are businesses that file suit to recover money owed by others. Increasingly, interest groups file lawsuits to promote public policies that favor their members. In this text we profile many interest groups, including the ACLU, NAACP, and NOW.

Social, Economic, and Political Forces

These three rings of the legal system operate within the larger society of which they are a part. The legal system is affected by social, economic, and political forces in a variety of ways. For example, as U.S. social attitudes toward marriage have changed over time, the number of divorce cases has increased. Moreover, the traditional notion of limiting marriage to persons of different genders is increasingly being called into question.

Some social and economic forces take the form of political demands. Concern over drunk driving has prompted demands that legislatures pass stiffer laws. Similarly, calls to get tough on illegal drug use have led to a decades-long War on Drugs. And concerns over the high price of medical and automobile insurance have prompted calls for tort reform. Courts are also involved in immigration issues, the War on Terror, and same-sex marriage.

Several decades of polling point to three somewhat contradictory sets of public assessments about the courts. The general public has a relatively shallow reservoir of knowledge about the courts. More citizens, for example, can identify by name, persons who play judges on TV than can identify the chief justice of the U.S. Supreme Court. The general public is also critical of the overall operations of the courts. Ordinary citizens believe that judges don't deal harshly enough with criminals and that lawyers file too many frivolous lawsuits. Although citizens express widespread dissatisfaction with the courts' performance, the typical American citizen is highly supportive of courts and judges. Far more than legislators or executives, judges retain the public's respect and confidence. It is amid contradictions like those that public sentiments influence government policy. The judiciary is no exception. We can best assess the larger environment that courts operate within by focusing on courts as political institutions.

COURTS AS POLITICAL INSTITUTIONS

Although courts are clearly legal institutions, social theories of law point out that courts are also political institutions. The courts, which interpret and apply the laws, do not exist in a vacuum. Rather, the creation, application, and interpretation of law exist within a political and social context. Courts are one governmental agency among many, and their activities are influenced, directly and indirectly, by what other branches of government do or do not do. Understanding the legal and political context within which courts operate is important in studying their role within American society (George and Epstein 1992).

Courts and Politics: How They Are the Same

Law and courts cannot be understood without understanding their roots in U.S. politics. Narrow definitions of politics that focus on partisan influences, popular elections, and political parties cloud this vital process. A more comprehensive view is provided by David Easton, who defines **politics** as "the authoritative allocation of values for a society" (1965, 50).

Applying Easton's definition to the judiciary's activities highlights several political features of its operation. Certainly, courts' decisions must be considered authoritative. Only courts have the legal power to sentence a convicted offender to prison, impose a monetary award in a civil case, or declare an act of Congress unconstitutional.

These **court decisions** often involve discretion. The judge may decide to sentence the offender to probation, award the amount of monetary damages requested by the injured party, or interpret a vague statute in a way that passes constitutional muster. In short, because laws are unclear, court officials must make important discretionary choices.

Finally, by stressing who gets what, Easton's definition calls attention to the fact that court decisions determine winners and losers and, therefore, allocate societal resources. Criminals sentenced to prison, defendants in civil cases who have to pay damages for the accidents they caused, and supporters of the legislation declared unconstitutional are losers in the judicial process. Their opposite numbers are winners. We see the allocative function of courts most dramatically when the stakes are high: The death penalty is imposed; companies are ordered to pay billions of dollars in damages; or acts of Congress affecting thousands of people are declared unconstitutional. Decisions like those have immediate, dramatic consequences. Most of the time, however, the stakes are low—a few months in jail or a few thousand dollars in damages. Cumulatively, though, those low-stake decisions are important. As judges sentence more defendants to prison for longer periods, the prison population swells, prompting demands for change. As judges and juries are increasingly willing to find defendants liable and to award greater damages, demands arise to reform how the courts handle accident cases, medical malpractice, and the like.

Courts and Politics: How They Differ

Because courts are both legal and political institutions, their operations differ from those of other governmental bodies. One difference is in how they get their business. Legislative and executive branches of government are proactive institutions: They do not wait for others to bring problems to their attention. Rather, they seek out problems and, therefore, in large measure, control their own agenda. Courts, however, are passive and reactive. Judges can act only when they are called on by parties having no connection to the judiciary. Because they depend on others to bring matters to their attention, courts have a limited ability to control their agenda. Once a lawsuit is filed, the judge is expected to make a decision.

Therein lies another difference: Unlike other governmental officials, judges typically do not enjoy the luxury of *not* making a decision. Legislative and executive bodies normally do not take an action that they do not have to take. Through a variety of devices, they can decide not to decide politically charged issues. Indeed, at times, other branches of government deliberately let the judiciary handle important questions and then criticize them for the decisions they make; this adds to the controversy surrounding the courts.

Courts also differ from other governmental institutions in how they make decisions. The legislative and executive branches are very responsive to elections, public opinion, and partisan pressure. Lobbying and direct contacts are of critical importance. By contrast, the judiciary is insulated from these standard practices of the political process. Writing letters, placing phone calls, or promising to deliver votes on election day are legitimate ways of trying to influence officials in other branches of government. But attempting those tactics with a judge will be met at best with a rebuff (the secretary will politely but forcefully suggest that the judge is unavailable) or at worst with a citation for contempt of court.

Because the judiciary is largely insular within the broader political system, politically disadvantaged groups often turn to the courts to seek redress. It is no accident, therefore, that many of the highly controversial Supreme Court decisions involve groups with little or no political influence. Prisoners, racial minorities, members of small religious groups such as Black Muslims and Jehovah's Witnesses, sexual minorities, and so on have too few votes to influence elected officials, but, armed with legal arguments, they have been able to gain important victories in the courts.

Yet another way that the judiciary differs from other governmental institutions is in the type of information presented. Before making a decision, the legislative and executive branches elicit a wide array of information from diverse points of view. By contrast, information in court is presented through the adversary process, which narrows and isolates the evidence. In addition, because a lawsuit typically involves only two sides, arguments to the courts tend to stress directly opposite points of view rather than the middle ground that is so important to other governmental institutions.

The relationship between courts and other political institutions differs in important ways around the world. In some nations, the courts are independent of the government;

in others, they are subservient. In some nations, courts largely confine themselves to handling routine decisions, but, on occasion, court decisions have wide ramifications.

COURTS AND CONTROVERSY

Viewing courts as a part of the government and as both legal and political institutions illustrates the major impact that courts have on the U.S. political and social landscape. As Alexis de Tocqueville observed in 1835, "There is almost no political question in the United States that is not resolved sooner or later into a judicial question" (257). During the era in which he wrote, the Court was wrestling with matters such as the creation of a national bank and the legal status of slaves.

De Tocqueville's observation is as relevant now as it was then. Every year, the roll call of important Supreme Court decisions captures the major social and political issues facing the nation. In turn, many Supreme Court decisions have become lightning rods for controversy, with the winning side loudly applauding the Court's judgment and the losing party harshly criticizing the ruling. Controversy, however, is not limited to decisions of our nation's highest court. Decisions at all levels—state, federal, trial, and appellate—are regularly praised or damned (depending on which side won). Such controversy underscores the increasing importance of courts as policy makers.

A growing range of controversial issues is being brought to the American judiciary. Citizens across the nation are divided on how those issues should be decided. The same holds true for the judges who must decide them. In major cases, for example, the nine justices of the Supreme Court are seldom unanimous; indeed, they often decide cases by a single-vote margin (5–4). The same also holds true if one compares the decisions of state supreme courts and other appellate bodies on similar sets of legal questions—there is often disagreement about how they should be settled.

Differences of opinion on how to decide controversial policy matters before the American judiciary often reflect the ideological differences readily apparent in the other two branches of government. Votes cast by legislatures and decisions made by presidents and governors are regularly described in terms of liberalism and conservatism. Alas, those terms have little precise meaning in the United States. They have become merely labels rather than categories for analysis. Nonetheless, they do capture the flavor of many issues debated in American politics, including many coming before the courts.

We can loosely organize many of the controversial issues that come before the judiciary under the headings of social policies, criminal justice issues, and civil justice issues. Table 1.1 provides an overview of contrasting ideological positions on some of these issues.

Social Policies

In the aftermath of *Brown v. Board of Education* (1954), which ordered an end to racial segregation in the public schools, numerous groups have turned to the courts to redress grievances once settled by other government and social institutions. Judges have ordered sweeping changes in state prisons, for example. Critics argue that courts are ill suited to resolve these types of disputes and have overstepped their proper

---

TABLE 1.1   Liberal and Conservative Positions on Issues That Come Before the Courts

The terms *liberal* and *conservative* are used as though everyone knows what they mean, but, at times, it is hard to effectively define these political beliefs. This table presents a simplified version of liberal and conservative stances on some of the issues discussed in this book.

	Liberals	Conservatives
Social Policies		
Abortion	Support "freedom of choice."	Support "right to life."
Posting the Ten Commandments	Oppose.	Favor.
Gay and lesbian rights	Support equal treatment.	Oppose erosion of societal values.
Criminal Justice Issues		
Death penalty	Oppose.	Favor.
Sentencing	Favor rehabilitation.	Favor tough sentences.
Innocents on death row	The possibility of error necessitates expansion of appellate review.	Unnecessary appellate review merely weakens the justice system.
Exclusionary rule	Safeguards vital rights.	Lets crooks go on technicalities.
War on drugs	Skeptical.	Strongly favor.
Gun control	Favor.	Oppose.
Civil Justice Issues		
Tort reform	Plaintiffs have a right to sue for damages.	Favor placing limits on who may sue.
Product liability lawsuits	Manufacturers should be held responsible for defective products.	Unnecessary and unreasonable litigation harms our nation's economy.

boundaries by unnecessarily treading on the toes of other institutions. Proponents counter that such decisions are part of an ongoing process of adapting law to changing circumstances and ensuring equal justice under the law. A number of these social policies center on issues of race, ethnicity, gender, and sexual preference. Some of the social policies discussed in this book include abortion, gun ownership, posting of religious symbols in public places, and same sex marriage.

Criminal Justice Issues

Since the 1960s, getting tough on crime has become a staple of U.S. political dialogue at the local, state, and national levels, and the courts, much more so than police departments or prisons, are held responsible. Moreover, appellate courts are charged with releasing guilty defendants on technicalities. Some of the most prominent issues to be examined include the war on drugs, proposals to abolish the exclusionary rule, concerns over innocents on death row, the continuing debate over the death penalty, and gun control.

Civil Justice Issues

More recently, attention has also been directed toward how the courts process civil cases. The American legal system is increasingly portrayed as suffering from a "litigation explosion." A lawsuit over a coffee spill at a McDonald's restaurant in Albuquerque,

New Mexico, quickly became the focus of extensive national debate and a rallying cry for those who argue that an unprecedented growth in case filings is overwhelming the courts and increasing delay. Excessive jury verdicts are blamed for driving up the costs of insurance. The medical profession calls for changes in the rules governing medical malpractice lawsuits. The insurance industry sponsors national advertising campaigns denouncing "lawsuit abuse." Those issues have prompted both state and federal legislatures to pass tort reform laws. The methods used to process civil (as well as criminal) filings have become a staple of U.S. political rhetoric. Some of the topics to be discussed in this book include the litigation explosion, tort reform, and caps on punitive damages.

Conclusion

The nation's biggest environmental disaster also spawned the nation's largest amount of litigation (measured in dollar terms). The numbers are staggering. Compensation and clean-up costs are calculated in the tens of billions of dollars. Potential civil fines are estimated in the tens of millions of dollars. The number of lawsuits tallied are in the tens of thousands.

We've included a discussion of the Gulf of Mexico oil spill in virtually every chapter of *Judicial Process: Law, Courts and Politics* because it illustrates many of the topics in this book. The actions of lawyers and litigants, to say nothing of the decisions of judges and juries will shape the eventual outcome of this environmental disaster. Some will be filed in federal court, others in state venues, and just as interesting—a process outside of the courts has been established—BP agreed to create a $20 billion claims fund to which over 800,000 claims have been made. Whether this will prove to be a viable alternative to the judicial process remains to be seen. Much of the litigation is civil in nature but criminal prosecutions are also possible. Trials are almost a certainty and lengthy appeals inevitable.

We've also included discussions of the BP oil spill because it illustrates the nexus between law and politics. Government officials, both elected and appointed, will make numerous discretionary decisions over the next years that will shape not only which lawsuits will be brought but also where they will be heard and how they will be settled. In arguing that how the judiciary responds to oil spill lawsuits needs to be considered as part of the political process, we are not suggesting that decisions in individual cases will be less fair and impartial. What we are suggesting is that at a minimum the political system sets the outer limits on what is considered fair and just. For example, from the beginning Congressional leaders of both parties made it abundantly clear that BP would not be allowed to wiggle out of its responsibility by claiming the $75 million cap in existing liability legislation.

The impact of the Deepwater Horizon oil spill is ongoing. By the time this is read, new developments will certainly have occurred, but hopefully what we write about now will help the reader put future events into perspective. Toward that end, the web page accompanying this book will contain semi-regular updates on what is happening and where to turn for analysis.

The controversy over the Gulf of Mexico oil spill and its impact on the legal system is just one example of how law, courts, and politics intersect in the United States.

Every day, newspapers and television cover reactions to court decisions on important issues such as stays of execution for condemned murderers, businesses that are suing and being sued over stock manipulations, and big-name entertainers being arrested for drunk driving or being involved in messy (and often expensive) divorces. The judicial process pervades our society.

We begin our study of U.S. courts by recognizing that they are both legal and political institutions—hence, the title "Law, Courts, and Politics." Idolizing courts as purely legal agencies ignores the fact that, in interpreting the law, judges often make choices based on criteria other than the letter of the law. That intersection of law and politics is what makes the U.S. judiciary such a fascinating and lively subject. In a fundamental sense, the legal and political contexts in which courts operate are often in considerable tension. Some forces and issues tug to make the courts more insular; others pull to make them more accountable to society. The analysis of those forces is the focus of this text.

CRITICAL THINKING QUESTIONS

1. How does Easton's definition of politics differ from popular notions of politics?

2. In what ways are courts different from other governmental and political institutions?

3. Are courts more involved in policy making today than they were two or three decades ago? Why or why not?

Search Terms

courts   judiciary

Useful URLs

http://www.supremecourtus.gov
  Supreme Court of the United States: This official site includes up-to-date Court opinions, biographies of the justices, and much more.

http://www.house.gov
  U.S. House of Representatives: This site offers access to members' official Web pages.

http://www.senate.gov
  United States Senate: Provides information on the history of the Senate, information on current senators, contact information, and information on the Capitol building, including a virtual tour.

http://www.whitehouse.gov
  President of the United States: The official White House site offers texts of presidential speeches, press briefings, and executive orders.

http://www.ncsconline.org
  National Center for State Courts: This nonprofit organization is dedicated to improving court administration.

http://www.abanet.org
The American Bar Association (ABA), the largest organization of lawyers in the United States, provides ready access to a variety of material about the nation's legal system.

REFERENCES

Banks, Christopher, and John Green. 2001. *Superintending Democracy: The Courts and the Political Process.* Akron, Ohio: University of Akron Press.

Campbell, Colton, and John Stack. 2001. *Congress Confronts the Court: The Struggle for Legitimacy and Authority in Lawmaking.* Lanham, Md.: Rowman & Littlefield.

Easton, David. 1965. *A Framework for Political Analysis.* Englewood Cliffs, N.J.: Prentice Hall.

Friedman, Lawrence. 1975. *The Legal System: A Social Science Perspective.* New York: Russell Sage Foundation.

George, Tracey, and Lee Epstein. 1992. "On the Nature of Supreme Court Decision Making." *American Political Science Review* 86: 323–337.

Geyh, Charles. 2008. *When Courts & Congress Collide.* Ann Arbor: University of Michigan Press.

Gibson, James L., Gregory A. Caldeira, and Vanessa Baird. 1998. "On the Legitimacy of National High Courts." *American Political Science Review* 92: 343–358.

Howard, J. Woodford. 1981. *Courts of Appeals in the Federal Judicial System: A Study of the Second, Fifth, and District of Columbia Circuits.* Princeton, N.J.: Princeton University Press.

Jacob, Herbert. 1995. *Law and Politics in the United States.* 2d ed. New York: HarperCollins.

Johnson, Charles, and Bradley Canon. 1984. *Judicial Policies: Implementation and Impact.* Washington, D.C.: CQ Press.

Kritzer, Herbert M. 2001. "The Impact of *Bush v. Gore* on Public Perceptions and Knowledge of the Supreme Court." *Judicature* 85: 32–38.

Milner, Neal. 1986. "The Dilemmas of Legal Mobilization: Ideologies and Strategies of Mental Patient Liberation Groups." *Law and Policy* 8: 105.

Sherwin, Richard. 2002. *When Law Goes Pop: The Vanishing Line Between Law and Popular Culture.* Chicago: University of Chicago Press.

Tocqueville, Alexis de. 1835. In *Democracy in America,* edited by Harvey C. Mansfield and Delba Winthrop. Chicago: University of Chicago Press.

FOR FURTHER READING

Bamberger, Michael. 2000. *Reckless Legislation: How Lawmakers Ignore the Constitution.* New Brunswick, N.J.: Rutgers University Press.

Bergman, Paul, and Michael Asimov. 1996. *Reel Justice: The Courtroom Goes to the Movies.* Kansas City, Mo.: Andrews McMeel Publishing.

Freeman, Robert. 2000. *Popular Culture and Corrections.* Lanham, Md.: American Correctional Association.

Friedman, Lawrence. 2004. *American Law in the Twentieth Century.* New Haven, Conn.: Yale University Press.

George, Robert. 2000. *Great Cases in Constitutional Law.* Princeton, N.J.: Princeton University Press.

Kesselman, Mark, Joel Krieger, and William Joseph. 2010. *Introduction to Comparative Politics,* 5th edition. Boston, MA: Wadsworth.

Perry, Barbara. 2010. *The Supreme: An Introduction to the U.S. Supreme Court Justices, 2nd edition. New York:* Peter Lang.

Ryden, David. 2001. *The U.S. Supreme Court and the Electoral Process.* Baltimore: Georgetown University Press.

Stevens, Dennis. 2011. *Media and Criminal Justice: The CSI Effect.* Sudbury, MA: Jones and Bartlett.

Slotnick, Elliot. 2006. Judicial Politics: Readings from Judicature, 3rd edition. Washington, DC: CQ Press.

Tarr, G. Alan. 2010. *Judicial Process and Policymaking.* Boston, MA: Cengage.

LAW AND LEGAL SYSTEMS

In common-law countries such as the United States, law books are numerous. These volumes of English Reports underscore the English heritage of our nation's legal system.

David Neubauer

"… the middle of nowhere" is how Chief Justice John Roberts described the location of an 8-foot-tall cross during oral argument in yet another Supreme Court case that examines the relationship between the government display of religious symbols and the First Amendment. The Court ultimately sided with the government and said the presence of the cross, which had been on display since 1934 in a remote part of the Mojave Desert National Preserve, did not violate the Establishment Clause of the constitution. But along the way the case generated two lawsuits filed by the same plaintiff, five court decisions, several congressional laws, and shortly after the decision the cross disappeared.

   Salazar v. Buono (2010) involves a Supreme Court interpretation of the nation's most basic law—the Constitution. But, as this chapter shows, constitutional law is only a small part of American law. The law of the land can be found not only in constitutions but also in statutes enacted by Congress, rules written by bureaucrats, and decisions rendered by courts. In turn, these various sources of law regulate everything from how fast we drive our cars to what happens when the car we drive gets in an accident. As stressed throughout this chapter, American law is both voluminous and subject to different interpretations.

This chapter provides a brief overview of law from the vantage point of the courts. It begins by asking, "What is law?" and then examines how most of the world organizes their legal systems. Knowledge of other legal systems better highlights distinctive features of American common law, including the use of precedent and the adversary system. The latter part of the chapter examines the numerous components of law found in the United States and how this law often involves discretionary choices.

Religion and politics is the substantive theme of this chapter. Case Close-Up: *Salazar v. Buono* (2010) examines the Court's most recent decision dealing with the Establishment Clause of the First Amendment. Courts in Comparative Perspective: The French Republic and the Code Napoléon examines France, with a brief discussion of the government's decision to ban Muslim women from wearing scarves to school.

What Is Law?

Law pervades every aspect of our lives, but only a small part of this law is readily apparent: stoplights and press coverage of a local murder trial, for example. Mainly, though, the law operates behind the scenes. Few of us are aware that the radio we listen to and the milk we pour on our cereal are controlled by governmental rules and regulations. Often the law appears to be relevant only when we face a problem like a stolen television or an automobile accident. But, in indirect ways, the law affects how fast we can drive and the agreements we sign when purchasing cars or taking out loans for college tuition. To an even greater extent, the law regulates the public and private institutions that are a central part of our lives. In short, law is an inescapable part of our complex industrialized society.

With so much law surrounding us, we would think the term *law* would be easy to define, but the opposite proves to be true. In the words of law professor Lawrence Friedman (1984), law "is a word of many meanings, as slippery as glass, as elusive as a soap bubble." Mainly because law is a dynamic force in society, scholars have debated its definition for centuries but have yet to arrive at a consensus on its meaning. Although definitions of law vary, they agree on four essential features. As used in this book, **law** is a body of rules enacted by public officials in a legitimate manner and backed by the force of the state. This working definition incorporates features that most scholars agree on.

First, law is a body of rules governing the relationships between members of society. These rules and regulations provide predictability in the conduct of human affairs.

Second, rules are enacted by public officials. Thus, by definition, law is connected with government. Many private institutions, such as schools, churches, and businesses, operate on the basis of rules and regulations, but under our definition those rules and regulations are not considered law unless they are recognized by a governmental institution.

Third, law must be enacted by public officials in a legitimate manner. What distinguishes legal compulsion from terrorism or extortion is that legal force is applied by a legitimate party, for a legitimate cause, in a legitimate way, at a legitimate time.

Fourth, law is backed by the force of the state. There can be no law without sanctions. As the *Law Dictionary for Non-Lawyers* (Oran and Tosti 2000) puts it, law is "that which must be obeyed." Simply put, the law has teeth to it. Failure to abide by the rules and regulations can lead to confiscation of property, fines, awards of monetary damages, or physical punishment (incarceration or, on rare occasions, death). In most instances, however, it is not necessary to apply sanctions; the threat of sanctions often is enough to influence people's behavior in the desired manner.

Law and Justice

In a representative democracy, public perceptions of law embody fundamental notions of justice, fairness, and decency (Walker 2006; Tyler 1988). This potential linking of law and justice (in the form of unjust laws) also makes law difficult to define. But law and morality do not necessarily equate. Our working definition of law deliberately excludes any reference to justice because there is no precise legal or scientific meaning to the term. Rather, justice is a general term used to support particular political and social goals. In the public arena, justice is used in several ways.

At times, justice is simply defined as winning. Whether a court's decision is labeled just or unjust often depends on which party prevailed. Consider a hotly contested murder trial that ends in a not-guilty verdict. The defendant and his friends are quick to say that they knew all along that "justice" would prevail. At the same time, the family and friends of the deceased express outrage that "justice" was not done because a monstrous murderer has been freed to prey on other innocent citizens. Reaching an objective conclusion in this battle of competing justice clichés is impossible.

Justice is often (as noted previously) equated with achieving desired results. In this sense, prohibition is widely regarded as a "bad" law because it did not eliminate the use of alcoholic beverages, it produced widespread disrespect for law among average citizens, and it spawned criminal organizations headed by notorious criminals such as Al Capone. Thus, trying to define good or bad law on the basis of whether the law achieved its intended results is problematic. Citizens, lawmakers, and scholars disagree over the criteria to use in defining intended impact and, therefore, often disagree on whether the law was "good" or "bad."

Sometimes, however, justice is equated with normative values. *Roe v. Wade* (1973) (Chapter 14) provides the clearest contemporary example of how defenders and critics of a policy use deeply held societal values to bolster their respective positions. Pro-choice groups, stressing the right to privacy, support abortion because it respects the right of a woman to control her own body. Pro-life groups, stressing the rights of the unborn, condemn abortion as murder.

Clearly, there are varying and conflicting views on what constitutes good law or bad, just law or unjust. Attempting to include any such standards in a working definition of law serves only to muddy the waters. By adopting a bare-bones definition of law that most agree on, however, we can approach the debate over the link between law and justice as an important topic for study in its own right. Throughout this book, we discuss topics—such as abortion, posting of the Ten Commandments, school desegregation, plea bargaining, gay marriage, and the death penalty—that provoke debate over the interface between law and justice.

LEGAL SYSTEMS

Americans equate legal systems with lawyers questioning witnesses, judges ruling on the basis of precedent, and jurors deciding guilt or innocence. All of these are considered fundamental rights in the United States. Yet these practices are not found in the majority of the countries in the world.

Each of the nearly 200 nations of the world has its own distinct legal system. The role of law in each society varies because of very different social and political environments. But some important commonalities exist among legal systems. The French scholar René David (David and Brierley 1978) classifies legal systems primarily on the basis of the following question: Could a lawyer educated in one nation's law handle, without much difficulty, another nation's law? If the answer is "yes," then the legal systems are considered similar. For example, a lawyer trained in the United States would find it easy to converse with his or her counterparts in London, Sydney, and New Delhi. But the same cannot be said if he or she travels to Paris, Moscow, or Beijing. The language barrier aside, American lawyers would find they share few similarities with the lawyers in these countries. Table 2.1 summarizes some of the most important differences among the four major legal systems of the world: civil law, socialist law, Islamic law, and common law. Understanding these alternative legal systems and the social environments that shaped their development can provide a better understanding of our own legal system (Cole, Frankowski, and Gertz 1987). The following discusses each in some detail.

CIVIL LAW

Civil law is also referred to as Roman law, Romano-Germanic law, or continental civil law. It is the oldest family of law, tracing its origins to the Roman Empire. This legal tradition was preserved after the fall of the Roman Empire by the universities of both Latin and Germanic countries in Europe. Beginning in the twelfth century, law professors developed codes of law based on the compilation of Roman law by the Roman emperor Justinian.

Civil law is a body of law characterized by a compilation of laws in writing. Civil law is contrasted with common law, which is a compilation of judicial opinions. Unlike a typical U.S. law book, which is filled from beginning to end with judicial decisions, the code is a systematic collection of interrelated articles written in a terse, staccato style. For example, the Code Napoléon (named after Emperor Napoléon Bonaparte, who extensively revised French law) consists of three parts: "Of Persons," "Of Things and the Different Modifications of Ownership," and "Of the Different Modes of

TABLE 2.1	Major Legal Systems of the World			
	Common Law	**Civil Law**	**Socialist Law**	**Islamic Law**
Other names	Anglo-American, judge-made	Continental, Roman	Communist	Religious law
Source of law	Judicial interpretation and legislation	Code	Marxism-Leninism	Sacred religious Document
Lawyers	Control courtroom	Judges dominate trials	Party members	Secondary role
Judges' qualifications	Former practicing lawyers	Career bureaucrats	Party members	Religious as well as legal training
Degree of judicial independence	High	Insulated from regime	Courts an extension of the state	Very limited
Juries	Often available at trial level	Mixed tribunals in serious cases	Often used at lowest level	Not allowed
Policy-making role	Courts share in balancing power	Courts have equal but separate power	Courts are subordinate to the legislature	Courts and other governmental branches are subordinate to the Shari'a
Examples	Australia, England, Canada, India	France, Germany, Israel, Japan, Mexico, Ecuador	China, Russia	Saudi Arabia, Nigeria

Acquiring the Ownership of Things." Thus, the code expresses rules of law as general principles phrased in abstract language.

The code serves as a source of law that provides answers for all disputes. The tradition is that those rules will be interpreted broadly. Therefore, judges and lawyers emphasize abstract concepts rather than concrete cases. In interpreting the codes, judges reason deductively, guided by the presumed intent of the drafters of the code. Thus, the common-law approach, which emphasizes precedent (discussed later), is largely unknown. Indeed, previous court decisions are not considered to be sources of law. This means that, in searching for an answer to a legal problem, lawyers and judges in the civil legal system look to provisions of the code rather than to prior court decisions. One consequence is that, by American standards, law books are short and a judge's working library is small.

From the perspective of U.S. common law, several features of civil law are distinctive:

- Judges, not lawyers, dominate court hearings. Thus, judges call witnesses and question them.
- Judges are career bureaucrats who have not been practicing lawyers.
- Juries are not used. Rather, mixed tribunals consisting of both judges and lay citizens are used, but only for serious crimes.

Civil law is the most widely used in the contemporary world, forming the basis of the law in most of the European nations. Through colonization by France and Spain,

COURTS IN COMPARATIVE PERSPECTIVE

■ *The French Republic and the Code Napoléon*

Motivated by the French principle of secularism, the government in April 2010 banned the wearing of a "burqa"—a common Islamic head-to-toe covering. The ban included fines for women who went out in public wearing a burqa and stiff fines for men who forced women to wear one. Previously the French government banned Islamic head scarves in public schools. In the United States, such policies would quickly be challenged in court, stressing the importance of "freedom of religion." But no such lawsuits will be filed in France because that nation's constitution has a strong prohibition against mixing religion and politics. The ban on the wearing of burqas is but one example of the different roles that courts and constitutions play in France and in the United States.

France's 62 million inhabitants reside in a land mass approximately twice the size of Colorado. France boasts one of the four strongest Western European economies and is known both for its agricultural products and for its highly developed industrial sector.

France is a unitary state with a highly centralized form of government. All major decisions are made through a national bureaucracy located in Paris. Since the French Revolution in 1789, France has had 15 constitutions. The most recent was adopted in 1958 and created the Fifth Republic.

Contemporary French law is associated with its leading historical figure, Napoléon Bonaparte, a general in the French army who seized power in 1799. When Napoléon was not waging war, he took the lead in modernizing the legal system. The Code Napoléon, or Code Civil, the first modern legal code of France, was promulgated in 1804. It is a revised form of Roman law, dividing civil law into personal status (e.g., marriage), property (e.g., real estate), and the acquisition of property (e.g., wills and contracts). With amendments, the Code Napoléon is still in force in France today.

At the trial level, cases are heard by police courts (minor matters) and correctional courts (serious matters). Assize courts are reserved for rare crimes that carry a sentence of life imprisonment. At the appellate level, France does not have the equivalent of a constitutional court like the U.S. Supreme Court. Rather, review is split among three courts. The Supreme Court of Appeals (Cour de Cassation) hears appeals from the lower appellate courts in regular legal areas. The Constitutional Council (Conseil Constitutionnel) gives advisory opinions about the constitutionality of legislation that has been passed but has not yet gone into effect. Finally, the Council of State (Conseil d'État) reviews decisions of the nation's all-powerful bureaucracy.

From the perspective of U.S. common law, several features of the French legal system are distinctive:

- The civil and criminal proceedings are combined—the same court can hear both civil and criminal cases.
- Lawyers (who wear black robes in court) speak only when spoken to (Mauro 1997).
- Judges (who wear red robes) are civil servants who must compete for entry after graduating from the National School of Magistrature.
- In crimes carrying a sentence of life imprisonment, the defendant is tried by a court of three professional magistrates and a nine-member jury. No juries are used in any other courts.
- The nation's highest court occasionally engages in policy making. For example, France's highest court established in law a disabled child's "right not to be born" (BBC News 2001).

The difference between the French and the U.S. legal systems extends far beyond court procedures and the relative power of judges and lawyers. A case in point is the tragic death of Princess Diana. Shortly after she died in an automobile accident in downtown Paris, nine photographers were taken into custody and held without charges being filed. Moreover, they had no right to see their lawyers during initial questioning. The nine photographers, for example, faced potential criminal charges of failure to aid someone in danger, which is not a crime in the United States. Nor are publications protected by "freedom of the press"; indeed, French publications often are ordered to pay high amounts of damages in libel cases.

As for the nine photographers, the French prosecutors dropped all charges two years later. But that did not end the matter: The final decision was in the hands of the investigating magistrates. They eventually concurred, holding that the accident was caused by the driver, who was speeding, inebriated, and on drugs ("Driver Blamed ..." 1999).

Roman law spread to other nations as well, including Central and South America, Turkey, and Japan. (See Courts in Comparative Perspective: The French Republic and the Code Napoléon.)

Socialist Law

The socialist family of laws originated in the former Soviet Union following the Russian Revolution of 1917 and was used primarily in what were once called the Eastern Bloc nations. For that reason, it is often referred to in the United States as communist law. It is currently used in both Russia and China. The foundations of socialist law reflect two contradictory forces. On the one hand, the legal systems of Eastern Europe were formerly part of the civil law legal system and have retained some of those characteristics. Codes, for example, provide the source of general rules of conduct. Moreover, legal terminology and legal procedures reflect, to a large extent, their civil law heritage.

On the other hand, the originality of **socialist law** stems from its birth in revolution. Unlike the emphasis in common law and civil law on maintaining order, socialist law is premised on creating a radically different society. The blueprint for this new society is the philosophy of Karl Marx and Vladimir Lenin; the guiding principle is societal ownership of the major means of production. Marxist-Leninist doctrine viewed law in capitalist nations as suppressing the underprivileged and saw the new socialist law as a tool for building the new state.

From the perspective of U.S. common law, several features of socialist law are distinctive:

- Socialist law rejects the common-law and civil law notions that law is the fundamental basis for society. Rather, law is deemed the arbitrary work of an autocratic sovereign. One extension is, therefore, the withering away of the state—after the workers' regime is established—because there would be no need for law.
- The primary goal of socialist law is the protection of the state; only limited protection is afforded private property. Crimes against private property, for example, are viewed as far less serious than those against the state.
- Law has an educational role; it is an instrument for educating citizens about the new socialist society. As a result, crime is viewed not primarily as the failure of individuals (as it is in the United States) but as the failure of the state—because the government failed to properly educate its citizens. Thus, it was common to order that political dissidents undergo political re-education.

With the breakup of the Soviet Union and the demise of many communist regimes, socialist law is rapidly changing. Many Eastern European nations are adopting property rights and providing criminal defendants more protections. The nature of the changes and their extent vary from country to country. In short, socialist law remains in effect, and its influence is likely to persist (Fairchild and Dammer 2006).

ISLAMIC LAW

Most of the legal systems in the modern world are secular—the law is not directly related to religion or any religious body. By contrast, religious legal systems are based directly on religious beliefs. The Torah (the first five books of the Old Testament) serves as the core of Israeli law. Similarly, Hinduism influences the legal system in India, and the impact of Confucius is readily apparent in China.

The primary contemporary example of a legal system directly reflecting religious tenets is **Islamic law**. What is perhaps most distinctive about Islam is the extent to which it dominates all aspects of life. Islamic law is called the *Shari'a*, which consists of two parts: the Qur'an (sometimes spelled Koran), which sets out principles revealed by God through Muhammad; and the Sunna, which contains the practices and decisions made by Muhammad. Islamic law is intrinsic to Islamic faith (Reichel 2001).

From the perspective of U.S. common law, several features of Islamic law are distinctive:

- Judges undergo religious as well as legal training.
- Lawyers do not assert independence from the legal system or the government.
- Juries are not allowed.

The extent to which Islam influences the law varies significantly among Muslim countries. In Saudi Arabia and Iran, Islam is the only legal tradition; Islamic law and Islamic clerics dominate political and social life. By contrast, Jordan and Kuwait have both civil and Islamic aspects to their legal systems. Moreover, some nations, such as Kenya and Nigeria, combine Islamic law and local custom (Fairchild and Dammer 2006). (See Courts in Comparative Perspective: The Kingdom of Saudi Arabia: Pure Islamic Law, in Chapter 8.)

COMMON LAW

The other major legal system is the common law, also referred to as Anglo-American law. The common law is utilized in English-speaking nations, including England, Australia, New Zealand, Canada, and the United States. (In the Canadian province of Quebec, however, the law is based on French civil law. Similarly, Louisiana civil law, but not criminal law, is based on the civil legal system.)

The **common law** traces its roots to medieval England. (Table 2.2 displays key legal developments in relation to the development of the common law and other legal systems.) After the Norman Conquest of 1066, the new rulers gradually introduced central governmental administration, including the establishment of courts of law. Initially, the bulk of the law was local and was administered in local courts. A distinct body of national law began to develop during the reign of Henry II (1154–1189), who expanded the jurisdiction of the royal courts. The king's courts applied the common customs of the entire realm rather than the parochial traditions of a particular shire or village. Thus, the term *common law* meant general law as opposed to special law; it was the law common to the entire land.

TABLE 2.2	Key Developments in the Law	
Hammurabi	1792–1750 B.C.E	First written code of law.
Moses	1200–1080	Old Testament lawgiver often associated with the Torah and the Ten Commandments.
Code of Justinian	533 C.E.	The Roman Code became the basis for much of European law.
Muhammad	570	Birth of the Prophet who founded Islam.
Norman conquest	1066	Beginnings of the English common law.
Magna Carta	1215	The English king is forced to limit some of his powers.
Blackstone	1765	*Commentaries on the Laws of England* published.
Declaration of Independence	1776	One of the world's greatest documents of liberty.
U.S. Constitution	1787	Philadelphia Convention drafts the Constitution.
Bill of Rights	1791	Bill of Rights ratified.
	1804	Napoleonic Code.
Karl Marx	1848	*Communist Manifesto* published.
Civil War amendments	1865–1870	Thirteenth, Fourteenth, and Fifteenth Amendments ratified.
	1917	Russian Revolution overthrows the czar.
Vladimir Lenin	1917	Lenin becomes chairman of the Soviet government.
Berlin Wall dismantled	1989	Communist regimes in Russia and Eastern Europe begin to collapse.
	1991	Soviet Union dissolved.

But common law was not the only source of law in England. A multiplicity of types of laws, and therefore judges to interpret those laws, were used. Admiralty courts developed and interpreted maritime (sea-going) law. These courts of admiralty were obviously important for the nation's economy, because England was a great sea power. For ordinary citizens, the ecclesiastical or church courts governed vital matters such as marriage and divorce. Perhaps the most important were the Courts of Chancery (which applied equity law).

Equity

Initially, common law exhibited considerable flexibility, but by the late Middle Ages, judicial interpretations stressed a static conservatism. The courts became increasingly costly and complex because judges emphasized procedural technicalities. Thus, the common law evolved into a hard and limited law; despite significant changes in society, the courts of common law refused to recognize new forms of legal redress.

To cite but one example, common-law remedies were largely limited to monetary damages, but in many situations either the **plaintiff** could not get relief from the common-law courts or the relief available was clearly inadequate. Consider the following situation: Farmer Jones decides that the best way to use his land is to build a dam across the stream that runs through his property. Unfortunately, the resulting pond will flood some of Farmer Smith's best pastureland. Under common law, Smith would have to wait until the land was flooded before he could sue for damages. Clearly, Farmer Smith doesn't want to wait for the possible award of monetary damages years later; he wants to preserve his pasture right now.

The refusal of judges to adapt the common law to changing societal conditions gave rise to its principal rival—**equity**. Plaintiffs who could not get redress before the common-law courts petitioned the king, who was considered the fountainhead of justice. He, in turn, referred those petitions to the chancellor, who, over time, began to exercise considerable judicial power. Later, a separate Court of Chancery emerged, whose decisions were based on broad principles of justice and reason (that is, equity) rather than on rigid standards of common law. Thus, equity became a systematized body of law distinct from the common law that began where the common law ended. In its broadest sense, equity meant fair dealing. Therefore, equitable remedies (injunctions, primarily) were more flexible and relatively nontechnical compared with the common law. To return to our example, the Court of Chancery would issue an injunction forbidding Farmer Jones to build the dam. Because equity presumed to correct their work, common-law judges viewed this alternative system of law with suspicion.

As the history of equity illustrates, law in England and later in America did not develop at one time and in one piece but, rather, emerged gradually. Unlike the coherent whole that characterizes civil law, the common law resembles a fabric woven by the royal judges of England with the slow, hesitant persistence of a tortoise (Post 1963).

English Heritage; American Adaptations

The colonists brought the principles of British common law to America. The influence of Anglo-American law is clearly seen in the language of the U.S. Constitution: Article III defines federal judicial power as extending to "all Cases in Law and Equity … [and] of admiralty and maritime jurisdiction." Similarly, the Seventh Amendment begins, "In suits at common law …" But although the colonists brought with them the terms and procedures of the common law, they did not always apply the substance of the law as had been done in British law. Rather, they adapted common law to the changing conditions of a frontier society. In Britain, for example, land was scarce, and the common law made it difficult to sell, virtually guaranteeing that land would remain in the same family for generations. In the colonies, land appeared plentiful, and the law made it easy to buy and sell (thus fostering land speculation, which became one of the principal occupations in many of the emerging states).

In ways large and small, Americans adapted the heritage of the English common law to the social context of, first, the colonies and, later, the states. Early in the nineteenth century, U.S. courts abandoned the complex rules of civil procedure in favor of simpler ones. By the late nineteenth century, most states had merged their separate courts of law and equity. By the early twentieth century, judge-made law was rapidly being replaced by legislatively passed laws. Thus, over time, the American usage of the term *common law* focused on the case method rather than on specific English practices.

KEY CHARACTERISTICS OF THE COMMON LAW

The common-law heritage is strikingly different from that of European civil law. Whereas civil law developed in the antiseptic atmosphere of the university, Anglo-American law grew out of the muck and mire of courtroom battles over real disputes involving living human beings. Through the centuries, three key characteristics of this common-law heritage emerged: (1) judge-made law, (2) use of precedent, and (3) uncodified regulations.

Judge-Made Law

Common law is predominantly judge-made law rather than legislatively enacted law. Until the late nineteenth century, there was no important body of statutory law in the United States. Instead, the task of organizing social relationships through law was largely performed by judges. For example, the common-law courts developed the rights and obligations of citizens in important areas such as property, torts, wills, and contracts. Similarly, the courts defined felonies, such as murder, manslaughter, robbery, larceny, and rape.

Common law's most distinctive feature is the development of a system of law from judicial decisions on a case-by-case basis. By the end of the thirteenth century, unofficial reports of cases were published in annual yearbooks, which were frequently referred to by lawyers and gradually came to serve as a source of precedent. Given that Parliament was rarely in session, the judges formulated most of the rules of law.

Precedent

Precedent is a court decision that serves as authority for deciding a similar question of law in a later case with similar facts. Precedent is also referred to as **stare decisis** ("let the decision stand").

Precedents are established in appellate court opinions, which discuss the legal questions in the case and examine previous court decisions. Those points of law decided by a court to resolve a legal controversy constitute the holding of the case—in other words, the court decides that a certain rule of law applies to the given factual situation and renders a decision accordingly. The rule of law as applied to the facts of the case constitutes precedent. Sometimes, in their opinions, courts make comments that go beyond what is necessary to decide the case. These extraneous judicial expressions are referred to as **obiter dicta** (often, simply **dicta** [pl.] or **dictum** [sing.]). Although they have no value as precedent, they are often good guides to how a court will decide future similar cases.

The reliance on precedent is central to the common law's approach to problem solving. Rather than issue an opinion that attempts to solve the entire range of a given legal problem, common-law courts decide only as much of the case as they must to resolve the individual dispute. Thus, in sharp contrast to the deductive approach of the civil legal system, common law employs inductive logic. Broad rules and policy directives emerge only over time through the accumulation of court decisions. Precedent provides stability, coherence, and predictability. As Justice Louis Brandeis once wrote, "Stare decisis is usually the wise policy, because in most matters it is more important that the applicable rule of law be settled than that it be settled right" (*Burnet v. Coronado Oil and Gas Co.* 1932).

Uncodified Rules and Regulations

Common-law rules and regulations are uncodified; that is, there is no one place where an individual can find an official statement of the whole of the law or even a major portion of it. Instead, the law emerges through precedent found in court decisions.

When are two cases similar? That is the catch in the notion of precedent, and there is no correct answer. Legal rules found in precedents are generalizations that emphasize certain facts while discounting or ignoring others. In a short but influential book, Edward Levi (1948), then a law professor and later U.S. attorney general, argued that "the pretense is that the law is a system of known rules applied by a judge." In deciding whether the facts in the present case are sufficiently like the facts in an earlier case, common-law judges and lawyers reason by analogy. Analogies are neither correct nor incorrect, but only more or less persuasive. Reasoning by analogy affords leeway in formulating new legal rules or modifying old ones to fit changing political, economic, social, and technological developments (Ducat 1988).

This reasoning by example provides the "indisputable dynamic quality of law" (Levi 1948). Judges may distinguish the current case from previous decisions: They may find that the facts of the current case differ from previous ones and, therefore, that the rule of law found in the earlier cases doesn't apply to this one. They may also apply existing doctrines of law to new and emerging problems. The Court's decision in *Roe v. Wade* (1973), for example, reflected the efforts of the Court to confront modern realities, particularly contemporary notions of a right to privacy. And, on very rare occasions, courts may even overturn their previous decisions. Two of the cases highlighted in this book involve Supreme Court reversals of their own prior decisions: *District of Columbia v. Heller* (2008) reversed *United States v. Miller* (1939); *Gideon v. Wainwright* (1963) reversed *Betts v. Brady* (1942).

THE ADVERSARY SYSTEM

Truth is elusive. Two people witness the same event, yet relate different versions of what happened. Some of those differences stem from how near to the event, or how far from it, the person was. On other occasions, however, different versions of the same event stem from self-interest. A defendant in a criminal case often remembers events radically differently than the alleged victim does. Legal systems require a method of establishing the facts (truth) of the matter. The two great families of law differ not only in how law is interpreted but also in the procedures used in court to ascertain the facts of the case.

Essentially, two approaches exist—inquisitorial and adversarial—to the question of how best to establish the facts of a particular case. Civil law is inquisitorial in style: The judge is responsible for calling witnesses and asking questions. (Inquisition refers to a judicial examination; unfortunately, Americans tend to equate the inquisitorial style of justice with church-based inquisitions that sometimes used torture to ferret out and punish heresy.) In sharp contrast, common law is confrontational in style: The opposing parties are responsible for calling witnesses and asking questions.

The common law uses the **adversary system**, in which a judge acts as a neutral decision maker presiding over a battle between two opposing parties. Each side presents its case to the court, and a decision is reached between the two alternative versions of fact and law. This clash between opposing sides is viewed as the best way to ensure that the legal rights of all parties are protected. Defenders of the adversary system are suspicious of the inquisitorial system, under which a judge is responsible for eliciting facts that are favorable to both sides. To the common-law mind, concentrating such power in the hands of a single person places too much responsibility on an individual, no matter how well motivated. According to the American Bar Association (1970, 3), the guiding principle is that when two parties approach "the facts from entirely different perspectives and objectives … [they] will uncover more of the truth than would investigators, however industrious and objective, seeking to compose a unified picture of what had occurred." Civil lawyers counter that U.S. trials are hardly bastions of truth. American lawyers will sometimes admit in private (rarely in public) that witnesses at trial don't always tell the whole truth and sometimes are known to engage in fabrication. According to Europeans, such dishonesty is much less likely to occur in their courts.

The two key elements of the adversary system are (1) party prosecution and (2) a neutral and passive decision maker (Landsman 1988).

Party Prosecution

The adversary system pits the prosecuting attorney against the defense attorney. Although the term *prosecution* is popularly associated with criminal cases, the law employs a broader definition: Prosecution means the process of engaging in a lawsuit, whether civil or criminal. It is the responsibility of the opposing parties, not the judge or the jury, to define the legal issues in the case and present the evidence supporting their positions. The principle of party prosecution focuses attention on the legal questions and facts that are most important to the litigants. It also encourages each side to present its most persuasive evidence. Placing the responsibility on each party also means that each side has its day in court. Regardless of the eventual verdict, each side has the opportunity to present its case.

The principle of party prosecution indicates that a legal system is more than rules on paper. It is also a plan for distributing power among judges, juries, plaintiffs (or prosecutors), and defendants (whether civil or criminal). The adversary system diffuses power: Each actor is granted limited powers, and, in turn, each has limited powers to

LAW AND POPULAR CULTURE

■ *Brokedown Palace* (1999)

To celebrate their high school graduation, two American teenagers plan an exotic trip. Telling their parents that they are off to Hawaii, they instead go to Bangkok, Thailand. When a third friend suggests a quick trip to Hong Kong, the two friends quickly agree—only to be arrested at the airport for possessing heroin.

After they are arrested, the girls are taken to jail, where they are basically told they are guilty. When Alice claims that she has a right to talk to a lawyer, the officer replies, "Yeah and a phone call." After making a statement to the police, Darlene signs a document that, she has been assured, has been accurately translated, but it turns out that the paper is actually a confession.

The two are sentenced to 33 years in a hideous prison ruefully described by its inmates as the "Brokedown Palace." They sleep on a bamboo mat on the floor in a crowded room. They have to earn their food by cutting grass, which they must do by sitting on the ground and breaking the blades of grass off with their fingers. Insects are an ever-present problem, and Darlene develops an infection after a cockroach crawls into her ear.

This movie is a stark reminder that Americans traveling abroad should not expect to find American-style justice if they get into trouble. The story is partly based on true experiences.

After watching this movie, discuss the following questions:

1. Would U.S. police use similar or different tactics in a situation like this?

2. Would the outcome have been different if the adversary system were used in Thailand?

3. Would the prison sentence have been different in the United States? After all, drug smuggling is a serious offense in this country.

4. What does this movie have to say about prison conditions? Chapter 9 discusses often-controversial prison litigation reform in the United States. Were the prison conditions depicted in this movie similar to or different from those in the United States (before federal court orders regarding conditions in state prisons)?

counteract the powers of other actors. If the judge appears to be biased or unfair, the jury has the ability to disregard the judge and reach a fair verdict. The opposite is also true: If the judge believes that the jury has acted improperly, then he or she has the power to set aside the jury verdict and order a new trial. By diffusing power, the adversary system builds in a series of checks and balances aimed at curbing abuse or misuse of the judicial process.

Neutral and Passive Decision Maker

The adversary system relies on a neutral and passive decision maker to decide disputes between the opposing parties. The judge serves as a neutral arbitrator, ensuring that each side battles within the established rules. Moreover, the judge is expected to be passive, letting the opposing attorneys call the witnesses and ask them questions. The underlying theory of the adversary system is that neutral, passive decision makers are essential to ensure evenhanded consideration of each case and to convince society that the judicial system is trustworthy and legitimate. When a decision maker becomes an active questioner or otherwise participates in a case, he or she is likely to be perceived as biased rather than neutral. Thus, neutrality and passivity help ensure the reality and appearance of fairness.

To function effectively, neutral and passive decision makers must be free from outside pressures. Thus, judicial independence is a crucial normative value of the

U.S. legal system. Judicial independence has been defined as "judges who are free from potential domination of other branches of government" (*United States v. Will* 1980). For that reason, the judiciary is institutionally separate from the legislative and executive branches of government. In addition, it is difficult to remove judges from office. Federal judges and some state judges are appointed for life. Even where judges are elected, they serve for relatively long periods, typically 10 years. Institutional separation and long terms of office are designed to shield the judge from elected officials or the voting public, no matter how unpopular his or her decisions may be.

Whereas Americans view threats to judicial independence in terms of freedom from political interference from other branches of government, in some nations judicial independence is threatened by intimidation and violence. The experiences of these countries are a constant reminder that law, courts, and the judicial process do not always work as they do in the United States. (See Law and Popular Culture: *Brokedown Palace*.)

THE MAJOR COMPONENTS OF U.S. LAW

U.S. law consists of numerous bits and pieces. It is helpful to view these bits and pieces as consisting of eight components (Table 2.3). These components summarize the way lawyers and judges think about the law. In a basic sense, they are the intellectual sources of the law (although technically speaking "sources of law" has a more narrow meaning). These components are interrelated and overlapping (Jacob 1995). For example, criminal law is found at all levels of government, it is found in several sources, and it can be both substantive and procedural.

Federalism

One of the most important features of the U.S. Constitution is **federalism**, which divides power between the national government and state governments. Federalism produces a complicated and somewhat intricate distribution of powers among the three levels of government—federal, state, and local. The end result is a fragmented set of laws.

Federal law, the term popularly used to refer to the law of the national government, is the only law that applies throughout the entire nation. Thus, the law passed by the U.S. Congress that prohibits robbing a federal bank is the same in California as it is in Florida. (California and Florida laws on robbery, on the other hand, differ.)

State law occupies the next level. Each state enacts laws that govern the citizens within its territory. State law is extensive and diverse. The clearest illustration of this is Nevada: Faced with a rather desolate environment, the state survives and prospers by creating legal loopholes not found in most other states. Gambling is legal, divorces are easy to obtain, and laws prohibiting prostitution are a local option. Less well known is the fact that the Nevada legislature has made the state a good place to do business by making it easy for businesses to incorporate and levying low taxes on inventories. In less dramatic ways, laws between the other states differ as well. State laws, however, are subordinate to federal law.

TABLE 2.3	Major Components of U.S. Law	

Federalism

National

State

Local

Multiple Sources of Law

Constitutions

Statutes

Administrative regulations

Judicial Decisions

Case law

Public Law and Private Law

International

Administrative

Constitutional

Criminal

Tort

Contract

Property

Inheritance

Civil Law and Criminal Law

Divorce

Felony

Property

Misdemeanor

**Substantive Law and
Procedural Law**

Rights

Responsibilities

Due process of law

Rules of court

Remedies

Judgment

Monetary damages

Injunction

Doctrines of Access

Jurisdiction

Standing to sue

Political question

Justiciability

Class action

Local law constitutes the lowest level of law. These laws emanate from numerous local governments. State governments are unitary; that is, all power rests at the state level. But state governments create local units of government such as cities, counties, school boards, and park districts. Each local unit is empowered to enact rules and regulations that have the force of law within their limited geographical or functional area.

Multiple Sources of Law

Federal, state, and local laws are found in multiple sources. Depending on the issue, the applicable rules of law may be found in constitutions, statutes, administrative regulations, or court decisions.

Constitutions   Within the hierarchy of law, constitutions occupy the top rung. A **constitution** is the document that establishes the underlying principles and general laws of a nation or a state. The U.S. Constitution is the fundamental law of the land. All other laws—federal, state, or local—are subsidiary. Similarly, each state has a constitution that is the "supreme law of the state." State courts may use their state constitution to invalidate the actions of state legislators, governors, or administrators.

Constitutions define the powers that each branch of government may exercise. For instance, Article III of the U.S. Constitution creates the federal judiciary. Constitutions also limit governmental power. Some limitations take the form of prohibitions. Thus, Article I, Section 9, states, "No Bill of Attainder or ex post facto law shall be passed." Other limitations take the form of specific rights granted to citizens. The clearest example is the first ten amendments to the Constitution, known collectively as the **Bill of Rights**. For example, the First Amendment begins, "Congress shall make no law respecting an establishment of religion, or prohibiting the free exercise thereof...."

State constitutions also contain bills of rights, many of which are modeled after their national counterpart.

Constitutions also specify how governmental officials will be selected. The U.S. Constitution provides that federal judges shall be nominated by the president, be confirmed by the Senate, and serve for "good behavior." Similarly, state constitutions specify that state judges will be selected by election, appointment, or merit.

Statutes   The second rung of law consists of **statutes**. Laws enacted by federal and state legislatures are usually referred to as statutory law. The statutory law enacted by local units of government is commonly called a municipal ordinance.

Until the latter part of the nineteenth century, U.S. legislatures played a subsidiary role in the formulation of law. It was American courts, for example, that developed almost all rules of law governing industrial accidents. About the time of World War I, however, state legislatures began to pass workmen's compensation laws, which effectively shifted the locus of lawmaking from the judiciary to the legislatures (Friedman 1984). Similar shifts from judge-made to legislatively enacted laws have occurred in most other areas as well.

One reason for the growing importance of legislatively enacted statutes was the conservative nature of the common law. In the realm of private property, American judges placed great emphasis on the common-law concept of economic laissez-faire (Abraham 1993)—that is, minimal government interference. With the twentieth-century rise of the modern state, legislative bodies began to place greater emphasis on broader definitions of the public interest, changing some of the age-old concepts of the common law in the process. The growth of statutory law also reflected the new types of problems facing a rapidly industrializing society. Questions of how to protect the interests of workers and consumers were much broader in scope than those typically handled by the courts. It took decades for the common law to develop and refine legal rights and obligations, but the growing needs of an increasingly complex society could not afford the luxury of such a lengthy time frame. Legislators could enact laws that were not only much broader in scope than those adopted by judges but also more precise and detailed. Thus, a great deal of law today is statutory.

Administrative Regulations   The third rung of American law consists of **administrative regulations**. Legislative bodies delegate rule-making authority to a host of governmental bureaucracies variously called agencies, boards, bureaus, commissions, or departments. At all levels of government—federal, state, and local—administrative agencies are authorized to issue specific rules and regulations consistent with the general principles specified in the statute or municipal ordinance. The Internal Revenue Service (IRS), by rule, decides what constitutes a legitimate deduction. State boards, by rule, set standards for nursing homes. Local zoning boards, by rule, decide where restaurants may be built.

Administrative regulations are the newest, fastest-growing, and least understood source of law. The rules and regulations promulgated by governmental agencies are extensive. The federal bureaucracy alone issues thousands of rules each year. Law professor Kenneth Culp Davis once calculated that after 25 years of publishing the actions of federal agencies, the *Federal Register* already occupied more library shelf space than all the laws passed by Congress since it first met in 1789 (Carter 1988).

Controlling the actions and inactions of unelected bureaucrats has always been a major concern in the United States. Besides the substantive laws promulgated by administrative agencies, there are also rules and regulations relating to procedure. **Administrative law** concerns the duties and proper running of an administrative agency. At the federal level, some principal statutes governing procedure are the Freedom of Information Act, the Privacy Act, and the Administrative Procedure Act. At the state level, one also finds an extensive body of administrative law governing state administrative agencies.

Judicial Decisions

Appellate court decisions also remain an important source of law. According to the common-law tradition, courts do not make law; they merely find it. (Table 2.4 shows how to locate court decisions.) But this myth, convenient as it was for earlier generations, cannot mask the fact that courts do make law. This tradition nonetheless suggests a basic difference between legislative and judicial bodies: Legislative bodies are free to pass laws boldly and openly. Moreover, their rules are general and all encompassing. Courts make law more timidly, on a piecemeal basis, and operate much more narrowly. To paraphrase law professor Lawrence Friedman (1984), legislatures make law wholesale, whereas courts make it retail.

TABLE 2.4	How to Read a Legal Citation for a Supreme Court Case
This Cite	**Means**
Bush v. Gore, 531 U.S. 98 (2000)	Volume 531 of the *United States Supreme Court Reports*, page 98. Case decided in 2000.

Supreme Court opinions can also be found online at:
  http://www.supremecourtus.gov/opinions/info_opinions.html

  http://www.findlaw.com/casecode/supreme.html
  Findlaw.com has an entire section devoted to the United States Supreme Court.

  http://www.law.cornell.edu/supct/index.html
  The Legal Information Institute provides access to many court opinions and other legal information. It is maintained by Cornell Law School.

Although U.S. law today is primarily statutory and administrative, vestiges of judge-made law persist. The law governing personal injury (tort law) remains principally judge-made law, as do procedural matters such as rules of evidence and doctrines of access. The major influence of case law, however, is seen in interpreting the law of other sources. The Constitution is a remarkably short document, consisting of only some 4,300 words, and it is full of generalizations such as "due process of law," "equal protection of the laws," "unreasonable searches and seizures," and "commerce among the several states." The authors of the Constitution left later generations to flesh out the operating details of government. Supreme Court decisions have been primarily responsible for adapting constitutional provisions to changing circumstances. Through an extensive body of case law, the Court has supplied specific meaning to these often-vague phrases. For that reason, the Court has often been termed an ongoing constitutional convention.

Case law is highly important in determining the meaning of other sources of law as well. Statutes, for example, address the future in general and flexible language. The interpretations that courts provide can either expand or contract the statute's meaning. No lawyer is comfortable with his or her interpretation of a statute or an administrative regulation without first checking to see how the courts have interpreted it.

Public and Private Law

U.S. law also draws a distinction between public law and private law. **Public law** directly involves government. One branch of public law is international law, which is the customary law that applies to the relationships and interactions between countries. Other branches relate to the operations of government itself—the most prominent examples being administrative law and constitutional law. Yet other branches of public law spell out the rights and duties of citizens vis-à-vis the government. Criminal law, for example, specifies public wrongs that will be punished, and tax laws delineate how much money a citizen is required to pay the government.

Private law governs relationships between private citizens and falls into several major divisions. **Tort** law involves the legal wrong done to another person. Suits over injuries suffered during automobile accidents are prime examples of tort law. When lawyers speak of an **injury**, they do not necessarily mean a physical injury. Rather, the term has a broader meaning, including any wrong, hurt, or damage done to a person's rights, body, reputation, or property. Another type of private law covers **contracts**, or agreements between two or more persons involving a promise (termed a consideration in legal proceedings). Insurance policies and bank loans are considered contracts. **Property**, which centers on the ownership of things, is another division of private law. Property is usually divided into **real property** (land and things attached to it) and **personal property** (everything else). Personal property can range from stocks and patents to automobiles and the right to use a famous person's name. Property received from a person who has died is governed by laws on inheritance. The best-known application is a **will**, a written document telling how a person's property should be distributed after his or her death.

Private law is, of course, not really private. In fact, it relies heavily on the actions of public agencies. Legislatures often pass laws governing private actions. Thus, legislatures enact **divorce** laws allowing couples to legally end their marriages. More-over, breaches of private law can be brought to a public forum (the courts) for resolu-tion. Such governmental activities indicate that private law involves public policy of great importance to the rest of society. Yet the laws dealing with torts, contracts, prop-erty, inheritance, and divorce are considered private because they do not depend pri-marily on public agencies for their application and execution. Private law, therefore, grants individuals, businesses, and groups considerable discretion in shaping general provisions that govern the specific details of private life.

Civil and Criminal Law

The distinction between civil and criminal law is a fundamental one in U.S. law. A civil suit involves a dispute between private parties. (In this context, the government is con-sidered a private party. Thus, governments can sue civilly to recover back taxes, gain title to private property needed to build a park, or stop a chemical plant from dischar-ging noxious liquids into a river.) Although virtually all disputes are potentially disrup-tive to the overall functioning of society, some are viewed as so disruptive that civil remedies are not enough. A criminal suit, therefore, involves a violation of a govern-ment's penal laws.

One difference between civil and criminal law centers on who has been harmed. Civil suits are considered private matters, whereas criminal violations involve public wrongs, which harm all society. A second difference involves prosecution. Unlike the civil law, in which private parties file suit in court, violations of public wrongs are pros-ecuted by the state. The types of remedies also differ. In civil law, the injured party receives compensation. Violators of the criminal law, however, are punished by being sentenced to prison, ordered to pay a fine, or placed on probation. The type of sen-tence provides one basis for distinguishing between types of criminal violations. In general, a **felony** is a more serious criminal offense and thus results in a more severe sentence than a **misdemeanor**, which is a lesser crime usually punishable by no more than one year in prison.

Civil and criminal are distinct bodies of law, yet they can overlap. A single event may involve both a civil and a criminal lawsuit. Consider, for example, a drunk driver who kills someone. The driver can be prosecuted criminally for the offense of driving under the influence of intoxicating liquor and can also be sued civilly for the tort of wrongful death.

Substantive and Procedural Law

Law can also be characterized as either substantive or procedural. **Substantive law** is the part of the law that defines rights. When lawyers speak of "a right," they mean a legal right, not a moral one. Thus, a legal **right** is the ability to control certain actions of other people. Every right has a corresponding duty. For example, pedestrians have the right to cross the street on a green light, and drivers have a duty to avoid hitting those people with their cars. In creating rights (and their corresponding duties), the law defines the legal relationship between the citizen and the state, and among citizens themselves. Prime examples of substantive law include contracts, property, torts, wills, and criminal prohibitions.

Procedural law, on the other hand, establishes the methods of enforcing legal rights. Thus, it involves the rules by which cases are heard and decided. To ensure the fair and orderly administration of justice, procedural laws govern the conduct of cases in court. **Rules of court** specify how lawsuits are filed, procedures for exchanging information prior to trial, applicable time frames, and the like. Similarly, the rules of evidence seek to ensure that decisions will be made on the basis of reliable facts. The main rules of court governing the federal judiciary are the Federal Rules of Civil, Criminal, and Appellate Procedure and the Federal Rules of Evidence. These rules also serve as models for many states. In addition, most courts have adopted local rules of court governing specific practices in their locality.

The principal purpose of procedural law is to protect against arbitrary actions. Quite literally, procedural law prevents people from taking the law into their own hands. In U.S. law, the most essential procedures are captured by the phrase "due process of law," which is specified in several places in the U.S. Constitution and most state constitutions as well. No exact definition of due process applies to all situations, but the central idea of **due process of law** is fundamental fairness: A person should always have notice and a real chance to present his or her side in a legal dispute, and no law or governmental procedure should be arbitrary or unfair. Procedural due process should not be confused with substantive due process which is the idea within American jurisprudence that there are certain rights derived from the Constitution that must be carefully protected from government intervention and regulation.

Remedies

A court's official decision about the rights and claims of each side in a lawsuit is known as a **judgment**. If the plaintiff wins, the judgment also contains a **remedy**, which is the relief granted by the court. The remedies granted depend on whether the case involves law or equity.

Under common law, some litigants seek a **declaratory judgment**, which is a judicial determination of the legal rights of the parties. At other times, litigants seek the **restitution** of goods that they are rightfully entitled to. But mainly parties suing under common law seek monetary damages, that is, money that a court orders paid to a person who has suffered a legal injury. The two principal types of **monetary damages** in American law are (1) **compensatory damages**—payments for the actual harm suffered, which may include medical bills, lost income, or pain and suffering—and (2) **punitive damages**—monies awarded to a person who has been harmed in a particularly malicious or willful way. The latter are not related to the actual cost of the injury or the harm suffered but are designed to serve as a warning to keep that sort of act from happening again. (Thus, both the civil and the criminal law involve deterrence.)

Under equity, litigants seek a very different type of remedy called an **injunction**, which is a court order that requires a person to take an action or to refrain from taking action. For example, a court may issue an injunction prohibiting a company from

DEBATING LAW, COURTS, AND POLITICS

▪ The Law and Politics of Constitutional Interpretation

How to apply the Constitution, a document written 220 years ago, to contemporary society is not readily apparent. Although the Supreme Court is the principal governmental institution interpreting the Constitution, the other political branches are involved, too.

Disagreements over how to interpret the Constitution are most immediately debates about law. And constitutional law is extensive and complex. The Supreme Court decisions have weaved layers of concepts and subconcepts around the bare bones of the Constitution. But debates over how to interpret the Constitution are also political. Each side uses the language of law in ways to send political messages. In the public forum, questions about how to interpret the Constitution are typically reduced to a few bumper sticker slogans like following precedent, strict constructionism, and judicial activism.

Following Versus Overturning Precedent

Precedent figures prominently in court opinions explaining why the decision reached was the proper one. But understanding Supreme Court decision making solely on the basis of precedent has serious limitations. For one, many of the cases reaching the Supreme Court have precedent on both sides. Moreover, a Supreme Court justice's propensity to support precedent is often directly proportional to whether he or she agrees with the holding in the previous case. For example, President Bush's two nominees—Roberts and Alito—at times vote to overturn precedent.

Judicial Activism Versus Judicial Restraint

Discussions about "judicial activism" focus on law-making authority. There has been a long-standing debate on when unelected federal judges should overturn laws passed by popularly elected legislatures. A judiciary that always deferred to the actions of popularly elected officials, however, would be separate but hardly independent.

Today, judicial activism has become a code phrase used by conservatives to condemn a range of Supreme Court decisions they oppose. In this vocabulary, activism is simply another word for liberal. But others point to conservative judicial activism. Thus, to some political scientists, the doctrine of judicial restraint is nothing more than a rhetorical cover for deferring to policies that a justice happens to agree with (Keck 2005; Segal and Spaeth 1993).

Strict Constructionism Versus a Living Document

Allegations that courts, particularly the Supreme Court, have overstepped their proper role of interpreting law (rather than making it) are often linked with charges that justices are interpreting the Constitution in the wrong way.

Two broad schools of thought exist. Strict constructionists argue that the Constitution should be interpreted on the basis of what the text meant at the time it was adopted. This means that the Court should not create rights not in the Constitution. Justice Scalia is the leader of this school of thought on the current Court. To others, the Constitution should not be frozen in time but instead should be viewed as a living document. The job of the justices, therefore, is to discern the purposes behind constitutional provisions and apply them to modern circumstances that the founders never envisioned. Justice Breyer is most often identified with this view on the current Court.

The Language of Law and the Rhetoric of Politics

Public discourse about interpreting the Constitution illustrates the creative dynamics of law and politics in the United States. Clearly, the law matters. All participants speak of the Constitution with reverence and acknowledge its importance. The complexity and subtlety of interpreting the Constitution get swept aside in the rhetoric of politics, however. Bumper sticker slogans are not much help in deciding how the often-vague phrases of the nation's founding law have meaning in solving contemporary problems. But these political slogans underscore the importance of debating the political and legal meaning of the Constitution.

The tension between law and politics is often expressed in the legal terms of reason and result. The reasoning about law is what both sides point to. But, in turn, each side thinks the reasoning will lead to a result that they desire. In turn, the public respects the Court because they perceive it to be a legal institution, but at the same time they care about the outcomes of court decisions.

DEBATING LAW, COURTS, AND POLITICS

■ Deepwater Horizon Litigation Scorecard

Thousands of lawsuits have been filed in the wake of the Deepwater Horizon oil spill. Here we present a scorecard of the types of claims and lawsuits that have been filed and might be filed in state or federal court. The many types of lawsuits generate different political dynamics for changing the law after the Gulf of Mexico oil spill. The laws covering oil spills illustrate a major point in Chapter 2: there is uncertainty in interpreting emerging areas of law. Lawyers and litigants differ as to the application of existing laws meaning that judges (and sometimes juries) have discretionary choices. The laws covering the oil spill also reinforce the central theme of this book (discussed in Chapter 1): how discretionary choices that are made within the legal system that are influenced by the other branches of government.

Personal Injury and Wrongful Death Claims

The survivors of the eleven men who perished the night that the Deepwater Horizon exploded, plus any workers who were injured, can file suit in federal court under the Jones Act of 1920 which was passed in response to the sinking of the Titanic. They can recover monetary damages if they can prove that BP or any other defendants were negligent (Chapter 11 discusses the disputes between defendants over liability). However, the amount of monetary damages that can be recovered are significantly less than if the accident occurred on land and the lawsuit were filed under state tort law. The survivors may collect economic damages such as loss of future earnings but not punitive damages or loss of society (an obscure term used in Maritime law which roughly translates to relationships with wife, children, etc.). These limits are but one indication that maritime law is archaic and often bears little resemblance to domestic law (Sloan July 26, 2010). The widows of several of those killed in the explosion have petitioned Congress to change the law retroactively but these efforts are opposed by the oil and natural gas industry as well as cruise ship lines (NBC August 2, 2010).

Clean-Up Costs

The oil spill fouled water, beaches and marshes from Florida to Texas. Under the Oil Pollution Act of 1990, BP and other defendants are responsible for paying all clean-up costs. In the immediate aftermath of the oil spill, BP directly paid many of the clean-up costs by hiring workers, unemployed fishermen, etc. But the law also requires the defendants to pay the expenses incurred by state, local and federal governments during the clean-up. How much is owed may prove to be contentious. After Hurricane Katrina, local and state governments sued FEMA over disputes about damages and there is every reason to expect similar lawsuits after the oil spill. In anticipation of potential lawsuits, some local governments retained lawyers who are experts in oil and natural gas litigation (Rainey August 4, 2010).

Restoring the Environment

The Oil Pollution Act of 1990 also requires the rehabilitation of damaged natural resources. The varying standards that courts have used in calculating the "reasonable cost of those damages" (Findley and Farber 2008) plus the likelihood that experts hired by the government are likely to differ with experts paid for by BP about the extent of damages suggests that litigation extending over many years is quite possible.

Liability

In the wake of the 1989 Exxon Valdez oil spill in Alaska, Congress passed the Oil Pollution Act of 1990. A key provision of this law limits liability to "total of all removal costs" of the spill plus $75 million. (Chapter 12 examines the Supreme Court's decision in the Exxon Valdez case.) There is, however, a very important exception to the $75 million cap—it does not apply to claims under state law or maritime law. As a result most victims and potential plaintiffs will sue BP and other parties in state courts where the liability limits do not apply. To critics the oil spill exposed major limitations in this legislative scheme. One was the small cap on liability. A number of Congressional Democrats introduced the Big Oil Prevention Liability Act of 2010 to raise the cap to $10 billion but it is opposed by many Republicans.

Investor Stockholder Lawsuits

The oil spill was a disaster not only for the Gulf Coast but also for the economic value of BP. BP, one of the

(continued)

largest companies in the world, saw its stock prices plummet by a third. Investors in the United States (Baldas June 9, 2010) as well as overseas (Baldas June 10, 2010) have filed suit in various federal courts alleging BP made false and misleading statements concerning its safety protocols and safety record, thus harming investors. Large pension funds are also expected to file suit.

Mounting Fines

BP and its corporate partners potentially face billions of dollars in fines (separate from paying for clean-up of the oil and compensating those who suffered economic losses). The Clean Water Act sets a civil fine of $1,100 for every barrel of oil released in a spill. However, if the government can prove that the spill was the result of "gross negligence" the fine becomes a criminal fine and the amount jumps to $4,300 per barrel. Moreover, if the

government determines that the spill was the result of negligence, royalties at the rate of 18.75% would also be due. The worst case scenario is BP would owe $18 billion in fines (Hargreaves 2010). But no one knows how many gallons were spilled. Given the potentially large amount of dollars involved, litigation over how much is owed in fines will likely last years.

$20 Billion Compensation Fund

The oil spill negatively affected the livelihood of a wide variety of people who live on the coast or make their living indirectly through commerce related to the coast. BP created a compensation fund administered by Kenneth Feinberg as an alternative to filing suit. The Compensation fund is the largest ever Alternative Dispute Resolution program. How well it works in practice is examined in Chapter 10.

---

dumping industrial wastes into a river. To qualify for an injunction, the suing party must demonstrate to the court that it will suffer irreparable damages—in this case, that dumping will pollute an important natural resource. Consistent with the preventive and remedial heritage of equity, a judge may issue a preliminary or temporary injunction to stabilize an emergency situation. A permanent injunction is granted only after the issues have been fully tried in court. An injunction is very powerful and can be enforced by the contempt power of the court. Thus, a person who violates an injunction can be fined or sent to jail.

Doctrines of Access

Although the judiciary is a passive institution (as discussed in Chapter 1), that does not mean that judges are required to hear all disputes brought to them. An extensive body of law, much of it created by courts themselves, governs which types of cases courts may (or may not) decide. These **doctrines of access** partially control the flow of cases into the judiciary. Thus, before a judge decides a case, several criteria must be met: (1) The court must have jurisdiction over the matter; (2) the controversy must be a real dispute, rather than a hypothetical one; and (3) the plaintiff must have standing to sue. In ordinary lawsuits, those requirements are well understood and have changed little over the last decades. In policy lawsuits, however, the requirements may change. Much like the bellows of an accordion, Supreme Court decisions have alternately expanded and contracted access to the courts. In 1946, the Court ruled that how legislative bodies create representative districts was a political question and, therefore, not subject to federal judicial scrutiny (*Colegrove v. Green*). That view was later changed in *Baker v. Carr* (1962), which resulted in a series of decisions on legislative reapportionment.

INTERPRETING THE LAW

Citizens typically misunderstand how judges and lawyers interpret and apply the eight components of law described in the previous section. The public perceives law as a vast collection of unconnected rules that law students must memorize. From that grows a common myth that the law is a series of precisely written and readily located rules that cover all eventualities. In essence, the legal system is perceived as a giant computer, programmed to deal with the problems that litigants feed into it, with lawyers and judges merely serving as technicians. That view is misleading. As Justice Douglas once wrote: "The law is not a series of calculating machines where definitions and answers come tumbling out when the right levers are pushed" (1948, 104). Law is more than a collection of rules and regulations; it is a process of reasoning about the meaning of words, concepts, and doctrines. The craft of U.S. judges and lawyers lies in the common-law heritage, which provides a way of interpreting and applying the vast array of legal rules.

The legal reasoning employed by lawyers and judges to make sense out of the words found in constitutions, statutes, administrative regulations, and previous court decisions is vastly different from the thought process employed by average citizens in conducting their lives. As Chapter 5 will show, a good deal of law school focuses on teaching students to think like lawyers. On the basis of that specialized, professional training, lawyers on opposite sides of a case are often able to agree on what the law means; those cases rarely go to court. Many areas of the law are settled, and the rules are widely known. There the doctrine of precedent provides an excellent guide to how judges will decide. But, in emerging areas of the law, there is flux. Thus, lawyers for the opposing parties cite law that supports their conflicting positions; these cases are very likely to end up in court. Here the law presents the necessity for discretionary choices by legal actors such as judges, lawyers, and juries. Debating Law, Courts, and Politics: Deepwater Horizon Scorecard examines these discretionary choices following the well disaster. The three following situations illustrate the interplay between legal reasoning and discretionary choices in the law.

The Meaning of Words

One type of discretionary choice involves interpreting the meaning of words. The law attempts to be precise, but it doesn't always succeed. The U.S. Constitution uses phrases such as "equal protection," "due process," and "interstate commerce." Legislatures likewise pass statutes—and judges write decisions—employing vague language. Thus, the law is unpredictable at times because of what law professor Zechariah Chafee calls "the disorderly conduct of words" (1941, 381).

Words and statements that seem clear in the abstract have different meanings to different people because of their varied experiences (Carter 1988). The words of the law do not have fixed meanings; rather, words are interpreted within specific contexts.

Nowhere is the debate over the meaning of the words more important than in interpreting the U.S. Constitution. Debating Law, Courts, and Politics: The Law and Politics of Constitutional Interpretation examines the interplay between law and politics in interpreting the Constitution.

Conflicting Laws

A second type of discretionary choice involves conflicting laws. Given the large and ever-growing volume of law, it is not uncommon to find one law conflicting with another. Thus, judges must decide that one law is applicable but another is not, or they must find a way to reconcile the conflicting laws.

Some of the most controversial Supreme Court decisions stem from clashing provisions of the Bill of Rights. The First Amendment states, "Congress shall make no law respecting an establishment of religion, or prohibiting the free exercise thereof...." Those provisions have sparked controversy over matters such as posting the Ten Commandments in public spaces. (See Case Close-Up: *Salazar v. Buono* 2010.) Faced with controversies like those, the Court typically attempts to balance the competing principles. In *Lemon v. Kurtzman* (1971), the Court offered the following three-prong test to strike a balance between establishment of religion and freedom of religion:

- The state law must have a secular rather than a religious purpose.
- The primary effect of the law neither advances nor inhibits religion.
- State programs aiding religious schools must avoid excessive entanglement of religion and the state.

But tests like this one are not necessarily accepted by all justices. Indeed, several conservative justices have attacked the standards set forth in *Lemon*, preferring an accommodationist approach, which stresses that the First Amendment prohibition of an establishment of religion should not be allowed to interfere with another First Amendment freedom—freedom of religion (*Lee v. Weisman* 1992; *Santa Fe v. Doe* 2000).

Gaps in the Law

The third type of discretionary choice involves gaps in the law. Even though American law is voluminous, situations still arise that were not contemplated by previous law writers. Judges, legislatures, and bureaucrats, therefore, are called on to apply existing law to new situations. Consider two examples drawn from the field of biology—the AIDS epidemic and DNA evidence. These developments have, in turn, produced considerable changes in the law.

A century ago, Oliver Wendell Holmes (1897) observed: "It is revolting to have no better reason for a rule of law than that it was so laid down in the time of Henry IV

CASE CLOSE-UP

■ *Salazar v. Buono* (2010)

Does a Cross in a National Park in the Mojave Desert Violate the First Amendment Ban on an Establishment of Religion?

The first amendment to the United States Constitution begins, "Congress shall make no law respecting an establishment of religion…" To some this phrase means a ban on the official establishment of a religion by the government, but to others it simply means that government may not endorse a particular religion. It is hard to imagine a more remote and unpopulated place than the 1.6 million acre Mojave National Preserve in California generating a controversy over the government's establishment of religion, but that is exactly what happened when Frank Buono filed a lawsuit arguing that a Christian cross that had been placed in the park in 1934 by the Veterans of Foreign Wars (VFW) violated the establishment clause of the first amendment. The case had all the elements of law and politics even before a lawsuit was filed. In 1999 a citizen asked the National Park Service if they could erect a Buddhist memorial at the same location. The National Pak Service denied this request and stated that it planned to remove the existing cross. That action resulted in Congress passing a law that prohibited using governmental funds to remove the cross—religion and politics at work. In 2001 Mr. Buono filed a lawsuit. Further complicating matters, in 2002, Congress passed a new law designating the cross as a national monument. Clearly the courts were going to have to sort this out.

The lawsuit would take a decade to make its way to the Supreme Court. And when it ultimately did what started out as a fairly simple question of did the National Park Service having a cross displayed on public land violate the establishment clause had become a complex set of questions, including whether Mr. Buono even had standing to sue (he did). *Salazar v. Buono* 2010 generated six different opinions, a 5-4 majority opinion by Justice Anthony Kennedy, concurring opinions by Chief Justice Roberts, Justice Alito and Justice Scalia, and dissenting opinions by Justice Stevens and Breyer. The first court to hear the case (a Federal district court) concluded that presence of the Cross violated the establishment clause. After the court's decision Congress passed a second law that banned the use of federal funds to

remove the cross. Then while the National Park Service was appealing the ruling Congress passed another law that instructed the Secretary of the Interior to transfer the land on which the cross is located to the VFW. The second court to hear the case (the Ninth Circuit Court of Appeals) agreed with the District Court's conclusion and ordered the cross removed. The National Park Service did not appeal the ruling and continued taking steps to transfer the land to the VFW as instructed by Congress. Mr. Buono filed a second lawsuit in response arguing that the land transfer was an attempt to avoid complying with the decision of the District and Appeals Courts. The District Court and Circuit agreed with Mr. Buono and the case was ultimately appealed by Secretary of the Interior to the U.S. Supreme Court. The Supreme Court, with Justice Kennedy writing for the majority, concluded that the government had not acted improperly and that the presence of the cross did not constitute an "establishment of religion," at one point writing "the Constitution does not oblige government to avoid any public acknowledgement of religion's role in society." But Justice Stevens argued in dissent that Congress's efforts to create a land swap may have constituted the establishment of religion because they were undertaken with the motivation to protect the display of a religious symbol. He wrote that "The cross is not a universal symbol of sacrifice. It is the symbol of one particular sacrifice, and that sacrifice carries deeply significant meaning for those who adhere to the Christian faith." At the end of the day the relationship between government and religious symbols appeared as confusing as it has been since the founding of this country, with the Court divided 5-4 about the main issues.

Salazar is not the first establishment clause case and it most certainly will not be the last. For years, social conservatives have opposed prohibitions of prayer in public schools and at school events such as football games. More recently, conservatives have fought the teaching of evolution in high school biology classes. Is it permissible to label evolution as a theory, or are efforts to include alternative views such as "intelligent design" merely efforts to introduce religion into the curriculum? And during the holiday season, efforts to erect nativity scenes and place other religious symbols on public grounds have often provoked lawsuits from groups such

(continued)

as the American Civil Liberties Union, charging that such efforts are banned by the Establishment Clause. At the center of virtually all these cases since *Lemon v. Kurtzman* (1971) has been the "endorsement test." Which as later adapted by Justice Sandra Day O'Connor essentially asks whether a reasonable person would consider the religious display as being "endorsed by the government." If not, then the display can remain; if so, then

it has to be removed. The Court concluded in this case that it did not. But what do you think? Can the government erect or maintain any religious symbol without violating the basic principle of the First Amendment that "Congress shall make no law..." *Salazar* illustrates the complex interactions between the branches of government and brings into stark relief the tension between religion and politics in the United States.

[1367–1413]. It is still more revolting if the grounds upon which it was laid down have vanished long since, and the rule simply persists from blind imitation of the past." More recently, Gary Will (1984) made the same point: "Fitting the law to a technologically dynamic society often is like fitting trousers to a 10-year-old: adjustments are constantly needed." Unlike tailoring trousers to fit a growing body, however, adjusting the law to meet new problems in society invariably produces choices, and choices lead to conflicts. The discretionary choices courts make about these matters are integral to the political dynamics of the nation.

CONCLUSION

The Supreme Court's split decisions on cases involving religious symbols on government property typically draw immediate praise or condemnation. Although Salazar went largely unnoticed by the public, Court watchers saw it as another example of the Court's uncertainty about how to interpret what the First Amendment really means regarding the establishment of religion only that much harder.

Split decisions on religious symbols enable each side in the larger debate over religion in the public square to claim a measure of victory. They also serve to guarantee that all sides will file future lawsuits to test the limits. But as Justice O'Connor said in a previous First Amendment case dealing with the public display of the Ten Commandments, "...we do not count heads before enforcing the First Amendment." The current approach, she believes, has worked well both to protect religious liberties and to avoid religious violence, a fact of life in some nations of the world such as Nigeria (Chapter 7), Saudi Arabia (Chapter 8), India (Chapter 10), Israel (Chapter 11), and Russia (Chapter 12).

U.S. law is complex, fragmented, and voluminous. Compared with law in most other nations of the world, it is also unique. Americans have a hard time understanding other legal systems; the opposite is equally true. Thus, one way to focus on the unique features of the American legal system is to view it from the perspective of an observer from a non-common-law country.

Foreign observers are bewildered by the diversity of American law. In their countries, a single body of law governs the entire nation, and one set of courts applies that law. Thus, if you ask a German lawyer to define theft, he (rarely she) can quite definitively cite the meaning that applies throughout the nation. In sharp contrast, the

United States has 51 separate and distinct legal systems, each with its own body of laws and its own court structure. Thus, if you ask a U.S. lawyer to define theft, she or he can provide only a general statement qualified by the observation that the specifics vary depending on the jurisdiction you are talking about.

Foreign observers also find the common-law heritage strikingly different from their legal traditions. The common law and the civil law differ in fundamental ways. The growing interface between technology and the law also underscores the importance of a global approach to law and courts. In recent years, computer users in foreign nations, many from Asia, have mounted concerted virus attacks upon U.S. websites. Users in Russia have developed computer software that allegedly attempts to circumvent copyright law. On the other side of the equation, many European nations, Germany for one, objected to the Communications Decency Act because material that was legal in the host country might violate U.S. law. Whereas Anglo-American judges played a major role in developing the law, their European counterparts did not. Under European civil law, the laws (termed codes) were passed by the legislature, and past judicial decisions are simply not important. Another fundamental difference is in how the law is interpreted. Anglo-American judges look to past court decisions, but their European counterparts interpret the law on the basis of the intent of the framers and not on the basis of precedent.

Foreign visitors are also unaccustomed to the American adversary system. In civil legal systems, trials differ greatly from those of our adversary system. The most striking contrasts occur in criminal prosecutions. Police investigations of criminal violations are supervised by a judicial official or an impartial state's attorney in some countries. A dossier is prepared that contains the evidence gathered in the case and the formal charges drafted by the prosecutor. In essence, the trial is a public verification of the dossier, not an independent inquiry. As a result, trials are often brief, lasting no more than a half hour. Witnesses do not recite what they know about the case but are simply asked to verify the statement they previously gave to the police or the prosecutor. Moreover, judges are active participants who search for the truth of what happened independent of the opposing parties' contentions. The judges, not the lawyers, interrogate witnesses. Indeed, lawyers cannot directly cross-examine witnesses.

Foreign observers also find the U.S. jury system hard to understand. The reaction of one German law student is typical: After a morning spent observing a trial in an American courthouse, her voice reflected absolute disbelief as she asked, "How can you allow twelve people, totally unlearned in the law, to make such important decisions? In my country, we only allow highly trained and very experienced judges to decide guilt or innocence in a murder case." That question highlights the fundamentally different role of lay jurors in the two legal systems. Under European civil law, jurors are used only in the most serious criminal cases, and their functions are very different from those of their common-law counterparts. They are not independent decision makers but, rather, members of a mixed tribunal composed of several judges and several lay citizens. Sitting together, judges and jurors preside over the trial, discuss the law and the evidence together, and render a joint decision.

Finally, foreign visitors are struck by the unique role of the Supreme Court in U.S. politics. All legal systems have a high court that has the final say in interpreting the law. In most nations, the high court decides rather narrow legal issues. In the United States, the courts do more. They are also called on to decide some of the most pressing social and political issues of the day. Foreign observers would be particularly struck by the amount of media attention to the judiciary. In their countries, court decisions are rarely controversial.

CRITICAL THINKING QUESTIONS

1. All the non-English-speaking industrial democracies use the civil law. Would you prefer being tried in one of those countries or in a nation that uses the common law?

2. One of the biggest societal changes in recent years has been the rapid expansion of computer technology. How have legislatures and courts responded to perceived misuse of the Internet, such as computer crimes and pornography?

3. How do the multiple components of law lead to conflicts in law? How do policy leaders use the multiple components of law to support or defend their positions on controversial legal issues?

4. What components of law are most likely to be criticized in public debates? Which components are least likely to be criticized?

Search Terms

common law   Islamic law   law

Useful URLs

http://memory.loc.gov/ammem/amlaw/lawhome.html
A Century of Law Making for the New Nation, from the Library of Congress, provides ready access to all the important legal documents involved in creating the United States.

http://www.nolo.com/glossary.cfm
Nolo.com provides "Everybody's Legal Dictionary."

http://www.aallnet.org
American Association of Law Libraries site provides easy access to case law.

http://www.duhaime.org/law_museum/hallfame.aspx
The Law's Hall of Fame includes biographical information about some of the most important people in the history of law.

REFERENCES

Abraham, Henry. 1993. *The Judicial Process: An Introductory Analysis of the Courts of the United States, England, and France.* 6th ed. New York: Oxford University Press.

American Bar Association. 1970. *Standards Relating to the Prosecution Function and the Defense Function.* Chicago: American Bar Association.

Baldas, Tresa, June 9, 2010. "BP Shareholders Bring Latest Class Action in Western Louisiana." *Wall Street Journal.*

Baldas, Tresa, June 10, 2010. "Class Action Seeks to United Angry BP Investors around the World." *Wall Street Journal.*

BBC News. 2001. "France Upholds 'Right Not to Be Born.'" July 13.

Blumenthal, Ralph. 2005. "Split Rulings on Displays Draw Praise and Dismay." *New York Times*, June 28, p. A17.

Carter, Lief. 1988. *Reason in Law*. 3d ed. Glenview, Ill.: Scott, Foresman.

Chafee, Zechariah. 1941. "The Disorderly Conduct of Words." *Columbia Law Review* 41: 381.

Cole, George, Stanislaw Frankowski, and Marc Gertz. 1987. *Major Criminal Justice Systems: A Comparative Survey*. 2d ed. Newbury Park, Calif.: Sage.

David, René, and John Brierley. 1978. *Major Legal Systems in the World Today*. New York: Free Press.

Douglas, William O. 1948. "Dissent: A Safeguard of Democracy." *Journal of the American Judicature Society* 32: 104–105.

"Driver Blamed for Diana Death Crash." 1999. *Bath Chronicle*, September 4.

Ducat, Craig. 1988. "Precedent." *The Guide to American Law*. St. Paul, Minn.: West.

Fairchild, Erika, and Harry Dammer. 2006. *Comparative Criminal Justice Systems*. 3d ed. Belmont, Calif.: Wadsworth.

Friedman, Lawrence. 1984. *American Law: An Introduction*. New York: Norton.

Hargreaves, Steve. July 20, 2010. "BP's fine could hit the Billions." CNN.

Hirsch, Masako. July 22, 1010 "Oil Spill Cleanup Causes Mess of its Own." TPSI.

Holmes, Oliver Wendell. 1897. Address reprinted 1920 in *Collected Legal Papers*. Boston: Harcourt.

Jacob, Herbert. 1995. *Law and Politics in the United States*. 2d ed. New York: Harper Collins.

Keck, Thomas M. 2005. *The Most Activist Supreme Court in History: The Road to Modern Judicial Conservatism*. Chicago: University of Chicago Press.

Landsman, Stephan. 1988. *Readings on Adversarial Justice: The American Approach to Adjudication*. St. Paul, Minn.: West.

Levi, Edward. 1948. *An Introduction to Legal Reasoning*. Chicago: University of Chicago Press.

Mauro, Tony. 1997. "The French Legal System." *USA Today*, September 4.

Oran, Daniel, and Mark Tosti. 2000. *Law Dictionary for Non-Lawyers*. 2d ed. St. Paul, Minn.: West.

Post, C. Gordon. 1963. *An Introduction to the Law*. Englewood Cliffs, New Jersey: Prentice Hall.

Rainey, Richard. August 4, 2010. "Jefferson Parish Looking for a Lawyer for BP Litigation." *Times Picayune*.

Reichel, Philip L. 2001. *Comparative Criminal Justice Systems: A Topical Approach*. 3d ed. Upper Saddle River, New Jersey: Prentice Hall.

"Seeking Justice." August 2, 2010 NBC Nightly News.

Segal, Jeffrey, and Harold J. Spaeth. 1993. *The Supreme Court and the Attitudinal Model*. New York: Cambridge University Press.

Sloan, Karen. July 26, 2010. "Maritime law is all at Sea." *National Law Journal*.

Tyler, Tom. 1988. "What Is Procedural Justice? Criteria Used by Citizens to Assess the Fairness of Legal Procedures." *Law and Society Review* 22: 103–135.

Walker, Samuel. 2006. *Sense and Nonsense About Crime and Drugs: A Policy Guide*. 6th ed. Belmont, Calif.: Wadsworth.

Will, Gary. 1984. "Fitting Laws to Dynamic Society Likened to Trousers on 10-Year-Old." *Lawrence Journal-World*, January 22, p. 6.

FOR FURTHER READING

Adams, David, ed. 2005. *Philosophical Problems in the Law*. 4th ed. Belmont, Calif.: Wadsworth.

Altman, Andrew. 2001. *Arguing About the Law: An Introduction to Legal Philosophy*. 2d ed. Belmont, Calif.: Wadsworth.

Berkman, Michael, and Eric Plutzer. 2011. *Evolution, Creationism, and the Battle to Control America's Classrooms*. West Nyack, New York: Cambridge University Press.

Debs, Richard. 2010. *Islamic Law and Civil Code: The Law of Property in Egypt*. New York: Columbia University Press.

Drakeman, Donald. 2009. *Church, State, and Original Intent*. New York: Cambridge.

Dwyer, Daisy Hilse. 1990. *Law and Islam in the Middle East*. New York: Bergin and Garvey.

Feinberg, Joel, and Jules Coleman. 2008. *Philosophy of Law*. 8th ed. Belmont, Calif.: Wadsworth.

Friedman, Lawrence. 1990. *The Republic of Choice: Law, Authority, and Culture*. Cambridge, Mass.: Harvard University Press.

Ginsburg, Tom. 2003. *Judicial Review in New Democracies: Constitutional Courts in Asian Cases*. Cambridge, U.K.: Cambridge University Press.

Hall, Kermit, and Peter Karsten. 2008. *The Magic Mirror: Law in American History*. New York: Oxford University Press.

Koopmans, Tim. 2003. *Courts and Political Institutions*. Cambridge, U.K.: Cambridge University Press.

Merryman, John. 1985. *The Civil Law Tradition*. 2d ed. Stanford, Calif.: Stanford University Press.

Russell, Peter, and David O'Brien, eds. 2001. *Judicial Independence in the Age of Democracy: Critical Perspectives from Around the World*. Charlottesville, Virginia: University of Virginia Press.

Schneier, Edward. 2006. *Crafting Constitutional Democracies: The Politics of Institutional Design*. Lanham, Maryland: Rowman & Littlefield.

Schubert, Frank. 2012. *Introduction to Law and the Legal System*, 10th ed. Belmont, Calif.: Cengage

Sloan, Lawrence. 2010. The Language of Statutes: Laws and Their Interpretations. Chicago, Ill.: University of Chicago Press.

FEDERAL COURTS

U. S. COURTHOUSE

JOHN H. WOOD, JR.
UNITED STATES COURTHOUSE
655 E. DURANGO

The U.S. courthouse in San Antonio, Texas, is named in honor of the first federal judge assassinated in the twentieth century. Although the design of this building is modern, the federal courts date to 1789.

David Neubauer

It is "not in the public interest" for Arizona to enforce parts of its recently passed law aimed at curbing illegal immigration wrote U.S. District Court judge Susan Bolton. Arizona has been frustrated by the seeming inability of the federal government to curb illegal immigration, estimated at nearly 11 million, so they decided to take action. The Arizona law was particularly far reaching, authorizing law enforcement officials to arrest and detain any person if they had reasonable suspicion that the person was in the country illegally. The Ninth Circuit U.S. Court of Appeals upheld the District Court injunction preventing the enforcement of the law. But in August 2010 Arizona's Governor, Jan Brewer, on behalf of Arizona, filed a 41 page appeal with the United States Supreme Court. In the appeal Arizona argued, "it is widely recognized that the federal immigration laws are not adequately enforced" and that "this broken system leaves the people and government of Arizona to bear a disproportionate share of the burden for a national problem" (Vicini 2011). Arizona's request falls under the Court's discretionary jurisdiction so now the Supreme Court will decide whether to hear the case. Should states have the power to enforce federal law in this way? How the Supreme Court will rule on this and other state immigration laws remains to be seen, but a previous case frames the battle lines. During oral argument over an earlier Arizona law that imposes hash penalties on businesses that hire illegal immigrants, Justice Scalia said such state laws were a necessary response to federal inaction. Justice Breyer countered that the federal law had struck a careful balance between enforcing immigration laws and avoiding employment discrimination, a balance that the Arizona law undermined (Liptak 2010).

The numerous immigration cases being head in virtually every part of the country is but the latest illustration of a major part of U.S. history: the federal courts have been a major factor in deciding the balance between state and national power in a federated nation. Not surprisingly some have argued then and now that the federal courts have too much power. Indeed, the interplay between politics and the judiciary goes back to the early days of the republic. Throughout our history, there have been disputes over which cases federal courts should hear. Indeed, the Founding Fathers were deeply divided over creating any federal courts besides the U.S. Supreme Court. The principal tasks of this chapter, therefore, are to explain the organization of U.S. courts and to discuss how the current federal judicial structure—district courts, appellate courts, and the U.S. Supreme Court—is a product of 200 years of political controversy and compromise about the proper role of the federal judiciary. The remainder of the chapter focuses on the three-tier system of federal courts, specialized courts, and the administrative structure. Finally, a discussion of the contemporary debate over how many cases are too many for the federal courts to handle will illustrate that the controversies continue.

PRINCIPLES OF COURT ORGANIZATION

The U.S. court system is complicated and technical. Even lawyers who use the courts regularly sometimes find the details of court organization confusing. Court nomenclature includes many shorthand phrases that mean something to those who work in the courts daily but can be quite bewildering to the outsider who tries to read the words in their literal sense. Learning the language of courts is like learning any foreign language—some of it can come only from experience. Before exploring the specifics of federal and state courts, this section will discuss the basic principles of court organization. Three concepts—jurisdiction, the dual court system, and trial versus appellate courts—underlie the structure of the American judiciary.

Jurisdiction

Court structure is largely determined by limitations on the types of cases a court may hear and decide. **Jurisdiction** is the power of a court to decide a dispute. A court's jurisdiction can be further subdivided into geographical, subject matter, and hierarchical jurisdiction.

Geographical Jurisdiction   Courts are authorized to hear and decide disputes arising within a specified geographical jurisdiction. Thus, a California court ordinarily has no jurisdiction to try a person accused of committing a crime in Oregon. Courts' geographical boundaries typically follow the lines of other governmental bodies such as cities, counties, or states.

Two principal complications arise from geographical jurisdiction. First, events that occur on or near the border of different courts may lead to a dispute over which court has jurisdiction. If the law of the two jurisdictions differs significantly, then determination of which law applies can have important consequences for the outcome of the case. Second, a person accused of committing a crime in one state may, for whatever reason (flight or happenstance), be in another state when he or she is arrested. **Extradition** involves the surrender by one state (or country) of an individual accused of a crime outside its own territory and within the territorial jurisdiction of the other. If an American fugitive has fled to a foreign nation, then the U.S. secretary of state will request the return of the accused under the terms of the extradition treaty the United States has with that country. (A few nations do not have such treaties.)

Subject Matter Jurisdiction   Court structure is also determined by subject matter jurisdiction. Trial courts of limited jurisdiction are restricted to hearing only a limited category of cases, typically misdemeanors and civil suits involving small sums of money (termed small claims). U.S. bankruptcy courts, for example, are restricted to hearing bankruptcy cases. State courts typically include traffic courts and juvenile courts, both of which are examples of subject matter jurisdiction. Trial courts of general jurisdiction are empowered to hear all other types of cases within the jurisdictional area. In state court systems (discussed in Chapter 4), the county trial court fits here.

Hierarchical Jurisdiction   This subdivision refers to differences in the courts' functions and responsibilities. Original jurisdiction means that a court has the authority to try a case and decide it. Appellate jurisdiction means that a court has the power to review cases that have already been decided by another court. Trial courts are primarily courts of original jurisdiction, but they occasionally have limited appellate jurisdiction, for example, when a trial court hears appeals from lower trial courts (such as mayor's courts or a justice of the peace court). Appellate courts often have a very limited original jurisdiction. The U.S. Supreme Court has original jurisdiction involving disputes between states, and state supreme courts have original jurisdiction in matters involving disbarment of lawyers.

Dual Court System

America has a **dual court system**: one national court system and separate court systems in each of the 50 states, plus the District of Columbia and the U.S. territories. The result is more than 51 separate court systems. You will find federal courts in every state and territory of the union. Furthermore, a federal court in Alabama operates in essentially the same way as its counterpart in Wyoming. However, the structural uniformity does not mean that actual practices are identical. On the contrary, these courts exhibit important variations in how they interpret and apply the law—an

FIGURE **3.1**
The Court Systems of the United States and the Routes of Appeal

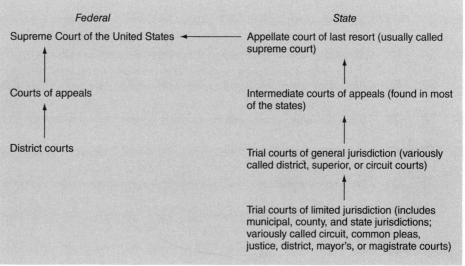

indication of the federal courts' heritage of independence, decentralization, and individualism. Figure 3.1 shows the ordering of cases in the dual court system. The division of responsibilities is not as clear-cut as it looks, however. State and federal courts share some judicial powers. Some acts, such as selling drugs or robbing banks, are crimes under federal law and under the laws of most states, which means that the accused could be tried in either a federal or a state court. Furthermore, litigants in state court may appeal to the U.S. Supreme Court, a federal court.

Trial and Appellate Courts

The third concept embodied in the American court system is the relationship between trial and appellate courts. Virtually all cases, whether civil or criminal, begin in the **trial court**. In a criminal case, the trial court arraigns the defendant, sets bail, conducts a trial (or takes a guilty plea), and, if the defendant is found guilty, imposes sentence. In a civil case, the trial court operates in much the same fashion, ensuring that each party is properly informed of the complaint, supervising pretrial procedures, and conducting a trial or accepting an out-of-court settlement. Because only trial courts hear disputes over facts, witnesses appear only in trial courts. Trial courts are considered finders of fact, and the decision of a judge (or a jury) about a factual dispute normally cannot be appealed.

The losing party in the trial court generally has the right to request an appellate court to review the case. The primary function of the **appellate court** is to ensure that the trial court correctly interpreted and applied the law. In performing that function, appellate courts perform another important function: They re-examine old rules, devise new ones, and interpret unclear language of past court decisions or statutes.

Appellate and trial courts operate very differently, because their roles are not the same. In appellate courts, no witnesses are heard, no trials are conducted, and juries are never used. Moreover, instead of a single judge deciding (as in trial courts), a group of judges makes appellate court decisions, typically a three-judge panel but there may be as many as 28 judges, as in the U.S. Court of Appeals for the Ninth Circuit. In addition, appellate judges often provide written reasons justifying their decisions; trial court judges rarely write opinions.

The principal difference between a trial and an appeal is that a trial centers on determining the facts, whereas an appeal focuses on correctly interpreting the law. This distinction is not absolute, however. Fact finding in the trial courts is guided by law, and appellate courts are sensitive to the facts of a case.

THE HISTORY OF THE FEDERAL COURTS

The organization of the federal judiciary has been a major political issue for more than 200 years. The current structure of district courts, courts of appeals, and the U.S. Supreme Court reflects a long-standing debate over the organization of U.S. government. Questions about the jurisdiction of the federal courts are not mere details of procedure. Rather, they go to the heart of the federal system of government and affect the allocation of governmental power between the national government and the state governments.

Any study of the federal courts in the twenty-first century must begin with two eighteenth-century landmarks: Article III of the U.S. Constitution and the Judiciary Act of 1789. Although important changes have occurred since, the decisions made at the very beginning of the republic about the nature of the federal judiciary have had a marked impact on contemporary court structure.

The Constitutional Convention

One major weakness of the Articles of Confederation was the absence of a national supreme court to enforce federal law and resolve conflicts and disputes between courts of the different states. Thus, when the delegates gathered at the Constitutional Convention in Philadelphia in 1787, there was widespread agreement that a national judiciary should be established. Early in the convention, a resolution was unanimously adopted that "a national judiciary be established." Considerable disagreement arose, however, on the specific form that the national judiciary should take. Article III was the subject "of more severe criticism and greater apprehension than any other portion of the Constitution" (Warren 1926, 7).

Two schools of thought arose as to whether there should be a federal court system separate from the state systems. Advocates of states' rights (later called Anti-Federalists) feared that a strong national government would weaken individual liberties. More specifically, they saw the creation of separate federal courts as a threat to the power of state courts. As a result, the Anti-Federalists believed that federal law should be adjudicated first by the state courts and that the U.S. Supreme Court should be limited to hearing only appeals from state courts. On the other hand, the

Nationalists (who later called themselves Federalists because they favored ratification of the Constitution) distrusted what they saw as the provincial prejudices of the states and favored a strong national government that could provide economic and political unity for the struggling new nation. As part of that approach, the Nationalists viewed state courts as incapable of developing a uniform body of federal law that would allow businesses to flourish. For those reasons, they backed the creation of lower federal courts.

The conflict between states' rights advocates and Nationalists was resolved by one of the many compromises that characterized the Constitutional Convention. Article I set out the authority of Congress in considerable detail, and Article II described the executive authority, albeit somewhat less specifically. But Article III is brief and sketchy, providing only an outline of a federal judiciary: "The judicial Power of the United States, shall be vested in one Supreme Court, and in such inferior Courts as the Congress may from time to time ordain and establish." The brevity of that provision left Congress with the task of filling in much of the substance of the new judicial system. As one observer of the period commented, "The convention has only crayoned in the outlines. It is left to Congress to fill up and color the canvas" (Goebel 1971, 280).

The Judiciary Act of 1789

Once the Constitution was ratified, action on the federal judiciary came quickly. Indeed, the first bill introduced in the Senate dealt with the unresolved issue of inferior federal courts. The congressional debate included many of the same participants, who repeated all the arguments heard in the judiciary debates at the Constitutional Convention. After extensive debate, Congress passed the Judiciary Act of 1789, which laid the foundation for the current U.S. national judicial system by creating a complex three-tier system of federal courts. At the top was the U.S. Supreme Court, consisting of a chief justice and five associate justices. At the base were 13 district courts, each presided over by a district judge. In the middle was a circuit court in every district, each composed of two Supreme Court justices, who rode the circuit, and one district court judge. Figure 3.2 shows the location of the district and circuit courts in 1789.

The Judiciary Act of 1789 represented a major victory for the Federalists: They were successful in creating separate federal district courts. At the same time, the act was a compromise that allayed some of the Anti-Federalists' fears. In at least three ways, the organization of the federal judiciary supported state interests (Richardson and Vines 1970).

First, the boundaries of the district courts were drawn along state lines; no district encompassed more than one state. Thus, from the outset, the federal judiciary was "state contained." Even though district courts enforced national law, they were organized along local lines with each district court responsible for its own work under minimal supervision.

Second, by custom, the selection process ensured that federal district judges would be residents of their districts. Although nominated by the president, district judges were to be (and are today) local residents, approved by senators from the state, presiding in their home area, and, therefore, subject to the continuing influence of the local social and political environment.

FIGURE 3.2
The Federal Judiciary in 1789

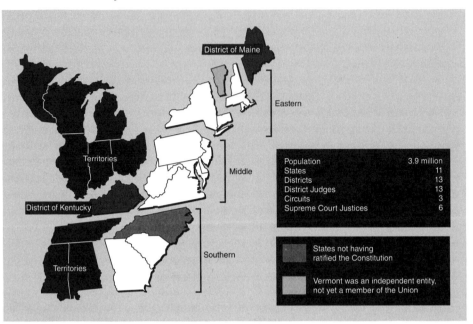

Third, the act gave the lower federal courts only limited jurisdiction. The Federalists wanted the full range of federal jurisdiction granted by the Constitution to be given to district and circuit courts. However, to achieve a lower federal court system, they were forced to reduce that demand greatly. The 1789 act gave the newly created lower courts far less jurisdiction than outlined in the Constitution.

1789 to 1891

The Judiciary Act of 1789 provided only a temporary compromise on the underlying issues between Federalists and Anti-Federalists. The Federalists pushed for expanded powers for the federal judiciary. Those efforts culminated in the passage of the Judiciary Act of 1801, which eliminated circuit riding, created many new judgeships, and greatly extended the jurisdiction of the lower courts. The Federalist victory was short-lived, however. With the election of Thomas Jefferson as president, the Anti-Federalists in Congress quickly repealed the act and returned the federal judiciary to the basic outlines of the previous circuit court system. The 1801 law is best remembered for the resulting lawsuit of *Marbury v. Madison* (1803).

Between 1789 and 1891, observers generally agreed on the inadequacy of the federal judicial system, but the underlying dispute persisted. Congress passed numerous minor bills that modified the system in a piecemeal fashion. Dissatisfaction centered on two principal areas: circuit riding and the appellate court workload.

One of the most pronounced weaknesses of the 1789 judicial structure was circuit riding. The Supreme Court justices, many of them old and ill, faced days of difficult and often impossible travel. In 1838, for example, the nine justices traveled an average of 2,975 miles. Justice McKinley, whose circuit included Alabama, Louisiana, Mississippi, and Arkansas, traveled 10,000 miles a year, yet found it impossible to make it to Little Rock. The justices complained about the intolerable conditions that circuit-riding duties imposed on them—which occasionally included physical danger. In 1888, while traveling in his home state of California, Justice Stephen Field was almost murdered by an unhappy litigant.

Beyond the personal discomforts some justices encountered, the federal judiciary confronted a more systemic problem—mounting caseloads. Initially, the federal judges of the newly created trial courts had relatively little to do because their jurisdiction was very limited. The Supreme Court also had few cases to decide. But the initially sparse workload began to expand as the growth of federal activity, the increase in corporate business, and the expansion of federal jurisdiction by court interpretation created litigation for a court system that was ill equipped to handle it. From the end of the Civil War until 1891, it was not uncommon for a case to wait two or three years after being docketed before it was argued before the Supreme Court. Indeed, by 1890, the high court's docket contained more than 1,800 cases. The essential cause was that the high court had to decide every case appealed to it.

Court of Appeals Act of 1891

Some historians have viewed the creation of the court of appeals as a response to increased federal litigation resulting from a rapidly expanding population and the growth of business following the Civil War. That explanation suggests that the court of appeals appeared on the American scene as a logical, painless, almost automatic response to changing social conditions. Such an assumption is erroneous. The creation of the court of appeals in 1891 was the culmination of "one of the most enduring struggles in American political history" (Richardson and Vines 1970, 26). There was no debate over the difficulties facing the federal court system. All parties in the controversy agreed that the federal judiciary needed relief; what was in dispute, as in 1801, was the nature of the relief. (See Table 3.1.)

To relieve the burden of mounting litigation in the federal courts, the supporters of states' rights wanted to return cases to the state level by reducing the jurisdiction of federal courts. The supporters of national power, on the other hand, argued for expanding the jurisdiction of federal courts by creating a system of federal appellate courts that would take a great deal of the burden off the high court and also allow the trial courts to function as true trial courts.

The landmark Court of Appeals Act of 1891 represented the climactic victory of the Nationalist interests. The law created nine new courts known as circuit courts of appeals. Under this new arrangement, most appeals of trial decisions went to the circuit court of appeals, although, in some instances, the act allowed direct review by the Supreme Court. In short, the creation of the circuit courts of appeals released the high court from hearing many types of petty cases. The high court now had much greater control over its workload and could concentrate on deciding major cases and controversies.

TABLE 3.1	Key Developments in the Federal Judiciary	
U.S. Constitution	1787	Article III creates U.S. Supreme Court and authorizes lower federal courts.
Judiciary Act of 1789	1789	Congress establishes lower federal courts.
Marbury v. Madison	1803	The Supreme Court has the authority to declare an act of Congress unconstitutional.
Courts of Appeals Act	1891	Modern appellate structure created.
Judges Bill	1925	Supreme Court given control over its docket.
Court Packing Plan	1937	FDR's attempt to pack the Court is defeated.
Administrative Office Act	1939	Current administrative structure created, including judicial conference and judicial councils.
Federal Judicial Center	1967	Research and training unit created.
Federal Magistrate Act	1968	Commissioners replaced by U.S. magistrates. (Later, the name is changed to magistrate judges.)
Sentencing Commission	1984	Charged with developing sentencing guidelines.
Congressional Act of 1988	1988	Some mandatory appeals to the Supreme Court are eliminated.
Antiterrorism and Effective Death Penalty Act	1996	Severely limits rights of state prisoners to file habeas corpus petitions in federal court.
USA Patriot Act	2001	Expands the government's ability to gather domestic antiterrorism intelligence, allowing for less court scrutiny and closing some court proceedings to the public.
Military Commissions Act	2006	Restrictions on habeas corpus rights of alien enemy combatants.
Boumediene v. Bush and *Al Odah v. United States*	2008	The Supreme Court invalidated the provision of the Military Trials for Enemy Combatants Act that deprived the detainees of their constitutional right to habeas corpus review in the federal courts.

The period from 1891 to the present has been referred to as principally a "mopping up" operation (Richardson and Vines 1970). In 1925, Congress passed the Judges Bill, which, among other things, gave the Supreme Court much greater control over its docket. In 1988, Congress eliminated even more mandatory appeals to the high court (Chapter 14). The basic structure and jurisdiction of the federal courts have not changed much since the Judges Bill of 1925, which finalized the current organizational arrangement of district courts, courts of appeals, and the Supreme Court. To be sure, there have been some modifications: Several important administrative structures have been created, and from time to time, specialized courts have been added. But those changes are essentially refinements on the eighteenth-century organizational structure first created by the Judiciary Act of 1789 and modified by the Court of Appeals Act of 1891.

UNITED STATES DISTRICT COURTS

The current court system includes 94 U.S. district courts. There is at least one district court in each state and one each in the District of Columbia, Puerto Rico, the Virgin Islands, Guam, and the Northern Mariana Islands. Furthermore, based on the compromise that produced the Judiciary Act of 1789, no district court crosses state lines (see Figure 3.3). Some states have more than one district court: California, New York, and Texas, for instance, each have four. Because district courts often encompass large geographical areas, some hold court in various locations, or divisions. Some districts have only one division; others have as many as eight. In the U.S. territories, the district courts may also be responsible for local and federal matters.

Congress has authorized 677 district court judgeships for the 94 districts. The president nominates district judges, who must be confirmed by the Senate. Once they take the oath of office, they serve during "good behavior," which, for practical purposes, means for life. The number of judgeships in each district depends on the amount of judicial work as well as the political clout of the state's congressional delegation and ranges from 1.5 in sparsely populated eastern Oklahoma to 28 in densely inhabited southern New York (Manhattan) and central California. Judges are assisted by an elaborate supporting cast consisting of clerks, secretaries, law clerks, court reporters, probation officers, pretrial services officers, and U.S. marshals. The larger districts also have a federal public defender. Another important actor at the district court level is the U.S. attorney. There is one U.S. attorney in each district, nominated by the president and confirmed by the Senate, but, unlike the judges, he or she serves at the pleasure of the president. The U.S. attorney and his or her staff prosecute

FIGURE **3.3**
The Federal Judiciary in 2005

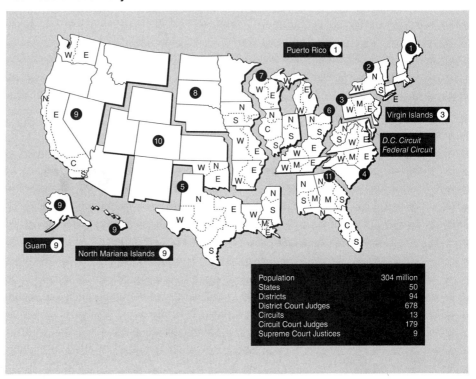

Population	304 million
States	50
Districts	94
District Court Judges	678
Circuits	13
Circuit Court Judges	179
Supreme Court Justices	9

violations of federal law and represent the U.S. government in civil cases, which constitute about one-third of all civil lawsuits.

U.S. district courts also incorporate three special types of courts and/or judges. Depending on the nature of the lawsuit, a case may be decided by three-judge district courts, magistrate judges, or bankruptcy judges. Their roles are discussed next.

Three-Judge District Courts

Three-judge district courts illustrate how public policy issues interact with court structure. Special three-judge district courts were first created early in the twentieth century at a time when federal district judges were striking down state and federal laws regulating social and economic conditions. Congress, deciding to apply some brakes to that process, prohibited single federal judges from making such decisions and provided that when litigants challenged certain types of laws as unconstitutional, they would have to try to persuade three judges, not just one. Through the years, Congress extended the limited jurisdiction of such three-judge courts in statutes covering civil rights and voting rights. Three-judge district courts are created on an ad hoc basis and disbanded after the case has been decided.

For many years, three-judge district courts were a rarity (Burger 1975). The advent of widespread civil rights litigation changed that pattern, however. The decisions of these courts figured prominently in many of the most controversial issues reaching the federal judiciary, such as racial discrimination, reapportionment, and abortion (Carp and Stidham 1990).

The increased use of three-judge courts led critics, such as Chief Justice Warren Burger, to question whether the conditions that led to the enactment of the three-judge court statutes continued to exist. Their principal argument was that this hybrid body made poor use of judicial personnel and review by the court of appeals was readily available. (Wright 1970).

In 1976, in response to calls for complete abolition, Congress greatly restricted the use of three-judge district courts. A three-judge district court can now hear cases only if the litigation involves legislative reapportionment or if the cases are specifically mandated by Congress in legislation such as the 1964 Civil Rights Act or the 1965 Voting Rights Act. (Chapter 14 discusses Supreme Court jurisdiction in these special cases.) This change in jurisdiction has had a dramatic effect. From a high of 320 three-judge district court cases in 1973, the number dropped to just 7 in 2009 (1 reapportionment case and 6 civil rights cases).

United States Magistrate Judges

The work of the district judges is significantly aided by a system of U.S. magistrate judges, who are the federal equivalent of state trial court judges of limited jurisdiction. In passing the Federal Magistrates Act of 1968, Congress sought "to provide a new first echelon of judicial officers in the federal judicial system and to alleviate the increased workload of the United States District Courts" (Puro 1976, 141). But the magistrates were unhappy over their title, and in 1990, Congress responded to their concerns by including the word *judge*; thus, they are now known officially as magistrate judges (Smith 1992).

Magistrate judges are selected by the district court judges. Full-time magistrate judges are appointed for eight-year terms and part-time magistrate judges for four years. They may, however, be removed for "good cause." Except in special circumstances, all must be lawyers and members of the state bar. In 2011, there were a total of 567 magistrate judges, a few of whom are part time.

Magistrate judges play an increasingly important role in helping district court judges dispose of their growing caseloads. In a typical year, for example, they handle almost 1,000,000 matters for the federal courts.

Creation of the office raised several constitutional issues. Although magistrate judges perform quasi-judicial tasks and work within the judicial branch of government, they are not Article III judges. (That is, they are not nominated by the president or confirmed by the Senate and do not serve for life.) The major question is, When does the involvement of a magistrate judge in a case reflect the exercise of judicial power, rather than mere administrative functions? Several Supreme Court decisions limited the powers of the magistrates, holding that only Article III judges were authorized to perform certain judicial functions. In response, Congress passed the 1976 and 1979 Federal Magistrates Acts, which clarified and expanded the scope of the magistrates' power and authority.

Magistrate judges are now authorized to perform a wide variety of duties, such as conducting the preliminary stages of all criminal cases, sentencing misdemeanor offenders, supervising civil discovery, reviewing Social Security disability benefit appeals, and even conducting full civil trials with the consent of the litigants. In short, under specified conditions and controls, magistrate judges may perform virtually all tasks carried out by district court judges, except trying and sentencing felony defendants (Smith 1987).

Bankruptcy Judges

The work of the district judges is also significantly aided by 352 bankruptcy judges. The bankruptcy workload of the district courts is enormous: Historically, well over one million petitions were filed annually. In 2005, however, Congress passed the Bankruptcy Abuse Prevention and Consumer Protection Act in an attempt to limit consumers from filing bankruptcy. The vast majority (97 percent) of those bankruptcy filings are consumers who cannot pay their bills. The others are filed by businesses— big and small. Indeed, companies valued in the billions have declared bankruptcy; obviously, such mega-filings create much more work for the judiciary than a bankruptcy petition filed by an individual consumer.

In an earlier era, district judges delegated the processing of these cases to bankruptcy referees (the title was upgraded to bankruptcy judge in 1973), who were appointed by district court judges for six-year terms. But, by the early 1970s, the continuing increase in bankruptcy filings, pressures from bankruptcy referees, and disagreements between debtors and creditors created pressure for systemic change.

Ultimately, Congress passed the Bankruptcy Reform Act of 1978. Besides changing the substance of bankruptcy law, the new legislation significantly altered court procedures, including (1) requiring bankruptcy cases to be filed in bankruptcy courts rather than in district courts; (2) providing for presidential appointment, with Senate approval, of bankruptcy judges; (3) increasing the term of bankruptcy judges to fourteen years; and (4) expanding the jurisdiction of bankruptcy judges. A system of bankruptcy courts separate from the district courts was seemingly in place, but this new structure provoked strong opposition from some federal judges who had sought to keep bankruptcy judges in a clearly subordinate role (Baum 1998).

The increased power and authority of bankruptcy judges led to legal challenges. In 1982, a deeply divided Supreme Court struck down the law, holding that certain powers granted to bankruptcy judges could be exercised only by Article III judges, who are insulated from political pressures by life tenure and protection from pay cuts (*Northern Pipeline Construction Co. v. Marathon Pipeline Co.* 1982). The Court asked Congress to quickly pass remedial legislation, but a compromise bill was enacted only after two years of stalemate. Bankruptcy judges would remain adjuncts of the district courts, but they would be appointed for 14-year terms by the court of appeals in which the district is located.

In 2005, Congress passed a sweeping new bankruptcy law making it easier for creditors such as credit card companies to collect from debtors. The result was a dramatic drop in filings in 2007 to 800,000. But the national economic downturn a year later has caused filings to skyrocket with almost 1.6 million bankruptcy cases filed in the most recent year.

Caseload of the U.S. District Courts

In the federal system, the U.S. district courts are the federal trial courts of original jurisdiction. Table 3.2 provides an overview of the federal courts' case volume, which is large and growing. In 2009, just over 350,000 criminal and civil cases were filed in the U.S. district courts (not including bankruptcy, misdemeanors, and the like). Those numbers reflect a dramatic increase over the caseload in the 1960s.

The district courts are the trial courts for all major violations of federal criminal law. (Magistrate judges hear minor violations.) For many years, federal prosecutions remained fairly constant (roughly 30,000 per year), only to shoot up dramatically beginning in 1980—partly because of a dramatic increase in drug prosecutions. In 2009, U.S. attorneys filed 76,655 criminal cases against 97,982 defendants. Criminal cases reached the highest level since 1932, the year before the Prohibition Amendment was repealed. In a major shift, immigration cases (33 percent) now constitute the single largest category of criminal prosecutions, followed by drug violations (22 percent) embezzlement, and fraud.

TABLE 3.2	Case Filings in U.S. Courts, 2009				
	Total	**Criminal**	**Civil**	**Prisoner Petitions**	**Minor Criminal**
Courts of appeals	57,740	13,710	14,716	16,249	n/a
District courts	353,052	76,655	276,397	52,304	n/a
Magistrate judges	982,295	171,226	257,266	22,163	118,510

n/a not applicable.
Source: Data from Administrative Office of the U.S. Courts, *2009 Annual Report of the Director: Judicial Business of the United States Courts* (Washington, D.C.: U.S. Government Printing Office, 2009). The most recent statistics are available at http://www.uscourts.gov/Statistics.aspx.

Although there are almost four times more civil filings than criminal ones, in some districts the number and the complexity of criminal filings limit the ability of the district courts to address promptly the more numerous civil cases. Although only a small percentage of all civil cases are filed in federal courts, those cases typically involve considerably larger sums of money than the cases filed in state court. Federal court jurisdiction deals primarily with questions of federal law, diversity of citizenship, and prisoner petitions.

Federal Questions   Article III provides that federal courts may be given jurisdiction over "Cases, in Law and Equity, arising under this Constitution, the Laws of the United States, and Treaties made, or which shall be made under their authority." Cases that fall under this type of jurisdiction are generally referred to as involving a federal question. Most federal question cases are filed alleging a violation of a congressional statute, principally Social Security, labor, civil rights, truth-in-lending, and antitrust laws.

A major reason for the dramatic increase in the civil caseloads is the passage by Congress of social welfare policies that extend the civil rights and privileges of persons residing in the United States. Thus, the federal trial courts hear a diverse array of federal question cases arising from laws such as the Age Discrimination in Employment Act, the Voting Rights Act, the Family and Medical Leave Act, the Violence Against Women Act, and the Americans with Disabilities Act.

Diversity Jurisdiction   Diversity-of-citizenship cases involve suits between citizens of different states or between a U.S. citizen and a foreign country or citizen. For example, a citizen from California claims to be injured in an automobile accident in Chicago with an Illinois driver and sues in federal court in Illinois, because the parties to the suit were of "diverse citizenship." (However, the injured California driver also has the option of suing in state court in Illinois.) In deciding diversity-of-citizenship cases, federal courts apply state (not federal) law (Sloviter 1992). Overall, diversity cases constitute 35 percent of the civil docket of the district courts, thus making a significant contribution to their workload.

Federal jurisdiction over diversity-of-citizenship cases reflects a debate that began more than 200 years ago and continues today (Curry 2007; Kramer 1990). This jurisdiction was first established by the Judiciary Act of 1789 because of fears that state courts would be biased against out-of-state litigants. According to the Nationalists, only federal courts could be counted on to provide a fair and impartial hearing for disputes between citizens of different states. Through the years, many have questioned whether the conditions that existed in 1789 are relevant to the contemporary necessity for diversity jurisdiction. In particular, the United States has become more centralized and also more homogeneous, thus eliminating the parochial state prejudices that characterized the colonial period. To modern-day critics, diversity jurisdiction unnecessarily adds to the caseload of already-overburdened federal district courts. Furthermore, critics believe that state courts are better equipped to decide these matters, given that most diversity cases involve automobile accidents, which state judges already handle on a day-to-day basis. For those reasons, a majority of federal judges and many legal commentators have called for eliminating, or significantly reducing, federal court jurisdiction in diversity-of-citizenship cases.

But some lawyers remain concerned about local favoritism in state courts. They prefer to retain diversity jurisdiction because in some circumstances it allows them to pick which court, state or federal, will decide the case. A survey of practicing attorneys reported that the choice of courts depends somewhat on how expeditiously a court will be able to process the case, a preference for federal rules of procedure, and a desire to appear before high-quality judges (federal courts are given higher ratings) (Bumiller 1980–1981).

In 1988, Congress added another chapter to the ongoing debate over diversity jurisdiction. In an effort to restrict the types of minor disputes that may be filed in federal court, the amount-in-controversy threshold was raised from $10,000 to $50,000 and later to $75,000. Despite some speculation to the contrary, this change in jurisdictional amount has indeed significantly decreased the number of diversity cases filed in federal courts each year. In Illinois, Indiana, and Nevada (states with many diversity lawsuits), the federal caseload was reduced by half, as had been predicted. But in states such as California and Pennsylvania, the change has had a smaller impact because, even before 1988, the majority of diversity cases involved $50,000 or more in damages (Flango 1991). Overall, total diversity filings in 2009 reached nearly 100,000 and appear to be on the increase.

Prisoner Petitions   An interesting and controversial area of district court jurisdiction involves prisoner petitions. Prisoners incarcerated in either federal or state penitentiaries may file a civil suit in federal court alleging that their rights under federal law are being violated (Neubauer and Fradella 2011). Of the five types of prisoner petitions, the best known is the writ of *habeas corpus* which contends that the prisoners is being illegally held, because they were improperly convicted; for example, they were denied the effective assistance of counsel at trial (discussed further in Chapter 13). Another commonly filed prisoner petition relates to the conditions of confinement; for example, the penitentiary is overcrowded or provides inadequate medical assistance (see Chapter 9).

Petitions from state and federal inmates have increased significantly, from about 3,500 filings in 1960 to more than 52,000 today. Those numbers are being driven by the sharp increase in the prison population. United States magistrate judges hear the vast majority of these prisoner petitions but are limited to making a recommendation to the U.S. district judge (who typically follows the recommendation). Thus, these cases add volume but take little of the district judges' time. In 1996, Congress greatly restricted the number of prisoner petitions that can be filed in federal court.

UNITED STATES COURTS OF APPEALS

In 1891, Congress created the courts of appeals to relieve the Supreme Court from having to hear the growing number of appeals. The courts of appeals are the intermediate appellate courts of the federal system. Originally called circuit courts of appeal, they were renamed and are now officially known as the United States Court of Appeals for the_____Circuit. Eleven of the circuits are identified by number, one is called the D.C. Circuit, and another is called the Federal Circuit. (The latter two are located in Washington, D.C.; see Figure 3.3.) The skyrocketing volume of cases filed in the courts of appeals has prompted a debate over how large circuits can become and still remain effective. (See Debating Law, Courts, and Politics: When Will the Ninth Circuit Be Overturned Next?)

The courts of appeals are staffed by 179 judges nominated by the president and confirmed by the Senate. As with the district courts, the number of judges in each circuit varies—from 6 (First Circuit) to 28 (Ninth Circuit)—depending on the volume and complexity of the caseload. Each circuit has a chief judge (chosen by seniority), who has supervisory responsibilities. Several staff positions aid the judges in conducting the work of the courts of appeals. A circuit executive assists the chief judge in administering the circuit. The clerk's office maintains the records. Each judge is also allowed to hire three law clerks. In addition, each circuit has a central legal staff that screens appeals and drafts memorandum opinions.

In deciding cases, the courts of appeals normally use rotating three-judge panels. Along with active judges in the circuit, these panels may include visiting judges (primarily district judges from the same circuit) and senior judges (who are retired from active service but still participate in cases). By majority vote, all the judges (or a larger subset, such as fifteen in the Ninth Circuit) in the circuit may sit together to decide a case or rehear a case already decided by a panel. Such **en banc** hearings are relatively rare, however; in a typical year, fewer than 100 are held throughout the entire nation.

Caseload of the U.S. Courts of Appeals

The courts of appeals have very limited original jurisdiction in cases coming from some administrative agencies. Thus, their principal responsibility is appellate jurisdiction to review decisions made in some other forum. Congress has granted the courts of appeals jurisdiction over basically two categories of cases: (1) reviews of criminal and civil cases from the district courts, which constitute approximately 90 percent of all filings; and (2) appeals from administrative agencies, such as the Securities and Exchange Commission and the National Labor Relations Board. Over 8,000 administrative agency appeals are filed annually. Because so many of these administrative and regulatory bodies are based in Washington, D.C., the D.C. Circuit Court of Appeals hears an inordinate number of such cases. This court is considered the second most important court in the nation (after the U.S. Supreme Court), because its decisions function as a check on the regulatory agencies' behavior.

In 2007, 57,740 cases were filed in the U.S. courts of appeals. Over the last three decades, the caseload has grown rapidly. This growth has not been uniform, however. Criminal appeals shot up dramatically from 1963 to 1973 but have since leveled off, today constituting 24 percent of all appeals. Thus, the largest increase has been in civil appeals. This increase in caseload has not been matched by an equivalent increase in judgeships, however. In 1960, there were 68 judgeships, compared with 179 today (Administrative Office 2009). As a result, the number of cases heard per panel has steadily increased.

A decision by the court of appeals exhausts the litigant's right to one appeal. Although the losing party may request that the Supreme Court hear its case, such petitions are rarely granted. As a result, the courts of appeals are the "courts of last resort" for virtually all federal litigation. Their decisions end the case; only a very small percentage will be heard by the nation's highest court.

THE UNITED STATES SUPREME COURT

The U.S. Supreme Court is the highest court in the nation. It is composed of nine justices: eight associate justices and one chief justice, who is nominated specifically to that post by the president. Like other judges appointed under Article III of the Constitution, Supreme Court justices are nominated by the president, require confirmation by the Senate, and serve for life.

Cases proceed to the Supreme Court primarily through the **writ of certiorari**, an order to the lower court to send up the case records so the Supreme Court can determine whether the law has been correctly applied. The Court reviews decisions from the U.S. courts of appeals and state appellate courts of last resort. Although the Supreme Court is the only court in the nation to have authority over all 51 separate legal systems, in reality its authority is rather limited.

Caseload of the Supreme Court

With few exceptions, the Court selects which cases it will decide out of the many it is asked to review each year. In deciding to decide, the Court employs the **rule of four**: Four judges must vote to hear a case before it is placed on the docket. As a result, only a small percentage of the requests for appeals are ever granted. By law and custom, a set of requirements must be met before a writ of certiorari (or cert, as it is often called) is granted. In particular, the legal issue must involve a "substantial federal question." That means state court interpretations of state law can be appealed to the Supreme Court only if there is an alleged violation of either federal law or the U.S. Constitution. For example, a suit contending that a state supreme court has misinterpreted the state's divorce law would not be heard because it involves an interpretation of state law and does not raise a federal question. As a result, the vast majority of state cases are never reviewed by the Supreme Court.

Through its discretionary powers to hear appeals, the high court limits itself to deciding about eighty cases a year. The Court does not operate as the court of last resort, attempting to correct errors in every case in the nation, but, rather, marshals its time and energy to decide the most important policy questions of the day (see Chapter 14). The cases granted certiorari reflect conflicting legal doctrines; typically, lower courts have decided similar cases in very different ways. Although the Supreme Court decides only a small fraction of all cases filed in the courts, those decisions set major policy for the entire nation. In this way, the Court's role may be unique when compared with the role of high courts in other countries. (See Courts in Comparative Perspective: The Federal Republic of Germany.)

COURTS IN COMPARATIVE PERSPECTIVE

■ The Federal Republic of Germany

Religious objects may not be hung in school classrooms, decided the nation's highest court—and a southern legislature immediately took action to circumvent the decision. With the exception of a few details, the scenario seems straight out of a chapter in American politics. But, in this case, the religious object was a crucifix, and the legislature was the state of Bavaria in southern Germany. The Constitutional Court of Germany had held that crucifixes violate the religious freedom enshrined in the German constitution. The legislature in predominantly Roman Catholic Bavaria promptly passed a new law requiring crucifixes in classrooms, pointing to the history and cultural character of Bavaria ("Bavarian Law …" 1995). This decision highlights important issues in a nation where law has been autonomous and seldom intruded into politics.

As Western Europe's richest and most populous nation (82 million), Germany remains a key member of the continent's economic, political, and defense organizations. With the advent of the Cold War, two German states were formed in 1949: the western Federal Republic of Germany (FRG) and the eastern German Democratic Republic (GDR). The decline of the USSR and the end of the Cold War allowed German reunification in 1990.

In Germany, the presidency is largely a ceremonial post, and executive power is concentrated in the hands of the chancellor, who is a party leader elected in the most recent election. Germany has a bicameral legislature: The Federal Assembly, or Bundestag, consists of 669 members elected by popular vote under a system combining direct and proportional representation. The Federal Council, or Bundesrat, has sixty-nine members selected by state governments.

Germany, like the United States, is a federated nation with power divided between the national government and the state governments (called Laenders). How power is divided between national and state governments is fundamentally different in the two countries, however. For example, Germany has no dual court system—the only federal courts are at the national level. Germany also has an extensive series of specialized courts dealing with administration, labor, social security, and taxes.

Germany has a civil legal heritage. Lawyers and judges consider themselves autonomous from politics. Judges are career civil servants—after receiving an undergraduate law degree, they attend a judicial college, and then become career civil servants. Thus, unlike U.S. judges (except for a few at the highest appellate levels), they have not been practicing lawyers.

The German constitution (called the Basic Law) consists of 146 articles, the first 17 of which spell out the rights of German citizens. Some of those rights parallel the U.S. Bill of Rights, including freedom of religion, freedom of speech, and freedom from unreasonable search and seizure. Other rights, however, are different, including the right to "free development of … personality" and the right to choose one's own trade or profession (Dammer and Albanese 2011).

The highest court in Germany is the federal constitutional court (the Bundesverfassungsgericht), which sits in two divisions. The 16 judges are selected by a commission of the two houses of the federal parliament. Party affiliations are apportioned; the court has the reputation of standing above party politics. As in the civil law tradition, dissent is not encouraged. During the court's first 22 years of existence, no dissenting votes were recorded. More recently, though, the internal conflict on the court is apparent, and the writing of dissenting opinions is becoming customary (Blankenburg 1996).

In recent years, decisions made by the German constitutional court have caused ripples in German society, but hardly the contentious waves of protest that often break out in the United States. Among the debated decisions are:

- Same-sex marriages do not violate constitutional provisions protecting marriage and the family (Associated Press 2002).
- Jehovah's Witnesses have the right to be recognized as a religious public body, as do the two main Christian churches ("Jehovah's Witnesses …" 2000).
- Abortion is unconstitutional because it violates the Basic Law's protection of human life (but violators should not be prosecuted) (Kinzer 1993).

Those few examples aside, it remains rare that German courts are called on to decide divisive political and social issues (Kesselman, Krieger, and Joseph 2010). This contrasts sharply with the situation in the United States, where federal courts are involved in so many political and social issues of the day.

SPECIALIZED COURTS

The Judiciary Act of 1789 established the three levels of the federal court system in existence today. The district courts, the courts of appeals, and the Supreme Court handle the bulk of federal litigation and, therefore, are a principal focus of this book. To round out the discussion of the federal judicial system, however, a brief discussion is needed on the several additional courts that Congress has periodically created. These courts are called **specialized federal courts** because they are authorized to hear only a limited range of cases—taxes or patents, for example. They are created for the express purpose of helping administer a specific congressional statute.

The specialized federal courts are summarized in Table 3.3, which highlights two important distinctions. First, most specialized courts have permanent, full-time judges appointed specifically to that court. A few specialized courts, however, temporarily borrow judges from federal district courts or courts of appeals as specific cases arise (Baum 1991).

TABLE 3.3	**Specialized Federal Courts**		
Courts with Permanent Judges			
Court	**Status**	**Level**	**Jurisdiction**
Tax Court	Article I	Trial	Tax disputes
Court of Federal Claims	Article I	Trial	Monetary claims against the federal Government
Court of Veterans Appeal	Article I	Trial	Federal veterans' benefits
Court of International Trade	Article III	Trial	Imports of foreign goods
U.S. Court of Appeals for the Armed Forces	Article I	Appellate	Uniform Code of Military Justice
Court of Appeals for the Federal Circuit	Article III	Appellate	Trademarks, patents, foreign trade, claims against the federal government

Courts with Judges Borrowed from Other Federal Courts		
Court	**Level**	**Jurisdiction**
Alien Terrorist Removal Court	Trial	Decides whether an alien should be deported on the grounds of being an alien terrorist
Foreign Intelligence Surveillance Court	Trial	Electronic surveillance of foreign intelligence agents
Foreign Intelligence Surveillance Court of Review	Appellate	Electronic surveillance of foreign intelligence agents

Source: Adapted from Lawrence Baum, *Specializing the Courts*. Chicago: University of Chicago Press, 2011. For further details on courts visit the web site of the Federal Judicial Center at http://www.fjc.gov/history/home.nsf/page/courts.html

Article I and Article III Status

The second distinction relates to the specialized courts' constitutional status. Judicial bodies established by Congress under Article III are known as **constitutional courts**. The Supreme Court, the courts of appeals, and the district courts are, of course, constitutional courts. Judicial bodies established by Congress under Article I are known as **legislative courts**. Bankruptcy judges and U.S. magistrate judges are examples of legislative courts. The constitutional status of federal courts has important implications for judicial independence. Article III (constitutional court) judges serve for a period of good behavior, which amounts to a lifetime appointment. Article I (legislative court) judges, on the other hand, are appointed for a specific term of office. Moreover, Article III judges are protected against salary reductions while in office. Article I judges enjoy no such constitutional protection. In short, constitutional courts have a greater degree of independence from the other two branches of government.

Many of the specialized federal courts were originally established by Congress as Article I courts. During the 1980s, several of these courts were reorganized, given new names, and "officially transformed into constitutional courts" (Ball 1987, 75). The U.S. Court of Appeals for the Federal Circuit illustrates those developments. It was created in 1982 by combining the existing Court of Claims and the U.S. Court of Customs and Patent Appeals. Today, this specialized court hears cases involving patents, copyrights, trademarks, claims against the U.S. government, and international trade.

Although specialized federal courts are largely unknown to the general public, they are very important to the business community. For example, the Court of Appeals for the Federal Circuit hears high-stakes battles over such issues as government contracts, international trade disputes, and intellectual property. Indeed, for patent lawyers, the court is, in effect, the court of last resort, because the Supreme Court rarely accepts patent cases for review (Schmitt 1993). But their low-profile, specialized nature does not mean they are without political significance. Decisions to create or expand the jurisdiction of specialized federal courts typically have been the product of interest groups trying to secure advantages for themselves. The most prominent of these special interest groups has been the federal government, which has been far more successful than private interest groups. In short, creation and expansion of specialized courts appears to affect the substance of judicial policies and, therefore, needs to be understood in terms of winners and losers (Baum 1991).

Military Justice

In the wake of the terrorist attacks on September 11, 2001, the specialized court that has attracted the most attention involves military justice. The military actions in Afghanistan and Iraq have led to a number of cases that have landed in the courts of military justice.

Military law provides the legal mechanism for controlling the conduct of military personnel. Congress adopted the Uniform Code of Military Justice in 1950, extending significant new due process rights in courts-martial. The law created the Court of Military Appeals, composed of five civilian judges appointed for 15-year terms by the president. The intent was clearly to extend civilian influence to military law. The Military Justice Act of 1968 contributed to the further civilianization of courts-martial. The 1950 code covers criminal acts but also can punish acts that are not criminal for civilians (for example, disrespect of an officer). Moreover, on a military base, military justice applies not only to members of the armed services but also to civilian employees, and it covers acts committed on and off a military base (Sherman 1987).

Like other systems of criminal law, the objective of military justice is to provide a forum for determining guilt or innocence. In addition, courts-martial enforce order and discipline in the military. In the words of the U.S. Army: "The purpose of military law is to promote efficiency and effectiveness in the military establishment, and thereby to strengthen the national security of the United States." Thus, although military justice is not exempt from the Constitution, it is certainly distinctive. Military justice differs from state and federal justice in the following ways:

- The jury is composed of three or five persons.
- The jurors are military personnel.
- The burden of proof is less than that in a civilian court.
- A two-thirds majority is sufficient to convict (as opposed to civilian cases, which require a unanimous vote).
- Convictions are automatically appealed to a higher military court.

Ultimately, the case may be appealed to the U.S. Supreme Court, but such cases are rare.

In recent years, a few high-profile cases have thrust military justice into the news. Following are some of the more prominent cases:

- In 2011 the Army accused a unit of forming a "kill team" that killed Afghan civilians for sport.
- In 2009 Major Hasan was accused of massacring recruits at Ft. Hood.
- Lieutenant Colonel Terrance Lakin was found guilty of failing to follow a lawful order; Lakin contended President Obama was not a legal citizen and therefore could not be commander and chief.

Although military tribunals have low visibility in American society, some of their activities have been dramatized in the media. (See Law and Popular Culture: *A Few Good Men*.)

Enemy Combatants

In response to September 11, the United States invaded Afghanistan, capturing hundreds of persons suspected of being members of the al Qaeda terrorist organization. The military decided that those captured did not qualify as prisoners of war (and therefore they were not subject to the Geneva Convention) but instead would be considered *enemy combatants*. Hundreds were held at the Navy base in Guantanamo Bay, Cuba, because they were not subject to the jurisdiction of the U.S. federal courts

By 2003 the Bush administration decided that these enemy combatants would be tried in military courts, where the proceedings would be secret and the potential punishments could include the death penalty. The government's strategy suffered a major blow in Supreme Court decisions in June 2004. The Court did not immediately confront the president, who faced a major re-election fight in a few months. But the tone and the rationale of the Court's opinions undermined the administration's

LAW AND POPULAR CULTURE

■ *A Few Good Men* (1992)

"You can't handle the truth!" thunders Colonel Nathan Jessup (portrayed by Jack Nicholson), highlighting the fact that "truth" can be a multilayered concept. Jessup is base commander at Guantánamo, Cuba. He is one of the Marines' "few good men" and on the fast track to being promoted to general. His view of truth highlights a clash between the code of the professional soldier and the canons of civilian society. His response also shows that, to some, higher principles should prevail over mundane realities. Corporal Dawson (Wolfgang Bodison) and Private Louden Downey (James Marshall) are charged with killing Willie Santiago, a fellow Marine who is not only disgruntled but wants out of the Marine Corps altogether.

The Judge Advocate General (JAG) appoints Lieutenant Daniel Kaffee (Tom Cruise) to defend the two young Marines. This seems a curious choice, because Kaffee has never tried a case and often boasts that he plea-bargained 44 cases in a row. But this time, two fellow lawyers—Lieutenant Commander JoAnne Galloway (Demi Moore) and Lieutenant Weinberg (Kevin Bacon)—goad Kaffee to probe behind the obvious.

The dramatic action hinges on whether the two young Marines were acting on their own or whether their superiors ordered a Code Red (Marine lingo for severe hazing as a punishment for failure to perform duties). As the investigation proceeds, it becomes obvious that lies (like truth) are multilayered. With but one exception, the top brass is lying. Documents have been forged. And a key witness disappears, only to mysteriously reappear just when the defense seems to have hit rock bottom.

How closely the movie matches reality is impossible to tell, because trials in military court are closed to the public. But it does point to a key tension between military law and broader notions of justice. After World War II, a number of top German officials, military

officers included, were tried for war crimes. The Nuremberg War Trials established the principle that soldiers cannot rely on illegal orders as a defense against wrongdoing. (See the movie *Judgment at Nuremberg* [1961].) Thus, the attempt by the defense to show that Corporal Dawson and Private Downey should be acquitted because they were merely following orders is not legally recognized. If the orders were illegal, they had a duty to refuse to follow them. In the real world, however, low-ranking soldiers like Downey and Dawson are unlikely to be schooled in such legal niceties. In the end, they stand by their principles as proud Marines, whereas those higher up seem to be ethically challenged. The movie is also rife with unethical activity by the lawyers.

After you watch this movie, be prepared to answer the following questions:

1. What image does this movie project about plea bargaining (discussed in Chapter 9)? The case goes to trial, but would the defendants have been better served if they had pled guilty?
2. Defense attorney Daniel Kaffee rejects the plea bargain offered by the prosecutor. Was Kaffee representing the best interests of his clients or only flattering his own ego?
3. What image does this movie project about judicial independence? Would a civilian judge act the same way as does the military judge?
4. How does this military court trial differ from a similar trial in a civilian court? How does this trial differ from trials in other movies?
5. Would the outcome of this trial have been different in a civilian court than in a military court? If so, how and why?
6. What image does this movie project about female lawyers?
7. What image does this movie project of legal ethics?

---

position, declaring that "a state of war is not a blank check for the president" (*Rasul v. Bush* 2004; *Al Odah v. United States* 2005).

The military responded by creating an elaborate system of military tribunals that did not mirror the processes and procedures used in federal courts. Federal district and appellate courts would subsequently disagree about the legality of these military tribunals, setting up another Supreme Court confrontation. The Supreme Court rejected the Bush administration's argument that the president, as commander-in-chief of the military, had the authority to create such military commissions (*Hamdan v. Rumsfeld* 2006).

Up until this point, the debate had largely been between the executive branch and the courts. But following *Hamdan*, Congress became involved and passed the Military Trials for Enemy Combatants Act, which allows the president to identify enemies, imprison them indefinitely, and interrogate them beyond the reach of the full court reviews traditionally afforded criminal defendants and ordinary prisoners. The Supreme Court declared these processes unconstitutional in *Boumediene v. Bush* (2008). As a result, a number of enemy combatants have been released either by order of courts reviewing their detention in Guantanamo Bay.

Where to try defendants held at Guantanamo Bay remains a hotly debated topic. President Obama proposed trying them in federal court in New York City, close to the site of the terrorist attack, but this idea was withdrawn after considerably negative comments.

The issue of enemy combatants is but one example of the debate over the role of courts in the war on terrorism. (See Debating Law, Courts, and Politics: Are the Federal Courts Obstructing the War on Terrorism, or Are They Protecting Civil Liberties?)

Foreign Intelligence Surveillance Court

The Foreign Intelligence Surveillance Court has authority over electronic surveillance of foreign intelligence agents. Because it was created by the Foreign Intelligence Surveillance Act (FISA) it is popularly referred to as the FISA Court. This court has no permanent judges; rather, the chief justice appoints 11 justices who hear requests for warrants as needed. The courtroom is inside the U.S. Department of Justice, and only the judge is allowed to review the requests submitted by the Justice Department. By statute, the judge is authorized to sign a search warrant for electronic eavesdropping based on "clear and convincing evidence," a legal standard that is less stringent than that required for a normal search warrant. The difference in standards means that any evidence gathered by a FISA warrant may not be used in a criminal prosecution.

For years, the work of the FISA Court labored in obscurity (Baum 2011). Indeed, the only visible public role came in year-end reports, which invariably indicated that the court had approved all warrant requests. This lack of public attention changed greatly with the revelation in late 2005 that the National Security Agency (NSA) was conducting warrantless surveillance of domestic phone conversations of suspected foreign terrorist groups like al Qaeda. The Bush administration contended that the president had inherent war powers under the Constitution to order eavesdropping without warrants even though some in Congress disputed this interpretation. In the wake of controversy, a Republican-controlled Congress enacted the Protect America Act of 2007. The law mandated that telecommunications providers assist the government in intercepting international phone calls and e-mails for national security purposes. The law was upheld in 2008 over a Fourth Amendment challenge by a decision of the Foreign Intelligence Surveillance Court of Review, although the decision was not made public until early 2009. That court has appellate review over decisions of the Foreign Intelligence Surveillance Court. The court reasoned that requiring the government to obtain

CASE CLOSE-UP

■ Where to Hear the Deepwater Horizon Lawsuits?

The BP oil spill cast the public light on a little known judicial body called the United States Judicial Panel on Multi-district Litigation (2011). Created in 1968 the panel consists of seven judges appointed by the Chief Justice. The panel meets several times a year to determine whether civil cases filed in different district courts involve common questions of fact or law and therefore should be transferred to one federal district and consolidated. The purpose of this centralization of cases is to avoid duplication of discovery and prevent inconsistent pretrial rulings between courts. The panel is busier than one might expect, deciding over 22,000 civil actions in the most recent year for which statistics are available. These cases rarely make headlines because where these matters are litigated seldom matters. But where the oil spill cases are litigated does matter.

Plaintiff lawyers lobbied hard to have the cases consolidated in New Orleans because it is closest to where the accident occurred and convenient for the plaintiffs. Left unspoken, but present nonetheless is the desire for the plaintiffs to try cases before jurors who were most affected by the spill and therefore most supportive of recovery efforts.

Defense lawyers lobbied hard to have the cases consolidated in Houston because it is where BP maintains its U.S. headquarters and where key witnesses and vital documents are located. Left unspoken, but present nonetheless, was the desire for the defendants to try cases in an area with a long history of supporting the oil and natural gas industry.

The panel met in Boise, Idaho three months after the well explosion amidst an almost carnival atmosphere. Normally attorneys are granted only 20 minutes for arguments but because the oil spill cases are so large the panel allotted an hour. Behind the scenes lawyers argued among themselves over who should argue the cases (thus garnering free publicity useful in attracting clients (Thomas 2010). According to the Los Angeles Times, part of the hearing resembled city boosters promoting the advantages of their city much like competition for hosting the Olympics (Williams 2010).

In a written opinion the panel chose to consolidate the 300 plus cases involving wrongful death and economic and environmental damage in New Orleans because it was the "geographic and psychological center of gravity" for the oil spill. The panel also chose U.S. District Court Judge Carl Barbier to preside over the cases. The Fifth Circuit had earlier refused to ask Barbier to recuse himself from spill-related cases even though he previously owned corporate bonds issued by two of the defendants. To avoid the appearance of a conflict of interest Barbier divested himself of the holdings.

In the end, the importance of appearing to be fair won out. Some of the 23 attorneys who appeared before the panel suggested that sending the cases to the oil-and-gas hub of Houston would appear unfair to the fishermen, property owners, restaurateurs and others suing for spill related economic damages (Anderson 2010).

---

a warrant would impair its ability to gather time-sensitive information, thereby potentially putting national security interests at risk. The opinion concluded by saying that as long as the executive branch has "several layers of serviceable safeguards to protect individuals against unwarranted harms and to minimize incidental intrusions, its efforts to protect national security should not be frustrated by the courts" (*In re Directives Pursuant to Section 105B of the Foreign Intelligence Surveillance Act* 2008, 29).

FEDERAL JUDICIAL ADMINISTRATION

The history of the federal courts suggests a haphazard administrative structure. The roots of the problem can be traced to the nature of the judicial system created by the first Congress.

> From the Judiciary Act of 1789 and subsequent measures pertaining to the structure of the federal judiciary emerged three important characteristics: independence, decentralization, and individualism. These characteristics were particularly apparent in judicial administration. Here, courts in all three tiers enjoyed virtual autonomy. Judges in administrative matters were not only independent of Congress and of the president but of each other as well. (Fish 1973, 7)

In essence, Congress had created a hierarchy of courts that was without direction and without responsibility. "Each judge was left to himself, guided in the administration of his business by his conscience and his temperament" (Frankfurter and Landis 1928, 220).

An important catalyst for administrative reform was Chief Justice William Howard Taft. In 1922, at Taft's urging, Congress expanded the power of the chief justice to assign district judges where they were needed and created the Judicial Conference, an administrative mechanism that provided advice (Stumpf 1988). The changes of the early 1920s were followed by the passage of the Administrative Office Act of 1939, which largely created the current administrative structure of the federal judiciary. This law once more illustrates the interplay between judicial administration and politics. During the mid-1930s, the conservative majority on the Supreme Court declared many pieces of New Deal legislation unconstitutional.

After his re-election in 1936, President Franklin Delano Roosevelt put forth his famous plan to "pack" the Court with additional judges who presumably would rule in favor of congressional legislation that Roosevelt supported. (His proposal never passed.) At the same time, he accused the federal court of administrative inefficiency, a criticism that carried over to the entire federal judiciary. To solve that problem, FDR proposed that a national court administrator be appointed by the chief justice and have absolute authority to manage the judicial system. The judiciary opposed the initial legislation as an attack on its heritage of independence, decentralization, and individualism. But, at the same time, some judges were dissatisfied with the old system of court management because it was managed by the Department of Justice, an executive agency. Thus, a movement arose among federal judges and national court reformers to clean their own house. The result was a compromise plan: The Administrative Office Act of 1939 was the judiciary's substitute for FDR's court bill. The act expanded the responsibilities of the Judicial Conference, created the Administrative Office of the U.S. Courts, and established the judicial councils. Those agencies, along with the office of the chief justice and the more recently created Federal Judicial Center, are the main units involved in administering the federal courts.

Chief Justice

The chief justice is the presiding officer of the Supreme Court and has supervisory authority over the entire federal judicial system. To help fulfill those duties, the chief justice is allotted an extra law clerk and an administrative assistant to help with the administrative tasks both for the Court and for the judicial system as a whole. In his role as head of the federal judiciary, the chief justice is an ex officio member of several important administrative organizations and also appoints people to key administrative posts. Chief Justice Warren Burger (1969–1986) devoted considerable effort to judicial administration. Chief Justice William Rehnquist (1986–2005) often spoke about the need for Congress to increase the number of federal judges, increase the salaries of judges to be competitive with the private practice of law, and reduce the workload of the courts. Chief Justice John Roberts (2005–) appears to act like his predecessor, highlighting the needs of the judiciary but not being particularly outspoken.

Judicial Conference of the United States

The Judicial Conference of the United States is the administrative policy-making organization of the federal judicial system. Its membership consists of the chief justice, the chief judges of each of the courts of appeals, one district judge from each circuit, and the chief judge of the Court of International Trade. The conference meets semiannually for two-day sessions. Because these short meetings are not sufficient to accomplish a great deal, most of the work is done by about twenty-five committees, which consist of judges and a few lawyers who are appointed by the chief justice. In spite of the long hours and unpaid labor, appointments to these committees are coveted as a status symbol through which judges gain esteem among their peers (Fish 1973). The recommendations of the committees set the agenda for the conference.

The Judicial Conference directs the Administrative Office in administering the judiciary budget and makes recommendations to Congress concerning the creation of new judgeships, increases in judicial salaries, and budgets for court operations. The Judicial Conference also plays a major role in the impeachment of federal judges (see Chapter 6). Probably the most important function of the conference is revising the various rules of federal procedure. Proposed changes in the federal rules originate with the Judicial Conference. The Supreme Court can approve, modify, or disapprove those recommendations. Once adopted, the recommendations are transmitted to Congress and automatically become law in ninety days unless Congress acts adversely. In short, the Judicial Conference is a vehicle through which federal judges play a major role in developing policy for the federal judiciary.

Administrative Office of the U.S. Courts

From 1870 to 1939, the U.S. Department of Justice handled the day-to-day administrative tasks of the federal courts. That arrangement generated persistent conflict, because administrative control over the judiciary was in the hands of an executive (that is, a political) agency. Department of Justice field auditors, for example, examined books, records, and accounts and performed "a communication function as well as an investigative one" (Fish 1973, 93). Against that backdrop, the Administrative Office Act of 1939 created the Administrative Office of the U.S. Courts, a judicial agency.

Appointed by the chief justice, the director reports to the Judicial Conference. Acting as the Judicial Conference's official representative in Congress, the Administrative Office's lobbying and liaison responsibilities include presenting the annual budget requests for the federal judiciary, arguing for the need for additional judgeships, and transmitting proposed changes in court rules. The Administrative Office (AO) is also the housekeeping agency of the judiciary, responsible for allotting authorized funds and supervising expenditures. Throughout the year, local federal court staff send the AO a vast array of statistical data on the operations of the federal courts, ranging from the number of filings to the speed of the disposition of cases. The data are

published in several formats and are readily available on the Internet at http://www.
uscourts.gov.

Federal Judicial Center

The Federal Judicial Center, created in 1967, is managed by a director appointed by
its board, which consists of the chief justice, the director of the Administrative Office,
and judges from the U.S. district courts, courts of appeals, and bankruptcy courts

One of the principal activities of the Federal Judicial Center is education and
training of federal judicial personnel, including probation officers, clerks of court,
and pretrial service officers. For example, seminars for newly appointed federal judges
are held whenever there is a sufficient number of judges to justify them. The center
also conducts research on a wide range of topics, including the work of the magistrate
judges, ways of measuring the workload of the courts, and causes of delay.

Judicial Councils

The judicial council (sometimes referred to as the circuit council) is the basic administrative unit of a circuit. Originally, the judicial councils were composed of all the
active-duty judges of the courts of appeals; in effect, the circuit councils consisted of
the courts of appeals sitting en banc but wearing administrative rather than judicial
hats. The judicial councils were restructured and strengthened by congressional legislation in 1981. No longer are all active-duty circuit judges automatically members of
the council; rather, they decide by majority vote who will sit. In addition, half of the
membership of the council consists of district judges.

A judicial council is given sweeping authority to "make all necessary and appropriate
orders for the effective and expeditious administration of justice within its circuit."
Working within that broad mandate, the councils monitor district court caseloads and
judicial assignments. Although the law specifies that "all judicial officers and employees
of the circuit shall promptly carry into effect all orders of the judicial council," their
actual enforcement powers are limited. The major weapons at the councils' disposal are
persuasion, peer group pressure, and publicity directed at the judge or judges who are
reluctant to comply with circuit policy. At times, for example, circuit councils have
ordered that a district judge receive no new cases until his or her docket has been
brought up to date. Judicial councils are also authorized to investigate complaints of
judicial disability or misconduct (a topic probed in greater detail in Chapter 6).

United States Sentencing Commission

The U.S. Sentencing Commission is an independent agency in the judicial branch of
government. The commission was created by the Sentencing Reform Act provisions
of the Comprehensive Crime Control Act of 1984. Its principal purpose is to establish
sentencing policies and practices for the federal courts, including detailed guidelines
prescribing the appropriate form and severity of punishment for offenders convicted
of federal crimes. The development, monitoring, and amendment of the sentencing
guidelines is the centerpiece of the agency's work, but the commission also provides

DEBATING LAW, COURTS, AND POLITICS

■ Are the Federal Courts Obstructing the War on Terrorism, or Are They Protecting Civil Liberties?

The events of September 11, 2001, have forever changed American politics. How best to respond and prevent terrorism has sparked a spirited debate (Gottlieb 2009). Broadly speaking, conservatives believe that the government should be given wide latitude to adjust policy and liberty during time of emergency (Posner and Vermeule 2007; Thornburgh 2005), while liberals argue that amorphous threats are no reason to restrict the rights and privacy of citizens. Amidst these different policy paths the president launched a War on Terrorism that included the creation of a giant new federal bureaucracy—the Department of Homeland Security. Congress passed the Patriot Act, which expanded the powers of federal law enforcement officials to investigate suspected terrorists. The War on Terrorism has also been fought in the nation's courts. Decisions of federal courts have been at the forefront of defining the proper boundaries of the United States in conducting the War on Terrorism. Those decisions have often proven to be controversial, because judges are the ones asked to strike a balance between the legitimate needs of government to provide security and the need to protect the values of individual liberties.

As discussed earlier President Bush' strategy for trying enemy combatants in military courts as opposed to civilian courts suffered numerous setbacks before the Supreme Court. The administration's record is likewise mixed in other legal battles in the War on Terrorism. The Bush administration hailed the conviction of four North African immigrants living in Detroit as a major victory against terrorism. But a year later, the case was dismissed because of prosecutorial misconduct. Moreover, the first Guantanamo detainee Ahmed Khalfan Ghailani, to face a trial in civil court was acquitted of all but one of the hundred counts he faced (Weiser 2010). And the youngest detainee, Omar Khadr who was only 15 when arrested, was allowed to plead guilty and be sent back to Canada within a year (Rosenberg 2010).

Zacarias Moussaoui was the only person indicted in connection with the September 11 terrorist attacks.

The legal proceedings against the suspected twentieth hijacker were particularly lengthy and difficult. At one point, the judge imposed major sanctions on the federal government for its refusal to grant Moussaoui's lawyers access to certain government evidence (but the Fourth Circuit Court of Appeals sided with the Bush administration). Throughout the proceedings, Moussaoui fought with the prosecutors, the judge, and even his own lawyers. Eventually, he pled guilty. In 2006, he was sentenced to life in prison.

The government has won on some occasions, however. In a case pitting free speech against national security, the Supreme Court upheld a federal law that makes it a crime to provide material support to foreign terrorist organizations, even if the help takes the form of training for peacefully resolving conflicts (*Holder v. Humanitarian Law Project* 2010).

These contemporary decisions are consistent with historical patterns. During times of national emergency, courts have been far more lenient in interpreting the scope of government power (Clark 2006: Epstein et al. 2005). During the Civil War, President Lincoln ordered military detention of suspected Confederate sympathizers; during World War I, the government imprisoned leaders who opposed the war; during World War II, the government interned Japanese Americans in concentration camps; and during the Korean conflict, McCarthyism became associated with anticommunist hysteria (Mayer 2002). But, over time, the nation's courts have become less responsive to governmental insistence on providing security and more responsive to claims that individual liberties have been violated.

The "enemy combatant" issue is but the latest dispute over what cases federal courts should, or should not, hear. The actions by Congress to strip the federal courts of jurisdiction over enemy combatants are consistent with the recent efforts by Congress to strip the federal courts of jurisdiction over other controversial matters such as abortion and the death penalty. Rarely has Congress acted to expand the federal courts' jurisdiction.

training; conducts research on sentencing-related issues; and serves as an information resource for Congress, criminal justice practitioners, and the public.

The commission's seven voting members are nominated by the president, confirmed by the Senate, and serve six-year terms; no more than four can be from the same political party. The commission is charged with the ongoing responsibilities of evaluating the effects of the sentencing guidelines on the criminal justice system, recommending to Congress appropriate modifications of substantive criminal law and sentencing procedures, and establishing a research-and-development program on sentencing issues (further examined in Chapter 9).

The Ongoing Federal Courts Caseload Controversy

The emotional battle over whether the federal courts should review the detention status of alien enemy combatants is but the latest example of a long-running battle over what cases should (or should not) be heard in federal court. At first, state courts handled almost all of the nation's judicial business—federal jurisdiction was tightly limited by the Judiciary Act of 1789. But with the onset of the Industrial Revolution, the caseload of the federal courts began to grow. That increase in federal judicial business was accelerated by Prohibition, then by the New Deal, and even further by federal lawmaking often associated with President Johnson's Great Society programs. As stressed throughout this chapter, increasing caseloads have, in turn, prompted changes and additions to the federal judiciary—appellate courts have been added and specialized courts created.

Federal caseload growth, therefore, is nothing new; what is new, however, is the pace of that expansion. For most of U.S. history, the growth in federal cases was gradual. No longer! Over the last thirty years, district court filings have risen by 75 percent; court of appeals cases have increased more than 150 percent. Although this rate of increase is somewhat less than the previous three decades, the absolute numbers are what is important.

Many federal judges believe that the federal courts have too many cases to decide and emphasize that in some districts it is very difficult to bring a civil case to trial because of the press of criminal prosecutions. The judiciary has called for a significant increase in the number of federal judges, but Congress is unlikely to do so because of sharp partisan differences (see Chapter 6). The problem is particularly acute in some metropolitan jurisdictions, where federal judges must postpone civil trials for months and even years to accommodate criminal trial schedules (particularly of major drug dealers) in accordance with the Speedy Trial Act. There are also pressing caseload problems in the five southwestern district courts that border Mexico where drug importation and illegal smuggling cases dominate the court's docket.

Congressional Expansion

Under federalism, one of the powers reserved to the states is the power to regulate persons and property in order to promote the public welfare (commonly referred to as police powers). Based on those police powers, state governments and their local subdivisions pass laws to promote the public health, welfare, and safety. Thus, most crimes are

FIGURE **3.4**
Federal Court Filings and Appeals, 1940–2007

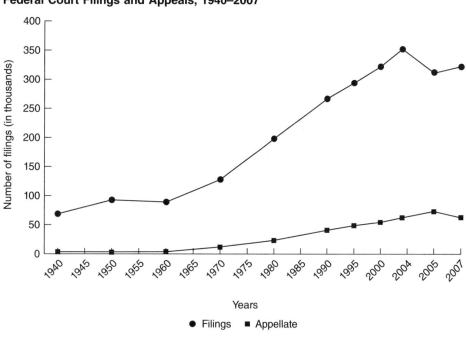

Source: Data from various editions of the *Annual Report of the Director: Judicial Business of the United States* (Washington, D.C.: Government Printing Office).

defined by the states (see Chapter 2). Over the years, Congress has extended federal criminal jurisdiction beyond the basics centering on federal property and interstate commerce. The underlying motivation has been public concerns (some would say public hysteria) about public morality (Meier 1994). Thus, the Mann Act of 1910 prohibited the interstate transportation of prostitutes, the Harrison Act of 1914 outlawed drugs associated with deviants, and the Volstead Act ushered in Prohibition in 1919.

Contemporary demands to expand federal criminal jurisdiction typically reflect contrasting partisan and ideological positions. Conservatives generally favor reducing federal court caseloads but have called for increasing federal criminal jurisdiction to include gang crimes, carjacking, and transferring numerous gun cases from state to federal courts. If these efforts are successful, it is possible that numerous violent offenders who were armed with a weapon will be prosecuted in federal, not state, court.

Democrats oppose such efforts but tend to support expansion of federal criminal law to cover citizens with limited political power. Thus, they favor expanding federal criminal legislation to cover hate crimes, stalking, and violence against women.

Judicial Reduction

Federal judges, whether appointed by Republican or Democratic presidents, almost uniformly oppose the federalization of state crimes (Schwarzer and Wheeler 1994). Chief Justice Rehnquist (1993) decried what he called the near transformation of some federal courts into national narcotics courts. Two Supreme Court decisions have challenged congressional expansion of federal criminal court jurisdiction.

- Lopez was convicted in federal court of carrying a pistol in a high school. The Court reversed and, in doing so, set limits on what crimes Congress may federalize. Chief Justice William Rehnquist's majority opinion stressed that in passing the Gun-Free School Zones Act in 1990, Congress "did not issue any findings showing a relationship between gun possession on school property and commerce" (*United States v. Lopez* 1995).
- In the same vein, a conservative majority of the Court declared part of the Violence Against Women Act of 1994 unconstitutional (*United States v. Morrison* 2000). In particular, victims of rape and other violent felonies "motivated by gender" no longer may sue their attackers in federal court (although state remedies are still available).

These decisions have sparked intense debate. To some, concern about overexpansion of federal jurisdiction is a genuine concern in matters like these. To others, the concern over caseload appears to be a façade, masking conservative antipathy toward gun control and toward the protection of the rights of vulnerable members of society.

ATTACKS ON THE FEDERAL JUDICIARY

In recent years, attacks on the federal judiciary have paralleled discussions of expanding or reducing federal court jurisdiction. But the political rhetoric is hardly consistent—supporters of expanding federal court jurisdiction in one area may also employ fiery political rhetoric to call for reduction of federal court jurisdiction in other areas. That is what happened as Terri Schiavo lay in a coma in a Florida hospital while the courts, the governor, and the legislature fought about whether her husband would be allowed to remove the feeding tube that was keeping her alive. The Florida courts had repeatedly said the feeding tube could be removed; the Florida governor and legislature tried to prevent its removal with legislation that the Florida Supreme Court ruled unconstitutional. The controversy expanded beyond Florida when President Bush signed a hastily drafted law passed by Congress that was carefully tailored to allow the federal courts to review her case. Prominent congressional supporters of Schiavo succeeded in passing legislation allowing federal court review of her case even though they strongly oppose federal court review of prisoners on death row (Chapter 13). Moreover, they have been in favor of removing same-sex marriages and other issues from federal court review (Chapter 14).

After the U.S. district court refused to order that the feeding tube not be removed from Terri Schiavo, then–House Majority Leader Tom Delay launched a strong attack, calling the federal judiciary an "arrogant, out-of control, unaccountable judiciary." Various conservative Republicans offered the following suggestions:

- Creation of an inspector general to conduct investigations of judges
- A tougher disciplinary mechanism for judges
- Limitation on lifetime appointments
- Impeachment of judges who render unpopular decisions

- Elimination of some lower federal courts
- Reduction in federal court funding

These attacks upon the federal judiciary have prompted concern that the independence and legitimacy of the judiciary may be undermined. In his state of the judiciary speech, Chief Justice Rehnquist cautioned that judges must be protected from political threats. "Judges are expected to administer the law fairly, without regard to public reaction. A judge's judicial acts may not serve as a basis for impeachment. Any other rule would destroy judicial independence." In a similar vein, Margaret Marshall, chief justice of the Massachusetts Supreme Judicial Court, argued: "I worry when people of influence use vague, loaded terms like 'judicial activism' to skew public debate or to intimidate judges. I worry when judicial independence is seen as a problem to be solved and not a value to be cherished" (quoted in Russell 2005).

CONCLUSION

What is unusual about the "enemy combatant" and Terri Schiavo cases is not the nature of the issue but, rather, how the issue became packaged. Disputes over what types of cases should or should not be heard in federal court are as old as the nation itself. The authors of the Constitution debated whether business cases should be heard in state or federal courts. Today, the nation debates whether federal courts should be able to hear cases involving abortion and school prayer. Seldom, however, do these major issues have a specific face attached to them. Ultimately, what was unique about the Terri Schiavo case was that the public could focus on a specific person, thus escalating the emotional content of the debate.

The Terri Schiavo case also highlights the importance of interest groups (to be discussed in Chapter 7). The Life Legal Defense Foundation (a conservative pro-life interest group) funded the legal bills (estimated at over $300,000) of Terri Schiavo's parents. Without such funding, the case probably would not have gained a national profile.

The "enemy combatant" cases from Guantánamo Bay illustrate a different, but no less important, aspect of the debate about the role of the federal courts. At the core of the debate is whether enemy combatants in the War on Terrorism will be granted access to the federal courts or will have to settle for military tribunals—but the debate is also about the balance of power among the federal courts, the military, the president, and Congress.

Justice Antonin Scalia, speaking about the deterioration of the federal courts, noted that in the 1960s, the federal courts had a few judges and small caseloads, but the cases they did hear were "by and large ... cases of major importance." Today, the federal courts have more judges and larger caseloads, but many of those cases are "minor" and "routine" ones concerning "mundane" matters of less import or even "overwhelming triviality" (1987). Thus, to one of the Court's leading conservatives, the federal courts should be returned to their rightful role of deciding only the nation's most significant cases.

We can only speculate about how the Founding Fathers would react to the concerns expressed by Justice Scalia. The Federalists would certainly agree that the federal courts should hear cases brought by big business, but at the same time, they would also wonder why a conservative would want to limit (rather than expand) federal jurisdiction. The Anti-Federalists would likely applaud limiting federal court jurisdiction but might be troubled by notions of shutting out ordinary citizens. But both sides would agree that the federal judiciary—like our entire nation—is certainly much bigger and more important than they could have imagined. Somehow, the almost ancient concerns of eighteenth-century America have survived to handle the issues of the twenty-first century. In short, arguments about what types of cases should be heard by federal courts are as old as the nation.

CRITICAL THINKING QUESTIONS

1. To what extent are contemporary debates over the role of the federal courts similar to debates in the eighteenth century? To what extent does the contemporary debate differ?

2. How would the U.S. judiciary be different today if the Founding Fathers had decided not to create a separate system of federal and state courts? How would U.S. politics be different?

3. In the wake of the terrorist attacks of September 11, 2001, does national security require that more cases be tried in the specialized courts and the military courts, or do those courts fail to provide sufficient protections for defendants?

4. How would you reduce federal court caseloads? What types of cases don't belong in federal court? What types of cases should be shifted to federal court from state court? What do your choices reflect about your political values?

Search Terms

federal courts   federalization of crime

Useful URLs

http://www.uscourts.gov
   The federal judiciary homepage includes the most recent statistics on federal court activity.

http://www.ussc.gov
   The official site of the U.S. Sentencing Commission.

http://www.supremecourtus.gov
   The official site of the Supreme Court of the United States; very good for recent opinions, arguments, schedules, and so on.

http://www.fcca.ws
   The official site of the Federal Court Clerks Association.

http://www.fedjudge.org
   The official site of the Federal Magistrate Judges Association.

http://www.fjc.gov/federal/courts.nsf
   Inside the Federal Courts is an educational website offered by the Federal Judicial Center.

http://jurist.law.pitt.edu/terrorism.htm
   This is the site of Terrorism Law and Policy

REFERENCES

Administrative Office of the U.S. Courts 2007. *Annual Report of the Director: Judicial Business of the United States Courts.* Washington, D.C.: U.S. Government Printing Office.

Anderson, Curt. 2010. "Panel Seeks Right Place to Consolidate Spill Lawsuits." *Houston Chronicle* July 29.

Associated Press. 2002. "German Court Upholds Legality of Gay Marriages." July 18.

Ball, Howard. 1987. *Courts and Politics: The Federal Judicial System.* 2d ed. Englewood Cliffs, N.J.: Prentice Hall.

Baum, Lawrence. 1990. *American Courts: Process and Policy.* 2d ed. Boston: Houghton Mifflin.

———. 2011. Specializing the Courts. Chicago: University of Chicago Press.

———. 1991. "Specializing the Federal Courts: Neutral Reforms or Efforts to Shape Judicial Policy?" *Judicature* 74: 217–224.

———. 1998. *American Courts: Process and Policy.* 4th ed. Boston: Houghton Mifflin.

"Bavarian Law Orders Crucifixes for Schools." 1995. *New York Times,* December 14.

Blankenburg, Erhard. 1996. "Changes in Political Regimes and Continuity of the Rule of Law in Germany." In *Courts, Law and Politics,* edited by Herbert Jacob. New Haven, Conn.: Yale University Press.

Bumiller, Kristin. 1980–1981. "Choice of Forum in Diversity Cases: Analysis of a Survey and Implications for Reform." *Law and Society Review* 15: 749–774.

Burger, Warren. 1975. "Reducing the Load on 'Nine Mortal Justices.'" *New York Times,* August 14, p. A1.

Carp, Robert, and Ronald Stidham. 1990. *The Federal Courts.* 2d ed. Washington, D.C.: CQ Press.

Clark, Tom. 2006. "Judicial Decision Making During Wartime." *Journal of Empirical Legal Studies.* 3: 397–419.

Curry, Brett. 2007. "Institutions, Interests and Judicial Outcomes." *Political Research Quarterly* 60: 454–467.

Dammer, Harry and Jay Albanese. 2011. *Comparative Criminal Justice Systems,* 4th Ed. Belmont: Wadsworth.

Dilworth, Donald. 1998. "Blue Ribbon Judicial Panel Will Recommend Fate of Federal Ninth Circuit." *Trial* 34: 92.

Epstein, Lee, Daniel Ho, Gary King, and Jeffrey Segal. 2005. "The Supreme Court During Crisis: How War Affects Only Non-War Cases." *New York University Law Review* 80: 1–116.

Fish, Peter. 1973. *The Politics of Federal Judicial Administration.* Princeton, N.J.: Princeton University Press.

Fisher, Louis. 2005. *Military Tribunals and Presidential Power: American Revolution to the War on Terrorism.* Lawrence: University Press of Kansas.

Flango, Victor. 1991. "Did Increasing the Federal Jurisdictional Amount Have the Predicted Impact on State Courts?" *State Court Journal* 15: 21–24.

Frankfurter, Felix, and James Landis. 1928. *The Business of the Supreme Court.* New York: Macmillan.

Goebel, Julius. 1971. *History of the Supreme Court of the United States: Vol. 1, Antecedents and Beginnings to 1801.* New York: Macmillan.

Gottlieb, Stuart(ed.). 2009. *Debating Terrorism and Counterterrorism: Conflicting Perspectives on Causes, Contexts, and Responses.* Washington, DC: CQ Press.

Hellman, Arthur. 1990. *Restructuring Justice: The Innovations of the Ninth Circuit and the Future of Federal Courts.* Ithaca, N.Y.: Cornell University Press.

"Jehovah's Witnesses Score Partial Success Before German Court." 2000. *New York Times,* December 20, p. A14.

Kesselman, Mark, Joel Krieger, and William A. Joseph. 2010. *Introduction to Comparative Politics.* Boston, MA: Wadsworth.

Kinzer, Stephen. 1993. "German Court Restricts Abortion." *New York Times,* May 29, p. A1.

Kramer, Larry. 1990. "Diversity Jurisdiction." *Brigham Young University Law Review* 1990(1): 97–129.

Liptak, Ada. 2010. "Judges, Minus One, Hear Challenges to Arizona Law on Hiring Immigrants." *New York Times* December 8.

Mayer, Jeremy. 2002. *9-11: The Giant Awakens.* Belmont, Calif.: Wadsworth.

Meier, Kenneth J. 1994. *The Politics of Sin: Drugs, Alcohol, and Public Policy.* New York: Sharpe.

Posner, Eric, and Adrian Vermeule. 2007. *Terror in the Balance: Security, Liberty, and the Courts.* New York: Oxford University Press.

Puro, Stephen. 1976. "United States Magistrates: A New Federal Judicial Officer." *Justice System Journal* 2: 141–156.

Rehnquist, William. 1993. *Year-End Report on the Federal Judiciary.* Washington, D.C.: Supreme Court of the United States.

Richardson, Richard, and Kenneth Vines. 1970. *The Politics of Federal Courts*. Boston: Little, Brown.

Rosenberg, Carol. 2010. "Child al-Qaida Soldier is Guilty." *The Times-Picayune* October 26.

Russell, Jenna. 2005. "Marshal Defends Bench Independence." *Boston Globe*, May 23.

Scalia, Antonin. 1987. "Remarks … Before the Fellows of the American Bar Foundation and the National Council of Bar Presidents." New Orleans, February 15.

Schmitt, Richard. 1993. "Battle Erupts Over Federal Circuit Seat." *Wall Street Journal*, October 21, p. B8.

Schwarzer, William, and Russell Wheeler. 1994. *On the Federalization of the Administration of Civil and Criminal Justice*. Washington, D.C.: Federal Judicial Center. Banks, Christopher. 2000. "The Politics of Court Reform in the U.S. Courts of Appeals." *Judicature* 84: 34–43.

Sherman, Edward. 1987. "Military Law." In *Encyclopedia of the American Judicial System*, edited by Robert Janosik. New York: Scribner's.

Sloviter, Dolores. 1992. "Diversity Jurisdiction Through the Lens of Federalism." *Judicature* 76: 90–93.

Smith, Christopher. 1987. "Who Are the U.S. Magistrates?" *Judicature* 71: 143–150.

———. 1992. "From U.S. Magistrates to U.S. Magistrate Judges: Developments Affecting the Federal District Courts' Lower Tier of Judicial Officers." *Judicature* 75: 210–215.

Stumpf, Harry. 1988. *American Judicial Politics*. New York: Harcourt Brace Jovanovich.

Thomas, Philip. 2010. "Oil Plaintiff Lawyers Battle over Who Gets to Argue at the MDL Hearing." *Mississippi Litigation Review and Commentary*. July 15.

Thornburgh, Dick. 2005. "The USA Patriot Act and Civil Liberties." *Albany Law Review* 68: 801–814.

United States Judicial Panel on Multidistrict Litigation. 2011 http://www.jpml.uscourts.gov/

Vicini, James, 2011. "Arizona Appeals to Supreme Court on Immigration Law." Reuters August 10.

Warren, Charles. 1926. *The Supreme Court in United States History*. Boston: Little, Brown.

Weiser, Benjamin. 2010. "Detainee Acquitted on Most Counts in '98 Bombings." *New York Times* November 17.

Williams, Carol. 2010. "Lawyers Promote Cities for Oil Trials." *Los Angeles Times* July 30.

Wright, Charles Alan. 1970. *Law of Federal Courts*. St.Paul, Minn.: West.

For Further Reading

Ball, Howard. 2007. *Bush, the Detainees, and the Constitution: The Battle Over Presidential Power in the War on Terror*. Lawrence: University Press of Kansas.

Buckman, Jeremy. 2003. "Judicial Lobbying and the Politics of Judicial Structure: An Examination of the Judiciary Act of 1925." *Justice System Journal* 24: 1–22.

Cross, Frank B. 2007. *Decision Making in the U.S. Court of Appeals*. Palo Alto, Calif.: Stanford University Press.

Fisher, Louis. 2005. *Military Tribunals and Presidential Power: American Revolution to the War on Terrorism*. Lawrence: University Press of Kansas.

Foster, Nigel, and Satish Sule. 2009. *German Legal System and Laws*. New York: Oxford University Press.

Giles, Michael W., Virginia Hettinger, Christopher Zorn, and Todd C. Peppers. 2007. "The Etiology of the Occurrence of En Banc Review in the U.S. Court of Appeals." *American Journal of Political Science* 51(3): 449–463.

Haynes, Wendy. 2004. "Seeing Around Corners: Crafting the New Department of Homeland Security." *Review of Policy Research* 21: 369–395.

Howard, Robert. 2009. *Getting a Poor Return: Courts, Justice, and Taxes*. Albany, NY: SUNY Press.

Hudson, Barbara. 2009. "Justice in a Time or Terror" *British Journal of Criminology* 49:702–717.

LoPucki, Lynn. 2005. *Courting Failure: How Competition for Big Cases Is Corrupting the Bankruptcy Courts*. Ann Arbor: University of Michigan Press.

Richards, Peter Judson. 2007. *Extraordinary Justice: Military Tribunals in Historical and International Context*. New York: New York University Press.

Shortell, Christopher, and Charles Smith. 2005. "The Institutional Stability of the Judiciary in the Aftermath of Terrorism." *Judicature* 88: 172–177.

Yackle, Larry. 2009. *Federal Courts, 3rd edition*. Durham, NC: Carolina Academic Press.

STATE COURTS

The reconstructed colonial courtroom in Constitution State Park in Danville, Kentucky. Clerks used quill pens to record entries in the docket book.

David Neubauer

"You have a daughter. Why is it important to get a handle on this drug problem?" queries the anonymous female reporter. "Because it is an issue that affects all families," responds Robert Wakefield, a justice of the Ohio Supreme Court and soon to be the nation's next drug czar. But, while Wakefield is busy being briefed by high-level officials about how to wage the War on Drugs, his teenage daughter Caroline is secretly being educated by a group of underachievers about how to become addicted to drugs.

The movie *Traffic* puts a face on the complex issues in the War on Drugs and raises serious questions about U.S. drug policy. The War on Drugs has led to rapidly increasing court dockets across the United States and has filled jail cells across the nation. In an effort to cope with rising case volume, many communities created drug courts that respond in a therapeutic way to drug offenders and, at the same time, seek to reduce prison populations.

Common state court cases include armed robberies and automobile accidents, but that is only part of the workload. State judges must also adjudicate cases involving citizens who speed while they drive and others who drink while they drive; wives who want divorces from unfaithful husbands and husbands who physically abuse their wives; juveniles who rob liquor stores and juveniles who simply drink liquor. In many ways, the multiple perspectives on the War on Drugs presented in *Traffic* reflect the contemporary realities of state courts—the number of cases placed on the dockets increases, and societal expectations about how justice is to be administered demand stiffer penalties; yet, staffing levels remain constant. Thus, whereas an earlier generation viewed court reform in terms of a neater organization chart, contemporary discussions are more likely to focus on reforms such as creating drug courts.

This chapter examines the structure and the functions of state courts, beginning with a discussion of the development of American courts and continuing with a discussion of the somewhat confusing four levels of state courts: trial courts of limited jurisdiction, trial courts of general jurisdiction, intermediate appellate courts, and courts of last resort. The chapter then examines the lower courts in some depth, discussing justice of the peace courts, municipal courts, and juvenile courts. The efforts of court reformers to reorganize state court structure—traditionally identified with efforts to create a unified court system—are explored. An extended discussion of drug courts illustrates current thinking about court reform.

The History of State Courts

Just as American law borrowed heavily from English common law, so the organization of American courts reflects their English heritage. Although certain traditions persist, court structures have also changed over time. Such alterations, though, were far from automatic; issues such as the clash of opposing economic interests, the debate over state versus national power, and outright partisanship have shaped the development of America's 50 diverse state court systems.

Colonial Courts

During the colonial period, political power was concentrated in the hands of the governor, an appointee of the English king. Governors performed executive, legislative, and judicial functions. The courts were rather simple institutions whose structure replicated English courts in form but not in substance. The numerous, complex, and highly specialized English courts were ill suited to the needs of a small group of colonists trying to survive on the edge of the wilderness, so the colonists greatly simplified the English procedures.

The county courts stood at the heart of American colonial government. Besides adjudicating cases, they also performed important administrative functions (Friedman 1985). As towns and villages became larger, new courts were created so people would not have to travel long distances to have their cases heard. Through the years, each colony modified its court system according to variations in local customs, different religious practices, and patterns of commercial trade. Those early variations in legal rulings and court structures have persisted and contribute to the great variety of U.S. court systems today (Glick and Vines 1973).

Early American Courts

After the American Revolution, the functions of state courts changed markedly. Their governing powers were drastically reduced and taken over by legislative bodies. The former colonists viewed judicial action as coercive, distrusted lawyers, and harbored major misgivings about English common law. They were not anxious to see the development of a large, independent judiciary. Thus, judicial decisions were often scrutinized by state legislatures, and in response to unpopular court decisions, some judges were removed from office or specific courts were abolished.

The distrust of the judiciary increased when courts declared unconstitutional legislative acts favoring free money. Such actions were a major source of political conflict between legislatures and courts representing opposing interests. Legislators were more responsive to policies that favored debtors, usually small farmers. Courts, on the other hand, reflected the views of creditors, often merchants. Out of that conflict over legislative and judicial power, though, the courts gradually emerged as an independent political institution.

Courts in a Modernizing Society

Rapid industrialization following the Civil War produced fundamental changes in the structure of American courts. Increases in population, the growth of cities, and the rise of industrialization greatly expanded the volume of litigation. Moreover, the types of disputes coming to the courts changed. Not only did the growth of industry and commerce result in disputes over this new wealth, but also the concentration of people in the cities (many of whom were immigrants), coupled with the pressures of industrial employment, meant the courts were faced with a new set of problems. The American courts, still reflecting the rural society of the early nineteenth century, were inadequate in the face of rising demands for services (Jacob 1984).

States and localities responded to the increased volume of litigation in a number of ways. City courts were created to deal with new types of cases in the urban areas. Specialized courts were formed to handle specific classes of cases (for example, small-claims courts, juvenile courts, and family relations courts). Additional courts were often created by specifying the geographic boundaries of a city court's jurisdiction. The development of courts in Chicago illustrates the confusion, complexity, and administrative problems that resulted from that sporadic and unplanned growth. In 1931, Chicago had 556 independent courts; the majority were justice of the peace courts that handled only minor offenses (Glick and Vines 1973).

In Chicago and elsewhere, the jurisdiction of those courts was not exclusive; that is, a case could be brought before a variety of courts, depending on the legal and political advantages that each one offered. Moreover, each court was a separate entity; each had a judge and a staff. Such an organizational structure meant there was no way to shift cases from an overloaded court to one with little to do. Each court also produced patronage jobs for the city political machines.

Courts Today: A Complex Court Structure

The haphazard expansion of the American court system resulted in an often-confusing structure. Each state system is different. Although some states have adopted a unified court structure, others still have numerous local courts with overlapping jurisdictions. Moreover, there may be major variations in court jurisdiction within a state: The jurisdiction of courts in one county may differ from those in the adjoining county. To examine the many state courts, it is useful to divide them into four levels: trial courts of limited jurisdiction, trial courts of general jurisdiction, intermediate appellate courts, and courts of last resort.

TRIAL COURTS OF LIMITED JURISDICTION: LOWER COURTS

At the first level are **trial courts of limited jurisdiction**, sometimes referred to as **inferior courts** or, more simply, **lower courts**. The country contains over 13,000 trial courts of limited jurisdiction, staffed by more than 18,000 judicial officers. Thus, the numerous lower courts constitute 85 percent of all judicial bodies in the United States. The number of trial courts of limited jurisdiction varies from none (in California, the District of Columbia, Illinois, Iowa, Minnesota, and Puerto Rico) to more than 2,000 (in New York and Texas). Several states, including California—which has one of the largest court systems in the world—have adopted a unified court system in which limited and general jurisdiction courts are combined. (See the section on trial courts of general jurisdiction.)

Variously called county, city, district, justice of the peace, magistrate, municipal, or probate courts, the lower courts decide a restricted range of cases. Most are created by local government—city or county—and, therefore, are not part of the state judiciary. Thus, lower courts are typically controlled only by the local governmental bodies that create and fund them. The lower courts are rarely **courts of record**; that is, no official verbatim transcript is kept of the witnesses' testimony or the judges' rulings. Appeals of lower-court decisions are heard in a trial court of general jurisdiction, not in a state's appellate courts. Such an appeal is termed **trial de novo** because the case must be heard again in its entirety, taking the testimony of the same witnesses and hearing the identical arguments of the attorneys as the lower court did. The caseload volume of the lower courts is staggering—more than 100 million matters a year. An overwhelming number of these lower-court cases (more than fifty million in 2008) are traffic related (Table 4.1).

TABLE 4.1	Case Filings in State Trial Courts, 2008 (in millions)					
	Traffic	**Civil**	**Criminal**	**Domestic**	**Juvenile**	**Total**
General/unified jurisdiction	14.1	8.7	6.6	4.1	1.4	34.9
Limited jurisdiction	43.5	10.8	14.7	1.6	0.7	71.3
Total	57.6	19.5	21.3	5.7	2.1	

Source: R. LaFountain, R. Schauffler, S. Strickland, W. Raferty, and C. Bromage, *Examining the Work of State Courts: An Analysis of 2008 State Court Caseloads* (Williamsburg, Va.: National Center for State Courts, 2010).

Criminal Cases

On the criminal side, the lower courts hear an eclectic mix of ordinance violations and misdemeanor criminal cases. Thus, these courts process the millions of Americans accused each year of disturbing the peace, shoplifting, public drunkenness, and speeding. Generally, lower courts are restricted to imposing a maximum fine of $1,000 and no more than a year in jail. In some states, though, they are authorized to levy fines as high as $5,000 and to sentence defendants to up to five years in prison. (Later, this chapter will discuss in greater detail the quality of justice dispensed by the nation's lowest and most neglected courts.)

In addition, many lower courts are responsible for the preliminary stages of felony cases: After a felony arrest, a judge in a trial court of limited jurisdiction will hold arraignments, set bail, appoint counsel for indigents, and conduct preliminary examinations. Later, the case is transferred to a trial court of general jurisdiction for trial (or plea) and sentencing.

Civil Cases

On the civil side, the lower courts decide a range of disputes that may include torts, contracts, real property, and sometimes even domestic relations cases. The determination of whether a civil case is heard by a limited or a general jurisdiction court is made by the amount of damages being requested—smaller amounts (for example, generally up to $10,000) go to limited jurisdiction courts, and larger amounts go to general jurisdiction courts. A large category of cases falls under the label **small claims**—which refers not to a substance but to a process. Small claims involve cases under a certain money limit, which ranges from a low of $1,500 in some states (Kentucky) to a high of $10,000 (Alaska), with the most common maximum of $5,000. In most states, streamlined procedures to provide quick, inexpensive processing by dispensing with written pleadings, strict rules of evidence, and the right to trial by jury have been adopted (Goerdt 1992). Accordingly, small-claims cases are less formal and less protracted than other civil cases. Ten states do not allow lawyers, and most (41) do not allow jury trials. Small claims constitute a large portion of civil filings every year; thus, they are examined in greater depth in Chapter 11.

TRIAL COURTS OF GENERAL JURISDICTION: MAJOR TRIAL COURTS

At the second level are the **trial courts of general jurisdiction**, usually referred to as **major trial courts**, which currently number more than 2,000 and are staffed by over 11,000 judicial officers (*Examining the Work of State Courts* 2008). The phrase *general jurisdiction* means that these courts have the legal authority to decide all matters not specifically delegated to the lower courts. The division of jurisdiction between the lower courts and the major trial courts is specified by law—statutory or constitutional or both. The names used for these courts in all states are listed in Table 4.2. Anyone interested in understanding the judicial process as it is carried out in the fifty states (and the District of Columbia and Puerto Rico) should be aware of the great variation in court names and functions. Tables 4.2, 4.3, and 4.4 profile the court systems of the United States to highlight that variation.

TABLE 4.2	Major Trial Courts in the United States
Name of Court	**States**
Circuit court	Alabama, Arkansas, Florida, Hawaii, Illinois, Indiana,[a] Kentucky, Maryland, Michigan, Mississippi, Missouri, Oregon,[b] South Carolina, South Dakota, Tennessee,[c] Virginia, West Virginia, Wisconsin
Circuit court and family court	Hawaii
Court of common pleas	Ohio, Pennsylvania
District court	Colorado,[d] Idaho, Iowa, Louisiana,[e] Minnesota, Montana,[f] Nebraska, Nevada, New Mexico, North Dakota, Oklahoma, Texas, Utah, Wyoming
Superior court	Alaska, Arizona,[b] California, Connecticut, Delaware,[g] District of Columbia, Georgia, Maine, Massachusetts, New Hampshire, New Jersey, North Carolina, Rhode Island, Vermont,[h] Washington
Supreme court	New York[i]

[a]Indiana also uses superior and probate courts.
[b]Oregon and Arizona also use a tax court.
[c]Tennessee also uses probate, chancery, and criminal courts.
[d]Colorado also uses the Denver Probate, Juvenile, and Water Court.
[e]Louisiana also uses a juvenile and family court.
[f]Montana also uses the Water and Worker's Compensation Court.
[g]Delaware also uses a chancery court.
[h]Vermont also uses district and family courts.
[i]New York also uses county courts.
Source: Court Statistics Project, *State Court Caseload Statistics, 2008* (Williamsburg, Va.: National Center for State Courts, 2010).

The geographical jurisdictions of the major trial courts are typically defined along existing political boundaries, counties primarily. Each court has its own support staff consisting of a clerk of court, a sheriff, and so on. In most states, the trial courts of general jurisdiction are also grouped into judicial districts or circuits. In rural areas where districts or circuits encompass several adjoining counties, the trial court judges are true generalists who hear a wide variety of cases. They literally "ride the circuit," holding court in different counties on a fixed schedule. More populated counties have only one circuit or district court for the area, often with numerous judges. Here, judges are frequently specialists assigned to hear only certain types of cases, such as criminal, family, juvenile, and civil. Table 4.1 provides workload data on the major trial courts.

The lion's share of the nation's judicial business exists at the state, not the federal, level. More than 100 million civil and criminal cases are filed each year in the nation's state courts, compared with just over 300,000 cases in the federal district courts (over 1 million if bankruptcy filings are included). Moreover, the types of cases filed in the state courts differ greatly from those going to the federal courts. Litigants in federal courts are most often big businesses and governmental bodies. In sharp contrast, litigants in state courts are most typically individuals and small businesses.

Criminal Cases

Federal courts hear a high percentage of white-collar crimes, whereas state courts decide primarily street crimes. The more serious criminal violations are heard in the trial courts of general jurisdiction. The public associates felonies with crimes of

TABLE **4.3**	State Intermediate Courts of Appeals in the United States
Name of Court	**State (Number of Judges)**
Appeals court	Massachusetts (25)
Appellate court	Connecticut (9), Illinois (52)
Appellate division of superior court	New Jersey (34)
Appellate divisions of supreme court	New York (55)
Appellate terms of supreme court	New York (15)
Circuit court of appeals	Puerto Rico (33)
Commonwealth court	Pennsylvania (9)
Court of appeals	Alaska (3), Arizona (22), Arkansas (12), Colorado (16), Georgia (12), Idaho (3), Indiana[a] (15), Iowa (9), Kansas (14), Kentucky (14), Michigan (28), Minnesota (16), Mississippi (10), Missouri (32), Nebraska (6), New Mexico (10), North Carolina (15), Oregon (10), South Carolina (9), Tennessee[b] (12), Utah (7), Virginia (11), Washington (22), Wisconsin (16)
Courts of appeal	California (105), Louisiana (53), Ohio (68)
Courts of appeals	Texas (80)
Court of civil appeals	Alabama[b] (5), Oklahoma[b] (12)
Court of criminal appeals	Alabama[c] (5), Tennessee[c] (12)
Court of special appeals	Maryland (13)
District courts of appeal	Florida (62)
Intermediate court of appeals	Hawaii (4)
Superior court	Pennsylvania (15)
None	Delaware, District of Columbia, Maine, Montana, Nevada, New Hampshire, North Dakota, Rhode Island, South Dakota, Vermont, West Virginia, Wyoming

[a]Indiana also uses a tax court.
[b]Civil only.
[c]Criminal only.
Source: Court Statistics Project, *State Court Caseload Statistics, 2008* (Williamsburg, Va.: National Center for State Courts, 2010).

violence, such as murder, robbery, and rape, but 90 percent of criminal violations heard by state courts are nonviolent crimes, such as burglary and theft (discussed in Chapter 8). In addition, state courts must process an increasing number of drug-related offenses, ranging from the simple possession of small amounts of illicit drugs to the sale of large quantities of cocaine and heroin. In an analysis of thirteen states for the period 1976–2002, the National Center for State Courts reports that felony dispositions have increased 124 percent (*Examining the Work of State Courts* 2003). Most criminal cases (77 percent) do not go to trial, because the defendant pleads guilty. Thus, the dominant issue in the trial courts of general jurisdiction is not guilt or innocence but, rather, what penalty to apply to the guilty.

Civil Cases

In major trial courts, civil cases outnumber criminal cases by two to one (regardless of the media focus on criminal cases). Press attention also suggests that personal injury lawsuits dominate civil filings. In reality, tort cases make up only a relatively small percentage of the docket, about 5 percent! The most common types of civil litigation illustrate the diversity of people and issues in state civil courts: domestic relations, estate, personal injury, and contracts.

Domestic relations cases filed in the major trial courts include issues such as petitioning for divorce, determining child custody, setting levels of child support, allocating economic resources (homes, cars, and savings accounts), and, in some states, providing for spousal support (alimony and the like). Domestic relations cases account for about 30 percent of case filings. In recent years, the percentage of domestic relations cases has remained relatively unchanged.

Estate cases (often referred to as **probate**) are the second most common type of case filed in the states' major trial courts. For those who made a will before their death, the courts supervise the distribution of assets according to the terms of the will. For those who failed to make out a will before dying, the courts determine which heirs will inherit the estate. Most estate matters, therefore, present the judge with little if any controversy.

Personal injury cases constitute the third most common type of case filings. Tort law covers a wide range of legal injuries. Most involve a physical injury, which can vary from a sprained ankle to wrongful death. Although tort cases may involve a wide range of activities, most stem from accidents involving motor vehicles. Tort cases constitute only about 5 percent of all filings in trial courts of general jurisdiction, but they are the most likely to go to trial. Nearly two-thirds of all cases going to trial in general jurisdiction courts involve tort claims (Ostrom, Kauder, and LaFountain 2001). Though increasing recently by small amounts, the overall rate of tort filings for the past decade appears to be mostly steady, perhaps because of tort reform. Despite that, media coverage of a "litigation explosion" continues.

Other types of civil cases include contract cases, where one party claims that the other party failed to live up to the terms of a contract and asks for monetary damages as compensation, and property rights cases, which typically involve mortgage foreclosures.

INTERMEDIATE COURTS OF APPEALS

A century ago, state court systems included only a single appellate body—the state court of last resort. Like their federal counterparts, state courts experienced a significant growth in appellate cases that threatened to overwhelm their state supreme courts. Officials in 39 states responded by creating **intermediate courts of appeals**, or ICAs (Table 4.3). The only states that have not followed suit are either sparsely populated or geographically compact. These courts must hear all properly filed appeals. Subsequent appeals are at the discretion of the state supreme court. Thus, a decision by the state's intermediate appellate court is the final one for most cases.

The structure of the intermediate courts of appeals varies in several ways. Twenty-four states organize their ICAs on a statewide basis, and the rest on a regional basis. In most states, these bodies hear both civil and criminal appeals. Alabama and Tennessee, however, have separate courts of appeals for civil and criminal cases. The number of intermediate courts of appeals judges ranges from a low of 3 in Idaho to a high of

105 in California. Like their federal counterparts, these courts typically employ rotating three-judge panels for deciding cases.

The ICAs handle the bulk of the caseload in the appellate system, and their workload has increased dramatically in the last decade. States created these courts and allotted them additional judgeships in hopes of relieving the state supreme courts from crushing caseloads, only to find that the ICAs experience the same problems (Chapter 13). Numerous efforts are being made to increase the efficiency of the appellate process, but not all agree on where to draw the line between needed efficiencies and the requirement that justice be done.

Criminal defendants are increasingly likely to appeal their convictions but find appellate courts markedly unsympathetic to their legal arguments. Even though appellants in civil cases are more likely to persuade a panel of three judges that the trial court erred, trial court decisions are typically affirmed. As discussed later, the intermediate appellate courts represent the final stage of the process for most litigants—only a relative handful of cases will be heard by the state's highest appellate court.

COURTS OF LAST RESORT: STATE SUPREME COURTS

The court of last resort is generally referred to as the **state supreme court**. The specific names, however, vary from state to state, and to further complicate the picture, Texas and Oklahoma have two courts of last resort—one for civil appeals and one for criminal appeals. The number of supreme court judges varies from a low of five to as many as nine; the most common number is seven (see Table 4.4). Unlike the intermediate appellate courts, most of these courts sit **en banc** (that is, all judges hear all cases), though a few use rotating panels for some cases. All state supreme courts have a limited amount of **original jurisdiction** in dealing with matters such as disciplining lawyers and judges. In most states, the high court has primarily **discretionary**

TABLE 4.4	State Courts of Last Resort in the United States
Name of Court	**State (Number of Judges)**
Court of appeals	District of Columbia (9), Maryland (7), New York (7)
Court of criminal appeals	Oklahoma (5), Texas (9)
Supreme court	Alabama (9), Alaska (5), Arizona (5), Arkansas (7), California (7), Colorado (7), Connecticut (7), Delaware (5), Florida (7), Georgia (7), Hawaii (5), Idaho (5), Illinois (7), Indiana (5), Iowa (7), Kansas (7), Kentucky (7), Louisiana (7), Michigan (7), Minnesota (7), Mississippi (9), Missouri (7), Montana (7), Nebraska (7), Nevada (7), New Hampshire (5), New Jersey (7), New Mexico (5), North Carolina (7), North Dakota (5), Ohio (7), Oklahoma[a] (9), Oregon (7), Pennsylvania (7), Puerto Rico (7), Rhode Island (5), South Carolina (5), South Dakota (5), Tennessee (5), Texas[a] (9), Utah (5), Vermont (5), Virginia (7), Washington (9), Wisconsin (7), Wyoming (5)
Supreme court of appeals	West Virginia (5)
Supreme judicial court	Maine (7), Massachusetts (7)

[a] Civil appeals only.
Source: Court Statistics Project, *State Court Caseload Statistics, 2006* (Williamsburg, Va.: National Center for State Courts, 2007).

jurisdiction, much like the U.S. Supreme Court. It selects a small number of cases to hear, but those cases tend to have broad legal and political significance. In states without an intermediate court of appeal, however, the supreme court has no power to choose which cases will be placed on its docket.

The state supreme courts are the ultimate review board for matters involving interpretation of state law. The only other avenue of appeal for a disgruntled litigant is the U.S. Supreme Court, but successful applications are rare and must involve important questions of federal law. Although state supreme courts vary greatly in the details of their internal procedures used to decide cases, most are roughly similar to the U.S. Supreme Court.

State Supreme Courts: A Research Agenda

During the last two decades, political scientists have increasingly turned their attention to studying state supreme courts (Hall 2001). State supreme courts have become important policy makers (Bosworth 2001) and are historically understudied because political scientists have focused almost exclusively on the federal courts. State supreme court research is directed at getting beyond the simple description of these legal entities. The focus is on explaining why state supreme courts operate the way they do. For example, Langer (2002) examines how state supreme courts interact with other branches of government using a separation-of-powers framework. She finds that the justices' ideology, along with institutional aspects of the courts, helps us understand why the courts reach the decisions they do. Such research is often referred to as neo-institutionalist, and the researcher focuses on such institutional characteristics as selection method and size of court to explain the behavior of state supreme courts. Researchers such as Melinda Hall and Paul Brace have exploited this approach to show us that there is much to understand about state courts of last resort, including that state supreme court justices react to both case facts and institutional constraints (Hall 2001, 1992; Brace, Langer, and Hall 2000; Brace and Hall 1997). These authors were instrumental in the establishment of the State Supreme Court Data Project, which currently contains valuable information on all 50 state courts and is a useful research tool (http://www.ruf.rice.edu/~pbrace/statecourt).

THE LOWER COURTS: A CLOSER LOOK

Although the cases heard in the nation's lowest tribunals are minor, these judicial bodies are nonetheless quite important, for it is here that the vast majority of ordinary citizens have contact with their nation's judiciary (Table 4.1). Overall, three out of four cases filed yearly in state court are decided in the less prestigious trial courts of limited jurisdiction. The caseload numbers are truly staggering: 50 million traffic violations, 21 million criminal cases, 19 million civil matters, and just over 2 million juvenile cases.

For decades, the problems of the lower courts have been at center stage in the efforts of reformers to improve the nation's judiciary. What troubles court reformers the most is the apparent lack of the adversary model of justice. Defendants are rarely represented by an attorney, trials are rare, and judgments are often entered with lightning speed. Informality, rather than the rules of courtroom procedure, predominates. Is that justice? Nearly forty years ago, the President's Commission on Law

Enforcement and Administration of Justice (1967, 128) asked that question and expressed outrage:

> The commission has been shocked by what it has seen in some lower courts. It has seen cramped and noisy courtrooms, undignified and perfunctory procedures, and badly trained personnel. It has seen dedicated people who are frustrated by huge caseloads, by the lack of opportunity to examine cases carefully, and by the impossibility of devising constructive solutions to the problems of offenders. It has seen assembly-line justice.

The nonjudicial atmosphere of lower-court proceedings, it is said, does little to instill respect for the law in the minds of defendants, plaintiffs, and witnesses. Yet, these courts have been treated as a judicial stepchild and have suffered from long-term neglect (Ashman 1975).

Few doubt that the lower courts do not always administer justice as well as they might, but two major factors affect their work. First, they are not simply major trial courts with a higher volume of less serious cases. Lower courts demonstrate greater flexibility because the judges and the prosecutors focus directly on trying to produce substantive justice, rather than just adhering to procedures. Second, lower courts exhibit immense variation. For example, the drug courts found in the nation's largest cities operate very differently from justice of the peace courts located in rural areas. The dominating factor, then, is that the lower courts are locally controlled and are not generally part of the state judiciary. Stated another way, the lower courts truly reflect local customs. Given this wide-ranging disparity, it is best to consider several different categories of lower courts existing in the United States: justice of the peace courts, municipal courts, and juvenile courts. Each occupies a very different position within the judiciary and, therefore, warrants separate treatment.

JUSTICE OF THE PEACE COURTS

Lower courts in rural areas are historically called **justice of the peace courts**, and the officeholder is usually referred to simply as a **JP**. This system of local justice traces its origins to fourteenth-century England, when towns were small and isolated. The JP system developed as a way to dispense simple and speedy justice, with local land-owners (squires) deciding disputes more according to their knowledge of the local community than to their reading in the law.

In some ways, the small-town flavor of the JP system persists today (even in large urban places such as Harris County, Texas, which includes Houston). In the past, the vast majority of JPs were part-time nonlawyers who conducted court at their regular places of business—in the back of the undertaker's parlor, at the front counter of the general store, or next to the grease rack in the garage. Today, however, JPs tend to be more professional and hold court in a courthouse or another government building. A common list of qualifications might include the following for the state of Texas.

To be eligible to hold the office of justice of the peace, a person must:

- be a citizen of the United States;
- be at least 18 years of age on the day the term starts or on the date of appointment;
- not have been determined mentally incompetent by a final judgment of a court;
- not have been finally convicted of a felony from which the person has not been pardoned or otherwise released from the resulting disabilities;

- as a general rule, have resided continually in Texas for one year and in the precinct for the preceding six months; and
- must not have been declared ineligible for the office.

(State of Texas Justice of the Peace Manual 2002)

Today, many of the JPs have been replaced with magistrates. Magistrates assume the same kinds of responsibilities as traditional JPs but do not use that title. Magistrates are more likely to be appointed than elected and tend to have better training than JPs. For example, North Carolina's justices of the peace were phased out in 1968–1970 and replaced with magistrates who are required to have more education and are appointed by the district court judge. The qualifications and the professionalism of justice of the peace courts have been a constant source of concern for critics.

The debate over the quality of justice of the peace courts continues today regardless of whether the officeholders are referred to as JPs or as magistrates. Typically, the salary is low, it is hard to attract qualified individuals, and they are frequently nonlawyers. That has led many to criticize the system and call for the abolition of nonlawyer judges; others believe that a law degree is less important at this stage of the judicial process.

Municipal Courts

Municipal courts are the urban counterparts of the justice of the peace courts. A century ago, the increasing volume of cases in large cities overwhelmed the ability of the rurally conceived JP system to dispense justice. Municipal courts were shaped by an important aspect of big cities—the political machine. Big-city political machines viewed the lower courts as opportunities for patronage. Party bosses controlled the selection of judges, appointed the bailiffs, and reserved the right to select clerks from the ranks of the party faithful. Not surprisingly, municipal courts were often tainted by corruption. In return for political favors or cash, charges would be dropped or files would mysteriously disappear. The judicial reformers of the 1920s and 1930s sought to clean up the courts by removing them from politics.

The Assembly Line

The overriding reality of big-city municipal courts is the need to move cases quickly (Ashman 1975). "Obstacles" to speedy disposition—warning of constitutional rights, presence of counsel, trials—are neutralized. In a process often labeled *assembly-line justice*, shortcuts are routinely taken to keep the cases moving. Thus, the municipal courts more closely resemble a bureaucracy geared to mass-processing cases than an adjudicative body that considers each case (Ryan 1980–1981).

In municipal courts, the defendant's initial appearance is usually the final one. Most people charged with a traffic violation or a minor misdemeanor plead guilty at the first appearance. The quick plea represents a fatalistic view of most defendants: "I've done it. Let's get it over with." Realistically, a defendant charged with a crime such as public drunkenness or disorderly conduct cannot raise a valid legal defense. What has struck all observers of these courts is the speed with which the pleas are processed.

Few trials are held in the lower courts. The general absence of attorneys and the minor nature of the offenses combine to make requests for jury trials rare. Municipal courts, in a sense, are not really trial courts, because few defendants contest their guilt; in actuality, they are sentencing institutions. The courtroom encounter is geared to making rapid decisions about which sentence to impose.

Lower-court judges have a wide range of alternative sanctions from which to choose; yet, they sentence few defendants to jail, requiring most (some two-thirds) to simply pay a fine. The result is a high degree of uniformity: By and large, a given defendant gets the same sentence as all others in the same category. To the casual observer, the process may appear to be an assembly line, but closer probing indicates that sentences can also be fitted to the specific defendant. Some individual attention to cases occurs during plea negotiations. Despite overall sentencing consistencies, exceptions are made (Ragona and Ryan 1983).

Is the Process the Punishment?

Some time ago, researchers started questioning the image of the lower courts as assembly-line operations. Susan Silbey (1981) argues that the standard picture of lower courts as wholesale, mechanical processors of a high volume of cases is only partially correct. The operations of the misdemeanor courts are not as chaotic, disordered, or unreasonable as they may first appear. A second consideration is that the lower courts do try to provide justice, but they do so by responding to problems rather than crimes, concentrating their efforts on producing substantive justice rather than focusing on purely formal (that is, due process) justice. Separate studies in New Haven, Connecticut (Feeley 1979), and Columbus, Ohio (Ryan 1980–1981), assessed the disparate functions served by the lower courts.

To Malcolm Feeley, the process was the punishment. That finding was based on several years studying the lower court in New Haven firsthand. The main punishment of defendants occurs during the processing of cases, not after a finding of guilt. Feeley contends that the pretrial process imposes a series of punishments ("price tags") on the accused. Those price tags often include staying in jail (briefly), paying a bail bondsman, hiring a private attorney, and losing time and perhaps wages because of repeated court appearances. Those costs far outweigh any punishment imposed after the defendant pleads guilty. Those price tags also affect the roughly 40 percent of the defendants eventually found not guilty. In short, the pretrial process itself is the primary punishment, according to Feeley.

To John Paul Ryan, the outcome is the punishment. A statistical analysis of court sentences in Columbus, Ohio, found that, unlike those in New Haven, lower-court judges in Columbus routinely impose fines on convicted defendants. Often those fines are substantial. Further, 35 percent of the guilty in Columbus are sentenced to jail—six times as many as in New Haven. Finally, defendants in traffic cases often have their driver's licenses suspended and/or are ordered to attend drunk driver's education classes. In short, Columbus defendants were more likely to be fined, to pay heavier fines, to go to jail, and to be required to participate in some sort of treatment program than their counterparts in New Haven.

Scholars disagree about whether the process or the outcome is the punishment, but they agree that the nation's lower courts are the nerve center of the U.S. legal system.

JUVENILE COURTS

Juvenile courts are a unique and distinctive type of judicial body. Technically, the proceedings are civil, but, in practice, they are a blend of criminal and civil. That duality is reflected in the multiple roles performed by the juvenile courts, a point highlighted by a former judge of the Denver Juvenile Court:

> This court is a far more complex instrument than outsiders imagine. It is law, and it is social work; it is control, and it is help; it is the good parent and, also, the stern parent; it is both formal and informal. It is concerned not only with the delinquent, but also with the battered child, the runaway, and many others.... The juvenile court has been all things to all people. (Rubin 1984, 79–80)

Juvenile courts were the product of the Progressive movement—turn-of-the-century, middle-class reformers who were concerned with the problems associated with growing urbanization. The children of the urban immigrant poor were of special interest (Tanenhaus 2004). The Progressives sought to use the power of the state to save children from a life of crime. They urged the creation of a separate juvenile justice system that would provide flexible procedures for the treatment of the underlying social problems that were seen as the basis of juvenile crime. The underlying philosophy of juvenile court was that the state should deal with a child who broke the law much as a wise parent would deal with a wayward child (Platt 1970). That philosophy is legitimized by the legal doctrine of **parens patriae** (state as parent), which allows the state to intervene to protect children's welfare.

Today, all states have juvenile courts, but their organizational relationship to other judicial bodies varies greatly. In some jurisdictions, the juvenile court is a specific division of the trial court of general jurisdiction. The judges are regular members of the bench who rotate in this assignment. In other jurisdictions, the juvenile court is an entirely separate court, whose judges are selected specifically to the position. There are numerous combinations of these two approaches, however. Some large cities, for example, have a family court that handles domestic relations cases as well as juvenile matters.

In 2003, an estimated 2.2 million juveniles were arrested by law enforcement authorities—some for serious crimes (aggravated assault, homicide, armed robbery, and rape). That reflects a continuing trend of decreasing juvenile arrest rates. During the period 1994–2003, juvenile arrests for violent crime dropped by 32 percent (*OJJDP Statistical Briefing Book* 2005). Age usually determines whether a person is processed through the juvenile court or the adult justice system. In most states, a child is a juvenile until the age of 18, but, in some states, it is 17 or 16. In most states, children charged with serious offenses such as murder, rape, or armed robbery or who have a history of repeated offenses may be tried as adults, not as juveniles (Singer 1993). As the public's frustration with crime continues to grow, and as children seem to commit serious crimes at even younger ages, public pressures mount to lower the age at which a child is considered an adult in the eyes of the criminal law.

There is enormous variation in the types of matters that can be brought before juvenile courts. These problems fall into three categories: delinquency, status offenses, and child victim.

Delinquency is a violation of a criminal law that would be a crime if the act were committed by an adult. Common examples include theft, burglary, sale or possession of drugs, and criminal damage to property. A child found to be **delinquent** may be placed on probation or committed to a juvenile institution. The period of confinement may exceed that for an adult.

Status offenses involve acts illegal only for juveniles. Common examples include runaway, truancy, possession of alcohol, and curfew violations. Juveniles found to be status offenders may be sent to the same juvenile correctional institutions as are those found to be delinquent. Status offenses constitute 14 percent of juvenile filings.

Juvenile courts also deal with child-victim petitions involving neglect or dependency. Thus, the child is before the court for no fault of his or her own. Common examples include battered children, children abandoned by their parents, and children who are not receiving proper education or proper medical care. Neglected or dependent children cannot be sentenced to juvenile institutions. Rather, the court has a broad mandate to order social services, foster home or group home care, or medical or mental health services.

Juvenile court statutes set forth two standards for deciding the appropriate disposition for a child: the best interests of the child and the best interests of the community. Because the concept of the juvenile court was to aid—not punish—children, the due process guarantees of the adult criminal court were absent. Procedures were more administrative than adversarial, stressing the informal, private, and noncombative handling of cases. The nature of the juvenile court process remained unchanged until the 1960s. When the Warren Court began to scrutinize procedures in adult criminal courts, its attention also turned to juvenile courts. In a groundbreaking decision, the Supreme Court held in **In re *Gault*** that the due process clause of the Fourteenth Amendment applied to juvenile court proceedings. The court emphasized that "under our Constitution the condition of being a boy does not justify a kangaroo court." The opinion specified that juveniles have (1) the right to notice, (2) the right to counsel, (3) the right to confront witnesses, (4) privilege against self-incrimination, (5) the right to transcripts, and (6) the right to appellate review. The *Gault* decision points to the constant tension within the juvenile court system between those who think children should be given all the due process guarantees accorded adults and those who reason that children must be handled in a less adversarial, more treatment-oriented manner so legal procedures will not interfere with efforts to secure the justice that is in the children's best interest (Grisso and Schwartz 2000). Briefly, more formal procedures may interfere with the juvenile court's traditional ability to provide individualized justice. *Gault* signaled that the juvenile court must become a real court, and its procedures must be regularized in accordance with constitutional requirements (Rubin 1984). *Gault* and subsequent Supreme Court rulings have had a marked effect on juvenile court procedures, changing many of its traditional characteristics and, in some respects, causing it to resemble criminal court (Manfredi 1998). Indeed, Joseph Sanborn (1993) concludes that it is time for juvenile courts to provide defendants whom the court seeks to punish the right to a public jury trial.

Today, the focus of juvenile justice court reform is often on the concept of restorative justice. Juvenile courts that embrace this concept focus on these principles:

- Healing the victim, the community, and the offender
- Involving stakeholders (e.g., victims, community members)
- Transforming traditional views of justice

A recent study of nearly 1,000 juvenile justice programs finds that these principles are being embraced by juvenile courts though implementation is often difficult (Bazemore and Schiff 2004).

COURT UNIFICATION

For more than a century, the organization of American courts has been a central concern of court reformers who believe the multiplicity of courts is inefficient (because judges cannot be shifted to meet the caseload needs of other courts) and also inequitable (because the administration of justice is not uniform). Historically, court reform has been associated with implementing a unified court system. Figure 4.1 provides a diagram of a unified state court system (using Illinois as an example), and Figure 4.2 offers a contrasting diagram of the limited-unification system used in New York.

The principal objective of a **unified court system** is to shift judicial administration from local control to centralized management. The loose network of independent judges and courts would be replaced by a coherent hierarchy, with authority concentrated in the state capital. Although court reformers differ about the exact details of a unified court system, their efforts reflect five general principles: a simplified court structure; centralized administration, rule making, and budgeting; and statewide financing (Berkson and Carbon 1978).

Simplified Court Structure

Court reformers stress the need for a simple, uniform court structure for the entire state. In particular, the multiplicity of minor and specialized courts, which often have overlapping jurisdiction, would be consolidated in one county-level court. That would mean that variations between counties would be eliminated and replaced by a similar court structure throughout the state. Overall, the court reformers envision a three-tier system: a state supreme court at the top, intermediate courts of appeal where the volume of cases makes it necessary, and a single trial court.

Centralized Administration

Reformers envision the state supreme court, working through court administrators, as providing leadership for the state court system. The state court system would embody a genuine hierarchy of authority, with local court administrators required to follow the policy directives of the central office and, in turn, being held accountable by the state supreme court. Thus, a centralized state office would supervise the work of judicial and nonjudicial personnel.

Centralized Rule Making

Reformers argue that the state supreme court should have the power to adopt uniform rules that would be followed by all courts in the state. Examples of such rules would include procedures for disciplining errant attorneys and time standards for disposing of cases. In addition, judges could be temporarily assigned to other courts to alleviate backlogs and reduce delay. Centralized rule making shifts control from the legislatures to judges and lawyers.

CASE CLOSE-UP

■ *Kimbrough v. United States* (2007)
Crack Cocaine v. Powder—Which Deserves More Punishment?

The War on Drugs starts in the neighborhoods and streets of America, but ultimately the battle ends up in the state and federal courts where judge are faced with imposing penalties that result in prisons being crowded with inmates who are, these days, incarcerated more often than not for drug crimes. Members of the legal system and the public have displayed mixed feelings over the last 40 years about the proper penalties that should be associated with drug crimes, especially nonviolent ones.

There is so much variation and uncertainty about what the proper penalty should be that in 2007 the United States Sentencing Commission Sentencing Guidelines still included a sentencing disparity of 100:1 for crack cocaine v. powder cocaine. This disparity originated in the Anti-Drug Abuse Act of 1986 where a defendant found guilty of a crime that involved crack cocaine resulted in a much stiffer sentence than powder cocaine—regardless of other circumstances. Were the guidelines really intended to guarantee consistency in sentencing decisions or were they being used to try and achieve a social outcome? How much discretion should judges have to assign penalties that fit the crime, or should they be forced to apply certain penalties regardless of their judgment about the appropriateness of the penalty in that case.

In 2004, Derrick Kimbrough was arrested in Norfolk, VA by police in a part of town known for drug crimes. In 2005 he pled guilty to a number of drug charges, including distributing crack cocaine and possession of a firearm during a drug-trafficking crime. Based on the sentencing guidelines in place he should have been sentenced to a minimum prison sentence of 19 years, but he district court judge, Raymond Jackson, sentenced him to 15 years in prison, a more lenient punishment that the guidelines recommended. The Fourth Circuit Court of Appeals found the sentence unreasonable and ordered resentencing. In the meantime Kimbrough filed a writ of certiorari to the U.S. Supreme Court where his case would ultimately call into question the voluntary versus mandatory nature of the sentencing guidelines for the federal courts.

Nearly half of the states have Sentencing Guideline Systems in place that provide mandatory or advisory guidance on what penalties to impose for various criminal convictions.

"Sentencing guidelines provide structure at the criminal sentencing stage by specifically defining offense and offender elements that should be considered in each case. After considering these elements using a grid or worksheet scoring system, the guidelines recommend a sentence or sentence range." (NCSC…). State judges are expected to consult, and if they guidelines are mandatory, apply sentences accordingly.

The Federal Sentencing Guidelines are established by the United States Sentencing Commission, and approved by Congress. The original intent was that the guidelines would be mandatory but in 2005 the Supreme Court ruled in *United States v. Booker* (2005) that they could not be mandatory because that would violate the Sixth Amendment so they became essentially advisory or voluntary. In 2007 the Supreme Court heard Derrick Kimbrough's case; essentially to decide the question whether federal judges could deviate from the sentences recommended by the sentencing guidelines. The government argued that the guidelines represent the intent of Congress and therefore must be applied uniformly. Attorneys for Kimbrough argued that judges should have discretion in applying the sentences and should be able to take into consideration factors about the case they deem relevant to the proper punishment.

The Court ruled 7-2 in Kimbrough that the sentence handed down by the District Court Judges was appropriate and constitutional. Ruth Bader Ginsburg's opinion for the majority affirmed the reasonableness of the punishment and reasserted that, according to *Booker*, the Federal Sentencing Guidelines are advisory.

This case illustrates the complexity of restricting the discretion judges have in imposing penalties. It also brings attention to the disparity present when, in this case drug laws, sentencing guidelines are used to try and achieve a social outcome. Are crimes involving crack cocaine really that much different than those using powder? In 2010 the Congress eliminated the sentencing disparity for crack and powder cocaine in the Fair Sentencing Act.

FIGURE **4.1**
Example of a Unified State Court Structure

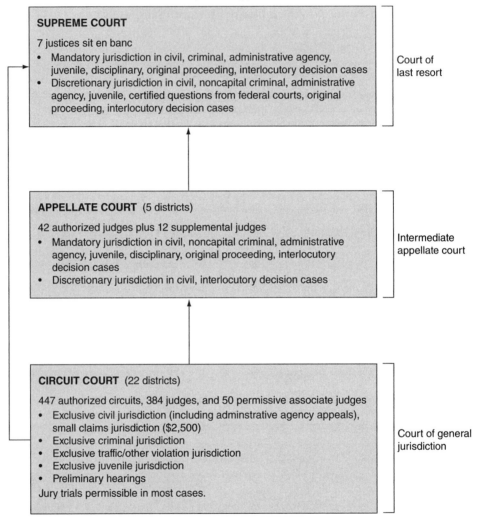

ILLINOIS COURT STRUCTURE
Arrows show paths of appeal.

SUPREME COURT

7 justices sit en banc
- Mandatory jurisdiction in civil, criminal, administrative agency, juvenile, disciplinary, original proceeding, interlocutory decision cases
- Discretionary jurisdiction in civil, noncapital criminal, administrative agency, juvenile, certified questions from federal courts, original proceeding, interlocutory decision cases

Court of last resort

APPELLATE COURT (5 districts)

42 authorized judges plus 12 supplemental judges
- Mandatory jurisdiction in civil, noncapital criminal, administrative agency, juvenile, disciplinary, original proceeding, interlocutory decision cases
- Discretionary jurisdiction in civil, interlocutory decision cases

Intermediate appellate court

CIRCUIT COURT (22 districts)

447 authorized circuits, 384 judges, and 50 permissive associate judges
- Exclusive civil jurisdiction (including adminstrative agency appeals), small claims jurisdiction ($2,500)
- Exclusive criminal jurisdiction
- Exclusive traffic/other violation jurisdiction
- Exclusive juvenile jurisdiction
- Preliminary hearings
Jury trials permissible in most cases.

Court of general jurisdiction

Source: *Bureau of Justice Statistics State Court Organization, 1998* (Washington, D.C.: U.S. Department of Justice, 2000).

Centralized Judicial Budgeting

Centralized budgeting would give the state judicial administrator (who reports to the state supreme court) the authority to prepare a single budget for the entire state judiciary and send it directly to the legislature. The governor's power to recommend a judicial budget would be eliminated. Likewise, lower courts would be dependent on

FIGURE **4.2**
Example of Limited Unification of a State Court Structure

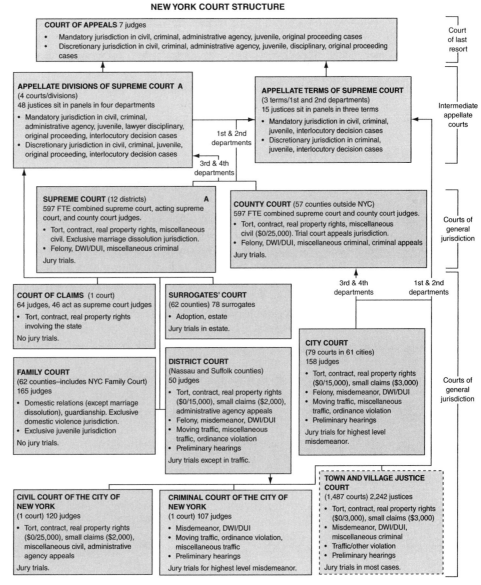

NEW YORK COURT STRUCTURE

COURT OF APPEALS 7 judges
- Mandatory jurisdiction in civil, criminal, administrative agency, juvenile, original proceeding cases
- Discretionary jurisdiction in civil, criminal, administrative agency, juvenile, disciplinary, original proceeding cases

Court of last resort

APPELLATE DIVISIONS OF SUPREME COURT A
(4 courts/divisions)
48 justices sit in panels in four departments
- Mandatory jurisdiction in civil, criminal, administrative agency, juvenile, lawyer disciplinary, original proceeding, interlocutory decision cases
- Discretionary jurisdiction in civil, criminal, juvenile, original proceeding, interlocutory decision cases

APPELLATE TERMS OF SUPREME COURT
(3 terms/1st and 2nd departments)
15 justices sit in panels in three terms
- Mandatory jurisdiction in civil, criminal, juvenile, interlocutory decision cases
- Discretionary jurisdiction in criminal, juvenile, interlocutory decision cases

Intermediate appellate courts

1st & 2nd departments

3rd & 4th departments

SUPREME COURT (12 districts)   **A**
597 FTE combined supreme court, acting supreme court, and county court judges.
- Tort, contract, real property rights, miscellaneous civil. Exclusive marriage dissolution jurisdiction.
- Felony, DWI/DUI, miscellaneous criminal
Jury trials.

COUNTY COURT (57 counties outside NYC)
597 FTE combined supreme court and county court judges.
- Tort, contract, real property rights, miscellaneous civil ($0/25,000). Trial court appeals jurisdiction.
- Felony, DWI/DUI, miscellaneous criminal, criminal appeals
Jury trials.

Courts of general jurisdiction

COURT OF CLAIMS (1 court)
64 judges, 46 act as supreme court judges
- Tort, contract, real property rights involving the state
No jury trials.

SURROGATES' COURT
(62 counties) 78 surrogates
- Adoption, estate
Jury trials in estate.

3rd & 4th departments

1st & 2nd departments

CITY COURT
(79 courts in 61 cities)
158 judges
- Tort, contract, real property rights ($0/15,000), small claims ($3,000)
- Felony, misdemeanor, DWI/DUI
- Moving traffic, miscellaneous traffic, ordinance violation
- Preliminary hearings
Jury trials for highest level misdemeanor.

Courts of general jurisdiction

FAMILY COURT
(62 counties–includes NYC Family Court)
165 judges
- Domestic relations (except marriage dissolution), guardianship. Exclusive domestic violence jurisdiction.
- Exclusive juvenile jurisdiction
No jury trials.

DISTRICT COURT
(Nassau and Suffolk counties)
50 judges
- Tort, contract, real property rights ($0/15,000), small claims ($2,000), administrative agency appeals
- Felony, misdemeanor, DWI/DUI
- Moving traffic, miscellaneous traffic, ordinance violation
- Preliminary hearings
Jury trials except in traffic.

TOWN AND VILLAGE JUSTICE COURT
(1,487 courts) 2,242 justices
- Tort, contract, real property rights ($0/3,000), small claims ($3,000)
- Misdemeanor, DWI/DUI, miscellaneous criminal
- Traffic/other violation
- Preliminary hearings
Jury trials in most cases.

Courts of general jurisdiction

CIVIL COURT OF THE CITY OF NEW YORK
(1 court) 120 judges
- Tort, contract, real property rights ($0/25,000), small claims ($2,000), miscellaneous civil, administrative agency appeals
Jury trials.

CRIMINAL COURT OF THE CITY OF NEW YORK
(1 court) 107 judges
- Misdemeanor, DWI/DUI
- Moving traffic, ordinance violation, miscellaneous traffic
- Preliminary hearings
Jury trials for highest level misdemeanor.

*Unless otherwise noted, numbers reflect statutory authorization. Many judges sit in more than one court, so the number of judgeships indicated in this chart does not reflect the actual number of judges in the system.
Source: *Bureau of Justice Statistics State Court Organization, 1998* (Washington, D.C.: U.S. Department of Justice, 2000).

the supreme court for their monetary needs and unable to lobby local representatives directly. Thus, decisions about allocating funds would be made at the state, and not the local, level. Issues of adequate funding levels for the judiciary become most politically prominent during periods of shrinking state revenues.

Statewide Financing

Along with centralized judicial budgeting, reformers argue for the adoption of statewide financing of the judiciary. Although courts are mandated by state law, they are often financed in whole or in part by local governments. Given that courts are often not a high priority for local government, they end up with less-than-adequate local financing. State government, in contrast, has more money and could better support necessary court services.

THE POLITICS OF COURT REORGANIZATION

Judicial reformers have achieved considerable success. Most states have substantially unified their court systems. Significantly, though, only a few states have adopted most or all of the principles suggested by court reformers (Baar 1993). Several states, for example, have adopted a four-tier system (rather than the recommended three tiers) by retaining the lower courts as a separate level rather than combining them with the major trial courts (Flango and Rottman 1992). Along those same lines, the principle of statewide financing has not fared well. In many states, the county (or an equivalent unit) still finances the major trial courts to a significant degree.

Why have some reform proposals been rejected? Why have the reformers' recommendations been significantly modified? The answer lies in the *political* dimensions of court reorganization. Battles over court organization are usually presented as dry technical issues involving case volume and efficiency, but such arguments mask the underlying political dynamics.

Support for court reform is concentrated among the elite of the legal profession. The American Bar Association is a longtime advocate of judicial reform. The American Judicature Society was formed in 1913 by elite members of the bar to campaign for improving the courts. Likewise, middle-class reform organizations, such as the League of Women Voters, endorse the ideals of court reform. More recently, judicial reform has achieved wide official recognition and has become the "government approved" approach to judicial administration. The National Institute of Justice within the U.S. Justice Department and the quasi-private National Center for State Courts reflect a trend toward greater government involvement and leadership in advocating the unified model of judicial administration (Glick 1988).

But the efforts of legal elites to drum up support for court reform are often greeted with disinterest or skepticism. Lawyers reflect divided sentiments over judicial reform. General practice and trial lawyers (who are less likely to be members of the American Bar Association) perceive that court reform would require unnecessary changes in their routines. Judges and other court personnel likewise resist the idea of being forced to learn new procedures if the courts are reorganized. Finally, many of the problems associated with the existing structure of courts are concentrated in large cities. Rural politicians and rural lawyers, because they see no problems in their own area, are not sympathetic to major overhauls that would not benefit them but might mean decreased control of local courts (Glick and Vines 1973). The general public has little interest in abstract notions of a cleaner-looking organization chart for the judiciary.

At times, court reform also engenders opposition. Court reform proposals can become a battleground between political parties (Glick 1988). The party in power often perceives quite correctly that court reform will mean the loss of important patronage positions. Any attempt to unify a state judiciary invariably brings opposition from local governments that wish to retain control of their local courts. Issues of local versus state authority also have important financial dimensions. As a result, most proposals to unify state court systems carry the provision that the state will pay all expenses of the local courts (thus relieving cities of millions of dollars in expenses) but allow municipalities to retain revenues derived from court fines and court fees. Finally, nonlawyer judges often oppose court reorganization because they fear their jobs would be abolished under plans requiring all judges to be lawyers. That is why many court reform proposals include "grandfather clauses" allowing nonlawyer judges to remain in office. (A grandfather clause is an exception that allows all those already doing something to continue that activity in spite of the new regulation.)

Despite those political obstacles, court reformers have made great strides in altering court structures. The changes adopted in a given state, however, reflect that state's political environment. Alaska and Hawaii have highly unified courts that reflect the way in which territorial courts developed before statehood. North Carolina's courts are highly consolidated, but elected county clerks remain powerful. Maryland was able to unify its minor courts into a statewide court of limited jurisdiction but was unable to overcome the resistance of the general jurisdiction trial courts, which remain locally funded and administered (Baar and Henderson 1982). Court reformers have been less successful in decoupling politics and court administration in the context of budgeting. States continue to struggle with how to fund court systems and how to manage the politics associated with budgeting (Hartley and Douglas 2003).

Court Reform: The Next Steps

The assumptions and the philosophy of traditional notions of court reform have been called into serious question. Many now believe that the old principles of court reorganization hamper creative thinking (Flango 1994; Lamber and Luskin 1992).

Modern critics argue that the concept of a unified court system reflects a classical view of public administration, which stressed a strong central administration (that is, policy flowed from the top down); contemporary theories of public administration, on the other hand, stress the active participation by those most affected (policies flow from the bottom up). As a result, the standard blueprint of court reorganization does not allow for a desirable diversity. Furthermore, the reformers fail to understand the realities of the courthouse (law in action, for short). In the words of Carl Baar (1980, 278), "The persistence of politics has been a failure not of court reformers but of those who have articulated reform arguments in the past." Some principles of a unified court system would not remove politics from the system but, rather, benefit some political actors more than others; for instance, court unification increases the influence of the legal profession (Scheb and Matheny 1988). Most important, court reformers suffer from elite bias. Their perceptions of the problems of the courthouse extend only to cases with policy significance involving major community actors and rarely to ordinary cases affecting average citizens. In the biting words of Laura Nader (1992), court reformers talk about "how to rid the ... courts of 'garbage cases' (e.g., consumer, environmental, and feminist issues)." The net result is that problems of battered women and abused children are not considered real court cases, and the difficult questions of child custody are ignored while judges concentrate on the issues raised by big business and big government.

Today, court reform concentrates more on how to improve the quality of justice meted out by American courts and less on how to provide a neater judiciary organization chart. The solutions proposed by lawyer elites seem unresponsive to the realities of ordinary cases heard in the nation's trial courts. A judiciary with a clearly delineated organizational structure staffed by judges selected on the basis of merit (selection processes are discussed in Chapter 6) will still face the same problems of large caseloads and types of cases—child custody, for example—that are difficult to decide. Community courts, domestic violence, family court, and mental health courts have sprung up all across the country in an effort to break away from traditional court room practices and find a better solution to mete out justice. A common example of this new reform agenda has been the the creation of drug courts.

Drug Courts

> The mission of the Dunkirk City Drug Court is to provide protection for the community from repeat drug and alcohol offenders by providing timely and effective treatment and supervision. The goal is to reduce the cost of the criminal justice system without increasing the risks to the public. In addition, the mission is to provide the tools so that defendants may become sober, productive citizens. (*Buffalo News* 2001)

That mission statement illustrates how the judiciary is responding to dramatic increases in drug cases. Beginning in the mid-1980s, drug caseloads rose across the nation. As a centerpiece of the so-called War on Drugs, elected officials at all levels—federal, state, and local—backed efforts to arrest, prosecute, and imprison persons possessing or selling illegal drugs. The result is nearly two million drug arrests every year. In the major urban areas of the United States, the impact of the War on Drugs has been particularly dramatic. (See Law and Popular Culture: *Traffic*.)

Some judges and court administrators feared that the first major casualty of the War on Drugs would be the nation's urban trial courts. "[T]he situation is desperate. The overload causes backlog; backlog feeds delay; and delay (along with the lack of jail and prison space) imperils rights to timely consideration, undermines deterrence, and breeds contempt for the law" (Lipscher 1989, 14). In some jurisdictions, civil cases were placed on the back burner because criminal filings (which increasingly meant minor drug cases) came first. Fears of a system breakdown, however, were somewhat overblown (Mahoney 1994). One reason was the creation of drug courts, which reflected a great deal of experimentation as judges, prosecutors, public defenders, and sheriffs, among others, sought to respond. Not surprisingly, different approaches were used (Davis, Smith, and Lurigio 1994)—but, over time, the treatment approach has become most prevalent (see Exhibit 4.1).

L A W   A N D   P O P U L A R   C U L T U R E

■ *Traffic* (2000)

As society changed and the nation's War on Drugs gathered steam, the courts became clogged with drug cases, and they reacted through organizational change. Few films do anything like spark a national debate, but the Academy Award–winning movie *Traffic* did just that. In *Traffic*, director Steven Soderbergh presents the complexity of America's War on Drugs through three divergent narratives that only occasionally overlap.

The first narrative is set in the morally hazy world of Tijuana, Mexico. The central figure is Rodriguez (Benicio Del Toro), an honest police officer who earns $316 a month. His efforts to curtail one of the two major drug cartels in the area run afoul of the ambitions of General Arturo Salazar (Tomas Milian). General Salazar is one of Mexico's toughest anticrime figures, but his reasons for asking Rodriguez and his partner, Manolo Sanchez (Jacob Vargas), to join his efforts are not immediately clear. However, Rodriguez knows that if he doesn't join General Salazar, his life will be in jeopardy.

The second narrative is set in the political ambiguity of Washington, D.C. The main figure is Robert Wakefield (Michael Douglas), a justice of the Ohio Supreme Court who has been selected to be the nation's drug czar. His briefings before officially accepting the job stress the political expectations of the job. His predecessor, for example, was removed because he lacked the capability to perform the "political component" of the job. But, as he tries to understand the official perspectives of the War on Drugs, a more personal view develops: His teenage daughter Caroline (Erika Christensen) is doing more than experimenting with drugs—she is becoming addicted. She escapes a drug treatment program and ends up in the inner city, where she is forced to prostitute herself to support her drug habit.

The third narrative is set in the socially snobby country clubs of La Jolla, California. The dominant person is Helena Ayala (Catherine Zeta-Jones), whose rich husband allows her to live the good life. But the Drug Enforcement Administration (DEA) has turned a mid-level drug dealer who fingers Helena's husband, Carl, as the area's major supplier. Suddenly, her husband is whisked away by the DEA, and she soon learns the truth about her husband's source of wealth. She also learns that her husband owes millions and, unless she can deliver the money, her children will be killed. Facing financial ruin, she soon takes command of the operation

and devises a way to make the government's key witnesses "unavailable to testify."

Traffic is a contemporary movie addressing a contemporary issue, to the extent of using cameos by current U.S. Senators Barbara Boxer (D-Calif.) and Orrin Hatch (R-Utah). It raised many issues about how our society and, ultimately, our courts deal with the drug issue. *Traffic* raised awareness about the difficulty of winning a drug war. The film prompted a *Chicago Tribune* editor to write, "*Traffic* lays bare the futility of a destructive war on drugs that has gridlocked our culture in the logic of law enforcement" (Muwakkil 2001). It was responsible at least in part for a special *Nightline* five-part series titled "Traffic: The War on Drugs." And the August 16, 2001, issue of *Rolling Stone* ran a special article on "America's War on Drugs," in which three commentators (including Senator Hatch and Robert Iger, president and chief operating officer of the Walt Disney Company) emphasized the importance of *Traffic* in bringing attention to the drug issue. Although the film and the subsequent commentary did not focus specifically on the issue of drug courts, such agenda setting by the media can lead to change in society that ultimately affects the courts.

Traffic depicts drug dealers very differently than did the 1971 movie *The French Connection*. In that movie, Gene Hackman starred as a New York detective trying to break up an organized crime gang smuggling heroin from Turkey through the French port of Marseilles. *The French Connection* presents no moral or policy ambiguities; it is an action movie about a good cop arresting bad guys. Thus, simply busting big-time drug dealers is the end in and of itself.

After watching *Traffic*, be prepared to answer the following questions:

1. How would a change in the legalization of drugs affect court dockets?
2. How does *Traffic*'s promotion of a more "therapeutic culture" contrast with the legal system's increasing use of drug courts?
3. The film displays the inherent discretion built into law enforcement. In what ways does such discretion contribute to the difficulty of running the drug war and, ultimately, managing drug courts?

To learn more about these movies, go to the website: http://www.trafficthemovie.com

---

EXHIBIT 4.1 **What Makes a Drug Court?**

According to a report by the National Association of Drug Court Professionals, 10 key components characterize the nation's drug courts:

1. Drug courts integrate alcohol and other drug treatment services with the justice system's case processing.
2. Using a nonadversarial approach, prosecution and defense counsel promote public safety while protecting participants' due process rights.
3. Eligible participants are identified early and promptly placed in the drug court program.
4. Drug courts provide access to a continuum of alcohol, drug, and other related treatment and rehabilitation services.
5. Abstinence is monitored by frequent testing for alcohol and other drugs.
6. A coordinated strategy governs drug court responses to participants' compliance.
7. Ongoing judicial interaction with each drug court participant is essential.
8. Monitoring and evaluation measure the achievement of program goals and gauge effectiveness.
9. Continuing interdisciplinary education promotes effective drug court planning, implementation, and operations.
10. Forging partnerships among drug courts, public agencies, and community-based organizations generates local support and enhances drug court effectiveness.

Source: U.S. Department of Justice, *Defining Drug Courts: The Key Components* (Washington, D.C.: U.S. Department of Justice, Office of Justice Programs, 1997). Available online at http://www.ncjrs.org/html/bja/define/welcome.html. Retrieved April 2, 2003.

Treatment Approach to Drug Offenders

The premise of most contemporary drug courts is that treatment will reduce the likelihood that convicted drug offenders will be rearrested (Hartley and Phillips 2001). Some courts tie the sentence to participation in drug treatment. Other courts defer adjudication of guilt while the defendant receives treatment; that is, the case is held in abeyance while the defendant participates in a drug program. If treatment is successful, the case is later dismissed. Defendants who successfully complete treatment thereby avoid the stigma associated with a felony conviction.

The Dade County (Miami) Circuit Court provides an example of a treatment approach to drug offenders. It has received extensive national publicity. To be eligible, defendants must have no prior felony convictions, must be charged with possession only (not sale), and must admit their drug problem and request treatment. These offenders are diverted into treatment. Miami's approach differs from traditional programs in other courts in two ways. First, the sentencing judge, rather than a probation officer, monitors offender progress. Participants must report to the drug court judge, who assesses their progress and moves them through the phases of the program. Second, defendants are usually allowed to stay in the program even when they violate its conditions of participation. Findings to date indicate that, compared with defendants not in the program, offenders in the Miami drug court treatment program have lower incarceration rates, less frequent rearrests, and longer times to rearrest (Goldkamp and Weiland 1993). A study of the Miami drug court by the National Institute of Justice reported a 33 percent reduction in rearrest rates for drug court graduates compared with other like offenders (Drug Court Clearinghouse 1997).

How the courts will deal with the continuing stream of drug cases continues to attract the attention of court administrators and the public. The recent changes in drug courts appear to point to what Nolan (2001) refers to as a move toward "therapeutic justice," in which the emphasis is on therapy rather than punishment. The "drug court family" is expanding, too, as jurisdictions have begun creating juvenile drug courts and family drug courts to emphasize the uniqueness of these special populations. In 2009, there were almost 500 juvenile drug courts and nearly 300 family drug courts in operation (Drug Court Clearinghouse 2009). For example, Ohio's family drug court is designed to deal with the unique aspects of adult drug offenders who are at risk of losing their children, thereby putting additional strains on the criminal justice system (Ritter 2001). These courts reflect the same goal of the more general drug courts but focus on special populations. (See Debating Law, Courts, and Politics: Marijuana: Evil Drug or Medicine?

Evaluating Drug Courts

The number of drug courts continues to grow. In 2009, there were over 1,500 drug courts in operation (Drug Court Clearinghouse 2009). Drug courts are not without detractors, though. In addition to those who object to the nonpunitive nature of the punishment are critics of the cost. The drug court in Montgomery County, Texas, for example, costs about $400,000 annually (Howie 2001). And, although federal and state grants have picked up some of those costs, the increased competition for funding means that jurisdictions increasingly have to pay their own way. The politics of funding drug courts has become increasingly complicated (Douglas and Hartley 2004).

But what if drug courts have the unintended consequence of increasing the number of prisoners in jail on drug charges? That is exactly what one Denver-area judge claims has happened. In the words of Judge Morris Hoffman (2000), "We grossly underestimated the enthusiasm with which our police and prosecutors would embrace the idea of a drug court." He claims that not only did court filings triple the year after the drug court was created but also the absolute number of convictions has risen. His numbers show that in 1993—before the drug court was created—256 drug defendants were sentenced to prison; in 1995—the year after the drug court was created—434 drug defendants received prison sentences. Thus, both filings and incarcerations went up. Hoffman refers to this as the "popcorn effect" and explains that the "very presence of the drug court, with its significantly increased capacity for processing cases, has caused police to make arrests in, and prosecutors to file, the kinds of ten- and twenty-dollar hand-to-hand drug cases that the system simply would not have bothered with before, certainly not as felonies."

The biggest questions surrounding drug courts, though, center on successes. A recent study or Oregon's drug courts concluded that their drug courts reduced recidivism and were cost effective (2010). But other evaluations—whose analysis goes beyond the blunt data of incarceration rates—have reported a different picture. In Washington, D.C., participation in the drug treatment program was poor—only forty-one of those eligible chose to participate. Moreover, completion of the program took much longer than anticipated; cases were open an average of eleven months as opposed to the six months estimated (Harrell, Cavanagh, and Roman

2000). Thus, the jury on drug courts is still out. Although it is difficult to compare drug courts across jurisdictions, it remains important to consider the wide range of criteria that can be used to evaluate their success or failure (Inciardi, McBride, and Rivers 1996).

DEBATING LAW, COURTS, AND POLITICS

■ Marijuana: Evil Drug or Medicine?

In the United States, marijuana is a Schedule I drug putting it in the same category as heroin, ecstasy, and LSD. To the federal government marijuana remains (at least as law on the books) an evil drug. Sale of the drug is illegal under federal law. But California in 1996 legalized the possession and sale of marijuana for medical reasons and in the fifteen years since then another 14 states and the District of Columbia have followed suit. How can a federal law exist that makes possession of any amount and sale of marijuana among the most serious crimes (even possessing one marijuana cigarette could lead to jail time), but states pass laws that allow doctors to write prescriptions for and patients to grow or possess marijuana if they have a variety of medical conditions? Such is the complexity of law in a federal legal system where there are national and state legislatures, federal and state courts, and national and state law enforcement.

Historically the prosecution of drug crimes has been a state responsibility with legislatures, law enforcement and courts making decisions about the appropriate penalties associated with the possession and sale of illegal drugs. Only in the most high profile trafficking or where other circumstances were present did the federal government get involved. But in 2001, partly in response to the "medical marijuana" movement, the United States Drug Enforcement Agency started making raids in California and, among others, arrested Diane Monson (CNN). Angel Raich later joined Monson in suing to block the application of the federal laws to their use of marijuana. Their case would ultimately end up in the United States Supreme Court and be the focus of *Gonzales v. Raich* (2005) where the Supreme Court ruled in a 6-3 decision that the Constitution's Commerce Clause gives the federal government the authority to regulate anything that has a substantial effect on interstate commerce. President Bush's director of national drug control policy in reacting to the outcome said "Today's decision marks the end of medical marijuana as a political issue." But California's attorney general at the time, Bill Lockyer, said "[the decision] shows the vast philosophical difference between the federal government and Californians on the rights of patients to have access to the medicine they need to survive and lead healthier lives" (*Washington Post*). The simple interpretation of Raich is that the federal government's laws covering marijuana trump any less restrictive law that a state might pass. In light of this decision marijuana growers and users, even in states where the law made it legal, could still be subject to federal prosecution.

But the Court's decision did not stop the push for the passage of medical marijuana laws in states and since the decision 6 states and the District of Columbia have passed laws making legal the use of marijuana for medical purposes. The two most recent states to pass laws include Arizona (April 2011) and Delaware (May 2011). In November 2010, 47% of California voters voted to legalize marijuana and just a month before the vote Governor Schwarzenegger signed a law that makes possession of less than one ounce of marijuana a civil infraction. So clearly voters and legislatures across the country continue to be taking the law in a different direction than the congress and the federal courts. In contrast to the Bush administration, the Obama administration originally indicated they would only attempt to prosecute individuals who violated both federal and state laws, giving hope to many marijuana dispensaries in states with medical marijuana laws that they would not be the target of federal raids. However, raids did continue and some U.S attorneys sent letters to state officials with medical marijuana laws emphasizing the rights of the United States government to prosecute individuals regardless of the state law. In June 2011 Attorney General Holder signaled again some possible changes in the way the federal government would prosecute individuals and dispensaries and Representatives Barney Frank (MA) and Ron Paul (TX) introduced legislation in the House of Representatives to remove marijuana from the list of Schedule I drugs. Even though it has no chance of being passed, its introduction, along with getting several co-sponsors, demonstrates that attitudes, even in Congress, are beginning to change.

(continued)

The fight over medical marijuana and to some degree the seriousness with which we should treat marijuana as a drug demonstrates the interplay between law, courts and the public. Marijuana has been a Schedule I drug since 1932, but popular opinion is constantly changing and voters and legislatures in states are making it legal for medical purposes and decriminalizing it for everyday use—making being caught with small amounts no different than receiving a traffic ticket. The fight over marijuana even demonstrates how different enforcement of laws can be from one political regime or party to another. At the end of the day how such legal issues ultimately get resolved in the United States will be sorted our through our laws and courts.

1. Discuss how it is possible for States to pass laws that contradict federal law and decisions of the United States Supreme Court.
2. Should popular opinion in states or the Constitution guide the Supreme Court in making decisions about whether state laws should be upheld or overturned?
3. What does it mean for a "nation of laws not men" when different political officials (presidents, attorneys general, drug enforcement agency officials) interpret and enforce the same law differently?

CONSEQUENCES OF COURT ORGANIZATION

How the courts are organized and administered has a profound effect on the way cases are processed and on the type of justice that results.

Decentralization and Choice of Courts

People frequently refer to the American legal system, but no such entity actually exists. Instead, there are 51 legal systems in America—the U.S. courts and separate courts in each of the fifty states. As stressed in Chapter 2, significant differences exist in the laws and rules applied by each legal system. As a result, lawyers sometimes try to maneuver cases into courts that are perceived to be favorable to their clients. Alternatively, they maneuver to avoid courts perceived to be less favorable. For example, some criminal offenses involve a simultaneous violation of state and federal law. As a general rule, federal officials prosecute major violations, leaving more minor prosecutions to state officials. Civil litigants may also have choices about where to file suit. For cases with federal jurisdiction, litigants may also choose which federal court to file in. The oil and natural gas industry, for example, prefers to litigate in the Fifth Circuit because that court has historically been supportive of the industry. By contrast, consumer groups prefer to file in the D.C. Court of Appeals, because that court has historically supported consumers.

The importance of choice of courts is illustrated by the lawsuit contesting the Texaco buyout of the Getty Oil Company. Pennzoil claimed that Texaco had interfered with its negotiations with Getty and sued Texaco in a Texas state trial court (*Pennzoil v. Texaco* 1985). A sympathetic home-state jury eventually awarded Pennzoil a staggering $10.5 billion. Some knowledgeable lawyers criticized Texaco for allowing itself to be sued in state, rather than in federal, court.

Local Control and Local Corruption

The fifty state court systems are often structured on a local basis. The officials who staff those courts—judges and lawyers, prosecutors and defense attorneys—are recruited from the local community they serve and, thus, reflect the sentiments of that community. As a result, the U.S. system of justice has close ties to local communities, and the application of "state" law often has a local flavor. For example, jurors in rural areas and jurors in urban areas often have markedly different opinions about who is at fault in an accident and the amount of damages that should be awarded.

COURTS IN COMPARATIVE PERSPECTIVE

■ The Federal Republic of Mexico

Agustín Vazquez Mendoza was on the Federal Bureau of Investigation's ten most wanted list for the 1994 murder of a U.S. undercover drug enforcement officer in Arizona when he was captured in Mexico City. After his arrest he sat in a Mexican prison because the Mexican Supreme Court blocked his extradition on grounds that he would be subjected to the death penalty. Was that decision an example of judicial corruption or a sign that the government was respecting judicial independence? On January 29, 2005, the DEA announced that Mendoza had finally been extradited to Arizona to stand trial. At trial he was found guilty and sentenced to life in prison.

Mexico and the United States share a long border and a long history of mutual suspicion. Today, the predominant issues are economic ones. Mexico has a free-market economy with a mixture of modern and outmoded industry and agriculture, increasingly dominated by the private sector. The average annual income is $13,900, and 47 percent of the population lives below the poverty line (CIA Factbook). The sharp contrast in economic conditions between the two nations leads to problems such as illegal immigration and drug smuggling.

The Mexican legal system traces its lineage to Spain. In its civil legal system, judges have more extensive responsibilities and power than do judges in common-law nations. For example, judges, rather than lawyers, direct investigations and take testimony. The highest court is the Supreme Court of Justice (or Corte Suprema de Justicia). Judges are officially appointed for life—in practice, however, judges resign at the beginning of each presidential election, allowing the incoming president to place his loyalists on the bench. Thus, although the Supreme Court of Justice officially has the power of judicial review, it rarely exercises such power (Hauss 2000).

Compared with the United States, Mexico does not have a tradition of judicial independence. Like many other countries in Latin America, Mexico is making a transition to electoral democracy, but its legal institutions remain mired in deep-rooted authoritarian legacies. There is an overall lack of rule of law, and the lack of commitment to the rule of law explains why constitutions tend to be hollow. For example, in 1994 it took then-President Ernesto Zedillo only one month after being elected to amend the Mexican constitution in a way that fundamentally transformed how the Supreme Court of Justice exercised judicial review (Schor 2000).

Mexico also has a legacy of governmental corruption that extends to the judiciary. There is a widespread perception that judges can be bought and sold. Although Mexico does not have a tradition of assassinating judges (as in Colombia), the possibility exists. Corruption is often associated with major drug cartels. The Mexican judiciary, police, and armed forces are thoroughly penetrated by *narcopolitica*, "the term first applied in Colombia to the fusion of politics and criminality portrayed in the film *Traffic*" (Whalen 2001). Thus, U.S. law enforcement agencies have been reluctant to share data with their Mexican counterparts.

The refusal to extradite Mendoza to the United States was one of more than seventy high-profile cases. The decision is rooted in the Mexican constitution, which forbids the death penalty and, thus, prohibits extraditing a Mexican citizen to a country where he or she may face the death penalty (Weiner 2002). In the past, the influence of the Mexican president might have been used to force a different decision, but at the time, Mexico's President Vicente Fox made respect for judicial independence a cornerstone of what he called a "transition to democracy" (Stevenson 2002). President Fox's attempt to change 100 years of national disregard for law was an important first step. Mexico's current president Felipe Calderon launched a crackdown on the drug cartels in 2006 but data from Mexico suggest that between 2006 and 2010 over 30,000 people have died from drug violence, continuing to present a serious challenge to Mexico's political and legal institutions.

Local control of justice has the obvious advantage of closely linking courts to the people they serve. But local control has also been the incubator for corruption and injustice. Every state invariably has a town or two where gambling and prostitution flourish because the city officials agree to look the other way. Not surprisingly, the officials often receive monetary benefits for being so nearsighted. Increasingly, though, such activities attract the attention of state police, state attorneys general, and federal prosecutors. (See Courts in Comparative Perspective: The Federal Republic of Mexico.)

The locally administered criminal justice system has also been marked by pockets of injustice. At times, the police and the courts have been the handmaidens of the local economic elite. In the South, the police and the courts hindered efforts to exercise civil rights by arresting or harassing those who sought to register to vote, eat at the whites-only lunch counter, or simply speak up to protest segregation.

The dual court system has provided a safety valve for checking the most flagrant abuses of local justice. Often, it is federal—not state or local—officials who prosecute corrupt local officials.

CONCLUSION

"I'm not sure I made the slightest difference," confides the nation's drug czar to his heir apparent. The movie *Traffic* makes it crystal clear that the general was being removed not for lack of zeal but for his failure to master the political dimensions of the War on Drugs. Publicly elected officials treat the War on Drugs like a third rail—touch it and you die. Privately, however, many governmental officials (some even in law enforcement) have serious doubts that this war is winnable.

Regardless of whether you agree with the portrayals in the movie *Traffic*, it brings home the fact that the War on Drugs is both a legal and a political issue (the theme sounded in Chapter 1). It also reminds us that the War on Drugs has swollen felony dockets across the nation. Much of that burden has fallen on the state court system—the subject of this chapter.

State courts administer most of the justice dispensed in the United States. They process far more cases than the federal courts and present a dizzying array of court structures and processes. Much like the federal system, state courts today have trial courts (of limited and general jurisdiction), intermediate appellate courts, and state courts of last resort (often called the state supreme court). But they also have an array of specialized courts that deal with specific kinds of cases, such as juvenile matters and drug offenses.

At the local level stand the justice of the peace courts in rural areas and the municipal courts in urban jurisdictions. These lower trial courts dispense justice in rapid fashion and are a frequent target of criticism from judicial reformers who argue that the system moves too quickly and that the "process is the punishment." The process slows down as parties appeal lower-court decisions to the intermediate courts of appeals and, finally, the state supreme court. Most cases never get appealed, and, in those that do, the appellate court often affirms the lower-court decision. For most litigants, a decision by the intermediate court of appeals will be final. Today, state supreme courts possess great control over their dockets and have considerable discretion in deciding which cases they will consider.

Because state courts are where most justice is dispensed, they have also been frequent targets of judicial reformers. One of the first suggestions by court reform advocates was the creation of specialized courts to deal with juveniles who were thought to be poorly served by the adult court system. Later, they argued that the confusing structure of local courts should be better organized—advocating a unified court system with a simplified court structure, central administration, and statewide financing. Today, court reformers often focus on the creation of specialized drug courts to deal with the unique problems illicit drug use has created for state courts.

The War on Drugs highlights two key aspects of the American judiciary:

- Courts do not exist in splendid isolation, somehow removed from what is happening in the rest of society. Courts, and the cases they hear, reflect broader societal developments.
- American courts are capable of adaptation. As the War on Drugs escalated, local officials across the nation sought to respond not just by making more arrests but also by trying to shape appropriate treatment-oriented programs.

The courts in the United States, more so than their counterparts in other nations of the world, have a unique ability to change with the times (Neubauer 2003). Their dynamic nature makes them an endlessly interesting topic of study.

CRITICAL THINKING QUESTIONS

1. Although we typically talk about state courts (as opposed to federal courts), would it be better to talk about local courts? To what extent are there major variations within your state?

2. Compare your state's courts with Figures 4.1 and 4.2. How unified is your state court structure?

3. Court reform is an often-mentioned concept but a fairly difficult one to pin down. What types of court reforms have been suggested for your state? Which interest groups support/oppose those reforms and why?

4. In what ways do drug courts and other courts that use therapeutic jurisprudence challenge traditional notions of court reform? To what extent might these courts become the focus of court reform in the future? Why?

Search Terms

courts	National Center for State	state courts
drug courts	Courts	

Useful URLs

http://www.ncsconline.org
> National Center for State Courts

http://www.ajs.org
> American Judicature Society

http://spa.american.edu/justice/drugcourts.php
> American University Justice Office Programs Drug Court Clearinghouse and Technical Assistance Project

http://www.statejustice.org
> State Justice Institute, established by federal law to award grants for the improvement of state courts

REFERENCES

http://www.oregon.gov/CJC/docs/ORDC_BJA_Cost_and_-Best_Practices_Final_Report_Dec2010.pdf?ga=t

Ashman, Allan. 1975. *Courts of Limited Jurisdiction: A National Survey*. Chicago: American Judicature Society.

Baar, Carl. 1980. "The Scope and Limits of Court Reform." *Justice System Journal* 5: 274–290.

———. 1993. "Trial Court Unification in Practice." *Judicature* 76: 179–184.

Baar, Carl, and Thomas Henderson. 1982. "Organizational Design for State Court Systems." In *The Analysis of Judicial Reform*, edited by Philip Dubois. Lexington, Mass.: Lexington Books.

Bazemore, Gordon, and Mara Schiff. 2004. *Juvenile Justice Reform and Restorative Justice: Building Theory and Policy from Practice*. Portland, Ore.: Willan Publishing.

Berkson, Larry, and Susan Carbon. 1978. *Court Unification: History, Politics, and Implementation*. Washington, D.C.: National Institute of Law Enforcement and Criminal Justice.

Bertram, Eva, ed. 1996. *Drug War Politics: The Price of Denial*. Berkeley: University of California Press.

Bosworth, Matthew J. 2001. *Courts as Catalysts: State Supreme Courts and Public School Finance Equity*. Albany: State University of New York Press.

Brace, Paul R., and Melinda Gann Hall. 1997. "The Interplay of Preferences, Case Facts, Context, and Rules in the Politics of Judicial Choice." *Journal of Politics* 59(4): 1206–1231.

Brace, Paul, Laura Langer, and Melinda Gann Hall. 2000. "Measuring the Preferences of State Supreme Court Judges." *Journal of Politics* 62(2): 387–413.

Brown, Lee. 1995. "Why the United States Will Never Legalize Drugs: Protecting Our Children." *Vital Speeches* 61: 628–630.

Buffalo News. 2001. October 16.

Currie, Elliott. 1993. *Reckoning: Drugs, the Cities, and the American Future*. New York: Hill and Wang.

Davis, Robert, Barbara Smith, and Arthur Lurigio. 1994. "Court Strategies to Cope with Rising Drug Caseloads." *Justice System Journal* 17: 1–18.

Douglas, James W., and Roger E. Hartley. 2004. "Sustaining Drug Courts in Arizona and South Carolina: An Experience in Hodgepodge Budgeting." *Justice System Journal* 25(1): 75–86.

Drug Court Clearinghouse and Technical Assistance Project. 1997. Washington, D.C.: American University.

———. 1999. *Looking at a Decade of Drug Courts*. Washington, D.C.: American University. Available online at http://www.american.edu/academic.depts/spa/justice/publications/decade1.htm.

———. 2007. *Drug Court Activity: Summary Information*. Washington, D.C.: American University.

Examining the Work of State Courts. 2003. Williamsburg, Va.: National Center for State Courts. Available online at http://www.ncsconline.org/D_Research/csp/2003_Files/2003_Main_Page.html.

———. 2007. Williamsburg, Va.: National Center for State Courts. Available online at http://www.ncsconline.org/D_Research/csp/CSP_Main_Page.html.

Feeley, Malcolm. 1979. *The Process Is the Punishment*. New York: Russell Sage Foundation.

Flango, Victor. 1994. "Court Unification and Quality of State Courts." *Justice System Journal* 16: 33–56.

Flango, Victor, and David Rottman. 1992. "Research Note: Measuring Trial Court Consolidation." *Justice System Journal* 16: 65–74.

Friedman, Lawrence. 1985. *A History of American Law*. 2d ed. New York: Simon & Schuster.

Glaser, Howard. 1994. "*Wachtler v. Cuomo*: The Limits of Inherent Powers." *Judicature* 78: 12–24.

Glick, Henry. 1988. *Courts, Politics and Justice*. 2d ed. New York: McGraw-Hill.

Glick, Henry, and Kenneth Vines. 1973. *State Court Systems*. Englewood Cliffs, N.J.: Prentice Hall.

Goerdt, John. 1992. *Small Claims and Traffic Courts: Case Management Procedures, Case Characteristics, and Outcomes in 12 Urban Jurisdictions*. Williamsburg, Va.: National Center for State Courts.

Goldkamp, John, and Doris Weiland. 1993. "Assessing the Impact of Dade County's Felony Drug Court." *National Institute of Justice Research in Brief*. Washington, D.C.: U.S. Department of Justice.

Grisso, Thomas, and Robert G. Schwartz. 2000. *Youth on Trial: A Developmental Perspective on Juvenile Justice*. Chicago: University of Chicago Press.

Hall, Melinda Gann. 1992. "Electoral Politics and Strategic Voting in State Supreme Courts." *Journal of Politics* 54(2): 427–446.

———. 2001. "State Supreme Courts in American Democracy: Probing the Myths of Judicial Reform." *American Political Science Review* 95(2): 315–330.

Harrell, Adele, Shannon Cavanagh, and John Roman. 2000. *Evaluation of the D.C. Superior Court Drug Intervention Programs*. Washington, D.C.: U.S. Department of Justice, National Institute of Justice.

Hartley, Roger E. 2002. *Alternative Dispute Resolution in Civil Justice Systems*. New York: LFB Scholarly Press.

Hartley, Roger E., and James W. Douglas. 2003. "Budgeting for State Courts: The Perceptions of Key Officials Regarding the Determinants of Budget Success." *Justice System Journal* 24(3): 251–263.

Hartley, Roger E., and Randy Phillips. 2001. "Who Graduates from Drug Courts? Correlates of Client Success." *American Journal of Criminal Justice* 26: 107–120.

Hauss, Charles. 2000. *Comparative Politics: Democratic Responses to Global Challenges*. Belmont, Calif.: Wadsworth.

http://www.law.com/jsp/article.jsp?id=1197281074188&slreturn=1&hbxlogin=1

http://www.pewcenteronthestates.org/uploadedFiles/NCSC_Sentencing_Guidelines_profiles_July_2008.pdf

http://governmentprnews.com/government_articles/2011/05/difficulties-with-sentencing-in-drug-crimes-crack-v-powder-cocaine-215700.htm

Hoffman, Morris B. 2000. "The Drug Court Scandal." *North Carolina Law Review* 78: 1437–1534.

Howie, Bob. 2001. "County Opts to Keep Drug Court." *Houston Chronicle*, September 6, This Week, p. 2.

Inciardi, James A., Duane C. McBride, and James E. Rivers. 1996. *Drug Control and the Courts*. Thousand Oaks, Calif.: Sage.

Jacob, Herbert. 1984. *Justice in America*. 4th ed. Boston: Little, Brown.

Lamber, Julia, and Mary Luskin. 1992. "Court Reform: A View from the Bottom." *Judicature* 75: 295–299.

Langer, Laura. 2002. *Judicial Review in State Supreme Courts*. Albany: State University of New York Press.

Lipscher, Robert. 1989. "The Judicial Response to the Drug Crisis." *State Court Journal* 13: 13.

Mahoney, Barry. 1994. "Drug Courts: What Have We Learned So Far?" *Justice System Journal* 17: 127–133.

Manfredi, Christopher p. 1998. *The Supreme Court and Juvenile Justice*. Lawrence: University Press of Kansas.

Meier, Kenneth. 1994. *The Politics of Sin: Drugs, Alcohol, and Public Policy*. Armonk, N.Y.: Sharpe.

Muwakkil, Salim. 2001. "Can *Traffic* Loosen Drug-Court Gridlock?"*Chicago Tribune*, January 15.

Nader, Laura. 1992. "Trading Justice for Harmony." *National Institute for Dispute Resolution Forum* (Winter): 12–14.

Neubauer, David. 1983. "Improving the Analysis and Presentation of Data on Case Processing Time." *Journal of Criminal Law and Criminology* 74: 1589–1607.

———. 2003. "Therapeutic Jurisprudence in Comparative Perspective." Paper presented at the annual meeting of the Academy of Criminal Justice Sciences, Boston, March 6.

Nolan, James L., Jr. 2001. *Reinventing Justice: The American Drug Court Movement*. Princeton, N.J.: Princeton University Press.

OJJDP Statistical Briefing Book. 2005. Available online at http://ojjdp.ncjrs.org/ojstatbb/crime/qa05101.asp?qaDate520050228.

Ostrom, Brian, Neal B. Kauder, and Robert C. LaFountain. 2001. *Examining the Work of State Courts, 1999–2000*. Williamsburg, Va.: National Center for State Courts.

Platt, Anthony. 1970. *The Child Savers: The Invention of Delinquency*. Chicago: University of Chicago Press.

President's Commission on Law Enforcement and Administration of Justice. 1967. *Challenge of Crime in a Free Society*. Washington, D.C.: U.S. Government Printing Office.

Ragona, Anthony, and John Paul Ryan. 1983. "Misdemeanor Courts and the Choice of Sanctions: A Comparative View." *Justice System Journal* 8: 199–221.

Ritter, Kera. 2001. "Woman Is First Graduate of Family Drug Court." *Cleveland Plain Dealer*, October 12, p. B3.

Rubin, H. Ted. 1984. *The Courts: Fulcrum of the Justice System*. New York: Random House.

Ryan, John Paul. 1980–1981. "Adjudication and Sentencing in a Misdemeanor Court: The Outcome Is the Punishment." *Law and Society Review* 15: 79–108.

Sanborn, Joseph. 1993. "The Right to a Public Jury Trial: A Need for Today's Juvenile Court." *Judicature* 76: 230–238.

Scheb, John, and Albert Matheny. 1988. "Judicial Reform and Rationalization: The Diffusion of Court Reform Policies Among the American States." *Law and Policy* 10: 25–42.

Schor, Miguel. 2000. "The Rule of Law and Democratic Consolidation in Latin America." Available online at http://darkwing.uoregon.edu/~caguirre/schorpr.html. Retrieved April 1, 2003.

Silbey, Susan. 1981. "Making Sense of the Lower Courts." *Justice System Journal* 6: 13–27.

Singer, Simon. 1993. "The Automatic Waiver of Juveniles and Substantive Justice." *Crime and Delinquency* 39: 253–261.

Stevenson, Mark. 2002. "Mexican Court Blocks Handover of Suspect." Associated Press, January 18.

Tanenhaus, David S. 2004. *Juvenile Justice in the Making*. Oxford, U.K.: Oxford University Press.

Terry, W. Clinton. 1996. "Felony and Misdemeanor Rearrests of the First Year Cohort of the Drug Court in Broward County, Florida." Paper presented at the annual meeting of the Academy of Criminal Justice Sciences, Las Vegas, March.

U.S. Department of Justice. 1997. *Defining Drug Courts: The Key Components*. Washington, D.C.: U.S. Department of Justice, Office of Justice Programs. Available online at http://www.ncjrs.org/html/bja/define/welcome.html. Retrieved April 2, 2003.

Walker, Rob. 1995. "Justicia en Mexico. . ." *American Lawyer* (April): 80.

Weiner, Tim. 2002. "Extraditions Are Limited by a Ruling in Mexico." *New York Times*, January 20, p. A9.

Whalen, Christopher. 2001. "Mexico Drug War Has a U.S. Front." *Insight on the News*, April 2, p. 22.

For Further Reading

D'Angelo, Laura. 2003. "Women and Addiction: Challenges for Drug Court Practitioners." *Justice System Journal* 23: 385.

Domingo, Pilar, and Rachael Sieder. 2001. *Rule of Law in Latin America: The International Promotion of Judicial Reform*. London: Biddles.

Douglas, James W., and Roger E. Hartley. 2004. "Sustaining Drug Courts in Arizona and South Carolina: An Experience in Hodgepodge Budgeting." *Justice System Journal* 25: 75.

Feld, Barry. 1999. *Bad Kids: Race and the Transformation of the Juvenile Court*. New York: Oxford University Press.

Goerdt, John, and John A. Martin. 1989. "The Impact of Drug Cases on Case Processing in Urban Trial Courts." *State Court Journal* 13: 4.

Hall, Melinda Gann, and Chris W. Bonneau. 2008. "Mobilizing Interest: The Effects of Money on Citizen Participation in State Supreme Court Elections." *American Journal of Political Science* 52(3): 457–470.

Kelling, George, and Catherine Coles. 1997. *Fixing Broken Windows: Restoring Order and Reducing Crime in Our Communities*. New York: Martin Kessler.

Langer, Laura, Jody McMullen, Nicolas P. Ray, and Daniel D. Stratton. 2003. "Recruitment of Chief Justices on

State Supreme Courts: A Choice Between Institutional and Personal Goals." *Journal of Politics* 65(3): 656–675.

Lukemeyer, Anna. 2003. *Courts as Policymakers: School Finance Reform Litigation*. New York: LFB Scholarly Publishing.

Manfredi, Christopher. 1998. *The Supreme Court and Juvenile Justice*. Lawrence: University Press of Kansas.

Wice, Paul. 1995. "Court Reform and Judicial Leadership: A Theoretical Discussion." *Justice System Journal* 17: 309–322.

———. 1995. *Court Reform and Judicial Leadership*. Westport, Conn.: Praeger.

LAWYERS AND LEGAL REPRESENTATION

Lawyers are the gatekeepers of the judicial process, and law schools, such as this one at Duke University in Durham, North Carolina, are the gatekeepers' gatekeepers.

David Neubauer

"Your cost cutting put BP at risk, didn't it, Mr. Hayward?" asked Robert Cunningham from Mobile, Alabama and one of 15 lawyers appointed by the federal district court to the plaintiffs' steering committee in the cases arising from the BP Deepwater Horizon oil spill in the Gulf of Mexico. The forum was a deposition in London and the subject was Tony Hayward, BP's chief executive at the time of the oil spill. Mr. Hayward countered that he always emphasized to his employees that 'reliable operations come first, whatever the cost'—and insisted that the corporate budget-cutting affected operations, not safety. But Mr. Cunningham scoffed, 'if the first words out of your mouth every time you open it were I am Superman, that wouldn't make you Superman, would it?" To which a lawyer for BP voiced a strong objection (Schwartz 2011).

The American judicial system is built around lawyers representing clients. The victims of the oil spill did not have a difficult time finding lawyers to represent them. The same applies to BP who hired numerous lawyers along the Gulf Coast within days of the spill. But such is not always the case every criminal defendant or civil complainant. Clarence Earl Gideon was forced to defend himself against a charge of burglary with the inevitable result that he was convicted. But his hand written petition from his prison cell resulted in major changes for indigent defendants like him.

Evelyn Arkebauer, Tairay Sewell, Elizabeth Riley, and Kathleen Osberger were luckier and found a lawyer to represent them. They are among the thousands of people every year who file medical malpractice lawsuits for such things as the failure of an anesthesiologist to respond to a page, errors made during childbirth, and paralysis resulting from failure to correctly diagnose a brain aneurysm (Ritter 2005). Every day, citizens become plaintiffs and defendants in civil court and count on lawyers to help them navigate the complexities of cases that deal with personal injury, family law, class action lawsuits, and many other legal matters. Access to lawyers for civil courts is even more important, because it is not a constitutional right and, therefore, the government is not required to provide parties in civil cases with an attorney as it is in criminal court.

What the BP oil spill victims, Clarence Earl Gideon, and the medical malpractice litigants have in common above all is their need for access to the legal system. Lawyers serve as gatekeepers of this system; decisions to take a dispute to a public forum for resolution often depend on the advice of counsel (Zemans and Rosenblum 1981). But who should have access to lawyers and at what price is one of the most controversial issues facing the American legal system. Lawyers like Robert Cunningham stand at the center of the tort wars which pit plaintiff lawyers against business interests, and in recent years businesses have been somewhat successful in winning the tort wars (Chapter 10).

This chapter examines the role of lawyers in gaining access to the legal system. First, the legal profession is considered from a macro perspective, looking at legal training, licensing requirements, disciplinary procedures, and bar associations. The next sections adopt a micro perspective, looking at what lawyers do, where they work, and the stratification of the legal profession. Finally, the availability of lawyers is examined, with special attention given to the unequal distribution of legal services.

LEGAL EDUCATION

The path to becoming a lawyer today involves a long, rigorous process beginning with an undergraduate college degree (four years), continuing through law school (three years), and culminating in passing the state bar examination. In an earlier era, however, this path was shorter and less demanding.

Legal Training Before 1870

Lawyers were a scarce commodity during the colonial period. Few English lawyers wished to move to the colonies, and even fewer Americans could afford to train in

England, where legal education centered in the four Inns of Court located in London: Lincoln's Inn, Gray's Inn, Inner Temple, and Middle Temple. The Inns of Court were combination trade guilds, bar associations, and institutions for instruction in the law. Students wishing to pursue a career in law entered one of the inns and, after several years of apprentice study, became qualified to practice in the courts. The costs of entering an Inn of Court and the length of time required guaranteed that barristers came from the English nobility (Abraham 1986). The English method of training lawyers was ill suited to the realities of a new and struggling nation.

To meet America's need for lawyers, entry into the profession was relatively open (Friedman 2005). Some lawyers learned their craft through self-study. As late as 1858, a prominent member of the Illinois bar, Abraham Lincoln, wrote to a friend that "the cheapest, quickest and best way into the legal world was to read Blackstone's *Commentaries*, Chitty's *Pleadings*, Greenleaf's *Evidence*, Story's *Equity*, and Story's *Equity Pleadings*, get a license and go to the practice and still keep reading" (Nortrup 1968). Many self-taught lawyers practiced on the frontier, where a quick wit was frequently of greater service than extensive legal knowledge.

Self-study often occurred in conjunction with an apprenticeship. An aspiring young lad would associate himself with a practicing lawyer, who provided instruction and granted access to his library. In return, the student paid a fee, performed legal research, and copied documents, much as paralegals or legal assistants do today. The quality of the apprenticeship varied greatly. Thomas Jefferson expressed the popular opinion when he said, "The services expected in return have been more than the instructions have been worth" (McKay 1985). Other tutors, though, provided reading materials, conducted tutorials on the great legal works, and commented on the important cases of the day.

Before the Civil War, law schools played only a minor role in the training of lawyers. The teaching of law in American universities dates back to 1779, when Thomas Jefferson chose his former tutor, George Wythe, to be the first professor of law at the College of William and Mary. Yale, Columbia, Harvard, and the University of Maryland soon followed that lead. But, by 1850, only fifteen university law programs were in existence, and their combined enrollments were probably less than 1,000 (Friedman 2005). Early university-based legal education was closely tied to the study of such allied disciplines as philosophy, political economy, and ethics. Those who chose to enter the practice of law through that route were being educated to become public leaders. University education, although viewed as prestigious, was also perceived as impractical.

Distinct from the study of law in a university setting was the growth of **proprietary** (for profit) **law schools**. The Litchfield School was the first independent law school in the United States, established in Connecticut in 1784. Litchfield introduced the first systematic and coherent program of legal instruction. Proprietary law schools were concerned with the needs of practitioners, and the instruction offered differed substantially from that received in universities. Whereas university professors were devoted to the broad study of law, the instructors in proprietary law schools focused on the actual practice of law.

Advent of the Modern Law School

Law schools began to play a prominent part in the training of U.S. lawyers only after the Civil War. With the appointment of Christopher Columbus Langdell as dean of the Harvard Law School in 1870, legal education changed dramatically. In an effort to professionalize legal education, Langdell tightened admission standards and raised graduation requirements. But his most important innovation was the introduction of the **case method** of instruction. Lectures on the law were replaced by reading what Langdell considered the essence of the law: appellate court opinions.

The case method approach soon became the standard form of law school instruction throughout the United States. Universities adopted the case method because it was very cost effective: One professor instructing large classes was economical. But the introduction of the case method also laid the foundation for a countertrend. Beginning in the late nineteenth century, many night law schools were founded. Whereas the leading law schools were raising their admission and graduation standards, night law schools welcomed any applicants who could pay the tuition. Thus, night law schools became an avenue of upward mobility for second-generation ethnic groups. Again, the nature and the quality of the instruction differed substantially from their university counterparts: The prestigious or near-prestigious law schools moved toward a national curriculum, but streetcar colleges, as they were often called, focused on the law of their state. In 1900, thirty-two of the most prestigious law schools in the nation organized the Association of American Law Schools (AALS); most night law schools remained outside the organization.

LAW SCHOOLS TODAY

If lawyers are the gatekeepers of the judicial process, then law schools are the gatekeepers' gatekeepers. In stark contrast to the nineteenth century, today virtually every new lawyer is a law school graduate. Therefore, observers and practitioners take an active interest in who is admitted, what is taught, and what (if any) differences exist between law schools.

Admissions

More students are pursuing a law degree today than ever before. According to the American Bar Association (ABA), 145,239 full- and part-time students were enrolled in the 200 ABA-approved law schools in the fall of 2009 (www.americanbar.org). Forty-seven percent were women. Compare that with 1967, when only 61,084 students were enrolled to earn a juris doctorate, and 2,769 were women—just 5 percent of the total!

Students face stiff competition for their seats, because law school admission requirements have come a long way since the turn of the century—when a high school graduate could enter most law schools directly. Today, law schools require a bachelor's degree. Admission is based primarily on the applicant's score on the Law School Admission Test (LSAT) and his or her undergraduate grade point average.

DEBATING LAW, COURTS, AND POLITICS

■ Thinking About Law School?

Every year, thousands of first-year college students start their academic studies with the intention of becoming lawyers. The steps to achieving that goal are straightforward:

1. Graduate from college.
2. Take the LSAT.
3. Apply to law school.

However, the path is a challenging one, for each step requires a different set of skills and concentration on unique objectives. There are many resources available to help students who are pursuing law as a career. Ask your prelaw adviser about a local university or college prelaw website. Some good examples of prelaw information include The University of Florida: http://www.advising.ufl.edu/prelaw/ and Pre-Law at the University of Michigan at http://www.lsa.umich.edu/advising/advisor/prelaw.

Graduate from College

Today, the first step toward becoming a lawyer is earning a bachelor's degree. It is recommended that your undergraduate course of study be academically rigorous, emphasizing critical thinking and writing skills. The depth and breadth of your undergraduate experience is more important than a narrowly tailored or vocation-oriented program of study. The ABA has developed a set of guidelines on how to prepare for a legal education, available online at http://www.abanet.org/legaled/prelaw/prep.html. Prelaw majors are less common than in the past; now prelaw students favor a wide array of academic degree programs. You should consult the prelaw adviser at your college or university, who can provide you with important information about law school and help you make decisions about how to choose a rigorous program of study that will help you succeed in law school.

Take the LSAT

The LSAT is administered by the Law School Admission Council (LSAC) four times a year (June, October, December, and February) at many locations across the country. Information about testing dates and cost is available on the LSAC website at http://www.lsac.org. The test assesses reading and verbal reasoning skills. It has

five sections, each lasting 35 minutes. They include one analytical reasoning section, one reading comprehension section, two logical reasoning sections, and one section that is experimental and may be any one of the other three types used on the test. (The experimental section is not used in calculating the score.) At the end of the test, a 30-minute writing section is administered. Scores on the test range from 120 to 180. Typically, a student takes the LSAT during the summer (June) or fall (October) preceding his or her senior year in college.

LSAT preparation varies drastically across applicants. Your prelaw adviser can help you develop a test preparation strategy. Some students prepare on their own, others take professional preparation classes, and some do both. A free sample test is available on the LSAC website, and numerous other preparation materials are available on the Web. The LSAC also sells a large number of tests that were previously given but are no longer used. Before you spend any money, investigate fully the available resources. Regardless of the test preparation strategy you choose, plan to prepare fully and adequately before taking the test.

A good place to start is the Law School Admission Council at http://www.lsac.org. The LSAC is a nonprofit organization made up of law schools in the United States and Canada. It administers the LSAT and the Law School Data Assembly Service (LSDAS) and also provides a variety of other resources for those interested in pursuing a legal education and joining the legal profession. Its website serves as a portal to sites for member law schools across the country and offers free information about the LSAT and the other resources it provides.

Apply to Law School

After taking the LSAT, you will begin the law school application process. Applications for law schools are available from the schools themselves, and the LSAC also provides electronic access to law school applications from its website (http://www.lsac.org). The application window usually runs from November to March. The application process naturally involves selecting schools. In recent years, law school rankings have received a great deal of attention. Information about ABA-accredited law schools

(continued)

is available on the Web and also in the ABA/LSAC official guide to law schools. *U.S. News & World Report* publishes annual rankings that recently attracted the derision of the LSAC, prelaw adviser associations, and the ABA, which maintain that the best law school is determined by the needs of the applicant, not by a set of rankings. In the past, law school deans have published statements opposing commercial rankings of law schools.

To learn more about going to law school, visit any of the following sites:

http://www.lsac.org
   Law School Admission Council
http://www.abanet.org/legaled/prelaw/prep.html
   American Bar Association
http://officialguide.lsac.org
   The Official Guide to ABA Approved Law Schools
http://www.accessgroup.org
   The Access Group offers financial aid information.

The LSAT is administered by the Law School Admission Council (LSAC) four times a year at many locations across the country. Information about testing dates, cost, and preparation is available on the LSAC website at http://www.lsac.org. (See Debating Law, Courts, and Politics: Thinking About Law School?)

The LSAC started the Law School Data Assembly Service (LSDAS) as a means of simplifying the application process to law schools. Nearly all ABA-approved law schools require the applicant to use the LSDAS. Through this centralized service, a single report is generated on the applicant that includes an undergraduate academic summary; copies of the applicant's academic transcripts, LSAT score, and writing sample; and, if the applicant chooses, copies of his or her letters of recommendation. After the applicant applies to a law school, the school contacts the LSDAS, which forwards a report to the requesting school. This has greatly reduced the burden on the student of organizing and coordinating many law school applications at the same time.

For the 2010-11 academic year, 155,050 LSATs were administered, a 9.6% decrease from 2009-10, which saw the highest number of test takers in the history of the exam, 171,514. However, the number today is still dramatically larger than it was in 1963–1964, when only 37,598 tests were taken. Legal training in universities has historically been restricted to the academic elite. The legal profession was almost exclusively a white male enclave that explicitly discriminated against both African Americans and women. Some law schools denied entry to women altogether, and those few women who were admitted found only limited job opportunities after graduation. In 1910, for example, there were only 558 female lawyers in the entire nation. And, as late as 1970, less than 5 percent of the profession were women. The same pattern held true for African Americans: Segregation prevented them from enrolling in southern law schools, and only a few were admitted by northern law schools. Only a handful of predominantly African-American law schools, such as Howard, prevented the profession from being all white. In the late 1960s, there were only three African-American lawyers in the state of Mississippi and only twenty-seven in Louisiana, a state with more than a million African-American citizens. Overall, African Americans constituted only 1 percent of the legal profession (Abel 1986).

Amid the national focus on equal protection during the 1960s, law schools began to revise their admission policies to admit more women and minorities. Those changes produced a more diverse law school population: Today, women constitute nearly 50 percent of enrolled students and receive 46 percent of the law degrees conferred by

ABA-approved law schools (although women made up just 25 percent of practicing attorneys in 2010). Minority groups have made much smaller gains: In 2008-09, 22 percent of the students enrolled were minorities, and they received about 22 percent of the degrees conferred. Obviously, there is still much to be done in creating a diverse legal profession.

Curriculum

Turn-of-the-century law schools offered one or, at most, two years of instruction. Today, three years are required (except for a handful of ABA-approved law schools that offer a part-time curriculum lasting four years). One purpose of legal education is to train students as generalists. Because the legal needs of clients are diverse, the curriculum stresses the fundamental background that all lawyers will need in practice. A second purpose is to teach students to think like lawyers—that is, to think objectively about what the law requires, not what they think is right or just. Problems are approached from a legal rather than a philosophical, moral, or personal viewpoint.

Those two interrelated purposes of legal education are reflected in the standardized curriculum offered in virtually all U.S. law schools. First-year students are required to take civil procedure, constitutional law, contracts, criminal law, property, torts, and legal research and writing. Not until midway through the second year are students allowed some freedom to choose courses. Electives vary from school to school, but common choices include administrative law, bankruptcy, business associations, civil rights law, comparative constitutional law, copyright law, environmental law, evidence, First Amendment law, taxation, media law, tax policy, trial advocacy, and trusts and estates. According to the ABA, some of the fastest-growing electives include intellectual property, international law, business law, and health law.

The most distinctive feature of law school education is the case method of instruction, which is designed to teach students legal reasoning through the analysis of appellate opinions. **Casebooks** organize appellate court decisions by major topics, along with explanatory notes and questions. Materials from other disciplines (for instance, history, ethics, economics, or public policy) are notably absent. Casebooks make law students easy to spot as they lug large green or brown tomes titled *Cases and Materials* on torts, wills, and contracts across campus and develop strong biceps in the process. Most law school professors continue to use the **Socratic method** (at least in the first year) to encourage the student to explore the facts of the case, to determine the legal principles applied by the judges, and to analyze the reasoning used. The professor often plays the devil's advocate, challenging students to defend their reasoning. Thus, a law student

> … learns to relate one case to another, to harmonize the outcomes of seemingly inconsistent cases so that they are made to stand together. By taking and putting together different cases, the student acquires a way of thinking and working with cases that constitutes the fundamentals of legal reasoning, as well as knowledge of doctrinal rules presented by these cases. (Loh 1984, 15)

The case method approach recognizes no single correct way of analyzing opinions. It is the process, not the outcome, that counts.

Over the years, critics have attacked legal education on three fronts. The first set of concerns focuses on teaching methods. The case method approach to learning is unlike anything students have experienced. Because this method requires independent, critical thought, it places a heavy demand on the student. In *One L* (1977), Scott Turow recorded his frustrations as a first-year Harvard Law School student: "I keep waiting for things to relent somehow. I'm blown out. I've never experienced mental exhaustion like what I felt by the end of each day this week. The ceaseless concentration on books and professors ... left me absolutely blithering when I got home each evening" (p. 61). Similarly, some object to the rigidity of the casebook and class recitation method of teaching. The confrontational manner of the Socratic method of legal instruction does continue to dominate first-year law classes, but second- and third-year courses are increasingly taught in seminar style. In *Letters from Law School: The Life of a Second-Year Law Student*, Lawrence Dieker (2000) describes these changes in the second year of law school and the changes since Turow wrote about his Harvard experience by noting that "law school today is, with little doubt, a kinder gentler place than the experience simultaneously criticized and glorified by Scott Turow" (p. 134).

A second set of criticisms focuses on the content of contemporary legal education. These critics believe that law schools are so preoccupied with having their students pass the bar examination that they neglect the public policy role of law and the legal profession. Nuts-and-bolts courses are emphasized, and insufficient attention is devoted to the law's political and social impact. Thus, law schools have been criticized for presenting inherently value-laden materials as if they are value-free.

A third set of criticisms points in the opposite direction. To some, law schools emphasize the theoretical, abstract aspects of law to the exclusion of the pragmatic realities of the practice of law (Zemans and Rosenblum 1981). Traditionally, law students have no direct contact with clients, nor do they even enter a courthouse. Faced with those criticisms, many law schools have established clinical training programs, which attempt to provide an educational bridge between the theoretical and the pragmatic. Under a professor's supervision, third-year law students deal directly with indigents who have legal problems. The students provide legal advice, draft documents, file lawsuits, and, in most states, even argue cases in court. Through those experiences, law students learn skills needed to translate real-life disputes into legal issues.

Differences Between Law Schools

Today, there are over 200 law schools in the United States. They are very similar in curriculum, but there are fundamental differences in the students served and the training provided. The most important difference involves accreditation: The American Bar Association is recognized by the U.S. Department of Education as the national accreditation body for law schools. The ABA sets minimal standards for accreditation, including the professional qualifications of professors, the faculty-student ratios, the number of holdings in the law library, and the required courses. A law degree from an ABA-approved law school ensures eligibility for taking the bar exam in any state. Typically, a graduate of an unapproved law school can take the bar exam only in the state in which the law school is located. In 2010, there were 200 ABA-approved law schools.

Another difference centers on the law schools' institutional affiliation. Most are affiliated with a university. A few, however, are freestanding, typically proprietary law schools in the tradition of the Litchfield School. Only a small number of law schools not associated with a university are accredited by the American Bar Association.

The availability of an evening course of instruction is another area of divergence. About one-third of the ABA-accredited law schools and virtually all independent law schools offer a night program. Evening students tend to be older than their daytime counterparts and are more likely to be employed—therefore preferring to attend law school on a part-time basis. Evening instructors often differ from the daytime faculty as well. They are frequently practicing attorneys who teach part time and offer a practical orientation.

Finally, law schools differ greatly in prestige. About twenty are consistently referred to as the most prestigious law schools in the nation. Many of these elite national law schools are private institutions that are part of equally prestigious universities, such as Chicago, Columbia, Cornell, Duke, Harvard, New York, Northwestern, Stanford, and Yale. But state universities are also prominent on the list—California at Berkeley and Los Angeles, Illinois, Michigan, Minnesota, North Carolina, Texas, Virginia, Washington, and Wisconsin. Faculty from these elite schools are typically graduates of other national elite schools.

Most law schools fall in the middle of the stratification system. These national law schools are part of state or private universities. Top graduates of these law schools are hired by national law firms.

At the bottom of the stratification system are the direct descendants of the turn-of-the-century night law schools. These local law schools are rarely affiliated with a larger university. Their approach to legal education is practical, stressing career-oriented concerns. In particular, local law schools concentrate on the specifics of the law of their state so their students can pass the bar examination. By contrast, other law schools are national in their orientation, providing a theoretical overview of legal concepts so their graduates can pass the bar exam in any state.

The most well known law school rankings are performed by *U.S. News & World Report*. Each year, their highly anticipated rankings create interest in "Which school is the best?" But efforts to rank schools, or to choose a school based on such rankings, are not without criticism. The Law School Admission Council urges potential students to find the best law school for themselves using as many criteria as possible, rather than relying on a single summary. Information about law schools is widely available on the Web. (See Debating Law, Courts, and Politics: Thinking About Law School?)

Cost of Law School

The high cost of law school has come into focus recently as critics allege that students are graduating with mounting debt that limits their career options. Paying for law school continues to challenge students. Nearly 90 percent of law students rely on education loans, and three years of law school can cost as much as $150,000. Data from the American Bar Association indicates that in 2009 the typical public school law school graduate had borrowed $46,499 and private school graduates $70,147. And that does not include any loans for undergraduate degrees. Some states are beginning to create loan repayment assistance programs that help law school graduates who take government or public sector positions. The cause of the increased borrowing is the rapid rate of increasing tuition and fees, which are growing as fast as or faster than undergraduate educational expenses. Since 2000 tuition has increased by 92 percent at public universities. Critics allege that amassing such debt will force students to choose positions in private practice, which provide higher starting salaries, rather than more modest-paying positions in public service or government. Although the impact of increasing costs on legal careers is difficult to demonstrate, the NALP survey at least suggests that student debt does constrain career choice, with two-thirds of the respondents reporting that law school debt was preventing them from considering a public sector law career.

Traditionally, the cost of law school has been seen as an investment in a professional degree that would easily repay itself. But the cost-benefit calculation has become more difficult for students, because the average salary of lawyers has not grown as fast as the expense of legal education combined with the rapidly increasing cost of an undergraduate degree. Many of today's first-year law students face financial challenges that rival those real-life situations described in their casebooks.

LICENSING REQUIREMENTS

After graduation from law school, a student must pass a state bar examination before being licensed to practice law. This requirement represents an effort to improve on the loose, easy admission to the bar that characterized the nineteenth century.

The haphazard nature of nineteenth-century legal education was matched by the lack of strict standards for admission to the bar. In a few states, the high court controlled all admissions to the bar, but, in most, each county admitted its own attorneys. As a result, the standards of the most lenient judge in the state set the criteria for admission throughout the state. Typically, the bar exam consisted of oral questioning by the judge in open court, and anecdotal evidence suggests that the process was loose at best. Salmon P. Chase (later to be chief justice of the Supreme Court) provided one such account. In 1829, he appeared before a Maryland judge, and, after some perfunctory questioning, the judge indicated that Chase needed to "study another year." But Chase begged for a favorable ruling, stating he had already made all arrangements to go to the "western country" and practice law. The judge relented and swore him in (Friedman 2005).

The lack of standards for admission to the legal profession attracted the attention of bar associations for several reasons. Easy admission allowed the entry of unqualified and unscrupulous attorneys, thus blemishing the reputation of all members of the profession. Easy admission also allowed too many lawyers to compete for the available legal work, thus depressing the income of current practitioners. Bar associations sought to improve the quality of the profession by upgrading legal education and by making licensing requirements more stringent. Today, the fitness and the character of an applicant to the bar are judged through the collection of background information, and virtually all states require applicants to pass some configuration of standardized bar examinations. A typical combination involves a standardized exam that covers basic areas of law, a second exam that covers knowledge of the law of that state, and a third that addresses legal ethics. Increasingly, states are using common standardized tests for all three of those areas. Information about the specific bar exam requirements of your state and others can be found in the Comprehensive Guide to Bar Admission Requirements, available online at http://www.abanet.org/legaled/publications/ compguide2005/compguide2005.html. The centerpiece of most bar requirements is the Multistate Bar Examination (MBE), used by fifty-three jurisdictions. (Washington, Louisiana, and Puerto Rico do not use the MBE.) The MBE is six hours in length and tests general legal knowledge (that is, contracts, torts, constitutional law, criminal law, evidence, and real property). It is offered twice a year in most states (February and July) and consists of 200 essay and multiple-choice questions. Both the number of test takers and their success vary across states. In 2010, of the 79,953 individuals who took bar exams nationwide (60,658 for the first time), 68 percent passed. Data on bar passage rates are collected and published by the National Association of Bar Examiners, and many law schools report the bar passage rates of their graduates. In 2010, New York administered 15,588 tests, just slightly more than California, which administered 12,788; together they represented nearly a third of all tests given. Students who fail one part of the exam can often retake just that section. Thus, the odds are good that anyone who persists will finally pass.

The other standardized exams that are now required by various states include the Multistate Professional Responsibility Exam (MPRE) (required everywhere except in Maryland, Washington, and Wisconsin), which is a two-hour multiple-choice exam covering legal ethics and professional responsibility, and the Multistate Essay Examination (MEE) (required in 21 jurisdictions), a three-hour essay exam covering more specific areas of law. The Multistate Performance Test (MPT) is also used by thirty-three jurisdictions; it tests the applicant's ability to perform basic lawyer tasks. To prepare for these exams, many recent law school graduates attend bar review courses. For a fee, these cram courses focus on the specific rules and doctrines of the state in which the attendees wish to practice.

Consistent with federalism, the specifics of licensing requirements vary from jurisdiction to jurisdiction. Attorneys who are licensed in one state are not automatically granted the right to practice law in other states. A court, though, will usually grant permission for an attorney who is licensed in one state to appear in a single case in another state. In many jurisdictions, a lawyer can be admitted to the bar on the basis of experience as a practicing lawyer in another state. But in one-third of the states, outsiders must pass all or part of the state bar examination before being admitted to practice law. Federal courts also establish their own requirements. However, by custom, admission to the bar of a state is typically a sufficient condition for admission to practice before the U.S. district court(s) sitting in that state.

LEGAL ETHICS AND DISCIPLINE

Rightly or wrongly, lawyers suffer from a bad image (Galanter 2005; Galanter 1992). American folklore associates adjectives such as *dishonest*, *unscrupulous*, and *conniving* with attorneys. Lawyers are the butt of endless jokes, which seem to strike a responsive chord among listeners. A recent ABA study rated the public's confidence in the legal profession behind the medical profession and doctors; members of the executive branch of government, the U.S. Supreme Court, the U.S. justice system in general, and federal courts other than the Supreme Court; the judiciary and judges; state and local courts; and Congress; and only slightly ahead of the media (ABA 2002). Evaluating those negative images is difficult, of course. Although individual examples of less-than-exemplary behavior are easy to come by, there is no convincing evidence that, as a group, lawyers are less ethical or honest than other professionals. In fact, during the past 25 years, law schools have focused increased attention on legal ethics, and some observers believe that this has paid off, with lawyers and judges who are more sensitive to ethical concerns (Gillers 2002). Attention to legal ethics has also reached across the Atlantic. In their 1999 book *The Ethics and Conduct of Lawyers in England and Wales*, Boon and Levin argue that the legal profession in England needs an ethics requirement comparable to the MPRE taken by bar applicants in the United States.

Bar associations have always insisted that lawyers are mostly honest, skilled, and aboveboard. Those groups define any problem associated with lawyers as a version of the rotten-apple theory—although there is one in every barrel, overall the quality is good. The legal profession has sought to improve its image in several ways. Public relations is one approach: Bar associations sponsor programs, such as Law Day, that project a positive image of lawyers. Preventive medicine is another way: Law students are required to take a course on legal ethics, and it constitutes a separate section of the bar exam in most states. Inevitably, however, some lawyers fail to behave honestly or ethically toward their clients. Thus, the most important mechanism for regulating the conduct of lawyers is disciplinary procedures.

The primary responsibility for establishing and enforcing professional standards of conduct for the legal profession rests with the highest court of each state. The state supreme court establishes standards of conduct that are based on the American Bar Association's *Model Rules of Professional Conduct* (2003). The model rules center on eliminating misrepresentation, dishonesty, and fraud from the legal profession. Enforcement is largely delegated to a state bar association standing committee on professional conduct. Local bar associations may also have professional codes of conduct that attorneys can be sanctioned for violating. Lawyers policing their own is not without critics and may even contribute to some of the public's misgivings about attorneys. A recent study published by the ABA confirms this point, noting that "bar associations are not viewed as protectors of the public or the public interest, but as clubs to protect lawyers" (ABA 2002, 4). In this report, just 26 percent of respondents to a survey thought the "legal profession does a good job of disciplining lawyers" (ABA 2002, 7).

Disciplinary proceedings typically begin with the filing of a complaint by a disgruntled client, although judges, lawyers, citizens, or the committee itself can initiate action. Three types of allegations of misconduct are most common: misuse of a client's funds; acceptance of money for services that are never rendered; and, finally, a felony conviction. (A lawyer convicted of a felony may lose his or her license to practice law, even if the conviction is unrelated to his or her activity as a lawyer.)

Complaints about attorney misconduct are investigated in secret. A few states—including Oregon, West Virginia, and Florida—have complaint processes that are partially or fully public. Most complaints are dismissed because of insufficient evidence. When there is evidence of an ethical violation, the committee files formal charges and conducts a private hearing. If the charges are proved, the committee recommends disciplinary action—a reprimand (either private or public), a suspension of the license to practice law for a given period of time, or restitution to the client. The most severe sanction is disbarment, which permanently revokes a lawyer's right to practice law. These recommendations may be appealed to the state supreme court, which, after a public hearing, may accept, modify, or reject them. Rather than face this public hearing, however, some lawyers voluntarily resign from the bar.

Because only a small number of complaints result in any kind of sanctions, some observers criticize the disciplinary process. One area of concern is the laxity with which judges and lawyers deal with the misconduct of their colleagues. Bar associations seem to punish their peers for flagrant violations but are gentle or "understanding" when it comes to minor transgressions or plain incompetence (Rhode 1981).

Critics also charge that bar associations are more concerned with the activities of the less prestigious members of the profession than with the shortcomings of the elite lawyers. Nonetheless, bar associations spend considerable time investigating their own. In 2006, more than 123,000 complaints were received by disciplinary agencies, of which nearly 80,000 were investigated and approximately 5,000 lawyers were sanctioned after a probable cause determination (Center for Professional Responsibility 2006).

Besides filing a complaint with the state bar association, a client dissatisfied with his or her lawyer can sue for legal malpractice. Part of the so-called litigation explosion (discussed in Chapter 10) has been a major increase in malpractice suits against lawyers. Not so long ago, lawyers lived by an unwritten professional code that made them reluctant to sue one another. That has changed in the past decade: By one estimate, 8 to 10 percent of the nation's practicing lawyers are sued each year (Kahler 1991).

BAR ASSOCIATIONS

In the formative years of the American republic, the handful of educated citizens who called themselves lawyers banded together largely for social purposes. In the face of popular hostility toward lawyers, however, those local bar associations virtually disappeared after 1830. A rebirth began in 1870 when a few lawyers, calling themselves "the decent part" of the profession, formed the Association of the Bar of the City of New York to fight judicial corruption wrought by the Tweed ring. Following that lead, lawyers in other major cities grouped together in similar organizations. In like manner, the first national organization of lawyers, the American Bar Association, was founded in 1878.

Initially, these organizations were elitist, allowing only the most respected members of the profession to join. Gradually, however, membership was opened to all practicing lawyers. Today, hundreds of legal associations are organized at the local, state, and national levels. In addition, each legal specialty has its own national association. From the perspective of the profession as a whole, however, the two most important types of bar associations are state and national.

State Bar Associations

Initially, membership in a state bar association was voluntary, and most lawyers chose not to join. In the 1920s, for example, barely one-quarter of the profession belonged to state bar associations. Legal reformers recognized that to have sufficient political influence to improve courts and upgrade the profession, lawyers needed to organize themselves more effectively. Thus, when Herbert Harley and other prominent lawyers formed the **American Judicature Society** in 1913, one of their proposals was compulsory membership in bar associations. Rather than call that system a closed shop (which had a negative connotation because of its association with labor unions), Harley campaigned for what he termed an **integrated bar**, which required all attorneys to join the state bar association, pay its dues, and subject themselves to its rules. Currently, 33 states have adopted an integrated (or unified) state bar, either by statute or by state supreme court decision. In the other jurisdictions, a lawyer may practice law without being a member of the state bar association.

American Bar Association

Membership in the **American Bar Association (ABA)** grew slowly. By 1920, only 12 percent of all lawyers belonged. A more aggressive approach resulted in a significant increase in membership. Today, the ABA claims more than 400,000 members (note there are an estimated 1,225,452 licensed lawyers in 2010). Headed by a president elected at its annual meeting, the ABA adopts major policy positions through its House of Delegates, which consists of representatives from all the state bar associations and from many large local bar associations as well. A good deal of the ABA's activities are conducted by committees (called sections) that reflect a broad array of topics ranging from antitrust to criminal justice to legal ethics.

Although the ABA claims to speak for the entire legal profession, historically membership consisted almost exclusively of white male Protestants. Racial discrimination was practiced as late as the 1940s: African Americans were excluded, and Jews were suspect (Auerbach 1976). Consistent with that membership base, the ABA established a record of support for conservative causes, adopting policy positions favoring big business over labor and Republicans over Democrats. The ABA was also vehemently anticommunist, supporting Senator Joseph McCarthy and the House Un-American Activities Committee. Since the 1960s, the ABA has sought to modify that conservative image, but its membership is still skewed toward attorneys practicing in large elite law firms. In particular, many of the ABA sections are dominated by attorneys whose major clients would be affected by the committee's proposed legislation (Green 1976).

Bar Association Activities

Originally concerned with political corruption, bar associations began to engage in numerous types of other activities central to the legal profession. Bar associations have been at the forefront of efforts to upgrade the quality of the legal profession by improving legal education, raising standards for admission to the bar, and removing dishonest lawyers through disciplinary actions. A closely related activity is promoting the overall image of the bar. The ABA conducts regular assessments of the public's views of the legal profession.

Bar associations see themselves as acting in the public interest. In the often-repeated words of the presidents of the ABA, "The Bar … is guided by a desire to serve the country and not itself…" (Green 1976). The ABA, for example, actively advocates improvements in the administration of justice, including court reorganization (Chapters 3 and 4) and judicial selection (Chapter 6). Some of those efforts do reflect a true attempt to serve the public interest by promoting the ideal of better justice, but bar associations are not totally disinterested parties. Some policies advocated by the ABA have molded the conditions under which courts are available to the public in ways that favor the legal profession.

Like other trade organizations, bar associations promote the economic well-being of their members. Efforts to protect citizens from inferior legal services often result in making the practice of law more lucrative for existing members. To regulate the supply of legal services, bar associations historically restricted entry into the profession by tightening licensing requirements. To keep fees high, bar associations restricted competition by imposing minimum fee schedules and prohibiting advertising.

The clearest example of how the legal profession has sought to improve its economic status centers on defining the unauthorized practice of law. Lawyers enjoy a monopoly over providing legal services, and bar associations have sought to protect that monopoly. As a state-regulated profession, lawyers have the authority to perform services that are prohibited to others. Just as only medical doctors can practice medicine, only licensed attorneys can practice law. Individuals who cross those boundaries are subject to criminal penalties. Unlike medicine, however, legal work is not so easily defined and separated from similar activities. Bar associations have been successful in persuading state legislatures to write very general statutes prohibiting the **unauthorized practice of law** and allowing bar associations and courts (composed of lawyers, of course) to interpret those laws. As a result, U.S. lawyers have gained a monopoly over many activities that nonlawyers perform in other societies. In Great Britain, for example, accountants deal with tax matters, and real estate agents handle the exchange of property. In the United States, in contrast, only lawyers can argue tax matters in court and, in some states, are necessary to complete real estate transactions.

Advocates of a professional bar argue that a legal education is necessary to adequately represent clients. However, in one study, Herbert Kritzer (1998) set out to examine whether that is actually the case. He found that in four specialized courts in Wisconsin where nonlawyers are permitted to represent clients, it was the advocate's experience, not legal training, that predicted success. Although not conclusive, this study suggests that a certain amount of skepticism is appropriate when proponents of a professional bar downplay the ability of nonlawyer advocates.

The legal profession's market is also threatened by lay competitors and the Internet. Some types of legal tasks are routine and may occur during the life of many average citizens. Prime examples include uncontested divorces, adoptions, name changes, and writing wills. These tasks are not particularly complicated; all one has to do is fill in the correct form, file the document in the courthouse, and get a judge's signature. To help citizens perform these routine legal tasks, nonlawyers publish handbooks, produce forms, and offer advice. Some of the most popular topics include how to handle your own divorce, plan your estate with a living trust, and patent it yourself. The modern do-it-yourself legal trade is also available through computer software and the Internet. Although these routine legal tasks do not appear to require the type of expertise usually associated with lawyers, bar associations have tried to prevent nonlawyers from providing these services. Thus, a Florida secretary was prosecuted for the unauthorized practice of law for furnishing and typing routine legal forms for individuals. Upon conviction, she was sentenced to 30 days in jail. The governor and the cabinet intervened, however, and granted clemency on the basis that the bar association seemed more concerned with prosecuting nonlawyers than with disciplining licensed attorneys who had committed even graver offenses (Glick 1988). More often than not, those prosecuted for the unauthorized practice of law are former attorneys who have been disbarred and are now attempting to practice law again. Those political overreactions aside, bar associations caution that there are limits to being your own lawyer. Mari Frank, vice chair of the California Bar Association's standing committee on legal services to middle-income persons, makes the point as follows: "The problem is that a book can't ask questions, can't read minds. The books can help give you a background, and from there, you have the basis from which to ask questions of an attorney" (Eisinger 1993). In the end, it is no surprise to learn that laypeople and lawyers have markedly different perceptions about what kind of simple legal matters can be handled by the average citizen, and what complicated tasks require the attention of a licensed lawyer.

THE WORK OF LAWYERS

The word *lawyer* usually evokes the image of an individual arguing before a jury. Until the twentieth century, that was a good description. The most famous lawyers of the past—Daniel Webster and Clarence Darrow, for example—were skilled trial orators. But times have changed. The vast majority of U.S. lawyers never try a case. Rather, most of their work occurs not in the courtroom but in the shadows of the courthouse. England draws a formal distinction between types of lawyers (Abel 2003): **Solicitors** are office attorneys who advise clients about the law but can argue cases only in the lower courts. **Barristers** are litigators who argue cases in the major trial courts. The United States makes no such formal distinction, but there is an informal one.

The major activities of U.S. lawyers can be grouped into five somewhat overlapping categories: litigating, representing, negotiating, drafting documents, and counseling clients (Neubauer 2005; Baum 1986; Mayer 1967).

Litigating

Litigating involves presenting cases before a judge or jury. A trial lawyer must be a fighter who likes to question witnesses, object to other lawyers' questions, and, at times, argue with the judge as well. A case does not arrive in a lawyer's office neatly packaged and awaiting the summoning of a jury. One of the most vital skills of a trial attorney is organizing a raw dispute for trial, which requires numerous tactical decisions. Will this person make a good witness? How can I highlight the strongest points of my case while minimizing the weaknesses? What type of case is the opposition likely to mount, and how can I counter it? Obviously, a mastery of the rules of evidence is essential, but perhaps equally important is insight into the psychological and sociological dynamics of juries, clients, witnesses, and other lawyers. Because of the dramatic value inherent in trials, fictional accounts in television dramas and movies focus on lawyers as courtroom advocates. But, in reality, only a small number of attorneys are litigators. Indeed, many lawyers never try a case during their professional careers.

COURTS IN COMPARATIVE PERSPECTIVE

■ Italy

"It is shameful. It is a ruling without any logic… It is not possible to hold a fair trial here" argued Niccolo Ghedini the lead lawyer for Italian Prime Minister Silvio Berlusconi, the three-term Italian Prime minister (CNN 2011). Berlusconi is charged with paying Karima El Mahruog (aka Ruby the Heart Stealer) for sex while she was under 18 and for trying to get her released from a Milan police station after she had been arrested, offenses that could result in 15 years in prison. Ghedini's ultimate objective is to have the case transferred to Rome's Tribunal of Ministers, which hears cases related to public officials, instead of being heard in a Milan Criminal Court (Voice of America 2011).

Besides facing criminal charges, Mr. Berlusconi's media companies are in court in two other cases. He is certainly in need of good legal help and he can afford the best. One can safely assume that Mr. Berlusconi did not have any trouble finding a lawyer to represent him— after all he is the longest-serving prime minister since World War II and wealthy. But the types of lawyers available in Italy are fundamentally different in term of training and career choices from those in the United States.

In Europe, every major university (excepting technical ones) has a College of Law. But law is an undergraduate major (much like chemistry or political science) which means that a law degree is not a professional degree as in the U.S. Indeed many law school graduates choose to become public bureaucrats or work in the private sector. Those who wish to pursue a legal career must make a career choice immediately after they graduate from law school and decide whether to become a lawyer, a judge or a prosecutor. Each has its own distinct educational system which ends in passing (hopefully) a rigorous exam. Italy has one important variation on the typical European pattern. Prosecutors are part of the judicial system and trained in the same way. Thus judges may become prosecutors and vice versa but a person is limited to only four career changes (Fabri 2007).

Italian law is based on Roman law and is modified by statutes. The system is inquisitorial in style but has elements of the adversary system, mainly in its appeal process (Grande 2000). They have an independent judiciary that was established by the 1948 Constitution.

Lawyers are referred to as (avvocato) and Judges (giudici). Judges are civil servants and once appointed serve for life. The court system has three general levels, inferior courts that hear criminal and civil cases, appellate courts, and a single Constitutional Court. Political Scientist Mary Volcansek's (2000) careful examination of Italy's highest court concludes that it is political and occasionally acts in a way that is consistent with American norms of judicial review, including responding to external political forces. Perhaps this tendency will help Berlusconi when the Constitutional Court makes the final decision whether he will be tried as an ordinary criminal or as a public official.

The Berlusconi trial highlights some unique features of Italian justice that Americans are likely to find distinctive and perhaps disquieting:

• The defendant was not required to attend his own trial;
• Defendants are not under oath when they testify and do not have to testify truthfully;
• Two of Mr. Berlusconi's top lawyers are also members of parliament and Mr. Berlusconi's ruling political party the Democrat Liberal Party (PDL). They receive salaries from the state at the same time they are representing the prime minister against criminal charges;
• The lawyers publicly denounced the trial judges in ways that would be unthinkable for all except the most radical of American lawyers;
• Appeals are quite lengthy and constitute a trial de nova (a new trial).

The three giant photos that hung outside the Milan courthouse during the trial of Berlusconi highlight a darker side of Italian justice (AFP 2011). The photos are of two Milan judges and a prosecutor displayed as an expression of thanks to judges and police who have been killed doing their job. During the 1970s a total of 26 judges and prosecutors were killed by the left-wing Red Brigades, extreme rightists groups, or the mafia (AFP 2011). Nor are such threatens of violence against the judiciary a part of the past; as recently as 2010 a bazooka was discovered near a courthouse when Italian police conducted raids prompted by mafia threats against the judiciary (UPI).

Representing

Representing clients before the growing number of state and federal regulatory agencies is somewhat similar to litigating. Businesses or individuals dealing with these agencies typically hire lawyers to represent their interests in matters such as securing a license (or preventing its revocation), urging changes in administrative regulations (or opposing any alterations), or requesting variances in zoning rules (or protecting existing zoning provisions). Representation is most visible during public hearings but also occurs during informal discussions with administrative staff, who usually are also lawyers. Lawyers lobby on behalf of clients seeking advantageous amendments to tax laws or the passage (or defeat) of regulatory legislation concerning the environment, consumer protection, and the like. As the scope of governmental regulation increases, so does the demand for lawyers to represent clients before various and sundry governmental agencies.

Negotiating

Of the millions of lawsuits filed each year, only a small percentage are ever tried; most are voluntarily settled. Indeed, lawyers for the opposing parties are expected to meet before the trial to try to **negotiate** a settlement. Thus, a third major activity lawyers engage in is negotiating. In other types of social conflicts, working out a settlement to a lawsuit ultimately involves finding the range of possible outcomes within which each party would rather make a concession than fail to reach agreement at all (Schelling 1960). Armed with a realistic assessment of possible outcomes, lawyers seek to gain the best possible settlement for their clients. In a tort action, for example, the plaintiff's attorney is typically able to negotiate an out-of-court financial settlement with the defense attorney representing the insurance company. Negotiations in criminal cases are often referred to in more pejorative terms (such as *plea bargaining* or *copping a deal*), but they reflect dynamics similar to their civil counterparts.

Drafting Documents

Trial outcomes confirm the old saying that "an oral contract isn't worth the paper it is written on"; courts typically will not enforce oral agreements, because the parties have conflicting interpretations of what was agreed on. Thus, one of the critical skills of the lawyer is the drafting of documents. The difference between a properly written will and a badly drafted one means the difference between order and chaos, between the quick settlement of an estate during probate and litigation over competing claims. Because of the technical aspects of this kind of work, the ability to write documents such as mortgages and articles of incorporation has been referred to as "the most legal of the lawyer's skills" (Mayer 1967). A properly drafted document can avoid potential lawsuits, but not all lawsuits can be avoided. Lawyers also draft important documents during all phases of litigation.

In filing a case, the plaintiff's attorneys must state precisely the nature of the claim. In finalizing an out-of-court settlement, lawyers for all parties need to specify the agreements in detail. After the trial, judges prepare judgments and write court orders. For appellate judges, of course, writing opinions explaining the court's decision is a major activity.

Counseling Clients

Another important task is counseling clients. Part of this role requires attending to the client's emotional needs, particularly during stressful events such as divorce or criminal prosecution. Just as patients evaluate their doctors' friendly bedside manner, clients measure their lawyers' courteous and understanding demeanor.

The most important counseling role, however, centers on advising clients about the dictates of the law. As professionals educated in the law, lawyers are expected to provide advice about the possible legal consequences stemming from their clients' actions or inactions. Thus, lawyers must fully and dispassionately evaluate the strengths and the weaknesses of the client's case, as well as assess the position of the opposing party.

The counseling role can lead to tension between lawyer and client. As advocates, attorneys are expected to champion their client's case. As counselors, however, lawyers interpret the law for their clients, appraising risks and outlining options. Thus, at times, a lawyer must offer advice that the client does not want to hear. In a criminal case, for example, the defendant's preferred outcome is a disposition of not guilty. But the defense attorney, having weighed the evidence for both sides, may advise the client that the chances of acquittal are slim and a plea of guilty with a short prison term is the best possible outcome. The amount of conflict is often a product of the client's knowledge about the legal system. Some types of clients, particularly businesses and other institutions, are quite knowledgeable about the law. But others, especially individuals with no prior experience with the law and courts, are often unversed in what the law considers important.

Cause Lawyering

In addition to the conventional tasks of lawyers—which include litigating, representing, negotiating, drafting documents, and counseling clients—a subset of lawyers practice what is referred to as cause lawyering (Sarat and Scheingold 2006; Scheingold and Sarat 2004). Cause lawyering involves mobilization of the law combined with political calculations. It adds an element of political and social advocacy to the toolkit of lawyers. Cause lawyering emerged in the 1960s and now includes activities on both the political left and the political right as groups try to advance their causes through the use of litigation. In *Lawyers of the Right* Ann Southworth (2008) writes about how lawyers played leading roles not just as advocates for conservative causes but also as chief strategists and spokespersons.

WHERE LAWYERS WORK

Nineteenth-century lawyers worked alone in offices near the courthouse and earned their livelihood from the fees paid by the clients they represented on a case-by-case basis. The traditional "small-town lawyer" has not disappeared altogether, but that historical image fits less well today (Zemans and Rosenblum 1981). Law is increasingly an urban profession, with lawyers setting up offices in high-rise buildings close to their business clients but far from the courthouse. Slightly more than 25 percent of the lawyers in the United States are located in just two states—California and New York. An additional 25 percent work in Illinois, Florida, Massachusetts, Pennsylvania, and Texas. Thus, half of the profession work in just seven states (ABA 2008b). Moreover, rather than working alone, the majority work in law firms that have ongoing arrangements with their clients. Besides private practice, lawyers work for businesses and government.

Private Practice

Private practice remains the dominant area in which lawyers work. According to the latest survey, nearly three-quarters of lawyers are actively engaged in the private practice of law (Table 5.1). As in an earlier era, some work alone, but the proportion of solo practitioners has been steadily declining since World War II. Today, less than half of the private bar work by themselves (ABA 2011). Solo practitioners, however, are still an important segment of the bar, particularly in small cities, where they constitute the backbone of the profession.

Increasingly, lawyers in private practice are associated with other lawyers. Law firms vary in size from two to hundreds. Internal governance arrangements range from a splitting of office expenses to an elaborate written agreement specifying layers of authority. Economy of scale is one reason for the rise of the law firm: Groups of lawyers can more easily bear the costs of overhead (office rent and law books) and support personnel (secretaries, clerks, and paralegals). Law firms are also able to provide a wider array of legal expertise to serve the diverse needs of their clients. Despite the trend toward working together, most lawyers still work by themselves or in small firms—63 percent work by themselves or with fewer than six colleagues.

Business

The increasing complexity of the business environment has produced a growing demand for legal services by businesses. Much of that legal advice is provided by private practitioners. Major corporations retain large law firms to serve as outside counsel. Similarly, small to medium-size law firms often practice exclusively civil law, representing small to medium-size businesses. But, increasingly, large businesses are also hiring attorneys as

TABLE 5.1	Where Lawyers Work, 2010
Type of Practice	**Percent**
Private practice	74
Private industry	8
Government	8
Judiciary	3
Legal aid/public defenders	1
Legal education	1
Retired/inactive	5

Source: *Lawyer Demographics* (Chicago: American Bar Association, 2011). Available online at http://www.americanbar.org/content/dam/aba/migrated/marketresearch/PublicDocuments/lawyer_demographics_2011.authcheckdam.pdf. Retrieved: July 8, 2011.

salaried employees. A house counsel works directly for a company and handles that company's routine legal matters; this position has been a major growth area for the legal profession. In recent years, the number of lawyers working directly for businesses has almost doubled, particularly in areas such as manufacturing, transportation, utilities, banking, and insurance (Curran 1986). Some companies employ only one or two lawyers, but others employ considerably more. Indeed, one-third of all lawyers employed by business work with fifty or more other lawyers.

Many large corporations have a legal division headed by a general counsel, who is also a senior management official. The general counsel supervises the myriad legal concerns that are part of modern corporate activity—including monitoring business activities to ensure compliance with statutory and regulatory requirements such as civil rights, safety regulations, and securities—and serving as the corporation's liaison with the law firm that is on retainer to the corporation (Blish 1992). When litigation arises, however, outside counsel usually represents the corporation.

Government

A substantial number of lawyers work for the government. Today, 8 percent of the bar are employed by a wide variety of public agencies. Although we commonly think of government lawyers as courtroom advocates arguing for the conviction or acquittal of persons accused of crime, that image only partially captures the variety of tasks performed. Less than half the lawyers employed by the government work as prosecutors or public defenders. The majority work in noncriminal justice areas processing liability claims, drafting administrative regulations, and serving as hearing officers.

The federal government employs attorneys in almost every department and agency. Predictably, the largest share work in the Department of Justice. With thousands of lawyers, it is the nation's largest law firm, employing many of the nation's best and brightest attorneys. But a significant number of lawyers are employed by other federal agencies, such as the Internal Revenue Service, Congress, the National Labor Relations Board, the Department of Defense, and the Department of Health and Human Services.

State governments employ even more lawyers than the federal government. The majority work in offices of local prosecutors or for the state attorney general. The rest are employed by a variety of departments or agencies at the state, county, or local level.

Law Clerks

Many lawyers work for the government in the capacity of judging—which will be examined in the next chapter. However, closely related to judging is the practice of clerking for a judge. Law clerks conduct legal research and engage in legal writing for the judge with whom they work (Oakley 1981). The most high profile are those who clerk for the Supreme Court (Peppers 2006, Ward and Weiden 2006), but all federal judges and many state judges have law clerks. Law clerkships may be for a specified term or career, though the vast majority are term positions. Judicial clerkships are highly prized by law students and viewed as prestigious by potential employers. Three of the current Supreme Court justices previously clerked for the Supreme Court: Breyer (Justice Arthur Goldberg), Kagan (Justice Thurgood Marshall), and Roberts (Justice William Rehnquist).

DEBATING LAW, COURTS, AND POLITICS

■ BP Faces Off Against Its Old Foes

"Have you suffered from loss of income due to the oil spill and negligence? Our aggressive team of oil spill damage lawyers at Fitts Zehl can help get back what you deserve" (Oil Spill Damage Lawyer 2010). After the explosion on the Deepwater Horizon oil rig, ads like this quickly appeared on television, radio, newspapers and bill boards along the coastline of the Gulf of Mexico. The only distinctive feature about this particular ad is that it appeared on the Internet, a sign that lawyers are now comfortable searching for clients using a newer form of mass media—the Internet (see Chapter 7).

Criticism of the lawyers representing those who suffered damages because of the oil spill followed almost as quickly as the ads the lawyers were running. Louisiana Republican Senator David Vitter's campaign for re-election was quick to blast his opponent for attending a conference in Canada where trial lawyers were planning how to get rich off of the victims of the oil spill. His radio ad proclaimed that "the trial lawyers want to benefit from the victims of the oil spill" and proposed capping lawyer's fees at five percent. The same theme was sounded in business publications like the *Wall Street Journal* which immediately labeled them part of the plaintiff bar. Indeed they wrote that BP "is facing many of its old foes" (Baldas 2010).

The oil spill litigation represents another round in the battle between plaintiff lawyers and defense lawyers (Chapter 10) and this long standing battle spilled over to legislative chambers. In Louisiana the business lobby was successful in blocking a plan by the state attorney general to hire private lawyers on contingency to represent the state in the oil spill litigation (Barrow 2010). In Alabama, the Governor signed an executive order limiting attorney fees that the Attorney General may pay ("Alabama Governor…" 2010). To critics such limits only work to the advantage of the oil industry because state governments will be unable to hire lawyers with the needed expertise in suing the oil and natural gas industry.

The lawyers seeking to represent the victims of the oil spill are diverse in background and prior legal practice. A few have a long track record of suing oil companies; one was noted for winning millions in damages following the Texas City oil refinery explosion in 2005 (Baldas 2010). Others were veterans of major class action lawsuits against tobacco manufacturers and drug makers (Chapters 10 and 11); the business community has heavily criticized these lawyers individually and collectively in the past. Finally may of the lawyers were essentially neighborhood lawyers that make a living representing those hurt in car wrecks and the like.

The diversity aside, plaintiff lawyers are seldom shy about talking about themselves and this trait was on display in the federal courthouse in New Orleans. In multidistrict litigation, such as the oil spill, the federal judge selects a Plaintiffs Steering Committee. This small group of lawyers will coordinate the litigation, conduct pretrial discovery, and either settle or try the case. The few lawyers selected often earn very lucrative attorney fees which means that there is intense jockeying between plaintiff lawyers to be selected. Robert Cunningham of Mobile, Alabama was one of those selected and he took the lead in taking the deposition of Tony Hayward, BP's chief executive when the oil rig exploded (Schwartz 2011).

But so much like all the other repercussions of the oil spill it is difficult to predict whether the oil spill will be as lucrative for the plaintiff's bar as they hope and others fear. Many of the potential law suits were pre-empted when BP created the $20 billion dollar fund, which refused to pay attorney's fees. Although plaintiffs could file lawsuits, many opted for a quicker and surer settlement (Chapter 10). Indeed within a year the tone of the lawyer ads had changed to stress that you needed a lawyer if you thought you weren't being treated fairly by BP and the settlement fund. The oil spill lawyers became the principal critics of the compensation fund.

As for defense lawyers the oil spill has been a major bonanza. BP and others quickly signed on many local lawyers (no doubt partly out of fear that they might sign with plaintiffs).

DIVERSITY AND STRATIFICATION OF THE LEGAL PROFESSION

By now, it should be clear that the law is not a single, unified profession. There are important differences within the legal profession based partially on the law school one attended and where one works. The litigation following the BP oil spill highlight some of these differences. (See Debating Law, Courts, and Politics: BP Faces Off Against Its Old Foes.)

But how significant are those differences? That was the guiding question in a comprehensive study of the diverse tasks that characterize the social role of lawyers. In 1975, the interdisciplinary team of law professor John Heinz and sociologist Edward Laumann conducted extensive interviews with more than 800 practicing attorneys. In *Chicago Lawyers* (1982), Heinz and Laumann reported dramatic differences among lawyers. Their original work was updated and revisited in the Chicago Lawyers II project, conducted by John Heinz and Robert Nelson in 1995, once again interviewing more than 800 lawyers (American Bar Foundation n.d.).

Those studies found that one difference in structure of the practicing bar is based on the fields of law one practices. Demands for legal services are arrayed along a continuum from very general to highly specific. At one end of the continuum are fields of law that are likely to arise during the course of the daily affairs of many individuals and businesses. People of even moderate means, as well as businesses of any size, buy and sell property, write and probate wills, negotiate contracts, and resolve the consequences of accidents or other misadventures. The demand for such legal services is large and dispersed throughout society. At the other end of the continuum are fields of law that serve the needs of a narrow range of individuals or businesses. Some lawyers concern themselves only with antitrust or admiralty matters.

Practice in these latter fields requires specialized training and experience often not acquired in law school. Heinz and Laumann found that a handful of lawyers characterized themselves as true generalists who perform general, unspecified legal work. The majority also practice in several areas of law. Some lawyers, however, are highly specialized: Twenty-two percent reported that they practice exclusively in one field. Only a few lawyers, for example, practice patent, antitrust, or admiralty law, but when they do, that is all they practice.

Another difference in the structure of the bar relates to which party the lawyer represents. The adversary system creates clearly distinguishable specialties representing the two sides of a case. In labor, environmental, personal injury, criminal, and consumer law, lawyers consistently represent either plaintiffs or defendants. Only rarely will they represent someone in the opposing position. Finally, the original Chicago study found that the most important differentiation within the legal profession centered on the types of clients served. Lawyers' work clusters on the basis of problems associated with particular types of clients. Some lawyers represent large organizations—corporations, labor unions, or government. Others represent mainly individuals. By and large, lawyers operate in one of these two hemispheres of the profession; seldom, if ever, do they cross the line separating these very different types of legal work. However, by 1995, these distinctions were less clear. The authors attribute the declining differences to such factors as "increasing specialization in law practice, broader recruitment by law firms, and the diminishing significance of ethnoreligous identification" (ABA 2002).

On the basis of these differences, Heinz and Laumann reported that Chicago lawyers fell into two groups. The corporate client sector consists of lawyers whose clients are large corporations, regulatory agencies, or governmental bodies. The personal client sector is divided into personal business and personal plight lawyers. Far from being random, these groupings are related to other important distinctions in the legal profession. Lawyers serving the corporate client sector are more likely to work in large law firms, represent stable clients, handle intellectually challenging tasks, earn substantial incomes, have graduated from elite or prestigious law schools, come from Protestant backgrounds, and be regarded by fellow lawyers as the most prestigious members of the bar. In sharp contrast, attorneys serving the personal client sector are more likely to work alone or with a single partner, represent clients on a one-shot basis, handle repetitive and dull legal tasks, earn moderate incomes, have attended local law schools, come from Catholic or Jewish backgrounds, and be ranked by fellow lawyers at the bottom of the profession in terms of prestige. These groupings have important implications for the courts. Corporate sector attorneys are rarely found in the courthouse and average only a single state court appearance per month. Personal client sector attorneys, on the other hand, are frequently in the courthouse, averaging fifteen state court appearances each month. Since 1975, the corporate client sector has grown more rapidly than the personal client sector. In 1975, the distribution of lawyers' time was 54 percent corporate and 40 percent personal client. By 1995, it was 61 percent corporate and just 29 percent personal client. The trend is clear: We can best capture the flavor of this diversity by focusing on the opposite ends of the continuum of practicing lawyers in big cities.

Large Law Firms

The most distinctive place where lawyers work is the large law firm. Because the first firms were founded in New York, home of the greatest concentration of U.S. corporate headquarters, lawyers in large law firms are collectively called Wall Street lawyers. Today, these firms are found in every large U.S. city as well (Smigel 1969). Their offices, located in large downtown office buildings, are dressed in plush carpets, walnut furniture, and tasteful modern art. The largest is Chicago's Baker & McKenzie, with 3,774 attorneys, many of whom staff offices as far afield as Hong Kong, Paris, and Rio de Janeiro. The second largest is DLA Piper Rudnick Gray and Cary, also in Chicago, with 3,448 attorneys, followed by Jones Day (Washington), with 2,515 attorneys, Hogan Lovells (Washington), with 2,345 attorneys, Latham & Watkins (New York), 2,006 attorneys, and Skadden, Arps, Slate, Meagher & Flom (New York), 1,886 attorneys.

Although only a small percentage of lawyers work in large law firms, such organizations generally exert a disproportionate influence on U.S. law and politics. The clientele consists of the corporate elite of the United States—the companies listed on *Fortune*'s annual list of the 500 largest businesses. As James Stewart (1984) points out, "Only such clients can afford the elite corporate law firms and the kind of practice for which the firms pride themselves—one in which no stone is left unturned, no matter how seemingly insignificant, and with virtually no regard for time or money" (p. 14). Thus, the Wall Street lawyers are advisers to corporate America, but their role extends beyond merely providing legal advice and appearing in court. They also manage uncertainty for their clients (Flood 1991), which often requires playing a directly political role. Because the interests of their corporate clients are affected by legislative and administrative policy, lawyers in large firms often function as lobbyists and seek to influence governmental decisions.

Large law firms represent the same businesses year in and year out. Indeed, they emphasize maintaining strong ties, and hence trust, with their clients. This ongoing relationship between lawyer and client is secured through a yearly retainer. How much law firms charge their corporate clients is a closely guarded secret, but the fees are substantial.

One service that Wall Street law firms provide their clients that is not easily matched by other lawyers is the coordinated services of highly specialized legal experts in all fields important to large institutions. Thus, any major legal problem confronting a large business—taxation, corporations, antitrust, and securities regulation, for example—can be handled by the firm. Another distinctive feature of Wall Street law firms is the ability to provide high-quality legal expertise: Large law firms recruit the top graduates from the elite, prestigious law schools, offering prime attractions of challenging legal issues coupled with high salaries. Traditionally, large law firms hired only white, Anglo-Saxon, Protestant men, but that pattern is changing.

Lawyers working in large firms are divided into associates and partners. Recent law school graduates begin as associates and function in a subordinate role, providing legal assistance to partners but rarely having contact with clients. In essence, firms engage in a "promotion-to-partner tournament" (Galanter and Palay 1991).

After five to eight years, some associates are promoted to partners; others leave the firm, sometimes finding jobs with the firm's clients. Partners hold a permanent position in the law firm and participate in its management. Besides their annual salary, they are entitled to a share of the year-end profits. Through the years, partners come to do less strictly legal work. One senior Wall Street lawyer aptly summarized the division of labor in terms of "finders, minders, and grinders." Finders are the senior partners who bring in clients, minders are the managers who organize the work of the firm, and grinders are the associates and junior partners who do legal research (Nelson 1981). Typically, partners earn increasingly larger incomes and charge clients increasingly higher rates for their services. Thus, lawyers in large firms are the best paid in the profession and enjoy the greatest prestige. They are also counted among the profession's leaders, holding important leadership positions in the ABA.

Solo Practitioners

Law offices of the solo practitioners are a permanent feature of urban architecture. They can be found near the imposing stone edifice of the courthouse or in neighborhoods close to their clients. The offices are almost barren, with only a few old magazines scattered in the small waiting room (Wice 1978).

Unlike corporate lawyers, who represent the same organizations year in and year out, the clients of solo practitioners are one-shotters—individuals who rarely hire a lawyer. Thus, solo practitioners spend a fair amount of their time drumming up business. During the day, they are often found in the courthouse corridors soliciting clients, sometimes in violation of bar association ethics. In the evening, they can be found at local bars mingling with people who might one day need a lawyer or participating in neighborhood organizations in hopes that one day a member might need their services.

The cases these clients bring to solo practitioners often involve divorce, criminal law, immigration, and personal injury—the very types of legal matters that are deemed too unsavory or too unprofitable for other members of the bar to handle. Given that the fees in these cases are individually quite small, solo practitioners are wholesalers; to make a living, they must handle a large number of cases each year. Still, their incomes fall at the bottom range of the profession (Carlin 1962). Overall, solo practitioners enjoy the least amount of prestige among fellow lawyers, rarely participate in bar association activities, and are the most often cited for ethical violations. They are, however, the most likely to appear as counsel in court on a regular basis.

Lawyer Employment and Salaries

Geography plays an important role in the employment patterns of the legal profession. Although lawyers work everywhere, the largest number of lawyers practice in urban areas. According to the LSAC, nearly 43 percent of all new jobs in 2005 with a known location were in just twenty cities. The states with the largest number of new law jobs continue to be New York, California, and Texas, with the most jobs in the South Atlantic, Mid-Atlantic, East North Central, and Pacific regions of the country (LSAC 2007).

To the critics, those numbers are irrelevant. They worry that too many lawyers encourage unnecessary litigation. Another concern is "meter running," in which lawyers spend useless time that they bill to rich clients. As Deborah Rhode (1985, 576) succinctly observes, "Most lawyers will prefer to leave no stone unturned, provided, of course, they can charge by the stone." Even though everyone supposedly knows these types of behaviors do happen, Lawrence Friedman (1985) argues that it is hard to find any large-scale evidence of lawyers stirring up unnecessary work. He concludes that the growth in the legal profession reflects the economic market, with demand pushing supply. After all, most lawyers work for businesses that seem willing to pay the fees. We find empirical support for this in recent trends; not all the 40,000 men and women who graduate from law school each year find jobs practicing law. The tightening of the job market for lawyers indicates that, indeed, demand, not supply, fuels the growth (and, by implication, litigation) in the legal profession.

Related to geography are lawyer salaries. It is no surprise that lawyers in the largest urban areas earn, on average, the largest salaries, but there remains substantial variation across the type of employment. The median starting salary of lawyers in the ten cities with the largest number of jobs is $114,020 for positions in private practice, $65,250 for business, and $49,769 for government jobs (LSAC 2007). The U.S. Bureau of Labor Statistics reports that in 2010 the median salary for lawyers in the United States was $112,760, with 25 percent of lawyers earning $77,200 or less. Locations with the highest-paid lawyers in order of salary are the District of Columbia, California, New York, Delaware, and Georgia. The Bureau of Labor Statistics (http://www.bls.gov/bls/blswage.htm) provides data on the number of lawyers in your state (along with all other occupations) as well as up-to-date salary information.

ACCESS TO LEGAL SERVICES

Some critics are concerned about access to legal services. The availability of lawyers in the United States represents both a paradox and a contradiction. The paradox is that whereas there are many lawyers (1,162,124 in 2008), some citizens facing legal problems can't find a lawyer to represent them. A recent ABA report found that although seven in ten households reported having an occasion during the past year that might have led them to hire a lawyer, more than half of those households reported that they did not plan to follow through and hire an attorney. This imbalance can be traced primarily, but not exclusively, to the high monetary costs of legal services. Most lawyers work for businesses, which write off the costs of legal services as business expenses. Similarly, wealthy individuals can clearly afford the best legal advice to help them shelter their incomes to reduce their taxes or plan for passing on their wealth after their death. The poor, however, cannot afford to hire a lawyer to help them with their legal problems. Even some middle-income individuals have difficulty finding a lawyer they can afford. Indeed, one study reports that the unmet legal needs are greater than had been thought. Some 40 percent of low-income people encounter at least one legal problem during a year, yet 70 percent of them don't turn to a lawyer for help (Montes 1994).

The imbalance in the availability of legal services produces a contradiction in the normative values of society. Based on law on the books, the U.S. legal system prides itself on providing wide access for redress of ills. Based on law in action, however, the allocation of court access is left to market mechanisms. This disparity is of particular concern in a democracy that prides itself on equal justice under the law. The next two sections examine government programs and legal mechanisms that seek to overcome economic barriers to the availability of legal services.

Criminal Defense Services for the Poor

In criminal prosecutions, legal representation is a **right**, not a privilege. *Gideon v. Wainwright* (1963) held that indigent defendants charged with a felony were entitled to the services of a lawyer paid by the government. (See Case Close-Up: *Gideon v. Wainwright* 1963.) This right to counsel affects a substantial number of defendants. In big cities, as many as two out of three felony defendants are legally indigent. The two primary methods for providing indigents with counsel are assigned counsel and the public defender.

CASE CLOSE-UP

■ *Gideon v. Wainwright* (1963)

Right to Counsel

Clarence Earl Gideon had been in and out of prison since the age of fourteen. His brushes with the law had been minor—public drunkenness and petty theft primarily—but now he faced a much more serious charge—burglarizing a poolroom in Bay Harbor—and "he had a fierce feeling that the State of Florida had treated him wrongly" (Lewis 1972, 6). He demanded that the court appoint a lawyer to defend him, telling the trial judge that the Supreme Court had made a decision to the effect that all citizens tried for a felony crime should have aid of counsel, but the lower court ignored that plea. After he was convicted and imprisoned, he petitioned the Supreme Court to hear his case.

Every year, hundreds of pauper petitions like Gideon's are sent to the Supreme Court; few are ever heard. But this petition struck a responsive chord. In what became officially known as *Gideon v. Wainwright* (1963), the Court forcefully noted that "in our adversary system of criminal justice, any person, hauled into court, who is too poor to hire a lawyer, cannot be assured a fair trial unless counsel is provided for him. This seems to us to be an obvious truth...." The Sixth Amendment states that "in all criminal prosecutions, the accused shall enjoy the right ... to have the assistance of counsel for his defence." As written by the framers more than 225 years ago, this constitutionally protected right to counsel meant only that the judge could not prevent a defendant from bringing a lawyer to court. (In England, defendants had been convicted despite their plea to have their lawyer present.) Thus, the Sixth Amendment affected only those who could afford to hire their own lawyer. Beginning in the 1930s, the Supreme Court took a more expansive view of the right to counsel. Criminal defendants in federal cases were entitled to a court-appointed lawyer if they were too poor to hire their own.

But a different rule prevailed in the state courts. Only defendants accused of a capital offense were entitled to court-appointed counsel; indigent defendants charged with ordinary felonies or misdemeanors were not (*Betts v. Brady* 1942). Thus, a significant number of defendants in state courts had to face the legal maze of criminal proceedings by themselves. The inequity of that situation was spelled out by the Supreme Court in *Griffin v. Illinois* (1956): "There can be no equal justice where the kind of trial a man gets depends on the money he has."

Gideon v. Wainwright (1963) significantly expanded the legal meaning of the right to counsel. As occasionally happens, the Supreme Court reversed its earlier precedent in *Betts*:

> Governments, both state and federal, quite properly spend vast sums of money to establish machinery to try defendants accused of crime. Lawyers to prosecute are everywhere deemed essential to protect the public's interest in an orderly society. Similarly, there are few defendants charged with crime, few indeed, who fail to hire the best lawyers they can get to prepare and present their defenses. That government hires lawyers to prosecute and defendants who have the money hire lawyers to defend are the strongest indications of the widespread belief that lawyers in criminal courts are necessities, not luxuries. The right of one charged with crime to counsel may not be deemed fundamental and essential for fair trials in some countries, but it is in ours.

As a result, all indigent defendants charged with a felony were entitled to the services of a lawyer paid by the government, irrespective of whether they were on trial in state or federal court.

A later decision partially extended the Sixth Amendment to cover misdemeanor cases in lower courts (*Argersinger v. Hamlin* 1972). Moreover, the right to counsel is not limited to trial but extends throughout the criminal prosecution. Indigent defendants are entitled to court-appointed counsel during critical stages of the proceedings, including interrogation in the police station, police lineups, and the preliminary hearing. After conviction, the right to counsel extends to appeal (but not to habeas corpus proceedings). *Gideon* proved to be a transforming event in the U.S. criminal justice system. It was the first major decision of the Warren Court's revolution in criminal justice, but, unlike other decisions, it proved not to be controversial. The Court's rationale, focusing on basic fairness and the importance of lawyers, gave it widespread legitimacy. Moreover, *Gideon* focused on the need for a lawyer at the trial itself. Later decisions—*Miranda v. Arizona* (1966) in particular—restricted police gathering of evidence and proved to be highly contentious.

Assigned Counsel

The oldest and most widely used program for providing the poor with counsel is the **assigned counsel system**. It reflects the traditional way in which professions such as the law have responded to charity cases: Lawyers represent indigent defendants on a case-by-case basis. Historically, in many areas, serving as an assigned counsel was considered part of a lawyer's professional obligation (**pro bono publico**, meaning "for the public good"), and, therefore, the attorney was not paid.

Today, lawyers are paid, but less than the normal rate. Critics contend that assigned counsel systems provide the least qualified lawyers to defend the poor. There is no guarantee that the lawyer appointed is qualified to handle the increasing complexity of the criminal law. Moreover, those appointed are often either young lawyers seeking courtroom experience or, in big cities, the least skilled members of the bar, who need numerous appointments to earn a living. As a practical matter, the assigned counsel system is also easy to administer in courts with few cases.

Public Defender

The **public defender** is a twentieth-century response to the problem of providing legal representation for indigents. Under a public defender system, salaried lawyers paid by local or state government represent all criminal indigents in the jurisdiction. In the wake of *Gideon*, public defender programs have increasingly been adopted. Today, the public defender system is used in most big cities and in most medium-size jurisdictions as well. A few states have established statewide, state-funded programs.

Proponents cite several arguments in this system's favor. One is that a lawyer paid to represent indigents on a continuous basis will devote more attention to cases than a court-appointed attorney who is either not compensated or paid minimally. A second advantage is that the system provides more experienced, competent counsel. Because public defenders concentrate on criminal cases, they can keep abreast of changes in the law, and the day-to-day courtroom work keeps their trial skills sharp. Finally, a defender system assures continuity and consistency in the defense of the poor. Issues that transcend individual cases are more likely to be considered by a permanent, ongoing organization than by lawyers working under appointment systems.

Civil Representation for the Poor

In civil procedures, legal representation is considered a **privilege**, not a right. No constitutional protections guarantee indigents access to legal services in civil matters. But the poor, and the not-so-poor, can potentially obtain legal representation in several ways, such as contingency fees, legal clinics, and the Legal Services Program.

Contingency Fee In most types of legal matters, a lawyer requires an advance payment and bills the client regardless of the outcome. The specific amount of the fee is based either on a flat amount for performing a specific legal service or on the number of hours spent on the case (Brickman 2003; Barker 1994; Litan and Salop 1994). In one type of case, lawyers work on the basis of a **contingency fee**, wherein the lawyer is paid only if the case is won. The fee is a proportion, typically one-third, of the monetary damages recovered by the plaintiff. Lawyers representing plaintiffs in personal injury cases typically work under a contingency fee arrangement.

Contingency fees clearly increase lawyers' availability to represent people who have suffered injuries (Kritzer 2005). They shift the economic risks of prosecuting a lawsuit from the client to the lawyer. If a substantial fee were required before taking a personal injury case, many people would be discouraged from hiring a lawyer when their rights had been violated, no matter how great their chances of winning in court. A contingency fee arrangement also forges a tight bond between a lawyer's income and winning. Indeed, some lawyers advance money to their clients to tide them over until a good settlement is reached rather than settle early, because the client needs the money right away. Thus, the contingency fee largely ensures that ordinary citizens can find a lawyer willing to take their case, provided, of course, that the lawyer perceives that the case has a good chance of being won and that the winnings will be greater than the expenses.

The contingency fee is a distinctive feature of U.S. law (Karsten 1998). In Europe, England, and Canada, for example, this practice is prohibited. The contingency fee is also controversial (Passell 1994). By and large, the current controversy pits trial attorneys, who represent accident victims, against Wall Street lawyers, who represent insurance companies. Opponents of the system say that, first, the contingency fee can be unfair to clients—a person may win a substantial court judgment only to find much of it paid to the lawyer. Second, lawyers' earnings can be a windfall, far out of proportion to the actual time invested or skills used (Brickman 2003). Third, the possibility of winning big also means that personal injury attorneys engage in techniques to funnel business their way. Some of these methods for drumming up business are perfectly legal and ethical, but others appear to violate the canons of legal ethics. Because of these concerns, some states have limited contingency fees, often as a means of redressing a host of imagined problems with the legal system. As with many reform proposals, however, there is a notable absence of good empirical analysis in the debate. Political scientist Herbert Kritzer (2005) carefully examines the issues surrounding the use of the contingency fee and concludes that lawyers who use the contingency fee do not benefit so much more financially than lawyers who are paid by the hour and that they turn away plenty of cases. Thus, the suggestion that contingency fee lawyers take frivolous lawsuits in the hopes of winning may be unfounded. In an empirical analysis of tort reform limits, economists Tabarrok and Helland (2005) find that contingency fees benefit plaintiffs and do not cause higher awards. They conclude that reforms may not have the anticipated results and that careful empirical analysis is necessary to evaluate how the contingency fee system currently in place operates.

LAW AND POPULAR CULTURE

■ *Boston Legal*

Boston Legal (ABC Television, 2004–2008).
Welcome to the law firm of Crane, Poole, & Schmidt, the fictional firm at the heart of *Boston Legal*. While the plots of many episodes differ, most of the storylines center around Alan Shore (played by James Spader), an ethically-challenged attorney who, with the help of Denny Crane (played by William Shatner), a senior partner in the firm, gains recognition as an attorney of last resort – the guy who can win cases that no other attorney in private practice would ever want to take. Crane, however, possess an eccentric personality and engages in bizarre conduct as a function of being in early stages of Alzheimer's. Shirley Schmidt (played by Candice Bergen) is the firm's star litigator and managing partner. In that latter role, she not only has to make major decisions for the firm, but also has to supervise the questionable behaviors of the arrogant and narcissistic team of Shore and Crane.

Crane's own outrageous behavior helps to mentor Shore in his unethical ways. Indeed, it becomes clear that Shore's knack for winning is a function of his highly questionable methods. Shore will not "let trivial things like honesty and integrity get in the way of winning a case" (Smitts 2004). For example, in one episode, he had an unlicensed physician remove a potentially life-threatening bullet from a client who had refused to see medical treatment in a hospital for fear that the evidence gathered through traditional medical channels would lead to his being criminally convicted.

Television portrayals of fictional lawyers like Alan Shore and Denny Crane create unreasonable expectations in viewers who may need to hire a lawyer. After all, who would not want to be represented by attorney-gladiator ready to "fight the battle for them" (Slocum 2009, p. 516)? But such expectations are not realistic.

In real life, attorneys who practiced law the way Alan Shore and Denny Crane did on *Boston Legal* would find themselves in a lot a trouble with judges and their state bar association. Lawyers who are bound by codes of professional responsibility and the rules of court to behave in ways that conform to a set of legal ethics. The fictional defense attorneys of yesterday, like Perry Mason, Matlock, or Atticus Finch in *To Kill a Mockingbird* were consistently depicted as highly ethical attorneys who won cases not by ignoring the rules of professional responsibility, but rather by exercising their superior lawyering skills with uncompromised integrity. It is interesting to ask why media portrayals of fictional defense attorneys have changed so much in a generation or two? Moreover some argue that fictional depictions of unethical lawyers like those portrayed on *Boston Legal* contribute to the image of the unethical criminal defense attorneys?

Despite the media portrayal of lawyers as angry, avenging gladiators, such a role is less common than most clients think. In real life, lawyers like the ones we see on TV and in the movies often end up costing their clients money. The "litigation-as-war" mentality usually ratchets up the attacks and counterattacks, with the clients becoming even angrier and more frustrated as the litigation escalates into all-out war. "And the end result is not only that the lawsuit ends up costing both parties a lot of money in legal fees, but also that clients often end up pretty unhappy with the whole legal process, even if they end up getting much of what they wanted in terms of a financial outcome" (Slocum 2009 p. 517). Far from getting the justice they wanted and believe they deserve, they end up feeling that the legal system let them down.

Advertising and Legal Clinics   Two long-standing bar association practices—minimum fees and prohibitions on advertising—affected the market for lawyers. Under minimum fee schedules, bar associations established the lowest fee that lawyers could charge for a particular service. That type of price fixing promoted the economic well-being of the profession but eliminated price competition as a consideration in a client's effort to hire a lawyer. In *Goldfarb v. Virginia State Bar* (1975), the Supreme Court struck down minimum fee schedules as a violation of antitrust laws. Similarly, in the interests of projecting a professional image, lawyers were forbidden from advertising their services. In *Bates v. State Bar of Arizona* (1977), the Court found that those restrictions violated the First Amendment. But the Court later ruled that states can place limits on advertising. Florida, for example, prohibits lawyers from mailing letters to accident victims or their relatives within 30 days of a mishap.

As a practical matter, few lawyers have taken advantage of these changes. Legal fees often reflect informal price setting, and advertising is irrelevant to lawyers who work for businesses. Every big city has at least one lawyer who makes regular television appearances to tell citizens he or she is willing and able to fight their legal battles.

Abolishing minimum fee schedules and allowing lawyers to advertise have also led to the development of legal clinics, which pioneered the mass production of routine legal services for middle-class individuals through price cutting (Abel 1986). Clinics advertise extensively and try to make themselves accessible by locating in places frequented by average citizens—shopping malls, for example (Baum 1986). Clinics specialize in uncomplicated legal matters—divorce, personal injury, wills, bankruptcy, and traffic offenses—that can be handled primarily by standard forms. By making extensive use of **paralegals**, clinics are able to handle a large volume of cases at reasonable rates (Wice 1991). During the past few years, however, the clinics have fallen on hard economic times: High overhead has forced many of them to close (France 1994).

Legal Services Program   The legal aid movement began in New York City in 1876 with the founding of the German Aid Society, a group of laypeople dedicated to aiding indigent German immigrants. Similar groups were soon formed in other big cities. In 1911, the National Legal Aid Association (now the National Legal Aid and Defender Association) was formed to provide a public forum. The movement grew slowly. As late as 1964, nine cities with populations of a million or more had no programs, and fifteen slightly smaller communities had no civil legal aid at all. Moreover, these programs suffered from a number of major limitations:

- Budgets were small. Funds were derived from private donations, bar associations, and community chests. As a result, only a few poorly paid lawyers were employed in legal aid clinics.
- Financial eligibility levels for clients were stringent, sometimes falling below the government poverty level.
- The types of cases handled were limited. Legal aid clinics could not sue institutions such as banks and department stores that contributed to the community chest or bring suit against governmental agencies such as housing authorities. Similarly, divorce cases were not accepted because divorce was viewed as a right for the well-to-do but only a privilege for the poor. In short, one had to be truly "deserving" to qualify for legal aid assistance (Stumpf 1975).

The creation of the Legal Services Program in 1965 as part of President Lyndon Baines Johnson's War on Poverty represented a dramatic departure. No longer was legal aid to be restricted to the "deserving." Key features of the program included the following:

- Neighborhood offices were established to provide direct access to indigent clients.
- Programs were structured to ensure independence from local businesses, governmental bodies, and private groups (including bar associations) that might have opposing interests.
- Emphasis was placed on aggressive advocacy in addressing systemic issues that affected the poor, stressing reform rather than treating individual legal problems.
- Major increases in funding were provided (Stumpf 1975).

Opposition to the Legal Services Program was substantial and intense. Among the leading critics was then-Governor Ronald Reagan of California, who strongly objected to the efforts of the California Rural Legal Assistance Program to help migrant farmworkers. Similarly, during the 1968 presidential campaign, Vice President Spiro Agnew attacked legal services programs that sued state or local governments. As a result, Congress and President Nixon created an independent entity with specific legislative guidelines limiting acceptable types of advocacy. Thus, the Legal Services Corporation (LSC) was formed in 1974. The LSC is a private, nonprofit corporation established by Congress. It is run by an eleven-member board appointed by the president and confirmed by the Senate. It currently has a $420 million budget that helps fund 138 programs across the country that provide legal aid to more than one million people. Program focus varies depending on the locale. Attorneys in rural areas in California and Texas devote much of their time to representing migrant farmworkers in labor disputes. In urban areas, the focus is on housing, employment, and government benefits.

For a small organization with a modest budget, the Legal Services Corporation continues to generate an extraordinary amount of controversy. President Reagan tried unsuccessfully for eight years to eliminate the LSC but was successful only in reducing its budget (Masci 1994). President Clinton attempted to resurrect the agency, but his efforts failed when the Republicans gained control of Congress in 1994. In 1996, the Republican majority in Congress not only cut the LSC budget substantially but also added a wide variety of restrictions on LSC operations. Those restrictions prohibit funding for organizations that file class action lawsuits, challenge welfare reform, litigate on behalf of prisoners or aliens, represent those evicted from public housing for drug-related reasons, or deal with abortion rights. Some of the restrictions have since been overturned by the Supreme Court, most notably the restriction against funding welfare reform challenges in the case of *Legal Services v. Valazquez* (2001).

The troubled history of the Legal Services Corporation is the product of intense ideological wrangling. Conservatives argue that federal dollars should not finance political attacks on government programs and institutions. Rather, legal aid should go to assist individuals with routine civil cases. Thus, conservative groups such as the American Farm Bureau Federation continue to insist that the efforts of legal aid lawyers should be confined to prosaic legal work such as filing divorces and negotiating landlord-tenant disputes but should not include class action suits and other forms of social engineering (Jost 1990). Liberals counter that the poor are entitled to the same broad range of legal services as other citizens. In particular, case-by-case litigation is often less effective in solving the problems of the poor than lobbying or filing class action lawsuits.

The ideological wrangling at the national level is matched by political divisions at the local level. Although the American Bar Association supports legal aid programs, state and local bar associations, often in conjunction with local businesses and political interests, wage major attacks on program activities. Advocacy programs that threaten established economic interests are not acceptable. Powerful local interests employ a variety of mechanisms to constrain poverty lawyers who wish to raise issues of social reform in trial courts. In one study, poverty attorneys in four out of five programs studied were unable to spend much of their time working on reform cases. Because of their subordinate political position in the local community, they were forced to establish and maintain ties to groups opposing legal challenges to the political and economic status quo. When, occasionally, attorneys in those programs considered mobilizing reform issues, established business groups and wealthy individuals were able to force "nondecisions" (Kessler 1990).

Despite a relatively constant budget (not shrinking during the recent past), some commentators believe that the Legal Services Corporation is in a strong position relative to its thirty-year history (Vivero 2002). Support in Congress for the LSC has become institutionalized and mostly bipartisan. The tumultuous political back-and-forth of the 1990s appears to have been replaced by a general consensus that civil legal services for those in need is an important responsibility of the federal government, a view that is supported by a wide majority of citizens. In a Harris poll commissioned by the LSC in 1999, 66 percent of adults agreed that federal funding should be used to provide legal assistance to low-income people in a wide range of civil cases. Even more, 80 percent, agreed that federal funds should be used to provide legal assistance to low-income victims of domestic violence. Both Congress and citizens appreciate the need for legal assistance in accessing criminal and civil courts.

CONCLUSION

The legal story is still unfolding for the individual plaintiffs suing BP for the Deepwater Horizon oil spill. Their cases will be heard in 2012 and the legal judgments and appeals will almost certainly linger on for many years to come. They have talented lawyers from reputable firms yet they are up against a company with billions of dollars and an army of lawyers.

It is unlikely that any single plaintiff will become a household name the way that Clarence Earl Gideon has become. Overnight, Gideon went from defending himself to having Abe Fortas—one of the nation's most prestigious lawyers—represent him. Following the Supreme Court reversal of his conviction, Gideon was given a new trial. His court-appointed lawyer discovered evidence suggesting that the man who had accused Gideon of burglarizing the poolroom had himself committed the crime. Moreover, thousands of other prison inmates in Florida and elsewhere were freed as a result of *Gideon*. Nor could Gideon have realized that his name would become associated with a landmark Supreme Court decision. He achieved no small degree of legal immortality. His case, which was chronicled by *New York Times* reporter Anthony Lewis (1964) in *Gideon's Trumpet*, transformed the law, signaling a due process revolution in the rights of criminal defendants. Gideon himself was not transformed, however. He avoided any more major brushes with the law, but he died penniless on January 18, 1972, in Fort Lauderdale, Florida.

But Gideon is not alone; every day, citizens become involved in criminal and civil legal matters and need access to the legal system. Lawyers are the gatekeepers of the legal system and provide that much-needed access. Thus, access to a lawyer translates directly into access, or lack thereof, to the courts. Access to a lawyer is so important that the Supreme Court has said that a lawyer is necessary in serious criminal cases, and Congress reacted to the importance of having lawyers to help the poor access the civil justice system by creating the Legal Services Corporation.

Becoming a lawyer requires a legal education and a rigorous examination. Earning a license to practice law gives lawyers the right to practice law, and it comes with great responsibility. Through the years, the legal profession in the United States has become more professional and, some would argue, more ethical. At the same time, not everyone appreciates lawyers, and their public image is not always consistent with their level of training. In part, that may be a function of the wide range of roles lawyers play—from working in private practices to holding positions in private industry and government. The practice of law continues to attract students and evolve as the legal system and its needs change.

CRITICAL THINKING QUESTIONS

1. Many lawyers go into government. Should law schools train students in politics and government, in addition to the law? Why or why not?

2. How many lawyers are in your state, and where are they located? How does that compare with the number of lawyers in nearby states and across the nation?

3. Does your state have a legal ethics requirement? How does your state discipline lawyers?

4. Should low-income people be provided a free attorney? What kind of civil representation is available in your area for indigents?

Search Terms

adversary system	*Gideon v. Wainwright*	public defender
defense attorneys	indigent defense	right to counsel

Useful URLs

http://www.abanet.org
  American Bar Association is the nation's largest organization of lawyers.

http://www.nlada.org
  National Legal Aid and Defender Association, a nationwide network of people, programs, and organizations committed to equal access to justice for the poor.

http://www.lsc.gov
Legal Services Corporation, whose mission is to promote equal access to the courts by making grants to provide civil legal assistance.

REFERENCES

Abel, Richard. 1986. "The Transformation of the American Legal Profession." *Law and Society Review* 20: 7–17.

———. 2003. *English Lawyers Between Market and State: The Politics of Professionalism*. New York: Oxford University Press.

Abraham, Henry. 1986. *The Judicial Process: An Introductory Analysis of the Courts of the United States, England, and France*. 5th ed. New York: Oxford University Press.

AFP. 2011. "Berlusconi Slams Judges in 'False Testimony' Trial." May 9.

"Alabama Governor Limits Attorney Fees in Oil Spill Lawsuit." 2010. Law.com August 17.

American Bar Association. 2002. *Public Perceptions of Lawyers: Consumer Research Findings*. Chicago: American Bar Association.

———. 2003. *Model Rules of Professional Conduct*. Chicago: American Bar Association.

———. 2008a. *Lawyer Demographics*. Chicago: American Bar Association. Available online at http://www.abanet.org/legaled/statistics/charts/stats%20-%201.pdf. Retrieved August 12, 2008.

———. 2008b. Available online at http://www.abanet.org/marketresearch/2008_NATL_LAWYER_by_State.pdf. Retrieved August 12, 2008.

American Bar Foundation. n.d. "The Legal Profession: Chicago Lawyers II." Available online at http://www.abf-sociolegal.org/1998rep/legalprof.html. Retrieved April 2003.

Auerbach, Jerold. 1976. *Unequal Justice: Lawyers and Social Change in Modern America*. New York: Oxford University Press.

Baldas, Tresa. May 14, 2010. "Oil spill suits pit BP against old foes." *National Law Journal*.

Barker, Sarah Evans. 1994. "How the Shift from Hourly Rates Will Affect the Justice System." *Judicature* 77: 201–202.

Barrow, Bill. 2010. "House Cutoff Kills Attorney Measure." *Times-Picayune* June 22.

Baum, Lawrence. 1986. *American Courts: Process and Policy*. Boston: Houghton Mifflin.

Blish, Nelson. 1992. "In-House Staffing Plan Needs Fresh Approach." *National Law Journal* (December 14): S13.

Boon, Andrew, and Jennifer Levin. 1999. *The Ethics and Conduct of Lawyers in England and Wales*. Oxford, U.K.: Hart Publishing.

Bowen, Lauren. 1995. "Advertising and the Legal Profession." *Justice System Journal* 18: 43–54.

Brickman, Lester. 2003. "Effective Hourly Rates of Contingency Fee Lawyers: Competing Data and Non-Competitive Fees." *Washington University Law Quarterly* 81: 653–736.

Carlin, Jerome. 1962. *Lawyers on Their Own: A Study of Individual Practitioners in Chicago*. New Brunswick, N.J.: Rutgers University Press.

Center for Professional Responsibility. 2006. *Survey on Lawyer Discipline Systems: 2006 Data*. Chicago: American Bar Association. Available online at http://www.abanet.org/cpr/discipline/sold/home.html.

CNN. 2011. "Judge Rejects Berlusconi Objections In Sex Case." July 18 available at http://edition.cnn.com/2011/WORLD/europe/07/18/italy.berlusconi.cases/

Curran, Barbara. 1986. "American Lawyers in the 1980s: A Profession in Transition." *Law and Society Review* 20: 19–52.

Dieker, Lawrence. 2000. *Letters from Law School: The Life of a Second-Year Law Student*. Carlsbad, Calif.: Writer's Club Press.

Eisinger, Jana. 1993. "Nonlawyers Claim a Growing Swath of Legal Turf." *New York Times*, July 16, p. D6.

Fabri, Marco. 2007. "Criminal Procedure and Public Prosecution Reform in Italy: A Flash Back." Available at http://www.essex.ac.uk/ecpr/events/generalconference/pisa/papers/LPP14.pdf

Flemming, Victor. 1993. "About Real Lawyers." *Trial* 29: 84–85.

Flood, John. 1991. "Doing Business: The Management of Uncertainty in Lawyers' Work." *Law and Society Review* 25: 41–72.

France, Mike. 1994. "Legal Clinics: Lights Go Out for Storefronts." *National Law Journal* (October 17): 251.

Friedman, Lawrence. 1985. *Total Justice: What Americans Want from the Legal System and Why*. Boston: Beacon Press.

———. 2005. *A History of American Law*. 3d ed. Carmichael, Calif.: Touchstone.

Galanter, Marc. 1992. "Public View of Lawyers: Quarter-Truths Abound." *Trial* 28: 71–73.

———. 2005. *Lowering the Bar: Lawyer Jokes and Legal Culture*. Madison: University of Wisconsin Press.

Galanter, Marc, and Thomas Palay. 1991. *Tournament of Lawyers: The Transformation of the Big Law Firm*. Chicago: University of Chicago Press.

Gaudron, Mary. 1997. Speech to Launch Australian Women Lawyers. Retrieved April 2, 2003, from http://www.hcourt.gov.au/speeches/gaudronj_slasp.htm.

Gillers, Stephen. 2002. *Regulation of Lawyers: Problems of Law and Ethics*. New York: Aspen.

Glick, Henry. 1988. *Courts, Politics, and Justice*. 2d ed. New York: McGraw-Hill.

Grande, Elisabetta. 2000. "Italian Criminal Justice: Borrowing and Resistance." *Journal of Comparative Law* 48 (Spring).

Green, Mark. 1976. "The ABA as Trade Association." In *Verdicts on Lawyers*, edited by Ralph Nader and Mark Green. New York: Thomas Crowell.

Heinz, John, and Edward Laumann. 1982. *Chicago Lawyers: The Social Structure of the Bar*. New York: Russell Sage Foundation.

Jost, Kenneth. 1990. "LSC Returning to Normalcy, but Skirmishes Continue." *Congressional Quarterly*, June 2, pp. 1728–1731.

Kahler, Kathryn. 1991. "More Lawyers Being Sued for Malpractice." *New Orleans Times-Picayune*, August 10, p. 8.

Karsten, Peter. 1998. "Enabling the Poor to Have Their Day in Court: The Sanctioning of Contingency Fee Contracts, a History to 1940." *DePaul Law Review* 47: 231–260.

Kessler, Mark. 1990. "Legal Mobilization for Social Reform: Power and the Politics of Agenda Setting." *Law and Society Review* 24: 121–144.

Kritzer, Herbert M. 1998. *Legal Advocacy: Lawyers and Nonlawyers at Work*. Ann Arbor: University of Michigan Press.

———. 2005. *Risks, Reputations, and Rewards: Contingency Fee Legal Practice in the United States*. Stanford, Calif.: Stanford University Press.

Law School Admission Council. 2007. *ABA-LSAC Official Guide to ABA-Approved Law Schools 2008*. Newtown, Pa.: Law School Admission Council.

Lewis, Anthony. 1964. *Gideon's Trumpet*. New York: Random House.

———. 1972. *Clarence Earl Gideon and the Supreme Court*. New York: Random House.

Litan, Robert, and Steven Salop. 1994. "Reforming the Lawyer-Client Relationship Through Alternative Billing Methods." *Judicature* 77: 191–197.

Loh, Wallace. 1984. *Social Research in the Judicial Process: Cases, Readings, and Text*. New York: Russell Sage Foundation.

Marongiu, Pietro. "Italy." *World Factbook of Criminal Justice Systems* available at http://bjs.ojp.usdoj.gov/content/pub/ascii/WFBCJITA.TXT viewed July 25, 2011.

Masci, David. 1994. "Legal Services Reauthorization Gets Early Nod from Panel." *Congressional Quarterly*, May 28, pp. 1397–1398.

Mayer, Martin. 1967. *The Lawyers*. New York: Harper & Row.

McKay, Robert. 1985. "Legal Education." In *The Guide to American Law*. St. Paul, Minn.: West.

Montes, Jorge. 1994. "New Study Explores Unmet Legal Needs." *Passport* 12: 1–2.

Nelson, Robert. 1981. "Practice and Privilege: Social Change and the Structure of Large Law Firms." *American Bar Foundation Research Journal* 95: 97–140.

Neubauer, David. 2005. *America's Courts and the Criminal Justice System*. 8th ed. Belmont, Calif.: Wadsworth.

Nortrup, Jack. 1968. "The Education of a Western Lawyer." *American Journal of Legal History* 12: 294–347.

Oakley, John. 1981. *Law Clerks and the Judicial Process: Perceptions of the Qualities and Functions of Law Clerks in American Courts*. Berkeley: University of California Press.

Oil Spill Damage Lawyer. 2010. http://www.oilspilldamage-lawyer.com/?_vsrefdom=ppc&gclid=CLHhnKy foKMCFRafnAodnGpMrg

Passell, Peter. 1994. "Contingency Fees in Injury Cases Under Attack by Legal Scholars." *New York Times*, February 11, p. A1.

Peppers, Todd C. 2006. *Courtiers of the Marble Palace: The Rise and Influence of the Supreme Court Law Clerks.* Stanford: Stanford University Press.

Rhode, Deborah. 1981. "Why the ABA Bothers: A Functional Perspective on Professional Codes." *Texas Law Review* 59: 689–724.

———. 1985. "Ethical Perspectives on Legal Practice." *Stanford Law Review* 38: 567–610.

Ritter, Jim. 2005. "I Wanted to Work for the Little Guy." *Chicago Sun Times*, March 13.

Sarat, Austin, and Stuart A. Scheingold. 2006. *Cause Lawyers and Social Movements.* Stanford, Calif.: Stanford University Press.

Scheingold, Stuart, and Austin Sarat. 2004. *Something to Believe In: Politics, Professionalism, and Cause Lawyering.* Stanford, Calif.: Stanford University Press.

Schelling, Thomas. 1960. *The Strategy of Conflict.* Cambridge, Mass.: Harvard University Press.

Schwartz, John. 2011. "BP's Ex-Chief and Plaintiffs' Lawyers Spar over Safety." New York Times. Online: http://www.nytimes.com/2011/07/02/us/02gulf.html.

Searcey, Dionne. July 1, 2010. "Lawyers Scramble for BP Claim Funds." *Wall Street Journal.*

Searcey, Dionne. September 27, 2010. "Lawyer Bluster on Display in Oil Spill Litigation." *Wall Street Journal.*

Slocum, R.W. 2009. "The Dilemma of the Vengeful Client: A Prescriptive Framework for Cooling the Flames of Anger." *Marquette Law Review,* 92: 481–549.

Smigel, Erwin. 1969. *The Wall Street Lawyer: Professional Organization Man?* 2d ed. Bloomington: Indiana University Press.

Smitts, Todd. 2004. "Plot Summary for *Boston Legal.*" *Internet Movie Database.* Available online at http://www.imdb.com/title/tt0402711/plotsummary

Southworth, Ann. 2008. *Lawyers of the Right: Professionalizing the Conservative Coalition.* Chicago: University of Chicago Press.

Stewart, James. 1984. *The Partners: Inside America's Most Powerful Law Firms.* New York: Warner.

Stumpf, Harry. 1975. *Community Politics and Legal Services: The Other Side of the Law.* Newbury Park, Calif.: Sage.

Tabarrok, Alexander, and Eric Helland. 2005. *Two Cheers for Contingent Fees.* Washington, D.C.: American Enterprise.

Thornton, Margaret. 1996. *Dissonance and Distrust: Women in the Legal Profession.* Melbourne: Oxford University Press.

———. 1998. "Authority and Corporeality: The Conundrum for Women in Law." *Feminist Legal Studies* 6(2): 147–170.

Thorson, Carla. 1998. "Review of Dissonance and Distrust: Women in the Legal Profession." *Law and Politics Book Review* 8(4): 180–181.

Turow, Scott. 1977. *One L: An Inside Account of Life in the First Year at Harvard Law School.* New York: Penguin.

UPI. 2010. "Mafia Threatens Italian Judges." October 6.

Vivero, Mauricio. 2002. "'Renegade' Agency to Institution of Justice: The Transformation of Legal Services Corporation." *Fordham Urban Law Journal* 29: 1323.

Voice of America. 2011. "Milan Court Turns Down Berlusconi Request to Move Sex Trial to Rome." http://blogs.voanews.com/breaking-news/2011/07/18/milan-court-turns-down-berlusconi-request-to-move-sex-trial-to-rome/

Volcansek, Mary L. 2000. *Constitutional Politics in Italy: The Constitutional Court.* New York: Palgrave Macmillan.

Ward, Artemus and David L. Weiden. 2006. *Sorcerers' Apprentices: 100 Years of Law Clerks at the United States Supreme Court.* New York: New York University Press.

Wice, Paul. 1978. *Criminal Lawyers: An Endangered Species.* Newbury Park, Calif.: Sage.

———. 1991. *Judges and Lawyers: The Human Side of Justice.* New York: HarperCollins.

Zemans, Frances, and Victor Rosenblum. 1981. *The Making of a Public Profession.* Chicago: American Bar Foundation.

FOR FURTHER READING

Auchincloss, Louis. 1974. *The Partners*. Boston: Houghton Mifflin.

Bennett, Robert S. 2008. *In the Ring: The Trials of a Washington Lawyer*. New York: Random House.

Davis, Kevin. 2007. *Defending the Damned: Inside Chicago's Cook county Public Defender's Office*. New York: Atria.

Delsohn, Gary. 2003. *The Prosecutor: A Year in the Life of a District Attorney*. New York: Dutton/Penguin.

Galanter, Marc. 2005. *Lowering the Bar: Lawyer Jokes and Legal Culture*. Madison: University of Wisconsin Press.

Granfield, Robert and Lynn Mather. 2009. *Private Lawyers and the Public Interest: The Evolving Role of Pro Bono in the Legal Profession*. New York: Oxford University Press.

Grisham, John. 1991. *The Firm*. New York: Doubleday.

Harris, Beth. 2004. *Defending the Right to a Home: The Power of Anti-Poverty Lawyers*. Burlington, Vt.: Ashgate.

Meinhold, Stephen, and Charles Hadley. 1995. "Lawyers as Political Party Activists." *Social Science Quarterly* 76: 364–380.

Monsma, Karl, and Richard Lempert. 1992. "The Value of Counsel: 20 Years of Representation Before a Public Housing Eviction Board." *Law and Society Review* 26: 627–668.

Mossman, Mary Jane. 2006. The *First Women Lawyers: A Comparative Study of Gender, Law and the Legal Profession*. Oxford, U.K.: Hart Publishing.

Perez-Perdomo, Rogelio. 2006. *Latin American Lawyers: A Historical Introduction*. Stanford, Calif.: Stanford University Press.

Rhode, Deborah L. 2005. *Pro Bono in Principle and in Practice: Public Service and the Professions*. Stanford, Calif.: Stanford University Press.

CHAPTER
6

JUDGES

Judges have their own entrance to the old federal courthouse in Denver, Colorado. Although judges are the most important actors in the courthouse, lawyers and litigants shape how they make decisions.

David Neubauer

Gregory Wersal, a longtime member of the Minnesota Republican Party, planned to run for a seat on the Minnesota Supreme Court. He was motivated to run by a dislike of the court's decisions on issues such as crime, welfare, and abortion. But how far could he go in criticizing the Court's decisions to convince voters he would make a better judge? Not very far, as he soon found out. The Minnesota canon of judicial ethics prohibited judicial candidates from announcing their views on disputed legal or political issues. Fearful of losing his license to practice law, Wersal dropped out of the race, but, joined by a variety of conservative and liberal interest groups, he later filed suit in federal court, arguing that the Minnesota rule violated his freedom of speech. The Supreme Court's decision cast new legal and public attention on judges in the United States: their role, how we select them, and whether they can be impartial.

This chapter untangles the conflicting notions about who judges are, what they do, and how they do it. It first examines the debate over how judges are chosen and whether some methods result in better judges. Next, it discusses how judges learn their jobs, some of the benefits and frustrations of the office, and the tasks that judges perform. In light of persistent concerns over whether judges are as qualified as they should be, the last part of this chapter examines mechanisms for removing unfit judges.

JUDICIAL SELECTION

The quality of justice is commonly equated with the quality of the judges who dispense it. In turn, most discussions of the quality of the judges begin (and all too often end) with a discussion of judicial selection. The long-standing debate over which method of judicial selection produces the best judges is shaped by three general questions: What are the characteristics of a good judge? Whom do we trust to select judges? Where do we draw the line between judicial independence and political accountability?

What Are the Characteristics of a Good Judge?

The noted American jurist Benjamin Cardozo once wrote, "In the long run, there is no guarantee of justice except the personality of the judge" (1921, 149). Alas, no agreed-upon set of criteria details the personality of good judges—to say nothing of their legal talent or their insight into human behavior. "Scratch the average person's idea of what a judge should be and it's basically Solomon," says Yale law professor Geoffrey Hazard (quoted in Jackson 1974, 7). Judges are expected to be fair, honest, patient, wise, tolerant, compassionate, strong, decisive, and courageous. In short, they are expected to exhibit "appropriate judicial temperament" (Di Pietro, Carns, and Cotton 2000, 198).

Because society expects so much of its judges, there are clear difficulties in establishing the qualities of a good judge and in determining what constitutes a poor judge. "Although it is possible to identify such factors as professional incompetence, laziness, or intemperance which should disqualify a lawyer from becoming a judge, it is much more difficult to choose confidently the potentially superior judge from among a number of aspirants who appear generally qualified" (President's Commission 1967, 66). Gauging the optimal judicial personality is particularly perplexing because of the wide array of jobs judges must perform. A number of those tasks—keeping the docket moving comes to mind—are not directly related to legal wisdom or other seemingly obvious legal qualifications. Thus, although a strong reform movement proposes recruiting better-quality (which often means more learned) men and women to the bench, many of those who become judges have more modest credentials that are probably better suited to the actual functions that judges perform (Jacob 1973). In the modern era, public perceptions of judges are increasingly influenced by television. (See Law and Popular Culture: *Judge Judy*: Justice with an Attitude or Just Plain Nonsense?)

Who Should Select Judges?

Just as there is no agreement on what constitutes a good judge, so there is no consensus on whom we should trust to select good judges. Strong cases can be made for a variety of actors. Lawyers regularly interact with other lawyers in the courthouse, so as a group they should know best which colleagues have the legal knowledge and social skills to make good judges. Elected officials are chosen by the voters to decide important policy questions, so they should also know which local lawyers are best suited to a judgeship. Voters select other governmental officials, so why shouldn't they be entrusted with the task of deciding who is best qualified to wear the black robes?

However, an equally strong case can also be made *against* each of these actors. Bar associations may select judges who promise to make life easier for lawyers but place little emphasis on the needs of the litigants. Elected officials may appoint judges to reward their political cronies with little regard for the public good. Voters may easily be swayed by irrelevant campaign promises to select lawyers who do not possess the necessary background and knowledge for the job. The bottom line is that Americans don't really trust any of these actors. As a result, judicial selection is a highly unstructured process that allows participation by lawyers, judges, elected officials, voters, and, increasingly, interest groups as well. As discussed shortly, various methods of judicial selection give some actors greater influence than others.

Judicial Independence or Political Accountability?

Judicial selection is further complicated by the fact that Americans hold contradictory expectations about judges. On the one hand, judicial independence is vital for neutral and impartial decision making (discussed in Chapter 2). If judges are to be free to decide cases unfettered by the whims of the current regime, then they should be selected in ways that maximize their independence so that they can follow the law as they see it. But, at the same time, Americans place a heavy emphasis on the political accountability of their governmental officials. If judges are important policy makers—and they are—then judges should be selected and retained in ways that make them accountable to the public they serve.

To some, elections are the most appropriate method for guaranteeing the popular accountability of judicial policy makers. Critics, on the other hand, assert that elections are fundamentally inconsistent with the principle of judicial independence. The tension between the contrasting goals of judicial independence and political accountability plays a prominent role in debates over which method of judicial selection is best (Wasmann, Lovrich, and Sheldon 1986). In essence, American-style judicial selection represents a compromise between those two goals. No matter how they are selected, American judges enjoy terms of office that are considerably longer than those of other public officeholders.

Varying Roads to a Judgeship

The debate over what characterizes good judges, who should select them, and how independent or accountable judges should be produces a crazy quilt of judicial

LAW AND POPULAR CULTURE

■ Judge Judy: Justice with an Attitude or Just Plain Nonsense?

Straight-talking Judge Judy (aka Judy Sheindlin) stormed onto the television screen on September 16, 1996, and quickly became the boss of syndicated courtroom television show ratings. She is reportedly paid $30 million a year. Her show is regularly among the top 10 syndicated shows in the country, and you've probably seen it. Before starting her own show, Judge Judy served as a judge in New York, hearing more than 20,000 cases. She is the author of three books aimed at a general audience—*Don't Pee on My Leg and Tell Me It's Raining* (1996), *Beauty Fades, Dumb Is Forever* (1999), and *Keep It Simple, Stupid: You're Smarter Than You Look* (2000)—and a children's book, *Win or Lose by How You Choose* (2000). On the bench, she was known for her outspoken behavior and for being one of New York's toughest judges—attributes she brings to her syndicourt (syndicated courtroom) television show with sayings such as "I'm the BOSS, Applesauce."

Some observers see *Judge Judy* and other law-related television shows as beneficial because they reveal to viewers information about how the legal system works. Others disagree and see Judge Judy's behavior and that of her fellow syndicourt show judges as unrepresentative of the real-world job of judging, describing it as "sarcastic, accusatory, and opinionated" (Podlas 2002, 41).

A fair question might be, what difference does it make who's right? If people enjoy the entertainment, what damage could these shows possibly do? Kimberlianne Podlas suggests four troubling implications of these shows: (1) They may reduce respect for the bench, (2) they may lead to general misinterpretation of judicial behavior and temperament, (3) they may alter expectations about the legal system, and (4) participants in real cases may adopt inappropriate models of behavior.

To test whether any of those negative consequences of watching too much syndicourt TV exists, Podlas conducted a survey of 241 potential jurors in three jurisdictions in the Northeast. She asked them about their syndicourt viewing behavior and about their views of judges. Her findings reveal that frequent viewers of syndicourt programs, when compared with nonviewers, are far more likely to believe that "judges should have an opinion regarding the verdict, judges should make their opinion clear, judges should ask questions during trial, they should be aggressive with litigants or express displeasure with their testimony," and perhaps most shockingly, "a judge's silence indicates belief in a litigant" (Podlas 2002, 41). Moreover, prior court service or experience did nothing to diminish the impact of watching these programs on attitudes about the judiciary.

Judge Judy may have an admirable goal, for she says on her website, "For 24 years, I tried to change the way families deal with problems on a very small scale, one case at a time. Now I can use the skills I have developed and take my message to more people every day." But it may also be the case that in taking her message to the people—which is inconsistent with the normal behavior of judges and the actual day-to-day operations of America's courts—she is doing more harm than good to the credibility and legitimacy of the judiciary.

After watching one or more episodes of *Judge Judy*, be prepared to discuss the following questions:

1. Compare the behavior of Judge Judy with that normally expected of judges as described in this chapter.

2. Write down three things you think you know about the legal system based on your own experience watching law-related shows such as *Judge Judy* and then discuss whether your observations are indeed true.

3. In what way might the popularity of *Judge Judy* be related to the public desire to be able to see actual courtroom proceedings?

To read more about these topics, visit the following websites:

http://www.judgejudy.com

selection procedures. Three principal methods are used to select judges in the United States: appointment (either by the executive or by the legislative branch of government), elections (either partisan or nonpartisan), and merit selection. But there are numerous permutations to these three methods. Most states use one method for selecting trial judges and another for choosing appellate court judges.

Moreover, many states use one method for *initial* selection and a different one for *retention*.

Formal methods of judicial selection, however, are far less influential in choosing judges than are informal dynamics. (That distinction mirrors the discussion of law and politics in Chapter 1.) Formal methods (laws) establish who the principal actors in judicial selection are. Informal dynamics (politics) determine the influence of those actors in judicial selection. Thus, the political dynamics of a jurisdiction, much more so than legal institutions, map the actual routes by which some lawyers become judges and others continue practicing law (Graham 1990a). Fortunately, political scientists have studied both the formal and the informal dimensions of judicial selection extensively and know quite a bit about how various methods of judicial recruitment work in practice. Examining the appointment of federal judges, judicial elections, and merit selection will illustrate how judicial selection involves both law and politics.

APPOINTMENT OF FEDERAL JUDGES

The U.S. Constitution establishes a straightforward method for selecting judges to preside in federal court: Judges are nominated by the president, confirmed by the Senate, and after appointment serve for life. The informal dynamics of federal judicial selection, however, are considerably more complex than the formal rules suggest. For one, the politics of federal judicial selection differ by level of court. The process for selecting district and circuit court judges is somewhat different from that used to determine who will be a justice on the U.S. Supreme Court. A vacancy on the Supreme Court presents the president with an opportunity to leave an enduring mark on this important policy-making body, and the president is typically personally involved. (The unique processes of nominating and confirming a Supreme Court justice are discussed in detail in Chapter 15.)

The formal process of judicial selection gives the president considerable power. According to the Constitution, only the president can nominate. Other actors may suggest deserving candidates, but in the end the president must make the choice. Presidents, therefore, value vacant judgeships, because they are opportunities to reward the party faithful, pursue political objectives, and appear presidential in the process. But valuable as judicial vacancies are, presidents have little control over when they will occur (Massie, Hansford, and Songer 2004). Federal judges are appointed for life, which generally means that vacancies occur when a judge dies or retires or when Congress authorizes additional judgeships. For example, in 2011 16 percent of Federal judges on the bench were appointed by President Reagan (1980–88) or President Bush (88–92). Presidents exert little influence over when they will have positions to fill. Traditionally, senators and especially home-state senators (meaning those representing the states in which the federal district court judicial vacancies are located) exerted considerable influence over both whom the president considered (suggesting potential nominees) and the ultimate confirmation. The practice of senatorial courtesy meant that the president would consult with home-state senators of his party about acceptable nominees before the nomination, and the use of the blue slip in the judiciary committee allowed home-state senators from either party to stall a president's choice (Denning 2002). Both of those senatorial powers have been diminishing over time. The White House has become the primary player in the federal judicial nomination process (Goldman et al. 2005). The Obama administration has elevated the role of the White House and the White House Counsel's office over the participation of the Department of Justice's Office of Legal Policy, which is now used primarily to vet potential nominees (Goldman, Slotnick, and Schiovani 2011). The administration also benefitted from the advice and involvement of Vice President Joe Biden who previously served on the Senate Judiciary Committee. Obama returned the tradition of vetting federal court candidates with the American Bar Association (ABA) prior to nomination. Obama has nominated the most diverse group of federal judges in the nation's history with 7 out of every 10 nominees representing nontraditional groups (Biskupic 2010).

The Demise of Senatorial Courtesy?

In nominating a candidate to fill a judicial vacancy, presidents are not free to do as they wish. The Constitution gives the Senate the power of advice and consent, an institutional prerogative that it jealously guards. The unwritten tradition of **senatorial courtesy**, which began under George Washington in 1789, allows senators to influence presidential appointments. Senators expect to be *consulted* before the president nominates a person to a federal judicial vacancy in their state. Thus, under the tradition of senatorial courtesy, a senator from the president's political party may declare a nominee from his or her state personally unacceptable, and senators from other states—finding strength in numbers—will follow their colleague's preference and not approve the presidential nominee. Thus, when senators exercise their objection to a nominee, it usually prevents that nominee from being confirmed; if the senator allows the nomination to go forward, it will likely result in confirmation. In the Senate, it is the Senate Judiciary Committee that reviews nominations forwarded by the president. But the influence of senators in general over judicial nominations has been declining (Binder and Maltzman 2004), and recently the committee has adopted procedural changes designed to limit the practice of senatorial courtesy; yet, senators continue to play a role. So much so that President Obama made it a high priority to consult with Senators of states with judicial vacancies to try and minimize delay and increase the chances of his choices being confirmed (Goldman, Slotnick, and Schiovani 2011).

The impact of senatorial courtesy depends, in part, on the respective political parties of the senator and the president. For district court vacancies, if the president and the senator belong to the same political party, the senator may have more influence on who is nominated. Senators have been known to make specific recommendations as to who they think is qualified or exercise a veto over persons they find unacceptable. If, however, the president and the senator belong to different political parties, the senator from the state in question has considerably less influence, because he or she has no veto power.

Senatorial courtesy plays a lesser role in nominations to the courts of appeals. Although these judgeships are informally allocated to individual states, they are not subject to senatorial courtesy. In turn, the president has the greatest political freedom of action in deciding on nominations to the federal courts in the District of Columbia because the district has no senator and, therefore, senatorial courtesy does not apply to vacancies on these judicial bodies. Indeed, on occasion, presidents make appointments to the District of Columbia courts to circumvent the invocation of senatorial courtesy. Illustrative of that situation was the 1962 appointment of Louisiana federal district judge J. Skelly Wright to the Court of Appeals for the District of Columbia rather than to the Fifth Circuit Court of Appeals. Wright was very unpopular in the South because of his consistent record of supporting integration (including at the University of New Orleans, where one of the authors teaches). For that reason, Senator Russell Long of Wright's home state opposed his nomination to the Fifth Circuit Court of Appeals, which includes Louisiana. Rather than antagonize a powerful senator, President Kennedy nominated Wright to a vacancy on the D.C. court (Grossman 1965), which greatly pleased white southern senators—because now Wright would be deciding cases somewhere else.

Interest Group Involvement

Presidential nominations and Senate confirmations of judicial candidates are increasingly the object of great attention by interest groups (Steigerwalt 2010; Scherer 2005; Bell 2002). The Federalist Society, the Judicial Selection Project, Common Cause, the National Association for the Advancement of Colored People (NAACP), the National Women's Political Caucus, and People for the American Way are examples of interest groups that seek to influence who is selected and confirmed for a federal judgeship.

Historically, the private group with the most influence on federal judicial selection was the legal profession. Until recently, the American Bar Association (ABA) Standing Committee on the Federal Judiciary held an unusual position in the selection process. It had no constitutional or statutory basis, yet presidents consulted the committee before making a nomination, and the Senate Judiciary Committee regularly requested its opinion before confirmation (Slotnick 1983). The committee consists of fourteen prominent members of the legal profession who are appointed by the ABA president for staggered three-year terms. After consulting with lawyers and law professors, the committee ranks judicial nominees as "well qualified," "qualified," or "unqualified." After initial selection (but before official nomination), the nominee would complete an ABA questionnaire. The committee would then consider the nominee, vote, and send a letter to the Justice Department giving its evaluation. That would allow the president and his advisers to avoid nominating someone who would later be declared unqualified.

The relationship between the ABA and the president has frequently varied by political party, with Democrats usually being more hostile than Republicans to the ABA's views. In a highly unusual step President Bush in 2001 suspended the traditional process, which dates back to the Eisenhower administration, of submitting the names of potential candidates to the ABA prior to a public announcement. President Obama restored that tradition and seeks the ABA committee's ranking prior to making a public announcement of a candidate.

Until somewhat recently, interest groups were more influential on the nomination side than on the confirmation side of the process. That appears to be changing (Bell 2002). Interest groups from both sides of the ideological spectrum appear to have decided that federal judgeships are critical to their policy agenda and have begun pulling out all the stops to try to influence senators. Some believe the effect of this is an increase in the bombastic and personal nature of the attacks on judicial nominees and the heightened sense of obstruction and delay of some judicial confirmations.

Despite the rancorous debate and slow nomination process, President Obama has been generally successful, as have his predecessors, in securing the confirmation of his nominees to the federal bench. After a hearing before the Senate Judiciary Committee, the full Senate usually confirms the nominee, typically without a dissenting vote. But, if the nomination is controversial, the committee hearings and the Senate vote become the focus of intense political activity. However, the Senate has refused to confirm a presidential nominee only on rare occasions. During the eight years of the Clinton administration, including six years when Republicans controlled the Senate, only Ronnie White's nomination to the federal bench was defeated on the floor of the Senate. Instead of outright rejection, recent presidents have found that a Senate controlled by the opposite party subjects their nominations to long delays.

Presidential Political Goals

Who becomes a federal judge is a direct result of who the president is at the time. Early-twentieth-century presidents employed three contrasting motivations in selecting judicial nominees. Presidents Warren Harding and Theodore Roosevelt were primarily concerned with patronage and used the appointment process to reward the party faithful. Presidents William Taft and Herbert Hoover were primarily motivated by a desire to maximize professionalism and used the appointment process to select truly distinguished jurists. Finally, Presidents Woodrow Wilson and Franklin Roosevelt reflected a major concern with governmental policies and used the appointment process to stock the bench with judges who reflected their presidential philosophies (Solomon 1984). Since World War II, presidents have increasingly fallen into the last category. Whether Democratic or Republican, they link judicial nominations with their domestic policy agenda (Slotnick 1988). Republican President Richard Nixon stressed appointing strict constructionists to the Supreme Court (discussed in Chapter 15). Democratic President Jimmy Carter was the first president to try to make the federal bench more representative of the American public, resulting in an unprecedented number of "nontraditional" appointees (that is, nonwhite males) to the federal bench (Goldman 1981).

According to some, Jimmy Carter began the modern-day politicization of the judiciary, as evidenced by his appointments of "activist" judges who used their personal views as a guidepost for interpreting the law (Cohodas 1988). Elliot Slotnick has pointed to the Carter administration as the tipping point for the use of "policy motivations" by presidents to advance their influence in the federal judiciary (2002). Others counter that President Reagan was the first president to institutionalize a systematic philosophical screening process for prospective appointments to the lower federal courts. President Clinton continued that tradition, although commentators argue that his appointments were some of the most ideologically conservative ever appointed by a Democratic president (*Judicature* March–April 2001). President Bush's nominees were largely viewed as being politically conservative. And Obama's first two years of appointments have seen the most diverse group of candidates ever nominated for federal judgeships (*Judicature* May–June 2011). Whichever president began the change in the appointment politics, it is now clearly in full effect.

The partisan nature of the appointment process during the Obama administration has taken its toll on both the president and the Senate, causing a higher level of scrutiny and rhetoric around the appointment of federal judges than has ever been seen before.

Filibuster Threats

The increasingly partisan battles over who should sit on the federal bench is readily apparent when one party in the Senate filibusters, or at least threatens to filibuster, a presidential nomination. During President Bush's tenure Democrats in the Senate blocked some of his more controversial nominations. A group of senators known as the "Gang of 14" and included seven Republicans and seven Democrats announced that they would oppose future judicial nominees only under "extreme circumstances." In November 2006, the Democrats won control of the 110th Congress and, thus, were once again in the majority, making the power of the "Gang of 14" questionable.

President Obama has found his nominees stymied by Republican opposition in the Senate. At the end of his first two years only 56 percent of Obama's District Court nominees and 68 percent of his Appeals Court nominees had been confirmed by the Senate. While observers note that the Senate's approval process appears less dysfunctional, the delay in nominations keeps getting worse. Goldman, Slotnick, and Shiovani (2011) have created an "Index of Obstruction and Delay" and demonstrate that it was worse for Obama's first two years than for any other Congress/President two year term ever, although the last two years of the Bush administration when the Democrats held a majority in the Senate was a close second.

The Obama Judiciary

In just two years President Obama has already begun to leave his imprint on the Federal judiciary. He has appointed the most diverse group of judges ever. Notably over 50 percent of his district court appointments have been women. President George W. Bush was said to have made judicial nominations one of his most important domestic priorities. President Obama appears to be taking them just as seriously but he also has a wide ranging legislative agenda that requires political persuasion and although he has a Democratic majority in the Senate, it is not filibuster proof. Indeed President Obama is well schooled in the use of the filibuster as he is a former Senator who supported a filibuster during the confirmation of current Supreme Court Justice Samuel Alito. President Obama was a law professor at the University of Chicago Law School for 12 years prior to being elected to the Senate so it is most certain that he has spent time thinking about the role of the president in judicial nominations and recognizes the lasting impact his choices will have. The Democratic majority in the Senate dwindled after the 2010 elections, and as a result fewer of Obama's nominees are being approved, which has prompted Chief Justice Roberts to ask Democrats and Republicans to find a long-term solution to selecting federal judges, particularly given the rising number of federal court vacancies (Holland 2011).

TABLE 6.1	Characteristics of District Court Judges Appointed by Recent Presidents					
	Obama[a]	G. W. Bush	Clinton	G. H. W. Bush	Reagan	Carter
Occupation						
Politics/government	11	13	12	11	13	5
Judiciary	52	48	48	42	37	45
Large law firm	14	19	16	25	18	14
Medium firm	14	10	13	15	19	19
Small firm	4	6	9	4	10	14
Law professor	2	1	2	1	2	3
Experience						
Judicial	55	52	52	47	46	54
Prosecutorial	48	47	41	39	44	38
Law School Education						
Public	46	49	40	53	45	52
Private	41	39	41	33	43	31
Ivy League	14	12	20	14	12	17
Gender						
Male	46	79	72	80	92	86
Female	55	21	29	20	8	14
Ethnicity/Race						
White	59	82	75	89	92	78
African American	25	7	17	7	2	14
Hispanic	5	11	6	4	5	7
Asian	11	2	1	0	1	1
Native American	0	0	0	0	0	1
ABA Rating						
Extremely well qualified/well qualified	75	70	59	57	54	51
Qualified	25	28	40	43	47	48
Not qualified	0	2	1	0	0	2
Party Identification						
Democrat	89	8	88	6	5	91
Republican	0	83	6	89	92	5
Past Party Activism	55	53	50	64	60	61
Net Worth						
<$200,000	2	5	13	10	18	36
$200,000–499,999	9	18	22	31	38	41
$500,000–999,999	23	22	27	26	22	19
>$1 million	66	55	38	32	23	4
Average Age at Nomination	50	50	50	48	49	50
Total Number of Appointees	44	261	305	148	290	202

[a] Through 2010.
Source: Adapted from Sheldon Goldman, Elliot Slotnick and Sara W. Schiavoni. "The Confirmation Drama Continues" *Judicature* 94(6) (2011): 262–303.

Backgrounds of Federal Judges

When exploring differences between presidents, political scientists have been particularly interested in the background characteristics of federal judges they appoint. The profile of recent appointees to the U.S. district court in Table 6.1 is useful in assessing similarities and differences between appointing presidents.

Republican and Democratic nominees to the federal bench share some interesting similarities. The lawyers who become federal judges often have a political background: They are members of the president's political party, have been active in party politics, and have held prior governmental positions (either as judge or as prosecutor). And, up until President Obama, no matter which president makes the appointments, federal judges tend to be white male Protestants educated at elite law schools (Haire et al. 1994). More than half of President Obama's appointments have been women.

Clearly, presidents differ in their policy goals, the procedures employed in making their selections, and the backgrounds of the judges who are appointed. Chapter 13 examines the important question of whether those differences have actually produced changes in how the federal courts allocate values; briefly, an impressive body of research concludes that judicial behavior is systematically related to the president who made the appointment. For example, recent research suggests that George W. Bush's appointees are among the most conservative of any modern president and in the same league as those of Reagan (Carp, Manning, and Stidham 2004). And considerable research has found that both district and courts of appeals judges appointed by Democratic presidents hand down a greater percentage of liberal decisions than jurists selected by GOP presidents (Carp, Manning, and Stidham 2001; Rowland and Carp 1996; Wenner and Ostberg 1994; Songer and Haire 1992; Songer and Davis 1988; Goldman 1966). In 2011, 52 percent of all federal judges had been appointed by a Republican president, compared to just 38 percent appointed by a Democrat (with the remaining 10 percent of judgeships currently vacant) (Goldman, Slotnick, and Schiovani 2011).

Another way to look at the president's influence on the federal bench is to look at how many judicial vacancies he filled. The absolute number of justices appointed is particularly important at the court of appeals level, where the judges do the overwhelming majority of their work in three-judge panels. The idea is that if a president has appointed enough of the justices on a circuit to dominate the panels (2–1), there is a greater likelihood that his preferences can be translated into favorable decisions. In 2011, just over 50 percent of all active Federal Appeals Court judges were appointed by G.W. Bush, G.H.W. Bush or Reagan (Goldman, Slotnick and Schiovani 2011).

JUDICIAL ELECTIONS

In contrast to the federal judges, the majority of state judges are initially selected or retain their position through popular elections. The concept of an elected judiciary emerged during the early 1800s and began to take hold during the Jacksonian era as part of a larger movement aimed at democratizing the political process. At the time of the Civil War, 24 of the 34 states had an elected judiciary (Berkson 1980). Populists, who believed that an elitist judiciary did not square with the ideology of a government controlled by the people, spearheaded the movement (Dubois 1980). According to that philosophy, there should be no special qualifications for public office; the voters should decide who is most qualified. At the start of the twentieth century, a countertrend began: Concerned about widespread corruption in city governments, the Progressive movement sought to weaken the influence of political parties by instituting **nonpartisan elections**, in which officials run for office not on the basis of party affiliation but on the basis of personal qualifications.

Currently, seven states initially choose all or most of their judges in **partisan elections** (Table 6.2), in which candidates are listed by party affiliation. Partisan ballots make it easy for party leaders to use judicial posts as patronage to reward the party faithful. Fourteen states initially choose some or all of their judges in nonpartisan elections. Nevertheless, even where nonpartisan elections are employed, partisan influences are often present. A fair estimate is that, in half of the states using "nonpartisan" judicial ballots, the political parties play some role (Jacob 1984). Judicial candidates are endorsed by parties, receive party support during campaigns, and are readily identified with party labels (Glick and Vines 1973).

Formal selection methods are not always a guide to how judges are actually selected, however. States using popular elections (either partisan or nonpartisan) also employ interim selection methods to "temporarily" fill judicial vacancies. **Gubernatorial appointment** and merit selection predominate in filling these temporary vacancies.

TABLE 6.2	Initial Selection of State Judges			
Partisan Election	**Nonpartisan Election**	**Combined (Merit with Some Elections)**	**Merit Selection for All Judges**	**Appointment**
Alabama	Arkansas	Arizona	Alaska	California (G)
Illinois	Georgia	Florida	Colorado	Maine (G)
Louisiana	Idaho	Indiana	Connecticut	New Jersey (G)
Ohio	Kentucky	Kansas	Delaware	South Carolina (L)
Pennsylvania	Michigan	Missouri	District of Columbia	Virginia (L)
Texas	Minnesota	New York	Hawaii	
West Virginia	Mississippi	Oklahoma	Iowa	
	Montana	South Dakota	Maryland	
	Nevada	Tennessee	Massachusetts	
	North Carolina		Nebraska	
	North Dakota		New Hampshire	
	Oregon		New Mexico	
	Washington		Rhode Island	
	Wisconsin		Utah	
			Vermont	
			Wyoming	

G = gubernatorial, L = legislative.

Source: *Judicial Selection in the States: Appellate and General Jurisdiction Courts* (Chicago: American Judicature Society, 2007). Available online at http://www.ajs.org/selection/docs/Judicial%20Selection%20Charts.pdf. Retrieved August 8, 2008.

Therefore, the combination of formal selection and interim selection methods accounts for how many trial judges first arrive on the bench.

Judicial Campaigns

Traditionally, judicial elections in the United States have been low-key, low-visibility affairs marked by the absence of controversy (Arbor and McKenzie 2011; Hojnacki and Baum 1992; Dubois 1986). Ethical rules and cultural values prevent judicial candidates from discussing specific issues during the campaign; a lawyer would hardly appear to be judicial timber if he or she promised that once he or she was elected, Jones would be convicted or Smith found liable no matter what the evidence showed (Dubois 1980; Ladinsky and Silver 1967). As a result, candidates for a seat on the bench confine themselves to generalities: They promise to be tough on criminals and pledge to be fair and just; they vow to improve the efficiency of justice without, of course, denying any litigant a fair and impartial hearing. Forced to wage essentially issueless campaigns, candidates for judicial office attempt to persuade voters that they are best qualified for the job because of their impeccable legal credentials, years of experience as a practicing attorney, endless hours devoted to charitable causes, and membership in legal groups with impressive names (the American Judicature Society, for example). Those qualifications are reinforced by political ads featuring the lawyer poring over law books late into the night and the smiling candidate sitting in his (or her) living room surrounded by a loving spouse and several adorable children. (Adding a dog or a cat to the picture is considered good for attracting the animal lovers' vote.) Alas, from the voters' perspective, all the judicial candidates are virtually indistinguishable from one another. All the aspirants for the bench stress that they will be fair, efficient, and, above all, just, while on the bench. Moreover, all the candidates appear to be equally well qualified for the office. Traditionally, the result has been a bland judicial campaign that provides voters with limited information (Baum 1999; Sheldon and Lovrich 1999; McKnight, Schaefer, and Johnson 1978;). Voter turnout for judicial elections is typically low, with fewer people participating in the judicial election than those voting in the top of the ballot races. The more heated campaigns at the top of the ballot attract a higher voter turnout than the relatively low-key judicial elections found at the end of the ballot.

What is perhaps particularly interesting about the confusing nature of the public mind-set is that nonpartisan elections lead to the lowest level of information and voter interest, thus providing **incumbent** judges with important advantages when running for re-election. In a poll commissioned by the interest group Justice at Stake, just 13 percent of voters reported knowing a great deal about judicial candidates (Greenberg and DiVall 2002). And that comports with previous social scientific research in this area. The prestigious title of judge is listed on the ballot in front of the judge's name. Given their lack of knowledge, voters are more likely to find a reason for pulling the lever in favor of the sitting judge. This important voting cue means that few local lawyers wish to challenge a sitting judge, because if the election is lost (and in all probability it will be), the challenger may not receive favorable considerations from the incumbent. Likewise, local bar associations discourage challenges to incumbent judges for purely partisan or personal reasons if they think the sitting judge is performing adequately. Therefore, once a judge is selected, either through an election or through an appointment to fill a midterm vacancy, the chances of being voted out of office are small. Few sitting judges are even opposed for re-election, and, of those challenged, few are ever voted out of office (Dubois 1984; Baum 1983). Indeed a recent study finds that over three-quarters of elections fail to provide voters a choice (Nelson 2011).

Once in a while incumbents are opposed for re-election, and sometimes incumbents are voted out of office (Kiel, Funk, and Champagne 1994). This is most likely to occur when judges receive an unusual amount of negative publicity centering on advanced age, alleged incompetence, a decision in a highly controversial case, or allegations of improper or immoral behavior. Incumbent judges are also more likely to be turned out of office in states that use partisan elections to choose judges. The use of party labels serves as a major cue for distinguishing among policies and officials. If the voters are dissatisfied with the party in power, they are likely to vote against many or all candidates who share that label, and judges are not always immune when a party is swept out of office (Dubois 1984, 1980, 1979). It is important to recognize, however, that incumbency rates for judges in retention and partisan elections are roughly equivalent to those of members of other elected branches, such as the U.S. House of Representatives, which frequently has incumbent re-election rates in the 95 percent range. Thus, judicial elections do not appear to be very much different from some other election systems in their tendency to return incumbents to office.

Elections do have an impact on judicial behavior, however. Having decided in mid-life to change careers, sitting judges do not relish the thought of having to re-establish a law practice. Moreover, if a challenger surfaces, they will have to raise funds and wage a campaign. Judges in elected systems realize that the best way to avoid such possibilities is to work closely with the local lawyers. After all, challenges to sitting judges are likely to be mounted only if the lawyers are dissatisfied with the judges' performance. Thus, maintaining close ties to local lawyers is perhaps the best insurance policy a judge can have against having to wage a potentially costly campaign for re-election.

Nastier, Noisier, and Costlier

Times are changing. Judicial campaigns are becoming "nastier, noisier, and costlier" (Schotland 1998). Compared with other electoral contests, judicial campaigns have tended to be relatively inexpensive. Nonetheless, judicial candidates do need to raise funds to finance their campaigns. How much it costs to run varies considerably across the states; among the most expensive states in which to campaign for a Supreme Court judgeship are Alabama, Illinois, Michigan, Mississippi, and Ohio. In the 2000 election cycle, data on 146 candidates from states that elect their supreme court justices show they raised a combined $45.6 million, double the amount spent in 1994 (Goldberg, Holman, and Sanchez 2002). Clearly, judicial elections are becoming more expensive. How important is this money? An analysis of Texas Supreme Court elections from 1980 to 1998 finds that money is more important than traditional factors such as partisanship, coattails, and incumbency in predicting the electoral success of state supreme court candidates (Cheek and Champagne 2000).

Judicial elections are getting noisier, too, especially when it comes to television ads. A report on the 2000 state Supreme Court elections covering the 75 largest media markets identified 22,646 commercials. Granted, all of the advertising examined occurred in four states (Alabama, Michigan, Mississippi, and Ohio) that were among those in which the most money was raised. Nonetheless, judicial campaigns focusing on issues are increasing in the aftermath of the Supreme Court decision in *Republican Party v. White* (2002), which ruled that state rules requiring candidates for judgeships not to discuss political issues was an unconstitutional violation of the First Amendment. So far, however, the evidence does not support the claim that White dramatically changed the rhetoric of judicial campaigns (Salokar 2005; Hall and Bonneau 2009). In a recent study of lower court elections in six states Arbour and McKenzie (2011) conclude that the campaign messages are composed or statements largely allowable in the pre-White era.

Who contributes to campaigns and why raises important issues of ethics and fairness. In Illinois, many contributors do so for reasons other than ensuring the election of qualified candidates. The bulk of the funds are raised by sure winners thus, it is fair to assume that some contributors believe they are getting something for their money, which usually means they are trying to curry favor with judges (Nicholson and Nicholson 1994). In 2007, candidates for the Pennsylvania Supreme Court raised over $5 million, setting a state record, and in 2006, candidates for Alabama's supreme court raised $8.2 million (Barnes 2007). In the 2000 elections, lawyers and business interests made up 50 percent of the campaign contributions to state supreme court candidates (Goldberg, Holman, and Sanchez 2002), but by 2005 and 2006, according to the National Institute on Money in State Politics, nearly 50 percent came from business interests alone (Barnes 2007).

The relationships among elections, money, and noise in judicial campaigns appear to be resonating with voters. Recent data from two polls show that "two-thirds of American voters feel that individuals or groups who give money to judicial candidates often get favorable treatment" (Greenberg and DiVall 2002) and "almost three out of four people believe that raising campaign money compromises impartiality" (ABA 2002). At the same time, people continue to think elected justices are more fair and impartial than those who are appointed, and the public favors nonpartisan elections (63 percent in favor; 24 percent opposed) as a selection method (ABA 2002). The Supreme Court, in a divided opinion, address the issue of elections and money, holding that a state supreme court justice must recuse himself because he had received major contributions from a litigant (*Caperton v. Masseey Coal*, 2009). (See Case-Close-Up *Caperton v. Massey* and Campaign Cash.)

Nastier, noisier, and costlier judicial races are by and large confined to races for a seat on the state supreme court (Abbe and Herrnson 2002). Even though less money is spent and the volume is turned down in lower-court judicial elections, there *is* action. Abbe and Herrnson (2002) find that nearly 44 percent of trial and appellate court races were competitive in 1998. If the trend at the state supreme court level trickles down to the lower-court elections, we can expect some very exciting judicial contests ahead. Most of the activity today focuses on the supreme court, particularly decisions on tort reform (see Chapter 9). The high level of publicity challengers receive and the attractiveness of the office make justices of a state's highest court more susceptible to being opposed and attract a better-qualified challenger (Bonneau and Hall 2003). Today, it is expected that state supreme court races will be hard fought, whereas, a decade ago, only a few were bitter partisan battles. Thus some argue that we entered an era of "the new politics of judicial elections" (Sample, Hall, and Casey 2010).

CASE CLOSE-UP

■ *Caperton v. Massey Coal Co.* (2009)

Campaign Cash

In 2002 a Boone County, West Virginia jury awarded $50 million to Hugh Caperton, finding that Massey Coal took illegal actions that put Caperton's company, Harman Mining Company, out of business. Massey Coal appealed the case to the West Virginia Supreme Court, which reversed the original judgment in a 3-2 vote. Eventually the Supreme Court of the United States would take up the case and you might think that it would be because the facts were in dispute or because of the size of the jury's award, but it actually had to do with one of the judges on the West Virginia Supreme Court—in particular Justice Brent Benjamin who was one of the 3 judges who ruled against Caperton. The controversy was whether he should be allowed to hear the case.

Justice Benjamin was elected to the West Virginia Supreme Court of Appeals in 2004. Prior to becoming a judge Mr. Benjamin was a lawyer with the law firm of Robinson and McElwee. West Virginia elects their Supreme Court justices and during the 2004 election Mr. Benjamin was running against incumbent justice Warren McGraw. During the campaign the CEO of Massey Energy spent an estimated $3 million on a campaign to defeat Mr. McGraw; this was reported to be nearly 60 percent of the entire amount spent on the race between both sides (Biskupic 2009). Mr. Benjamin won and when the case, which originally resulted in a trial verdict of $50 million for Mr. Caperton, got to the West Virginia Supreme Court, the trial verdict was overturned and Mr. Benjamin was a member of the 3 person majority. Opponents of the outcome argued that Mr. Benjamin should have recused himself because the apparent conflict of interest. But he refused to do that. Now the case would go to the Supreme Court.

Caperton comes in the midst of a dramatic rise in campaign spending in state supreme court elections (Bonneau 2007). Critics of this spending argue that it gives the public the impression of impropriety and impacts views of judicial impartiality (Wohl 2000). Now the U.S. Supreme Court would make a statement about the large amount of money being spent in these elections. The principal issue before the Supreme Court was whether Justice Benjamin should have recused himself.

Anthony Kennedy authored the 5-4 opinion for the majority and based the decision on the Due Process Clause and pointed to the standard of recusal from *Withrow v. Larkin* as being when "the probability of actual bias on the part of the judge or decision maker is too high to be constitutionally tolerable." Kennedy wrote, "In an election decided by 50,000 votes, Blankenship's campaign contributions—compared to the total amount contributed to the campaign, as well as the total amount spent in the election—had a significant and disproportionate influence on the outcome. And the risk of that Blankenship's influence engendered actual bias is sufficiently substantial that it 'must be forbidden if the guarantee of due process is to be adequately implemented ... Just as no man is allowed to be a judge in his own cause, similar fears of bias can arise when—without the other parties' consent—a man chooses the judge in his own cause." Chief Justice Roberts and Justice Scalia both authored dissenting opinions. Chief Justice Roberts listed 40 uncertainties that made him disagree with the outcome and wrote that they were only a few. The first question was "How much money is too much money? What level of contribution or expenditure gives rise to the probability of bias?" and the 40th question was "What if the parties settle a Caperton claim as part of a broader settlement of the case? Does that leave the judge with no way to salvage his reputation?" Justice Scalia was direct "In the best of all possible worlds, should judges sometimes recuse even when the clear commands of our prior due process law do not require it? Undoubtedly. The relevant question, however, is whether we do more good than harm by seeking to correct this imperfection through expansion of our constitutional mandate in a manner ungoverned by any discernable rule. The answer is obvious." The case was reversed and remanded. The case was reargued and in November 2009 the West Virginia Supreme Court without Justice Benjamin, ruled the same way; Caperton would not get any compensation.

Does this all sound too much like fiction? In 2008 Matt Lauer of the Today show asked popular author John Grisham about his bestselling book "The Appeal" and Grisham told him it was based on this story "It happened a few years ago in West Virginia. A guy who owned a coal company got tired of getting sued. He elected his guy to the Supreme Court ... So it happens." (Biskupic 2009). Critics of the decision argue that it will open up the courts to many challenges by lawyers that judges should recuse themselves based on campaign spending or contributions, but supporters of the decision reply that judicial impartiality must be protected.

MERIT SELECTION

"Remove the courts from politics" has been the long-standing cry of **judicial reformers**, who point to three adverse effects of electing judges: First, popular elections discourage qualified lawyers from running for a vacant judgeship, because they do not wish to subject themselves to the messy realities of campaigning. Second, popular elections suggest the appearance of impropriety, because candidates for office may appear to promise to decide cases in a popular manner. Third, popular elections are a contest in which the electorate is least likely to be informed about the legal merits of the competing candidate. Implicit in those and other reformers' arguments is identifying poor judges as political hacks who are subservient to the party that initially chose them for a judgeship.

To cure these ills, legal reformers advocate **merit selection**, also known as the nonpartisan court plan, the merit plan, or the **Missouri Bar Plan** because Missouri was the first state to adopt it in 1940. Merit plans are actually hybrid systems incorporating three elements from other judicial selection methods: gubernatorial appointment, popular election, and citizen involvement. Most important, merit plans include a formalized role for the legal profession. In its present form, merit selection calls for the establishment of a judicial nominating commission composed of lawyers and laypeople who suggest a list of qualified nominees (usually three to five) (Henschen, Moog, and Davis 1990). From those names, the governor makes the final selection, and after a short period of service on the bench (typically one year), the new judge faces an uncontested **retention election**. The sole question for the voters to decide is "Should Judge X be retained in office?" If the incumbent wins a majority of affirmative votes, he or she earns a full term (Aspin and Hall 1994). Each subsequent term is secured through another uncontested retention ballot (Hall and Aspin 1992).

Voters invariably return incumbents to office, typically with healthy margins of more than 80 percent. Only a handful of judges have been removed from office (Baum 1983). Between 1964 and 1998 in 10 states that hold retention elections, only 52 judges out of 4,588 judicial elections were not retained. That's a retention rate of 99 percent! And more than half of those defeated—28—were in Illinois, which requires a 60 percent affirmative vote (Aspin 1999). Interestingly, minority judges fare as well in retention elections as do white judges (Luskin et al. 1994).

Some evidence, however, points to an increasing politicization of judicial retention elections for state supreme court judges, with special interest groups engaging in aggressive campaigns to unseat judges seen as politically unacceptable (Reid 1999). During the Fall 2010 elections, three Justices of the Iowa Supreme Court were defeated in retention elections after a socially conservative group called Iowa for Freedom targeted them because they had voted to legalize same-sex marriages. Overall, however, judges are still overwhelming retained. Opposition campaigns are most likely to succeed when there is a clear issue that is important to a large portion of voters (Aspin 2011).

To counter criticism that retention elections are largely toothless tigers, a growing number of states are creating judicial performance evaluation programs to help voters make informed decisions (Brody 2004; Keilitz and McBride 1992a, 1992b). Since 1975, Alaska voters have had access to a detailed evaluation of sitting judges approximately one month before the retention election. The evaluation includes assessments of the judge's legal ability, impartiality, integrity, temperament, and diligence and an overall ranking. The evaluation is performed by attorneys, peace officers, jurors, court employees, and court watchers and is overseen by a nonpartisan citizens' commission (Di Pietro, Carns, and Cotton 2000).

Merit selection has won increasing acceptance. A number of states now utilize the plan to select either all the judges in the state or those on the appellate bench (see Table 6.2). In addition, several other states, including Ohio, Pennsylvania, and Texas, have actively considered adopting merit selection. The growing importance of merit selection is demonstrated by the fact that all states that have altered their judicial selection techniques in recent years have adopted some form of the Missouri Bar Plan. Moreover, even in states that have not formally adopted merit selection, some governors use "voluntary merit plans" to fill temporary vacancies (Dubois 1980). In recent years only a few efforts to adopt merit selection have succeeded. In 2008, however, merit selection was adopted in Green County, Missouri and two counties in Alabama approved a modified merit selection plan for interim appointments (Anderson 2009).

Why have some states adopted merit selection but not others? To answer that question, Judith Haydel (1987) examined changes in judicial selection techniques over a 30-year period. She found several forces at work, but not necessarily the ones usually posited. The adoption of merit selection is related to strong support by the state bar for judicial reform, a professional legislature, changes in the electorate, and a governor with "weak" power. Although judicial reformers advocate merit plans as an apolitical method for placing qualified lawyers on the bench, these findings suggest that states adopt merit selection for political reasons. Some of the broad political forces involved reflect efforts to professionalize state government. But, at the same time, these changes are most attractive when the electorate is unstable (voting turnout is decreasing and the level of education is increasing). Adoption of merit reform is a mechanism by which governmental officials may shield themselves from an unstable political environment while retaining the partisan status quo.

The importance of the political context associated with the adoption of merit selection is reinforced by studies of the political realities of judicial selection under merit plans. Although judicial reformers contend that merit selection will significantly improve the quality of judges and remove the courts from politics, that is not necessarily the case. The most far-reaching study of the actual operations of merit selection focused on Missouri and found that politics still played a role. Political conflicts intrude into the selection of the judicial nominating commission. Lawyers in Missouri are divided between plaintiff lawyers and defense lawyers; those two factions compete to elect their representatives to the judicial nominating commission. Some commission members also think and act, at least in part, in partisan terms. Missouri governors often appoint their political supporters to the commission, and, in turn, those lay members look to the governor, or his or her political associates, for cues about which candidates they should support for nomination. Ultimately, of course, the governor must choose, and, typically, the successful candidate has some political ties to that administration. In short, merit plans appear to alter the politics of judicial selection but do not remove them. In fact, removing politics from judicial selection does not seem possible. What the reformers presumably mean is the removal of "partisan" politics. In operation, merit selection has reduced the influence of political parties and greatly increased the power of the legal profession (Watson and Downing 1969). (See Courts in Comparative Perspective: Judges in the United Kingdom.)

COURTS IN COMPARATIVE PERSPECTIVE

■ Judges in the United Kingdom

Male judges, opined Cherie Blair (wife of Prime Minister Tony Blair), "either view women as weak and vulnerable and in need of protection, or as brazen and wicked and deserving of harsher treatment." The British press interpreted public comments like those as signs that Ms. Blair was no longer pursuing a judicial career. In sharp contrast to the United States, in the United Kingdom, public visibility is a detriment to being appointed a judge. To quote a former lord chief justice, "The best judge is the man who is least known to readers of the *Daily Mail*" (Rozenberg 2002).

Great Britain was the dominant industrial and maritime power of the nineteenth century. At its zenith, the British Empire stretched over one-fourth of the earth's surface. But, during the twentieth century, its strength was seriously depleted by two world wars, and its empire was dismantled. Today, 60 million citizens live in the United Kingdom—which consists of England, Wales, and Northern Ireland.

The United Kingdom is both a constitutional monarchy (with the queen playing a largely ceremonial role) and a parliamentary democracy (with legislative, executive, and judicial powers all residing in the Parliament). The principal legislative body is the House of Commons. The nation's chief executive is the prime minister (the leader of the majority party in the House of Commons). The nation's highest court is the House of Lords (another legislative branch). Thus, unlike the United States, which divides governmental power among three branches of government, the United Kingdom concentrates it in just one.

Magistrate courts decide minor offenses, and crown courts hear major crimes. ("The Old Bailey" is the informal name for the criminal crown court in London.) Convicted offenders may appeal to the criminal division of the court of appeals. The ultimate review body is the House of Lords (the upper house of Parliament).

Although legal matters technically are the responsibility of the entire House of Lords, they actually are handled by nine to twelve law lords. The House of Lords is different from the Supreme Court of the United States because England does not have a written constitution—which means that the courts cannot review acts of Parliament (Fairchild and Dammer 2001).

Although the United States adapted its legal system from English common law, judicial selection is markedly different in the two nations. At the magistrate court level, there are a few full-time stipendiary magistrates sitting alone. More commonly, three lay magistrates preside. They are unpaid, work part-time, and are not required to be legally trained (but are advised by a legally qualified clerk). The more than 30,000 lay magistrates are selected by local panels. Although attempts are made to balance the bench in terms of sex, age, political affiliation, and ethnic origin, some criticize this system because the lay magistrates are not representative of the general population. Middle-class, middle-aged, white professionals dominate the magistracy. Although women are well represented (45 percent), ethnic minorities are not (Davies, Croall, and Tyrer 1995).

The crown courts' judges are chosen by the Lord Chancellor (the nation's highest judge) in a highly secretive process. According to a high-ranking barrister (a trial lawyer in the British system), "The Lord Chancellor sounds out the leading members of the judiciary to determine which barristers have been most impressive." Not surprisingly, those most often considered impressive resemble current judges—white males who have graduated from Oxford or Cambridge and have expressed no left-wing sentiments. This "old boys' club" has been criticized for being out of touch with society (Darnton 1993). Clearly, judicial selection in England maximizes independence but perhaps builds in undue isolation as well.

WHICH SYSTEM IS BEST?

The debate over the best method for selecting judges has raged for decades. Elections are supported by those who believe the vote of the people is the most appropriate method for guaranteeing the popular accountability of judicial policy makers. Merit plans are supported by those who believe that elections are fundamentally inconsistent with the principle of judicial independence. Less philosophically, these competing perspectives reflect a political tug of war over which group will be most influential in choosing judges. Different methods of judicial selection heighten or diminish the influence of political parties or the legal profession (Sheldon and Maule 1997). Elections give political parties a greater voice in judicial selection, whereas merit selection provides the organized bar with a special influence.

Evaluating the Systems

In evaluating which method of judicial selection is best, a key criterion is whether one system produces better judges than another. To judicial reformers, merit plans place the greatest emphasis on legal and judicial credentials and reduce the impact of partisan political values in recruitment. Opponents of merit selection counter that elective systems select judges who are equally qualified for office. Moreover, elective systems are claimed to be more open to minorities and legal outsiders, because merit systems tend to be biased toward higher-status lawyers. At one level, it is difficult to examine this argument, because it is impossible to evaluate a normative concept such as "best." Therefore, for research purposes, it is necessary to rephrase the question empirically. Thus, researchers ask, do judges selected by one method differ from those selected by others? When the question is phrased in this way, measurable judicial credentials such as prior legal experience and education are used as surrogate indicators of judicial quality. Two different conclusions emerge from this extensive body of literature.

For individuals who wish to become judges, methods of judicial selection do make a slight difference. Former legislators are clearly more likely to be selected in states where legislators appoint judges. Similarly, a higher proportion of people who have held local political office become judges in states that elect their bench. By contrast, lawyers who have held state office (such as legislators) have a better chance of becoming judges in states where the governor appoints judges. We can perhaps best evaluate these differences by asking what systems appear to favor candidates with local political office experience—which typically means the district attorney. Under the Missouri Bar Plan and elective systems, former district attorneys are more often selected as judges. Where the executive or the legislature makes the selection, though, fewer district attorneys become judges. The differences within systems are also pronounced. In California, for example, which governor makes the appointment has an impact on who becomes a judge (Dubois 1985).

From a broader perspective, methods of judicial selection have only a marginal influence on the types of lawyers who becomes judges. Whether elected by the voters, appointed by the governor, or selected through merit plans, state judges are more alike than different. In personal background characteristics such as prior political experience, ties to the local community, political party affiliation, and quality of legal education, the systems of judicial selection are not very different (Emmert and Glick 1988, 1987; Flango and Ducat 1979). Today, the bench is changing and beginning to more closely resemble the American electorate (Bonneau 2001). However, the jury is still out with regard to whether the method of selection results in different kinds of justices. Research continues to find that methods of judicial selection do not have the impact on personal characteristics of the judges that the debate in the literature would have us believe (Nagel 1973; Canon 1972). Nor do judges selected by different methods appear to behave differently on the bench (O'Callaghan 1991). Thus, no systematic evidence (yet) indicates that one selection system produces better judges than another.

Similarities in Judges' Backgrounds

Political scientists have collected information mostly about state supreme court judges. It used to be easy to summarize their background characteristics: white, Protestant, and male. But, over the past twenty years, things have changed substantially. In the most comprehensive data collection effort to date, Bonneau (2001) demonstrates that in twenty years female representation has gone from 3 percent to 26 percent of all state supreme court justices; high-status Protestant identifiers have decreased from 30 percent in 1980 to just 20 percent in 2000; and, perhaps most important, former elected official experience has become less important among justices today than it was twenty years ago.

Finally, judges are seldom newcomers to political life. Three out of four state supreme court judges held a prior nonjudicial political office. Trial court judges also have held prior office, with the modal category being district attorney or state legislator (Glick and Emmert 1986). Thus, before donning the black robes, judges have had some familiarity with the range of public issues that governments and courts must address. Those factors mean that few political mavericks survive the series of screens that precede becoming a judge. The selection process tends to eliminate those who hold views and exhibit behavior widely different from the mainstream of local community sentiment. In short, both selection systems recruit judges whose attitudes reflect those of the local community (Levin 1988).

Diversity and the Judiciary

The United States is experiencing a revolutionary change in composition of the bench. The dominant profile of judges as white male Protestants has begun to change, but, to some, change has not come fast enough. Women and racial minorities historically have faced tremendous obstacles to becoming lawyers and judges. Before 1961, only two women, one African-American male, and one male with a Mexican father had served as Article III judges. Few women and minorities were appointed to federal judgeships until the Carter administration (Goldman and Saronson 1994). Since Carter, however, progress has been made, albeit slowly, toward diversifying the federal judiciary. George W. Bush was been particularly vocal about his goal of diversity, and although the absolute number of minorities serving as federal judges has increased, the improvement remains modest (Solberg 2005). On January 1, 2005, 24 percent of federal judges were women, 11 percent were African Americans, and 7 percent were Hispanics. A combined 37 percent of federal judges could be considered nontraditional (Schiavoni 2005).

The picture of diversity among state judges is significantly more complicated. Until the twentieth century, the number of women judges in America was so small it could be counted on one hand. The twentieth century began witnessing changes, though not very quickly. By 1950, women had achieved at least token representation on the bench. It was not until 1979, however, that every state could report that its bench included at least one woman judge (Carbon 1984). Today, an estimated 24 percent of the American bench is staffed by women. That growth parallels increases in

DEBATING LAW, COURTS, AND POLITICS

■ 3/9th is Two Votes Away from a Majority

Elena Kagan is the 112th person to become a Supreme Court justice—Harvard law trained, supervising editor of the law review, law clerk for a federal judge, professor of law at the University of Chicago, advisor to President Clinton, and 45th Solicitor General of the United States during Obama's administration. On Monday, May 4, 2010 when the newest justice took a seat for the Supreme Court's 2010–11 term her credentials looked in most every way like those of the other eight justices. But in one important way something was very different. The previous year President Obama had appointed Sonia Sotomayor to replace retiring justice David Souter. On this significant day with Kagan joining Sotomayor and 17-year veteran on the Court justice Ruth Bader Ginsburg, the Supreme Court would have three women judges. Everyone took notice.

Justice Ginsburg commented on the change, "The major difference is going to be the public perception of where women are in the justice system … the three of us, we are here to stay … when the schoolchildren file in and out of the court and they look up and they see three women, then that will seem natural and proper—just how it is." (Barnes 2010). But beyond demographic and gender representation, which may contribute to the institutional legitimacy of the court (Epstein, Knight, and Martin 2003), will it matter for the litigants who come before the court and the legal questions they present? It is not possible to know yet how often Kagan will vote with her reliably liberal colleagues Ginsburg and Sotomayor and it is worth noting that Ginsburg frequently disagreed with justice Sandra Day O'Connor, the first female Supreme Court justice. But O'Connor was appointed by Republican President Ronald Reagan and was involved in Republican politics in her home state of Arizona. Ginsburg was appointed by Democratic President Clinton, Sotomayor and Kagan by Obama so the odds they will vote together more frequently seem higher. But is that because of their gender or their political ideology or both?

Justice Ginsburg has said "in the typical case—that I'm a woman, that I was raised a Jew—that doesn't play into the decision" (Barnes 2010). Her view is backed up by recent studies of judicial voting that show that in most areas of law the decisions of female and male judges are rarely different. Boyd, Epstein, and Martin (2010) find that in 12 out of 13 areas of law (with sex discrimination showing effects) male and female federal judges do not different in their decisions. But in the one area where they found effects, sex discrimination, they concluded "not only do males and females bring distinct approaches to these cases, but the presence of a female judge on a panel actually causes male judges to vote in way they otherwise would not – in favor of the plaintiffs." (Boyd, Epstein, and Martin 2010).

The Supreme Court is not the only judiciary where the number of women judges is increasing, women are 26 percent of state judges, 22 percent of federal judges and perhaps more importantly in 2010, 20 States had a woman serving as the chief justice of the State's High Court, and even in the South, 8 of the 13 State High Courts were led by a woman—the highest regional percentage in the country (Curriden 2010). Women still have a long way to go to be represented on the bench the way they are in the general population, but the trend is going in the right direction with nearly 50 percent of law school graduates being female and politicians and voters selecting more and more women for judgeships.

the number of women lawyers. Significant growth in the number of women lawyers began in the 1970s, and, by 1984, approximately 13 percent of the legal profession were women. There is every expectation that the proportion of women on the bench will continue to grow as women continue to make up an ever-larger percentage of law students. In 2000, women were 49 percent of first-year law students and received 46 percent of the law degrees conferred (ABA 2001). As a result, scholars are increasingly probing the "difference" women may bring to the bench (Martin 1993). One study found that women on the U.S. courts of appeals were more likely than their male counterparts to favor the claimant in employment discrimination cases and the

CASE CLOSE-UP

■ *Chisom v. Roemer* (1991)

Diversity and the Bench

Janice Clark had always wanted to be a judge. As a practicing lawyer, she seemed to possess the education and experience necessary to don the black robes, but she still faced an insurmountable barrier. The problem was not gender—after all, women were being elected to the bench on a regular basis all over the United States. Rather, the insurmountable barrier was race. White voters rarely vote for African-American candidates; indeed, as an African-American candidate for a judgeship, Clark received only 3.2 percent of the white vote. So, as lawyers often do, she filed suit in 1988 in the U.S. District Court for the Middle District of Louisiana. Joined by African-American voters and lawyers throughout Louisiana, her class action lawsuit alleged that electing judges from multimember districts diluted African-American voting strength in violation of the Voting Rights Act.

The lawsuit was joined by local civil rights groups as well as several national organizations, including the Voter Information Project and the Lawyers' Committee for Civil Rights Under Law. The nominal defendant was the governor of the state and all other governmental officials connected with judicial elections. Also appearing for the defendants were attorneys representing the Louisiana District Judges Association and the Orleans Trial Judges Association (*Clark et al. v. Edwin Edwards et al.* 1988).

U.S. district court judge John Parker's opinion stressed that of all the 156 district court judgeships in Louisiana, only 2 were held by African Americans. The reason was that judgeships were elected from the entire judicial district, which had the effect of "diluting black voting strength," a violation of the Voting Rights Act.

This case was one of several filed in the federal courts, and the underlying legal issue was eventually settled at the appellate level in *Chisom v. Roemer* (1991) and *Houston Lawyers' Association v. Attorney General of Texas* (1991). The basic legal issue hinged on an interpretation of the Voting Rights Act of 1965, as amended in 1982. The Voting Rights Act covers representatives.

Clearly, legislators are considered representatives, but what about judges? The Fifth Circuit said "no," but, in *Chisom*, the Supreme Court held otherwise, finding that judges were indeed covered by the Voting Rights Act.

Crossing this important threshold means that in the drawing of election districts (either for legislatures or for judges), the lines may not dilute minority voting. That conclusion is based on repeated findings of the existence of racially polarized voting; that is, in an election contest pitting a black candidate against a white one, white voters are very unlikely to cast their ballot for the black candidate (Engstrom 1989). But the future of this line of decisions is cloudy. In a 5–4 decision, the Supreme Court ruled that race is an impermissible consideration in drawing congressional voting districts (*Miller v. Johnson* 1995). Nonetheless, challenges to judicial election and selection procedures under the Voting Rights Act have been mounted in fifteen states (Scruggs, Mazzola, and Zaug 1995).

Janice Clark's legal argument eventually became the law of the land. The series of Supreme Court cases firmly established the principle that judges cannot be elected in ways that place minority candidates at an unfair disadvantage. But the eventual impact is far from certain. Each of the states with a significant minority population differs somewhat in tradition and method of judicial selection, factors that shape the emerging systems of judicial selection. But, for Janice Clark, the outcome was both immediate and positive. She ran again for the major trial court bench in Baton Rouge and won, taking the oath of office on January 1, 1993. She continues to generate headlines. When a high-ranking state police official publicly complained about one of her decisions, she took to the bench and scolded the official, explaining that the problem was not her interpretation of the law but how poorly the legislature had written the state's gaming law in the first place. Her unusual candor aside, it will be many years before we know if minority judges have a long-term impact on the type of justice meted out in courthouses across America.

defendant in search-and-seizure matters. Nonetheless, the authors argue that drawing conclusions about the difference women make on the bench is still problematic (Davis, Haire, and Songer 1993). The appointment of Elena Kagan as the 112th person to serve on the Supreme Court focused public attention on the changing demographics of America's judiciary (See Debating Law, Courts, and Politics: 3/9th is Two Votes Away from a Majority).

The American Judicature Society reported in 1973 that slightly more than 1 percent of state judges were African American. By the mid-1980s, the percentage had increased to 3.8 percent. Thus, Barbara Luck Graham (1990b) found 714 African-American state court judges covering 41 states in 1986. This underrepresentation on the bench is partially a reflection of the relative paucity of African-American attorneys and of how judges are selected. African-American judges are more likely to be found in states using the merit plan (Sheldon and Maule 1997) and are less likely to be selected in states using elections (Graham 1990a). A study of state supreme court justices in 1999 found that 9 percent were African American (Martin and Pyle 2002). In 1991, the Supreme Court held that the Voting Rights Act of 1965, as amended in 1982, applies to judicial elections (*Chisom v. Roemer* 1991; *Houston Lawyers' Association v. Attorney General of Texas* 1991). The rulings paved the way for major changes in the 41 states, particularly in the South, that use elections for at least some of their judges (Smith and Garmel 1992). (See Case Close-Up: *Chisom v. Roemer* 1991.)

JUDGES AT WORK

The formal powers of judges extend throughout the judicial process. In criminal cases, the accused face judges whenever decisions affecting their futures are made. Judges set bail, rule on pretrial motions to suppress evidence, accept pleas of guilty, and, after conviction, set punishment. In civil cases, the parties are not necessarily required to go to court, because they can negotiate a settlement on their own. But often the judge is called on to rule on motions, participate in settlement discussions, and, if there is a trial, rule on the admissibility of evidence. If the case is appealed, the judges of the reviewing court question the attorneys during the hearings, read the briefs, and, most important, decide whether the decision of the lower court should be affirmed or reversed. The work of trial judges differs dramatically from that of their peers on the appellate courts. The appellate courts are covered in depth in later chapters; hence, the following discussion focuses on trial judges.

Trial Judges at Work

Although trial court judges' work is much more varied, we think of them primarily as presiding at trials. During a trial, serving as an umpire is the judge's primary task: He or she mainly reacts to the activities of the lawyers in his or her courtroom. Judges are expected to be neutral and not intervene to the undue advantage of either side. Because no legal code can furnish clear, unambiguous rules for every situation, judges exercise discretion in determining how the law applies to the particular facts of the case.

Most case dispositions result not from a jury verdict but from the voluntary actions of the parties: Criminal defendants plead guilty, and civil defendants negotiate a settlement. Thus, negotiating activities form a common part of the judge's workday. Judges vary greatly in the extent to which they participate in negotiations. Some are active participants, freely discussing with lawyers the weight of the evidence and likely trial outcomes. Others, however, refuse to participate, lest they give the impression of being biased.

Only on rare occasions do trial judges write legal opinions setting forth the reasons for their decisions. But they often must rule on motions filed by the attorneys. In criminal cases, they must rule on defense motions to exclude evidence because of improper police conduct or to change the site of the trial because of prejudicial pretrial publicity. In civil cases, they must rule on motions for summary judgment or on disputes over discovery.

Judges must also be administrators. They try to keep their **dockets** (the calendar of cases scheduled to be heard) current. One major management task is the scheduling of cases. How generously judges grant attorneys' requests for continuances (additional time) greatly affects how speedily or slowly cases reach disposition. Another major management problem is keeping track of the cases and all the papers involved in a specific case. Lost cases and lost papers can have serious consequences. Bailiffs, clerks, and law clerks assist judges in those administrative tasks. In large courts, the administrative tasks are so time consuming that one judge (or sometimes more than one) is designated chief judge and devotes almost full time to administering the court. In a growing number of courts, particularly in large ones, court administrators may also be present.

Benefits of the Job

Judges enjoy some distinct benefits of their position. For some lawyers, a judgeship represents the capstone to a successful career. After all, the position is surrounded with a high level of prestige and respect. Lawyers address the judge as "Your Honor," and everyone in the courtroom stands when the judge enters or leaves. Many judgeships control patronage positions, such as bailiffs, clerks, commissioners, reporters, probation officers, and secretaries. Because those positions are usually not covered by civil service regulations, judges can award them to friends, relatives, campaign workers, and party leaders. In some areas, judicial staff positions are a significant reservoir for party patronage.

Judicial salaries are not the highest incomes of the legal profession, but they are higher than the national average. In 2010, annual salaries of judges of trial courts of general jurisdiction ranged from $104,170 to $178,835. The average was $132,500 (National Center for State Courts 2011). For some lawyers, a judicial salary represents an increase over that received in private practice and is certainly more secure. For others, however, a judgeship represents a significant decrease in earning power. With states facing dire budget short falls, the judiciary has been cut with predictable results. The State of New York has not raised judicial salaries in 12 years with the result that judges are leaving the bench in record numbers, not to retire but to return to the practice of law (Glaberson 2011).

It is not at all unusual in federal court, for example, to find lawyers who are paid more than the judges. Through the years, Congress has responded to public displeasure with court decisions by keeping judicial salaries low. As a result, a number of young judges have resigned from the bench for more lucrative careers in private legal practice (Greenhouse 1989). Today, judicial salaries continue to be a major source of controversy. In testimony before the National Commission on the Public Service, former Chief Justice Rehnquist testified that "inadequate compensation seriously compromises the judicial independence fostered by life tenure." Federal district court judges are currently paid $174,000; appeals judges, $184,500; Supreme Court associate justices, $213,900; and the chief justice, $223,500.

Frustrations of the Job

The pressures of today's court system mean that the ideals surrounding the position of judge are not always borne out by reality. Trial court judges in the nation's largest cities often face staggering caseloads. Instead of having time to reflect on challenging legal questions, trial judges must move the docket, acting more like administrators in a bureaucracy than like judicial sages.

Moreover, the judge's actions are limited by the system—lawyers are late, court documents get lost, jails are crowded. The public believes judges are the principal decision makers in courts, but often they are not. Instead, they defer to the judgments of other courtroom actors—prosecutors and defense attorneys, lawyers for the plaintiff or the defendant in civil cases, clerks, psychiatrists, jail wardens, sheriff's deputies—who may have a greater knowledge about particular cases. Thus, in criminal cases, judges often accept plea agreements struck by the defense and prosecution and sentences recommended by the probation officer. In civil cases, judges routinely approve divorce decrees negotiated by the litigants and their attorneys. In short, although judges retain the formal legal powers of their office, they must informally share those powers with other participants in the courtroom.

Added to those general constraints is the overall low prestige of criminal court judges, who occupy the lowest rung within the judicial system. Like the other actors in the criminal justice system, the judge becomes tainted by close association with defendants who are perceived to be societal outcasts. The frustrations of trial judges assigned to the criminal docket are particularly pronounced. Some judges prefer the relative peace of civil court, where dockets are less crowded, courtrooms quieter, legal issues more intriguing, and witnesses more honest, to the criminal court atmosphere of too many cases, too much noise, too many routine (and often dull) cases, and too many fabricated stories.

JUDGING THE JUDGES

In recent years, considerable political attention has focused on selecting the right types of people for judgeships. A troublesome question still remains, however: What should be done about unfit judges? Despite the lack of clarity about what attributes a good judge should possess, one central conclusion stands out: A few judges fall short of expectations (Exhibit 6.1). A few are senile, prejudiced, vindictive,

---

| EXHIBIT 6.1 | **Examples of Judicial Misconduct** |

- Since 2008, at least 16 judges in Georgia have resigned rather than face ethics hearing before the Judicial Qualifications Commission (Torpy and Rankin 2010).

- Chief Judge Sharon Keller of the Texas Court of Criminal Appeals was charged with incompetence, violating her duties, and casting public discredit on the judiciary for refusing to delay the closing of the clerk's office for an emergency appeal for a man facing the death penalty. The man was executed several hours later (Kovach 2009).

- Judge Calvin Hotard of Second Parish Court, Jefferson Parish (Louisiana), retired from the bench in the wake of judiciary commission allegations of helping five criminal defendants in exchange for sexual favors (Louwagie 2000).

- Philadelphia Traffic Court Judge Willie F. Singletary was charged with misconduct after a YouTube video showed him soliciting campaign funds (Elliott-Engel 2008).

- New Hampshire Superior Court Judge Patricia C. Coffey was disciplined for serious misconduct relating to helping her husband protect assets from the reach of creditors (NHCaseLaw.com 2008).

---

tyrannical, lazy, and sometimes corrupt. Proper judicial conduct is indispensable to the people's confidence in their judiciary, confidence that itself is indispensable to the rule of law.

A critical issue in judging the judges is how to devise a system for removing unfit judges while guaranteeing an independent judiciary. The need for such protection is illustrated by attempts of the ultraconservative John Birch Society to impeach Chief Justice Earl Warren. The Impeach Earl Warren campaign attempted to remove the chief justice not because of his lack of integrity as a judge but because they disagreed with the Court's decisions on racial integration, freedom of religion, and criminal procedure. Protections against unpopular court rulings constitute the hallmark of an independent judiciary. Yet, judicial independence is not an end in itself. Provisions protecting judicial independence were not created for the benefit of the judges, but for the benefit of the judged (Byrd 1976).

Systems for removing or disciplining unfit judges must also grapple with the wide range of misbehavior encompassed by the phrase *judicial misconduct* (Begue and Goldstein 1987). Most directly, judicial misconduct involves corruption. For example, in recent years, judges in cities such as Chicago, New York, and Philadelphia have been accused of (and sometimes convicted of) criminal offenses—taking bribes or fixing traffic tickets, for example. But not all judicial misconduct is so venal (Wice 1991); sometimes it involves improper or bizarre behavior on the bench. The most difficult situations involve judges of advanced years. After years of dedicated service to the community and exemplary conduct on the bench, a judge might show symptoms of Alzheimer's disease, for example. Deciding what to do with judges who are too old and too senile to continue to dispense justice is no easy task. In that regard, a growing number of states impose mandatory retirement ages for judges. The Supreme Court has ruled that state laws requiring judges to retire at seventy years of age do not violate the federal Age Discrimination in Employment Act (*Gregory v. Ashcroft* 1991).

Formal methods for removing unfit judges—recall elections and impeachment proceedings—are generally so cumbersome that they have seldom been used. Moreover, those techniques are better directed at corrupt judges than at those whose behavior is improper or whose advanced age has caught up with them. A more workable method for dealing with judicial misconduct is the judicial conduct commission.

State Judicial Conduct Commissions

In 1960, California became the first state to adopt permanent and practical machinery for disciplining its judges. In response to mounting public clamor for accountability of governmental officials, all fifty states have now followed that pioneering lead, either replicating the California model or borrowing key elements from that state's approach (Gray 2007; Brooks 1985; Tesitor 1978).

Judicial conduct commissions are created as an arm of the state's highest court. The commission typically consists of judges, lawyers, and prominent laypeople who investigate allegations of judicial misconduct and, when appropriate, hear testimony. If the commission finds in favor of the judge, the investigation is closed and the matter is permanently concluded (Miller 1991). This confidentiality is essential lest a judge's reputation be tarnished by a crank complaint. Many complaints are issued against judges by disgruntled litigants whose charges are no more serious than that the judge did not rule in their favor (Gray 2007). Alternatively, the commission may recommend a sanction of private admonishment, public censure, retirement, or removal. The state supreme court retains the final power to discipline errant judges (Gardiner 1986).

Although commissions are armed with the potent weapon of a public recommendation, they typically prefer to act privately. If the information gathered suggests judicial misconduct, the commission holds a confidential conference with the judge, who has an opportunity to rebut the charges. The commission may try to correct the matter; a judge with a substance abuse problem, for example, is encouraged to enroll in a treatment program. If the problems are serious, continuous, or not immediately solvable, the commission usually requests voluntary retirement. The informal pressures and the threat of bringing public proceedings are often powerful enough to force the judge in question off the bench. The complaints and investigations remain confidential unless the commission finds it necessary to seek a reprimand or removal before the state supreme court.

Increasingly, unsatisfied litigants and groups are heading to the Internet to describe their complaints. Web pages dedicated to perceived misconduct are now common and videos of potential misconduct are starting to appear on sites such as YouTube. Moreover, some are calling for judicial conduct commissions to hold public hearings (Tembeckjian 2007).

The Federal Conduct and Disability Act

Congress passed major changes in the self-governance mechanism of the federal judiciary in 1980. The Judicial Councils Reform and Judicial Conduct and Disability Act establishes a formal process for acting on complaints of misconduct by federal judges (Burbank 1987; Neisser 1981). In 2002 Congress amended the act and gave it a separate chapter in the U.S. Code, Chapter 16 (Hellman 2007).

TABLE 6.3	Selected Federal Judges Who Have Faced Disciplinary Action	
Judge	**Allegations**	**Outcome**
Harry Claiborne (District of Nevada)	Jury acquitted Claiborne of accepting a bribe but convicted him of income-tax evasion.	While serving a two-year sentence in federal prison, Claiborne was found guilty on three of four impeachment articles by the required two-thirds vote in the Senate, and he was removed from the bench (1986).
Walter Nixon (Southern District of Mississippi)	Convicted of perjury for falsely denying before a federal grand jury that he had intervened in a state narcotics case involving the son of a friend.	While serving his sentence at Eglin Air Force Base in Florida, Nixon was removed from the federal bench (1989).
Alcee Hastings (Southern District of Florida)	Jury acquitted Hastings of soliciting a $150,000 bribe from two convicted racketeers but found the co-defendant guilty.	The Judicial Council of the Eleventh Circuit and the Judicial Conference concluded that Hastings not only was guilty but also had fabricated his defense. The House of Representatives, by an overwhelming margin, voted seventeen articles of impeachment, and the Senate ousted Hastings from office in 1989.
Robert Aguilar (Northern District of California)	Convicted in 1990 on two counts of obstructing justice for telling a friend about a government wiretap; the Ninth Circuit reversed, but the Supreme Court reinstated the wiretap conviction (*United States v. Aguilar* 1995).	The judge remained on the bench during his appeal but was limited to trying civil cases. After another conviction and yet another appellate reversal, Aguilar resigned from the bench, apparently in exchange for criminal charges being dropped.
Robert Collins (Eastern District of Louisiana)	First federal judge in history to be convicted of bribery for taking a $100,000 bribe from a drug smuggler.	While serving a seven-year prison sentence and facing impeachment proceedings, Collins resigned from the bench before formal Senate action was taken.
Brian Duff (Northern District of Illinois)	Displayed erratic temper and shoot-from-the-hip courtroom manner; highest rate of reversal in the Chicago courthouse.	Amid reports of a Justice Department complaint filed with the Judicial Council of the Seventh Circuit, the judge stepped down with the possibility of a reduced caseload after three years. Judge Duff cited medical problems (Robinson 1996).
Samuel Kent (Southern District of Texas)	Accused of sexually molesting his case manager.	Reprimanded by the Judicial Council of the Fifth Circuit (Olsen 2008). In August 2008, Kent pled guilty to obstruction of justice for lying to judges who investigated sexual misconduct complaints. He was sentenced to 33 months in federal prison. The House impeached the judge but he resigned before a Senate trial.
Thomas Porteous (Eastern District of Louisiana)	Accused of taking cash from lawyers when he was a state trial court judge and lying under oath.	Impeached by the House and overwhelmingly convicted by the Senate.

Complaints are initially heard by the judicial councils (the administrative arm of each federal circuit court of appeals). Most result in either a finding of no misconduct or the imposition of nonpublic sanctions. In 2008, the Judicial Conference adopted policies to end the differences across circuits in the way that misconduct complaints are handled (Mauro 2008). However, if substantial evidence of serious misconduct is shown, the judicial council sends a written report to the Judicial Conference, which may recommend that the House of Representatives begin impeachment procedures.

Article II of the Constitution provides for the removal of high-ranking federal officials such as judges for "treason, bribery, or other high crimes and misdemeanors." The House must first vote articles of impeachment specifying the charges of wrongdoing, which is roughly equivalent to a grand jury indictment. The trial on the articles of impeachment is conducted before the Senate. Conviction requires a two-thirds vote of the senators present and carries with it removal from office. In functioning as both judge and jury in impeachment trials, historically all senators have observed the testimony and cross-examination of witnesses. But, in the modern era, the pressure of legislative business makes this time-consuming process unworkable. Therefore, during the Claiborne impeachment trial in 1986, the Senate made the historic decision to establish a twelve-person impeachment committee to receive evidence and take testimony before trial on the Senate floor (Gerhardt 1996; Heflin 1987). That shortcut was upheld by the Supreme Court (*Nixon v. United States* 1993).

An unprecedented series of allegations of misconduct against several federal judges highlights the interlocking relationships among criminal prosecutions, impeachment, and the new statutory scheme (Table 6.3). The impeachment proceedings against Judge Alcee Hastings (Southern District of Florida) presented the most difficult questions, because he was never convicted of a criminal offense. Hastings, the first African-American federal judge ever appointed in Florida, was indicted for soliciting a $150,000 bribe from two convicted racketeers. A jury acquitted the judge but found the co-defendant guilty. Nonetheless, the Judicial Council of the Eleventh Circuit and the U.S. Judicial Conference concluded that Hastings not only was guilty but also had fabricated his defense. Hastings argued that racial motivations were behind the impeachment proceedings. By an overwhelming margin, the House of Representatives voted seventeen articles of impeachment, and the Senate ousted him from office in 1989. (In a bizarre twist, Hastings subsequently was elected to the U.S. House of Representatives.)

The cases presented in Table 6.3 are truly exceptional. Since John Pickering was impeached and convicted in 1803 (the first such U.S. district court judge to be removed) on charges of mental instability and intoxication from the bench, only five more judges have been removed from the bench. And all but one of those has occurred since 1936. No appellate court judges have been impeached by the U.S. House of Representatives, but these statistics obscure the fact that many misconduct and disability problems are resolved informally by the judiciary itself or when the judge resigns (Fitzpatrick 1988).

It is important to underscore the fact that issues about judicial misconduct are far different from questions about judicial ethics. Because of their special role in the adversary system, judges are subject to additional ethical constraints beyond those imposed on lawyers. The BP oil spill highlights one such issue of judicial ethics—when does a judge's past legal practice disqualify him or her form hearing a case (See Debating Law, Courts, and Politics: Can we Find Fair and Impartial Judges to Preside over the BP Oil Spill Cases?).

DEBATING LAW, COURTS, AND POLITICS

■ Can We Find Fair and Impartial Judges to Preside Over the BP Oil Spill Cases?

The BP oil spill cast a strong spotlight on the nexus between lawyers, judges, and the political influence of the oil and natural gas industry. Before coming to the federal bench many of the federal judges in New Orleans had represented the oil and natural gas industry which raised the fundamental question: can judges with close ties to an industry be fair and impartial?

Oil and natural gas is a dominant industry in the states of Louisiana and Texas (which along with Mississippi compose the Fifth Circuit). Not surprisingly the U.S. senators from these states, irrespective of their party label, have through the years been strong champions of the industry. In turn they have often received campaign contributions from the industry. The identification of these Senators with oil and natural gas interests has also extended to the appointment of federal judges. But at the same time, because oil and natural gas companies are interwoven with the economic, social and political fabric of the community, so are the lawyers. Many lawyers work directly or indirectly for the very types of companies that now find themselves as defendants in multi-billion-dollar lawsuits (Chapter 11).

For decades, the Fifth Circuit has been known as a court supporter of the oil and natural gas industry. After the BP oil spill, numerous judges in the federal court in New Orleans as well as the Fifth Circuit immediately recused themselves because of their ties to the oil industry or investments in it. As the oil spill was unfolding the Fifth Circuit found itself unable to hear an appeal in a global-warming suit because 8 of the 16 active judges on the Fifth Circuit recused themselves. Without a quorum the court could not hear an *en banc* appeal. Some wonder whether similar conflicts of interest will prevent the Fifth from hearing appeals in the BP oil spill cases.

Potential conflicts of interest are also apparent at the District level. Seven of the 12 active judges recused themselves and others might were faced with a similar prospect because their spouses were representing one of the parties involved (Baldas 2010). National attention focused on U.S. District Court Judge Marvin Feldman, who ordered an end to the government moratorium on drilling. Several environmental groups asked the judge to disqualify himself because he has extensive investments in companies that operate pipelines, develop natural gas deposits. Judge Feldman refused to recuse himself, but just before issuing his ruling he sold his stock in Exxon Mobile which left some wondering if he had a conflict of interest when he wrote the opinion (Mufson and Stephens 2010).

Questioning the fairness and impartially of judges based on the law they practiced before they came to the bench has important political consequences. To some, attaching a judge's decision on the basis of the law the judge practiced before coming to the bench undermines the integrity of the judiciary. In the words of two lawyers who specialize in professional responsibility: "it is imprudent for us to question the basis upon which we place faith in the judiciary whenever a judge makes a ruling we don't like" (Cohen and Helm 2010). Liberal groups, for example, attached Judge Feldman's ruling on the moratorium (which was very unpopular nationwide) because he had ties to the oil and natural gas industry. Conversely conservative groups attached some of President Obama's nominees to the Justice Department because they had provided *pro bono* representation of Guantanamo detainees when in private practice. Decisions at this level will prove, almost by definition, to be politically controversial. And just because a decision proves controversial, doesn't mean that the integrity of the judge should be impugned. After all, former prosecutors are allowed to preside over criminal cases.

CONCLUSION

The Supreme Court's decision in *Republican Party v. White* (2002) focused increasing public attention on how the United States selects its judges, who does the selecting, and what role judges should perform once on the bench.

Should judges be elected? To former Supreme Court justice Sandra Day O'Connor and many legal reformers, popular election erodes judicial independence and impartiality. But, as stressed in this chapter, allegations that judges have not been impartial are often made by interest groups that have lost a case before the judge in question. But contrast O'Connor's argument with the evidence marshaled by Hall and Bonneau (2009) *In Defense of Judicial Elections* which led Bonneau (2011) to write in the Washington Post:

1. There is no evidence that judicial elections cause voters to view judicial institutions as less legitimate.
2. There is no difference, other things being equal, in the quality of judges who emerge from elections as opposed to appointments.
3. Campaign spending makes elections more competitive.
4. There is no proof that elected judges are for sale.

Should judges be appointed? Merit selection is the principal alternative to judicial elections, but merit appointment does not eliminate politics. Under merit selection, politics is simply shifted from external electoral politics to internal bar association politics.

What should be the role of political parties in judicial selection? An earlier generation of judicial reformers sought to remove political parties from the selection process, but that idyllic fiction has been punctured. In *Republican Party v. White* (2002), the state Republican party brought the lawsuit in its own name because it wanted more influence over judicial elections.

What should be the role of interest groups in judicial selection? Conservative and liberal groups alike view court decisions as important and seek to influence who will make those decisions. (Chapter 7 will discuss more fully the increasing importance of interest groups in the judicial process.)

Are judges political actors? From the perspective of political scientists, critics' concerns seem out of touch. As stressed in Chapter 1, judges make decisions in ways that differ from the ways of legislative and executive governmental officials, but their decisions nonetheless have an impact on politics.

Would changing the rules of judicial selection have an impact? One of the criticisms of *Republican Party v. White* (2002) is a projection that lawyers will be mounting the same types of election campaigns now used for legislative and executive offices. A long literature on studying judicial elections, however, suggests that tinkering with the rules is unlikely to have a major impact on who become judges. In the states, elected judges look very similar to appointed ones.

In the aftermath of *Republican Party v. White* (2002), the public dialogue over judicial selection remains as confusing as ever. Perhaps that confusion is a strong indication that judicial selection remains a complicated and divisive issue.

CRITICAL THINKING QUESTIONS

1. Which method of judicial selection do you think is best? What does your choice reveal about your personal attitudes?

2. In the wake of *Republican Party v. White* (2002), will judicial elections change?

3. At what point are efforts to remove "unfit judges" really efforts to remove judges because of decisions they have made?

4. Does underrepresentation of women and racial minorities on the bench hurt justice?

5. Would citizens' views of the fairness of courts improve if more nontraditional people became judges?

Search Terms

judges   judicial misconduct

Useful URLs

http://www.ajs.org
     American Judicature Society

http://www.uscourts.gov/vacancies/judgevacancy.htm
     Administrative Office of the United States Courts (vacancy information)

http://judiciary.senate.gov
     U.S. Senate Committee on the Judiciary

http://www.usdoj.gov/olp/judicialnominations.htm
     U.S. Department of Justice, Office of Legal Policy

http://aja.ncsc.dni.us
     American Judges Association

http://www.judicialwatch.org
     Judicial Watch is an ethical and legal "watchdog" over our government, legal, and judicial systems with a conservative orientation.

http://www.afj.org
     The Alliance for Justice stresses securing access to justice.

REFERENCES

Abbe, Owen G., and Paul S. Herrnson. 2002. "How Judicial Election Campaigns Have Changed." *Judicature* 85: 286–295.

American Bar Association (ABA). 2001. *ABA-LSAC Official Guide to ABA-Approved Law Schools, 2002 Edition.* Chicago: American Bar Association.

———. 2002. Press release, August 13. Available online at http://www.manningproductions.com/ABA245/OMK/release.html. Retrieved April 4, 2003.

Anderson, Seth (Moderator). 2009. "Anatomy of a Merit Selection Victory." *Judicature* 93: 6–13.

Arbour, Brian K. and Mark J. McKenzie. 2011. "Campaign Messages in Lower-Court Elections after Republican Party of Minnesota vs. White." *The Justice System Journal* 32(1):1–23.

Aspin, Larry. 1999. "Trends in Judicial Retention Elections, 1964–1998." *Judicature* 83: 79–81.

———. 2011. "The 2010 Judicial Retention Elections in Perspective: Continuity and Change from 1964-2010. *Judicature* 94: 218–232.

Aspin, Larry, and William Hall. 1994. "Retention Elections and Judicial Behavior." *Judicature* 77: 306–315.

Baldas, Tresa. 2010. "Another Federal Judge Recuses from Oil Spill Cases." *The National Law Journal.* June 3

Barnes, Robert. 2007. "Judicial Races Now Rife with Politics." *Washington Post*, October 28, p. A1.

Barnes, Robert. 2010. "Supreme Court opens term with three women, potential for partisan divide." Washington Post, October 3, 2010. http://www.washingtonpost.com/wp-dyn/content/article/2010/10/02/AR2010100203382.html

Baum, Lawrence. 1983. "The Electoral Fates of Incumbent Judges in the Ohio Court of Common Pleas." *Judicature* 66: 420–430.

———. 1999. "Electing Judges." In *Contemplating Courts*, edited by Lee Epstein, 18–43. Washington D.C.: CQ Press.

Begue, Yvette, and Candace Goldstein. 1987. "How Judges Get Into Trouble." *The Judges Journal* 26: 8.

Bell, Laura Cohen. 2002. *Warring Factions: Interest Groups, Money, and the New Politics of Senate Confirmation.* Columbus: Ohio State University.

Berkson, Larry C. 1980. "Judicial Selection in the United States: A Special Report." *Judicature* 64: 176–193.

Biskupic, Joan. 2009. "Supreme Court case with the feel of a best seller." *USA Today.* 2/16/2009. http://www.usatoday.com/news/washington/2009-02-16-grisham-court_N.htm

Biskupic, Joan. 2010. "Obama's Push For Diversity Hits a Snag" *USA Today* 6/15/2010. http://www.usatoday.com/news/washington/judicial/2010-06-15-diversity-lower-courts_N.htm

Binder, Sarah A., and Forrest Maltzman. 2004. "The Limits of Senatorial Courtesy." *Legislative Studies Quarterly* 29(1): 5–22.

Bonneau, Chris W. 2001. "The Composition of State Supreme Courts." *Judicature* 85: 26–31.

Bonneau, Chris W. 2007. "Campaign Fundraising in State Supreme Court Elections." *Social Science Quarterly* 88: 68–85.

Bonneau, Chris W. 2011. "Why We Should Keep Judicial Elections." *Washington Post* May 26, 2011. http://www.washingtonpost.com/opinions/why-we-should-keep-judicial-elections/2011/05/26/AGt08HCH_story.html

Bonneau, Chris W., and Melinda Gann Hall. 2003. "Predicting Challengers in State Supreme Court Elections: Context and Politics of Institutional Design." *Political Research Quarterly* 56: 337–349.

Boyd, Christina L., Lee Epstein and Andrew Martin. 2010. "Untangling the Causal Effects of Sex on Judging." *American Journal of Political Science* 54(2): 389–411.

Brody, David C. 2004. "The Relationship Between Judicial Performance Evaluations and Judicial Elections." *Judicature* 87: 168–177, 192.

Brooks, Daniel. 1985. "Penalizing Judges Who Appeal Disciplinary Sanctions: The Unconstitutionality of 'Upping the Ante.'" *Judicature* 69: 95–102.

Burbank, Stephen. 1987. "Politics and Programs in Implementing the Federal Judicial Discipline Act." *Judicature* 71: 12–28.

Byrd, Harry. 1976. "Has Life Tenure Outlived Its Time?" *Judicature* 59: 266.

Canon, Bradley. 1972. "The Impact of Formal Selection Processes on the Characteristics of Judges—Reconsidered." *Law and Society Review* 6: 579–594.

Carbon, Susan. 1984. "Women in the Judiciary." *Judicature* 65: 285.

Cardozo, Benjamin. 1921. *The Nature of the Judicial Process.* New Haven, Conn.: Yale University Press.

Carp, Robert A., Kenneth L. Manning, and Ronald Stidham. 2001. "President Clinton's District Judges: 'Extreme Liberals' or Just Plain Moderates?" *Judicature* 84: 282–290.

———. 2004. "The Decision-Making Behavior of George W. Bush's Judicial Appointees." *Judicature* 88: 20–28.

Champagne, Anthony, and Greg Thielemann. 1991. "Awareness of Trial Court Judges." *Judicature* 74: 271–277.

Cheek, Kyle, and Anthony Champagne. 2000. "Money in Texas Supreme Court Elections: 1980–1998." *Judicature* 84: 20–25.

Cohen, Joel, and Katherine Helm. 2010. "The BP Mess: Judging Judges' Impartiality." Law.Com August 2.

Cohodas, Nadine. 1988. "Reagan's Legacy Is Not Only on the Bench." *Congressional Quarterly*, November 26, p. 3392.

Curriden, Mark. 2010. "Tipping the Scales: In the South, Women have made huge strides in the State Judiciaries." *ABA Journal* July 2010. http://www.abajournal.com/magazine/article/tipping_the_scales/

Darnton, John. 1993. "England's Judges (and Hiring System) Under Fire." *New York Times*, July 18.

Davies, Malcolm, Hazel Croall, and Jane Tyrer. 1995. *Criminal Justice: An Introduction to the Criminal Justice System in England and Wales*. London: Longman.

Davis, Sue, Susan Haire, and Donald Songer. 1993. "Voting Behavior and Gender on the U.S. Court of Appeals." *Judicature* 77: 129–133.

Denning, Brannon P. 2002. "The Judicial Confirmation Process and the Blue Slip." *Judicature* 85: 218–226.

Di Pietro, Susanne, Teresa W. Carns, and William T. Cotton. 2000. "Judicial Qualifications and Judicial Performance: Is There a Relationship?" *Judicature* 83: 196–204.

Dubois, Philip. 1979. "Voter Turnout in State Judicial Elections: An Analysis of the Tail of the Electoral Kite." *Journal of Politics* 41: 865–867.

———. 1980. *From Ballot to Bench: Judicial Elections and the Quest for Accountability*. Austin: University of Texas Press.

———. 1984. "Voting Cues in Nonpartisan Trial Court Elections: A Multivariate Assessment." *Law and Society Review* 18: 395–436.

———. 1985. "State Trial Court Appointments: Does the Governor Make a Difference?" *Judicature* 69: 20–28.

Elliott-Engel, Amaris. 2008. "Judge Charged with Misconduct After YouTube Video Shows Him Soliciting Campaign Funds." *The Legal Intelligencer*, June 20, 2008. Available online at http://www.law.com/jsp/article.jsp?id51202422419560. Retrieved August 11, 2008.

Emmert, Craig, and Henry Glick. 1987. "Selection Systems and Judicial Characteristics: The Recruitment of State Supreme Court Judges." *Judicature* 70: 228–235.

———. 1988. "The Selection of State Supreme Court Justices." *American Politics Quarterly* 16: 445–465.

Engstrom, Richard. 1989. "When Blacks Run for Judge: Racial Divisions in the Candidate Preferences of Louisiana Voters." *Judicature* 73: 87–89.

Epstein, Lee, Jack Knight, and Andrew D. Martin. 2003. "The Norm of Prior Judicial Experience and its Consequences for Career Diversity on the U.S. Supreme Court." *California Law Review* 91(4): 903–66.

Fairchild, Erika, and Harry Dammer. 2001. *Comparative Criminal Justice Systems*. Belmont, Calif.: Wadsworth.

Fitzpatrick, Collins. 1988. "Misconduct and Disability of Federal Judges: The Unreported Informal Responses." *Judicature* 71: 282–283.

Flango, Victor, and Craig Ducat. 1979. "What Differences Does Method of Judicial Selection Make? Selection Procedures in State Courts of Last Resort." *Justice System Journal* 5: 25–44.

Galberson, William. 2011. "Pay Frozen, More New York Judges Leave Bench." *New York Times* July 4.

Gardiner, John. 1986. "Preventing Judicial Misconduct: Defining the Role of Conduct Organizations." *Judicature* 70: 113–121.

Gerhardt, Michael J. 1996. *The Federal Impeachment Process: A Constitutional and Historical Analysis*. Princeton, N.J.: Princeton University Press.

Glick, Henry, and Craig Emmert. 1986. "Stability and Change: Characteristics of State Supreme Court Judges." *Judicature* 70: 105–111.

Glick, Henry, and Kenneth Vines. 1973. *State Court Systems*. Englewood Cliffs, N.J.: Prentice Hall.

Goldberg, Deborah, Craig Holman, and Samantha Sanchez. 2002. "The New Politics of Judicial Elections." Justice at Stake. Available online at http://www.justiceatstake.org/files/JASMoneyReport.pdf. Retrieved April 3, 2003.

Goldman, Sheldon. 1966. "Voting Behavior on the United States Courts of Appeals, 1961–64." *American Political Science Review* 60: 374–383.

———. 1981. "Carter's Judicial Appointments: A Lasting Legacy." *Judicature* 64: 344–355.

Goldman, Sheldon, and Matthew Saronson. 1994. "Clinton's Nontraditional Judges: Creating a More Representative Bench." *Judicature* 78: 68–73.

Goldman, Sheldon, Elliot Slotnick, Gerard Gryski, Gary Zuk, and Sara W. Schiavoni. 2005. "Bush Remaking the Judiciary: Like Father Like Son?" *Judicature* 86: 282–309.

Goldman, Sheldon, Elliot Slotnick and Sara W. Schiavoni. 2011. "The Confirmation Drama Continues" *Judicature* 94(6) (2011): 262–303.

Graham, Barbara Luck. 1990a. "Do Judicial Selection Systems Matter? A Study of Black Representation on State Courts." *American Politics Quarterly* 18: 316–336.

———. 1990b. "Judicial Recruitment and Racial Diversity on State Courts: An Overview." *Judicature* 74: 28–34.

Greenberg, Stan, and Linda A. DiVall. 2002. Available online at http://www.justiceatstake.org/files/PollingsummaryFINAL.pdf. Retrieved April 4, 2003.

Greenhouse, Linda. 1989. "Rehnquist, in Rare Plea, Asks Raise for Judges." *New York Times*, March 6, p. A1.

Gray, Cynthia. 2007. "How Judicial Conduct Commissions Work." *The Justice System Journal* 28: 405–418.

Grossman, Joel. 1965. *Lawyers and Judges: The ABA and the Politics of Judicial Selection*. New York: Wiley.

Haire, Susan, Gerard Gryski, Gary Zuk, and Deborah Barrow. 1994. "An Intercircuit Profile of Judges on the U.S. Courts of Appeals." *Judicature* 78: 101–103.

Hall, Melinda G. and Chris W. Bonneau. 2009. *In Defense of Judicial Elections*. New York: Routledge.

Hall, William, and Larry Aspin. 1992. "Distance from the Bench and Retention Voting Behavior: A Comparison of Trial Court and Appellate Court Retention Elections." *Justice System Journal* 15: 801–813.

Haydel, Judith. 1987. "Explaining Adoption of Merit Selection in the States, 1950–1980: A Multivariate Test." Paper presented at the annual meeting of the Southwestern Political Science Association, Dallas, March 18–21.

Heflin, Howell. 1987. "The Impeachment Process: Modernizing an Archaic System." *Judicature* 71: 123–125.

Hellman, Arthur. 2007. "Judges Judging Judges: The Federal Judicial Misconduct Statutes and the Breyer Committee Report." *The Justice System Journal* 28: 426–435.

Henschen, Beth, Robert Moog, and Steven Davis. 1990. "Judicial Nominating Commissioners: A National Profile." *Judicature* 73: 328–334.

Hojnacki, Marie, and Lawrence Baum. 1992. "Choosing Judicial Candidates: How Voters Explain Their Decisions." *Judicature* 75: 300–309.

Holland, Jesse. 2011. "Senate Urged to Fill Judicial Posts." *The Times-Picayune* January 2.

Jackson, Donald Dale. 1974. *Judges*. New York: Atheneum.

Jacob, Herbert. 1973. *Urban Justice: Law and Order in American Cities*. Englewood Cliffs, N.J.: Prentice Hall.

———. 1984. *Justice in America: Courts, Lawyers, and the Judicial Process*. 4th ed. Boston: Little, Brown.

Keilitz, Susan, and Judith McBride. 1992a. "Judicial Performance Evaluation Comes of Age." *State Court Journal* 16: 4–13.

———. 1992b. "Revised Chart for 'Judicial Performance Evaluation Comes of Age.'" *State Court Journal* 16: 30–33.

Kiel, L. Douglas, Carole Funk, and Anthony Champagne. 1994. "Two-Party Competition and Trial Court Elections in Texas." *Judicature* 77: 290–293.

Kovach, Gretel. 2009. "Mixed Opinions of a Judge Accused of Misconduct." *New York Times*, March 8.

Ladinsky, Jack, and Allan Silver. 1967. "Popular Democracy and Judicial Independence: Electorate and Elite

Reactions to Two Wisconsin Supreme Court Elections." *Wisconsin Law Review* 1967(1): 128–169.

Levin, Martin. 1988. "Urban Politics and Policy Outcomes: The Criminal Courts." In *Criminal Justice: Law and Politics*, 5th ed., edited by George Cole. Pacific Grove, Calif.: Brooks/Cole.

Louwagie, Pam. 2000. "Judge Ends His Tarnished Career." *New Orleans Times-Picayune*, September 15, p. A1.

Luskin, Robert, Christopher Bratcher, Christopher Jordan, Tracy Renner, and Kris Seago. 1994. "How Minority Judges Fare in Retention Elections." *Judicature* 77: 316–321.

Martin, Elaine. 1993. "Women on the Bench: A Different Voice?" *Judicature* 77: 126–128.

Martin, Elaine, and Barry Pyle. 2002. "Gender and Racial Diversification of State Supreme Courts." *Women & Politics* 24(2): 35–52.

Massie, Tajuana D., Thomas G. Hansford, and Donald R. Songer. 2004. "The Timing of Presidential Nominations to the Lower Federal Courts." *Political Research Quarterly* 57(1): 145–154.

Mauro, Tony. 2008. "Binding National Rules Adopted for Handling Judicial Misconduct Complaints." *Legal Times*, March 12.

McKnight, R. Neal, Roger Schaefer, and Charles A. Johnson. 1978. "Choosing Judges: Do the Voters Know What They Are Doing?" *Judicature* 62: 94–99.

Miller, Benjamin. 1991. "Assessing the Functions of Judicial Conduct Organizations." *Judicature* 75: 16–19.

Mufson, Steven and Joe Stephens. 2010. "Judge in Drilling Case Held Stock n Oil Company affected by Moratorium." *Washington Post*. June 26.

Nagel, Stuart. 1973. *Comparing Elected and Appointed Judicial Systems*. Newbury Park, Calif.: Sage.

National Center for State Courts. 2011. *Survey of Judicial Salaries*. Williamsburg, Va.

Neisser, Eric. 1981. "The New Federal Judicial Discipline Act: Some Questions Congress Didn't Answer." *Judicature* 65: 143–160.

Nelson, Michael. 2011. "Uncontested and Unaccountable? Rates of Contestation in Trial Court Elections." *Judicature* 94: 208–217.

NHCaseLaw.com. 2008.

Nicholson, Marlene, and Norman Nicholson. 1994. "Funding Judicial Campaigns in Illinois." *Judicature* 77: 294–299.

O'Callaghan, Jerome. 1991. "Another Test for the Merit Plan." *Justice System Journal* 14: 477–485.

Olsen, Lise. 2008. "Justice Department Broadening Investigation of Kent." *Houston Chronicle*, July 20. Available online at http://www.chron.com/disp/story.mpl/front/5897425.html. Retrieved August 9, 2008.

Podlas, Kimberlianne. 2002. "Should We Blame Judge Judy? The Messages TV Courtrooms Send Viewers." *Judicature* 86: 38–43.

President's Commission on Law Enforcement and Administration of Justice. 1967. *Task Force Report: The Courts*. Washington, D.C.: U.S. Government Printing Office.

Reid, Traciel V. 1999. "The Politicization of Retention Elections: Lessons from the Defeat of Justices Lanphier and White." *Judicature* 83: 68–77.

Robinson, Mike. 1996. "Abrasive, Erratic Judge Sidelined." *New Orleans Times-Picayune*, October 12.

Rowland, C. K., and Robert A. Carp. 1996. *Politics and Judgment in Federal District Courts*. Lawrence: University Press of Kansas.

Rozenberg, Joshua. 2002. "Will This Bar the Way to Judge Booth?" *Daily Telegraph*, June 19.

Salokar, Rebecca. 2005. "From the Benches and Trenches: After *White*: An Insider's Thoughts on Judicial Campaign Speech." *The Justice System Journal* 26:149.

Sample, James, Charles Hall and Linda Casey. 2010. "The New Politics of Judicial Elections." *Judicature* 94: 50–57.

Scherer, Nancy. 2005. *Scoring Points: Politicians, Political Activists and the Lower Federal Court Appointment Process*. Stanford, Calif.: Stanford University Press.

Schiavoni, Sara. 2005. "Diversity on the Bench." *Judicature* 88: 258–259.

Schotland, Roy. 1998. "Comment: Judicial Independence and Accountability." *Law & Contemporary Problems* 61: 149–150.

Scruggs, Anna, Jean-Claude Mazzola, and Mary Zaug. 1995. "Recent Voting Rights Act Challenges to Judicial Elections." *Judicature* 79: 34–41.

Sheldon, Charles H., and Nicholas P. Lovrich. 1999. "Voter Knowledge, Behavior and Attitudes in Primary and General Judicial Elections." *Judicature* 82: 216–223.

Sheldon, Charles H., and Linda S. Maule. 1997. *Choosing Justice: The Recruitment of State and Federal Judges*. Pullman: Washington State University Press.

Slotnick, Elliot. 1983. "The ABA Standing Committee on Federal Judiciary: A Contemporary Assessment." *Judicature* 66: 385–393.

———. 1988. "Federal Judicial Recruitment and Selection Research: A Review Essay." *Judicature* 71: 317–324.

———. 2002. "A Historical Perspective on Federal Judicial Selection." *Judicature* 86: 13–16.

Smith, Nancy, and Julie Garmel. 1992. "Judicial Election and Selection Procedures Challenged Under the Voting Rights Act." *Judicature* 76: 154–155.

Solberg, Rorie Spill. 2005. "Diversity and George W. Bush's Judicial Appointments: Serving Two Masters." *Judicature* 88: 276–283.

Solomon, Rayman. 1984. "The Politics of Appointment and the Federal Courts' Role in Regulating America: U.S. Courts of Appeals Judgeships from T.R. to F.D.R." *American Bar Foundation Research Journal* 8: 285.

Songer, Donald, and Due Davis. 1988. "Carter's Nominating Commissions for the U.S. Courts of Appeals: An End Run Around Senatorial Courtesy." *Southeastern Political Review* 16: 61–82.

Songer, Donald, and Susan Haire. 1992. "Integrating Alternative Approaches to the Study of Judicial Voting: Obscenity Cases in the U.S. Courts of Appeals." *American Journal of Political Science* 38: 673–696.

Steigerwalt, Amy. 2010. *Battle over the Bench: Senators, Interest Groups, and Lower Court Confirmations*. Charlottesville, VA: University of Virginia Press.

Tembeckjian, Robert. 2007. "Judicial Discipline Hearings Should be Open." *The Justice System Journal* 28: 419–425.

Tesitor, Irene. 1978. *Judicial Conduct Organizations*. Chicago: American Judicature Society.

Torpy, Bill, and Bill Rankin. 2010. "Off the Bench, In Disgrace." *The Atlanta Journal-Constitution*. August 22.

Wasmann, Erik, Nicholas Lovrich, and Charles Sheldon. 1986. "Perceptions of State and Local Courts: A Comparison Across Selection Systems." *Justice System Journal* 11: 168–185.

Watson, Richard, and Rondal Downing. 1969. *The Politics of the Bench and Bar: Judicial Selection Under the Missouri Nonpartisan Court Plan*. New York: Wiley.

Wenner, Lettie, and Cynthia Ostberg. 1994. "Restraint in Environmental Cases by Reagan-Bush Judicial Appointees." *Judicature* 77: 217–220.

Wice, Paul. 1991. *Judges and Lawyers: The Human Side of Justice*. New York: HarperCollins.

Wohl, Alexander. 2000. "Justice for Rent: The Scandal of Judicial Campaign Financing." *American Prospect* 11:34–37.

For Further Reading

Bushnell, Eleanore. 1992. *Crimes, Follies, and Misfortunes: The Federal Impeachment Trials*. Champaign: University of Illinois Press.

Carns, Teresa. 2009. "The Alaska Merit Selection System at Work, 1984-2007." *Judicature* 93: 102–108.

Carp, Robert, Donald Songer, C. K. Rowland, Ronald Stidham, and Lisa Richey-Tracy. 1993. "The Voting Behavior of Judges Appointed by President Bush." *Judicature* 76: 298–302.

Epstein, Lee, and Jeffrey Segal. 2005. *Advice and Consent: The Politics of Judicial Appointments*. New York: Oxford University Press.

Ford, Lynne. 2011. *Women and Politics: The Pursuit of Equality*, 3rd edition. Belmont: Wadsworth.

Goldman, Sheldon, Gerard Gryski, and Gary Zuk. 2001. "Clinton's Judges: Summing Up the Legacy." *Judicature* 84: 228–254.

Geyh, Charles. 2006. *When Courts and Congress Collide: The Struggle for Control of America's Judicial System*. Ann Arbor: University of Michigan Press.

Gryski, Gerard. 2005. "Partisan Makeup of the Bench." *Judicature* 88: 270–271.

Hettinger, Virginia, Stefanie A. Lindquist, and Wendy L. Martinek. 2006. *Judging on a Collegial Court: Influences on Appellate Decision Making*. Charlottesville: University of Virginia Press.

Jacobi, Tonja. 2005. "The Senatorial Courtesy Game: Explaining the Norm of Informal Vetoes in Advice and Consent Nominations." *Legislative Studies Quarterly* 30(2): 193–217.

Spohn, Cassia. 2009. *How Do Judges Decide? The Search for Fairness and Justice in Punishment*. Thousand Oaks, CA: Sage.

Volcansek, Mary. 1993. *Judicial Impeachment: None Called for Justice*. Urbana: University of Illinois Press.

Wheeler, Russell. 2010. "Changing Backgrounds of U.S. District Judges: Likely Causes and Possible Implications." *Judicature* 93: 140–149.

Williams, Margret. 2009. "Individual Explanations for Serving on State Courts." *The Justice System Journal* 30: 158–178.

MOBILIZING THE LAW: LITIGANTS, INTEREST GROUPS, COURT CASES, AND THE MEDIA

The war memorials outside the Ogle County, Illinois, courthouse illustrate that courthouses have always been at the center of the public square. Today, debates in the public square often result in lawsuits being filed in courthouses.

David Neubauer

The lawyers at the Cato Institute, a libertarian think tank in Washington, DC, were armed with a cause—bringing a right to bear arms lawsuit to the Supreme Court. The timing seemed right, outside funding had been promised and the lawyers possessed the needed type of expertise. But first they needed a plaintiff. By a process of attrition and elimination, Dick Heller emerged as the face of gun rights because he had a personally compelling story. Heller was a special police officer in Washington D.C., licensed to carry a handgun while working. But at the end of the day, when he left his job guarding the Federal Judicial Center, he had to turn in his gun because D.C.'s strict gun control law did not allow private citizens to possess a loaded weapon. Thus Heller became one of six handpicked, sympathetic plaintiffs who feared living in the dangerous parts of Washington, D.C. without a gun to protect themselves (Doherty 2008).

Every working day, people like Dick Heller file suit in court. Very few of those cases will have any broad social or political impact, however; most have consequences only for those directly involved. Thus, when one couple sues to end their troubled three-year marriage or another files suit against the drunk driver who injured them in an automobile accident, they don't expect their cases to end up in the Supreme Court. Indeed, they hope just the opposite: they want the matter settled quickly and, of course, in their favor.

These cases, real and hypothetical, illustrate that courts are passive institutions. As argued in Chapter 1, courts do not seek out cases to decide but, rather, depend on others to bring matters to their attention. How many cases are filed, as well as the kinds of cases brought to court, is determined by the decisions of others—victims of crime, merchants who are owed money, people injured in automobile accidents, for example. Thus, although the judicial process itself is dominated by professionals—the lawyers and the judges discussed in Chapters 5 and 6—the courts are not merely the private reserve of professionals. They serve ordinary people who bring criminal complaints via the prosecutor's office or who come to court to rectify some alleged wrong in civil court. Conversely, of course, half of those participants do not wish to be there. Thus, it is important to underscore the reality that when individuals, groups, or government officials voluntarily go to court, they compel the involuntary appearance of other individuals, groups, or governmental officials. For those who find themselves named as defendants in lawsuits, the experience can be an unpleasant one: If the case is criminal, the defendant may be found guilty and sentenced to prison; if it is civil, the defendant may be found negligent and ordered to pay monetary damages.

This chapter focuses on the consumers of the courts and the types of cases they bring for resolution. The chapter begins with a discussion of why people go to court. As we shall see, there are a host of other third parties who resolve disputes. Thus, many disputes never make their way to court, but many do. Every year, more than 100 million cases of very different types are filed. This chapter discusses three major conceptual differences among cases: the nature of the parties, the kinds of decisions judges must make, and traditional versus policy-oriented lawsuits. The judiciary's policy-making role accounts for the determination of interest groups in pursuing their objectives through the courts. Thus, this chapter also examines interest groups in the judiciary, as well as the relationship between the media and the legal system.

LEGAL MOBILIZATION

The term **legal mobilization** refers to the process by which a legal system acquires its cases (Black 1973). At times, legal mobilization stems from the direct involvement of public officials; for example, the police make an arrest or the IRS sues for nonpayment of taxes. More often, however, legal mobilization stems from citizen-initiated actions; for example, individuals call the police to report a burglary or file suit for damages suffered in an automobile accident. By invoking legal norms, private citizens employ the power of the state. Thus, users of the courts also play an important part in the judicial process. By defining a problem as a legal one, citizens make demands on the courts. Thus, individual litigants actually set the judicial branch's agenda (Marshall 1998; Zemans 1983). How often citizens sue or call the police largely determines how many cases courts must decide. The volume and the complexity of American law provide a uniquely democratic mechanism by which individuals, groups, and organizations may invoke public authority for their private benefit. Bear in mind that these are American patterns. Courts in other nations function in different ways because they face different tasks and challenges. (See Courts in Comparative Perspective: The Federal Republic of Nigeria.)

Individuals and groups, however, do not necessarily have to file suit in court in an effort to settle their disputes. Indeed, in the United States there are a variety of dispute settling institutions that do not involve the courts. The judiciary is merely one forum for dispute resolution; numerous other avenues are available (Menkel-Meadow 2003; Sarat 1989; Black and Baumgartner 1983; Yngvesson and Mather 1983). A wide variety of people serve as impartial third parties attempting to resolve disputes. Some are chosen because of their standing within a social community or the position of trust that they occupy. A priest, a minister, or a rabbi, for example, may be asked by a parishioner to mediate matrimonial difficulties. Others are selected because of their background, training, or expertise. The American Arbitration Association maintains an extensive list of economists, engineers, business professors, and the like who are available (for a fee) to mediate or arbitrate commercial disputes. Conversely, some third parties become involved because they are generalists. Lawyers and judges fall into this category.

Third parties vary in their settlement roles. Friendly peacemakers try to influence the individual or the group to abandon their hostilities. Without addressing the matter at issue, they strive merely to bring an end to the dispute, regardless of its causes or content. Like peacemakers, mediators refuse to take sides in the dispute, but they do delve into the problem and seek a solution. Mediators attempt to bring about an agreement by listening to each side and trying to get each party to understand the other's point of view (Kydd 2006; Greig 2005). By identifying areas of common concern, mediators may propose solutions. In a successful **mediation**, the parties reach an agreement that is satisfactory to each and with which they will comply. **Arbitration** operates similarly to mediation but with one important difference: Arbitrators, unlike mediators, have the authority to impose a binding determination. In arbitration, the parties agree ahead of time to be bound by the decision of the impartial third party. Moreover, that decision is enforceable in court (McDermott 1986). Aside from its well-known use in resolving labor disputes, arbitration is now widely used to settle disputes in industries such as textiles, construction, insurance, and sports (Abrams 2000; Cooley 1986).

COURT CASELOADS

Most disputes never mature into lawsuits; rather, they are handled by third-party alternatives. Nonetheless, many Americans do look to the courts to redress their grievances. The large and apparently growing volume of cases has prompted concern among citizens and academics about whether we are experiencing a litigation explosion (Haltom and McCann 2004). Whether Americans are indeed litigating more and enjoying it less is examined in greater depth in Chapter 10.

Large and growing caseloads, though, are nothing new to the American judiciary. As discussed in Chapters 3 and 4, the increasing number of demands has resulted in

COURTS IN COMPARATIVE PERSPECTIVE

■ The Federal Republic of Nigeria

For bearing a child out of wedlock, 31-year-old Amina Lawal Kurami must die by stoning—thus ruled an Islamic court in Funtua, one of the most conservative towns in Nigeria's predominantly Islamic north (Reuters 2002). The decision prompted international outrage and also highlights the divisiveness of religion in some nations. In Nigeria, major policy issues are not *interracial* (the vast majority of the population is black) but *intra-racial* (the nation is sharply divided between Christians [40 percent] and Muslims [50 percent]).

Nigeria, in western Africa, is the continent's most populous nation, with more than 155 million people living in a geographic area roughly twice the size of California. The oil-rich economy, however, has long been hobbled by political instability and corruption. Nonetheless, Nigeria is vitally important to the United States which imports 10 percent of the nation's oil.

Nigeria was a British colony from 1914 until it received independence on October 1, 1960. A few years later, an attempt by the Ibos (a Christian tribe) to secede resulted in the Biafran civil war, which left more than a million dead. Nigeria adopted a new constitution in 1999, following sixteen years of corrupt military rule. In 2007, Nigeria held its first successful "civilian-to-civilian transfer of power" (Central Intelligence Agency 2008). But increasingly elections are marred by violence. Nigeria's largest opposition party (based in the Muslim North) has challenged in court the reelection of President Goodluck Jonathan alleging election fraud (BBC 2011).

The structure of government roughly parallels that in the United States. The executive is the president, who is both chief of state and head of government. The legislature consists of two branches, a 108-member senate (with 3 members popularly elected from each state) and a house of representatives (with 360 members elected from individual districts). At the top of the judicial branch is the supreme court, whose members are appointed by the Provisional Ruling Council. And, like the United States, the nation is a federation, with 36 independent states. The legal system is based on English common law, but, increasingly, Islamic Shari'a law is being adopted in many of the northern states, a move

that was not allowed when Muslim generals ruled the nation.

Nigeria is composed of more than 250 ethnic groups, including the Hausa and Fulani (29 percent), the Yoruba (21 percent), and the Ibo (18 percent). These tribal divisions are exacerbated by religious differences. At times, Nigeria has been on the brink of a tribal and religious war. As a growing number of states adopt Islamic law, new clashes are breaking out. Following the terrorist attacks of September 11, 2001, for example, at least 500 people died and many more were injured in riots in various cities across the nation ("At Least 500 ..." 2001).

Nigeria also suffers from a reputation of corruption, which is "rampant" in the courts (Sobel 2001) and police (Gambrell 2010). Violence also undermines judicial independence. The 71-year-old Bola Ige, the nation's attorney general, was assassinated. Ige had been one of the most outspoken campaigners for democracy during the former military rule, and federal troops were dispatched to defuse the political tensions (McKenzie 2001).

Whether the nation, much less the judiciary, can function in this environment is problematic. The nation's constitution is secular, but Muslims point to provisions for freedom of religion as permitting the adoption of Muslim law. The president of Nigeria has verbally opposed those moves but has taken no other actions. On other matters, the supreme court has clearly backed the powers of the national government, but whether it has the legal authority and the political legitimacy to act in this matter is unclear.

As for Amina Lawal Kurami, Islamic judges ruled that she could not be stoned to death until her child is weaned at the age of two or three. A higher court later ruled that she could not be put to death. And over time similarly harsh sentences have also been moderated. Morality police that once had free reign have seen their powers limited. The practice of Islamic law has settled into a distinctively Nigerian compromise between the dictates of faith and the chaotic realities of modern life in an impoverished developing nation (Polgreen 2007).

the creation of new types of courts and has prompted significant court reform. Today, responses to caseload pressures are primarily alterations of court procedures— for example, instituting court-annexed arbitration in the trial courts (discussed in Chapter 10) or adopting expedited processing techniques in the appellate courts (covered in Chapter 13).

The raw statistics reveal that Americans readily look to the courts to redress their grievances. Without some important qualifications, however, those raw statistics provide a misleading impression of the judiciary's work. The tyranny of judicial statistics is that they treat all cases the same: A charge of disorderly conduct is counted the same as a murder prosecution; an uncontested divorce is tabulated the same as a tort. In fact, case filings may not necessarily require judicial action. Many cases are settled without ever having been heard by a judge. Moreover, cases vary in complexity: A civil suit may seek to recover $250 or $25 million; a criminal case may involve petty theft or first-degree murder. Of the 90 million plus cases filed in court annually, the vast majority are relatively minor: Almost 60 percent involve traffic violations, and a large number are misdemeanor and small-claims cases. As discussed in Chapter 4, those simple cases are heard by lower courts, where little of the adversary model of justice is present and dispositions are rapid. Cases also differ on the basis of the substance of the law: torts and contracts, divorce and small claims, and so on. Important as these legal categories may be, they provide little understanding about the dynamics of case dispositions. The next three sections discuss different ways of making sense out of court caseloads by focusing on the nature of the parties involved, the kinds of decisions judges must make, and whether the lawsuits are traditional or involve public policy.

PARTY CAPABILITY

Some litigants are more likely to win than others. Some are more likely to win their case because they have the facts and the law on their side. Perhaps other litigants are more likely to prevail because they hired a better lawyer than their opponent (Chapter 5). And perhaps some individuals, businesses or organizations are more likely to win because they have more resources than the other side. In a provocative essay, anthropologist and law professor Marc Galanter (1974) argues that party capability is important because some litigants possess advantages not enjoyed by other plaintiffs or defendants. In his analysis, one-shotters are litigants who only occasionally appear in court; repeat players, on the other hand, often bring cases to court. The distinction between one-shotters and repeat players largely parallels differences in the economic status of the parties. "Have-nots" consist of litigants who have relatively few economic resources, whereas "haves" consist of businesses and organizations that possess considerable economic resources. According to Galanter, repeat players (the haves) hold a series of advantages over one-shotters (the have-nots). Because they are frequent users of the courts, repeat players develop expertise in pressing their claims and often enjoy cozy, informal relationships with judges and other court personnel. Moreover, because of their superior power and resources, repeat players are better able to employ institutional tactics such as delay and discovery to manipulate the litigation process and achieve their goals. For those reasons, Galanter argues, repeat players are more likely to win in court. (That contention is further scrutinized in Chapter 11.) The next section examines how these configurations are tied to the types of cases coming to court.

Many lawsuits pit repeat players against one-shotters. All criminal cases fall into this configuration. Clearly, the government possesses many more institutional resources than does the accused individual (which is why constitutional provisions and criminal procedure provide the defendant with so many protections). On the civil side, the government often sues individuals for unpaid taxes, land condemnation, and so on. Other examples are businesses attempting to collect money owed by individuals—they represent many cases pitting the repeat players against the one-shotters. Small-claims cases, in particular, often involve merchants suing individuals for money owed.

When one-shotters sue repeat players, the power equation is seemingly reversed. Individuals with little, if any, experience in the legal system are asserting a claim against a major societal institution. Personal injury lawsuits provide the most important example, as when the injured party in an automobile accident sues the defendant's insurance company, seeking to recover damages for medical expenses, lost wages, pain and suffering, and the like.

One-shotters suing other one-shotters represents an interesting configuration, because neither is likely to have much familiarity with the law. The most common example involves divorce. As discussed in Chapters 10 and 11, an important consequence is that lawyers often must spend considerable time educating their clients about what the law considers reasonable and unreasonable.

Finally, a number of cases pit repeat players against other repeat players. Common examples include one level of government suing another level of government (for example, the U.S. Department of Justice suing to block the state of Arizona from enforcing its own immigration law and states suing the federal government to have the 2010 Health Care Reform declared unconstitutional). On the private side, big businesses regularly sue other businesses, big or small, for money owed, antitrust violations, and so on. As discussed in Chapter 3, the federal courts are most likely to be the forum for resolving disputes between repeat players.

Galanter's article has been so influential that several years ago a group of scholars met at a conference to celebrate its twenty-fifth anniversary and to consider whether his typology is still relevant (Kritzer and Silbey 2003). The answer appears to be "yes," but with some caveats. In a 1999 review of research presented at that meeting, Grossman, Kritzer, and Macaulay noted that (1) the government as a repeat player is far more important now than it was twenty-five years ago and may be different from other repeat players with regard to party capability; (2) the differences between repeat players and one-shotters is less dramatic now than when Galanter was writing, largely because of structural reforms such as the wider diffusion of legal knowledge; and (3) a dichotomous classification of win or lose may not represent the nuanced desires of litigants in many cases today. Not everyone finds support for the Galanter thesis. Songer, Kuersten, and Kaheny (2000) conclude that some of the benefits of upperdog status are diminished when underdog litigants are supported in court by the filing of amicus curiae briefs by interest groups.

In the end, whether one accepts the Galanter typology or not, the importance of party capability is widely agreed upon. Party capability has been shown repeatedly, and in a variety of contexts, to be an important predictor of litigation success and success more generally in the legal arena. Thus, it is useful to consider how the parties' relative capabilities may affect a lawsuit's outcome or process.

THE ADJUDICATORY PROCESS

Cases differ not only in the capabilities of the parties but also in the types of decisions the judge must make. Some so-called cases provide little or nothing for the judge to do. The lawyers have resolved all the issues and ask the judge only to sign his or her name to end the matter. Such cases represent routine administration for the judge. Other cases require some judicial action but not necessarily a full-blown trial. Rather, judges may engage in one of three types of adjudicatory activities—procedural, decisional, or diagnostic (Kerwin, Henderson, and Baar 1986). An understanding of these types of tasks explains why courts process lawsuits in fundamentally different ways.

Routine Administration

Many cases filed in court are not disputes at all or are resolved without much involvement by the legal system. In these types of cases, the task of the judge is not to resolve an actual dispute but simply to provide a formal authorization for a private settlement. **Routine administration** means the court has no disputed question of law or fact to decide; the court merely processes and approves undisputed matters (Friedman and Percival 1976).

Uncontested divorce provides the clearest example of routine administration. In most divorce filings, the parties do not go to court until they have agreed (often with the help of their lawyers) on the terms of the divorce. Once an agreement has been reached, the parties go before a judge seeking formal approval (the judicial rubber stamp, as it were). Such cases are quickly disposed of. After a brief hearing, the judge signs the court order granting the divorce. Other types of cases that fall into the category of routine administration include mortgage foreclosure and probating an estate.

Procedural Adjudication

If a case involves an actual dispute, we are accustomed to thinking of its resolution in terms of the adversarial model: lawyers in court arguing before judge or jury. This is **procedural adjudication**, which involves four key elements: (1) Judges and lawyers engage in a search for the applicable law (and often disagree about how to interpret that law); (2) the process places a heavy reliance on formal rules of evidence; (3) to ensure the just resolution of the case, there is an exhaustive exploration of all relevant questions of fact and issues of law; and (4) although trials are relatively rare, procedural adjudication assumes that all parties are preparing for a trial and are considering no other options. Thus, in procedural adjudication, the process is long and expensive, because considerable effort is devoted to tailoring a decision to the unique events surrounding the case. In essence, seeing that justice is done is more important than seeing that disposition is reached quickly and inexpensively.

Torts provide the most typical example of procedural adjudication. Lawyers spend time trying to discover the facts of the case and file motions contesting the law. They threaten trial but rarely deliver, choosing to settle out of court instead. Similarly, criminal cases with heavy penalties—armed robbery and homicide, for example—are most likely to apply procedural adjudication. Generally, the higher the stakes (dollar values in civil cases; prison terms in criminal cases), the more likely the case will involve procedural adjudication and the more likely it will actually go to trial. A corollary to this proposition is that, in most cases, the stakes are low to moderate, and, therefore, the litigants settle.

Decisional Adjudication

Unlike cases requiring procedural adjudication, many disputes that come to court are uncomplicated—the law is clear and the facts in the case are straightforward. Thus, in **decisional adjudication**, judges seek to rapidly establish the relevant facts and expeditiously apply the law. Speed is imperative because so many litigants are awaiting their day in court. Emphasis is placed on a quick resolution, so rules and procedures are simple and informal. Simplified rules also reflect the nature of the litigants—many of whom appear **pro se** (representing themselves) and lack the legal knowledge needed to understand or use more complex, formal techniques.

Small-claims courts are a prime example of decisional adjudication. Misdemeanors, ordinance violations, and traffic cases likewise fall into this category. Thus, decisional adjudication largely characterizes the work of the minor trial courts, which hear staggering numbers of cases in which the stakes are small and the issues relatively easy.

Diagnostic Adjudication

Diagnostic adjudication is largely devoted to determining the cause of a problem and devising the proper treatment to eliminate it or at least mitigate it. Little emphasis is placed on establishing guilt or innocence or in determining winners or losers; as a consequence, rules and procedures do not play a central role in the proceedings. Indeed, the law largely provides only a framework for decision making; it offers little guidance about the final decision itself. The most distinctive feature of diagnostic adjudication is the role of nonjudicial personnel in defining issues and securing outcomes. Experts with professional credentials in psychiatry or social work are central to the dispositional process.

The archetype of **diagnostic adjudication** is the juvenile court, but this adjudicatory style is also used in proceedings involving involuntary civil commitment to mental institutions (Lewis et al. 1984) and contested divorces where the spouses cannot agree on child custody. Diagnostic adjudication also characterizes sentencing wherein the judge, often aided by probation officers, must determine the proper penalty to be applied to the guilty. Diagnostic adjudication cases prove the most troublesome for the courts because the law offers little guidance. These types of cases constitute the fastest-growing area of litigation. And as we will discuss next, lawsuits that seek to make major policy changes are an important and growing form of diagnostic adjudication.

TRADITIONAL VERSUS POLICY LAWSUITS

A third way that court cases differ is in the scope of the lawsuit. Broadly speaking, lawsuits are either traditional or policy oriented (Chayes 1976). Following are the distinguishing features of **traditional litigation**:

- The lawsuit pits a single plaintiff against a single defendant. Although, on occasion, multiple parties may be involved, the litigation is organized as a contest between two individuals.
- Litigation is retrospective. The controversy is about events that occurred in the past and have now ended.
- The plaintiff seeks compensation for past wrongs. As discussed in Chapter 2, the plaintiff often wants monetary damages.
- The lawsuit is a self-contained episode. The judgment will affect only the immediate parties.
- Once the case has ended, judicial involvement ceases.

Most lawsuits are traditional—for example, contracts, divorces, personal injuries, and small claims.

But courts in the United States have never been limited to deciding traditional lawsuits. They have, through the years, been called on to decide challenges to the policies of private or governmental institutions. The characteristics of **policy litigation** are strikingly different from those of traditional lawsuits:

- The lawsuit involves multiple plaintiffs and/or multiple defendants. Thus, the party structure is sprawling and amorphous and often changes during the case as parties are added and dropped. Moreover, the multiple parties on one side may themselves have conflicting perspectives.
- Litigation is future oriented. The controversy includes past actions and ongoing practices.
- The plaintiff seeks more than compensation for past wrongs; the plaintiff wants to affect the future behavior of the defendant. In addition to undoing the damages done, the plaintiff requests affirmative relief (often involving equity).
- The lawsuit has broad ramifications. The judgment affects other sectors of society.
- The court order does not terminate judicial involvement. The continuing participation of the court is necessary to ensure that the defendant does indeed change policy.

Policy litigation is of enormous and growing importance. The cases that are the focus of public and professional debate are overwhelmingly policy litigation cases. Policy litigation may be either private or public.

Policy-oriented private lawsuits are vehicles for settling disputes between private parties about private rights. The government's role is limited to providing rules for resolving those disputes (the law) and a forum in which to decide the matter (the courts). Recent examples include suits alleging defective products (Chapter 11), gender discrimination policies in paying workers (*Wal-Mart v. Dukes* 2011) and deceptive practices by financial institutions. Viewed from this perspective, product liability suits and personal injury litigation have been used not merely to recompense persons hurt

DEBATING LAW, COURTS, AND POLITICS

■ Can Courts Bring About Social Change?

With an increasing number of interest groups going to court to pursue policy lawsuits, some ask whether the courts can indeed bring about social change. Political scientist and law professor Gerald Rosenberg has given a pessimistic view of the Supreme Court's influence. Starting with his groundbreaking book *The Hollow Hope: Can Courts Bring About Social Change?* and following up in a series of articles and book chapters, he argues that courts are quite limited in their ability to bring about social change. He does not question whether courts have impact in specific cases, for clearly they do. Rather, his concern is whether judicial actions can lead to "policy changes with a nationwide impact" (Rosenberg 1991, 4). His analysis emphasizes three constraints on courts (particularly the U.S. Supreme Court): (1) Constitutional rights are limited, which prevents courts from hearing many significant social issues; (2) the judiciary lacks the necessary independence from other branches of government; and (3) courts lack implementation power (they cannot appropriate money or use the police) to enforce their orders.

Working within that model of a constrained judiciary, Rosenberg examines many of the same areas of law highlighted in this book, including civil rights (this chapter), abortion (Chapter 14), and rights of criminal defendants (Chapters 5, 8, and 9). He concludes that, in each of those areas, social change has occurred but not necessarily because of judicial involvement; rather, social change came only after significant change had occurred in the legislative and/or administrative arenas. The Court's decision in *Brown*, for example, is often mentioned as the catalyst for school desegregation. Yet, Rosenberg stresses, it was years before a significant number of African-American children attended previously all-white southern schools. Overall, he concludes that a growing civil rights movement from the 1930s, economic changes, population shifts, electoral concerns, and increases in mass communications created the pressure that led to changes in civil rights policy. Thus, at best, the Court followed, rather than led, the move toward social change. Indeed, the author concludes, "while there is little evidence that *Brown* helped produce positive change, there is some evidence that it hardened resistance to civil rights among both elites and the white public" (Rosenberg 1991, 155).

But not all are convinced of his conclusions. In a wide-ranging critique of the Rosenberg thesis. Several authors contributed to an edited volume, *Leveraging the Law: Using the Courts to Achieve Social Change*, and attempted to show that courts are capable of social reform (Schultz 1998). The contributors all conclude that the power of the courts is greater than that suggested by Rosenberg. One might also observe in this context that if the law is dead (in the context of creating social change), as Rosenberg seems to suggest, then a healthier corpse has rarely been seen (Zalman 1995). As emphasized in earlier chapters, America has a great many lawyers, and litigants file a multiplicity of lawsuits—indicators that the law is far from dead. If groups seeking significant social change are foolishly wasting their resources by engaging in litigation, why have conservative groups joined liberal interest groups in going to court? Moreover, Rosenberg's analysis implies that who sits on the Court ultimately doesn't matter, a proposition rejected by the vast majority of political observers.

Making Rights Real also finds that litigation is more powerful than Rosenberg's notions of a hollow hope. Political Scientist Charles Epp (2009) finds that in three different policy areas—police use of force, sexual harassment in the workplace, and playground safety—legal activists and governmental bureaucrats had major impacts. Lawsuits and the threat of litigation, combined with bureaucrats who pushed for change, produced major change. Police departments across the nation, for example, implemented and enforced policies on the use of deadly force. In the end *The Politics of Rights* (Scheingold 2004) moved from symbolic politics to effective public policy.

We discussed the constraints on the American judiciary that Rosenberg stresses in Chapter 1. Ultimately, one's reaction to *Hollow Hope* reduces to a basic question: Is the cup half empty or half full? All commentators agree that the judiciary is part of a larger political system. In presenting a thought-provoking challenge to deeply held views that courts matter, Rosenberg challenges us to think about the conditions necessary for social change—whether through the judiciary or through other branches of government.

by industrial practices, but also in an attempt to change the business policy of these private firms (Cooper 1988, 13). Policy oriented private lawsuits often take the form of class action lawsuits which explains why they have become politically controversial (Chapter 11).

Policy-oriented public lawsuits, on the other hand, involve the government more directly. The grievance is about public policy, and the government is a party. The most prominent example is *Brown v. Board of Education* (1954). In these cases, individual citizens or groups contend that some governmental institution has violated a constitutional or statutory right. Typically, the plaintiff seeks both negative and positive relief: The plea for negative relief is generally a request that the judge declare past governmental actions illegal. The affirmative relief requested is for a decree that attempts to directly change the structure or practice.

In *Hard Judicial Choices*, Phillip Cooper (1988) explores policy-oriented public lawsuits, which clearly operate at the point where the political and legal systems meet. If the judge finds that the law has indeed been violated, then a decree must be fashioned to remedy past wrongs—a remedy that often proves extremely controversial and very divisive in the community. The cases themselves are also the subject of considerable debate. (See Debating Law, Courts, and Politics: Can Courts Bring About Social Change?) Several policy-oriented public lawsuits figure prominently in this book, including government regulation of gun ownership (this chapter), prison conditions (Chapter 9), same-sex marriages (Chapter 13), and abortion (Chapter 14). Policy-oriented public lawsuits are an indication that the law extends into virtually every facet of our lives. And, as discussed in the following section, many of those policy-oriented public lawsuits are filed by interest groups that believe the rights of their members have been violated.

INTEREST GROUPS IN COURT

Policy litigation highlights an important fact of American political life: Judges make policy and will continue to do so whether they are predominantly conservatives or liberals, Republicans or Democrats, elected or appointed. In fact, some people find it easier to go to court to get the law changed than to go through the long, drawn-out legislative process. Although most interest group activity focuses on the legislative and executive branches of government, **interest groups** also sue to promote public policies that favor their members. Thus, interest groups regularly bring cases to court specifically to develop legal doctrines useful to their cause. The most widely cited example is the NAACP, which sponsored a series of lawsuits that eventually led to the desegregation of schools, lunch counters, and public accommodations as well as to the removal of racial barriers to voting. Prompted by the NAACP's success, interest groups representing a diverse array of viewpoints now regularly pursue their political objectives in court. Numerous researchers have examined how organizations have used the courts to pursue their interests, among them racial discrimination (Tushnet 2005), religious freedom (Sorauf 1976), sex discrimination (George and Epstein 1991; O'Connor 1980), and same-sex marriage (Pinello 2006).

Why Interest Groups Litigate

Why do interest groups prefer litigation to other, more traditional forms of lobbying? The reason is typically that they are politically disadvantaged in traditional forums (Epstein 1985). That is, they turn to the courts because they lack access to the legislative and executive branches of government. Politically disadvantaged groups "are highly dependent upon the judicial process as a means of pursuing their policy interests, usually because they are temporarily, or even permanently, disadvantaged in terms of their abilities to attain successfully their goals in the electoral process, within the elected political institutions, or in the bureaucracy" (Cortner 1968, 287). Thus, if they are to achieve their goals, they are almost compelled to resort to litigation. In the wake of the success of the NAACP Legal Defense Fund in striking down segregation, groups representing gays and lesbians, the disabled, religious minorities, women's rights, and so on have sought redress through the courts.

More recently, interest groups have gone to court not because they are politically disadvantaged but because they perceive that they are disadvantaged in the judicial arena. After liberal groups began to use the courts and gained significant victories in the process, conservative interest groups formed in the 1970s to counteract the liberal groups' successes. Epstein (1985) suggests that the idea that only politically disadvantaged groups resort to litigation might have been true in the 1950s and 1960s but no longer holds. She argues that "a wide range of groups regularly resort to the judicial arena because they view the courts as just another political battlefield, which they must enter to fight for their goals. Courtrooms, in fact, may no longer be much different from legislative corridors, which often serve as arenas for competing group interests" (148).

In *The Rise of the Conservative Legal Movement*, Steven Teles (2010) argues that starting in the 1970s conservatives learned that electoral victory did not easily convert into a reversal of major liberal policies, especially in the law. Conservative foundations and groups built a network designed to dislodge liberalism from law schools and professional networks. Overall he finds that rather than pursuing a grand master strategy, the conservative legal movement learned from trial and error.

In contemporary America, litigation is part of a group's policy strategy and its efforts to maintain its membership and is frequently related to its financial resources (Solberg and Waltenburg 2006). In the view of many groups, it is better to have litigated and lost than never to have litigated at all. Indeed, interest groups are increasingly litigating in state courts as well as before federal judges (Kuersten and Songer 1994). Thus, powerful groups go to court to enforce gains won politically in other branches of government (Olson 1990). Even political parties have used the courts as a means to advance their agendas (Gillman 2002). Interest group litigation is not unique to America, either. A study of Canada's supreme court examines the role of interest groups there in gaining access to the justice system (Brodie 2002).

Litigation over the definition of *obscenity* illustrates the involvement of interest groups in important public policy matters. Libertarian groups such as the American Civil Liberties Union have filed lawsuits aimed at protecting First Amendment freedoms of speech and press. At the same time, conservative groups, including Citizens for Decency Through Law and Morality in Media, have filed lawsuits to restrict the dissemination of sexually explicit works (Kobylka 1991).

Exhibit 7.1 provides a partial listing of some of the more prominent interest groups that have filed suit in court to advance their group objectives. Just because

EXHIBIT 7.1 **Interest Groups That Often Appear Before the Supreme Court**

■ *Broad-Based/Liberal*

    American Association of University Women: www.aauw.org
    American Civil Liberties Union (ACLU): www.aclu.org
    Americans for Democratic Action: www.adaction.org
    Center for Constitutional Rights: www.ccr-ny.org
    Common Cause: www.commoncause.org
    League of Women Voters: www.lwv.org

■ *Broad-Based/Conservative*

    American Conservative Union: www.conservative.org

■ *Liberal Public Interest Law Firms*

    Public Citizen Litigation Group: www.citizen.org

■ *Conservative Public Interest Law Firms*

    Mountain States Legal Foundation: www.mountainstateslegal.org
    Pacific Legal Foundation: www.pacificlegal.org

■ *Business*

    Chamber of Commerce: www.uschamber.com
    National Association of Manufacturers: www.nam.org
    National Right to Work Legal Defense Foundation: www.nrtw.org/b/b_prime.htm

■ *Union*

    American Federation of Labor/Congress of Industrial Organizations (AFL/CIO): www.aflcio.org
    Consumer Center for the Study of Responsive Law: www.csrl.org

■ *Civil Rights*

    National Association for the Advancement of Colored People (NAACP): www.naacp.org
    National Urban League: www.nul.org
    Southern Poverty Law Center: www.splcenter.org

■ *Women*

    Human Rights for Women: www.hrw.org/women
    Legal Momentum: www.legalmomentum.org
    National Council of Negro Women: www.ncnw.org
    National Organization for Women (NOW): www.now.org

■ *Abortion/Pro-Choice*

    NARAL Pro-Choice America: www.naral.org
    Planned Parenthood Federation of America: www.plannedparenthood.org

■ *Abortion/Pro-Life*

    Americans United for Life: www.unitedforlife.org
    National Right to Life Committee: www.nrlc.org
    U.S. Conference of Catholic Bishops: www.nccbuscc.org

■ *Environment*

    Audubon Society: www.audubon.org
    Sierra Club: www.sierraclub.org

(continued)

- *Free Speech*

  American Booksellers Association: www.bookweb.org
  American Decency Association: www.americandecency.org
  Association of American Publishers: www.publishers.org
  Morality in Media: www.moralityinmedia.org

- *Religion*

  American Jewish Congress: www.ajcongress.org
  Americans United for Separation of Church and State: www.au.org
  Anti-Defamation League of B'nai B'rith: www.adl.org
  Baptist Church: www.abc-usa.org
  Jehovah's Witnesses: www.watchtower.org
  Presbyterian Church (USA): www.pcusa.org

- *Crime*

  Mothers Against Drunk Driving (MADD): www.madd.org
  National Rifle Association: www.nra.org

- *Legal*

  American Association for Justice: http://www.justice.org
  American Bar Association: www.abanet.org
  American Judicature Society: www.ajs.org
  National Bar Association: www.nationalbar.org

- *Native American Tribes*

  Navajo Tribe: www.navajo.org
  Ute Tribe: www.utemountainute.com

Source: Adapted from Gregory Caldeira and John Wright, "Amici Curiae Before the Supreme Court: Who Participates, When and How Much?" *Journal of Politics* 52 (1990): 782–806.

a group files suit in court, however, doesn't mean it will win. Indeed, a study of federal courts concluded that interest groups were no more successful than individuals (Epstein and Rowland 1991).

Interest Group Resources

Given that legal battles can be quite lengthy, interest groups require resources. Five resources appear to be critical in successful efforts to pursue strategies through litigation (Epstein 1985). The first, of course, is money. The amount of *money* an organization allots to litigation affects the strategies employed, the kinds of issues pursued, and the chances of success. Groups sponsoring litigation, for instance, require more money than those whose involvement is limited solely to filing amicus curiae briefs (Epstein 1985). The second resource is *support* by other organizations. Interest groups attempt to gain the support of other, like-minded private interest groups as well as the federal government. Federal government support (discussed in Chapter 14) also contributes markedly to success at the Supreme Court level. A third resource is *longevity* (Cortner 1988). Precedent building, the essence of interest group activity, is best achieved by the ability to bring a number of lawsuits over time. Closely related to longevity is *expert legal staff*. A group's recruitment of lawyers who are committed to the organization's goals and well versed in the law can be crucial to its success. Expert legal staff allows a group to keep abreast of ongoing case law and select appropriate cases for group intervention. A final resource is *extralegal publicity*. The NAACP Legal Defense Fund, for example, inundated law reviews with articles presenting constitutional justification for its cause. Conservative interest groups have been known to use more flamboyant lobbying devices, including the publication of their own books and monographs, although those are seldom cited by the justices.

Interest Group Strategies

In pursuit of their political, social, and economic interests through litigation, interest groups employ four principal strategies: direct sponsorship, the use of amicus curiae briefs, the filing of class action lawsuits, and attempts to influence judicial nominations.

Direct Sponsorship Interest groups prefer direct sponsorship of cases from the trial court level all the way through appeal. By providing litigants with attorneys early in the case, an interest group can shape the trial record to focus on issues of particular concern to the organization. And, by filing multiple cases raising the same or closely related issues in different courts, the organization can increase the likelihood of having a "good" case available for appeal (Wasby 1993). A recent example of direct sponsorship of litigation centers on the Right to Bear Arms (See Case Close-Up: *District of Columbia v. Heller* and the right to bear arms).

Part of the NAACP's overall success has been its ability to select appropriate test cases. In *For Caucasians Only* (1959), Clement Vose detailed how the NAACP Legal Defense Fund developed and implemented a litigation strategy to persuade the Supreme Court that government enforcement of racially restrictive covenants was unconstitutional. But litigation for social change is far from completely planned, and interest groups are not always in complete control. In studying civil rights litigation, for example, Stephen Wasby (1985) found that numerous factors affected both the planning and the execution of a coordinated campaign to use the courts. Similarly, the Legal Services Corporation was remarkably successful before the Supreme Court, even though the organization was highly disorganized and attorneys typically advanced whatever claims their clients happened to raise (Lawrence 1990).

Amicus Curiae Briefs One of the most visible ways that groups participate in the judicial system is through the **amicus curiae** (friend of the court) brief. A group that is not a direct party to a lawsuit may make its views known to the court by filing an amicus curiae brief. That happens most often when appellate courts are hearing arguments on policy-oriented lawsuits. Such legal arguments often adopt a different perspective or argue positions the principal litigants do not wish to emphasize. Thus, amicus briefs present the court with a range of viewpoints about the legal issues raised in the case.

Amicus is a less costly but also less effective strategy than sponsorship of test cases, because the interest group is not able to frame the issue before the court. Amicus activity does allow interest groups to publicly express their views, however—a strategy increasingly being used. A longitudinal study of interest groups' use of amicus curiae revealed that they participated in 53 percent of the noncommercial cases decided by

CASE CLOSE-UP

■ *District of Columbia v. Heller* (2008)
The Right to Bear Arms

Few provisions of the Constitution have engendered as much fiery political rhetoric (Spitzer 2012) and conflicting legal analysis (Chapter 2) as the Second Amendment which reads:

> A well regulated Militia being necessary to the security of a free State, the right of the people to keep and bear Arms shall not be infringed.

The Supreme Court had seemingly settled upon the meaning of these somewhat archaic words in 1939. Jack Miller drove from Oklahoma to Arkansas with a sawed-off shot gun in his possession. The reason for the trip remains unclear but one suspects that his purpose was not a peaceful one. Miller was arrested and charged with violating the National Firearms Acts but was released when the U.S. District Court ruled the federal law violated the Second Amendment and an appeal followed.

Writing for a unanimous court Justice James McReynolds (a jurist noted for his conservative views) explored the history of the Second Amendment, emphasizing that the drafters inserted the phrase "well regulated Militia" very purposefully. Noting that the sentiment at the time opposed a standing army, the Court concluded that the right to bear arms applied only to the militia (roughly today's national guard) and not to individual citizens.

Through the years guns rights advocates have alternatively ignored the Miller decision or denounced it as wrong. The leader of this movement has been the National Rifle Association, one of the most powerful interest groups in the nation. In 1964, for example, it financed a number of Republics who defeated Democratic Congressmen who had voted for gun control and helped usher in the Republic majority in Congress. Just as importantly the NRA, and associated groups, have won the battle of public opinion—a solid majority of Americans believe that the right to bear arms is an individual, not a collective right.

Even though a number of law review articles (many encouraged by gun rights groups) argued that *Miller* was wrong, litigating the matter seemed fruitless until it was revived in an arena where it counts the most—the federal courts of appeals. In a convoluted domestic violence case that resulted in a federal prosecution for illegal possession of a weapon, the Fifth Circuit seemed to agree that the Second Amendment created an individual right to bear arms but then upheld the conviction on different grounds (*U.S. v Emerson* 2001).

Sensing that the timing was now right, a loosely associated group of lawyers working with the Institute of Justice at the Cato Institute decided that now was the time to mount a direct legal challenge to *Miller*. The lawyers wanted a diverse range of sympathetic plaintiffs, people who were gun enthusiasts but not gun nuts. Dozens of names were discussed and eventually six were chosen. Finding multiple plaintiffs in public policy litigation like this is typical because lawyers never know when one or more plaintiffs will pull out thus threatening standing to sue requirements. Indeed by the time the case reached the Supreme Court, Dick Heller was the only one remaining (Doherty 2008). Five years later the original filing resulted in a major Supreme Court decision.

Justice Scalia's majority opinion in *District of Columbia v Heller* has all the hallmarks of his distinctive linguistic approach to interpreting the constitution. Scalia limits the *Miller* case as interpreting the type of weapon that can be legislatively regulated and not the constitutional right to bear arms. Heller holds that the Second Amendment protects an individual right to possess a firearm, reasoning that the clause about the militia was merely prefatory and therefore did not limit the operative clause. Justice Stevens's dissent stresses that for over 70 years hundreds of judges have relied upon *Miller* as precedent and it indeed finds the Second Amendment is all about the militia and not individual rights.

The Heller decision attracted significant interest group activity. Sixteen groups filed amici briefs in favor of upholding DCs gun control law and approximately four times that many filed in support of Heller. What is particularly interesting is that in the opinion itself, both sides make extensive reference to these briefs.

Heller was a path breaking decision but it was also limited because it only applied to the federal government and federal enclaves like Washington, DC. The bigger question was whether it applied to the states as well. Two interest groups, the Illinois State Rifle Association and the Second Amendment Foundation were

(continued)

determined to find out. As in Heller, the interest groups sought to carefully pick their plaintiffs. This time the target was Chicago's strict hand gun laws. Alan Gura, who had successfully argued *Heller*, spread the word that he was looking for litigants in Chicago. Gura interviewed a number of residents by phone, email and finally in person. He settled on Otis McDonald as the public face of gun rights (Ham 2010). As instructed, McDonald, a 76-year-old African-American resident of Chicago's south side, walked into a police station and applied for a permit to carry a .22 caliber Beretta for self-protection. When his request was denied the lawsuit was in motion (Mastony 2010). In the opinion of the court, Justice Alito virtually awards McDonald the good housekeeping seal of approval, writing that McDonald "lives in a high-crime neighborhood.... He is a community activist and his efforts to improve his neighborhood have subjected him to violent threats from drug dealers." *McDonald v. Chicago* held that indeed that the Second Amendment is fully applicable to the states.

Conclusion

In *Heller* and *McDonald* guns rights groups like the NRA gained significant legal victories but it remains to be seen whether the victories are more symbolic than substantive. Heller stresses that like most rights, the Second Amendment right to bear arms is not unlimited. Indeed, Scalia boldly stated, "We are aware of the problem of handgun violence in this county, and we take seriously the concerns raised by the many amici who believe the prohibition of handgun ownerships is a solution." In this context, writing his last opinion before he retired at 90, Justice Stevens predicted an avalanche of lawsuits. Hundreds of lawsuits have been filed across the nation testing the limits of these Second Amendment cases. In particular the legal battles are over what types of weapons governments can reasonably restrict.

The litigation over the right to bear arms also underscores the importance of understanding the judiciary within the context of the other branches of government. The meaning of this symbolic victory will be determined in no small measure by the actions or inactions of legislatures and city councils across the nation in passing gun control legislation. In turn the effectiveness of these laws will be determined by how vigorously or weakly governors and mayors enforce new legislation. In short, litigation in court must be viewed not as an end in and of itself but as part of an ongoing governmental process involving all branches of government.

Litigation over the meaning of the Second Amendment has a lot in common with other major policy areas discussed in this book, including immigration policy, health care, same-sex marriages, medical marijuana, and so on—all involve extensive interest group activity.

the Supreme Court between 1970 and 1980 (O'Connor and Epstein 1982). Amicus activity by states is also becoming increasingly common (Morris 1987). Thus, the Supreme Court is remarkably accessible to a wide array of interest groups. Participation is not restricted to prestigious individuals, large private law firms, major corporations, or governments. On the contrary, during one term, more than 40 percent of the amicus briefs were filed by citizen groups, businesses, unions, trade groups, or professional associations (Caldeira and Wright 1990), and recent research shows that amicus curiae briefs do influence the thinking of the Supreme Court justices (Collins 2007).

Class Actions   A **class action** is a lawsuit brought by a person or an interest group on behalf of all people similarly situated. Thus, in a class action lawsuit, the plaintiff claims to represent the interests of many people who are in the same social, political, or economic situation, even though they are not individually named in the lawsuit. The plaintiff, therefore, seeks redress not just for himself or herself but also for all members of the group or class (Garth 1992). The class action suit reflects our growing awareness that many important aspects of citizens' lives are dominated by large groups and large organizations. Thus, class action lawsuits illustrate the proliferation of well-organized groups in our society.

Class actions figure prominently in policy-oriented public lawsuits filed by interest groups. The most widely known example is *Brown v. Board of Education* (1954).

Oliver Brown sought desegregation of the local school system not only for his daughter but also for all other minority children in the school district. Beyond the area of civil rights, class action lawsuits are typically filed in matters such as gender discrimination and sexual harassment.

Class action lawsuits are also used in policy-oriented private lawsuits. The increasing complexity and urbanization of modern American society have magnified tremendously the importance of the class action as a procedural device for resolving monetary disputes that affect many people (Hensler et al. 2000). Class action makes litigation economically feasible in situations where a fragmented many have suffered a small injury. For example, if each member of the class has suffered a minor injury (say, a loss of $50 to $100), the cost of hiring a lawyer and going to court is too great to justify individual lawsuits. But, by consolidating those claims in one class action lawsuit, an attorney has a sufficient stake to make the lawsuit economically feasible and perhaps even profitable. In effect, an entrepreneurial lawyer can create a class solely for the purpose of litigation (Mather 1991). Thus, class action suits have been used in product liability cases to recover damages for defectively manufactured goods and by stockholders suing corporations for manipulating the price of stocks. Some of these cases make headlines because of the dollar amounts. One of the largest product liability settlements in U.S. history was a $4.25 billion pact between women and breast implant manufacturers. In another case, the A. H. Robins Company created a $2.3 billion trust fund for women who were injured through the use of the Dalkon Shield, an intrauterine device (IUD) manufactured and sold by the company (Sobol 1991).

Class action lawsuits have become part of the lightning-rod category of what some refer to as "frivolous lawsuits." (Chapter 10). Normally, this category is also meant to include medical malpractice lawsuits. Republicans have been criticizing the plaintiffs and especially the lawyers in these cases for their efforts to win multimillion-dollar awards in state courts for members of class action lawsuits. In 2005, Republicans succeeded in passing federal legislation that requires certain class action lawsuits to be heard in federal court—those seeking $5 million in damages and in which less than 30 percent of the plaintiffs are from one state. Republicans believe that federal juries will be less likely than state juries to award multimillion-dollar judgments such as those against the tobacco companies.

Judicial Nominations   Beyond the advocacy of cases in court, another venue open for interest group influence in the legal system is judicial nominations. There are many reasons interest groups would like to aid their most-preferred judges in (or at a minimum prevent their least preferred judges from) achieving appointment or election to the bench. At the appellate level, where judges are likely to hear policy-oriented lawsuits and may have some discretion over the court's docket, it is advantageous to interest groups to have judges who share their philosophical orientation. At the trial level, judges decide cases involving dollar amounts large and small—so interest groups spend money to influence voters to elect lawyers who are pro-plaintiff or pro-defendant.

In the same way that interest groups work to influence the political agenda of legislatures and executives, they are turning their attention to courts. Federal court nominations by the president that require confirmation by the Senate have become increasingly contentious, visible, and salient, and, as they have done so, interest groups have stepped up their efforts to influence who is appointed (Caldeira, Hojnacki, and Wright 2000; Caldeira and Wright 1998; Maltese 1995).

INTEREST GROUP LITIGATION AND THE OIL SPILL

Interest groups often go to court, we have argued, but the BP oil spill suggests that at times they are not always successful. Environmental interest groups, for example were unsuccessful in trying to intervene as third-party claimants with a right to be at the plaintiffs table during trial. Environmental groups such as Defenders of Wildlife and the Center for Biological Diversity filed suit under the Clean Water Act and other federal legislation but the federal judge dismissed their claims holding that plaintiffs must show that they have suffered legal injuries and they had not (Mowbray June 17, 2011).

Interest groups representing the oil and natural gas were only somewhat more successful. A month after the oil started leaking from the Deepwater Horizon well, the Obama administration issued a moratorium on drilling for oil in the Gulf of Mexico in more than 500 feet of water. (The Deepwater Horizon was drilling in about 5,000 feet). The economic consequences of this moratorium were potentially huge, affecting about 30 working rigs, the potential layoff of thousands of off-shore oil workers, and devastating the livelihood of others who depend on income from these workers. A number of businesses working in the oil industry quickly filed suit in federal district court but most of the legal work was done by industry trade associations such as the Offshore Marine Service Association, representing companies that provide boats and equipment to the offshore drilling industry. U.S. District Judge Feldman ordered the moratorium stopped but the ruling had little impact. The Department of the Interior argued that time was needed to issue new safety regulations and judge the rigs accordingly. Over a year later drilling was allowed to resume in the Gulf of Mexico but there was little indication that the lawsuit had sped up the permitting process.

THE MEDIA AND THE LEGAL SYSTEM

On December 11, 2000, the Supreme Court made history when it released an audiotape of oral arguments in *Bush v. Gore* (2000) at the conclusion of the attorneys' presentations. Media outlets across the country replayed some or all of the tape immediately. The Court has done this again with several other cases, including *Gratz v. Bollinger* (a 2003 case dealing with affirmative action policies at the University of Michigan) and *Ayotte v. Planned Parenthood of Northern New England* (a 2005 case dealing with abortion restrictions for minors). Although the Court's policy on releasing same-day audio appears to be relaxing, the Court remains steadfast in its opposition to broadcasting live its cases on television and radio.

The press plays an important role in shaping what citizens know about their government, the judiciary included (Yanus 2009). In the words of Linda Greenhouse (1996) the veteran Supreme Court reporter for the *New York Times*, "...[J]udges for the most part, speak only through their opinions, which are difficult for the ordinary citizen to obtain and understand." Since judges (unlike other governmental officials) almost never hold press conferences, and live media coverage of courts is often not allowed, press coverage of what courts do, and now they do, is limited. This void, though, is partially filled by the entertainment media. More people get their information about how the legal system operates from watching crime dramas like *Law and Order* or movies like *Chicago* than reading the morning paper or tuning into the nightly news. Which is why this book includes the Law and Popular Culture feature.

The Historical Relationship

The relationship between the media and the courts has always been an important one. Print journalists have been covering the legal system since American courts were created: The First Amendment's protection of the press and the Sixth Amendment's protection of public access to trials interacted to guarantee press coverage of courtroom proceedings (Haltom 1998). Wide access for print journalists was established early in the nation's history for all but the most extenuating circumstances and has been protected by numerous Supreme Court cases (Bunker 1997). Currently, many local newspapers assign a reporter to cover the local courthouse, and Supreme Court decisions have always been the focus of a great deal of media coverage (Slotnick and Segal 1998). Yet controversy remains about the appropriate balance between (1) ensuring free and open access to court activities and (2) guaranteeing that the parties involved get a fair trial without turning the proceedings into a circus.

Televised Coverage

Each time a new medium arrives, these debates are replayed. When CourtTV aired its first case—*Florida v. Robert Scott Hill*, on July 1, 1991—a debate about the impact of cameras in the courtroom ensued (discussed in Chapter 12). Would attorneys perform for the audience? Would judges behave differently? Today, trials are televised daily (even though CourtTV is no longer in business). This coverage relies on public access to courtrooms, but television cameras in the courtroom have not always been welcome (Cohn and Dow 2002). The debate over how much access to give cameras has largely been played out in the state courts, and there are now rules that permit, with varying levels of restrictions, cameras and audiotaping devices in state courts across the country. The Radio-Television News Directors Association offers a state-by-state guide regarding cameras in the courtroom (http://www.rtnda.org/pages/media_items/cameras-in-the-court-a-state-by-state-guide55.php).

Federal courts and the Supreme Court, however, continue to enforce a general ban on cameras and audiotaping devices, though individual courts are permitted to lift that. One reason that some courts are reluctant to grant access to trials is the fear that such coverage will result in even greater efforts by lawyers to try their cases in the media. (See Law and Popular Culture: *Chicago*.) But we should not confuse the newness of some forms of modern media with the concept of spinning the media. *Spinning the Law: Trying Cases in the Courts of Public Opinion*, argues that spinning the law has occurring since before we became a nation. Kendall Coffey, a lawyer who has handled a number of high profile cases, observes that the number of celebrated trials

LAW AND POPULAR CULTURE

■ *Chicago* (2002)

In an effort to remake the image of his client Roxy Hart (played by Renee Zellweger), lawyer Billy Flynn (played by Richard Gere) holds a press conference. He starts by calling on an obviously friendly reporter from a dry newspaper, Mary Sunshine, who poses a predictably softball question: "Do you have any advice for young girls seeking to avoid a life of jazz and drink?" "Absolutely," Flynn responds. "Mrs. Hart feels it was the tragic combination of liquor and jazz which led to the downfall." And then he launches into a song called the "Press Conference Rag," intended to influence how his client's story gets told.

The film *Chicago* (2002), based on the musical of the same name, is set during the Roaring Twenties, when jazz, illegal liquor, sin, and the city of Chicago seemed synonymous. What is somewhat unusual is that it focuses on women killing men, a topic not typically portrayed in works of fiction. What is not unusual, however, is how lawyers try to manipulate the press to influence judges and juries. From the nation's beginning, defendants have hired lawyers to improve their public standing, hoping that will translate into favorable treatment by the criminal justice system.

The fictional, media-savvy Billy Flynn uses the press in an effort to complete an extreme makeover of his client Roxy Hart, who suffered from very serious image problems. (She murdered her lover and then tried to have her husband take the fall.) Real-life celebrity lawyers, such as Mark Geragos, employ similar strategies for clients such as Michael Jackson and Scott Peterson, who also need extreme makeovers of their public images. The pop star Michael Jackson was charged with sexually molesting several young boys and then paying their families in a cover-up. Scott Peterson was accused of murdering his pregnant wife and unborn child and then concocting an elaborate cover-up story.

Formal press conferences and informal news leaks played key roles during the prosecutions of Peterson and Jackson. In an earlier era, lawyers often preferred to keep their clients and their legal woes out of the public eye. But, today, many lawyers seem to delight in calling public attention to their clients and their legal peccadilloes. Not surprisingly, high-profile lawyers are accused of playing to the cameras (and reporters) both inside and outside the courtroom. Indeed, an assistant district attorney suggested,

"It looks like Geragos is trying to manipulate the media and the jury and he's been pretty good at it" (CBS News 2004). At times, though, such complaints are little more than sour grapes; after all, police and prosecutors regularly use the media to project a negative image of defendants.

Trials are an obvious source of interest for journalists because they represent the classic "whodunit." Thus, it is not surprising that the press follow some trials closely. Most trials are too mundane to evoke much public interest, but the legal woes of Peterson and Jackson proved to be major news events that often displaced more serious material about the war in Iraq and the presidential election. What has changed over time is the advent of cable news channels, which provide twenty-four-hour coverage of celebrity trials. The challenge for the media is how to cover those trials when a legal team is trying to manipulate the press. In turn, the growth of electronic media has made the reporters as much of the story as the lawyers (and their clients). The O. J. Simpson trial, for example, made legal reporter Greta Van Susteren a household name in the same way the Peterson and Jackson trials contributed to Nancy Grace's rise to fame.

It is unclear whether efforts by celebrity lawyers such as Mark Geragos and Johnny Cochran (O. J. Simpson's lead attorney, now deceased) ultimately matter to either the jury or the rest of the public. Peterson was convicted of murder and sentenced to death (Chapter 9). Jackson, on the other hand, was acquitted (although Geragos had left the Jackson defense team before trial). One thing that is clear, though, is that the media appear more than willing to continue to cover these trials and the actions of the celebrity attorneys. Whether that is good for the legal system or for justice is a question that remains unanswered. As we will discuss in Chapter 12, prejudicial pretrial publicity is a major concern in high-profile cases.

What do you think? Do the media have an obligation to ignore events concocted by lawyers simply to put a favorable spin on their clients' situations? Should the media use the First Amendment to justify around-the-clock coverage of celebrity trials? How could you study whether television coverage of these trials has an influence on the trial or the verdict? In what ways do modern celebrity attorneys such as Mark Geragos resemble the fictionalized Billy Flynn in *Chicago*?

has been increasing because the variety of media outlets has been also increasing. And the verdict about the impact of this spinning is mixed.

New Uses for the Internet

The popularity of the Internet has inspired some courts to offer educational materials that supplement traditional media coverage. Not content to remain dependent on journalists for the portrayal of their activities, the courts themselves complement other Internet sites to increase public understanding of and ability to use the legal system. At the Indiana courts' educational website (http://www.in.gov/judiciary/education), the public can learn about the Indiana court structure and the history of Indiana courts, read about the justices, and even listen to live audiostreaming of Indiana Supreme Court oral arguments. Such direct educational activities by the courts, combined with live coverage of trial proceedings and oral arguments in appellate cases, may mollify critics of the way the legal system is covered by both the print and the visual media. Other websites, such as CourtTV's Crime Library (http://www.crimelibrary.com), profile the criminal justice system, and sites such as http://www.findlaw.com aim to provide general legal education about a variety of legal issues.

The Internet is also being used to mobilize the legal system—both by providing rapid, broad dissemination of legal information and by allowing attorneys and clients to gain greater access to others in similar situations. For instance, interest groups and attorneys developing class action lawsuits (who previously had to rely on print or television to get their message out) can now use the Internet to locate and correspond directly with similarly motivated people around the world.

Social Media and the Judicial Process

Social Media has changed how people communicate and these changes have affected the judicial process as well. Culled from recent headlines here are some important (and not so important) examples.

- Cameras on cell phones are used to photograph crimes in progress helping police make arrests and introduced as evidence during trial.
- Lawyers are using the Internet and social networking to seek clients (Koppel 2010).
- Florida judicial candidates cannot use personal Facebook pages to solicit campaign funds (but they can use a Facebook by their election committee) (Lipman 2010).
- As Facebook has become a tool for cheating spouses, matrimonial lawyers are increasingly using such evidence during divorce proceedings (CNN July 14, 2010).
- E-mails often prove powerful evidence during trials involving allegations of racial and gender discrimination in firing. They also can provide juicy details in sexual harassment cases.
- Jurors doing Internet research and messaging during trial are resulting in mistrials (Schwartz 2010).

In short, the judicial process has adapted to changes in mass communication, whether it be radio, television, the Internet, or Facebook.

CONCLUSION

Although courts are passive governmental institutions, they apparently have a great deal to do. Every year, individuals and businesses, interest groups, and the government file over 100 million cases, mostly in state courts. By filing, litigants mobilize the law, choosing to take their disputes to judges rather than rely on other third parties. This chapter emphasized that court cases vary tremendously: The parties vary; the types of decisions judges must make vary. Some cases are so routine that judges have little, if anything, to do; other cases call on the court to exercise procedural adjudication, decisional adjudication, or diagnostic adjudication.

Finally, lawsuits vary in the scope of the conflict: Traditional lawsuits involve bilateral disputes, and policy-oriented lawsuits challenge existing practices of government or industry. As is shown in subsequent chapters, the differences between cases affect their flow through the trial courts. In criminal filings, questions about the defendant's guilt provoke different issues than do questions about sentencing. In civil filings, small claims, divorces, and personal injury lawsuits are processed very differently because they represent different underlying dynamics.

CRITICAL THINKING QUESTIONS

1. Can you think of any legal controversies that pit organized interests against each other?

2. What are the implications of having two core institutions of law—courts and legislatures—at odds with each other?

3. Why would the legislative branch want to preempt certain types of litigation?

Search Terms

advocacy group
amicus curiae

class action lawsuits
interest group

Useful URLs

http://www.classaction.com
   At this reference site, you can ask questions about class action lawsuits.

http://www.lawsource.com/also/usa.cgi?usb
   American Law Sources On-line: U.S. Courts Amicus Curiae Briefs

http://www.rtnda.org/pages/media_items/cameras-in-the-court-a-state-by-state-guide55.php
   Radio-Television News Directors Association offers a state-by-state guide regarding cameras in the courtroom.

http://www.peopleslawyer.net/smallclaims/homepage.html
   The People's Lawyer: How to Sue in Small Claims Court

http://www.worldadvocacy.com
   World Advocacy presents a list of advocacy groups around the world.

REFERENCES

Abrams, Roger I. 2000. *The Money Pitch: Baseball Free Agency and Salary Arbitration*. Philadelphia: Temple University Press.

"At Least 500 People Died in Riots Between Muslims and Christians in Nigeria." 2001. *Christianity Today*, October 22.

Barker, Lucius, and Twiley Barker. 1994. *Civil Liberties and the Constitution*. 7th ed. Englewood Cliffs, N.J.: Prentice Hall.

BBC. 2011. "Nigeria Election: Muammadu Buhari's CPC goes to Court." May 9.

Black, Donald. 1973. "The Mobilization of the Law." *Journal of Legal Studies* 2: 125–149.

Black, Donald, and M. P. Baumgartner. 1983. "Toward a Theory of the Third Party." In *Empirical Theories About Courts*, edited by Keith Boyum and Lynn Mather. New York: Longman.

Brady Center to Prevent Gun Violence http://www.bradycenter.org

Brodie, Ian. 2002. *Friends of the Court: The Privileging of Interest Group Litigants in Canada*. Albany: State University of New York Press.

Bunker, Matthew D. 1997. *Justice and the Media: Reconciling Fair Trials and a Free Press*. Englewood Cliffs, N.J.: Lawrence Erlbaum.

Caldeira, Gregory, and John Wright. 1990. "Amici Curiae Before the Supreme Court: Who Participates, When and How Much?" *Journal of Politics* 52: 782–806.

———. 1998. "Lobbying for Justice: Organized Interests, Supreme Court Nominations, and the United States Senate." *American Journal of Political Science* 42: 499–523.

Caldeira, Gregory A., Marie Hojnacki, and John R. Wright. 2000. "The Lobbying Activities of Organized Interests in Federal Judicial Nominations." *Journal of Politics* 62: 51–69.

CBS News. 2004. "Scott Practiced Testifying." Available online at http://www.cbsnews.com/stories/2004/10/22/national/main650766.shtml. Retrieved November 1, 2004.

Central Intelligence Agency. 2008. *The World Factbook*. Available online at *https://www.cia.gov/library/publications/the-world-factbook/geos/ni.html*. Retrieved September 28, 2008.

Chayes, Abram. 1976. "The Role of the Judge in Public Law Litigation." *Harvard Law Review* 89: 1281–1316.

CNN July 14, 2010. "Is Facebook becoming a 'tool' for cheating spouses?"

Coffey, Kendall. 2011. *Spinning the Law: Trying Cases in the Court of Public Opinion*. Amherst, New York: Prometheus Books.

Cohn, Marjorie, and David Dow. 2002. *Cameras in the Courtroom: Television and the Pursuit of Justice*. Lanham, Md.: Rowman & Littlefield.

Collins, Paul M., Jr. 2007. "Lobbyists Before the U.S. Supreme Court: Investigating the Influence of Amicus Curiae Briefs." *Political Research Quarterly* 60(1): 55–70.

Cooley, John. 1986. "Arbitration vs. Mediation—Explaining the Differences." *Judicature* 69: 263–269.

Cooper, Phillip. 1988. *Hard Judicial Choices: Federal District Court Judges and State and Local Officials*. New York: Oxford University Press.

Cortner, Richard. 1968. "Strategies and Tactics of Litigants in Constitutional Cases." *Journal of Public Law* 17: 287–307.

———. 1988. *A Mob Intent on Death: The NAACP and the Arkansas Riot Cases*. Middletown, Conn.: Wesleyan University Press.

Epp, Charles. 2009. *Making Rights Real: Activists, Bureaucrats, and the Creation of the Legalistic State*. Chicago: University of Chicago Press.

Epstein, Lee. 1985. *Conservatives in Court*. Knoxville: University of Tennessee Press.

Epstein, Lee, and C. K. Rowland. 1991. "Debunking the Myth of Interest Group Invincibility in the Courts." *American Political Science Review* 85: 205–217.

Friedman, Lawrence, and Robert Percival. 1976. "A Tale of Two Courts: Litigation in Alameda and San Benito Counties." *Law and Society Review* 10: 267–301.

Galanter, Marc. 1974. "Why the 'Haves' Come Out Ahead: Speculations on the Limits of Legal Change." *Law and Society Review* 9: 97–125.

Gambrell, Jon. 2010. "Rights Group Condemns Nigerian Police as Corrupt." AP August 18.

Garth, Bryant. 1992. "Power and Legal Artifice: The Federal Class Action." *Law and Society Review* 26: 237–272.

George, Tracey, and Lee Epstein. 1991. "Women's Rights Litigation in the 1980s: More of the Same?" *Judicature* 74: 314–321.

Gillman, Howard. 2002. "How Political Parties Can Use the Courts to Advance Their Agendas: Federal Courts in the United States, 1875–1891." *American Political Science Review* 96 (September): 511–524.

Greig, J. Michael. 2005. "Stepping Into the Fray: When Do Mediators Mediate?" *American Journal of Political Science* 49(2): 249–266.

Greenhouse, Linda. 1996. "Telling the Court's Story: Justice and Journalism at the U.S. Supreme Court." *Yale Law Journal* 105: 1537.

Grossman, Joel B., Herbert M. Kritzer, and Stewart Macaulay. 1999. "Do the 'Haves' Still Come Out Ahead?" *Law and Society Review* 33(4): 803–810.

Haltom, William. 1998. *Reporting on the Courts: How the Mass Media Cover Judicial Actions*. Belmont, Calif.: Wadsworth.

Haltom, William, and Michael McCann. 2004. *Distorting the Law: Politics, Media, and the Litigation Explosion.* Chicago: University of Chicago Press.

Ham, Mary. 2010. "Meet Otis McDonald: The Man Behind the SCOTUS Chicago un Case." *The Weekly Standard*. March 2.

Hensler, Deborah R., Nicholas M. Page, Bonita Dombrey-Moore, Beth Giddens, Jennifer Gross, and Erik K. Moller. 2000. *Class Action Dilemmas: Pursuing Public Goals for Private Gain*. Santa Monica, Calif.: RAND Institute for Civil Justice.

Kerwin, Cornelius, Thomas Henderson, and Carl Baar. 1986. "Adjudicatory Processes and the Organization of Trial Courts." *Judicature* 70: 99–106.

Kobylka, Joseph. 1991. *The Politics of Obscenity: Group Litigation in a Time of Legal Change*. New York: Greenwood.

Koppel. Nathan. 2010. "Using Social Networking as Legal Tool." *Wall Street Journal* June 15.

Kritzer, Herbert M., and Susan Silbey. 2003. *In Litigation Do the "Haves" Still Come Out Ahead?* Stanford, Calif.: Stanford University Press.

Kuersten, Ashlyn, and Donald Songer. 1994. "Political Disadvantage Theory and Amicus Curiae Participation in Southern State Supreme Courts." Paper presented at the annual meeting of the Southern Political Science Association, Atlanta, November.

Kydd, Andrew H. 2006. "When Can Mediators Build Trust?" *American Political Science Review* 100(3): 449–462.

Lawrence, Susan. 1990. *The Poor in Court: The Legal Services Program and Supreme Court Decision Making*. Princeton, N.J.: Princeton University Press.

Lipman, Eric. 2010. "Federal Judicial Candidates Can't Solicit Donations on Personal Facebook Pages" Law.com Legal Blog Watch August 4, 2010.

Lewis, Dan, Edward Goetz, Mark Schoenfield, Andrew Gordon, and Eugene Griffin. 1984. "The Negotiation of Involuntary Civil Commitment." *Law and Society Review* 18: 629–650.

Maltese, John Anthony. 1995. *The Selling of Supreme Court Nominees*. Baltimore: Johns Hopkins University Press.

Marshall, Anna-Maria. 1998. "Closing the Gaps: Plaintiffs in Pivotal Sexual Harassment Cases." *Law and Social Inquiry* 23(4): 761–793.

Mastony, Colleen. 2010. "The Public Face of Gun Rights." *Chicago Tribune*. January 30.

Mather, Lynn. 1991. "Policy Making in State Trial Courts." In *The American Courts: A Critical Assessment*, edited by John Gates and Charles Johnson. Washington, D. C.: CQ Press.

McDermott, John. 1986. "Arbitration and the Courts." *Justice System Journal* 11: 248–255.

McKenzie, Glenn. 2001. "Gunmen Kill Nigeria's Justice Minister." *New Orleans Times-Picayune*, December 25.

Menkel-Meadow, Carrie. 2003. *Dispute Processing and Conflict Resolution: Theory, Practice and Policy*. Burlington, Vt.: Ashgate/Dartmouth.

Morris, Thomas. 1987. "States Before the U.S. Supreme Court: State Attorneys General as Amicus Curiae." *Judicature* 70: 298–304.

Mowbray, Rebecca. 2011. "Judge Rejects Groups' Claims in Spill." *Times Picayune States Item*. June 17.

National Rifle Association. http://www.nra.org.

O'Connor, Karen. 1980. *Women's Organizations' Use of the Courts*. Lexington, Mass.: D.C. Heath.

O'Connor, Karen, and Lee Epstein. 1982. "Research Note: An Appraisal of Hakman's 'Folklore.'" *Law and Society Review* 16: 701–711.

———. 1984. "The Role of Interest Groups in Supreme Court Policy Formation." In *Public Policy Formation*, edited by Robert Eyestone. Greenwich, Conn.: JAI Press.

Olson, Susan. 1990. "Interest-Group Litigation in Federal District Court: Beyond the Political Disadvantage Theory." *Journal of Politics* 52: 854–882.

Pinello, Daniel R. 2006. *America's Struggle for Same-Sex Marriage*. New York: Cambridge University Press.

Polgreen, Lydia. 2007. "Nigeria Turns from Harsher Side of Islamic Law.' *New York Times* December 1.

Reuters. 2002. "World Fury at Stoning Sentence." August 20.

Rosenberg, Gerald. 1991. *The Hollow Hope: Can Courts Bring About Social Change?* Chicago: University of Chicago Press.

Sarat, Austin. 1989. "Alternatives to Formal Adjudication." In *American Court Systems: Readings in Judicial Process and Behavior*, edited by Sheldon Goldman and Austin Sarat. New York: Longman.

Scheingold, Stuart. 2004. *The Politics of Rights: Lawyers, Public Policy, and Political Change.* Ann Arbor: University of Michigan Press.

Schultz, David A., ed. 1998. *Leveraging the Law: Using the Courts to Achieve Social Change.* New York: Peter Lang.

Schwartz, John. 2010. "As Jurors turn to web, Mistrials are Popping up." *New York Times* March 18, 2009.

Slotnick, Elliot E., and Jennifer A. Segal. 1998. *Television News and the Supreme Court: All the News That's Fit to Air?* New York: Cambridge University Press.

Sobel, Allan. 2001. "An Independent Judiciary Isn't to Be Taken for Granted." *Judicature* 85: 6.

Sobol, Richard. 1991. *Bending the Law: The Story of the Dalkon Shield Bankruptcy.* Chicago: University of Chicago Press.

Solberg, Rorie Spill, and Eric N. Waltenburg. 2006. "Why Do Interest Groups Engage the Judiciary? Policy Wishes and Structural Needs." *Social Science Quarterly* 87(3): 558–572.

Songer, Donald, Ashlyn Kuersten, and Erin Kaheny. 2000. "Why the Haves Don't Always Come Out Ahead: Repeat Players Meet Amici Curiae for the Disadvantaged." *Political Research Quarterly* 53(3): 537–556.

Sorauf, Frank. 1976. *The Wall of Separation: Constitutional Politics of Church and State.* Princeton, N.J.: Princeton University Press.

Spitzer, Robert. 2012. *The Politics of Gun Control*, 5th edition. Washington, DC: CQ Press.

Stewart, Joseph, and Edward Heck. 1983. "The Day-to-Day Activities of Interest Group Lawyers." *Social Science Quarterly* 64: 173–182.

Teles, Steven. 2010. *The Rise of the Conservative Legal Movement: The Battle for Control of the Law.* Princeton, N.J.: Princeton University Press.

Tushnet, Mark V. 2005. *The NAACP's Legal Strategy Against Segregated Education.* Chapel Hill: University of North Carolina Press.

Vose, Clement. 1959. *For Caucasians Only.* Berkeley: University of California Press.

Wasby, Stephen. 1985. "Civil Rights Litigation by Organizations: Constraints and Choices." *Judicature* 68: 337.

———. 1993. *The Supreme Court in the Federal Judicial System.* 4th ed. Chicago: Nelson-Hall.

Yanus, Alixandra. 2009. "Full-Court Press: An Examination of Media Coverage of State Supreme Courts." *Justice System Journal* 30: 180–194.

Yngvesson, Barbara, and Lynn Mather. 1983. "Courts, Moots, and Disputing Process." In *Empirical Theories About Courts*, edited by Keith Boyum and Lynn Mather. New York: Longman.

Zalman, Marvin. 1995. "Is the Law Dead?" Plenary address delivered at the Academy of Criminal Justice Sciences, Boston, March.

Zemans, Frances. 1983. "Legal Mobilization: The Neglected Role of the Law in the Political System." *American Political Science Review* 77: 690–702.

FOR FURTHER READING

Alexander, S. L. 1999. *Covering the Courts: A Handbook for Journalists.* Lanham, Md.: University Press of America.

Browning, John. 2010. "The Online Juror." *Judicature*: 93: 231–235.

Cleary, Edward. 1995. *Beyond the Burning Cross: A Landmark Case of Race, Censorship, and the First Amendment.* New York: Random House.

Davey, Chris, and Karen Salaz. 2010. "Survey Looks at new Media and the Courts." *Judicature* 94:137–138.

Goss, Kristin. 2006. *Disarmed: The Missing Movement for Gun Control in America.* Princeton: Princeton University Press.

Greenberg, Jack. 1994. *Crusaders in the Courts: How a Dedicated Band of Lawyers Fought for the Civil Rights Revolution.* New York: Basic Books.

Hacker, Hans. 2005. *The Culture of Conservative Christian Litigation.* Lanham, Md.: Rowman & Littlefield.

Haynie, Stacia, and Kaitlyn Sill. 2007. "Experienced Advocates and Litigation Outcomes: Repeat Players in the

South African Supreme Court of Appeal." *Political Research Quarterly* 60(3): 443–453.

Iaryczower, Matias, Pablo T. Spiller, and Mariano Tommasi. 2006. "Judicial Lobbying: The Politics of Labor Law Constitutional Interpretation." *American Political Science Review* 100(1): 85–97.

Klarman, Michael. 2007. *Brown v. Board of Education and the Civil Rights Movement.* New York: Oxford University Press.

McCann, Michael. 1994. *Rights at Work: Pay Equity Reform and the Politics of Legal Mobilization.* Chicago: University of Chicago Press.

Peters, C. Scott. 2007. "Getting Attention: The Effect of Legal Mobilization on the U.S. Supreme Courts

Attention to Issues." *Political Research Quarterly* 60: 561–572.

Sauvageau, Florian, David Schneiderman, and David Taras. 2006. *The Last Word: Media Coverage of the Supreme Court of Canada.* Vancouver, BC: University of British Columbia Press.

Teles, Steven. 2010. *The Rise of the Conservative Legal Movement: The Battle for Control of the Law.* Princeton: Princeton University Press.

Young, McGee. 2010. *Developing Interests: Organizational Change and the Politics of Advocacy.* Lawrence: University of Kansas Press.

TRIAL COURTS: THE PRELIMINARY STAGES OF CRIMINAL CASES

Bail bondsman, like this one in Crowley, Louisiana, help control the jail population. Those who can afford to pay the fee will be immediately released from jail while awaiting trial.

David Neubauer

Mike Nifong, candidate for district attorney, proclaimed that he would not allow Durham to become known for "a bunch of lacrosse players from Duke raping a black girl." After a 30-year career as an assistant prosecutor in Durham County, North Carolina, Nifong was running for election as district attorney in his own right, and his comments fanned the fires of what quickly became a sensational national case. Following a party thrown by the Duke lacrosse team, three team members were accused of sexually assaulting a woman who had been hired as a stripper. Nifong would win the election, but the charges would eventually be dismissed for lack of evidence and Nifong himself would be disbarred.

Although the Duke lacrosse sexual assault case was highly unusual, it illustrates several key factors about the criminal justice system. One is the tremendous power of the district attorney, who, more so than the judge, jury, or defense attorney, holds the keys to justice in his (or her) hands. Another is the key importance of the early stages of a criminal case—defendants are much more likely to be cleared of criminal charges during these early stages than during the later stages of trial. Finally, the Duke lacrosse case highlights the fact that frequently a court case takes center stage in the nation's debate over some of the most volatile domestic issues facing the country—race, class, and gender.

This chapter discusses the early stages of a criminal case, focusing on when and why case attrition occurs—beginning with an arrest and proceeding through the initial appearance, the setting of bail, the prosecutorial screening, the preliminary hearing, the grand jury review, and the exclusionary rule. The decisions made at these early points determine the tone, tenor, quality, and quantity of cases moving through the criminal court process. (See Table 8.1.)

Clearly, the volume of cases is directly tied to early screening decisions. In many areas, charges against roughly half of the defendants are dismissed during these stages. Moreover, later stages in the proceedings—plea bargaining, for example—reflect how cases were initially screened. It is a long-standing practice in many courts, for instance, for prosecutors to overcharge a defendant—that is, they file accusations more serious than the evidence indicates—to give themselves leverage to later offer the defendant the opportunity to plead guilty to a lesser charge.

The charging process also has important consequences for defendants. Once a suspect is formally charged with a crime, the full power of the criminal court process comes into effect. Unless bond is posted, the accused must await trial in jail. He or

TABLE 8.1	Steps of Criminal Procedure	
	Law on the Books	**Law in Action**
Crime	Any violation of the criminal law.	Over 13 million serious crimes reported to the police yearly. Property crimes outnumber violent offenses eight to one.
Arrest	The physical taking into custody of a suspected law violator.	About 3 million felony arrests each year.
Initial appearance	The accused is told of the charges, bail is set, and a date for the preliminary hearing is set.	Occurs soon after arrest, which means the judge and the lawyers know little about the case.
Bail	Guarantee that a released defendant will appear at trial.	Every day, the nation's jails hold over 650,000 pretrial detainees.
Preliminary hearing	Pretrial hearing to determine if probable cause exists to hold the accused.	Cases are rarely dismissed, but a hearing provides the defense attorney a look at the evidence.
Charging	Formal criminal charges against defendant stating what criminal law was violated.	Between arrest and the major trial court, half of cases are dropped.
Grand jury	A group of citizens who decide if persons accused of crimes should be charged (indicted).	Grand juries indict the defendants the prosecutor wants indicted.
Arraignment	The defendant is informed of the pending charges and is required to enter a plea.	Felony defendant's first appearance before a major trial court judge.

she may have to raise money to hire a lawyer. The person's reputation may be damaged. Thus, the criminal court process imposes significant penalties, even on defendants who are later acquitted or whose cases are dismissed.

CRIME

Beginning in the 1960s, the United States experienced a dramatic increase in crime. For two decades, crime reported to the police increased faster than the population. By the 1980s, the crime rate had reached a plateau, and then, in the 1990s, it declined significantly (Figure 8.1). Nonetheless, even the number of murders, which dominate headlines about crime and crime rates, remain at about the same level today as they were six decades ago.

The most widely known measure of crime is the Federal Bureau of Investigation's (FBI) annual publication, *Uniform Crime Reports*, which divides criminal offenses into two categories: Type I offenses include homicide, rape, arson, aggravated assault, robbery, burglary, auto theft, and larceny over $50. Those eight offenses are collectively

FIGURE 8.1
Crimes Known to the Police

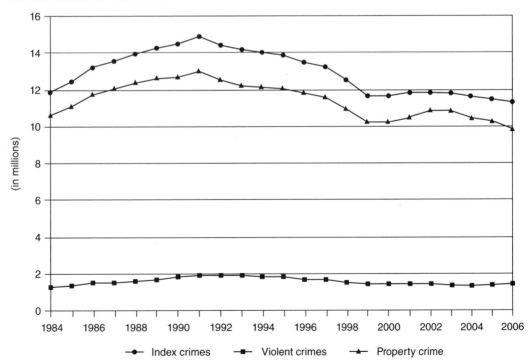

Source: Federal Bureau of Investigation, *Uniform Crime Reports*. Available online at http://www.fbi.gov/ucr/cius2006/offenses/index.html

known as index crimes, and they produce the headlines about high crime rates. Contrary to public perceptions, most felony arrests are for nonviolent offenses involving burglary and larceny. Fewer than one out of four arrests for Type I offenses involve a crime of personal violence. More frequent are Type II offenses, which range from theft to simple assault, public drunkenness to disorderly conduct. Important in the public debate is that drug offenses are included among the Type II crimes.

Crime has been a pressing national concern for over four decades. Newspapers headline major drug busts. Local television news programs show graphic footage of the latest murder scene. Not to be outdone, the national media offer tantalizing details on the latest sensational crime or prominent criminal. Those concerns often prompt governmental response. Candidates for public office promise that, if elected, they will get tough on criminals. Governmental officials, in turn, announce bold new programs to eradicate street crime, reduce violence, and end the scourge of drugs. Yet, despite all the attention and promises, street crime remains "a volatile, persistent, and intractable issue in American politics" (Scheingold 1991).

Certainly, one reason that crime has become such an important political issue is that crime is indeed a significant social problem. The United States has the highest crime rate of any Western industrial nation. Every year, more than twenty-four million Americans report they have been victims of a crime. Moreover, the violence rate is particularly high. Europeans, for example, are unaccustomed to reading about homicides and drive-by shootings, whereas Americans have become inured to the daily headlines about record murder rates and drug-related deaths. Many countries around the world respond to crime in ways that differ from U.S. methods. (See Courts in Comparative Perspective: The Kingdom of Saudi Arabia: Pure Islamic Law.)

High crime rates are reflected in high levels of fear of crime. A high percentage of Americans report they are afraid to walk in their neighborhoods at night because they might become crime victims. A closer look, however, shows that the fear of crime is not closely related to actual risk of crime: Citizens in small towns with quiet streets and virtually no crime are about as fearful of crime as residents of big cities with noisy streets and daily acts of public violence. Crime, therefore, is a perpetual political issue because it is a vague term—and purposefully so. It is an empty vessel that allows the listener to pour in his or her own content (Heinz, Jacob, and Lineberry 1983). In a basic sense, then, crime remains a political issue because it comes close to being all things to all people at all times. Nowhere is this more apparent than in the War on Drugs. (See Debating Law, Courts, and Politics: Marijuana: Evil Drug or Medicine? in Chapter 4.)

POLICING

In the United States, policing is even more decentralized than the courts. Whereas law enforcement in many European nations is centralized in one or more national agencies, in the United States it is spread out across more than 22,000 agencies. As Table 8.2 underscores, U.S. law enforcement is divided among federal, state, county, local, and special agencies. All told, approximately 850,000 full-time sworn law enforcement officers work in agencies that range from the small (2 or 3) to the gigantic (the New York Police Department consists of over 34,500 sworn officers).

COURTS IN COMPARATIVE PERSPECTIVE

■ The Kingdom of Saudi Arabia: Pure Islamic Law

According to the Saudi Ministry of Justice, the nineteen-year-old victim of a gang rape, known only as the "Girl from Qatif," deserved 200 lashes and six months in prison for violating the nation's strict sex segregation laws, which prohibit a woman from being in public with a male other than her husband. The case quickly drew international condemnation, and the Saudi government promised a review (Human Rights Watch 2007). This is but the latest example of a series of cases that have shocked Western observers:

- For the crime of armed robbery, the Saudi Arabian government beheaded four Sri Lankan citizens and left their headless bodies on public display in the capital of Riyadh (Human Rights Watch 2007).
- For smuggling several cases of liquor into the country, David Mornin, a fireman from Scotland, received 300 lashes and a year in jail.
- Over the years, many foreigners working in Saudi Arabia have experienced firsthand the harshness of this country's version of Islamic law (Murray 2001).

According to Human Rights Watch (2010), violations of defendants' rights are systemic in Saudi Arabia, including arrests without warrants; ill-treatment during interrogation; prolonged incommunicado detention; secret trials; and corporal punishment, including flogging and amputation of limbs, is imposed for even minor offenses.

Saudi Arabia, which lies on the Arabian Peninsula, is one of the richest nations in the world, thanks to oil. Of the 26 million people who live in the desert kingdom, 5.5 million are foreign nationals. Saudi Arabia is an absolute monarchy. In 1992, King Fahd implemented reforms, but the resulting constitutional government is radically different from Western-style governments. There are no elections, and political parties are not allowed. The new Consultative Council (or Shura Council) is subject to nomination and renomination by the king. Furthermore, many high officials, including the police and the judiciary, are members of the king's extended family (Dammer and Albanese 2011).

The Saudi Arabian legal system is based on the Shari'a, which consists of two parts: The Qur'an (sometimes spelled Koran) sets out principles revealed by God through Muhammad; and the Sunna contains the practices and decisions made by Muhammad. The dominance of Islam extends to judges, who are religiously rather than legally trained. Moreover, there are only 700 judges in the nation, because they are drawn from a strict sect of clerics with close ties to the royal family.

Significant changes have recently occurred In the Saudi Judicial System. The Judiciary Law of 2007 (effective in 2010) mandates a new judicial system with the courts assuming jurisdiction over most of the civil, commercial, and criminal disputes previously decided by various administrative committees. The first degree courts, similar to courts of general jurisdiction, will be located throughout the nation and include a wide variety of very specialized courts. At the next level are the Courts of Appeals created in each of the nation's 13 provinces. Most of the panels consist of three judges and have the power to overturn decisions of the first degree courts. A new court called the High Court will replace the former Supreme Judicial Council and hear appeals from the Courts of Appeals. Whether this new judicial system will function as a Western style legal system remains to be seen, particularly because the Minister of Justice, an appointee of the King, presides over the judicial system (Dammer and Albanese 2011). Moreover, the new court system will have to grapple with a long standing issue—Islamic law opposes modern business practices such as insurance and usury (charging interest on loans).

From the perspective of the United States, justice in Saudi Arabia is truly unique: Speeches in the 11,000 mosques are censored by administrative officials. Women are not allowed to acquire driving licenses. And corporal punishment is widely used. The lashings imposed on David Mornin typify the harshness of Saudi law, which is one of the purest Shari'a legal systems in the world (Moore 1996). In 1995, more than 150 delinquents were put to death by being publicly beheaded with a sword. Thieves have their right hand cut off. Allegations of torture are common. For those reasons, Saudi Arabia is of prime concern to Human Rights Watch and Amnesty International.

Following months of international condemnation and domestic outrage, King Abdullah pardoned the rape victim. The king is viewed as a modernizing influence who must walk a tightrope between those who want a strict interpretation of Islamic law and more progressive forces that push for democracy and increased international trade (Fleishman 2007).

TABLE 8.2	Profile of Law Enforcement in the United States	
	Number of Agencies	Number of Full-Time Sworn Officers
Federal	n/a	105,000
State	49	58,190
County	3,067	174,000
Local police	12,575	463,000
Special	1,481	49,398
Constable/marshall	5,133	2,323
TOTAL	22,305	851,911

Source: U.S. Department of Justice, Bureau of Justice Statistics, "Law Enforcement Statistics." Available online at http://bjs.ojp.usdoj.gov/index.cfm?ty=tp&tid=7 Retrieved July 7, 2011.

Historically, policing was a political issue for two interrelated reasons—patronage and corruption. Political machines often hired their own police in cities—big and small. Not surprisingly, some police departments were not known to be either efficient or even-handed. Generations of police reform sought to make law enforcement less subject to political influence. Those efforts have had major impacts. Today, policing is typically controlled by a civil service–oriented bureaucracy, and complaints of corruption have been greatly reduced. But efforts at greater police professionalism have, in turn, produced charges that the police are too aloof from the community they serve.

In the modern era, policing has become a political issue in the context of race relations. Charges of police brutality are often lodged by racial minorities, who perceive the police to be all too ready to use force—including deadly force—against African Americans and other racial minorities. Policing has also become an important political issue in terms of reorganization. Traditionally, policing was reactive—after a crime, the police investigated and sometimes made an arrest. Increasingly, though, police reforms stress that policing should be proactive—before a crime is reported, the police should be targeting potential criminals and known crime areas. Thus, policing today is increasingly oriented toward problem solving. The best known, but also the most ambiguous, reform strategy is community-oriented policing, which seeks to establish closer ties between the police and local residents. However, as it has been in the past, policing today is often measured by arrests made.

ARRESTS

Of the crimes brought to the attention of the police (the basis of the *Uniform Crime Reports*), only 20 percent result in an arrest. Police clearance by arrest varies greatly according to the type of crime involved: Forty-seven percent of violent crimes result

FIGURE **8.2**
Felony Arrests (in millions)

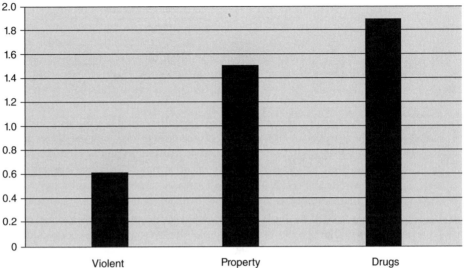

Source: Data from the Federal Bureau of Investigation, *Uniform Crime Reports for the United States—2009* (Washington, D.C.: U.S. Government Printing Office, 2010).

in arrest, compared with only 19 percent of property offenses (Federal Bureau of Investigation 2010). The low rate of crimes cleared by arrest means that a majority of crimes never reach the courts. Nonetheless, the workload of the criminal courts is heavy. The visible increase in crime during the 1960s and 1970s (and later the War on Drugs) swelled court dockets.

Every year, police **arrest** almost fourteen million people for nontraffic offenses—mostly minor ones such as simple assault, public drunkenness, petty theft, and possession of small amounts of marijuana. Of those, only a small percentage are for serious Type I offenses. Figure 8.2 highlights that arrests for property offenses are much more numerous than arrests for violent crimes and that drug arrests are by far the most common type of crime for which the police make an arrest. Drug arrests have increased sharply in recent years: In the 1980s, drug arrests increased rapidly and are now a staggering 1.6 million.

Police departments also vary in the quality of arrests referred to the district attorney, and some departments have a better record than others of forwarding sufficient evidence for a conviction (Holleran, Beicher, and Spohn 2010). Thus, when police are able to secure tangible evidence and cooperative witnesses for the prosecution (while honoring suspects' constitutional rights) the prosecutor is not only more likely to file charges, but also more likely to win a conviction (Albonetti 1987; Worrall, Ross, and McCord 2006). In turn, prosecutors perceive that some police agencies conduct more thorough investigations than others (Neubauer 1974b).

THE DEFENDANT

Those accused of violating the criminal law are a diverse lot. Although crimes of violence dominate the headlines, most **defendants** are charged with nonviolent offenses such as burglary, theft, or possession of drugs. Another indicator of the diversity of defendants is how often they are involved in the criminal justice system. At one end of the spectrum are those who are arrested once and are never involved again. At the other end of the spectrum are a small group of career criminals who are responsible for a disproportionate share of some offenses. In fact it is estimated that over 70 percent of all serious criminal offenses are committed by roughly 7 percent of offenders, a group commonly referred to as career criminals (Vaughn and DeLisa 2008; DeLisa 2005). Although many defendants are economically impoverished, a handful are middle or upper class. Accusations against high-ranking governmental officials, people in big business, and prominent local citizens demonstrate that defendants come from all social strata.

But that diversity aside, the vast majority of violators who get arrested form a distinctive profile. Compared with the average citizen, felony defendants are significantly younger, overwhelmingly male, disproportionately members of racial minorities, more likely to come from broken homes, less educated, more likely to be unemployed, and less likely to be married. By the time the court sorting process has ended, those sentenced to prison consist of an even higher proportion of poor, young, illiterate, and nonwhite males (Keen and Jacobs 2009; Haynie, Weiss and Piquero 2008). Thus, the typical felony defendant possesses few of the skills needed to successfully compete in an increasingly technological society (Table 8.3).

TABLE 8.3 Profile of State Prison Inmates	
Description	**Percent of Inmates**
Women	7
Racial or ethnic minorities	64
Thirty-five or younger	57
Raised primarily in single-parent home	43
Prior incarceration of immediate family member	36
Prior adult incarceration	55
Prior conviction	81
High school diploma or equivalent	57
Violent offense conviction	49
Property offense conviction	20
Drug conviction	21

Source: U.S. Department of Justice, Bureau of Justice Statistics, "Criminal Offenders Statistics." Available online at http://www.ojp.usdoj.gov/bjs/crimoff.htm.

Because most defendants are poor and uneducated, they are ill equipped to deal with the technical abstractions of the criminal law. A few defendants are incapable of understanding even the simplest instructions about their rights. Many are too inarticulate to aid their attorneys in preparing a defense. Some hold unfavorable attitudes toward the law and the criminal justice system and, thus, regard the judge and all other court personnel, including their defense attorneys, with hostility and distrust.

> As a result, the huge majority of defendants ... submit to the painful consequences of conviction but do not know for certain whether they committed any of the crimes of which they are accused. Such defendants are so unschooled in law that they form no firm opinion about their technical innocence or guilt. Neither do they actually agree or disagree that it is just to punish them. They do not know enough about themselves to tell the lawyers what to do (Rosett and Cressey 1976, 146).

Unlike many defendants depicted in the popular media, real-life defendants find themselves thrust into a court process that they are often incapable of understanding fully. This process begins shortly after arrest with the initial appearance.

INITIAL APPEARANCE

In the United States, the police must bring an arrested person before a judge "without unnecessary delay," which typically means forty-eight hours. This **initial appearance** is the defendant's first encounter with the courts and the judicial process. At this hearing, the judge advises the defendant of the right to remain silent, the right to counsel, the right to bail, and the right to a preliminary hearing (Ferdico, Fradella, and Totten 2008). Initial appearances typically last only a minute or two. Judges handle them in rapid-fire order, making little effort to determine whether the defendant understands what is being explained. In some high-volume, big-city courts, defendants are advised of their rights in groups.

For defendants accused of minor crimes (ordinance violations and most misdemeanors), the initial appearance is often the only courtroom encounter. Ninety percent of the nation's criminal cases are heard by trial courts of limited jurisdiction, which process the millions of Americans accused each year of disturbing the peace, shoplifting, drunkenness, and driving violations (Chapter 4). These minor crimes carry only fines or short jail sentences. Because the stakes are low, three out of four defendants plead guilty at the initial appearance and are immediately sentenced to either pay a small fine or serve a short jail term.

For defendants accused of major crimes (felonies and major misdemeanors), the initial appearance is largely a formality. In serious offenses such as murder, robbery, burglary, and the sale of drugs, only a judge of a trial court of general jurisdiction can accept a plea. During the initial appearance, therefore, lower-court judges only set bail, schedule the next court appearance, and appoint counsel for the indigent.

BAIL

Bail is a guarantee that, in return for being released from jail, the accused will return to court as needed. That promise is guaranteed by posting money or property with the court. If the defendant appears in court as required, the security is returned. If he or she fails to appear, however, the security can be forfeited. Virtually every defendant has the right to bail. On the theory that no amount of security is large enough to guarantee that a person facing the death penalty will not flee, defendants accused of a capital offense have no right to bail.

Bail procedures vary according to the seriousness of the crime. Those arrested for minor misdemeanors can be released quickly by posting bail at the police station. In most communities, the lower-court judges have adopted a fixed bail schedule that specifies an exact amount for each offense. Bail procedures for felony or serious misdemeanor cases are considerably more complex. The defendant must appear before the central court for the setting of bond.

Once bail has been set, a defendant can gain pretrial release in four ways. First, the accused may post the full amount of the bond in cash with the court. Second, the defendant (or friends or relatives) may post a property bond, which is a piece of property posted as collateral; typically, the equity must be at least twice the face amount of the bond. But few defendants have money or property. Many, therefore, must use the third method—the **bail bondsman**, who posts the amount of bond with the court and charges a nonrefundable fee, usually 10 percent of the bond's face amount. The fourth alternative is personal recognizance: Judges may release a defendant from jail without monetary bail if they believe the person is not likely to flee.

America's system of monetary bail means that defendants who are rich enough can buy their freedom and await trial at home. But the poor must await trial in jail. On any given day, almost 750,000 adults are held in jail (not prison), and approximately half of those have not been convicted of any crime. Despite declines in crime, America's jail population continues to grow.

In serious cases, judges have wide latitude in setting the amount of bail. Their decisions are based on two major factors, the more important being the seriousness of the crime (Karnow 2008; Flemming 1982). The more serious the crime, the higher is the amount of bail. Those practices reflect the philosophy that the more serious the crime, the greater the urge to forfeit bail, and, therefore, the greater the financial cost should be for such flight. A second factor in setting bond is the defendant's prior criminal record. Typically, bond for defendants with prior criminal records is set higher than normal for the offense charged (Wice 1974).

For decades, the monetary bail system has been the subject of extensive debate. Civil libertarians are concerned about apparent inequities. Requiring suspects to buy their freedom was viewed as unfairly discriminating against the poor. Moreover, some studies find that defendants held in jail awaiting trial are more likely to be convicted and also more likely to be sentenced to prison after conviction (Neubauer and Fradella 2011).

Conservatives, on the other hand, are concerned about the link between bail and crime. Allowing dangerous defendants to post bail is viewed as exposing the public unnecessarily to the risk of further victimization. Conservatives argue that current bail practices do not successfully restrain dangerous defendants, pointing to defendants who commit crimes while out of jail on pretrial release. To better protect the public, these critics urged the adoption of **preventive detention**, which allows judges to hold suspects without bail if they are accused of committing a dangerous or violent crime and if locking them up is deemed necessary for community safety. The federal government and three-fifths of the states have adopted some form of preventive detention. Moreover, in *United States v. Salerno* (1987), the Supreme Court upheld the constitutionality of such programs.

The merits of this ideological debate aside, the realities are that jails (like prisons, discussed in Chapter 9) are filled to overflowing. Abstract debates over which arrestees should be held in jail before trial must give way to practical decisions about a lack of available jail beds.

PROSECUTION

Prosecution, like courts and policing in the United States, is decentralized. Whereas some nations concentrate this power in one office, the prosecution function in this country is found at all four major levels of government: national, state, county, and local.

At the national level, the U.S. Department of Justice is in charge of prosecution in the federal courts. The criminal division handles a few high-profile cases, but the bulk of federal prosecution is in the hands of the U.S. attorneys in each of the district courts. U.S. attorneys are political appointees of the president who must be confirmed by the Senate.

At the state level, state attorneys general are in charge of prosecution, but in most states, this office has only limited criminal authority (often involving only criminal misdeeds of high-ranking state officials). Thus, most state attorneys general, who are elected officials, have come to champion the popular cause of consumer rights.

At the county level, the **prosecutor** (known as the district attorney in some jurisdictions and the state's attorney in most others) is the chief law enforcement official of the community. DAs, as they are often called, are typically elected officials who are responsible for prosecuting felonies and serious misdemeanors in the trial courts of general jurisdiction. Moreover, their activities are not monitored by the state's attorney general, which makes the prosecutor the most powerful official in the criminal courts. For a lawyer interested in a political career, the prosecutor's office offers a launching pad. Some lawyers lacking such political ambitions view the office as useful for gaining public visibility for a private law practice (Engstrom 1971).

At the local level, city attorneys (sometimes called solicitors) serve as local prosecutors. A recent estimate places their numbers at 5,700. Besides representing local government in a variety of civil matters, city attorneys also typically are responsible for prosecuting the large volume of minor criminal offenses in the minor trial courts.

Prosecution in the United States is characterized not only by decentralization but also by broad discretion. Through the years, courts have granted prosecutors wide leeway in deciding which cases to bargain out and which ones to try. From the time of arrest to the final disposition of the case, how the prosecutor chooses to exercise discretion determines to a large extent which defendants are prosecuted, the types of plea bargains that are struck, and the severity of the sentence imposed on the guilty. Nowhere is the broad discretion of American prosecutors more prominent than in the power to file criminal charges. (See Law and Popular Culture: *Law & Order.*)

FILING CHARGES

The criminal court process begins with filing a formal written accusation of the crime. The Sixth Amendment requires that a defendant be given information upon which to prepare a defense. Thus, the **charging document** includes the name of the person charged, a brief description of how and where the offense was committed, and the statute allegedly violated.

There are three major types of charging documents: complaint, information, and indictment. **Complaints**, which must be supported by oath or affirmation of either the victim or the arresting officer, are most commonly used in prosecuting misdemeanor offenses or city ordinance violations. An **information** is virtually identical in form to the complaint, except that it is signed by the prosecutor. In non–grand jury states, a bill of information is used to initiate felony prosecutions; in grand jury states, an **indictment** is used pending grand jury action.

One of the prosecutor's powers involves controlling the doors to the courthouse—that is, he or she decides whether charges should be filed and what the proper charge should be. Although the law demands prosecution for "all known criminal conduct," the courts have historically granted prosecutors wide discretion in deciding whether to file charges. No legislative or judicial standards govern which cases merit prosecution and which should be declined. Moreover, if a prosecutor refuses to file charges, no review of his or her decision is possible; courts have consistently refused to order a prosecutor to proceed with a case.

Although the prosecutor has the legal authority to dominate the charging process, some prosecutors choose to share that authority with the police. In those communities, the police file criminal charges with minimal supervision by the prosecutor. In essence, the prosecutors have transferred their decision-making power to the police (Mellon, Jacoby, and Brewer 1981). In communities where prosecutors choose to control the filing of criminal charges, a substantial percentage (one-third to one-half) of persons arrested are released without the filing of criminal charges (Collins 2007; O'Neill 2003; Boland et al. 1982; Neubauer 1974a). Police, however, resist prosecutorial control of the charging decision. Every arrest rejected by the prosecutor is viewed as an implicit criticism of the arresting officer.

LAW AND POPULAR CULTURE

■ *Law & Order*

Law & Order is the longest-running drama series to appear on network television. First aired in 1990, the show proved so popular that the producers have spun off shows such as *Law & Order: Special Victims Unit* and *Law & Order: Criminal Intent*. The shows are also replayed regularly on cable television. Indeed, it has been estimated that a viewer can watch a full 20 hours of these shows each week.

Part of the popularity of *Law & Order* stems from its ripped-from-the-headlines style. Each show is self-contained. The stripped-down quality means that plot is everything. And the stories often have a twist—the most obvious suspect is not necessarily the one who committed the murder. Although there are continuing characters, there is little effort at character development (Dempsey 2003). The entrapping sense of reality is reinforced by the video—outdoor scenes are shot on the streets of New York City, and indoor scenes are shot on a soundstage on the Hudson River.

At its best, *Law & Order* (and its numerous spinoffs) is willing to confront social issues, such as sexually transmitted diseases and gay sex, that typically go unmentioned in prime-time television. Unlike stereotypical crime stories in which most characters live stereotypical lives, the episode characters on *Law & Order* are more likely to experience issues associated with interracial dating and illegal immigration. Overall, the series seems best when its plots highlight the complexities of emotionally charged issues such as child molestation and child custody battles.

But how real is *Law & Order*? To scholars, the sense of realism projects a number of dubious images about policing and prosecution. *Law & Order* often distorts policing and prosecution beyond recognition. Investigation techniques are often bad, as, for example, in the episode in which the police searched the car of the murder victim on the street instead of impounding the vehicle inside a weather-free building. Interrogation techniques are equally faulty. Suspects are interrupted as they make statements instead of being allowed to tell their version before facing more probing questions. Plea-bargaining sessions also represent major distortions of reality. Typically on *Law & Order*, the defendant is in the same room as the prosecutor and the defense attorney. Overall, the program gives the impression that the law (particularly the part related to the constitutional rights of all citizens) is a nuisance. Indeed, disrespect for the law extends to police actions—some episodes show police brutality (minor but often unnecessary force in arresting a suspect).

Television shows such as *Law & Order* have had a major impact on the American legal system. Indeed The CSI Effect has become a major research topic (Stevens 2011). Professors teaching courses like violent crime scene analysis find that they must first help students unlearn what they learned incorrectly from watching television (Lacks 2007). Similarly, juries now demand forensic evidence (Surette 2011). Moreover, jurors have to be instructed that *Law & Order* is fiction, not fact. As a result, defense lawyers love the "*CSI* shows because they have caused juries to demand DNA analysis in nearly every two-bit 7-Eleven holdup. Prosecutors, meanwhile, feel hampered by the fact that ten eyewitnesses are not enough to satisfy *CSI*-watching jurors who crave the supposedly conclusive proof of hair follicles on a knife" (Goehner, Lofaro, and Novack 2004).

But all those sprays and lasers and high-tech microscopes, it turns out, are expensive. "DNA analysis is used every six seconds on *CSI*," says Robert J. Castelli, a professor at John Jay College of Criminal Justice who was a police officer for 21 years. "To analyze properly a sample of DNA can cost as much as $10,000. You're not going to be using DNA analysis in every burglary." So prosecutors are now spending a great deal of time trying to explain to juries that DNA evidence isn't always essential Baskin and Sommers 2010). Joshua Marquis, a pro–death penalty district attorney in Oregon, is worried that cops will have to start doing all sorts of unnecessary forensics work just to placate *CSI*-educated juries.

Concerns that fiction might dictate fact are not hypothetical. The Texas Appellate Court reversed the conviction of Andrea Yates (the Houston woman who drowned her children in a bathtub) because the prosecution psychiatrist falsely testified that he had consulted on a *Law & Order* episode with a similar theme (Liptak 2005). Frequent viewers of television crime dramas significantly increase concerns about crime (Holbrook and Hill 2005).

PRELIMINARY HEARING

The preliminary hearing (or preliminary examination, as it is called in some states) represents the first time a criminal case is reviewed by someone other than a law enforcement official. An arrested person is entitled to a timely hearing before a neutral judge to determine whether probable cause exists to detain the defendant prior to trial (*Gerstein v. Pugh* 1975; *County of Riverside v. McLaughlin* 1991). In grand jury states, the preliminary hearing binds over the accused for possible indictment. In non–grand jury states, the preliminary hearing is conducted by lower-court judges and is the sole procedure for determining whether sufficient evidence exists to justify holding the defendant. Beyond its legal rationale of protecting an innocent defendant from being held on baseless charges, the preliminary hearing often serves an important informal function as well. It gives the defense attorney an overview of the evidence against the client and provides the opportunity to learn more about the prosecutor's case (Prosser 2006).

During a preliminary hearing, the state does not have to prove the defendant guilty beyond a reasonable doubt, as would be required during a trial. Rather, all that is necessary is for the prosecutor to establish **probable cause** that a crime has been committed and that the defendant committed the crime. Typically, hearsay evidence (secondhand evidence) is admissible. Generally, the defense does not have the right to cross-examine witnesses, although some states and some judges permit attorneys to question witnesses (Gilboy 1984).

Although the legal purpose of the preliminary hearing is simple, the actual conduct of these hearings is quite complex (Washburn 2008). In a few jurisdictions, preliminary hearings are almost never held. In other jurisdictions, preliminary hearings resemble minitrials and last an hour or more. The most common practice is for preliminary hearings to be short and routine, with a police detective testifying from a police report he or she did not write to the effect that Mrs. Jones reported that a crime was committed. Then a minimal amount of information is given about why the police arrested Mr. Smith. The total time consumed is generally no more than five minutes. Such short and routine preliminary hearings typically result in a finding that probable cause is present. The study of Prairie City, Illinois, for example, documented that only 2 percent of the defendants had their cases terminated at the preliminary hearing (Neubauer 1974b).

Although in most jurisdictions, few cases are screened out of the criminal process during the preliminary hearing, it is a major stage of the proceedings in a few courts. For example, in Brooklyn, New York, 65 percent of felony cases receive a final disposition during the preliminary hearing (McIntyre and Lippman 1970). Where prosecutors choose not to review charges before filing, the judges must separate the strong cases from the weak ones during the preliminary examination.

GRAND JURIES

Grand juries differ from trial juries: Whereas trial juries decide whether the defendant is guilty or innocent of the charges, grand juries determine probable cause and return an accusation (an indictment). **Grand juries**, therefore, have two primary functions:

They serve as investigatory bodies, and they act as a buffer between the state and its citizens, preventing the government from using the criminal process against its enemies. Thus, if they are satisfied that the charges brought by the prosecutor are truthful and supported by sufficient evidence, they return an indictment or a **true bill** and the case continues. If, however, they find insufficient evidence to justify a trial, then they return a **no true bill**—and the case is dropped.

Provisions for the grand jury are included in the Fifth Amendment to the Constitution, which provides that "no person shall be held to answer for a capital, or otherwise infamous crime, unless on a presentment or indictment of a grand jury." The archaic phrase "otherwise infamous crime" has been interpreted to mean felonies. This provision, however, applies only to federal prosecutions. In *Hurtado v. California* (1884), the Supreme Court held that states have the option of using either an indictment or an information. As a result, the grand jury is the exclusive means of initiating all felony prosecutions in only nineteen states. In a few other states, a grand jury indictment is required only for capital offenses. In the remaining states, the grand jury is an optional investigative body (see Table 8.4).

The size of grand juries varies from as few as six jurors to as many as twenty-three. Grand jurors are normally selected randomly in a manner similar to the selection of trial jurors. In a handful of states, however, judges, county boards, jury commissioners, or sheriffs are allowed to exercise discretion. Grand juries are impaneled (formally created) for a set term (typically three months). During that time,

---

TABLE 8.4   Grand Jury Requirements

Grand Jury Indictment Required		Grand Jury Indictment Optional		Grand Jury Lacks Authority to Indict
All crimes	Missouri	Arizona	Montana	Connecticut
New Jersey	New Hampshire	Arkansas	Nebraska	Pennsylvania
South Carolina	New York	California	Nevada	
Tennessee	North Carolina	Colorado	New Mexico	
Virginia	Ohio	Georgia	North Dakota	
All felonies	Texas	Hawaii	Oklahoma	
Alabama	West Virginia	Idaho	Oregon	
Alaska	**Capital crimes only**	Illinois	South Dakota	
Delaware	Florida	Indiana	Utah	
District of Columbia	Louisiana	Iowa	Vermont	
Maine	Minnesota	Kansas	Washington	
Massachusetts	Rhode Island	Kentucky	Wisconsin[a]	
Mississippi		Maryland	Wyoming	
		Michigan		

[a] Wisconsin has not convened a grand jury in more than 30 years.
Source: David B. Rottman and Shauna M. Strickland. 2006. *State Court Organization, 2004.* Washington, D.C.

they meet periodically to consider the cases brought to them by the prosecutor and to conduct other investigations. If a grand jury is conducting a major and complex investigation, its time may be extended by the court.

The work of the grand jury is shaped by a number of unique legal dimensions (Alpert and Petersen 1985). Many legal protections found elsewhere in the criminal court process are not applicable to the grand jury. One of those is secrecy. Because the grand jury may find insufficient evidence to indict, it works in secret to shield those merely under investigation from adverse publicity. By contrast, the rest of the process is required to be conducted in public. Another unique aspect is that indictments are returned by plurality vote; in most states, one-half to two-thirds of the votes are sufficient to hand up an indictment. By contrast, trial jurors can convict only if the jurors are unanimous (or near unanimous in four states). Finally, witnesses before the grand jury have no right to representation by an attorney. By contrast, defendants have a right to have a lawyer present at all other vital stages of a criminal prosecution. Also, suspects do not have the right to go before the grand jury to protest their innocence or even to present their version of the facts.

The work of the grand jury is also shaped by its unique relationship with the prosecutor. Although, in theory, the prosecutor functions only as the legal adviser to the grand jury, in practice, the prosecutor dominates. Grand jurors hear only the witnesses summoned by the prosecutor. And, as laypeople, they are heavily influenced by the legal advice of the prosecutor. The net result is that grand juries often function as rubber stamps for the prosecutor. A study of Harris County (Houston), Texas, found that grand jurors spent only five minutes on the average case, discussed only 20 percent of the cases, rarely voiced dissent, and approved virtually all the prosecutor's recommendations (Carp 1975). Similarly, in one recent year, federal grand juries returned over 17,000 indictments, but only 68 no true bills. In short, grand juries indict whomever the prosecutor wants indicted (Washburn 2008). Moreover, the few no true bills voted typically reflect the prosecutor's assessment that these cases should not be prosecuted (Neubauer and Fradella 2010).

EXCLUSIONARY RULES

How the police investigate crimes and how district attorneys prosecute criminals are affected by a series of important Supreme Court decisions. The 1960s witnessed the first attempt by the nation's highest court to exercise strong policy control over the administration of criminal justice. Earlier opinions enunciating vague standards of "due process of law" were replaced by decisions specifying precise rules. Those sweeping changes in constitutional interpretation have been appropriately called the "due process revolution" (Graham 1970). The Court transformed the Bill of Rights from a collection of general constitutional principles to a code of criminal procedure. Those efforts to nationalize, rationalize, and constitutionalize the criminal justice system came at a time of rising crime, riots in the streets, and assassinations. To the public, there appeared to be a connection between the new trend of "judicial permissiveness" and the breakdown of law and order. The justices were accused of "coddling criminals" and "handcuffing the police."

The most controversial criminal justice decisions dealt with police gathering of evidence; otherwise valid and trustworthy evidence was excluded from trial. The **exclusionary rule** prohibits the prosecutor from using illegally obtained evidence during a trial. The Supreme Court's sole technique for enforcing several vital protections of the Bill of Rights, the rule's adoption has been justified on three grounds: (1) by a normative argument that a court of law should not participate in or condone illegal conduct, (2) by an empirical assessment that excluding evidence will deter law enforcement officials from illegal behavior, and (3) by experience that alternative remedies, such as civil suits for damages against police officers for misconduct, are unworkable.

The exclusionary rule is commonly associated with the search for and seizure of physical evidence, but, in fact, there are three distinct exclusionary rules.

The Identification of Suspects

During police lineups, defendants have the right to be assisted by counsel (*United States v. Wade* 1967). Moreover, if the lineup is improperly conducted, the trial judge may suppress (exclude) the identification of the suspect from the trial.

Confessions

Beginning in the 1930s, the Supreme Court rejected confessions based on physical or psychological coercion. The standards for interrogating suspects, however, were far from clear. In an attempt at greater precision, the Court adopted specific procedures for police interrogations. In what are widely known as *Miranda warnings*, the police are required to tell a suspect the following:

* You have a right to remain silent.
* Anything you say may be used against you.
* You have the right to have a lawyer present.
* You have the right to court-appointed counsel if you are indigent.

In addition, the Court shifted the burden of proof from the defense, which previously had to prove a confession was not "free and voluntary," to the police and the prosecutor, who now must prove they have advised the defendant of his or her constitutional rights. (See Case Close-Up: *Miranda v. Arizona* 1966.)

The composition of the Supreme Court changed significantly with the four Nixon appointments, and so did a number of interpretations of the scope of the *Miranda* warnings. For example, in *Harris v. New York* (1971), the Court held that a prosecutor may use a confession obtained without constitutional warnings to prove that a defendant who testifies is lying. Similarly, in *New York v. Quarles* (1984), Justice Rehnquist found that overriding considerations of public safety justified the police officer's failure to provide *Miranda* warnings before asking questions about the location of a weapon apparently abandoned just before arrest. Thus, the more conservative Burger Court somewhat limited the *Miranda* requirements by carving out exceptions. The Rehnquist Court rejected an opportunity to directly overturn *Miranda*, arguing that *Miranda* has become embedded in routine police practice to the point where the warnings have become part of our national culture (*Dickerson v. United States* 2000). The Roberts Court has continued the trend of limiting the scope of Miranda, holding that a suspect waives the right to remain silent unless they expressly invoke it (*Berghuis v. Thompkins* 2010).

Searches

The Fourth Amendment states, "The right of the people to be secure in their persons, houses, papers and effects against unreasonable search and seizure, shall not be violated." But what constitutes an unreasonable search and seizure? Historically, the gathering of physical evidence was governed by the common-law rule that "if the constable blunders, the crook should not go free." That meant that if the police conducted an illegal search (search without probable cause), the evidence obtained still could be used. Evidence was admitted in court if it was truthful and relevant. How the police obtained the evidence was treated as a separate issue. In essence, law enforcement officials who searched illegally faced no sanctions.

Early in the twentieth century, the Supreme Court modified the common-law tradition by adopting the exclusionary rule, but only in federal prosecutions. Years later, the exclusionary rule was extended to the states (*Mapp v. Ohio* 1961). As a result, evidence obtained during an illegal search and seizure is no longer admissible in state court.

The *Mapp* decision remains controversial nearly five decades later, but the nature of the debate has changed. Initially, critics called for its abolition, now, they just suggest modifications. Among the alternatives proposed have been a "substantial violation" test, an "egregious violation" standard, and a "good faith" exception. To the critics, modifications along those lines would reduce the number of arrests lost because of illegal searches, and the sanction would be more proportional to the seriousness of the Fourth Amendment violation (Jensen and Hart 1982). One variant or another of the good-faith exception to the exclusionary rule has been adopted by a few state and federal courts (Burkoff 1983). The Supreme Court, however, has recognized an "honest mistake" or a "good faith" exception to the exclusionary rule only in extremely narrow and limited circumstances (*United States v. Leon* 1984; *Illinois v. Krull* 1987). The high court is increasingly leaning in this direction. Thus, when Arizona police seized marijuana in the car of Isaac Evans, they were able to use it in court even though the arrest warrant was erroneously listed on a police computer. Rehnquist's opinion stressed that rights to privacy are not violated when there is a "good faith" exception for human error. But in a concurring opinion, three justices stressed that the ruling does not mean police can rely on a computerized system that "routinely leads to false arrests" (*Arizona v. Evans* 1995).

Through the years, a majority of Supreme Court justices have publicly expressed skepticism about *Mapp* but have been unable to agree among themselves on how to replace *Mapp*. The two most recently confirmed justices—Roberts and Alito—typically vote with the prosecutor most of the time (Greenhouse 2007). Thus, the Supreme Court, often finds that the police did indeed search legally (*Brendlin v. California* 2007), particularly if the suspect was found to in possession of illegal drugs. In *Kentucky v. King* (2011), for example the Roberts Court held that the smell of marijuana was sufficient to break down the door of an apartment without a search warrant.

CASE CLOSE-UP

■ *Miranda v. Arizona* (1966)

Limiting Police Interrogations

To Detective Carroll Cooley, Lois Ann Jameson's story of being raped in the desert was somewhat contradictory and offered few leads. She couldn't provide a very good description of her attacker. The only lead was her detailed description of the car, which eventually led Detective Cooley to a house on the west side of town, where he found a car exactly as described (Baker 1983). The subsequent interrogation and conviction of Ernesto Miranda was to change the landscape of American criminal justice.

By the time he was eighteen, Miranda's police blotter showed six arrests and four prison sentences. A stint in the military to turn his life around quickly degenerated into more problems in civilian life. But, at age 23, he appeared to have turned the corner. His boss at the produce company described him as "one of the best workers I ever had." Indeed, he had barely slept an hour after working a twelve-hour shift when the police knocked on the front door.

Stating that they didn't want to talk in front of his common-law wife, the police took Miranda to a Phoenix police station. Lois Ann Jameson (not her real name) viewed the lineup of Miranda and three other Hispanics from the city jail but could state only that Miranda's build and features were similar to those of her assailant. In the interrogation room, Miranda asked how he did, and Detective Cooley replied, "You flunked." At first, Miranda maintained his innocence, but after two hours of questioning, he signed a written confession admitting guilt. His subsequent trial was short and perfunctory. The only prosecution exhibit was the signed confession. The defense attorney offered no evidence and called no witnesses. Nor did the defense call the defendant, out of fear the jury would learn of his extensive criminal background. The jury quickly returned guilty verdicts for kidnapping and rape.

The interrogation of Miranda was in most ways unremarkable. It most certainly lacked the blatant brutality and duress at the center of earlier Supreme Court decisions on the limits of police interrogation. What was missing, however, was any advice to Miranda about his rights under the Constitution. Indeed, the police testified that they never told Miranda he didn't have to talk to the police, nor did they advise him of his right to consult with an attorney. (According to Miranda, the police promised to drop other charges if he confessed to the rape.) Those facts highlighted the giant chasm between the principles of the Constitution of the United States and the realities of U.S. police stations.

By 1966, the Supreme Court had been grappling with the issue of confessions for three decades. In the 1930s, the Supreme Court rejected confessions based on physical coercion (beatings with rubber hoses and the like). By the 1940s and 1950s, attention shifted to confessions produced as a result of psychological coercion (long periods of interrogation or improper promises, for example). Despite those numerous cases, the standards for interrogating suspects were far from clear.

Chief Justice Earl Warren's opinion in *Miranda* expressed concern over the "police-dominated" atmosphere of interrogation rooms and held that warnings were required to counteract the inherently coercive nature of station house questioning. But, in reality, *Miranda* created no new rights—under American law, suspects have never been required to talk to the police, and the right to counsel extends to the police station as well as to the courthouse. In essence, the Court held that the Fifth Amendment privilege against self-incrimination was as applicable to interrogation by the police before trial as to questioning by the prosecutor during trial.

Miranda v. Arizona (1966) is the Warren Court's best known, and also arguably the most controversial, decision extending constitutional rights to those accused of violating the criminal law. The four dissenting justices criticized the ruling on both constitutional and practical grounds. To Justice Byron White, the *Miranda* rule was "a deliberate calculus to prevent interrogation, to reduce the incidence of confessions, and to increase the number of trials." Police, prosecutors, and public officials likewise criticized the ruling, and it became a key plank in Richard Nixon's law-and-order campaign in 1968 (Chapter 15). With four Nixon-appointed justices, the Burger Court began narrowing *Miranda*, but the holding itself has not been overturned. Indeed, *Miranda* has now become settled law, deeply embedded in the constitutional fabric of the United States.

DEBATING LAW, COURTS, AND POLITICS

■ Should Criminal Charges be Filed in Response to the BP Oil Spill?

The explosion on the Deepwater Horizon rig not only caused the nation's largest oil spill but also created the deepest crime scene in the annals of crime. Almost a mile below the sea lay the blowout preventer, a giant piece of equipment designed to immediately close the well if pressure reached dangerous levels. But this last line of defense had obviously not worked and figuring out why it failed will prove to be of critical importance in assessing civil liability. Perhaps just as importantly it might also provide crucial evidence as to whether a crime had been committed. Four months after the rig exploded, a team of FBI agents supervised the lifting of the five-story tall, 300 ton blowout preventer from the ocean bottom to dry land. How the forensic examination would be conducted quickly became contentious. Indeed the U.S. District Court had to decide which civil defendants and government agencies would be allowed to have front row seats to monitor the investigation being conducted by a Norwegian company. The others were forced to watch on TV in another room and left out of the decision-making process.

Six weeks after the rig explosion, U.S. Attorney General Eric Holder announced that the Justice Department was launching a major criminal investigation. Earlier Exxon had faced criminal charges after its tanker, the Exxon Valdez, spilled oil in Alaska (Chapter 12). The federal investigatory team consists of numerous federal agencies including the FBI, Coast Guard, Environmental Protection Agency, and the Interior Department. The massive oil spill also spawned investigations conducted by federal regulatory agencies (the Coast Guard and Interior) aimed at finding out what went wrong and trying to prevent similar mishaps in the future. At the same time numerous civil lawsuits were filed by the various businesses working on the Deepwater Horizon with each legal entity accusing the other of negligence in causing the explosion (Chapter 11). Such parallel investigations are common after major disasters but they

inevitably produce tensions between the various parties. One such tension centered on whether witnesses would or would not testify. During administrative hearings aimed at establishing why the rig exploded, three BP engineers asserted their Fifth Amendment privilege against self-incrimination. Some argued that the pursuit of possible criminal charges was interfering with the broader issue of trying to prevent such accidents in the future. But asserting Fifth Amendment protections can work both ways. The chief counsel for the Joint Commission investigating the disaster made it clear to witnesses that it was in their best interests to cooperate. If they failed to do so, he stated, the Department of Justice would be notified and a likely criminal investigation would follow (Schliefstein 2010).

The question of whether criminal charges should be filed after the BP oil spill illustrates the interplay between law, courts, and politics. Even the decision to publicly announce that a criminal investigation was being launched represented a political balancing act. The government needed BP's efforts in stopping the oil flow while at the same time seemingly threatening to later prosecute some of the same officials for their earlier criminal negligence. Political balancing acts will be necessary in the future as well. The Attorney General (an appointee of the President) will have to decide whether criminal charges should be filed. And if charges are filed the Attorney General will later have to decide whether the case should be tried or settled.

Clashing editorials over the announcement of the launching of the criminal investigation illustrate how politically contentious decisions like this can be. *The Times-Picayune*, New Orleans's major newspaper, applauded the decision calling it an "important and necessary step" ("A Needed Probe" 2010). But business groups openly wondered whether such actions were both premature and counterproductive. An editorial in the *Wall Street Journal* termed the investigation a political persecution of BP (Gigot 2010).

PRETRIAL MOTIONS

Critics and supporters of the exclusionary rule agree on one central point: The grounds for a lawful search are complex, and appellate courts continually revise what constitutes an unreasonable search and seizure. Nonetheless, the police must often make immediate decisions about searching or interrogating a suspect. They don't have time to consult a lawyer about the complex and constantly evolving law governing search and seizure or confessions. Yet, those on-the-spot decisions may later be challenged in court as violations of the suspect's constitutional rights. Thus, even though the exclusionary rule is directed at the police, its actual enforcement occurs in the courts. A defense attorney who believes his or her client was subjected to an illegal search, provided a confession because of improper police activity, or was identified in a defective police lineup can file a motion to suppress the evidence.

Relatively few pretrial motions to suppress evidence are filed. An in-depth examination of nine jurisdictions found that only 8 percent of the cases involved a suppression motion. Moreover, once filed, pretrial motions are rarely successful. Challenges to identifications or confessions were granted only 5 percent of the time, and objections to the gathering of physical evidence succeeded only 17 percent of the time. Interestingly, not all defendants who successfully suppressed evidence escaped conviction (Nardulli 1983).

Costs of the Exclusionary Rule

A key question in the ongoing debate over the exclusionary rule centers on its costs. In the public's mind, *Miranda v. Arizona* (1966) and similar Supreme Court cases are the reasons for high crime rates in the United States. Such an interpretation oversimplifies a complex reality, however.

In a widely cited dissent, Chief Justice Warren Burger summed up the critics' position as follows: "Some clear demonstration of the benefits and effectiveness of the exclusionary rule is required to justify it in view of the high price it exacts from society—the release of countless guilty criminals" (*Bivens v. Six Unknown Federal Narcotics Agents* 1971). Assessing how many convictions are lost because of the exclusionary rule is difficult for reasons already discussed in this chapter: Case attrition occurs at numerous stages of the proceedings and for various reasons. Several studies, however, shed considerable light on the topic.

Exclusionary rules can lead to the freeing of apparently guilty defendants during prosecutorial screening. Prosecutors may refuse to file charges because of a search-and-seizure problem, a tainted confession, or a defective police lineup, but that occurs infrequently. The Government Accounting Office examined case rejections by U.S. attorneys and found that search and seizure was cited as the primary reason only 0.4 percent of the time (Comptroller General 1979). Similarly, a study of seven urban courts found that only 2.0 percent of the rejections were for *Mapp* or *Miranda* reasons (Boland et al. 1982). The most controversial study analyzed 86,033 felony cases rejected for prosecution in California. The National Institute of Justice (1982) found that 4,130 cases (4.8 percent) were rejected for search-and-seizure reasons. But the institute's conclusion that those figures indicate a "major impact of the exclusionary rule" has been challenged as misleading and exaggerated (Davies 1983).

Compared with lack-of-evidence and witness problems, *Mapp* and *Miranda* are minor sources of case attrition. Piecing together the various stages of the criminal court process leads to the conclusion that the exclusionary rule has a marginal effect on the criminal court system (Nardulli 1983). In a separate examination of case attrition data from California, Thomas Davies (1983) calculated that only 0.8 percent

(8 out of 1,000) arrests were rejected because of *Mapp* and *Miranda*. As for cases filed, Peter Nardulli (1983) calculated for his nine communities that 6 out of 1,000 convictions were lost because of exclusionary rules. Moreover, of the lost convictions, only 20 percent were for serious crimes.

CASE ATTRITION

Cases do not automatically move through the criminal justice process. Rather, at numerous stages in the proceedings, judges, prosecutors, and police officers exercise discretion, advancing some cases to the next step, diverting others for alternative dispositions, and dropping other cases altogether. Those screening decisions result in significant case attrition.

A detailed picture of case attrition during the court process emerges in a study of urban prosecutors summarized in Figure 8.3. For every 100 arrests, 24 are rejected, diverted, or referred to other jurisdictions during prosecutorial screening. Of those arrests that survive the initial hurdle, 21 are later dismissed by the prosecutor through a **nolle prosequi** (nonprosecution, which is often shortened to *nolle*). Overall, 55 of the initial 100 arrests survive to the trial stage. The high attrition rate of felony cases early in the process contrasts sharply with the small percentage of acquittals during the trial phase. Once cases reach the felony court, relatively few are dismissed. Most end in either a guilty plea or a trial verdict of guilty. The prosecutor's early decisions are, thus, much more important in terminating cases than the later activities of judges and juries.

Most courts exhibit a 50 percent case attrition rate. However, there are important variations among courts in the stage at which cases are dropped. An inverse relationship exists between early prosecutorial screening and later case dismissals. In some communities, for example, many cases are eliminated during prosecutorial screening, and only a handful are dismissed at later stages. Conversely, in other jurisdictions,

---

FIGURE 8.3
Case Attrition of Felony Arrests in Twenty-Eight Urban Prosecutors' Offices

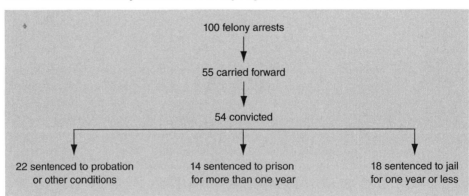

Source: Data from Barbara Boland, Paul Mahanna, and Ronald Sones, *The Prosecution of Felony Arrests, 1988* (Washington, D.C.: U.S. Department of Justice, Bureau of Justice Statistics, 1992).

few cases are initially declined by prosecutors, leading to a high rate of case dismissals later in the process. Thus, a critical stage for case screening and case attrition in one court may be of little importance in another jurisdiction.

The decisions made during the early stages of the criminal court process set the context for how cases are disposed of during plea bargaining or trial. After a case survives the initial hurdles, the courtroom work group operates on the assumption that the defendant is guilty. That produces an anomaly: The closer a case approaches to trial, the greater the likelihood the defendant will be found guilty. Once a case reaches the felony courts, the vast majority of defendants are found guilty. Thus, the important decisions about innocence or guilt are made early in the process by judges and prosecutors—not, as the adversary system projects, late in the process by lay jurors.

Case attrition is the product of a complex set of factors involving patterns of informal authority within the courtroom work group and the backlog of cases on the docket. Screening, however, is not random. Rather, case attrition is related to the sufficiency of the evidence, case priorities, and substantive assessments. As in any attempt to dissect discretion, these categories are not mutually exclusive—some screening decisions are based on more than one criterion.

Legal Judgments

Is there sufficient evidence to prove the elements of the offense? That is the most important question that prosecutors and court officials must answer in deciding whether to file charges initially or whether to dismiss the case if charges have already been filed (Miller and Wright 2008; Albonetti 1987). One assistant district attorney phrased it this way: "When I examine the police report I have to feel that I could go to trial with the case tomorrow. All the elements of prosecution must be present before I file charges" (Neubauer 1974b). That sufficiency of the evidence is an important consideration during prosecutorial screening is supported by a series of studies in Seattle, Chicago, San Diego, and Jacksonville, Florida (Neubauer and Fradella 2010). Similarly, when almost 900 prosecutors in 15 urban jurisdictions were asked whether they would accept or decline prosecution for 30 standard cases, the legal-evidentiary strength of the case emerged as the most important factor (Jacoby et al. 1982).

Two major types of evidence problems result in cases that are screened out of the process: One is insufficient evidence—the police investigation fails to uncover enough evidence to justify charging the defendant. Thus, insufficient evidence was the major reason for prosecutors refusing to file charges, with the percentage ranging from 61 percent in Manhattan to 30 percent in Washington, D.C. The second type of evidence problem stems from victims and witnesses who are reluctant to become involved in the criminal justice process. Some give the police incorrect addresses, refuse to sign a complaint, or fail to show up in court. Witness-related problems are, therefore, another important reason for declining prosecution (Boland, Mahanna, and Sones 1992).

Policy Priorities

Case attrition also results from general prosecutorial policies about case priorities. Prosecutors devote greater resources to offenses deemed more serious (Gilboy 1984). For example, a number of U.S. attorneys will not prosecute bank tellers who embezzle small amounts of money, get caught, and lose their jobs. The stigmatization of being caught and losing the job is viewed as punishment enough. Similarly, numerous local prosecutors have virtually decriminalized possession of small amounts of marijuana by refusing to file charges.

Substantive Assessments

The judicial process is expected to individualize justice. Substantive assessments of justice—attitudes of courthouse actors about what actions should not be punished—constitute the third category of criteria that guide screening. Some cases are dropped or reduced for reasons other than failure to establish guilt (Miller and Wright 2008; McIntyre 1968). Thus, even if evidence is strong, defendants might not be prosecuted if their conduct and background indicate they are not a genuine threat to society. Two commonly used phrases are that "prosecution would serve no useful purpose" and that prosecution would not be in the "interest of justice."

Substantive assessments of justice reflect a subjective decision on the part of the prosecutor that the case is not as serious as the legal charge suggests. Courthouse actors refer to these types of arrests as "cheap" or "garbage" cases. Arthur Rosett and Donald Cressey (1976) provide the following example: An old man stumbled drunkenly into a liquor store waving a cap pistol and demanding a bottle of whiskey. Even though the elements of the offense of armed robbery were clearly present, the judge, the complaining witnesses, and the prosecutor did not take the case seriously. It was viewed as a cheap robbery. Decisions not to file charges in cheap cases reflect the effort of court officials to produce substantive justice.

THE CRIMINAL JUSTICE WEDDING CAKE

The tyranny of criminal justice statistics is that they treat all cases in the same way. A homicide counts the same as a burglary, and rape is equivalent to a stolen car. Merely counting the number of criminal events gets in the way of understanding how and why court officials treat murder cases differently from burglaries and rape prosecutions receive more attention than charges involving stolen autos. To understand case attrition, Samuel Walker (2011) suggests that it is useful to view criminal justice as a wedding cake (Figure 8.4). The wedding cake model is based on the observation that criminal justice officials handle different kinds of cases very differently. Within each layer, there is a high degree of consistency; the greatest disparities are found between cases in different layers.

Celebrated Cases

The top layer of the wedding cake consists of a few very celebrated cases. The prosecution of O. J. Simpson represents one of the most celebrated cases of all time, but

FIGURE 8.4
The Criminal Justice Wedding Cake

Layer 1:
The celebrated cases

Layer 2:
The serious felonies

Layer 3:
The lesser felonies

Layer 4:
The misdemeanors

Source: From WALKER. Sense and Nonsense About Crime, Drugs, and Communities, 7th ed. © 2011 Wadsworth, a part of Cengage Learning, Inc. Reproduced by permission. www.cengage.com/permissions

every year a few other trials dominate headlines. Some recent examples that dominated the headlines include:

- The acquittal of Casey Anthony of murdering her daughter
- The prosecution of football star Michael Vick for dog fighting
- The filing and later dropping of charges against the Duke lacrosse players
- The conviction of Scott Peterson for murdering his wife and unborn baby

Equally newsworthy are those accused of bizarre crimes such as mass murder. Likewise, each year local communities have a few celebrated cases, either because a local notable was charged with a serious crime or because the crime itself was particularly heinous.

Celebrated cases are unusual because, from the moment the cases begin, criminal justice officials treat them differently, making sure every last detail of the judicial process is followed. The cases are also extraordinary because they involve the rarest of criminal court events—the full jury trial. To the fascination of the viewing and reading public, controversial matters are aired in public. As with morality plays of old and soap operas of today, public attention is focused on the battle between good and evil, although who is playing which role is not always obvious.

Because of the publicity surrounding them, celebrated cases have a tremendous impact on public perceptions of criminal justice. On one level, these cases reinforce civics book notions that defendants will receive their day in court, complete with a *Law & Order*–type defense counsel and an attentive jury. But, on another level, celebrated cases highlight the public's worst fears—the rich often get off scot-free because they can afford an expensive attorney. All too many seem to beat the rap. People assume that the court process ordinarily functions that way; clearly, it does not. Celebrated cases are atypical. They do not reflect how the courts operate on a day-to-day basis.

Serious and Lesser Felonies

The second layer of the wedding cake consists of serious felonies. The third layer includes lesser felonies. Although that distinction is often obvious, prosecutors and judges must engage in diagnostic adjudication at times. Courtroom actors differentiate between the second and third levels on the basis of three principal criteria: the seriousness of the crime, the criminal record of the suspect, and the relationship between the victim and the offender. The guiding question is, How much time is the case worth? Serious cases end up on the second layer, the "not-so-serious" ones on the third.

Analysis of the true seriousness of a case is part of the everyday language of the courthouse actors. Serious matters are routinely referred to as "heavy" cases or "real" crimes, the less serious ones as "garbage," "bullshit," or simply not real crimes. The practical consequences are that second-layer felonies are treated as serious indeed, with considerable attention given to their processing. Third-layer crimes, in contrast, receive less attention and are treated in a routine, lenient manner.

Misdemeanors

The bottom layer is a world unto itself, consisting of a staggering volume of misdemeanor cases, which far outstrip the number of felony cases. About half are "public order" offenses—disorderly conduct, public drunkenness, disturbing the peace, and so on. Only about a third involve crimes against property or persons, many of which are petty thefts or physical disagreements between supposed friends or acquaintances.

Rarely do these defendants have any social standing. In the eyes of the courtroom work group, few of these cases are worth much, and relatively little time is devoted to their processing. They are typically handled by a different court from the felony cases and processed in a strikingly different manner. Dispositions are arrived at in a routine manner, defendants are arraigned en masse, and guilt is rarely contested. Even less often are the punishments harsh. In short, cases in the lower layers are disposed of on the basis of decisional adjudication.

CONCLUSION

Prosecutors in the United States are powerful, but, as with all other governmental officials, there are limits. In the Duke lacrosse case, the state's attorney general took over the case and eventually dismissed all charges because of a lack of evidence. Moreover, the North Carolina Bar Association charged Nifong with lying to the judge, withholding key DNA evidence from the defense, and making inflammatory statements to the public. The North Carolina Supreme Court agreed and disbarred him.

In the end, the Duke lacrosse case was viewed as extraordinary. But it does illustrate the range of defendants appearing in criminal court. In many ways, the Duke students resemble those portrayed in television shows like *Law & Order*. Yet Ernesto Miranda fits the pattern more closely of those arrested by the police—a young minority male with little education and few job prospects. But the eventual outcome of his case was hardly typical. His case was heard by the nation's highest court, and he not only won the right to a new trial but also established new law in the process. Unlike the names of most defendants, whose cases are quickly forgotten, Miranda's name became a code word for crime and the rights of criminal defendants.

If *Miranda* the legal principle was to endure, Miranda the man was less fortunate. Initially, his chances of gaining an acquittal during retrial looked promising indeed. After all, the state's only evidence—the signed confession—had been ruled inadmissible. It turned out, however, that while in jail Miranda had admitted details of the crime to his common-law wife, who by now had grown afraid of him. She testified for the state and, after an hour and a half of deliberations, the jury found Miranda guilty of rape and kidnapping a second time. After serving his prison term, Miranda was living in a Phoenix flophouse when he became involved in a barroom quarrel over small change in a poker game. A large knife normally used to harvest lettuce ended his life. It is no small irony that the Phoenix police read Miranda's killer his *Miranda* rights when they arrested him.

America's courts process tens of millions of criminal cases every year. A few of them are celebrated and capture our attention, but most represent the routine work of police, prosecutors, judges, and juries. Today, crime rates continue to be a high-profile political issue even though they have stayed relatively constant for the last six decades. Criminal cases begin when police make arrests, and yet not all crimes result in arrests, and not all arrests end up going to trial. After being arrested, a defendant will appear in court and may get out on bail. During the process, charges will be filed against the defendant, and if the charge is a felony, a grand jury may issue an indictment.

The burden of responsibility on police and prosecutors to solve crimes and address our fears has sometimes led to controversial strategies that the Supreme Court has rejected. Over the years, the Supreme Court has made a number of high-profile decisions that expanded the protections afforded criminal defendants in areas such as confessions, searches, and pretrial motions. Together, those decisions illustrate the complexity of balancing protections for criminal defendants with the rights of citizens to be free from crime. *Miranda* now represents established law, but the Court remains free to reconsider its prior decisions in light of changes in society or the legal system.

CRITICAL THINKING QUESTIONS

1. Many discussions of crime suggest that smart defendants are able to beat the rap by pleading insanity, slanting their testimony at the urging of defense counsel, and exploiting legal loopholes such as the exclusionary rule. Given the profile of the typical criminal defendant, how realistic are those assumptions?

2. When the Court announced its decision in *Miranda v. Arizona* (1966), it sparked widespread controversy and was a major issue in the 1968 presidential campaign. Over time, however, it has become much more accepted than the Court's decisions in *Mapp v. Ohio* (1961) regarding search and seizure. What factors might explain this apparent shift in public assessments?

3. What are some recent examples of crimes that should be considered celebrated cases? Do any local cases fall into this category?

Search Terms

crime
police
prosecution

Useful URLs

http://www.fbi.gov/ucr/ucr.htm
  Federal Bureau of Investigation's *Uniform Crime Reports*.

http://www.ojp.usdoj.gov/bjs
  The Bureau of Justice Statistics provides comprehensive statistics.

http://www.ojp.usdoj.gov/ovc
  Office for Victims of Crime provides substantial funding to state victim assistance and compensation programs.

http://www.uncjin.org
  United Nations Crime and Justice Information Network (UNCJIN) offers information regarding crime and justice worldwide.

http://www.crimelibrary.com
  Crime Library offers major crimes, notorious criminals, and famous lawmen; also feature stories, photos, and daily reports on crimes of national and international interest.

REFERENCES

"A Needed Probe." 2010. *Times-Picayune* June 2.

Albonetti, Celesta A. 1987. "Prosecutorial Discretion: The Effects of Uncertainty." *Law & Society Review* 21: 291–313.

Alpert, Geoffrey and Thomas Petersen. 1985. "The Grand Jury Report: A Magic Lantern or an Agent of Social Control?" *Justice Quarterly* 2: 23–50.

Baker, Liva. 1983. *Miranda: Crime, Law and Politics*. New York: Atheneum.

Baskin, Deborah, and Ira Sommers. 2010. "Crime-Show Viewing Habits and Public Attitudes toward Forensic Evidence: The 'CSI Effect' Revisited." *Justice System Journal* 31: 97–113.

Boland, Barbara, Elizabeth Brady, Herbert Tyson, and John Bassler. 1982. *The Prosecution of Felony Arrests*. Washington, D.C.: Institute for Law and Social Research.

Boland, Barbara, Paul Mahanna, and Ronald Sones. 1992. *The Prosecution of Felony Arrests, 1988*. Washington, D.C.: U.S. Department of Justice, Bureau of Justice Statistics.

Burkoff, John. 1983. "Exclusionary Rules." In *Encyclopedia of Crime and Justice*, edited by Sanford Kadish. New York: Free Press.

Carp, Robert. 1975. "The Behavior of Grand Juries: Acquiescence or Justice?" *Social Science Quarterly* (March): 853–875.

Collins, Reed. 2007. "Strolling While Poor: How *Broken-Widows* Policing Created a New Crime in Baltimore." *Georgetown Journal on Poverty Law and Policy*. 14: 419–439.

Comptroller General of the United States. 1979. *Impact of the Exclusionary Rule on Federal Criminal Prosecutions*. Washington, D.C.: General Accounting Office.

Dammer, Harry, and Jay Albanese. 2011. *Comparative Criminal Justice Systems*, 4th edition. Belmont: Wadsworth.

Davies, Thomas. 1983. "A Hard Look at What We Know (and Still Need to Learn) About the 'Costs' of the Exclusionary Rule: The NIJ Study and Other Studies of 'Lost Arrests.'" *American Bar Foundation Research Journal* 83: 611–690.

Dempsey, John. 2003. "Wolf Pack Leads Cable with 'Law and Order.'" *Variety*, October 6, p. 26.

Engstrom, Richard. 1971. "Political Ambitions and the Prosecutorial Office." *Journal of Politics* 33: 190.

Federal Bureau of Investigation. 2004. *Uniform Crime Reports for the United States—2003*. Washington, D. C.: U.S. Government Printing Office.

Ferdico, John, Henry Fradella, and Christopher Totten. 2009. *Criminal Procedure for the Criminal Justice Professional*, 10th Edition. Belmont: Wadsworth.

Fleishman, Jeffrey. 2007. "Reform in Saudi Arabia Is Slow to Gain Ground." *Los Angeles Times*, December 17.

Flemming, Roy. 1982. *Punishment Before Trial: An Organizational Perspective on Felony Bail Process*. New York: Longman.

Forst, Brian, Frank Leahy, Jean Shirhall, Herbert Tyson, and John Bartolomeo. 1981. *Arrest Convictability as a Measure of Police Performance*. Washington, D.C.: U.S. Department of Justice, National Institute of Justice.

Fowler, Tom. 2010. "The Man Behind BP Engineers Taking the Fifth." *Houston Chronicle* August 30.

Gigot, Paul 2010 June 2, 2010 "A Political Prosecution of BP?" *Wall Street Journal* http://online.wsj.com/video/opinion-journal-a-political-prosecution-of-bp/3527A65A-9F9B-46AF-A488-D1E511DD78E3.html?KEYWORDS=bp+lawsuits

Gilboy, Janet. 1984. "Prosecutors' Discretionary Use of the Grand Jury to Initiate or to Reinstate Prosecution." *American Bar Foundation Research Journal* 9: 1–81.

Goehner, Amy, Lina Lofaro, and Kate Novack. 2004. "Where CSI Meets Real Law and Order." *Time*, November 8, p. 69.

Graham, Fred. 1970. *The Self-Inflicted Wound*. New York: Macmillan.

Greenhouse, Linda. 2007. "Passenger Granted Same Right as Driver." *New York Times*, June 19.

Heinz, Anne, Herbert Jacob, and Robert Lineberry, eds. 1983. *Crime in City Politics*. New York: Longman.

Holbrook, R. Andrew, and Timothy Hill. 2005. "Agenda-Setting and Priming in Prime Time Television: Crime Dramas as Political Cues." *Political Communication* 22: 277–295.

Holleran, David, Dawn Beichner, and Cassia Spohn. 2010. "Examining Charging Agreement between Police and Prosecutors in Rape Cases." *Crime and Delinquency* 56: 385–413.

Human Rights Watch. 2007. "Saudi Arabia: Four Sri Lankans Executed Without Warning." Available online at http://hrw.org. Retrieved February 27, 2007.

———. 2010. "Saudi Arabia: Criminal Justice Strengthened." January 14. http://www.hrw.org/en/news/2010/01/14/saudi-arabia-criminal-justice-strengthened. Retrieved July 8, 2011.

Jacoby, Joan, Leonard Mellon, Edward Ratledge, and Stanley Turner. 1982. *Prosecutorial Decisionmaking: A National Study*. Washington, D.C.: U.S. Department of Justice, National Institute of Justice.

Jensen, D. Lowell, and Rosemary Hart. 1982. "The Good Faith Restatement of the Exclusionary Rule." *Journal of Criminal Law and Criminology* 73: 916.

Kamisar, Yale. 1978. "Is the Exclusionary Rule an 'Illogical' or 'Unnatural' Interpretation of the Fourth Amendment?" *Judicature* 78: 83–84.

Karnow, Curtis E.A. 2008. "Setting Bail for Public Safety." *Berkeley Journal of Criminal Law* 13: 1–30.

Lacks, Robyn Diehl. 2007. "The 'Real' CSI: Designing and Teaching a Violent Crime Scene Class in an Undergraduate Setting." *Journal of Criminal Justice Education* 18: 2.

Liptak, Adam. 2005. "New Trial for a Mother Who Drowned 5 Children." *New York Times*, January 7.

McIntyre, Donald. 1968. "A Study of Judicial Dominance of the Charging Decision." *Journal of Criminal Law, Criminology and Police Science* 59: 463–490.

McIntyre, Donald, and David Lippman. 1970. "Prosecutors and Disposition of Felony Cases." *American Bar Association Journal* 56: 1154–1159.

Mellon, Leonard, Joan Jacoby, and Marion Brewer. 1981. "The Prosecutor Constrained by His Environment: A New Look at Discretionary Justice in the United States." *Journal of Criminal Law and Criminology* 72: 52.

Miller, Marc L., and Ronald Wright. 2008. "The Black Box." *Iowa Law Review*, 94: 125–196.

Moore, Richter. 1996. *Islamic Legal Systems*. Prospect Heights, Ill.: Waveland Press.

Murray, Martin. 2001. "300 Lashes for Scot in Audi Booze Racket." *Scottish Daily Record*, June 1.

Nardulli, Peter. 1983. "The Societal Cost of the Exclusionary Rule: An Empirical Assessment." *American Bar Foundation Research Journal*: 585–609.

National Institute of Justice. 1982. *The Effects of the Exclusionary Rule: A Study in California*. Washington, D.C.: U.S. Department of Justice.

Neubauer, David. 1974a. "After the Arrest: The Charging Decision in Prairie City." *Law and Society Review* 8: 495–517.

———. 1974b. *Criminal Justice in Middle America*. Morristown, N.J.: General Learning Press.

Neubauer, David and Hank Fradella. 2011. *America's Courts and the Criminal Justice System*. 10th ed. Belmont, Calif.: Wadsworth.

O'Neill, Michael Edmund. 2003. "When Prosecutors Don't: Trends in Federal Prosecutorial Declinations." *Notre Dame Law Review* 79: 221–290.

Prosser, Mary. 2006. "Reforming Criminal Discovery: Why Old Objections Must Yield to New Realities." *Wisconsin Law Review* 2006: 541–614.

Reagan, Ronald. 1981. Remarks at the annual meeting of the International Association of Chiefs of Police, New Orleans, September 28. Available online at http://www.reagan.utexas.edu/resource/speeches/1981/92881a.htm. Retrieved April 20, 2003.

Rosett, Arthur, and Donald Cressey. 1976. *Justice by Consent*. Philadelphia: Lippincott.

"Saudi Government: Rape Victim Had Illegal Affair." 2007. CNN, November 11.

Scheingold, Stuart. 1991. *The Politics of Street Crime: Criminal Process and Cultural Obsession*. Philadelphia: Temple University Press.

Schliefstein, Mark. 2010. "Oil Spill Panel Re-creates Failure of Well in 3-D." *Times Picayune* October 26.

Stevens, Dennis. 2011. *Media and Criminal Justice: The CSI Effect*. Sudbury, Mass: Jones and Barlett.

Surette, Ray. 2011. *Media, Crime and Criminal Justice: Images, Realities, and Policies*. 4th ed. Belmont: Wadsworth.

Walker, Samuel. 2011. *Sense and Nonsense About Crime and Drugs: A Policy Guide*. 7th ed. Belmont, Calif.: Wadsworth.

Washburn, K.K. 2008. "Restoring the Grand Jury." *Fordham Law Review* 76: 2333–2388.

Wice, Paul. 1974. *Freedom for Sale*. Lexington, Mass.: D.C. Heath, Lexington Books.

Worrall, John, and M. Elaine Nugent-Borakove (eds.). *The Changing Role of the American Prosecutor*. Albany, NY: SUNY Press. 2008.

FOR FURTHER READING

Bailey, Frankie, and Donna Hale. 2004. *Blood on Her Hands: The Social Construction of Women, Sexuality, and Murder*. Belmont, Calif.: Wadsworth.

Belknap, Joanne. 2007. *The Invisible Woman: Gender, Crime and Justice*. 3d ed. Belmont, Calif.: Wadsworth.

Davis, Angela. *Arbitrary Justice: The Power of the American Prosecutor*. New York: Oxford, 2007.

Delsohn, Gary 2003. *The Prosecutors: Kidnap, Rape, Murder, Justice: One Year behind the Scenes in a Big-City DA's Office*. New York: Plume.

Friedrichs, David. 2009. *Trusted Criminals: While Collar Crime in Contemporary Society*. Belmont, Calif.: Wadsworth.

Frohman, Lisa. *Prosecutors and Prosecution*. Burlington, VT: Ashgate. 2008.

Karmen, Andrew. 2010. *Crime Victims: An Introduction to Victimology*. 7th ed. Belmont, Calif.: Wadsworth.

Leo, Richard, and George Thomas. 2000. *The Miranda Debate: Law, Justice and Policing*. Boston: Northeastern University Press.

Messner, Steven, and Richard Rosenfeld. 2007. *Crime and the American Dream*. 4th ed. Belmont, Calif.: Wadsworth.

Simon, Jonathan. 2007. *Governing Through Crime: How the War on Crime Transformed American Democracy and Created a Culture of Fear*. New York: Oxford University Press.

Straus, Sarena. 2006. *Bronx D.A.: True Stories from the Sex Crimes and Domestic Violence Unit*. Fort Lee, NJ: Barricade Books.

TRIAL COURTS: HOW CRIMINAL CASES END: BARGAINING AND SENTENCING

Roughly 1.5 million adult inmates are housed in prisons in the United States. Federal prisons are most likely to house major drug dealers and white collar criminals whereas state prisons hold violent offenders and drug users.

David Neubauer

Scott Peterson returned from a Christmas Eve 2002 fishing trip to find his wife, Laci, missing. A frantic search by hundreds of volunteers failed to find the mother-to-be. The growing media coverage for the missing woman served only to focus attention on the husband, who was arrested four months later, after the remains of Laci Peterson and her unborn son washed ashore. The case fascinated America as few others in recent history have done, because it had all the elements of a tabloid sizzler: a beautiful wife, a cheating husband, hours of taped phone conversations, and a 10-month trial aggressively covered by the media. In the end, though, Scott Peterson's celebrity lawyers failed to convince a skeptical jury that someone else killed Laci Peterson (Ritter 2005).

Sensational cases such as the Scott Peterson murder trial, dramatic as they are, obscure two key realities of what happens in the criminal courthouse: Trials are rare, and sentences of death are even rarer. In the United States, criminal justice is popularly equated with trials. Yet, only a small percentage of defendants such as Scott Peterson are ever tried. The vast majority of convictions result not from a guilty verdict following a contested trial but, rather, from a voluntary plea by the accused. The second reality is that the death penalty is a tiny part of the sentences handed down. Of the more than seven million adults currently under correctional supervision, only about 3,000 are on death row. The political rhetoric of getting tough on crime has produced an unprecedented increase in prison populations. Thus, it is the dominant realities of plea bargaining and prison overcrowding that are the principal topics of this chapter.

The general substantive theme in this chapter is punishment. Law and Popular Culture: *The Shawshank Redemption* explores prison life as portrayed in the popular movie. Debating Law, Courts, and Politics: Should the Death Penalty Be Abolished? raises the question of abolishing the death penalty. Courts in Comparative Perspective: The People's Republic of China portrays the death penalty in China. Finally, Case Close-Up: *Roper v. Simmons* (2005) focuses on the Supreme Court decision sparing juveniles the death penalty.

THE COURTROOM WORK GROUP

Courtrooms are busy, noisy public places. The initial impression is of constant talking and endless movement. While the judge is granting probation to a defendant convicted of possessing a small amount of crack cocaine, a prosecutor and a defense attorney are engaged in an animated conversation about the terms of a plea bargain in a burglary charge. In more hushed tones, a public defender is briefing her client about the merits of the prosecutor's offer to a plea of simple robbery. All the while, police officers, bail agents, probation officers, and others are constantly moving in and out of the courtroom, exchanging social pleasantries along the way.

On the surface, courtrooms appear disorganized, but there is an underlying order to the diverse activities that occur (Maynard 1984). The group activity is best understood by the concept of the **courtroom work group**. The major participants are the prosecutors, defense attorneys, and judges who decide which defendants will be released on bail, what guilty pleas will be accepted, and, most important, what sentences will be imposed on the guilty (Flemming, Nardulli, and Eisenstein 1992).

The courtroom work group represents a complex network of ongoing social relationships. Every day, the same courthouse regulars assemble in the same courtroom, sit or stand in the same places, and perform the same tasks. The types of defendants and the nature of the crimes they are accused of committing also remain constant. Only the names of the victims and the defendants vary from day to day. Thus, although defendants and their cases come and go, the judges, prosecutors, and defense attorneys work together daily.

Interdependence governs the regular interactions among the members of the courtroom work groups. Judges, defense attorneys, and prosecutors represent separate and independent institutions, yet they are drawn together by their common task of disposing of cases. Each member of the work group can achieve individual goals and accomplish separate tasks only through the cooperation of the whole group. Judges are expected to move the docket and not allow backlogs of cases to develop. To accomplish that task, they depend on prosecutors and defense attorneys to plea-bargain cases. Assistant prosecutors are judged by their superiors on the basis of how many defendants are convicted. To achieve that goal, prosecutors depend on defense attorneys to convince their clients of the desirability of pleading guilty and on judges to accept those pleas. Defense attorneys seek to minimize the penalties imposed on their clients. To accomplish that objective, defense attorneys depend on prosecutors and judges not to hand out harsh sentences.

This mutual interdependence results in a level of cooperation not envisioned by the formal adversary model. Although we usually think of the criminal courts in terms of a conflict at trial, a more realistic appraisal is one of limited cooperation among the major participants. Cooperation, of course, is a two-way street. Those who work within the system can expect to receive some benefits. Defense attorneys who do not needlessly make additional work for prosecutors are granted access to important information about the case that might otherwise be withheld. On the other hand, those who challenge the system can expect sanctions. Defendants represented by uncooperative defense counsel sometimes receive longer prison terms than they would otherwise.

The hallmark of courtroom work groups is regularity of behavior. Normal penalties (the group's unwritten, agreed-upon sentences that are considered appropriate given the manner in which the crimes were committed and the backgrounds of defendants) provide a structure and framework to what appears to be an unstructured, almost chaotic process. Most of the matters before the courts are straightforward. Although no two crimes are exactly the same, most criminal cases fall into a limited number of categories. On the basis of past experiences, legal actors categorize crimes according to the typical manner in which they are committed, the social characteristics of the defendants, the settings of the crimes, and the types of victims (Sudnow 1965). Once a case has been placed into one of those categories, it is disposed of on the basis of a set pattern. The existence of such normal penalties allows the members of the work group to dispose fairly rapidly of the many routine cases that require their attention. The group forms a common orientation consisting of rules, understandings, and customs that accommodate the differing demands of the respective institutions. A group sense of justice is the result. Those shared norms establish boundaries for how cases will be plea-bargained as well as what sentences will be imposed on defendants who are found guilty. On the basis of normal penalties known to members of the courtroom work group, most cases are pled out (see Table 9.1).

TABLE 9.1	Steps of the Criminal Process	
	Law on the Books	**Law in Action**
Plea bargaining	The process by which a defendant pleads guilty to a criminal charge with the expectation of receiving some benefit from the state.	The majority of findings of guilt occur because of plea bargaining.
Charge bargaining	The defendant pleads guilty to a less serious charge than the one originally filed.	Some prosecutors deliberately overcharge so it appears that the defendant is receiving a break.
Count bargaining	The defendant pleads guilty to some, but not all, of the counts contained in the charging document.	In multiple-count charges, sentences are typically served concurrently (not consecutively), so the "sentence reduction" the defendant receives is largely illusionary.
Sentence bargaining	The defendant pleads guilty knowing the sentence that will be imposed.	Because the normal penalty for an offense is less than the maximum, defendants appear to get off lightly.
Sentencing		
Prison	A correctional facility for housing adults convicted of felony offenses, usually under the control of state government.	• Almost 1.5 million adults are in prison. • Sixty percent of prison inmates are African American or Hispanic.
Probation	Punishment for a crime that allows the offender to remain in the community without incarceration but subject to certain conditions.	Over 4,000,000 adults are under federal, state, or local jurisdiction on probation.
Fines	A sum of money to be paid to the government by a convicted person as punishment for an offense.	Often used in misdemeanors.
Capital punishment	The use of the death penalty (execution) as the punishment for the commission of a particular crime.	• Over 3,200 prisoners are on death row. • Fifty-five percent of death row inmates are white.

The Many Faces of Plea Bargaining

Guilty pleas are the bread and butter of the U.S. criminal courts. The data in Figure 9.1 demonstrate the pervasiveness of guilty pleas. Defendants are far more likely to be found guilty following a plea than following a trial (Covey 2008; Hashimoto 2008). **Plea bargaining** is the process through which a defendant pleads guilty to a criminal charge with the expectation of receiving some consideration (perhaps a more lenient sentence) from the state.

Plea bargaining is hardly new. Considerable evidence indicates that it became a common practice sometime after the Civil War (Sanborn 1986; Friedman 1979). Yet, for years, court officials persistently denied its existence. During the 1960s, however, plea bargaining emerged as a controversial national issue. The words used to describe negotiated settlements in criminal cases are one indication of that controversy. Currently, the two most popular terms—*plea bargaining* and *plea negotiations*—evoke

Trial Rates for Felony Defendants by Most Serious Charge

Trial rates for felony defendants in the 75 largest counties, by most serious arrest charge, 2002

Most serious arrest charge

Most serious arrest charge	Percent of defendants going to trial
Murder	(bar extends to ~44%)
Rape	
Weapons	
Robbery	
Assault	
Larceny/theft	
Drug trafficking	
Motor vehicle theft	
Burglary	
Fraud	
Forgery	
Driving-related	

Percent of defendants going to trial
(scale: 0%, 10%, 20%, 30%, 40%, 44%)

Source: Thomas Cohen and Brian Reaves, *Felony Defendants in Large Urban Counties, 2002* (Washington, D.C.: U.S. Department of Justice, Bureau of Justice Statistics, 2006).

negative images, suggesting that the courts are "bargaining with criminals" (Sanborn 1986). Other, even more pejorative phrases—copping a plea and striking a deal, for example—are sometimes used.

Types of Plea Agreements

The debate over semantics indicates that *plea bargaining* is a general term encompassing a wide range of practices. Even court officials cannot agree about what plea bargaining means: Some prosecutors, for example, refuse to admit they engage in bargaining; they simply call it something else. In the nation's courthouses, plea agreements take one of three forms: charge bargaining, count bargaining, or sentence bargaining.

One common type of plea bargaining is **charge bargaining**, wherein the defendant pleads guilty to a less serious charge than the one originally specified. For example, the defendant pleads guilty to robbery rather than to the original charge of armed robbery. The principal effect of a charge bargain is a reduction in the potential sentence. Some offenses carry a stiff maximum sentence, so a plea to a lesser charge greatly reduces the possible prison term the defendant will have to serve. Bargains for reduced charges are most commonly found in jurisdictions where prosecutors routinely overcharge to begin with. Thus, some charge reductions reflect the probability that the prosecutor would not be able to prove the original charge in a trial.

Another common type of plea bargaining is **count bargaining**, wherein the defendant pleads guilty to one criminal charge (or more than one), and the prosecutor dismisses all other pending charges. For example, a defendant accused of three burglaries pleads guilty to one burglary charge, and the two remaining accusations are dismissed. Like charge reduction agreements, a count bargain reduces the potential sentence but in a different manner. A defendant charged with many counts could theoretically receive a maximum sentence of, say, 60 years; that figure is arrived at by multiplying the number of charges by the maximum prison term for each. Such lengthy possible sentences are highly unlikely, however, because the judge will probably not sentence the defendant to serve the sentences consecutively (one after another). Consecutive sentencing is very rare; most sentences are imposed concurrently. Thus, count bargaining reflects the reality of the courthouse: Within limits, defendants will receive the same penalty no matter how few (or how many) charges exist to which they plead guilty.

The most common form of plea bargaining is **sentence bargaining**, wherein the defendant pleads guilty on the basis of the promise of a specific sentence. For example, the defendant is promised probation or a prison sentence not to exceed so many years. Typically, the defendant pleads to the original charge (called a "plea on the nose"), although in some areas sentence bargaining operates in conjunction with either count bargaining or charge bargaining. Invariably, in sentence bargaining the defendant receives less than the maximum penalty. To some critics, this is an indication that defendants get off too easily. Realistically, though, only defendants with long criminal records who have committed particularly heinous crimes receive the maximum penalty specified by law. In practice, courts impose sentence on the basis of normal penalties for specific crimes involving common types of defendants. Thus, the sentence agreed to is the one typically imposed in similar cases.

The Bargaining Process

The process by which a plea agreement is reached varies greatly from courtroom to courtroom. Who directly participates in plea bargaining varies as well. Some judges are major participants who agree ahead of time that if the defendant enters a plea of guilty, a specific sentence (sentence bargaining) will be imposed. Other judges refuse to participate at all; prosecutors dominate the bargaining process, negotiating deals on the basis of the judge's past practices. How negotiations are conducted also varies. At times, negotiations are rather casual, involving little more than a conversation in a corridor. By contrast, some courts have institutionalized plea bargaining: In a handful of courts, the defense attorney is required to sign a form specifying the plea bargain offered by the prosecutor.

Although plea bargaining is a complex process that varies among jurisdictions, numerous studies point to the following important similarities:

- The most important consideration is the seriousness of the offense: The more serious the crime charged, the harder the prosecutor bargains (Nardulli, Flemming, and Eisenstein 1984).

- The next most important consideration is the defendant's criminal record: Defendants with prior convictions receive fewer concessions during bargaining (Springer 1983).
- A key consideration is the strength of the prosecutor's case: The stronger the evidence against the defendant, the fewer the concessions offered (Adams 1983).

Why Cases Go to Trial

Although most defendants enter a plea of guilty, an important percentage of cases are tried. Cases go to trial when the parties cannot settle through bargaining. The decision to go to trial is influenced by two major factors: the strength of the prosecutor's case and the severity of the penalty on conviction. Defense attorneys recommend a trial when the risks are low or the possible gains are high. Based on that broad calculation, two different types of trial cases result. In one type, the defendant's possible gains are high because of the chance of an acquittal. There may be reasonable doubt that the defendant committed any crime, or two sets of witnesses may tell conflicting versions of what happened. The second type of trial involves situations in which the prison sentence will be severe. Even though a finding of not guilty is unlikely, the defendant may still decide the slim possibility of an acquittal is worth the risk of the trial penalty. However, not all trial cases are the result of such rational calculations. Some defendants want a trial no matter what. Judges, prosecutors, and defense attorneys label irrational those defendants who refuse to recognize the realities of the criminal justice system and insist on a trial even when the state has a strong case (Neubauer 1974).

The net effect of these plea-versus-trial considerations is that some types of cases are more likely to go to trial than others. Property offenses (burglary, theft, forgery) are unlikely to go to trial, because the state is apt to have a strong case (usually buttressed by physical evidence) and the prison sentence will not be long. Serious crimes such as murder, rape, and armed robbery are much more likely to be tried. In these crimes of violence, there may be reasonable doubt because the circumstances are often unclear. Moreover, a convicted defendant is likely to serve a long prison term and is, therefore, more disposed to take a chance on an outright acquittal.

PLEA BARGAINING AND COURTROOM WORK GROUPS

The portrayal of plea bargaining as a regrettable but necessary expedient for disposing of excessive caseloads contains a kernel of truth. Courthouses across the nation are indeed confronted with a large number of cases, a situation exacerbated by the War on Drugs (see Chapter 4). Moreover, courts, like other public agencies, possess inadequate resources for carrying out all their assigned tasks. But explaining plea bargaining in terms of the excessive caseload hypothesis suffers from numerous limitations. Most immediately, it cannot explain why plea bargaining is as prevalent in courts with relatively few cases as in courts with heavy caseloads (Eisenstein and Jacob 1977).

The principal weakness of the excessive caseload hypothesis is that it assumes a purely mechanical judicial process, suggesting that more judges, more prosecutors, and more courtrooms would result in more trials and harsher penalties. That view ignores the underlying reality of the criminal court process. Plea bargaining is a response to the situation facing the courthouse actors. Overall, plea-bargaining practices are more reflective of prosecutorial discretion than of the size of a court's docket (Church 1985). Thus, bargaining will likely continue, regardless of any increase in the number of legal actors, because the courtroom work group encourages coordination and cooperation.

Presumption of Factual Guilt

In the cases that survive after initial screening (Chapter 8), judges, prosecutors, and defense attorneys perceive that defendants are in serious trouble (Eisenstein and Jacob 1977). Indeed, throughout the history of a case, decisions on bail, indictment, and screening have been premised on the knowledge that the vast majority of defendants end up pleading guilty (Wright and Miller 2002). Stated another way, cases are cloaked with a presumption of factual guilt (Heumann 1978). "Dead bang" or "slam dunk" are terms court officials use to describe cases with very strong evidence and no credible demonstration of the defendant's innocence (Mather 1974). According to prosecutors, the strong evidence against the accused should indicate to any competent defense attorney that the defendant will be found guilty (Neubauer 1974). Although the courtroom work group spends a great deal of time discussing and analyzing how the crime was committed, in most instances there is little likelihood the defendant will be acquitted outright. The most likely outcome is that he or she will be convicted of a less serious offense. The question of what charge the facts will support is an important part of plea bargaining.

Costs and Risks of Trial

Trials are a costly and time-consuming means of establishing guilt. To try a single case requires the presence of a judge, a bailiff, a clerk, a defense attorney, a prosecutor, and a court reporter. During the trial, none of those court actors can devote much time to the numerous other cases requiring their attention. A trial also requires the presence of sundry noncourt personnel, including police officers, witnesses, victims, and jurors. For each of those people, a trial represents an unwanted intrusion into their daily lives.

Trials also represent uncertainties and risks. A number of unexpected events can occur during trial. The victim may refuse to cooperate. The testimony of a key witness may differ significantly from earlier statements made to the police. A witness may make an unfavorable impression on the jury. A mistrial may be declared. Even after a jury verdict of guilty, the appellate courts may reverse the decision, meaning the whole process must be repeated.

Because of the costs and the risks, all members of the courtroom work group have a common interest in avoiding unnecessary trials. To a large extent, a trial is seen as a shared penalty that all parties seek to avoid through plea bargaining. To be sure, not all trials can be avoided. But, through negotiations, scarce trial resources can be applied to the cases that need to be tried.

Jury Trial Penalty

In courthouses around the nation, it is a common assumption that defendants who do not plead guilty will receive a harsher sentence. That perception has been empirically documented (Brereton and Casper 1981–1982). One study concluded, "The cost of a jury trial for convicted defendants in Metro City [an unnamed major eastern city] is high: Sentences are substantially more severe than for other defendants" (Uhlman and Walker 1980, 337). Typically called the jury trial penalty, the notion reflects this philosophy: "He takes some of my time; I take some of his." Here "time" refers to the hours spent hearing evidence presented to a jury (King et al. 2005). The U.S. Supreme Court has clearly sanctioned the practice (*Bordenkircher v. Hayes* 1978).

Copping a Plea

"Your Honor, my client wishes at this time to withdraw his previous plea of not guilty and enter a plea of guilty." Using similar words, defense attorneys indicate that the case is about to end: The defendant is ready to plead. In limited circumstances, a defendant will enter a plea of **nolo contendere**, Latin for "I will not contest it." With that plea, the judge will find the defendant guilty, but the plea cannot be used in a civil proceeding as an admission of guilt. Thus, a plea of nolo contendere is usually entered when civil proceedings are likely. Most defendants, however, plead guilty to one or more charges listed in the information or the indictment.

For years, the taking of a guilty plea operated in an informal manner and largely depended on what local court officials believed should be done. The Supreme Court, however, set standards for the plea-bargaining process, holding that a plea of guilty is more than an admission of conduct; it is a conviction that also involves a defendant's waiver of the most vital rights of the court process: presumption of innocence, jury trial, and confrontation of witnesses (*Boykin v. Alabama* 1969). Thus, before a court can accept a defendant's plea of guilty, the judge must question the defendant to ensure that he or she understands the nature of the charge, comprehends the possible penalty on conviction, realizes a plea waives the right to a jury trial, and is satisfied with the services of the defense counsel. Such questioning ensures that the plea was not the product of threats, and that it reflects the defendant's own choice; it also provides an official court record, designed to prevent defendants from later contending they were forced to plead guilty. Some courts go a step further by requiring that a brief summary of the evidence against the defendant be entered into the record.

In seeking to regularize plea bargaining, the Court has also ruled that defendants have a limited right to withdraw a guilty plea. In *Santobello v. New York* (1971), the prosecutor agreed to permit the defendant to plead to a less serious offense and to make no recommendations as to sentencing. Months later, however, a new prosecutor, apparently unaware of his colleague's commitment, recommended the maximum sentence, which the judge imposed. The Supreme Court ordered that the defendant be allowed to withdraw the plea, arguing, "When a plea rests in any significant degree on a promise or agreement of the prosecutor, so that it can be said to be part of the inducement or consideration, such promise must be fulfilled."

Judges have discretion in deciding whether to accept the defendant's plea (Molesworth 2008). Some judges refuse to do so unless the defendant fully admits guilt.

If the defendant wishes to plead guilty but refuses to admit any wrongdoing, the judge may reject the plea and order the case to be tried. Other judges insist on a less stringent admission of wrongdoing (*Alford v. North Carolina* 1971).

FORMS OF PUNISHMENT

Flogging, exile, branding, and the stocks are just a few of the types of punishments historically inflicted on the guilty. Today, such sanctions constitute cruel and unusual punishment. In their place are imprisonment, probation, fines, and, on rare occasions, the death penalty. More than 7.2 million adults are currently under some form of correctional supervision. Although active discussion of sentencing alternatives is ongoing, these four are the principal forms of punishment from which the judge must choose. Because of the special issues surrounding the death penalty, it will be discussed at the end of the chapter.

Imprisonment

The United States relies on **imprisonment** more than any other Western nation. Over 1.6 million adult inmates are currently housed in state and federal prisons, and crime policies that stress getting tough with criminals have steadily been adding to the prison population over the years. Figure 9.2 dramatically underscores the tripling of the prison population over the last decades. Since 2000, however, the growth of the prison population has slowed significantly, increasing only 0.2 percent during the most recent

FIGURE 9.2
Increase in Adult Correctional Population, 1980–2009 (in millions)

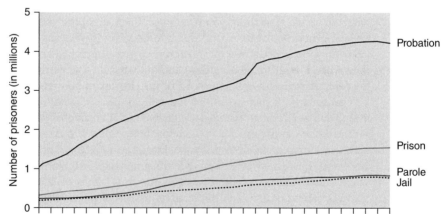

Source: Data from U.S. Department of Justice, Bureau of Justice Statistics. Available online at http://bjs.ojp.usdoj.gov/content/glance/corr2.cfm.

year when statistics are available (Sabol and West 2010). Nonetheless, the dominant reality in U.S. prisons today is overcrowding.

The problem of overcrowding has also been exacerbated by substandard prison conditions. In the 1970s, the federal courts began to examine closely the operations of correctional institutions to ensure compliance with the Eighth Amendment's protection against cruel and unusual punishment. The entire prison systems of at least nine states have been declared unconstitutional, and individual prisons have been found constitutionally defective in many others. As a result, in most states, prisons were operating under a federal court order, which typically specified a maximum prison population, required physical conditions to be upgraded, increased the number of prison guards, upgraded the quality of the food, and mandated minimal medical facilities (Rhodes 1992; Crouch and Marquart 1989). Those federal court orders transformed prison conditions, particularly in the South (Feeley and Rubin 1998).

It is now harder to challenge prison conditions in federal court, however. The Supreme Court created a higher standard for prisoners to allege Eighth Amendment violations, requiring "a deliberate indifference" on the part of prison officials (*Wilson v. Seiter* 1991). Moreover, in 1996, Congress passed the Prison Litigation Reform Act, which terminated federal court supervision of state prisons. Nonetheless, state correctional officials are aware that slipping back into old practices will result in future litigation. The Supreme Court, though, upheld a lower court decision ordering the state of California to reduce by up to 46,000 prison to alleviate unconstitutional conditions brought on by overcrowding (*Brown v. Plata* 2011).

Few prisoners serve their maximum terms of imprisonment. In a typical year more than 675,000 inmates leave prison, but only one out of four is released because his or her sentence has expired; the vast majority are released after serving only a part of the prison term imposed by the judge (West and Sabol 2010). The decisions made by governors, correctional officials, and parole boards play a major role in the early release of prisoners. (See Law and Popular Culture: *The Shawshank Redemption.*)

One form of early release is **parole**, the conditional release of an inmate from prison after a portion of the prison sentence has been served. Parole boards decide when to release prisoners, and parole officers supervise the parolees; rule violations or new crimes may result in a return to prison for the balance of the unexpired term. Clearly, parole decisions made by the executive branch of government affect how long an inmate must stay in prison. Furthermore, in all but four states (Hawaii, Pennsylvania, Tennessee, and Utah), prisoners are awarded **good time**, that is, days off their prison terms for good behavior or participation in various types of vocational, educational, or treatment programs. Correctional officials find these sentence reduction provisions necessary to maintain institutional order and reduce overcrowding.

How long an offender will be imprisoned also depends on the criteria parole boards use in granting conditional release and how correctional officials compute good time. The use of those powers is being questioned today. Critics charge that parole boards possess too much discretion. That questioning has produced significant changes in parole board authority in some jurisdictions in recent years. In 15 states, parole board authority to release all offenders has been abolished, and an additional five states abolished parole board authority to release certain violent offenders. Moreover, in fourteen other states and the District of Columbia, parole boards now have

LAW AND POPULAR CULTURE

■ *The Shawshank Redemption* (1994)

Bank executive Andy Dufresne (Tim Robbins) is falsely convicted of shooting to death his adulterous wife and her lover. Dufresne is to serve his two consecutive life sentences (one for each victim) in the maximum-security Shawshank Prison, where he soon meets Ellis Boyd "Red" Redding (Morgan Freeman), who has been denied parole after serving twenty years of his sentence. Red is the veteran convict who helps the new convicts adjust to the brutality of the guards and prisoners alike; he is also a smuggler who can get anyone just about anything. For Dufresne, the smuggled goods include a picture of the actress Rita Hayworth and a geologist's rock hammer.

At the center of the drama is Samuel Norton (Bob Gunton), the Bible-toting warden who lays down the cardinal rule: "No blasphemy. I'll not have the Lord's name taken in vain in my prison." But there is another side to the self-righteous warden—he runs several illegal businesses. Dufresne soon puts his business talents to work by keeping the warden's books (and documenting every detail of his corrupt enterprises).

Dufresne eventually escapes from prison using the rock hammer to tunnel his way out. He also smuggles out the warden's account records. He uses the passbooks to clean out the warden's secret bank accounts and mails the accumulated documentation to the local police. The police come to arrest the corrupt warden, who manages to escape justice by committing suicide.

Reflecting on prison movies such as *The Shawshank Redemption, Cool Hand Luke,* and *The Longest Yard,* Dr. Robert Freeman found himself cheering the inmates and detesting the sadistic guards, just as millions of other viewers have done. Unlike other viewers, he felt an element of disquiet as well—because (before embarking on a teaching career) he spent twenty years as an employee of the Pennsylvania Department of Corrections. Even though he had firsthand experience with the realities of prisons, Freeman found himself an avid consumer of the popular culture surrounding corrections.

Most of that culture is, of course, a negative one. In *Popular Culture and Corrections,* Freeman (2000) argues that prison movies have seven interwoven sets of negative imagery: systematic brutality in the service of inmate discipline; exploitation of inmates as a cheap source of labor; the degradation of female inmates; the condoning of homosexual rape; systematic racial prejudice; staff incompetence, corruption, and cruelty; and portrayal of guards as smug hacks who are indifferent to human suffering and obsessed with routine.

As you watch *The Shawshank Redemption,* ask yourself which of those themes are present and how are they portrayed. Also ask yourself why there is an apparent disconnect in the public mind between negative images of prisons in the popular media and pressures to lock up more prisoners for longer periods of time. You might also ponder how this movie contributes to federal court decisions that require upgrading conditions of confinement in the nation's prisons.

---

only limited discretion; explicit parole guidelines govern early release. Many states have also moved to reduce the amount of good time a prisoner may earn.

Nonetheless, the number of people on parole keeps increasing. Today, approximately 825,000 adults are under state parole supervision.

Probation

Probation is the principal alternative to imprisonment. It is the most commonly used sanction in the United States; indeed, more than three times as many adults are on probation as are housed in state and federal prisons (Auerhahn 2007). The problem of severe prison overcrowding has provoked another problem: a significant increase in probation. Approximately 4.2 million adults are on probation, which represents a doubling since the 1980s (see Figure 9.2).

Unlike incarceration, **probation** is designed to maintain control over offenders while permitting them to live in the community under supervision. Typical conditions of probation include keeping a job, supporting the family, avoiding places where alcoholic beverages are sold, reporting periodically to the probation officer, and not violating any law. Because probation is a judicial act, the judge may revoke it and send the defendant to prison if the conditions of probation are violated.

The use of probation is supported on two grounds: Prisons are inappropriate places for some defendants, and probation is significantly less expensive than imprisonment. State and federal laws grant judges wide discretion in deciding whether to place a defendant on probation. Typically, statutes allow probation when it appears the defendant is not likely to commit another offense, the public interest does not require the defendant to receive the penalty provided for the offense, and rehabilitation does not require the defendant to receive the penalty provided for the offense. Legislatures, however, often forbid the granting of probation for persons convicted of serious offenses such as murder, rape, and, in some states, armed robbery.

Fines

The imposition of a **fine** is one of the oldest and most widely used punishments. Used extensively for traffic offenses and minor ordinance violations, fines generate well over $1 billion annually for local governments. The imposition of a fine, however, is not confined to the lower courts. Many trial courts of general jurisdiction depend quite heavily on fines, alone or as the principal component in combination with another sanction (probation, for example), in sentencing criminal defendants for a wide variety of offenses, including some generally considered serious (Cole 1992). The BP oil spill has focused public attention on when fines in criminal cases are appropriate (See Debating Law, Courts, and Politics: Should Fines for the Deepwater Horizon Explosion be in the Millions or the Billions?)

NORMAL PENALTIES AND SENTENCING DECISIONS

Sentencing represents a joint decision-making process. Although only judges possess the legal authority to sentence a guilty defendant to prison, place him or her on probation, and/or choose a monetary penalty, other members of the courtroom work group are also influential. For example, where sentence bargaining predominates, the judge almost invariably imposes the sentence that the prosecutor and the defense attorney have already agreed on. Probation officers also play a role (Lurigio, Olson, and Snowden 2009). They prepare a **presentence investigation**, which typically includes a recommendation for an appropriate sentence. Although judges are not required to honor such recommendations, they almost invariably do (Clear and Latessa 1993).

In deciding on a sentence, members of the courtroom work group realize that each defendant and each crime are somewhat different. Overall, sentences are expected to be individualized—to fit the penalty to the crime and the defendant.

DEBATING LAW, COURTS, AND POLITICS

▪ Should Fines for the Deepwater Horizon Explosion be in the Millions or the Billions?

In a routine traffic violation or misdemeanor conviction fines are assessed in the hundreds of dollars. But in a major oil spill potential fines are calculated in the millions or the billions of dollars. From BP's perspective, the worst case scenario is a $21 billion civil and criminal fine, which suggests that the legal process of calculating and collecting these fines is likely to be a lengthy one (Hargreaves 2010). Three major issues will be litigated: how much oil was spilled? should criminal fines be levied? and which of the several corporations involved should pay these fines? (discussed in Chapter 11).

Determining how many barrels of oil spewed from the damaged well is a difficult task. Cameras and other devices monitored the blowout but they provide an imperfect guide to the volume of oil actually released. Estimates range from a flow of 35,000 to 60,000 barrels of oil per day but there were important variations from day to day. Moreover some of what was released were hydrocarbon byproducts that are not subject to a fine. The consensus government figure reported in the media was a total of 4.9 million barrels of oil spilled in the Gulf of Mexico but lawyers for BP hotly contest this number, suggesting that the government is overestimating by as much as 50 percent (Kunzelman 2011). Lawyers for the various corporations will also stress during negotiations how difficult it will be for the government to prove such numbers before a judge or jury.

The second contentious issue subject to court determination is whether gross negligence was involved. The Clean Water Act sets a civil fine of $1,100 for every barrel of oil released because of an oil spill. Based on an oil spill of 4.9 million barrels, the total fine would amount to $5.39 billion. If, however, the government determines that the spill was the result of "gross negligence" the fine virtually quadruples to $4,300 per barrel. It is important to note that the standard of gross negligence differs from the typical criminal standard of guilty intent. The industry is certain to argue that the accident was simply that, an accident that did not constitute gross negligence. But if the government can prove in court a criminal violation, the total potential fine calculates out to a staggering $21 billion.

No one expects such astronomical numbers to prevail in the end. Indeed fines are seldom leveled in rig accidents. Of 400 offshore incidents investigated by the Mineral Management Service (whose name was later changed to the Bureau of Ocean Energy Management, Regulation and Enforcement) only 16 resulted in a fine (Olsen and Nalder 2010).

The question of whether the fines for polluting the Gulf of Mexico should be assessed in the millions or the billions of dollars underscores the interaction of law, courts, and politics in the U.S. The beginning point is the law. The Clean Water Act creates the parameters for determining what the fine should be but also clearly creates discretion in how those fines will be calculated. In the federal courts the legal battles will be waged over how much oil was actually spilled and whether any of the parties were grossly negligent. But in the end highly ranking government officials (the Attorney General and others) will have to make a political judgment call whether it is better to settle out of court (ensuring fines are collected in a somewhat timely manner) or proceed to trial (a lengthy and uncertain trial process). And the amount of the final fine is certain to produce political fallout. Conservatives will probably object that the fines were punitive, designed to cripple the oil industry and in the end simply drive up the already high price of a gallon of gasoline. Liberals will no doubt suggest that the fines were lower than they should have been, and because they amount to only a tiny percentage of corporate profits and therefore do not deter.

Meanwhile another political battle is being waged in Congress. Proposals in Congress call for 80 percent of the money collected in fines to be devoted to coastal restoration projects in states along the Gulf of Mexico. But in a nation facing a major debt problem, prominent conservatives argue the money should go directly to balancing the federal budget.

TABLE 9.2	Sentences Imposed After Felony Convictions		
	Prison (%)	Jail (%)	Probation (%)
All offenses	41	28	31
Violent offenses	52	25	23
Murder	91	4	5
Sexual assault	59	23	18
Robbery	71	15	14
Aggravated assault	42	29	29
Other violent	42	35	23
Property offenses	38	28	34
Burglary	46	26	28
Larceny	36	31	33
Fraud	31	28	41
Drug offenses	39	27	34
Possession	34	28	38
Trafficking	42	26	32
Weapons offenses	45	28	27
Other offenses	35	35	30

Source: Matthew Durose and Patrick Langan, *State Court Sentencing of Convicted Felons, 2002* (Washington, D.C.: U.S. Department of Justice, Bureau of Justice Statistics, 2005).

Table 9.2 displays the range of sentences imposed after felony convictions. In seeking to standardize sentences, however, courtroom work groups employ normal penalties (Spohn 2009; Sudnow 1965). Using as a basis the usual manner in which crimes are committed and the typical backgrounds of the defendants who commit them, courtroom work groups develop typical sentences that are appropriate for given categories. Yet, typical sentences are not applied mechanically. Rather, they guide sentencing; upward and downward adjustments are made on the basis of the specifics of the crime and the defendant. Normal penalties vary from jurisdiction to jurisdiction. Nonetheless, two factors are consistently related to how courtroom work groups arrive at normal penalties: the seriousness of the offense and the prior record of the defendant.

Seriousness of the Offense

The most important factor in setting normal penalties is the seriousness of the offense (Spohn 2009; Steffensmeier, Ulmer, and Kramer 1998). The more serious the crime, the less likely the defendant will be granted probation. And the more serious the crime, the longer the prison sentence will be. When weighing the seriousness of the offense, courtroom work groups examine the "real offense" (what really happened, not the official charge). For example, if there has been a prior relationship between the victim and the defendant, courtroom work groups often perceive that the underlying crime was more a squabble between friends and, therefore, less serious than the official charge indicates (Wilmot and Spohn 2004; Vera Institute of Justice 1977).

Sentencing on the basis of seriousness is one of the major ways courts attempt to arrive at consistent sentences. Most courts employ a rank ordering that incorporates the full range of offenses from the most serious crimes of armed robbery and rape through the middle-level crimes of domestic violence to the lowest levels of forgery, theft, and burglary. One reason that sentences appear lenient is that most cases are distributed on the lowest levels of this ranking. Thus, when a judge is criticized for handing out too lenient a sentence, the usual response is that to give the defendant a longer prison term would necessitate an upward adjustment in all penalties.

Prior Record

The second most important factor in sentencing is the defendant's **prior record** (Spohn 2009; Albonetti 1997; Ulmer 1997). As it increases, so does the sentence. In considering whether to grant the defendant probation or place him or her in prison, the courtroom work group carefully considers the defendant's previous criminal involvement. Often, a single previous conviction is sufficient grounds for denying probation (Crow 2008; Welch and Spohn 1986). But that is hardly an automatic policy. Some courts grant probation for a minor felony even if the defendant has previously been convicted. Prior record also plays a role in setting the length of incarceration.

THE FAIRNESS OF SENTENCING

The sentences imposed by the courtroom work group have been the focus of heated debate for decades. Liberals and conservatives have expressed displeasure with sentencing but for fundamentally different reasons. Liberals are concerned that sentences handed down by courtroom work groups are unfair. Conservatives, on the other hand, are concerned that sentences handed down by the courtroom work group are too lenient. Those conflicting perspectives have prompted an extensive body of research, to which we now turn.

Sentences are expected to be fair, consistent, and unbiased. Numerous studies have investigated the extent of unwarranted variation in sentencing. Although terms such as *discrimination* and *disparity* overlap somewhat, they involve distinct behaviors. "Discrimination" refers to illegitimate influences in the sentencing process wherein the defendant's attributes are the primary focus. "Disparity," on the other hand, refers to inconsistencies in sentencing; here, the decision-making process is the principal topic of interest.

Sentencing Discrimination

The literature on **sentencing discrimination** focuses on extralegal variables (Hagan 1974). Considerable research has probed the extent to which the defendant's attributes of race, age, gender, and economic status pierce the judicial blindfold when sentences are imposed. The results are provocative not only because they raise important issues of equality before the law but also because they frequently appear to contradict one another (Walker, Spohn, and DeLone 2012). To cite only one example, whereas James Eisenstein and Herbert Jacob (1977, 301) conclude that "black defendants fared no worse than white defendants," Alan Lizotte (1978, 575) used some of the same data from Chicago to calculate that "the 'cost' of being a black laborer is an additional 8.06 months of prison sentence."

Race is the clearest example of an illegitimate criterion in sentencing. Critics of the criminal justice system view the arrest and imprisonment rates for minorities as evidence of racial discrimination. Although the law contains no racial bias, these critics claim that when criminal justice officials exercise discretion, discrimination can and often does enter in.

There are more studies of the effects of racial discrimination on sentencing than at any other decision point in the criminal justice system. Several major reviews of the literature have summarized and critiqued "what we know" about the impact of race on criminal sentencing (Pope and Clear 1994; Wilbanks 1987; Kleck 1981). Most of the research suggests that legal factors are more important than race in sentencing decisions. Regarding noncapital sentencing, the evidence is largely contrary to a hypothesis of general or widespread overt discrimination against African-American defendants. These studies fail to find a link between race and sentencing (D'Alessio and Stolzenberg 2009; Kramer and Steffensmeier 1993).

But conclusions that race plays only a minimal role have been called into question by some researchers (Spohn and Holleran 2000; Steffensmeier, Ulmer, and Kramer 1998). Zatz (1987) argues that discrimination has not disappeared but simply has become more difficult to detect. Kleck's review is sometimes misread as concluding there was no evidence of racial discrimination, when he actually found that the evidence was largely contrary to the discrimination theses and that discrimination was not general or widespread, not that it did not exist (Wilbanks 1987). There is evidence, for example, of discrimination for a minority of specific jurisdictions, judges, crime types, and so on (Miethe and Moore 1986; Welch, Spohn, and Gruhl 1985). In short, the research continues (Walker, Spohn, and DeLone 2012).

Sentencing Disparities

The literature on **sentencing disparities** examines not the attributes of the person being sentenced but, rather, the characteristics of the sentencing process itself (Forst 1982; Partridge and Eldridge 1974). The most frequently researched topics are geography (variations across jurisdictions) and judicial backgrounds and attitudes (variations between judges within the same jurisdiction).

What counts against defendants is not only what they do but also where they do it. Significant variations in sentencing patterns in different judicial districts within the same political jurisdiction are referred to as the **geography of justice** (Fearn 2005). For example, marked differences exist among states in prisoners per capita. Even after controlling for factors such as the number of crimes and the seriousness of those offenses, important geographical differences remain (Kautt 2002; Rengert 1989). Overall, the South imposes harsher sentences than other regions. Executions, for example, are concentrated there. Urban courts are marked by a greater use of probation and shorter prison terms than their rural counterparts. Such geographical patterns demonstrate that court officials, drawn as they are from the local communities, vary in their views of what offenses are the most serious as well as what penalty is appropriate (Tiede 2009; Johnson, Ulmer, and Kramer 2008; Myers and Talarico 1987).

Which judge imposes the sentence also counts. In any large community, it is an accepted fact that judges have different sentencing tendencies (Gibson 1980). One or two have reputations for handing out stiff sentences; one or two others are known for lenient sentences. Judges come to the bench from a variety of backgrounds. Studies of judicial decision making support the proposition that differences in judicial background are related to varying patterns of judicial behavior (Johnson, Ulmer, and Kramer 2008).

One comprehensive study of federal judges examined over 10,000 criminal cases and found district court judges appointed by Democratic presidents were more likely to decide for the defendant than judges appointed by Republican presidents. Similarly, judges from the North were more supportive of issues raised by defendants than judges from the South (Carp and Rowland 1983).

The public views judges as either harsh or lenient sentencers, but their actual practices are far more complex. Studies to date have found no single set of judicial sentencing attitudes (Steffensmeier and Hebert 1999). One study found that judges whose general sentences are in the middle range in most cases nonetheless varied in individual instances; each had imposed a sentence ranked among the ten most severe in at least one case and another sentence ranked among the ten least severe in another case (Partridge and Eldridge 1974).

The Severity of the Penalty

For decades, the public and their elected officials have expressed major concerns over high crime rates across the nation. The proposed solution is to get tough with criminals by increasing the severity of penalties. One way that legislatures have attempted to increase the severity of penalties is by increasing the maximum sentences. Another is to impose mandatory minimum prison sentences. Thus, through the years, legislative bodies have increased the severity of punishment for crimes such as dealing drugs, using a firearm while committing another offense, repeated drunk driving, child molestation, spousal abuse, and sexual assault. Those diverse crimes have little in common except that they were particularly unpopular at the time (Ditton and Wilson 1999). Such actions reflect the notion that harsher sentences will deter criminals and reduce crime. Those ideas are more often justified by moral claims than supported by valid scientific evidence. Researchers are skeptical of this deterrent effect. Numerous studies conclude that increasing the severity of the penalty does not result in lower crime rates (Zimring and Hawkins 1973).

Increasing the severity of the penalty, though, does have a major impact on the criminal justice system. Most immediately, more severe penalties have filled the prisons to overflowing. Less immediately, but just as important, harsher sentencing laws affect how members of the courtroom work groups exercise discretion.

Prison Overcrowding

Legislators and the public find raising penalties attractive because they appear to be fighting crime but do not have to increase appropriations; it is a policy apparently without costs. But, over the years, the economic costs have risen considerably. A rapidly rising prison population coupled with minimal standards for confinement means that prisons are expensive to build and even more costly to maintain. It costs more than $70,000 to build a single cell and about $25,000 to house a prisoner for a year. Stated another way, the construction of a new 500-cell prison costs over $337 million over a thirty-year period (Neubauer and Fradella 2011). Thus, state after state is finding it difficult to finance prisons. Some are now shifting funding from higher education to prison maintenance.

But the economic crisis in the late 2000s may have caused the American public to rethink its ever-more-punitive stance. Opinion research finds that the public "overwhelmingly favors spending more on policing, crime prevention programs for young people, and drug treatment for nonviolent offenders," while opposing additional funding for prisons (Gottschalk 2009, p. 456; see also, Cohen, Rust, and Steen 2006). States have been experimenting with different sentencing formulas aimed at rehabilitation, especially for nonviolent offenders (Gottschalk 2009; King 2008). But there can be no doubt that the increased severity of criminal penalties over the past 30 years or so still causes the United States to incarcerate more people per capita than any other country in the world.

Nullification by Discretion

Increases in the severity of punishments tend to be sidestepped by those who apply the law. As James Q. Wilson writes, "No one should assume that any judicial outcome can be truly 'mandatory'—discretion removed from one place in the criminal justice system tends to reappear elsewhere in it" (1975, 187). At a variety of points in the application of legal sanctions, discretion may be exercised to offset the severity of the penalty (Stith 2008; McCoy 1984). The police may reduce the number of arrests for violations subject to those penalties (Campbell and Ross 1968). Prosecutors often reduce the number of charges for that category (Merritt, Fain, and Turner 2006). Jurors may likewise decline to convict. Finally, after conviction, judges may be reluctant to apply the severe penalty (Robertson, Rich, and Ross 1973).

In short, punishment policy is only as harsh as the system that administers it. Through the discretionary actions of the police, prosecutor, judges, and juries, harsh penalties are nullified. The more severe the penalty, the less likely it is that it will be imposed when its severity exceeds the limits of punishment viewed as appropriate. The final result is that more produces less. Upping the severity of the punishment may not increase the threat of punishment and may even reduce it.

SENTENCING GUIDELINES

Concern about the fairness and/or severity of sentencing has prompted major changes in the sentencing process. Historically, legislatures gave judges wide powers to impose sentences. Legislatures created the forms of punishment (imprisonment, probation, and/or fines) but provided little guidance as to how judges should choose among those alternatives. Beginning in the 1980s, the nation began to rethink the purposes of punishment and the types of sentences created to carry out those purposes.

Opposition to traditional sentencing practices reflected an unusual political consensus. Liberals perceived the sentencing process as full of disparities and discrimination. Conservatives, on the other hand, saw the sentencing process as lacking severity and certainty. The two sides agreed that the central problem was excessive judicial discretion. As a result, numerous legislative bodies have enacted major changes in sentencing laws with the key objective of reducing the amount of discretion exercised by actors in the other branches of government. Thus, in many jurisdictions, legislatures have reined in the blank-check authority historically granted to judges by enacting, for example, sentencing guidelines.

State Sentencing Guidelines

Statewide **sentencing guidelines** are the most often mentioned procedure for ensuring fairness and appropriate severity in sentencing. They have been adopted in 21 states (Kauder and Ostrom 2008) and seriously considered in a few others (Reitz 2001).

Sentencing guidelines direct the judge to specific actions that should be taken. The sample sentencing grid in Exhibit 9.1 illustrates how they operate. The far left column ranks the seriousness of the offense according to ten categories. The top row provides a seven-category criminal history score for the defendant based on number of previous convictions, employment status, educational achievement, drug or alcohol abuse, and so on. Having determined the offense severity ranking and the criminal history score, the judge finds the recommended sentence in the cell where the applicable row and column meet. The cells below the bold black line call for sentences other than state imprisonment; these numbers specify months of supervision (that is, probation). The cells above the bold line contain the guideline sentence expressed in months of imprisonment. The single number is the recommended sentence. The range (shown below the single number) varies by plus or minus 5 to 8 percent from the guideline sentences and can be used for upward or downward adjustments.

State sentencing guidelines are best viewed as ranging along a continuum of more voluntary on one side and more mandatory on the other (Kauder and Ostrom 2008). Under voluntary sentencing guidelines, recommended sentencing ranges are derived by empirically analyzing the sanctions judges in the jurisdiction have usually imposed in various types of cases in the past. Thus, descriptive guidelines codify past sentencing practices as standards for future cases. Once adopted, these guidelines may voluntarily be used by judges but they are advisory only (Miethe and Moore 1989). Over the years some voluntary sentencing guidelines have fallen into such disuse that it is not always clear whether a particular state's guideline system is still operational (Kauder and Ostrom 2008).

Mandatory sentencing guidelines are used in a few states. The legislature delegates the authority for developing detailed sentencing criteria to a sentencing commission (Kramer, Lubitz, and Kempinen 1989). The resulting guidelines are prescriptive—that is, they express what sentence *should* be imposed, irrespective of existing practices. Once adopted, these guidelines must be followed by the sentencing judges. Mandatory

| EXHIBIT 9.1 | **Minnesota Sentencing Guidelines** |

IV. SENTENCING GUIDELINES GRID
Presumptive Sentence Lengths in Months

Italicized numbers within the grid denote the range within which a judge may sentence without the sentence being deemed a departure. Offenders with non-imprisonment felony sentences are subject to jail time according to law.

CRIMINAL HISTORY SCORE

SEVERITY LEVEL OF CONVICTION OFFENSE (Common offenses listed in italics)		0	1	2	3	4	5	6 or more
Murder, 2nd Degree (intentional murder; drive-by-shootings)	XI	306 *261–367*	326 *278–391*	346 *295–415*	366 *312–439*	386 *329–463*	406 *346–480*	426 *363–480*
Murder, 3rd Degree Murder, 2nd Degree (unintentional murder)	X	150 *128–180*	165 *141–198*	180 *153–216*	195 *166–234*	210 *179–252*	225 *192–270*	240 *204–288*
Assault, 1st Degree Controlled Substance Crime, 1st Degree	IX	86 *74–103*	98 *84–117*	110 *94–132*	122 *104–146*	134 *114–160*	146 *125–175*	158 *135–189*
Aggravated Robbery, 1st Degree Controlled Substance Crime, 2nd Degree	VIII	48 *41–57*	58 *50–69*	68 *58–81*	78 *67–93*	88 *75–105*	98 *84–117*	108 *92–129*
Felony DWI	VII	36	42	48	54 *46–64*	60 *51–72*	66 *57–79*	72 *62–84*
Controlled Substance Crime, 3rd Degree	VI	21	27	33	39 *34–46*	45 *39–54*	51 *44–61*	57 *49–68*
Residential Burglary Simple Robbery	V	18	23	28	33 *29–39*	38 *33–45*	43 *37–51*	48 *41–57*
Nonresidential Burglary	IV	12[1]	15	18	21	24 *21–28*	27 *23–32*	30 *26–36*
Theft Crimes (Over $5,000)	III	12[1]	13	15	17	19 *17–22*	21 *18–25*	23 *20–27*
Theft Crimes ($5,000 or less) Check Forgery ($251–$2,500)	II	12[1]	12[1]	13	15	17	19	21 *18–25*
Sale of Simulated Controlled Substance	I	12[1]	12[1]	12[1]	13	15	17	19 *17–22*

☐ Presumptive commitment to state imprisonment. First-degree murder has a mandatory life sentence and is excluded from the guidelines by law. See Guidelines Section II.E., Mandatory Sentences, for policy regarding those sentences controlled by law.

▨ Presumptive stayed sentence; at the discretion of the judge, up to a year in jail and/or other non-jail sanctions can be imposed as conditions of probation. However, certain offenses in this section of the grid always carry a presumptive commitment to state prison. See, Guidelines Sections II.C. Presumptive Sentence and II.E. Mandatory Sentences.

[1] One year and one day.

Source: Minnesota Sentencing Guidelines Commission available on line at http://www.msgc.state.mn.us/guidelines/guide10.pdf

guidelines have substantial legal authority. As you might expect, they achieve a much higher rate of judicial compliance and help reduce sentencing disparity.

Sentencing guidelines are complex in application (Kramer and Ulmer 2009). One major question asked by researchers and policy makers is whether sentencing guidelines do indeed result in fairer sentences. A three-state study concluded that in states that use sentencing guidelines, offenders are sentenced with more predictability, in a less discriminatory manner, and with increased transparency (Ostrom et al. 2008). Earlier studies reached similar conclusions. Racial, ethnic, and gender differences in sentencing generally decline (Kramer and Ulmer 1996; Parent et al. 1996). Disparity reductions, though, tend to erode somewhat over time (Griffin and Wooldredge 2006; Koons-Witt 2002). Researchers have also asked if sentencing guideline laws are associated with increases in sentencing severity, whether intended or not. This has been the experience in Minnesota (Tonry 1987) and Pennsylvania (Kramer, Lubitz, and Kempinen 1989). The same holds true at the federal level.

Since 2000, the U.S. Supreme Court has raised serious doubt about the constitutionality of sentencing guidelines, holding that other than the fact of a prior conviction, any fact that increases the penalty for a crime beyond the statutory maximum must be tried before a jury (*Apprendi v. New Jersey* 2000). On the basis of that reasoning, in 2004, the Court struck down sentencing guidelines in the state of Washington, holding that the Sixth Amendment gives juries (and not judges) the power to make a finding of fact beyond a reasonable doubt (*Blakely v. Washington* 2004). Some state supreme courts held that *Blakely* didn't apply to their state sentencing schemes (Lankford 2006) only to be firmly rebuffed when the Supreme Court struck down the California sentencing laws, holding that the statute gave judges authority that the U.S. Constitution places with juries (*Cunningham v. California* 2007).

Federal Sentencing Guidelines

The legal and political factors leading to the creation of state sentencing guidelines likewise led to the creation of the federal sentencing guidelines, which have become more visible and also more controversial than their state counterparts. In 1984, Congress created the U.S. Sentencing Commission (see Chapter 3) and charged it with developing guidelines for sentencing federal offenders. Those standards became law in 1987, and the Supreme Court subsequently upheld their legality (*Mistretta v. United States* 1989) only to rule them unconstitutional in 2005.

The federal sentencing guidelines proved to be highly controversial (Stithe and Cabranes 1998). Indeed, many federal judges, probation officers, defense attorneys, and even some prosecutors resent and resist the guidelines (Tiede 2009). According to Michael Tonry (1993), the federal sentencing guidelines "are a failure and should be radically revised or repealed." In support of that conclusion, he offers the following arguments. First, the guidelines are unduly harsh and, as a result, have produced a dramatic increase in the federal prison population. Second, the guidelines have failed to achieve their primary goal of reducing unwarranted disparities in federal sentencing. Indeed, the guidelines contribute to unfairness in sentencing because they are rigid and complex.

In a complex ruling, the Supreme Court has greatly altered how federal guidelines are used (*United States v. Booker* 2005). The first part of the opinion struck down federal sentencing guidelines as unconstitutional for the same reasons used to declare state sentencing guidelines unconstitutional—Congress improperly allowed judges and not juries to make key factual decisions in sentencing. But the second part of the opinion allows federal judges to continue to use the guidelines as advisory and appellate courts can review them for reasonableness.

The impact of *Booker* on federal sentencing practices was not as dramatic as some hoped and others feared. At the District Court level, the rate of within-range sentences remained the same and average sentence lengths remained constant. There were more downward departures, but these were largely due to actions of U.S. attorneys and not the judges (Hofer 2007). The U.S. courts of appeals varied in their approaches: Some adopted a wait-and-see attitude, others held that *Blakely* did not apply to the federal sentencing guidelines, and still others held that the guidelines were unconstitutional (Hurwitz 2006).

The Court revisited the issues, holding that sentences within the guidelines may be presumed "reasonable" but didn't require appellate courts to do so (*Rita v. United States* 2007) (Greenhouse 2007). Amid confusion about the impact of *Rita*, the Court again considered the issues, this time making it more difficult for courts of appeals to reverse a trial judge who imposes a sentence more lenient than the guideline recommendations (*Gall v. United States* 2007). At the same time, the high court, by a vote of 7–2, held that trial judges may narrow the sentencing gap between crack cocaine and powder cocaine (*Kimbrough v. United States* 2007). Although these decisions clearly restored some of the sentencing discretion taken away by the sentencing guidelines, they will likely result in only limited sentencing leniency. In all likelihood, federal judges will continue to use their sentencing power relatively sparingly, specialists in sentencing law predict (Liptak 2007). Moreover, in upcoming sessions, Congress might attempt to enact a new statutory sentencing scheme.

THE DEATH PENALTY

Of all forms of punishment, the death penalty is by far the most controversial and, therefore, merits separate attention. **Capital punishment** was once regularly applied to convicted felons in England and the United States. Since 1920, when statistics first began to be collected, executions declined from an annual average of 167 to only 21 per year between 1960 and 1967. From 1967 to 1972, an unofficial moratorium on executions existed. Today, only a small percentage of offenders potentially face the ultimate sanction that society can impose (see Figure 9.3).

Abolition of the death penalty has become a hot political topic. Opponents contend that it is morally wrong for the state to take a life, the death penalty has no deterrent value, and it is inherently discriminatory. Those arguments have led most Western democracies (except the United States) to abolish the death penalty. Supporters counter that retribution justifies the taking of a life and the death penalty serves as a deterrent. They are generally unconcerned or unconvinced about allegations of discriminatory impact. For more than three decades, the debate over the death penalty has focused largely on Supreme Court decisions.

FIGURE **9.3**
Prisoners on Death Row, 1953–2009

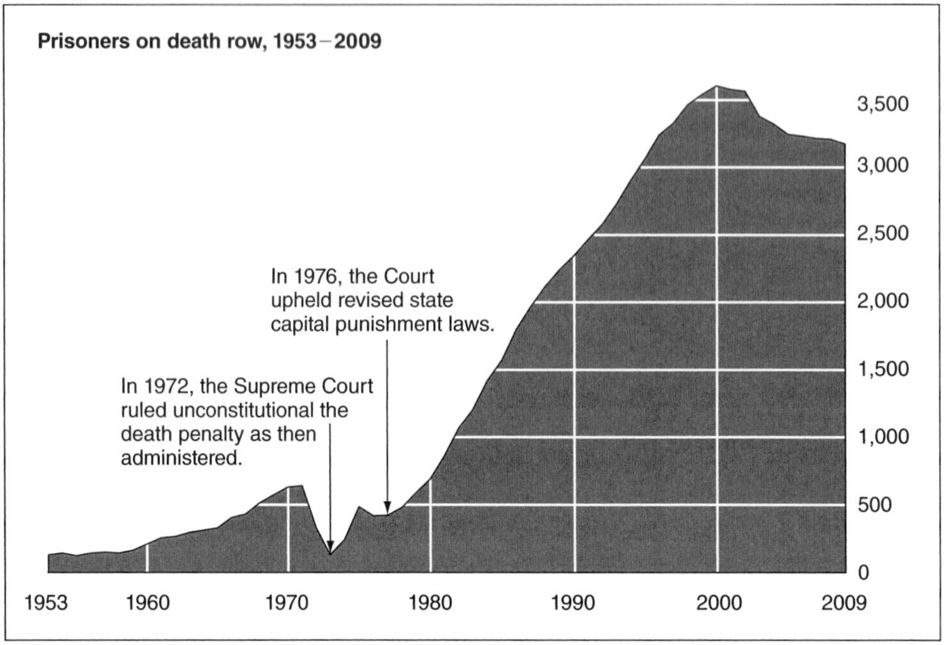

Source: Data from U.S. Department of Justice, Bureau of Justice Statistics. Available online at http://bjs.ojp.usdoj.gov/content/glance/dr.cfm

Eighth Amendment Standards

Is the death penalty consistent with the Eighth Amendment's prohibition against **cruel and unusual punishment**? The Supreme Court directly addressed that question for the first time in *Furman v. Georgia* (1972). A bare majority of the Court answered "yes," thus striking down all state death penalty statutes. But this case had limited precedential value. Among the five justices in the majority, two argued that capital punishment constituted cruel and unusual punishment under all circumstances. But the other three justices in the majority wrote more narrowly, expressing concern that the death penalty was selectively applied. The four dissenting justices (all Nixon appointees) likewise expressed divergent views about why they believed capital punishment was consistent with the Eighth Amendment.

In the wake of *Furman*, 37 states enacted new legislation that was tested in a series of five companion cases collectively known as the "death penalty cases" (*Gregg v. Georgia* 1976). A seven-justice majority agreed that the death penalty did not itself constitute cruel and unusual punishment. Next, the Court considered under what circumstances the death penalty may be imposed. The court struck down the laws in 21 states that made the death penalty mandatory—in those states, all discretion had been removed from the process by requiring that anyone convicted of a capital offense must be sentenced to death. However, the Court upheld guided discretion statutes, which allow judges and juries to weigh aggravating and mitigating circumstances in deciding whether a defendant should be sentenced to death. "The concerns expressed in *Furman* that the penalty of death not be imposed in an arbitrary or capricious manner can be met by a carefully drafted statute that ensures that the sentencing authority is given adequate information and guidance" (*Gregg v. Georgia* 1976). Exhibit 9.2 displays the key developments concerning capital punishment.

A death penalty law now must provide for a **bifurcated trial**. During the first, or guilt, phase of the trial, the jury considers only the issue of guilt or innocence. If the jury unanimously convicts for a crime carrying the death penalty, then the jury reconvenes. During the second, or penalty, phase of the trial, the jury considers aggravating and mitigating circumstances and must unanimously decide to impose the death penalty. In arguing for the imposition of the death penalty, the prosecutor points to aggravating circumstances—for instance, if the defendant was previously convicted of an unrelated murder or created a risk of death or great bodily harm to more than one person. Defense attorneys, on the other hand, highlight mitigating factors, such as the youth of the offender, lack of significant prior history of criminal activity, or mental illness.

Citing public opinion polls showing that a majority of citizens favor the death penalty for murder, many state legislatures quickly revised their laws to conform with those upheld in the "death penalty cases." Today, 34 states and the federal government have death penalty laws, thus covering roughly 75 percent of the population. The District of Columbia and the remaining thirteen states do not have capital punishment. In 2009, New Mexico became the most recent state to abolish the death penalty. (See Debating Law, Courts, and Politics: Should the Death Penalty Be Abolished?)

States exhibit important variations in their death penalty laws. Although all such laws encompass murder, some differ in the specific types of homicide cases considered death-eligible cases. It is important to realize that these and similar provisions are subject to change. Every year, some legislatures alter their death penalty laws, and some courts strike down laws. Thus, standards concerning the application of the death penalty continue to evolve. In the aftermath of *Gregg*, for example, the Court ruled that rape was not a grave enough offense to justify the imposition of the death penalty (*Coker v. Georgia* 1977). The Court also held that mentally retarded persons may be put to death (*Penry v. Lynaugh* 1989) but reversed itself in 2002 (*Atkins v. Virginia* 2002). Finally, the Court held that sixteen is the minimum age for executions (*Stanford v. Kentucky* 1989) but reversed itself in 2005, holding that eighteen is the minimum age for execution. (See Case Close-Up: *Roper v. Simmons* 2005.)

Discrimination and Capital Punishment

Capital punishment has figured prominently in studies of racial discrimination in sentencing. Marked racial differences in the application of the death penalty in the South provide the most obvious historical evidence of racial discrimination in sentencing. The racial gap was particularly pronounced in rape cases. Only the South executed

DEBATING LAW, COURTS, AND POLITICS

■ Should the Death Penalty Be Abolished?

The movie *Dead Man Walking* (1995) provides an intensely personal look at the people involved in a death penalty case. Sister Helen Prejean (Susan Sarandon) receives a desperate letter from a death row inmate named Matthew Poncelet (Sean Penn), asking her to help him avoid execution for murder. Her ministry to Poncelet also forces her to confront the emotional anguish and turmoil of the victim's family. While Sister Prejean desperately tries to gain a stay of execution from either the governor or the courts, the movie intersperses scenes of the brutal crime. Based on a true story and the book, *Dead Man Walking* by Sister Helen Prejean, the movie lays out the raw emotions underlying the debate over the death penalty.

The public debate over the death penalty also tends to be highly emotional, focusing on the pain an evil person has inflicted on the victim's survivors. By contrast, the academic debate over abolition of the death penalty centers on three deep-seated issues: morality, deterrence, and fairness. Not surprisingly, there are profound ideological differences on those three central issues.

To liberals, the death penalty is immoral, because the state should not take a life; conservatives counter that the death penalty is moral, because the defendant has already taken a life.

To liberals, the death penalty is not a deterrent, because many of those who commit murder are incapable of rational calculations. Conservatives respond that the death penalty is a deterrent, because some who might murder refrain from doing so because they know they might themselves die.

Liberals argue that the death penalty is unfairly administered. They stress that racial minorities are more likely than whites to be executed. They also believe that too many people on death row are innocent or that their trials involved procedural irregularities (discussed in Chapter 13). Conservatives counter that the fairness of the death penalty is unimportant or unproven. They believe that African Americans are no more likely to be executed than whites. They also argue that the review process works because appeals have freed the few innocents who were wrongfully convicted.

These issues form the background for the debate by the justices of the Supreme Court over how death penalty cases should be decided (*Kansas v. Marsh* 2006). At the end of its 2005–2006 term, the four liberal justices stopped short of calling for an end to capital punishment, but they pointed to studies finding that dozens of people condemned to death were later exonerated. Justice Souter stressed that we are in a period of new empirical arguments about how capital punishment is different. Justice Scalia responded that the studies were not proven. "Those ideologically driven to ferret out and proclaim a mistaken modern execution have not a single verifiable case to point to, whereas it is easy as pie to identify plainly guilty murderers who have been set free."

What do you think? Of the three main issues in the death penalty debate—morality, deterrence, and fairness—which provides the best argument for abolishing the death penalty? Which one is the most persuasive for keeping the death penalty? Do you think that the issue of innocents on death row justifies a moratorium on the death penalty?

---

rapists, and 90 percent of those executed for rape were African American. Those most likely to be executed were African Americans who had raped white women (Wolfgang and Riedel 1973). A variety of studies indicate that the use of the death penalty in the South was racially discriminatory (Ralph, Sorensen, and Marquart 1992; Baldus, Pulaski, and Woodworth 1983; Hindelang 1972). A different conclusion emerges for the North. Studies of the death penalty in northern states find no evidence of racial discrimination (Kleck 1981). Major racial differences in execution rates, together with studies finding racial discrimination in the application of the death penalty, figured prominently in the opinions of several justices when the Supreme Court struck down state death penalty laws in 1972 (*Furman v. Georgia*).

EXHIBIT 9.2	**Key Developments Concerning Capital Punishment**

Eighth Amendment	1791	Excessive bail shall not be required, nor excessive fines imposed, nor cruel and unusual punishments inflicted.
Witherspoon v. Illinois	1968	Prospective jurors cannot be excluded because they oppose the death penalty.
Furman v. Georgia	1972	All existing death penalty laws invalidated; five-judge majority expresses different reasons for this action.
Gregg v. Georgia	1976	Death penalty laws do not constitute cruel and unusual punishment under all circumstances. Mandatory death penalty laws struck down.
Coker v. Georgia	1977	Rape is not a grave enough offense to justify the imposition of the death penalty.
Pulley v. Harris	1984	The Eighth Amendment does not require states to assess whether a sentence of death has been compared to other cases to determine whether the sentence is proportional.
Lockhart v. McCree	1986	Potential jurors may be excluded if they oppose the death penalty. Thus, a death-qualified jury was upheld (overturning *Witherspoon v. Illinois*).
McClesky v. Kemp	1987	Statistical studies do not show that the application of the death penalty in Georgia is "wanton and freakish."
Thompson v. Oklahoma	1988	Defendants who were fifteen or younger at the time they committed murder may not be executed.
Stanford v. Kentucky	1989	It is not unconstitutional to apply the death penalty to persons who commit murder when they are sixteen or older.
Penry v. Lynaugh	1989	It is constitutional to execute mentally retarded persons.
Simmons v. South Carolina	1994	The defense may tell jurors that the only alternative to a death sentence is life without parole.
Harris v. Alabama	1995	States may give judges the power to sentence a capital defendant to death even if the jury votes not to impose the death penalty.
Ramdass v. Angelone	2000	Upheld sentence of death even though jurors were not told that defendant would not be eligible for parole if sentenced to life in prison.
Williams v. Taylor	2000	Upheld a section of the Anti-Terrorism and Effective Death Penalty Act intended to shorten the time between sentencing and execution.
Atkins v. Virginia	2002	Convicted defendants with an IQ of seventy or less may not be executed (overturning *Penry v. Lynaugh*).
Roper v. Simmons	2005	The Eighth Amendment forbids the imposition of the death penalty on offenders who were under age eighteen when their crimes were committed (reversing *Stanford v. Kentucky*).
Hill v. McDonough	2006	Death row inmates may challenge in federal court a state's method of lethal injection.
Kansas v. Marsh	2006	Upheld Kansas law requiring that when juries find that the arguments for and against capital punishment carry equal weight, the automatic sentence must be death.
Uttecht v. Brown	2007	Potential jurors who express reservations about the death penalty, but don't oppose it in all situations, may be removed from the jury.
Baze v. Rees	2008	Because the lethal injection process is not intended to cause unnecessary pain and suffering, it does not create an "objectively intolerable risk of harm" that qualifies as cruel and unusual punishment.
Kennedy v. Louisiana	2008	The death penalty is unconstitutional as a punishment for the rape of a child.

Research on the use of the death penalty post-*Gregg*, though, find that the race of the defendant is rarely associated with the imposition of a death sentence (Williams, Demuth, and Holcomb 2007). Rather, studies that find evidence of discrimination in the modern era report that black defendants who kill white victims are more likely to receive adverse treatment than those with similarly situated cases with non-black defendant—white victim cases (Paternoster and Brame 2008). Conclusions like this have emerged in states as diverse as Maryland, Florida, South Carolina, Georgia, and Colorado (Spohn 2009).

One stage in the process at which discrimination occurs, according to these studies, is the decision of the prosecutor to charge the defendant with a capital homicide (rather than a homicide that typically carries a life sentence) (Sorensen and Wallace 1999; Weiss, Berk, and Lee 1996; Radelet and Pierce 1985; Paternoster 1984). In Colorado, for example, prosecutors were more likely to seek the death penalty for homicides with white female victims (Hindson, Potter, and Radelet 2006).

These studies also find that jurors are more likely to choose a sentence of death rather than life imprisonment during the penalty phase of the trial. Indeed, when the U.S. General Accounting Office (1990, p. 6) reviewed the body of literature on racial discrimination in capital litigation in the post-Gregg era, it reported that in "82 percent of the studies, race of the victim was found to influence the likelihood of being charged with capital murder or receiving the death penalty, i.e., those who murdered whites were found to be more likely to be sentenced to death than those who murdered blacks." More recent studies have confirmed that this pattern has continued (Paternoster and Brame 2008; Baldus et al. 2002; Jacobs and Kent 2007; Jacobs et al. 2007; Baldus and Woodworth 2003).

Findings that the application of the death penalty remains racially biased despite the apparent protections required by *Gregg* have been challenged by a study of all death-eligible cases appealed to the Louisiana Supreme Court (Klemm 1986). The initial analysis revealed the impact of extralegal variables. More sophisticated analysis, however, highlighted the importance of legal variables. The prior relationship of the offender to the victim emerged as an important factor. Primary homicides are crimes of passion involving persons who knew each other. Nonprimary homicides occur during the commission of another felony (most typically, armed robbery), and the victim is a total stranger. Those convicted of nonprimary homicides were more likely to receive a sentence of death, regardless of the race of the offender or the race of the victim. Likewise, a study of the use of the death penalty in Texas before *Furman* found nonprimary homicides were more likely to result in the imposition of the death penalty (Ralph, Sorensen, and Marquart 1992).

Death Row Inmates

On the basis of the post-*Gregg* statutes, approximately 3,100 prisoners are under a sentence of death. The preponderance of those inmates awaiting execution are primarily in the South and secondarily in the West. Death row inmates are predominantly male (a scant 1.9 percent are female); disproportionally nonwhite, have never completed high school (50 percent), and have a prior felony conviction (two out of three) (Snell 2010).

CASE CLOSE-UP

■ *Roper v. Simmons* (2005)

Should Juveniles Be Sentenced to Death?

When he was seventeen years old, Christopher Simmons and a 15-year-old friend broke into a neighbor's house, hog-tied her with duct tape, and then shoved her over a railroad trestle into the Meramec River near St. Louis, Missouri. After the jury convicted Simmons of first-degree murder, they imposed the death penalty. The Supreme Court had earlier ruled that 17-year-olds could be put to death (*Stanford v. Kentucky* 1989), but the rationale for that decision had more recently been undermined when the Court declared that the mentally retarded could not be executed (*Atkins v. Virginia* 2002). But the justices waited almost three years to address for a second time the issue of the juvenile death penalty.

In *Roper v. Simmons* (2005), the Court held that the Eighth Amendment forbids the imposition of the death penalty on offenders who were under the age of 18 when their crimes were committed. The Court's decision affected 72 inmates on death row in twenty states. It also had an impact on untold numbers of future murder prosecutions.

Writing for the five-judge majority, Justice Kennedy (a Reagan appointee) argued that capital punishment must be limited to those offenders who commit "a narrow category of the most serious crimes" and whose extreme culpability makes them "the most deserving of execution." Those under 18 cannot with reliability be classified among the worst offenders. Citing factors such as juveniles' susceptibility to immature and irresponsible behavior, the Court concluded: "The differences between juvenile and adult offenders are too marked and well understood to risk allowing a youthful person to receive the death penalty." In finding a national consensus opposing the execution of juveniles, the Court set the age of 18 on the basis of state legislative determinations as to when one is old enough to vote, marry, or serve on a jury.

In a fiery dissent, Justice Scalia (joined by Justices Rehnquist and Thomas) blasted the majority opinion, arguing that it made a mockery of the vision of the federal judiciary set forth by the Founding Fathers and also that it ignored state legislatures. In short, the majority was off base for proclaiming itself the sole arbiter of our nation's moral standards. The finding of a national consensus was based on the flimsiest of grounds, he argued.

The decision in *Roper v. Simmons* (2005) highlights major differences of opinion over how the Constitution should be interpreted, as discussed in Chapter 2 (Debating Law, Courts, and Politics: The Law and Politics of Constitutional Interpretation). Six of the justices believe that the Eighth Amendment to the Constitution (and other critically important parts of the Bill of Rights) should be interpreted on the basis of "evolving standards of decency in a maturing society" (*Trop v. Dulles* 1958). In short, the meaning of the Bill of Rights is not frozen as originally drafted but should be interpreted in a common-law manner. To Scalia, Rehnquist, and Thomas, the interpretation of the Bill of Rights and other provisions of the Constitution should be based on their original meanings. Doctrines such as evolving standards make interpretation too subjective, they argue.

The decision in *Roper v. Simmons* (2005) also highlights major differences of opinion over the role of international law in interpreting the Constitution. The Court's opinion observed that only seven other countries—Iran, Pakistan, China, Saudi Arabia, Yemen, Nigeria, and Congo—allow the execution of juveniles. They concluded that "the overwhelming weight of international opinion against the juvenile death penalty is not controlling here, but provided respected and significant confirmation of the Court's determination that the penalty is disproportionate punishment for offenders under 18." That position provoked strong condemnation from the Court's three most conservative members. "[T]he basic premise of the Court's argument—that American law should conform to the laws of the rest of the world—ought to be rejected out of hand."

Amid the battles in the Senate over the confirmation of President Bush's nominations to the federal bench (see Chapter 6), *Roper v. Simmons* (2005) became the focal point for another round of judge bashing. House majority leader Tom Delay termed Justice Kennedy's work from the bench "outrageous" ("DeLay …" 2005).

COURTS IN COMPARATIVE PERSPECTIVE

■ The People's Republic of China

An old Chinese expression proclaims that one must "kill the chicken to frighten the monkey" (Reichel 2001). To some, that saying explains the frequent use of the death penalty in the world's most populous nation. During a worldwide scandal over unsafe Chinese products, Zheng Xiaoyu, who headed China's version of the Food and Drug Administration, was executed (Barboza 2007). Similarly, to mark a United Nations antidrug day, China executed at least 57 alleged drug traffickers (CNN 2001). How many are executed every year remains a state secret but according to Amnesty International (2011) China topped the world in the imposition of the death penalty.

China is one of the world's oldest civilizations, but the current government emerged in 1949, when Mao Tse-tung successfully led a revolution against the government. (The old regime under Chiang Kai-shek retreated to the island of Taiwan, where it continues to maintain a separate nation.) In recent years, the leaders of the People's Republic of China have quietly replaced the Soviet-style centrally planned economy with a socialist market-based one (Dammer and Albanese 2011). The result has been an economic boom; indeed, China now has the world's second-largest gross domestic productivity and is a major trading partner of the United States.

Reform of governmental units, however, has been more tentative. The primary governmental institution in China is the National People's Congress, which meets annually to approve the budget, make personnel changes, and adopt new policy directions. In reality, however, the National People's Congress, like all other governmental institutions, is subordinate to the Chinese Communist Party, which maintains firm control over the entire nation.

The legal system of the People's Republic of China is typically Marxist. The ideas of Karl Marx, Vladimir Lenin, and Mao Tse-tung (also spelled Mao Zedong) are the guiding principles of the present law. Consistent with Marxist ideology, legislators in the People's Republic of China reject the notion of the rule of law. Law is viewed instead as the tool of the ruling class (synonymous with the state) to repress the workers. Contemporary practice reverses that equation; the most serious crimes in China are defined as crimes of counterrevolution (antistate), which include crimes of undermining the socialist legal order (Guo et al. 1993). Thus, China made

headlines by its crackdown on dissidents, including U.S. scholars of Chinese ancestry who study in China and the Falun Gong, a popular religious movement that the Communist Party defines as a threat to internal order. Recently China ended the death penalty for 13 economic crimes but it remains to be seen if this will have any impact (BBC 2011).

Four levels of courts adjudicate criminal cases. The highest court in the nation is the Supreme People's Court, whose judges are appointed by the National People's Congress (Guo et al. 1993). Historically, these courts were merely instruments of the Communist Party, but a growing professionalism within the ranks of the Chinese bar suggests that there is cause for guarded optimism about the development of an independent judiciary (Melone 1998). Indeed, China recently enacted its first law to protect private property explicitly (Batson 2007). Moreover, China's highest court now must approve all executions, which might reverse a long-standing pattern of appellate courts rarely reversing death penalty cases (Magnier 2006).

From the U.S. perspective, the unique features of the Chinese legal system include the following:

- Criminal trials are conducted in secret, and defendants are rarely, if ever, found innocent.
- Defendants may be barred from discussing their case with defense attorneys before trial.
- Written criminal codes, typically found in Western nations, are scarce.
- Executions are swiftly carried out; four to six weeks from arrest to execution is not unheard of (Smith 2001).

Human rights advocates are concerned that China executes suspects after speedy trials wherein prisoners are sentenced in front of crowds reportedly as large as two million people. According to the Chinese penal code, "the death penalty is used only against those who have committed extremely serious crimes," but the code does not define what constitutes such a crime, leaving it up to the courts to decide (Agence France-Presse 2005). The crime rate in China is very low, so some suggest that periodic crackdowns are prompted by internal economic problems and growing demands by the intelligentsia for greater political freedom (Watson and Liu 1999).

(continued)

There is a momentous struggle going on in China over the role of the legal system. The ruling party in China sees the law as an instrument of control. Given that the judges are party members, they are expected to back the government. But a growing number of people believe that the legal system should be a check on authoritative governmental officials and a guardian of individual rights. Indeed, Chinese citizens are asserting their rights in record numbers. In the last decade, the number of civil court filings has doubled (to 4.4 million a year). Although those numbers are not high by American standards, this legal activity suggests a belief that everyone, even party officials, must be held accountable under the law (Pan 2004).

On January 16, 1977, the execution of convicted murderer Gary Gilmore by a Utah firing squad attracted considerable national and international attention, not only because he was the first person executed in the United States since the unofficial moratorium began in 1967, but also because Gilmore had opposed all attempts to delay the execution. Since the Supreme Court reinstated the death penalty, almost 1,200 people have been executed. A sentence of death does not necessarily mean the offender will be executed, however. Over 3,400 have had their death sentences vacated on appeal or commuted by the governor, or they have died in prison. The others remain on death row, pending the outcome of their appeals. (See Courts in Comparative Perspective: The People's Republic of China.) Some death row inmates have also been cleared of charges and released. According to the Death Penalty Information Center (www.deathpenaltyinfo.org), since 1973 there have been 138 death row exonerations. Recently researchers have started examining the challenges faced by these exonerees when they transition back into society (Westervelt and Cook 2008).

The wait on death row is lengthy—the time between the imposition of a sentence of death and its conclusion is approximately 14 years. Death penalty proponents are quick to condemn what they consider such unnecessary delay and advocate significant reductions in the ability of death row inmates to file habeas corpus appeals (see Chapter 13).

CONCLUSION

The trial of Scott Peterson highlights the dilemma defense attorneys face in a capital murder trial: Do you try to convince the jury that your client is innocent, or do you try to persuade them that your client should be spared the death penalty? Peterson's attorney evidently opted for the former, stressing to the jury that Scott Peterson might be a liar and a cheating husband but that didn't make him a murderer. But when the jury found him guilty of first-degree murder, he now faced the insurmountable task of convincing the jury that Peterson was really a good guy who didn't deserve to be executed. Unpersuaded, the jury recommended death. Like most of the other 713 condemned prisoners in California, Scott Peterson faces years on death row in San Quentin Prison while appellate courts review his trial and his sentence (see Chapter 13).

The issues raised in *Furman v. Georgia* (1972) 30 years ago are still with us. Although public support for the death penalty has increased, the United States as a nation executes very few defendants. Often unrecognized is the fact that murder (the only crime for which the death penalty is allowed) constitutes only a tiny percentage of crime. Perhaps more pressing is the lack of a national debate over prison overcrowding. The U.S. emphasis on getting tough on criminals is apparently a policy without costs until Americans total the bill for building and maintaining prisons. Although citizens and public officials want to send even more offenders to prison, they are unwilling to expend large sums of tax dollars to build the needed facilities. Thus, sentencing is likely to remain an important public policy issue for the foreseeable future.

The courtroom work group is involved in every stage of a criminal case. Once the case has passed the initial stages (see Chapter 8), the focus turns to negotiation and sentencing. Plea bargaining is much maligned but represents an important step in the criminal justice system. During this stage, members of the courtroom work group negotiate to avoid going to trial—whose costs and risks are frequently so great that members of the group share a common goal of settling the matter before a jury is involved. Of course, not all trials can be avoided, and some critics of plea bargaining argue that even more trials should be held. Others disagree, citing the importance of cooperation and negotiation among the courtroom work group for the process to move smoothly.

The courtroom work group is also involved in sentencing decisions. Once guilt is established, attention shifts to determining the proper penalty. There is much disagreement over who should determine the punishment that criminals receive. Should it be the legislative, executive, or judicial branch? Sentencing guidelines increase the power of the legislature and reduce that of judges. Increasingly, judges possess less discretion in matching the punishment to the crime committed. As legislatures and executive branch officials become more involved, the controversy will only grow.

CRITICAL THINKING QUESTIONS

1. Do defendants benefit from plea bargaining in receiving lower sentences, or is plea bargaining a shell game in which defendants are manipulated?

2. How have public demands to "get tough on crime" changed the sentencing process over the last several decades? What interest groups have contributed to those pressures? Why have interest groups that resist such pressures proven ineffective?

3. Have efforts to increase consistency in sentencing alleviated or exacerbated concerns over discrimination in sentencing?

Search Terms

| death penalty | prison | sentencing |
| plea bargaining | probation | |

Useful URLs

http://www.ojp.usdoj.gov/bjs
   This Bureau of Justice Statistics site provides numerous statistics on sentencing, prison, and the death penalty.

http://www.nicic.org

> This site covers the National Institute of Corrections, the federal agency that provides leadership in the areas of prisons, jails, and community corrections.

http://www.ussc.gov

> The U.S. Sentencing Commission is a federal agency that publishes the sentencing guidelines. Data are collected from probation offices in different judicial districts, the Judicial Conference Committee on Criminal Law, and the Administrative Office of U.S. Courts and compiled into statistical demographics. That information is published in its *Sourcebook of Federal Sentencing Statistics* and made available on the Web.

http://www.ncadp.org

> Site of the National Coalition to Abolish the Death Penalty, an interest group that began shortly after the Supreme Court decision in *Gregg v. Georgia* (1976) as an advocate for doing away with the death penalty and capital punishment. Today, thousands of people, and various federal, state, and local organizations across the nation, support them.

http://www.prodeathpenalty.com

> A pro–death penalty website.

REFERENCES

Adams, Kenneth. 1983. "The Effect of Evidentiary Factors on Charge Reduction." *Journal of Criminal Justice* 11: 525–538.

Agence France-Presse. 2005. "Chinese Legal Scholars Seek to Intervene on Death Penalty Usage." January 5.

Albonetti, Celesta. 1997. "Sentencing Under the Federal Sentencing Guideline: Effects of Defendant Characteristics, Guilty Pleas, and Departures on Sentence Outcomes for Drug Offenses, 1991-1992." *Law and Society Review* 31: 789–822.

Amnesty International. 2011. "China Human Rights." http://www.amnestyusa.org/our-work/countries/asia-and-the-pacific/china?id=1011134 accessed July 18, 2011.

Auerhahn, Kathleen. 2007. "Do You Know Who Your Probationers are? Using Simulation Modeling to Estimate the Composition of California's Felony Probation Population, 1980-2000." *Justice Quarterly* 24: 27–47.

Baldus, David, Charles Pulaski, and George Woodworth. 1983. "Comparative Review of Death Sentences: An Empirical Study of the Georgia Experience." *Journal of Criminal Law and Criminology* 74: 661–663.

Baldus, David C., and George Woodworth. 2003. "Race Discrimination in the Administration of the Death Penalty: An Overview of the Empirical Evidence with Special Emphasis on the Post-1990 Research." *Criminal Law Bulletin* 39: 194–226.

Barboza, David. 2007. "A Chinese Reformer Betrays His Cause, and Pays." *New York Times*, July 16.

Batson, Andrew. 2007. "China Builds Commerce Codes." *Wall Street Journal*, March 2.

BBC. 2011. "China Ends Death Penalty for 13 Economic Crimes." February 25.

Brereton, David, and Jonathan Casper. 1981–1982. "Does It Pay to Plead Guilty? Differential Sentencing and the Functioning of Criminal Courts." *Law and Society Review* 16: 45–70.

Bureau of Justice Statistics. 2000. *Correctional Populations in the United States*, 1997. Washington, D.C.: U.S. Government Printing Office.

Campbell, Donald, and H. Laurence Ross. 1968. "The Connecticut Crackdown on Speeding: Time-Series Data in Quasi-Experimental Analysis." *Law and Society Review* 3: 33–54.

Carp, Robert, and C. K. Rowland. 1983. *Policymaking and Politics in the Federal District Courts*. Knoxville: University of Tennessee Press.

Carrow, Deborah. 1984. "Judicial Sentencing Guidelines: Hazards of the Middle Ground." *Judicature* 68: 161–171.

Church, Thomas. 1985. "Examining Local Legal Culture." *American Bar Foundation Research Journal* 10: 449–518.

Clear, Todd, and Edward Latessa. 1993. "Probation Officers' Role in Intensive Supervision: Surveillance Versus Treatment." *Justice Quarterly* 10: 441–462.

CNN. 2001. "China Kills 57 on Anti-Drug Day." Available online at http://www.cnn.com. Retrieved June 26, 2001.

Cohen, Mark, Roland Rust, and Sara Steen. 2006. "Prevention, Crime Control or Cash?" Public Preferences Towards Criminal Justice Spending Priorities." *Justice Quarterly* 23: 317–335.

Cole, George. 1992. "Using Civil and Administrative Remedies to Collect Fines and Fees." *State Court Journal* 16: 4–10.

Covey, Russell D. 2008. "Fixed Justice: Reforming Plea Bargaining with Plea-Based Ceilings." *Tulane Law Review* 82: 1237–1290.

Crouch, Ben, and James Marquart. 1989. *An Appeal to Justice: Litigated Reform of Texas Prisons.* Austin: University of Texas Press.

Crow, Matthew S. 2008. "The Complexities of Prior Record, Race, Ethnicity, and Policy Interactive Effects in Sentencing." *Criminal Justice Review* 33: 502–523.

D'Alessio, Stewart, and Lisa Stolzenberg. 2009. "Racial Animosity and Interracial Crime." *Criminology* 47: 269–296.

"DeLay Criticizes Supreme Court Justice." 2005. Available online at http://www.cnn.com. Retrieved April 20, 2005.

Ditton, Paula, and Doris Wilson. 1999. *Truth in Sentencing in State Prisons.* Washington, D.C.: U.S. Department of Justice, Bureau of Justice Statistics.

Eisenstein, James, and Herbert Jacob. 1977. *Felony Justice: An Organizational Analysis of Criminal Courts.* Boston: Little, Brown.

Fearn, Noelle. 2005. "A Multilevel Analysis of Community Effects on Sentencing." *Justice Quarterly* 22: 452–486.

Feeley, Malcolm, and Edward Rubin. 1998. *Judicial Policy Making and the Modern State: How the Courts Reformed America's Prisons.* New York: Cambridge University Press.

Flemming, Roy, Peter Nardulli, and James Eisenstein. 1992. *The Craft of Justice: Politics and Work in Criminal Court Communities.* Philadelphia: University of Pennsylvania Press.

Forst, Martin. 1982. "Sentencing Disparity: An Overview of Research and Issues." In *Sentencing Reform: Experiments in Reducing Disparity*, edited by Martin Forst. Newbury Park, Calif.: Sage.

Freeman, Robert M. 2000. *Popular Culture and Corrections.* Lanham, Md.: American Correctional Association.

Friedman, Lawrence. 1979. "Plea Bargaining in Historical Perspective." *Law and Society Review* 13: 247–259.

Gibson, James. 1980. "Environmental Restraints on the Behavior of Judges: A Representational Model of Judicial Decision Making." *Law and Society Review* 14: 343–370.

Gottschalk, Marie. 2009. "The Long Reach of the Carceral State: The Politics of Crime, Mass Imprisonment, and Penal Reform in the United States and Abroad." *Law and Social Inquiry* 34: 439–472.

Greenhouse, Linda. 2007. "Justices Support Guidelines for Sentencing." *New York Times*, June 22.

Griffin, Timothy, and John Wooldredge. 2006. "Sex-Based Disparities in Felony Dispositions before versus after Sentencing Reform in Ohio." *Criminology* 44: 893–923.

Guo, Jianan, Quo Xiang, Wu Zongxian, Xu Zhangrun, Peng Xiaohui, and Lis Shuangshuang. 1993. "China." In *The World Factbook of Criminal Justice Systems: China.* Washington, D.C.: U.S. Department of Justice, Bureau of Justice Statistics. Available online at http://www.ojp.usdoj.gov/bjs/pub/ascii/wfbcjchi.txt.

Hagan, John. 1974. "Extra-Legal Attributes and Criminal Sentencing: An Assessment of a Sociological Viewpoint." *Law and Society Review* 8: 357–381.

Hargreaves, Steve. July 20, 2010. "BP's fine could hit the Billions." CNN.

Hashimoto, Erica. 2008. "Toward Ethical Plea Bargaining." *Cardozo Law Review* 30: 949–963.

Heumann, Milton. 1978. *Plea Bargaining: The Experience of Prosecutors, Judges and Defense Attorneys.* Chicago: University of Chicago Press.

Hindelang, Michael. 1972. "Equality Under the Law." In *Race, Crime and Justice*, edited by Charles Reasons and Jack Kuykendall, 312–323. Pacific Palisades, Calif.: Goodyear.

Hindson, Stephanie, Hillary Potter, and Michael Radelet. 2006. "Race, Gender, Region, and Death Sentencing In Colorado, 1980-1999." *Colorado Law Review* 77: 549–574.

Hofer, Paul. 2007. "*United States v. Booker* as a Natural Experiment: Using Empirical Research to Inform the Federal Sentencing Debate." *Criminology and Public Policy* 6: 433–460.

Hurwitz, Mark. 2006. "Much Ado About Sentencing: The Influence of *Apprendi*, *Blakely*, and *Booker* in the U.S. Courts of Appeals." *Justice System Journal* 27: 81–94.

Johnson, Brian, Jeffrey Ulmer and John Kramer. 2008. "The Social Context of Guidelines Circumvention: The Case of Federal District Courts." *Criminology* 46: 737–783.

Kauder, Neal and Brian Ostrom. 2008. *State Sentencing Guidelines: Profiles and Continuum*. Williamsburg, VA: National Center for State Courts.

Kautt, Paula. 2002. "Location, Location, Location: Interdistrict and Intercircuit Variations in Sentencing Outcomes for Federal Drug-Traffic Offenses." *Justice Quarterly* 19: 633–669.

Keil, Thomas, and Gennaro Vito. 1990. "Race and the Death Penalty in Kentucky Murder Trials: An Analysis of Post-*Gregg* Outcomes." *Justice Quarterly* 7: 189–207.

King, Ryan S. 2008. *The State of Sentencing 2007: Developments in Policy and Practice*. Washington, DC: The Sentencing Project.

King, Nancy J., David A. Soulé, Sara Steen, and Robert R. Weidner. 2005. "When Process Affects Punishment: Differences in Sentences after Guilty Plea, Bench Trial, and Jury Trial in Five Guidelines States." *Columbia Law Review* 105: 959–1009.

Kleck, Gary. 1981. "Racial Discrimination in Criminal Sentencing: A Critical Evaluation of the Evidence with Additional Data on the Death Penalty." *American Sociological Review* 46: 783–805.

Klemm, Margaret. 1986. "The Determinants of Capital Sentencing in Louisiana, 1979–1984." Unpublished Ph.D. dissertation, University of New Orleans.

Koons-Witt, Barbara. 2002. "The Effect of Gender on the Decision to Incarcerate before and after the Introduction of Sentencing Guidelines." *Criminology* 40: 297–328.

Kramer, John, Robin Lubitz, and Cynthia Kempinen. 1989. "Sentencing Guidelines: A Quantitative Comparison of Sentencing Politics in Minnesota, Pennsylvania, and Washington." *Justice Quarterly* 6: 565–587.

Kramer, John, and Darrell Steffensmeier. 1993. "Race and Imprisonment Decisions." *Sociological Quarterly* 34: 357–376

Kramer, John, and Jeffrey Ulmer. 1996. "Sentencing Disparity and Departures from Guidelines." *Justice Quarterly* 13: 81–106.

Kramer, John, and Jeffrey Ulmer. 2009. *Sentencing Guidelines: Lessons from Pennsylvania*. Boulder, CO: Lynne Rienner.

Kunzelman, Michael. 2011. "BP Can't Get White House Emails." Associated Press July 21.

Lankford, Jefferson. 2006. "The Effect of *Blakely v. Washington* on State Sentencing." *Justice System Journal* 27: 96–104.

Liptak, Adam. 2007. "Given the Latitude to Show Leniency, Judges May Not." *New York Times*, December 11.

Lizotte, Alan. 1978. "Extra-Legal Factors in Chicago's Criminal Courts: Testing the Conflict Model of Criminal Justice." *Social Problems* 25: 564–580.

Lurigio, Arthur, David Olson, and Jessica Snowden. 2009. "The Effects of Setting, Analyses and Probation Status." *Corrections Compendium* 34: 1–16.

Magnier, Mark. 2006. "China's High Court to Review Death Sentences." *Los Angeles Times*, November 1.

Mather, Lynn. 1974. "Some Determinants of the Method of Case Disposition: Decision-Making by Public Defenders in Los Angeles." *Law and Society Review* 8: 187–216.

Maynard, Douglas. 1984. *Inside Plea Bargaining: The Language of Negotiation*. New York: Plenum.

McCoy, Candace. 1984. "Determinate Sentencing, Plea Bargaining Bans, and Hydraulic Discretion in California." *Justice System Journal* 9: 256–275.

McDonald, Joe. 2004. "Report: China Carried Out Nearly 90 Percent of World's Executions in 2003." Associated Press, December 4.

Melone, Albert. 1998. "Judicial Independence in Contemporary China." *Judicature* 81: 256–261.

Merritt, Nancy, Terry Fain, and Susan Turner. 2006. "Oregon's Get Tough Sentencing Reform: A Lesson in Justice System Adaptation." *Criminology and Public Policy* 5: 5–36.

Miethe, Terance, and Charles Moore. 1986. "Racial Differences in Criminal Processing: The Consequences of Model Selection on Conclusions About Differential Treatment." *Sociological Quarterly* 27: 217–237.

———. 1989. "Sentencing Guidelines: Their Effect in Minnesota." *Research in Brief* (April). Washington, D. C.: U.S. Department of Justice, Bureau of Justice Statistics.

Molesworth, Claire L. 2008. "Knowledge versus Acknowledgment: Rethinking the *Alford* Plea in Sexual Assault Cases." *Seattle Journal for Social Justice* 6: 907–942.

Myers, Martha, and Susette Talarico. 1987. *The Social Contexts of Criminal Sentencing*. New York: Springer-Verlag.

Nardulli, Peter, Roy Flemming, and James Eisenstein. 1984. "Unraveling the Complexities of Decision Making in Face-to-Face Groups: A Contextual Analysis of

Plea-Bargained Sentences." *American Political Science Review* 78: 912–928.

Neubauer, David. 1974. *Criminal Justice in Middle America*. Morristown, N.J.: General Learning Press.

Olsen, Lise, and Eric Nalder. 2010. "Offshore Violations Net Few Fines." *Houston Chronicle* June 7.

Pan, Philip. 2004. "In China, Turning the Law Into the People's Protector." *Washington Post*, December 28.

Parent, Dale, Terrence Dunworth, Douglas McDonald, and William Rhodes. 1996. *The Impact of Sentencing Guidelines*. Washington, D.C.: U.S. Department of Justice, National Institute of Justice.

Partridge, Anthony, and William Eldridge. 1974. *The Second Circuit Sentencing Study: A Report to the Judges of the Second Circuit*. Washington, D.C.: Federal Judicial Center.

Paternoster, Raymond. 1984. "Prosecutorial Discretion in Requesting the Death Penalty: A Case of Victim-Based Racial Discrimination." *Law and Society Review* 18: 437–478.

Paternoster, Raymond, and Robert Brame. 2008. "Reassessing Race Disparities in Maryland Capital Cases." *Criminology* 46: 971–1007.

Pope, Carl, and Todd Clear. 1994. "Race and Punishment." *Journal of Research in Crime and Delinquency* 31: 132–134.

Radelet, Michael, and Glenn Pierce. 1985. "Race and Prosecutorial Discretion in Homicide Cases." *Law and Society Review* 19: 587–621.

Ralph, Paige, Jonathan Sorensen, and James Marquart. 1992. "A Comparison of Death-Sentenced and Incarcerated Murderers in Pre-*Furman* Texas." *Justice Quarterly* 9: 185–209.

Reichel, Philip L. 2001. *Comparative Criminal Justice Systems: A Topical Approach*. 3d ed. Upper Saddle River, N.J.: Prentice Hall.

Reitz, Kevin. 2001. "The Status of Sentencing Guidelines Reforms in the United States." In *Penal Reform in Overcrowded Times*, edited by Michael Tonry. New York: Oxford University Press.

Rengert, George. 1989. "Spatial Justice and Criminal Victimization." *Justice Quarterly* 6: 543–564.

Rhodes, Susan. 1992. "Review Essay: Prison Reform and Prison Life." *Law and Society Review* 26: 189–218.

Ritter, John. 2005. "Judge Sentences Peterson to Die." *USA Today*, March 17.

Robertson, Leon, Robert Rich, and H. Laurence Ross. 1973. "Jail Sentences for Driving While Intoxicated in Chicago: A Judicial Action That Failed." *Law and Society Review* 8: 55–68.

Sabol, William, and Heather West. 2010. *Prisoners in 2009*. Washington, DC: U.S. Department of Justice, Bureau of Justice Statistics.

Sanborn, Joseph. 1986. "A Historical Sketch of Plea Bargaining." *Justice Quarterly* 3: 111–138.

Smith, Craig. 2001. "China Justice: Swift Passage to Execution." *New York Times*, June 19, p. A1.

Snell, Tracy. 2010. *Capital Punishment, 2006—Statistical Tables*. Washington, D.C.: U.S. Department of Justice, Bureau of Justice Statistics.

Sorensen, Jon, and Donald Wallace. 1999. "Prosecutorial Discretion in Seeking Death: An Analysis of Racial Disparity in the Pretrial Stages of Case Processing in a Midwestern County." *Justice Quarterly* 16: 559–578.

Spohn, Cassia. 2009. *How Do Judges Decide?* Thousand Oaks, CA: Sage.

Spohn, Cassia, and Miriam DeLone. 2000. "When Does Race Matter? An Analysis of the Conditions under Which Race Affects Sentence Severity." *Sociology of Crime, Law and Deviance* 2: 3–37.

Spohn, Cassia, and David Holleran. 2000. "The Imprisonment Penalty Paid by Young, Unemployed Black and Hispanic Male Offenders." *Criminology* 38: 281–307.

Springer, J. Fred. 1983. "Burglary and Robbery Plea Bargaining in California: An Organizational Perspective." *Justice System Journal* 8: 157–185.

Steffensmeier, Darrell, and Chris Hebert. 1999. "Women and Men Policymakers: Does the Judge's Gender Affect the Sentencing of Criminal Defendants?" *Social Force* 77: 1163.

Steffensmeier, Darrell, Jeffrey Ulmer, and John Kramer. 1998. "The Interactions of Race, Gender, and Age in Criminal Sentencing: The Punishment Cost of Being Young, Black and Male." *Criminology* 36: 763–798.

Stith, Kate. 2008. "The Arc of the Pendulum: Judges, Prosecutors, and the Exercise of Discretion." *Yale Law Journal* 117: 1420–1497.

Stithe, Kate, and Jose Cabranes. 1998. *Fear of Judging: Sentencing Guidelines in the Federal Courts*. Chicago: University of Chicago Press.

Sudnow, David. 1965. "Normal Crimes: Sociological Features of the Penal Codes in a Public Defender Office." *Social Problems* 12: 254–264.

Tiede, Lydia. 2009. "The Impact of the Federal Sentencing Guidelines and Reform: A Comparative Analysis." *Justice System Journal* 30: 34–49.

Tiffany, Lawrence, Yakov Avichai, and Geoffrey Peters. 1975. "A Statistical Analysis of Sentencing in Federal Courts: Defendants Convicted After Trial, 1967–1968." *Journal of Legal Studies* 10: 369–390.

Tonry, Michael. 1987. *Sentencing Reform Impacts.* Washington, D.C.: U.S. Government Printing Office.

———. 1993. "The Failure of the U.S. Sentencing Commission's Guidelines." *Crime and Delinquency* 39: 131–149.

Uhlman, Thomas, and Darlene Walker. 1980. "He Takes Some of My Time, I Take Some of His: An Analysis of Judicial Sentencing Patterns in Jury Cases." *Law and Society Review* 14: 323–342.

Ulmer, Jeffrey. 1997. *Social Worlds of Sentencing: Court Communities under Sentencing Guidelines.* Albany: State University of New York Press.

U.S. General Accounting Office. 1990. "Death Penalty Sentencing: Research Indicated a Pattern of Racial Disparities." Gaithersburg, MD: Author. Available online at http://archive.gao.gov/t2pbat11/140845.pdf

Walker, Samuel, Cassia Spohn, and Miriam DeLone. 2012. *The Color of Justice.* 5th ed. Belmont, Calif.: Wadsworth.

Watson, Russell, and Melinda Liu. 1999. "Human Rights: China Kills a Few Chickens." *Newsweek*, January 11, p. 40.

Welch, Susan, and Cassia Spohn. 1986. "Evaluating the Impact of Prior Record on Judges' Sentencing Decisions: A Seven-City Comparison." *Justice Quarterly* 3: 389–408.

Welch, Susan, Cassia Spohn, and John Gruhl. 1985. "Convicting and Sentencing Differences Among Black,

Hispanic and White Males in Six Localities." *Justice Quarterly* 2: 67–80.

Westervelt, Saundra D. and Kimberly J. Cook. 2008. "Coping with Innocence After Death Row." *Contexts* 7 (4): 32–37.

Wilbanks, William. 1987. *The Myth of a Racist Criminal Justice System.* Pacific Grove, Calif.: Brooks/Cole.

Williams, Marian, Stephen Demuth, and Jefferson Holcomb. 2007. "Understanding the Influence of Victim Gender in Death Penalty Cases: The Importance of Victim Race, Sex-Related Victimization, and Jury Decision Making." *Criminology* 45: 865–891.

Wilmot, Keith Alan, and Cassia Spohn. 2004. "Prosecutorial Discretion and Real-Offense Sentencing: An Analysis of Relevant Conduct under the Federal Sentencing Guidelines." *Criminal Justice Policy Review* 15: 324–343.

Wilson, James Q. 1975. *Thinking About Crime.* New York: Random House.

Wolfgang, Marvin, and Marc Riedel. 1973. "Race, Judicial Discretion, and the Death Penalty." *Annals of the American Academy of Political and Social Science* 407: 119–133.

Wright, Ronald, and Marc Miller. 2002. "The Screening/Bargaining Tradeoff." *Stanford Law Review* 55: 29–118.

Zatz, Marjorie. 1987. "The Changing Forms of Racial/Ethnic Biases in Sentencing." *Journal of Research in Crime and Delinquency* 24: 69–92.

Zimring, Frank, and Gordon Hawkins. 1973. *Deterrence: The Legal Threat in Crime Control.* Chicago: University of Chicago Press.

FOR FURTHER READING

American Judicature Society. 2006. "The Effects of Capital Punishment on the Administration of Justice." *Judicature* 89: 244–305.

Christianson, Scott. 1998. *With Liberty for Some: 500 Years of Imprisonment in America.* Boston: Northeastern University Press.

Clear, Todd. 2007. *Imprisoning Communities: How Mass Incarceration Makes Disadvantaged Neighborhoods Worse.* New York: Oxford University Press.

Irwin, John, and James Austin. 1997. *It's About Time: America's Imprisonment Binge.* 2d ed. Belmont, Calif.: Wadsworth.

Lynch, Michael. 2007. *Big Prisons, Big Dreams: Crime and the Failure of America's Penal System.* New Brunswick, N.J.: Rutgers University Press.

Marquart, James, Sheldon Ekland-Olson, and Jonathan Sorensen. 1994. *The Rope, the Chair, and the Needle: Capital Punishment in Texas, 1923–1990.* Austin: University of Texas Press.

Messner, Steven, Zhou Lu, Lening Zhang, and Jianhong Liu. 2007. "Risks of Criminal Victimization in Contemporary Urban China." *Justice Quarterly* 24: 496–522.

Paternoster, Raymond, Robert Brame, and Sarah Bacon. 2007. *The Death Penalty: America's Experience with Capital Punishment*. New York: Oxford University Press.

Pollock-Byrne, Jocelyn M. 2002. *Women, Prison, and Crime*. 2d ed. Belmont, Calif.: Wadsworth.

Santos, Michael. 2006. *Inside: Life Behind Bars in America*. New York: St. Martin's.

Ulmer, Jeffrey T. 1997. *Social Worlds of Sentencing: Court Communities under Sentencing Guidelines*. Albany: State University of New York Press.

Vandiver, Margaret. 2006. *Lethal Punishment: Lynchings and Legal Executions in the South*. New Brunswick, N.J.: Rutgers University Press.

Vogel, Mary. *Coercion to Compromise: Plea Bargaining, the Courts, and the Making of Political Authority*. New York: Oxford University Press 2006.

Trial Courts: How Civil Cases Begin

In big cities like Seattle, Washington, municipal courts daily decide the largest category of civil cases—small claims. Although these cases rarely attract public attention, they are important to the individual litigants.

Stephen Meinhold

After returning home from Good Friday church services, Don Hubbard lay down to rest awhile. But when he couldn't get up, he was rushed to the hospital. Hubbard remembers the emergency room doctor raising an eyebrow when he said he had been taking the prescription drug Vioxx for over two years to treat chronic back pain (Finch 2007). Vioxx was used by an estimated 20 million people in the United States and was very profitable for its manufacturer. In September 2004, five months after Hubbard suffered his stroke, pharmaceutical giant Merck took Vioxx off the market after its researchers admitted that the painkiller doubled the risk of heart attacks and strokes.

Like tens of thousands of other Vioxx users across the nation, Hubbard sued. By rough count, Hubbard was one of 47,000 plaintiffs to file a lawsuit in state or federal court. Merck chose to fight every case and was successful in eight out of sixteen trials (Efrati, Koppel, and Heller 2007). But, in the end, the pharmaceutical giant chose to settle for $4.85 billion, one of the largest drug settlements ever (Johnson 2007).

Controversy surrounds how courts handle lawsuits involving large amounts of money (Vioxx, for instance) or relatively small dollar amounts (a minor automobile accident with injuries, for example).

This highly charged partisan rhetoric reflects the increasing attention being devoted to civil litigation. Although civil cases attract less attention from the media than do criminal cases, they affect individuals and society at least as much as criminal disputes do. Every year, over 19 million civil lawsuits are filed (LaFountain et al. 2010). The outcomes of those cases determine what compensation a person will receive for injuries suffered in an automobile accident, whether a manufacturer is liable for defective products, and which parent will have custody of the children after the breakup of a marriage. The fact that money or other important property considerations are involved means that, for the legal profession, civil cases are much more lucrative than criminal cases.

In the United States, there is a lively debate about the courts' role in deciding these civil disputes. To critics, in the United States too many lawsuits are filed, too many frivolous lawsuits appear on court dockets, civil cases are too expensive to process and as a result businesses (and ultimately consumers) are forced to pay unnecessary amounts. The principal remedy recommended is tort reform.

But such allegations about the deficiencies of the civil justice system, as well as the proposed remedies like tort reform, require close scrutiny. Therefore, this chapter explores how and why civil cases get to court in the first place by focusing on a few simple questions, such as who uses the courts, what kinds of cases get into court, and whether the courts are burdened with too many cases. Answering those questions requires looking at decisions made by litigants, advice offered by lawyers, legal standards imposed by the courts, and the availability of alternative dispute resolution programs. (Chapter 11 examines how civil cases end.)

DECIDING TO SUE

The place to begin assessing the so-called litigation explosion is not by counting the number of cases filed in court but, rather, by examining why so many disputes never make it to court in the first place. Litigation signals the arrival in the courthouse of disputes that have arisen elsewhere in society. Disputes are not simply static events that "just happen." Before being packaged in a lawsuit titled *Jones v. Smith*, a civil dispute undergoes a complicated process of transformation. For example, an auto accident is repackaged into a tort lawsuit over money damages, a quarrel between a landlord and a tenant is transformed into a small-claims suit over nonpayment of rent, and a child custody battle is redefined as a marital dispute. Negotiations over what a dispute is about are a critical dimension of the disputing process (Yngvesson and Mather 1983).

As we discussed in Chapter 8, criminal cases experience a high rate of attrition—for every 100 felony arrests, only 55 cases make it to the major trial courts. The same applies to civil matters: Only some disputes are actually filed as lawsuits, and others are dropped or are directed elsewhere. In an effort to provide baseline data about these phenomena, the Civil Litigation Research Project (CLRP) conducted a survey of 1,000 households asking respondents whether anyone in their household had experienced a dispute involving $1,000 or more (Miller and Sarat 1981).

The results are reported in Figure 10.1. Using these data, Galanter (1983) visualizes the civil justice process as a disputing pyramid consisting of several uneven layers. The concepts of grieving, claiming, disputing, hiring, and filing provide a good overview of the complicated process through which some disputes are transformed into lawsuits (see Table 10.1).

Grieving

All civil disputes begin as a grievance, which is an individual's belief that he or she (or a group) is entitled to a resource controlled by someone else (Miller and Sarat 1981). At one time or another, many citizens have felt grievances involving commercial transactions, work, family, accidents, or the like. Experiencing a significant grievance is by no means a rare or unusual event in American society. About 40 percent of the households sampled reported at least one grievance, and 20 percent reported two or more. Thus, the incidence of grievances provides a substantial potential for conflict.

FIGURE 10.1
The Disputing Pyramid for Civil Cases

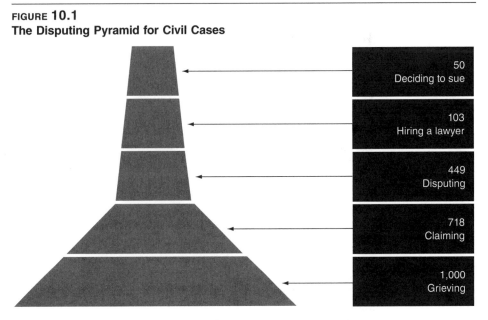

50
Deciding to sue

103
Hiring a lawyer

449
Disputing

718
Claiming

1,000
Grieving

Source: Richard Miller and Austin Sarat, "Grievances, Claims and Disputes: Assessing the Adversary Culture," *Law and Society Review* 15 (1981): 544. Reproduced with permission of Blackwell Publishing Ltd.

TABLE 10.1	Preliminary Steps in a Civil Lawsuit	
	Law on the Books	**Law in Action**
Grieving	A person (or a group) believes that he or she is entitled to a resource controlled by someone else.	Grievances are widespread in American society.
Claiming	The person (or the group) communicates the grievance to the other party.	Often, those experiencing a grievance choose to lump it, flee, or engage in harassment.
Disputing	The other party denies the claim in whole or in part.	At times, the other party accepts responsibility, meaning that there is no dispute.
Hiring a lawyer	This indicates that the person or group experiencing the grievance is serious.	Lawyers are often successful in resolving the dispute without litigation.
Deciding to sue (Filing a lawsuit)	Lawsuits transform grievances into legal terms understood by other lawyers and by judges.	Even after filing a lawsuit, the parties expect to settle the grievance without a trial.

Claiming

Faced with a grievance, a person may respond in several ways. One is by lumping it. Although the immediate reaction may be a threat to take action, within a day or two that initial anger may be replaced by the realization that pursuing the matter simply isn't worth the time, effort, and expense. To some people, taking their lumps and suffering a loss is preferable to pursuing the matter further (Felstiner 1974).

Another common response is flight. A tenant who experiences difficulties with a landlord, for example, may simply move out and rent from someone else. Still others respond to a grievance by engaging in harassment or even violence. This behavior occurs more often in poorer neighborhoods, where verbal abuse, vandalism, and assault may be the quickest way to settle the score. Although much of this behavior is criminal, it is often not reported to the police.

Lumping it, fleeing, or engaging in harassment are possible alternatives to taking further action. With those responses, the grievance goes no further. But other people are assertive and seek a remedy. Claiming refers to communicating a sense of entitlement to the party perceived to be responsible. Claiming is a frequent response to grievances: Seventy-two percent of the households sampled (shown as the second layer in Figure 10.1) reported that they had made some demand for satisfaction. The rate of claiming varies by the nature of the grievance: Those who have experienced discrimination are least likely to take further action; those who have experienced a problem with property or an unpaid debt are very likely to take further action.

Disputing a Claim

After a claim is made, the other party may accept responsibility and agree to redress the problem. If that happens, there is no dispute. Disputing occurs only when a claim is rejected, either in whole or in part. Almost two-thirds of the claims were rejected, thus resulting in a dispute (the third layer in Figure 10.1). The remaining one-third were settled without dispute. Interestingly, tort claims (typically automobile accidents) were the least likely to be contested; most were amicably settled by insurance companies according to well-established legal principles.

Making a claim does not necessarily mean going to court, however. Before filing a lawsuit, people are likely to try other alternatives. Some attempt to settle the dispute on their own through private negotiation and compromise. Others seek a third party—a mutual friend, a minister, or the like—to try to resolve the matter. In short, there are many alternatives to going to court in civil disputes. (The last part of this chapter explores the growing importance of alternative dispute resolution.)

Hiring a Lawyer

Another form of third-party intervention is the hiring of a lawyer. Relatively few disputants, however, use a lawyer's service. Less than one-fourth of those experiencing a dispute in the CLRP study reported using a lawyer. The two major exceptions to this pattern—postdivorce and tort problems—are explained by certain legal realities. The high involvement of lawyers in postdivorce disputes reflects the requirement of court action for problems such as nonpayment of child support or adjustments in visitation arrangements. The high use of lawyers in tort problems is tied to the contingency fee system, which facilitates and encourages the use of lawyers (Chapter 5).

Lawyers are a critical part of the disputing pyramid, serving as intermediaries (or gatekeepers) between clients and the legal system. Clients look to lawyers to define the law and explain how the legal system works. In turn, lawyers help clients relate legal rules to their individual problems. With the exception of minor matters such as small claims, few civil cases proceed to court without a lawyer.

Hiring a lawyer, however, does not automatically mean the dispute will result in a lawsuit. For example, a lawyer may facilitate a settlement without going to court. If nothing else, the act of hiring a lawyer indicates that the individual is serious and gets the attention of the other party. Thus, a letter written by a lawyer that threatens a lawsuit may prompt a previously unresponsive merchant to settle. Moreover, "lawyers often mediate between their clients and those not represented by lawyers. They seek to educate, persuade, and coerce both sides to adopt the best-available compromise rather than to engage in legal warfare" (Macaulay 1979, 117).

The interaction between lawyers and clients is a very important setting where law and society meet. In a basic sense, law is not just what judges write in appellate court opinions but also what lawyers say to their clients and other lawyers in their offices (Shapiro 1981). This "law talk" is of critical importance. Most litigants begin with a strong belief in "formal justice" that stresses an idealized notion of law in the abstract. But lawyers know how law is applied on a day-to-day basis and, therefore, attempt to teach their clients about the realities of the legal process (Merry 1985). "In the lawyer's office, the client is likely to be introduced to a system of negotiations in which formal hearings are rare, rights are no guarantee of remedies, unfamiliar rules of relevance are asserted, and the nature of their own disputes and objectives are transformed" (Sarat and Felstiner 1986, 126).

A study of lawyer-client conferences in divorce cases illustrates how lawyers socialize their clients to the realities of law in action as opposed to law on the books (Sarat and Felstiner 1988). Initially, clients insist on telling their lawyers why their marriage failed, often focusing on their spouse's character and personality. Lawyers avoid responding to those interpretations, because they consider who did what to whom during the marriage irrelevant to the legal task of dissolving the legal union. To get clients to move toward accepting settlement, lawyers may have to cool them down when they are at least partially inclined toward contest. Thus, lawyers deflect the client's desire for moral vindication and help him or her view the dissolution of marriage in instrumental rather than emotional terms. Lawyers focus on the business of securing the legal divorce and negotiating agreements about property and children. By and large, lawyers and clients are occupied with two different divorces: lawyers with a legal divorce, clients with a social and emotional divorce. The lawyers focus on legal norms and institutional practices, and the clients are oriented toward the social norms of their environment.

Filing a Lawsuit

If early efforts to resolve the dispute prove unsuccessful, the lawyer and client must decide whether to sue. Lawyers are critical agents in transforming societal disputes into viable lawsuits, translating clients' grievances into legal terms. A study of lawyers in a legal aid program found that, during the initial interview, the lawyer directed the client away from talking about legally irrelevant matters and steered the conversation toward eliciting information pertinent to the case at hand. The key part of the interchange is that the lawyer tells the client what the law says about the case, what can happen next in the normal course of events, and what the lawyer intends to do about the case. As one lawyer stated, "We don't care about what happened, we only care about what is going to happen" (Hosticka 1979, 601).

Nonlawyers often have profound misunderstandings about the civil justice system. Interviews with small-claims plaintiffs unrepresented by counsel highlight some of the unrealistic expectations that lawyers must overcome in advising their clients to file suit or not. Litigants view the facts of the dispute as straightforward and assume the court will readily accept their version of what happened. Thus, nonlawyers fail to appreciate the adversarial nature of civil litigation. Civil litigants must conceive their own case, assemble their own evidence, find their own witnesses, and present their own case in court, with a passive judicial system providing little assistance. (The criminal justice system, by contrast, has an important active component: A victim goes to the police, who investigate; if a defendant is charged, the prosecution is in the hands of the authorities; and the victim is often only a passive observer.) Thus, many litigants come to civil court with a model of procedure more appropriate to the criminal justice system they've seen on television. Moreover, most litigants have little awareness that they will encounter—and thus be required to overcome—a substantially different perspective on their case. Nonlawyers also know relatively little about the remedial authority of the civil courts. The civil system can compensate a litigant but rarely punishes one, whereas the criminal system punishes but rarely compensates. The civil system has no practical authority over a penniless defendant; but that perspective is lost on many litigants, some of whom base their decision to go to small-claims court on an overestimation of the court's remedial power (O'Barr and Conley 1988).

In deciding whether to litigate, lawyers and clients must also assess whether going to court will be worth the time, effort, expense, and hassle. Several factors, including psychological and emotional issues, influence the decision to litigate. Litigation creates or exacerbates conflict between the parties. A lawsuit pits one person against another in a very direct way. Most people find this direct conflict to be very unpleasant and also may be concerned that a lawsuit will have very practical and negative consequences. If, for example, the parties had a relationship prior to the case—such as two businesses that dealt with each other—it is unlikely the relationship will survive intact. To the extent that a relationship is important to either party, he or she may try to deal with the dispute in some other way. For that reason, litigation tends to be between parties who are strangers (Galanter 1983).

The decision to litigate is also influenced by assessments of real-world costs. A completely rational party will file suit only if the benefits of winning exceed the costs of losing. On one side of the equation are the expected benefits of winning. A crucial element is the probability of winning, which is estimated based on the applicable law and the factual strength of the case. At the same time, lawyer and client must calculate the potential monetary awards. On the other side of the equation are the potential costs of losing. Lawsuits can be expensive. Beyond the immediate costs of paying court fees, the plaintiff may also have to pay the attorney's fee and the expenses for expert witnesses, stenographers, and the like. If the lawsuit is lost, the plaintiff may have to pay those costs out of his or her own pocket. In purely economic terms, therefore, a plaintiff will litigate only if the expected benefits of winning are greater than the potential costs of losing (McLauchlan 1977).

RESOLUTION WITHOUT FILING A LAWSUIT

Few disputes eventually end up in court. In a study by Miller and Sarat (1981), only 50 out of 1,000 grievances ever made it as far as the filing of a lawsuit (see Figure 10.1). Moreover, even those disputes that reached the stage of hiring a lawyer did not necessarily result in a formal civil action in court. Note that, when the grievant used a lawyer, half of the grievances did not result in a lawsuit. Excluding postdivorce disputes (which virtually require court action), only 9 percent of all disputes eventually resulted in filing a case in court. A basic reason that disputes do not go to court is that most grievances are settled to the satisfaction of the party with a claim. Overall, 68 percent of those who made a claim eventually obtained part or all of what they originally sought.

This does not mean that courts, law, or lawyers play a trivial role in resolving disputes. On the contrary, claims are made, negotiated, and settled according to each party's understanding of its legal position and that of its opponents. The rights and remedies recognized by courts in the past are a powerful bargaining tool that may force an otherwise-reluctant party to settle short of going to court. Thus, most dispute processing takes place under the shadow of possible court action should negotiations fail. In short, bargaining occurs in the shadow of the courthouse.

If no bargain can be struck, the plaintiff must decide whether to file the lawsuit. (The process is described in "Steps in a Civil Lawsuit," in Chapter 11.) If the plaintiff does decide to file the suit, he or she becomes a statistic in the American "litigation explosion." The next section analyzes the origins of this highly publicized phenomenon.

Too Many Lawsuits?

With nearly 19 million civil lawsuits filed each year, some people wonder if the United States is becoming a nation of plaintiffs. The U.S. legal system is increasingly portrayed as suffering from judicial gridlock. An unprecedented growth in litigation is said to be overwhelming the courts, driving up costs, and increasing delay.

During the debate on health care reform, for example, critics argued that a major consequence would be a "litigation explosion" (Levey 2010). Several books have argued this point. Walter Olson (1991) wrote *The Litigation Explosion* and gave it the catchy subtitle *What Happened When America Unleashed the Lawsuit.* Patrick Garry (1997) penned *A Nation of Adversaries: How the Litigation Explosion Is Reshaping America.* More recently, Walter Olson (2003) published *The Rule of Lawyers: How the Litigation Elite Threatens the Rule of Law.* Indeed, a quick search of Amazon.com revealed the article "The Litigation Explosion, an Eye-Opening Expose ..." (Wagner 2005); alas, the content proved prosaic, offering advice to protect assets in case you are sued.

As in many discussions of emerging public policy issues, however, the problem of judicial gridlock is not readily defined. The colorful terms used to describe the problem are often so vague and elastic that their real meanings are hard to pin down (Neubauer 1986). It is important, therefore, to subject claims of a "litigation explosion" to close scrutiny (Johnston 2007; Schulhofer 1986).

At the heart of the concern about judicial gridlock is the assertion that, in recent years, U.S. courts have experienced an unprecedented growth in caseloads. Typically, the evidence cited consists of the following:

- Increased filings in federal courts
- Growth of the legal profession
- Atrocity stories citing petty or extravagant filings (the coffee-spill case serves as an example)

But each of those sources is highly suspect (Galanter 1983):

- Increases in federal court filings tell little about overall litigation rates, because only a handful of cases are ever heard in federal courts (Chapters 3 and 4).
- A rapidly expanding bar—even one that has increased much faster than the population—does not directly prove that courts are overburdened, because lawyers practice their trade in a variety of forums (Chapter 5).
- Selective recitations of atrocity stories hardly offer objective proof of overall patterns.

Probing Caseload Growth

Marc Galanter (1993) politely notes that the public discourse about civil justice reflects an environment in which "fibs and fables flourish" and knowledge is thin and spotty.

The polemical power of the litigation explosion argument springs from fond recollections of earlier times when courts had fewer cases and people were less likely to sue. Fortunately, a few excellent studies use rigor rather than nostalgia to probe litigation rates over time. It is difficult, of course, to form firm conclusions about the alleged litigation explosion, because of the diversity of the U.S. legal system. The existing studies, however, point to the following three broad conclusions.

Contemporary litigation rates are lower than those during the nineteenth century. That was certainly true of the St. Louis Circuit Court of Missouri. Interestingly, the litigation rate in the 1970s was half of what it was during the early nineteenth century (McIntosh 1980–1981). One reason that litigation rates have declined is the routinization of debt collection. Even though citizens today have high levels of debt and some have debt troubles, these cases are less likely to go to court for collection. Instead, many debt problems are handled by nonjudicial institutions such as the Federal Housing Administration, the Veterans Administration, the Small Business Administration, and various farm programs. In essence, debt collection cases have become "old" problems for the law (Kagan 1984).

A second conclusion is that, during most of the twentieth century, increases in the number of cases filed in court were directly related to the expansion of the U.S. population. There is ample evidence that, throughout the twentieth century, the absolute number of court cases increased, but so did the number of people living in the United States. At the turn of the twentieth century, the census counted 76 million Americans, a number that virtually doubled to 151 million in 1950 and by 2000 had swollen to more than 281 million. In short, the raw number of case filings must be adjusted for the size of the population. Viewed from this perspective, increases in case filings have paralleled expansion in population. For example, during most of the twentieth century, the absolute rise in federal district court filings barely kept pace with population growth (Clark 1981).

A third conclusion is that, toward the end of the twentieth century, case filings (adjusted for the size of the population) increased modestly but not dramatically. Beginning in the 1960s, federal case filings rose faster than increases in the population (Clark 1981). Similarly, in Los Angeles County, an upward trend was apparent after the mid-1970s (Selvin and Ebener 1984).

Shifts in Business and Political Institutions

To understand recent trends, we need to probe overall litigation rates to examine the kinds of cases filed (Hensler 1993). Focusing on the number of cases filed in court obscures important shifts in the kinds of cases contemporary courts must decide. At the turn of the twentieth century, market-related cases dominated; courts heard a great many disputes involving who owned a piece of property and how much money was owed to the terms of the contract. Today, nonmarket cases predominate; judges must decide who gets custody of the children after a divorce and how serious were the injuries suffered in an automobile accident (Daniels 1984). In addition, lawsuits challenging governmental actions (or inactions) constitute a higher proportion of court business (Lieberman 1983).

The Los Angeles Superior Court provides a close-up of these broad societal changes. In an earlier era, debt collection cases accounted for half of all court filings;

since the 1950s, their share of court business has dropped to only 10 percent. Those business cases have been replaced by disputes associated with one of the most significant inventions of the twentieth century—the automobile. In the 1930s, only 20 percent of the court's docket consisted of personal injury cases, compared with 60 percent in recent years. In combination, these changes suggest a more complex civil caseload today than in the past (Selvin and Ebener 1984).

In short, if there has been a litigation explosion, it has been a selective one. Filing statistics treat cases as interchangeable units, but, in reality, they are of different sizes and shapes. To revisit the concepts introduced in Chapter 7, courts today have fewer cases that require routine administration. Instead, they have more cases requiring diagnostic adjudication—child custody battles and juvenile proceedings are prime examples. Moreover, courts are hearing more policy lawsuits. It is the kinds of cases, not the number of cases, that really fuel the debate over the litigation explosion.

Recent evidence also suggests that tort filings are related to institutional characteristics of state judicial systems and state political culture. Yates, Tankersley, and Brace (2010) find a statistical relationship between case filings and "how judges are selected, how courts are administered, and the relative policy liberalism or conservatism of states." This line of scholarship is important because it requires us to consider that the supply of cases—deciding to sue—is influenced not just by the individual level characteristics of those involved and the type of dispute, but also by marc-level forces that impact the socio-legal culture.

Thus, to skeptics such as Marc Galanter and Stephen Daniels, claims of a litigation explosion are undocumented and grossly oversimplify a complex reality. On the basis of careful studies of court usage over time, the skeptics conclude that "we are not a litigious society" (Daniels 1985). In the same vein, a study of jury decisions in business cases concludes that plaintiffs often find civil juries a tough audience: "The urge to compensate innocent victims is balanced by jurors against their beliefs that plaintiffs often try to capitalize on sympathy and receive compensation that is not rightfully theirs" (Hans 2000, 47). Given those facts, where did public attitudes about lawsuit abuse originate?

Public Perceptions of the Litigation Explosion

At face value, the debate over the litigation explosion appears to be an argument over numbers. But that is not the real issue. It is not merely that the courts are doing more; it is also what they are doing more of that has produced so much sharp debate. In the aftermath of *Brown v. Board of Education* (1954), numerous disadvantaged groups turned to the courts to redress grievances that once would have been settled by other social institutions. In short, there has been a trend toward "legalization" or "judicialization" of disputes. Of particular concern are policy lawsuits that require judges to go far beyond traditional roles; contemporary examples include the legality of same-sex marriages, public displays of the Ten Commandments, and abortion.

Efforts by skeptics to debunk the myth of the litigation explosion have largely fallen on deaf ears among the general public, which persistently believes a litigation explosion exists. In a statewide poll of Louisiana voters, two out of three responded that Americans were indeed too quick to sue. Interestingly, responses were not related to factors such as social characteristics, previous litigation experience, or political attitudes of the respondents. Rather, the dominant explanatory variable was the race of the respondent. Whites overwhelmingly agreed that "people are too quick to hire a lawyer and go to court," whereas African Americans overwhelmingly agreed "anyone should be able to use the legal system to their advantage." In Louisiana, race is linked to a long past that may result in many African Americans feeling less a part of the dominant social paradigm. Thus, the have/have-not typology may help us understand the way people feel about lawsuits. In short, the haves appear quick to blame the have-nots for filing too many lawsuits (Meinhold and Neubauer 2001; Neubauer and Meinhold 1994; see also Brodsky et al. 1991).

Interpreting differences in opinion over legal attitudes in terms of haves versus have-nots fits with research on how community norms shape citizens' attitudes toward going to court. Through interviews and data collected from courthouse files, David Engel (1984) examined a small rural Illinois community. Concern about litigiousness was high, although there was relatively little litigation. Moreover, contract actions were ten times as frequent as personal injury cases, yet it was the latter that provoked concern. Personal injury cases challenge the community's core values of self-sufficiency and stoic endurance. Thus, lawsuits brought for breaches of contract (typically by the local establishment) were generally approved of, whereas lawsuits brought for personal injuries (typically by newcomers and outsiders) were generally condemned. Personal injury claimants were viewed as "quick to sue." Those views reflect traditional cultural norms stressing rugged individualism, reinforced by a farming community fatalism—accidents happen. Going to court, therefore, is perceived as attempting to escape individual responsibility by blaming someone else. Other countries have different standards for frivolous lawsuits and sanctions for those who pursue them. (See Courts in Comparative Perspective: The Republic of India.)

TORT REFORM

Every year the American Tort Reform Association (a business interest group), releases a colorful report on "judicial hellholes," identifying courts that it considers way too willing to award damages in civil lawsuits. These views are often shared by Republicans who argue that liability judgments against businesses (large and small) are a drag on the economy. The American Association for Justice (a trade association of plaintiff lawyers) counters that it is important to make sure any person who is injured by the misconduct and negligence of others can get justice in the courtroom. This perspective is often voiced by Democrats who see tort reform as little more than taking away the legal rights of American families in order to help powerful interests like the insurance industry.

The rhetoric of the litigation explosion is most visible in campaigns for tort reform. On one side, business groups denounce greedy lawyers who file unwarranted lawsuits that drive up the cost of doing business—to say nothing of driving up the cost of driving (as insurance premiums escalate). Lawyers counter that big businesses are the devious villains, trying to cheat citizens out of their right to sue while allowing businesses to make even greater profits by pocketing promised reductions in the cost

COURTS IN COMPARATIVE PERSPECTIVE

■ The Republic of India: The World's Largest Democracy

On an early December night in 1984, the wind silently blew a poisonous vapor across the city of Bhopal in central India. The chemical was forty tons of methyl isocyanate, leaking from a pesticide plant owned by Union Carbide. The victims were primarily the very young and the very old living in two shantytowns near the plant. Estimates of the number killed range from 3,000 to 12,000. Accounts of how many were injured vary from 20,000 to 200,000. No matter the precise numbers—Bhopal was history's worst industrial calamity. In short order, it would strain the legal and political systems of one of the few democracies in the developing world.

The Republic of India occupies only 2.4 percent of the world's land area but supports more than 15 percent of the world's population. Its billion-plus inhabitants are diverse indeed: Sixteen languages are spoken on the subcontinent, slightly more than one-third the size of the United States. Eighty percent of the people are Hindu, but religious minorities—particularly Muslims (14 percent), Christians, Sikhs, and Buddhists—play prominent roles, and religious violence periodically breaks out.

India was a British colony until it gained independence in 1947. An American-style constitution, adopted in 1950, provided for a president, a bicameral legislative branch, and a supreme court. Reflecting its British heritage, the government is headed by a prime minister. India is a federal nation with twenty-five states and other territories. Unlike the United States, however, India has only one court at the national level—the Supreme Court, which consists of thirty-one judges, who are appointed by the president from the career judiciary and remain in office until they reach the age of sixty-five. The Court typically sits in smaller benches of 2, 3, or 5 justices. State-level courts consist of a three-tiered system of high court, intermediate appellate courts, and district-level courts. The district-level courts do almost exclusively trial work, whereas the upper courts have both trial and appellate jurisdiction (Moog 1998).

The Indian Supreme Court is increasingly asserting itself as an independent branch of government particularly because citizens view the government as corrupt and not able to govern (Sharma 2011). In 1975, the Court found Prime Minister Indira Gandhi guilty of election violations. In response, her government declared a state of emergency, suspended judicial review, and ruled for two years by decree. In another prominent sign of political independence, the Court declared, in the early 1990s, that all citizens have a constitutional right to pollution-free air and water. More recently The Court has sanctioned the nation's sexual revolution, ruling that unmarried couples may live together (Page 2010). In short, the Indian Supreme Court, like its U.S. counterpart, is viewed by other branches of government as activist (Moog 1998). At the lower-court level, though, judicial independence has another face. Delays are endemic to the Indian legal system, yet judges show no inclination to reform the system (Moog 1992). Moreover, the Indian Supreme Court has been rocked by scandal in recent years.

Barely a week after the calamity, competing teams of American tort lawyers arrived in Bhopal. Their goal was to try the lawsuits in U.S. (not Indian) courts. Establishing jurisdiction in the United States offered several advantages:

- Damage amounts would be higher.
- Filing suit would be easier because India requires the plaintiff to pay high filing fees.
- Poor victims would be able to sue because Indian law does not allow for contingency fees.
- Suits involving hazardous materials are governed in the United States by the doctrine of "strict liability," whereas Indian law requires proof of negligence (Stevens 1984).

In 1986, however, federal courts in the United States ruled that the plaintiffs could not sue in U.S. courts. In 1989, the case was apparently settled when Union Carbide agreed to pay $470 million in damages. Within a few months, however, a new Indian government sought to set aside the agreement, arguing that the damage amount was too low. In another act of judicial independence, the Indian Supreme Court upheld the original civil settlement. In the end, the compensation for those killed ranged from $3,840 to $11,530. Those injured were to receive from $1,920 to $3,840 (Reuters 1992). Although the civil case has seemingly ended, there are still efforts to hold Dow chemical (which bought Union Carbide)

(continued)

financially liable (Shapoo 2010). Moreover criminal matters are still pending. The court is considering whether the two year sentences handed out to seven executives are too low (Shapoo 2010).

Over twenty five years later, the disaster lingers in and out of court. In 2007, Dow Chemicals offered to pay $470 million to clean up the site, but only if it is not subject to the legal liabilities of the disaster (Prasad 2007). Moreover, tens of thousands of survivors are still struggling. Some suffer ailments as diverse as tuberculosis, cancer, breathlessness, dizzy spells, and near-blindness. The survivors—mostly poor working-class people—are still seeking justice because they have been paid only 25,000 rupees ($560) (Reuters 2004).

---

of insurance. Lawyer bashing, which has long been a favorite pastime, has now become a national phenomenon (Hensler 1992). Conservative political columnists, for example, regularly headline the ills of "predatory lawyers" (Will 2007) and ask readers to "just say 'no' to the trial lawyers" (Atkins 2007). As a result, trial lawyers are a popular target in elections for local judgeships, votes in state legislatures, statewide referendums, and presidential elections.

The only thing new about these campaigns for tort reform is the amount of money being spent—it has increased greatly in recent years. What have not changed are the basic themes. Periodically, U.S. society experiences what is commonly called a "tort crisis," which, in turn, prompts legislatures to enact "tort reform." The crisis is said to consist of sharp increases in the cost of liability insurance and corresponding decreases in the availability of insurance. The response is based on an assumed relationship between litigation expenses and insurance costs; that is, insurance premiums are too high because courts have forced insurance companies to pay out excessive demands (Eaton and Talarico 1996). Following are examples of this cycle:

- During the 1960s, the tort crisis focused on automobile accidents, and the "reform" consisted of various types of no-fault insurance (Henderson 1977).
- In the 1970s, the perceived tort crisis and subsequent reforms concentrated on medical malpractice (Robinson 1986).
- In the 1980s, the tort crisis centered on the lack of availability of insurance for many types of businesses and governments.
- In the 1990s, the tort crisis had expanded to cut across a broad set of interests (Eaton and Talarico 1996).
- By the 2000s, the tort crisis was often linked to suits involving pharmaceuticals, medical providers like nursing homes, and financial institutions.
- In the 2010s tort reform is posed as an alternative to universal health care insurance.

A wide variety of proposals march under the general umbrella of tort reform including limiting the number of dollars a defendant must pay for an injury (termed caps on damages) and making it more difficult for plaintiffs to sue manufactures for injuries caused by using a defective product (termed product liability laws).

One of the most contentious tort reform proposals is placing limits on punitive damages, an issue that has reached the Supreme Court on several occasions. Discussions of punitive damages are at the forefront of the Gulf Coast oil spill because of the Supreme Court's decisions on the Exxon-Valdez oil spill. (See Case Close-Up: *Exxon v Baker*: Limiting Punitive Damages.) **Compensatory damages** are damages

CASE CLOSE-UP

■ *Exxon v. Baker* (2008)

Limiting Punitive Damages

The super tanker Exxon Valdez slipped anchor in Valdez, Alaska the night of March 24, 1989 and headed for the lower 48 states loaded with 53 million gallons of crude oil. In command was Joseph Hazelwood. Despite a known history of substance abuse and company mandated treatment programs, Hazelwood downed five double vodkas before the ship left port. Even though this quantity of alcohol (estimated at .241 blood alcohol content) would cause "a non-alcoholic to pass out," Hazelwood nonetheless was on the bridge. As the ship sailed down the icy outward passage Hazelwood inexplicably left the helm, failing to order a change in course.

The Exxon Valdez ran aground on Bligh Reef, tearing the hull open and spilling 11 million gallons of crude oil into Prince William Sound. The legal battles over the worst oil spill in the nation's history would frame many of the legal issues arising from the Gulf of Mexico oil spill 21 years later.

In the aftermath of the disaster, Exxon spent $2.1 billion in clean-up costs but even to this day oil oozes out of the shoreline and some wildlife have yet to return. In response, Congress passed the Oil Pollution Act of 1990 (see Chapter 2), under which BP was declared to be the responsible party.

Besides the damage to the environment, the Exxon Valdez spill affected the livelihood of many in the Prince William Sound, including commercial fishermen, seafood processors, landowners, Native Alaskans, and small businesses. Community disruption continues today with long term studies documenting chronic stress in households and occupations impacted by the spill (Picou, Gill, and Cohen 1997). After a lengthy trial a jury awarded $287 million in compensatory damages.

Beyond compensatory damages, 32,000 plaintiffs also sought punitive damages. The federal court judge hearing the case instructed the jury that the purpose of punitive damages were to punish and deter the defendants and the jurors could consider the reprehensibility of the defendant's conduct, including the failure of Exxon to properly supervise a captain it knew to have a serious history of alcoholism. In the end the jury awarded $5 billion in punitive damages, an amount reduced on appeal to the Ninth Circuit to $2.5 billion. Nearly two decades after the Exxon Valdez went aground, the Supreme Court ended the legal battles by slashing the punitive damages to $500 million. For many of the plaintiffs the stress associated with litigation from the oil spill has been as bad or worse as the oil spill itself (Gill, Picou, and Ritchie 2010).

The Court has wrestled with excessive punitive damages in earlier cases. The Court held that a punitive damage award of $145 million (compared with compensatory damages of $1 million) is excessive and violates the due process clause of the Fourteenth Amendment (*State Farm v. Campbell* 2003). The Court reinforced this trend in setting aside $79.5 million in punitive damages against tobacco giant Philip Morris, concluding that jurors might have improperly calculated the figure to punish the cigarette maker for the harm it causes to smokers other than the man whose widow brought the case. Compensatory damages totaled $821,000, so the ratio of punitive to compensatory damages was 97 to 1, which is far greater than the single-digit ratio that the Court had earlier adopted (*Philip Morris v. Williams* 2007).

In Exxon Valdez the Court noted "the stark unpredictability of punitive damages" as a major concern. Interestingly the Court cited a number of empirical studies by political scientists and other social scientists in justifying its holding that under maritime law punitive damages should not exceed compensatory damages (*Exxon v. Baker* 2008).

In the wake of the Gulf Oil disaster some in Congress vowed to undue this clear victory for big business and make BP pay by introducing "The Big Oil Polluter Pays Act" that would eliminate the 1:1 ratio of punitive damages to compensatory damages (Coyle 2010) but after Republican victories in the 2010 elections, the prospect of passing the law are doubtful. A lawsuit in federal court in New Orleans seeking punitive damages against BP and others involved in the gulf oil disaster is pending (Mowbray August 22, 2010).

The long delays in receiving compensatory damages from the Exxon Valdez spill and the relatively low amounts of punitive damages no doubt influenced the government to create a settlement fund in lieu of a protracted legal battle. Indeed an estimated 20 percent of those affected died before the Supreme Court heard the final appeal. The possibility of a protracted legal battle was the principal reason given for the creation of the BP settlement fund. (See Debating Law, Courts, and Politics: Is the BP Settlement Fund Indeed Fairer and Faster?)

directly related to the legal injury suffered by the plaintiff; they are typically based on medical expenses and lost wages but may also include monetary damages for intangibles such as pain and suffering and loss of consortium. **Punitive damages**, on the other hand, are awarded if the defendant was grossly negligent or intentionally committed the tort. Thus, punitive damages are above and beyond compensatory damages and are designed not only to punish the defendant for wrongdoing but also to deter others from doing the same in future cases.

Tort Tales

To the average citizen, the perception of a tort crisis comes from tort tales. Tort tales are moralistic parables that effectively drive home the point that something needs to be done about a legal system that is out of control. The specifics of tort tales change on a regular basis. But reduced to their basics, tort tales exhibit four characteristics. First, tort tales are short, often no more than three to five sentences long. This literary formula makes them easy to remember and, therefore, easy to retell. Second, tort tales emphasize the stupidity of the "victim." Invariably, the person suing did something foolish but won't admit to his or her shortcoming. Third, tort tales emphasize that the defendant is blameless. Typically, an individual (or a business) is doing something very ordinary when he or she is suddenly confronted by a meritless lawsuit. Finally, tort tales center on greed. Stupid "victims" are seeking outlandish monetary damages from ordinary folks like you and me, damages that are far in excess of any realistic injury (adapted from Haltom and McCann 2004).

In *Distorting the Law: Politics, Media, and the Litigation Crisis*, political scientists William Haltom and Michael McCann argue that tort tales distort reality. Indeed, the facts are usually far different from the tale that is being told. Nonetheless, efforts to refute tort tales often prove futile. Legal professionals and social scientists tend to publish their works in scholarly journals. The strong conclusion is that the nation is not facing a litigation explosion and that if there is a tort problem, it is a selective one. One reason that such analysis is drowned out by tort tales is that tort tales are closely connected to the moralistic "culture wars" waged in the United States. In particular, they reinforce popular notions that lawyers are greedy and the legal system has run amok (Haltom and McCann 2004). Perhaps the best-known tort tale involves a spilled cup of coffee at a McDonald's restaurant. (See Law and Popular Culture: Frivolous Lawsuits?)

State-Level Tort Reform

Efforts to enact tort reform have had some success. Many of the states that enacted tort reform in the 1980s have recently adopted new rules. According to the American Tort Reform Association (2010), since 1986 (the year the organization was formed) all states except Delaware and D.C. have enacted some sort of tort reform. Moreover in 34 states, legislatures have voted to limit punitive damages.

Tort reform at the state level reflects a political tug of war between two well-entrenched and well-funded interest groups—trial lawyers and insurance companies. Depending on how the issues are framed, consumer groups may also become involved. The 1988 California initiative on insurance reform illustrates the interplay between these powerful political interest groups.

Drivers in the most populous U.S. state pay the third-highest auto insurance rates in the nation. The insurance industry blamed those high rates on skyrocketing legal costs and supported regulatory reform that assigned most of the costs to trial lawyers. The California Trial Lawyers Association, on the other hand, ascribed the high cost of auto insurance to the oligopolist structure of the insurance industry and supported legal changes that assigned most of the costs to insurance companies. (Needless to say, each side accused the other of being greedy.) Both groups are among the most influential and best-financed lobbies in California; the battle of these titans in the legislature ended with the defeat of all attempts at so-called reform. The legislative stalemate led to a ballot initiative, where the debate expanded to include consumer groups who wanted lower insurance rates largely by removing the antitrust exemption of the insurance industry. The end result was that California voters were presented with five different insurance reforms on the November ballot. The only proposition to pass on Election Day was sponsored by the consumer activist group Voter Revolt (whose primary spokesperson was Ralph Nader). It called for removal of the insurance industry's antitrust exemption, for public hearings before rate increases, and for the setting of auto insurance premiums primarily by driving record rather than by the location of one's residence (Lupia 1994). In subsequent years, California voters were again called upon to decide similar issues (Price 1996).

In states like Alabama, Illinois, Indiana, Kansas, Kentucky, Georgia, New Hampshire, Oregon, Pennsylvania, and Washington legislatively passed tort reform has been struck down by state supreme courts. As a result, business interests are now spending unprecedented amounts of money in efforts to elect pro–tort reform judges (Chapter 6). Whether adoption of tort reform will, in the end, reduce the high costs of automobile insurance or medical malpractice insurance remains an open question.

At the macro level there is little doubt that tort reforms are having their intended impact—nationally tort filings declined a full 21 percent over the last decade for which statistics are available (LaFountain 2010). At the micro level, though, critics are concerned about hidden costs of making it harder to sue, arguing that children, the elderly, and women who work in the home are the "hidden victims" of tort reform, because plaintiff lawyers are no longer willing to handle their cases (Finley 2004).

National Tort Reform

Tort reform has historically been a state-level issue, because tort law is almost exclusively state law. In the 1990s, however, tort reform emerged as a potent national issue with clear partisan dividing lines.

During the 1992 presidential campaign, the George H. W. Bush administration condemned lawsuit abuse (Neubauer and Meinhold 1994). Two years later Republican candidates for the U.S. House of Representatives drafted a ten-point plan titled the "Contract with America." Among other things, it promised legal changes, including the Common Sense Legal Reform Act, which would make the losers pay for lawsuits, place limits on punitive damages, and reform product liability laws. Moderate

LAW AND POPULAR CULTURE

■ Frivolous Lawsuits?

Sharing stories about frivolous lawsuits has become as much a part of our popular culture as telling lawyer jokes. Just type in the phrase "frivolous lawsuits" on your favorite browser and you will find the latest story about an offbeat character or supposedly misguided policy nut. Indeed some feel compelled to provide a list of their top ten favorites.

Perhaps the most famous, but certainly the most enduring, example of a "frivolous lawsuit" is the dangerously hot cup of coffee. Stella Liebeck bought a cup of coffee at the drive-through window of an Albuquerque McDonald's. Having difficulty removing the top so she could add cream and sugar to her coffee, Liebeck put the cup between her knees. While she tried to dislodge the cap, scalding coffee gushed into her lap, causing second- and third-degree burns to the groin and inner thighs. Her lawsuit claimed the coffee was "defective" because it was so hot (more than 180 degrees Fahrenheit) that it was undrinkable.

First on radio talk shows and later in the print media, this tale of the dangerously hot cup of coffee became the best-known tort tale. Just examine the elements. First, the tale is short (and gets shorter the more it is retold). Second, it emphasizes the stupidity of the plaintiff—after all, she fumbled the cup of coffee. Third, it stresses the innocence of the defendant—buying coffee is an everyday occurrence and everyone should know that coffee is hot. Above all, this tort tale emphasizes greed—the jury awarded her $2.9 million dollars in damages. "When Stella Liebeck fumbled her coffee cup … she might as well have bought a winning lottery ticket…. That absurd judgment is a stunning illustration of what is wrong with America's civil justice system," opined the *San Diego Tribune*.

But was this really a frivolous lawsuit? After all in previous hot-coffee lawsuits, lawyers for McDonald's had settled out of court, but this time they decided to litigate, probably hoping to put an end to further lawsuits. Reporters from the *Wall Street Journal* (a pro-business publication that typically supports tort reform) discovered a very different reality to this tort tale.

Jurors initially scoffed at the idea of a lawsuit over a spilled cup of coffee, but they began to change their minds when lawyers presented gruesome photographs of the burns and proved that Mrs. Liebeck had spent seven days in the hospital undergoing painful skin grafts. Thus, the most interesting feature of the case is the transformation of jurors' attitudes from an initial assessment that this was a frivolous lawsuit to a later judgment that it was a serious matter (Hans and Lofquist 1992). The longer the case proceeded, the more the jurors saw McDonald's as callous and indifferent to the plight of an injured person. Witnesses for McDonald's testified that the giant fast-food corporation makes a considerable profit from selling one billion cups of coffee a year. Their officials seemed more interested in defending why their coffee is so hot (fully twenty degrees hotter than anyone else's) than apologizing to Stella Liebeck for the severe burns she suffered. In the end, jurors were struck by the fact that no one at McDonald's seemed to have the common courtesy, let alone the common sense, to say they were sorry. Thus, during trial, the case was transformed from a frivolous lawsuit to a case of the little guy fighting a giant corporation. Afterward, jurors pointed to the callous indifference of McDonald's as the key to their decision (Gerlin 1994).

The Albuquerque jury awarded Stella Liebeck a total of $2.9 million, of which $2.7 million was for punitive damages. The trial judge later reduced the jury award to $640,000; in the end, McDonald's settled the case out of court during the appeal for considerably less than the jury verdict. But this coffee-spill saga was literally heard in legislative chambers across the nation. Indeed every year a group calling itself The True Stella Awards (2011) features what it claims are true stories of "opportunists and self-described victims" suing "any available deep pockets and the U.S. Justice System."

The American public remains divided over going to court. Some lawsuits are viewed as "good" and others are regarded as "good" (Rhode 2004). But, like beauty, good lawsuits are in the eye of the beholder, and deciding which one to label frivolous ultimately depends on one's political perspective. In the battle over public opinion (which ultimately means the sympathies of jurors), one side wants to attach to the other side's actions the label "frivolous." The notion of frivolous lawsuits clearly advances the political agenda of conservative groups who want to restrict access to the legal system through policies like tort reform.

While colloquially a lawsuit may be termed frivolous based on one's view of the matter, legally frivolous

(continued)

litigation has a more precise legal meaning. It refers to filing a lawsuit that has little or no chance of winning. Federal and state rules of court provide that lawyers who file frivolous lawsuits may be sanctioned. These sanctions may take the form of requiring the payment of the other parties' legal fees. For example, a New Jersey judge ordered a major law firm to pay legal fees of $1.96 million for filing frivolous suits on behalf of billionaire Ronald Perelman in a family dispute (Longstreth 2010). Or the court may impose a fine. For example a federal judge fined Orly Taitz, a California lawyer and dentist, $20,000 for filing a "frivolous litigation alleging President Obama was not an American citizen." The judge held that Taitz attempted to misuse the federal courts to push a political agenda (AP 2010). But in the end backers of the birther movement labeled this a good lawsuit because it furthered their political cause.

Republicans in the Senate, however, found the changes too sweeping and their proposed changes were not acceptable to conservative House Republicans (Freedman 1995).

President George W. Bush also placed tort reform squarely on the national political agenda. In an effort to curtail multimillion-dollar class action lawsuits against companies, in 2005 the president signed the Class Action Fairness Act, which funnels class action suits with plaintiffs from multiple states out of state courts and into the federal courts. The objective in moving the suits to federal courts is to make it significantly more difficult for the lawsuits to be approved (CNN 2005).

Tort reform also emerged as a major issue in Republican efforts to defeat President Obama's health care reform. Republicans argued that reducing costs through limits on medical malpractice lawsuits should be the top priority.

One issue that divides conservatives is states' rights—traditionally, conservatives have supported states' rights, but, on the issue of tort reform, they seemingly want to override their long-standing opposition to federal regulation of traditionally state areas of lawmaking.

THE COMPLEX WORLD OF TORTS

It is very hard to talk intelligently about torts and tort reform because torts involve a variety of very different issues. Lawyers, of course, classify torts according to legal categories such as personal injury, libel, product liability, and medical malpractice. But, according to the RAND Corporation's Institute for Civil Justice (Hensler 1993), these legal terms suggest a single tort system, when, in reality, the tort liability system consists of multiple "worlds" of litigation. The multiple worlds of torts consist of routine, high-stakes, and mass torts (Ostrom, Rottman, and Hanson 1992).

Routine Tort Cases

Routine tort cases are epitomized by personal injuries suffered in automobile accidents and by other minor injuries (such as premises liability, commonly referred to as "slips and falls," which are allegations that the plaintiff slipped and fell because the property was improperly maintained). Routine cases statistically dominate tort filings in state court, accounting for 77 percent of all tort filings in the nation's largest counties. In routine tort cases, the extent of injuries is small, and these cases rarely, if ever, proceed to trial (Chapter 11).

TABLE 10.2 Median Final Awards in Tort Trial Cases	
Asbestos (47)	$682,000
Other Product Liability (52)	$500,000
Medical Malpractice (584)	$400,000
Premises liability (666)	$ 98,000
Other tort (305)	$ 83,000
Intentional tort (429)	$ 38,000
Slander/libel (80)	$ 24,000
All tort cases	$ 28,000
Motor vehicle (5,964)	$ 15,000

Source: Lynn Langton and Thomas Cohen, *Civil Bench and Jury Trials in State Courts, 2005* (Washington, D.C.: U.S. Department of Justice, Bureau of Justice Statistics, 2009).

As Table 10.2 highlights, the median verdict in an automobile tort case across the nation is $15,000. Here again, reality and perceptions of reality diverge. Individuals perceive that tort damage awards are much higher than they really are. One reason is that the media report verdicts that are on the order of ten to twenty times the size of the typical verdict (Kritzer 2001). Thus, the general public believes that million-dollar verdicts are typical, when they are, in reality, highly exceptional. One important consequence is that some clients believe that their injuries are worth considerably more than their lawyers do. In the words of one Wisconsin personal injury lawyer, "It is amazing how many clients come in and say that they are not trying to get rich off this case, but think they should get $100,000 for a whiplash or a slip and fall" (quoted in Kritzer 2001, 79).

Some automobile injury cases involve severe injuries and, therefore, are not handled in a routine manner. In high-stakes litigation, however, trials are more likely, and jury verdicts may be large.

High-Stakes Litigation

High-stakes litigation occurs when a plaintiff sues for a large amount of monetary damages. This category is typified by product liability and medical malpractice lawsuits. Although these cases figure prominently in discussions of tort reform, they are statistically somewhat rare, accounting for no more than 10 percent of tort filings. Indeed, lawyers are less willing to take on medical malpractice and product liability cases and less willing to carry them through trial, because they know these cases are, on average, expensive to litigate and difficult to win. In turn tort reform has made these cases even more expensive for plaintiffs to pursue. According to Dennis Peery, a San Antonio trial lawyer, he used to take four or five medical malpractice cases a year. But, in the wake of tort reform in the Lone Star State, "it is not economically feasible. It's not unusual to go to trial and spend $100,000 of my own money on a case, mostly to pay experts" (Donnelly 2007). Under the contingency fee system, plaintiff lawyers must front the costs, and if they lose the case, they must eat those costs. A study of Texas, which enacted medical malpractice reform in 2003, found that for these reasons few, if any, medical malpractice cases are now being filed in the Lone Star State (Daniels and Martin 2010).

Medical malpractice lawsuits are filed primarily against hospitals and are much more likely than automobile suits to reach trial. In medical malpractice cases, plaintiffs win only 23 percent of the time, compared with 64 percent of auto cases (Langton and Cohen 2009). But not all medical malpractice and product liability lawsuits involve high stakes. For example, although the public identifies medical malpractice cases with large verdicts, the median amount of damages awarded was $400,000, and cases that go to trial are typically much more serious than those that are settled out of court.

Mass Torts

Mass torts are most often associated with exposure to toxic substances and/or the use of pharmaceutical products. The Vioxx lawsuits clearly qualify as mass torts. Some of the major examples are presented in Exhibit 10.1. Mass torts differ from ordinary tort cases in the number of parties, the proximity of the event, and the money involved.

Instead of one plaintiff suing one defendant—such as in a dispute about an automobile accident—thousands of plaintiffs are involved in mass torts. More than 200,000 claimants came forth in the Dalkon Shield contraceptive device cases, and approximately 65,000 in the fen-phen cases (a drug used in weight loss).

Compounding the problem of multiple parties is the issue of causation. Instead of alleging that the injury was caused by a single event—a collision at an intersection, for example—mass tort plaintiffs are seldom able to pinpoint the precise time their medical problems began. The claims are for latent injuries caused by events that occurred years ago or over long periods of time. Decades may pass following exposure to a toxic

---

EXHIBIT 10.1   **Examples of Mass Torts**

- The explosion of the Deepwater Horizon oil rig led to 4.9 million barrels of oil polluting the Gulf of Mexico.

- Toyota owners in the U.S. and several foreign countries have filed class action law suits against the giant Japanese auto maker for injuries suffered during sudden acceleration.

- Defective brakes on Toyotas led to a massive recall and thousands of potential lawsuits.

- Thousands of homeowners in 38 states have complained that drywall (also called wallboard) purchased from China emits a toxic chemical that causes illnesses and corrodes appliances. Many of the foreign defendants have refused to appear in court.

- The Vioxx lawsuits. An estimated twenty million people took Vioxx with annual sales of $2.5 billion (Berenson 2007). Forty-seven thousand persons sued and will share in the $4.85 billion settlement.

- The asbestos lawsuits. Manufacturers of asbestos, a noncombustible and chemically resistant material widely used for years as a fireproof insulation, were sued after it was discovered that long-term exposure may produce asbestosis, a pneumonia-like disease that permanently destroys lung tissue.

- The breast implant lawsuits. Settled for $3.2 billion. Women claimed that they became ill after receiving silicone breast implants (Associated Press 1999).

- The Dalkon Shield lawsuits. Settled for $2.3 billion. Women claimed that the birth control device caused serious medical complications.

- The fen-phen lawsuits. Settled out of court for $3.75 billion. The manufacturer, American Home Products, took the combination diet drug off the market in 1997, following reports that users experienced serious heart valve disease (Peterson 2000).

- The Tobacco lawsuits. The tobacco industry settled claims that smoking cause cancer in 50 states for $246 billion, the largest civil settlement in U.S. history.

substance before a medical problem occurs. How do we know that the ailment was caused by the product in question and not some other circumstances? In the breast implant cases, for example, the American College of Rheumatology has firmly declared that there is no evidence that the devices cause the diseases attributed to them ("Doctors Dispute ..." 1995). In the Vioxx lawsuits, lawyers for Merck contended that factors like smoking and obesity caused the heart attacks and strokes, not the prescription drug.

Finally, mass torts differ from ordinary tort litigation in the staggering amount of money involved: Mass torts may involve billions of dollars rather than the thousands (or occasionally millions) of dollars awarded in ordinary tort cases (Feinberg 1991). Indeed, mass torts represent the largest product liabilities cases ever. In the silicone breast implant cases, for example, the initial settlement was $4.25 billion for more than 400,000 women who registered. The dollar amounts are so large that, in the big three of mass torts—asbestos, Dalkon Shield contraceptive devices, and silicone breast implants—the manufacturers filed for bankruptcy protection, claiming they faced potentially astronomical expenses from pending lawsuits. Eventually, 96 percent of the claims in the Dalkon Shield cases were paid. But those affected by asbestos haven't fared as well; by declaring bankruptcy, the Manville Corporation delayed paying claims for ten years or more, and many asbestos victims are being paid at the rate of 10 cents on the dollar. Others died before being paid at all. The largest and perhaps the most controversial of mass torts involve lawsuits against Big Tobacco.

In *Mass Torts in a World of Settlement*, law professor Richard Nagareda (2007) argues that the legal system has responded to mass torts by transforming them from individual adjudications to an administrative process which provides a systematized treatment of cases that vary in terms of geographical breadth, time frames and factual patterns. One significant factor in the emergence of mass torts is the emergence of an elite segment of the plaintiff's bar. These lawyers specialize in the identification, litigation and settlement of mass torts. Moreover they often use the media to recruit clients (see Chapter 5 on lawyer advertising). In turn these elite plaintiffs lawyers have often been the most fiercely criticized by the business community, portrayed as virtual demons in some circles.

The Gulf of Mexico oil spill clearly qualifies as a mass tort because so many people and businesses were affected and because of multiple types of issues ranging from loss of income, possible deleterious health consequences and environmental damages. Moreover, business interests were quick to attack plaintiff lawyers who participated in past mass torts. To understand more on how the oil spill cases are being treated in and out of court, we need to first examine alternative dispute resolution.

ALTERNATIVE DISPUTE RESOLUTION

Perceptions of a crisis in the courts have spurred efforts to employ informal, less adversarial means for resolving disputes than traditional legal processes (Coltri 2009; Nolan-Haley 2008; Goldberg et al. 2007). **Alternative dispute resolution (ADR)** was once considered a novelty but now has emerged as a major movement in the United States. Alternative dispute resolution enjoys widespread support. Indeed, many groups that are normally adversaries on other issues advocate alternatives to traditional litigation: For example, both businesses (represented by the U.S. Chamber of

Commerce) and consumers (exemplified by Ralph Nader) support ADR. Similarly, major legal organizations (the American Bar Association, for example) advocate alternatives to courts, as do groups that are suspicious of the law and lawyers. What unites these otherwise diverse groups is a shared concern that the courts are not adequately handling many types of civil and criminal cases.

But this apparent unity serves to mask widespread disagreement about the diagnosis of the problem and ways to cure it. The ADR movement incorporates divergent and contradictory goals. Some goals emphasize an improved process for case handling: ADR will provide more lasting, equitable resolutions for all parties by emphasizing mediation rather than the winner-take-all approach characteristic of the judicial process. Other goals focus on access to justice: ADR will increase accessibility to justice for the poor and the middle class. Other goals stress efficiency: ADR will improve the justice system by reducing caseloads, decreasing delay, and cutting litigants' costs.

Alternative dispute resolution is a label used to cover a broad range of options that share few characteristics aside from their common departure from traditional courtroom procedures. Nor are alternatives to the formal judicial processes new. Arbitration, juvenile courts, small-claims courts, and family courts are a few examples of long-standing activities that were established because it was felt they would be more effective than traditional court operations.

To provide a flavor of the range of techniques included under the ever-expanding ADR umbrella, we examine three types of programs: community courts, court-annexed arbitration, and settlement funds.

Community Courts

Community courts (formerly known as criminal justice–based mediation programs) process a range of minor civil and criminal matters through nonjudicial techniques. Typically, the stress is on mediation, not adjudication. Because community courts are government sponsored (either by a court or by a prosecutor), they receive the bulk of their case referrals from criminal justice agencies. The dominant goal is improving the justice system by removing minor cases from the court. In the view of the justice agencies, cases such as simple assault, petty theft, and criminal trespass are prime candidates for mediation and not formal processing in the lower courts (Williams 2007).

Initially, what are today called "community courts" began with a primary emphasis on misdemeanor criminal cases and later added civil matters from the local small-claims court and other sources. In a sense, they convert criminal matters to civil ones by treating the cases as matters for discussion between the individual disputants and not for processing between the state and the defendant. Like drug courts (see Chapter 4), community courts are problem-solving courts (Fagan and Malkin 2003). The Center for Court Innovation (2010) stresses that community courts are neighborhood-focused courts that attempt to harness the power of the justice system to address local problems. They can take many forms, but all focus on creative partnerships and problem solving.

The best-known community court in the nation is the Midtown Community Court in New York City. The Midtown experience was born of a profound frustration with quality-of-life crime in the neighborhood, particularly prostitution, vandalism, and low-level drug offenses. Offenders are sentenced to make restitution to the community through work projects in the neighborhood: removing graffiti, cleaning subway stations, and sorting cans and bottles for recycling. But, at the same time, the court attempts to link offenders with drug treatment, health care, education, and other social services. Perhaps one of the most unusual approaches is the inclusion in the courthouse of an entire floor of office space wherein social workers may assist offenders referred by the judge in the courtroom a few floors below. Thus, instead of an offender's being sent to a distant bureaucracy, he or she now has access to helping institutions within the courthouse itself (Clear and Cadora 2003).

Not all are convinced of the advantages of community courts, however. To some, these programs too closely parallel the faults of the justice of the peace courts (discussed in Chapter 4). In *Shadow Justice*, Christine Harrington (1985) argues that neighborhood justice centers reflect a return to the informalism that typified the lower courts before judicial reorganization.

Court-Annexed Arbitration

Early ADR programs were often portrayed as competing with the courts. Increasingly, however, ADR is being integrated into the U.S. judicial system. As the dispute resolution movement has gained legitimacy, attention has shifted to the use of alternative dispute resolution procedures within the courts. The most frequently adopted type of ADR program is court-annexed arbitration, which has been established in many state and federal courts (Cross and Miller 2009; Parrott 2007).

The primary goal of court-annexed arbitration is improving the justice system by providing litigants with a speedier, less expensive alternative to the traditional courtroom trial. Judges are authorized to require arbitration of civil suits that fall below a certain dollar amount (most commonly $50,000 or $100,000). The third-party arbitrator, usually an attorney in private practice, receives an honorarium. Arbitration hearings are brief, private, and informal. Relaxed rules of evidence are used; in particular, reports (medical records, for example) are usually sufficient as evidence, and, therefore, witnesses are not called. After hearing arguments and reviewing evidence, the arbitrator makes a decision on liability and damages. If neither party objects, the arbitrator's decision has the force of a court judgment. If either party is dissatisfied, however, he or she may reject the arbitrator's recommendation and request a trial de novo (from the beginning). To discourage frivolous appeals, disincentives are built into the process: Most commonly, the party rejecting the recommendation is required to reimburse the court for the arbitrator's fees and, in some instances, may be assessed court costs if the trial judgment is roughly equal to the arbitrator's award.

Amid this experimentation with ADR, a few empirical studies have probed the effectiveness of these programs and three tentative conclusions emerge.

First, court-annexed arbitration programs vary substantially, and that affects their outcomes (Hensler 1986). For instance, the North Carolina program targeted contract cases (Clarke, Donnelly, and Grove 1991), Atlanta included all cases involving money damages of less than $25,000 (Hanson and Keilitz 1991), and New Jersey focused solely on automobile tort filings (MacCoun 1991). Clearly, trying to draw conclusions about the supposed success of arbitration programs runs the risk of comparing the proverbial apples and oranges.

A second tentative conclusion is that arbitration works—but defining what works proves to be a tricky proposition (Boyum 1991). All too often, these programs are expected to accomplish so many goals that some parties are inevitably disappointed. Consider delay reduction. In asking what works, reformers typically have efficiency in mind. Thus, court-annexed arbitration is expected to reduce delay, cut court costs, and decrease the trial rate. In North Carolina, arbitration reduced case processing time by one-third; in Atlanta, arbitration cases were only modestly more expeditious; in New Jersey, there was a significant increase in disposition time for cases assigned to the program. Similar mixed findings appear in relationship to trial rates and litigation expenses.

A third tentative conclusion is that court-annexed arbitration appears to meet the goals of improving litigant satisfaction. Attorneys in Atlanta believe that the arbitration program helps to shape negotiations positively. Overall, they view outcomes as fair and satisfactory (Boersema, Hanson, and Keilitz 1991). Researchers also find that court-administered arbitration is viewed by most litigants as a fair way of resolving civil disputes (O'Leary and Raines 2001). Indeed, North Carolina litigants assigned to the arbitration program were more satisfied with their experience than were those in a comparison group—a finding that held no matter if the litigants won, settled, or lost (Clarke, Donnelly, and Grove 1991).

Evaluations to date suggest that court-annexed arbitration cannot, by itself, solve all the problems that characterize contemporary civil litigation (Hensler 1986). The establishment of an ADR program will not provide a "quick fix" for problems of delay (Mahoney et al. 1988). Indeed, some lawyers in New Jersey want to scrap their state's program. They complain that it results in unnecessary expense because 75 percent of the recommendations are rejected. Moreover, they fear that the program has been captured by repeat players (Chapter 7)—medical groups like HMOs hire a single firm to represent them in all arbitrations (Porter 2004).

Settlement Funds

ADR is most often identified with cases that have a small dollar value (community courts for example) and lawsuits involving medium ranged damages (court-annexed arbitration for example) but ADR is now directly and indirectly a factor in high profile and large dollar amount litigation as well. The central figure in this paradigm shift is Kenneth Feinberg (O'Keefe 2010).

Kenneth Feinberg is the senior partner of Feinberg Rozen, a D.C. and New York law firm that specializes in dispute resolution. Feinberg has become the go-to-guy for some of the nation's most emotionally and legally challenging questions facing the nation. In some of these cases Feinberg has worked as a special master appointed by the court (which means his settlement recommendations are reviewable by a judge). Here the influence of ADR is indirect—Feinberg seeks to bring together powerful and conflicting forces (Schwartz 2010). One such example is the Dalkon Shield birth control device lawsuits (a classic example of a mass toxic tort).

In recent years the impact of ADR has been more direct in the sense that a settlement fund was created before lawsuits were filed and the fund was administered separate from the courts. Eleven days after the terrorist attacks on September 11, 2001, Congress passed the Air Transportation Safety and Stabilization Act that largely shielded airlines from tort lawsuits and also created The September 11 Victim's

DEBATING LAW, COURTS, AND POLITICS

■ Is the $20 Billion BP Claims Process Faster, Fairer, and Fatter?

"You're crazy" to leave compensation up to the courts proclaimed Kenneth Feinberg. As the appointed claims administrator of the $20 billion BP Claims Fund, he promised that the process will be faster, the procedures fairer, and the payments fatter than traditional litigation (Alpert July 20, 2010). Although it will be years before any tentative conclusions can be reached whether these goals were indeed met, it is important to begin discussing these issues now because the BP Claims Fund represents the largest experiment in Alternative Dispute Resolution (ADR) ever attempted.

The nation's largest oil spill disrupted the livelihood of tens of thousands who are economically dependent upon the Gulf of Mexico, including the fishing and tourism industries. Within days of the Gulf of Mexico Oil Spill, BP pledged to pay "all legitimate claims," a commitment that became murkier the longer crude oil from the damaged well darkened the normally clear blue waters of the Gulf. Over the following weeks BP paid millions of dollars in claims but there were growing complaints that the process was too slow, too erratic and too dependent on trusting the oil giant, a commodity in very short supply among citizens living along the Gulf Coast.

Amidst mounting public displeasure that BP was not delivering, President Obama pledged to "make BP pay." After four hours of intense White House negotiations, BP promised to create a $20 billion claims fund, officially known as the Gulf Coast Claims Facility (http://www.gulfcoastclaimsfacility.com). Some supporters of the oil industry openly objected to what they called Obama's strong-armed tactics. Potential claimants include individuals, businesses and governments who suffered economic losses. However, the Fund does not cover clean-up costs or fines (see Chapter 9).

Faster Payments

Faster payments were a top priority of the GCCF because of the long delays in reimbursing Alaskans after the Exxon Valdez oil spill. (See Case Close-Up: *Exxon v. Baker* and Limiting Punitive Damages.) Waiting years, perhaps decades, for payments to cover economic losses was not a viable option following the explosion of the Deepwater Horizon drilling rig.

In the short term the GCCF was somewhat successful in making faster payments, dispensing almost $4.9 billion to 200,000 claimants during its first 11 months

in operation. The average emergency award for lost earnings and profits was $15,000. This appears to be a better track record than when BP was self-administering the claims process. Feinberg admitted, however, that he over-promised and under-delivered in terms of speed. But later the process hit its stride (Hammer June 21, 2011). Ordinary citizens and public officials alike complained about the need for a speedier process. The claims process was partially slowed by the unexpectedly large volume of claims—almost half a million claims were filed in the first few months. The payment process was also slowed by a large number of claims (roughly 40 percent) that lacked any documentation at all. The payment process was further slowed by an excessive number of fraudulent claims which were turned over to the FBI for possible criminal prosecution (Hammer December 15, 2010).

Fairer Process

A fairer process was the second pledge of the GCCF but assessing fairness is as difficult as divining justice (see Chapter 2). Deciding who should be paid and who doesn't deserve any money is a daunting task. No blueprint exists for deciding who suffered direct economic damages from the oil spill compared to those who suffered indirect damages and those who suffered economic losses for other reasons such as the economic recessions.

One measure of fairness in deciding who qualifies (and who doesn't) are standards set by state law, a factor that Feinberg stated he would follow. Toward that end, he commissioned John Goldberg (2010), a leading Harvard University Law Professor, to examine 16 hypothetical claimants and analyze their chances of winning damages in state courts. Commercial fishers, Gulf Coast hotel owners and their employees clearly qualified. But he concluded that dockside restaurants, beachfront real estate agents and store owners in coastal tourism towns were much less likely to win. Nonetheless, the fund was willing to pay (Hammer Nov. 26, 2010).

Another measure of fairness can be viewed in terms of flexibility. Initially, Feinberg proposed that claims would be limited to geographic proximity to the oil spill. But after a series of town hall meetings and criticisms from elected officials, he modified this standard and others (Clifford 2011). To some, Feinberg's flexible approach increased the fairness of the process but to

(continued)

others it merely added confusion; lawyers complained that changing standards meant they had a hard time advising business clients what was covered and what wasn't. Thus, some complain that the process has become arbitrary and capricious. In the words of Brent Coon, the prominent plaintiff's attorney who successfully sued BP following the explosion of its Houston refinery:

> The Fund pays one shrimper but not another, or pays a shrimper but not the shrimp processing plant which buys the shrimp (Mowbray December 18, 2010).

Fatter Payouts

Feinberg also promised that payments would be more generous than any state or federal court would award (Gonzalez 2010). This goal must be judged against two important restrictions the Gulf Coast Claims Facility placed on payments. First, the fund will not pay for punitive damages. Whether judges or juries would indeed determine that punitive damages were warranted is always speculative, but this restriction certainly reduces the size of the potential pot of money. Second the fund requires that any claimant who accepts a final settlement must agree not to sue BP or to sue any of the other potential defendants (see Chapter 11). Plaintiff lawyers have expressed great skepticism over this restriction, fearing that legitimate claims for long-term damages would be denied. Business interests have applauded this restriction because it provides some needed certainty during ongoing litigation.

Claims of fatter payouts must also consider who will ultimately pay. BP has hinted that it might treat the $20 billion pledged for the costs of the Claims Fund as a tax deductible business expense, which would mean that the U.S. taxpayers (rather than BP stockholders) would be footing part of the bill.

Ongoing Debate

The goals of a faster process, fairer procedures and fatter payments clearly suggest that there must be trade-offs if the BP Claims fund is ultimately better able to settle the mountains of claims better than a traditional courtroom approach. And these trade-offs are the center of the debate over this attempt at ADR. In many ways the debate mirrors the debate over tort reform. Plaintiff lawyers complain that the fast payout process only works to BP's advantage. Flexibility in determining who is eligible (and for how much) inevitably leads to claims that some got too much at the expense of those who received too little (or nothing at all). In defending the Claims Fund the *Wall Street Journal*, a consistent supporter of business interests, has likened Ken Feinberg to a piñata, you can tell what is happening by who is beating on the ball in the middle, and since it is the plaintiff's attorneys, he must be doing a good job (Gulf Claims piñata 2010). Other parts of the debate, however, reflect institutional differences in governments. Many state and local governments, for example have complained of strained finances because of the oil spill, claims as likely to be voiced by Republicans as well as Democrats.

On repeated occasions Feinberg shrugged off questions whether he needed outside guidance, declaring "ultimately it's my call" (Milbank 2010). This notion of an unaccountable czar raises troubling questions about the delegation of public authority to private institutions. The claims administrator is in reality performing a public function (very similar to a judge) but is a private individual. Moreover the decisions of the claims administrator are not appealable to a panel of judges (selected by the public or public officials) but rather to a panel of law professors (selected by the claims administrator). Nor are the ultimate standards for deciding which claimants get how much based on law enacted by government (see Chapter 2) but by a private lawyer. Amidst these concerns the federal courts (Hammer Feb 23, 2011) and the U.S. Department of Justice (Overseeing 2011) are exerting some oversight over the process.

Compensation Fund. Victims or their survivors could opt to accept compensation from the fund but they had to first waive any right to sue. In the end over $7 billion was paid by the federal government. Ken Feinberg was chosen administrator and developed a compensation schedule that ranged from a maximum of $250,000 for pain and suffering and between $500,000 to $7.1 million for death claims. Reactions to these settlements have varied. On one end of the spectrum, the conservative Federalist Society groused that the fund amounted to nothing more than a tax funded charity that made millionaires out of 9/11 victims (Maginnis 2002). Others expressed the opposite concern, noting that many who died in the 9/11 attack were important people whose survivors received less than they were worth (Tinari, Cahill, and Grivoyannis 2006).

The BP Settlement fund was modeled after the 9/11 Settlement Fund with the important difference that if was funded by a private company and not the government. This approach requires close scrutiny because it appears to be the wave of the future. For example after a gas line explosion in the San Francisco suburb of San Bruno, Pacific Gas and Electric Company established a $100 million victims compensation settlement fund. In essence the modern approach appears to be setting aside a certain dollar amount (its basis is not always clear) and then later figuring out who gets what. But this is done outside of the traditional courtroom and without all of the traditional characteristics of the judicial process. See Debating Law Courts and Politics: Is the $20 Billion BP Claims Process Fairer, Faster, and Fatter?

CONCLUSION

The Vioxx lawsuits illustrate the complex world of torts. Unlike routine torts, where the dollar amounts in question are seldom large, here upwards of $25 billion was at stake. Moreover, while most torts involve a single discrete event, mass torts like Vioxx are associated with exposure to a substance over long periods of time by many people. In some ways, though, Vioxx highlights the central feature of tort litigation: pitting repeat players against one-shotters (Chapter 7). Merck had deep pockets and spent upwards of $1 billion in legal fees, in the end saving about $20 billion. Plaintiffs like Don Hubbard are classic one-shotters, but what is somewhat unique to the American legal system, these one-shotters are represented by lawyers who have become themselves repeat players, suing deep-pocket defendants in industries as diverse as tobacco, pharmaceuticals, and finance. No wonder proponents of tort reform portray some of these lawyers as the devil among us.

Key to the public debate are tort tales, which resemble morality plays of old. One such tort tale centered on a spilled cup of coffee. Thus, Stella Liebeck became the unlikely and unwilling poster lady for the increasingly bitter battle over tort reform. No matter what the facts, her case became the rallying cry for supporters of tort reform, who believe it will solve all sorts of problems, whether real or imagined, that are said to afflict the U.S. system of civil justice. It was during the 1960s and 1970s that the criminal court process became part of the national debate. Since the 1980s, the civil court process has likewise been incorporated in the national debate over the numerous ills said to beset the U.S. judiciary.

Interest groups play a critical role in discussions of what ails the nation's judiciary. When President Bush denounced "judicial hellholes" he borrowed a phrase directly from an advocacy report prepared by the American Tort Reform Association, whose members stand to gain the most financially from tort reform. The battle over tort reform likewise highlights the importance of understanding the American judiciary in the context of the three branches of government. Businesses have sought to win favorable decisions in the nation's courts. But, when those efforts have proven less than satisfactory, they have sought to enlist the leadership of the executive branches of government (governors and presidents) to make their case before legislative bodies. In turn, courts in some states have struck down tort reform passed by either the legislatures or the voters. Consequently business groups have spent considerable sums trying to get their types of candidates elected, particularly to state supreme courts (Chapter 6). In short, the tug of war between the three branches of government continues.

Discussions of the so-called litigation explosion represent contemporary concerns about the legal health of U.S. society. Responsibility is laid at the feet of a wide variety of actors, including pathologically litigious plaintiffs, attorneys who are more concerned with their monthly billings than with their clients' best interest, juries that hand down excessive awards, activist judges, and misguided legislators who burden the courts with too many laws. In short, the list of who is responsible, and why, is now quite large. In an important sense, this expansion of the source of what is wrong is quite positive, because it incorporates many of the factors discussed in Chapter 1.

Efforts to understand and explain changes in court usage and the problems that result reinforce the utility of the definition of politics provided in Chapter 1, stressing the "authoritative allocation of values." Some observers have decried the lack of court remedies for the grievances of poor and middle-class U.S. citizens. Conversely, others see the need to limit access, not increase it. In short, the debate over the litigation explosion reflects a striking duality: Courts are being asked to resolve routine matters as well as social problems beyond their grasp.

CRITICAL THINKING QUESTIONS

1. Is the United States in the middle of a litigation explosion? Why or why not? Politically, who is advantaged by public perceptions of a litigation explosion? Who is disadvantaged?

2. What types of torts do tort reforms typically target and why? Which interest groups stand to gain from tort reform? Which interest groups stand to lose?

3. In what ways is alternative dispute resolution similar to or different from traditional court-based litigation? Why do liberals and conservatives seem to support ADR? In advocating ADR, do both have the same types of cases in mind?

Search Terms

alternative dispute resolution	mass tort	tort
litigation explosion	tobacco lawsuit	tort reform

REFERENCES

Alpert, Bruce. 2010. "Compensation for laid-off rig Workers Still Uncertain." *Times-Picayune* July 20.

American Tort Reform Association. 2010. "Tort Reform Record." Available online at http://www.atra.org. Retrieved August 27, 2010.

Associated Press. 1999. "Breast Implant Deal Is Approved." June 2.

Berenson, Alex. 2007. "Merck Agrees to Settle Vioxx Suits for $4.85 Billion." *New York Times*, November 9.

Boersema, Craig, Roger Hanson, and Susan Keilitz. 1991. "State Court-Annexed Arbitration: What Do Attorneys Think?" *Judicature* 75: 28–33.

Boyum, Keith. 1991. "Afterward: Does Court-Annexed Arbitration 'Work'?" *Justice System Journal* 14: 244–250.

Brodsky, Stanley, Ralph Knowles, Patrick Cotter, and George Herring. 1991. "Jury Selection in Malpractice Suits: An Investigation of Community Attitudes Toward Malpractice and Physicians." *Journal of Law and Psychiatry* 14: 215–222.

CBS New. 2010. "Supreme Court to Orly Taitz: Pay Up for 'Birther,' Litigation" August 17, 2010.

Center for Court Innovation. 2010. "Community Court." Available online at http://www.courtinnovation.org.

Clark, David. 1981. "Adjudication to Administration: A Statistical Analysis of Federal District Courts in the Twentieth Century." *Southern California Law Review* 55: 65–152.

Clarke, Stevens, Laura Donnelly, and Sara Grove. 1991. "Court-Ordered Arbitration in North Carolina: Case Outcomes and Litigant Satisfaction." *Justice System Journal* 14: 154–182.

Clear, Todd, and Eric Cadora. 2003. *Community Justice.* Belmont, Calif.: Wadsworth.

Clifford, Catherine. 2011. "BP Oil Claims; Many Complaints, Few Changes." CNN February 20.

CNN. 2005. "Bush Signs Class-Action Bill Into Law." February 18.

Coltri, Laurie. 2009. *Alternative Dispute Resolution: A Conflict Approach,* 2nd ed. Upper Saddle River, NJ: Pearson.

Coyle, Marcia 2010 "We're Going to Make Them PAY! Senators Target Exxon Ruling." *The National Law Journal* May 31.

Cross, Frank, and Roger Miller. 2009. *The Legal Environment of Business,* 7th ed. Cengage.

Daniels, Stephen. 1984. "Ladders and Bushes: The Problem of Caseloads and Studying Court Activities Over Time." *American Bar Foundation Research Journal* 751–795.

———. 1985. "We Are Not a Litigious Society." *The Judges' Journal* 24: 18–21.

Daniels, Stephen, and Joanne Martin. 2010. "It is no Longer Viable from a Practical and Business Standpoint: Damage Caps, 'Hidden Victims,' and the Declining Interest in Medical Malpractice Cases." *International Journal of the Legal Profession* 17:59–82.

"Doctors Dispute Implant Diseases." 1995. *New Orleans Times-Picayune*, October 25, p. A5.

Donnelly, John. 2007. "Malpractice Curbs Hailed, Faulted." *Boston Globe*, November 26.

Eaton, Thomas, and Susette Talrico. 1996. "A Profile of Tort Litigation in Georgia and Reflections on Tort Reform." *Georgia Law Review* (Spring): 427.

Efrati, Amir, Nathan Koppel, and Jamie Heller. 2007. "Vioxx Settlement's Next Big Question: How to Split It Up?" *Wall Street Journal*, November 12.

Eisenberg, Theodore, and James Henderson. 1990. "The Quiet Revolution in Products Liability: An Empirical Study of Legal Change." *UCLA Law Review* 37: 479.

———. 1992. "Inside the Quiet Revolution in Product Liability." *UCLA Law Review* 39: 731–810.

Engel, David. 1984. "The Oven Bird's Song: Insiders, Outsiders, and Personal Injuries in an American Community." *Law and Society Review* 18: 551–582.

Fagan, Jeffrey, and Victoria Malkin. 2003. "Theorizing Community Justice Through Community Courts." *Fordham Urban Law Journal* 30: 897.

Feinberg, Kenneth. 1991. "Do Mass Torts Belong in the Courtroom?" *Judicature* 74: 237.

Felstiner, William. 1974. "Influences of Social Organization on Dispute Processing." *Law and Society Review* 9: 63–94.

Finch, Susan. 2007. "$4.85 Billion Vioxx Deal Reached." *New Orleans Times-Picayune*, November 10.

Finley, L. 2004. "The Hidden Victims of Tort Reform: Women, Children and the Elderly." *Emory Law Journal* 53: 1263–1314.

Freedman, Allan. 1995. "Dole Retrenches in Defeat, Plans Narrower Bill." *Congressional Quarterly*, May 6, p. 1233.

Galanter, Marc. 1983. "Reading the Landscape of Disputes: What We Know and Don't Know (and Think We Know) About Our Allegedly Contentious and Litigious Society." *UCLA Law Review* 31: 4–71.

———. 1993. "The Tort Panic and After: A Commentary." *Justice System Journal* 16: 1–5.

Garry, Patrick. 1997. *A Nation of Adversaries: How the Litigation Explosion Is Reshaping America*. New York: Plenum/Insight.

Gerlin, Andrea. 1994. "How a Jury Decided That a Coffee Spill Is Worth $2.9 Million." *Wall Street Journal*, September 1, p. 1.

Gill, Duane A., Stephen J. Picou and Liesel A. Ritchie. 2010. "When the Disaster is a Crime: Legal Issues and the Exxon Valdez Oil Spill." In D.W. Harper and

K. Frailing (eds.) *Crime and Criminal Justice in Disaster*. Durham, NC: Carolina Academic Press.

Goldberg, John. 2010. "Liability for Economic Loss in Connection with the Deepwater Horizon Spill." Cambridge, Mass: Harvard Law School. Available online at http://nrs.harvard.edu/urn-3:HUL.InstRepos:4595438. Accessed November 22.

Goldberg, Stephen, Frank Sander, Nancy Rogers, and Sarah Cole. 2007. *Dispute Resolution: Negotiating, Mediation, and other Processes*. 5th ed. New York: Aspen.

Gonzalez, Angel. 2010. "Oil-Fund Czar Vows ample Payouts." *Wall Street Journal* August 23.

Haltom, William, and Michael McCann. 2004. *Distorting the Law: Politics, Media, and the Litigation Crisis*. Chicago: University of Chicago Press.

Hammer, David. 2010. "Paying Gulf Oil Claims Not Cut and Dried, Feinberg Admits." *Times Picayune* Nov. 26.

———. 2010. "Feds are going after Fraud Oil Spill Claims." *Times Picayune* December 15.

———. 2011. "Feinberg Waivers Challenged." *Times Picayune* February 23.

———. 2011. "Feinberg: Pace of Payment Quickens." *Times Picayune* June 21.

Hans, Valerie. 2000. *Business on Trial: The Civil Jury and Corporate Responsibility*. New Haven, Conn.: Yale University Press.

Hans, Valerie, and William Lofquist. 1992. "Jurors' Judgments of Business Liability in Tort Cases: Implications for the Litigation Explosion Debate." *Law and Society Review* 26: 85–116.

Hanson, Roger, and Susan Keilitz. 1991. "Arbitration and Case Processing Time: Lessons from Fulton County." *Justice System Journal* 14: 203–228.

Harrington, Christine. 1985. *Shadow Justice: The Ideology and Institutionalization of Alternatives to Court*. Westport, Conn.: Greenwood Press.

Henderson, Roger. 1977. "No-Fault Insurance for Automobile Accidents: States and Effects in the United States." *Oregon Law Review* 56: 287.

Hensler, Deborah. 1986. "What We Know and Don't Know About Court-Administered Arbitration." *Judicature* 69: 270–278.

———. 1992. "Taking Aim at the American Legal System: The Council on Competitiveness's Agenda for Legal Reform." *Judicature* 75: 244–250.

———. 1993. "Reading the Tort Litigation Tea Leaves: What's Going On in the Civil Liability System?" *Justice System Journal* 16: 139.

Hosticka, Carl. 1979. "We Don't Care About What Happened, We Only Care About What Is Going to Happen: Lawyer-Client Negotiations." *Social Problems* 26: 599–610.

Johnson, Linda. 2007. "Merck to Settle Vioxx Lawsuits." *Austin American-Statesman*. November 10.

Johnston, Michael. 2007. "The Litigation Explosion, Proposed Reforms, and their Consequences." *BYU Journal of Public Law* 21:2: 179–208.

Kagan, Robert. 1984. "The Routinization of Debt Collection: An Essay on Social Change and Conflict in the Courts." *Law and Society Review* 18: 323–372.

Koenig, Thomas, and Michael Rustad. 1993. "The Quiet Revolution Revisited: An Empirical Study of the Impact of State Tort Reform of Punitive Damages in Products Liability." *Justice System Journal* 16: 21–44.

Kritzer, Herbert. 2001. "Public Perceptions of Civil Jury Verdicts." *Judicature* 85: 79–82.

Kritzer, Herbert. 2004. *Risks, Reputations, and Rewards: Contingency Fee Legal Practice in the United States*. Stanford, CA: Stanford University Press.

LaFountain, Robert, Richard Schauffler, Shauna Strickland, Chantal Bromage, Sarah Gibson and Ashley Mason. 2010. *Examining the Work of State Courts*. Williamsburg, Va.: National Center for State Courts.

Langton, Lynn and Thomas Cohen, *Civil Bench and Jury Trials in State Courts, 2005* (Washington, D.C.: U.S. Department of Justice, Bureau of Justice Statistics, 2009).

Levey, Curt. 2010. "Health-Care Reform Could Create a Litigation Explosion." *Wall Street Journal* February 10.

Lieberman, Jethro K. 1983. *The Litigious Society*. New York: Basic Books.

Longstreth, Andrew. 2010. "Paul Weiss and Lowenstein Ordered to Pay $1.96 Million for Filing Frivolous Suit against Ron Perelman's In-Laws." *National Law Journal* August 26.

Lupia, Arthur. 1994. "Shortcuts Versus Encyclopedias: Information and Voting Behavior in California Insurance Reform Elections." *American Political Science Review* 88: 63–78.

Macaulay, Stewart. 1979. "Lawyers and Consumer Protection Laws." *Law and Society Review* 14: 115–171.

MacCoun, Robert. 1991. "Unintended Consequences of Court Arbitration: A Cautionary Tale from New Jersey." *Justice System Journal* 14: 229–243.

Maginnis, Joan. 2002. "The 9/11 Compensation Fund: Overview and Comment." Washington, DC: The Federalist Society for Law and Public Policy Studies, available online at http://www.fed-soc.org/doclib/ 20070326_VictimFund.pdf. Accessed March 27.

Mahoney, Barry, with Alexander Aikman, Pamela Casey, Victor Flango, Geoff Gallas, Thomas Henderson, Jeanne Ito, David Steelman, and Steven Weller. 1988. *Changing Times in Trial Courts*. Williamsburg, Va.: National Center for State Courts.

Marek, Lynne. 2007. "A Small Firm Wages '100 Years' War' on Tort Reform." *National Law Journal*, December 10.

McIntosh, Wayne. 1980–1981. "150 Years of Litigation and Dispute Settlement: A Court Tale." *Law and Society Review* 15: 823–848.

McLauchlan, William. 1977. *American Legal Process*. New York: Wiley.

Meinhold, Stephen, and David Neubauer. 2001. "Exploring Attitudes About the Litigation Explosion." *Justice System Journal* 22(2): 105–115.

Merry, Sally. 1985. "Concepts of Law and Justice Among Working Class Americans." *Legal Studies Forum* 9: 59.

Milbank, Dana. 2010. "Ken Feinberg, Czar of the Gulf." *Washington Post*. July 20.

Miller, Richard, and Austin Sarat. 1981. "Grievances, Claims and Disputes: Assessing the Adversary Culture." *Law and Society Review* 15: 525–565.

Mowbray, Rebecca. 2010. "Oil Spill Class Action calls for punitive Damages." *Times-Picayune* August 22.

———. 2010."Oil Firm Ordered to Give Up more Records." *Times-Picayune* December 18.

Moog, Robert. 1992. "Delays in the Indian Courts: Why the Judges Don't Take Control." *Justice System Journal* 16: 19–36.

———. 1998. "Activism on the Indian Supreme Court." *Judicature* 82(3): 124–132.

Nagareda, Richard. 2007. *Mass Torts in a World of Settlement*. Chicago: University of Chicago Press.

National Restaurant Association. 2008. "Frivolous Obesity Lawsuits." Available online at http://www.national restaurantassociation.com/government. Retrieved January 9, 2008.

Navarro, Mireya. 2010. "Sept. 11 Workers Agree to Settle Health Lawsuits." *New York Times* November 19.

Neubauer, David. 1986. "Are We Approaching Judicial Gridlock? A Critical Review of the Literature." *Justice System Journal* 11: 363–381.

Neubauer, David, and Stephen Meinhold. 1994. "Too Quick to Sue? Public Perceptions of the Litigation Explosion." *Justice System Journal* 16: 1–14.

Nolan-Haley, Jacqueline. 2008. *Alternative Dispute Resolution in a Nutshell*. St. Paul, Minn.: West.

O'Barr, William, and John Conley. 1988. "Lay Expectations of the Civil Justice System." *Law and Society Review* 22: 137–161.

O'Leary, Rosemary, and Susan Summers Raines. 2001. "Lessons Learned from Two Decades of Alternative Dispute Resolution Programs and Processes at the U.S. Environmental Protection Agency." *Public Administration Review* 61: 682.

O'Keefe, Ed. 2010. "Obama 'Pay Czar' Kenneth Feinberg to oversee Fund for Victims of BP oil Spill." *Washington Post* June 17.

Olson, Walter. 1991. *The Litigation Explosion: What Happened When America Unleashed the Lawsuit*. New York: Truman Talley Books/Dutton.

———. 2003. *The Rule of Lawyers: How the Litigation Elite Threatens the Rule of Law*. New York: St. Martin's Press.

Ostrom, Brian, David Rottman, and Roger Hanson. 1992. "What Are Tort Awards Really Like? The Untold Story from the State Courts." *Law and Policy* 14: 77–106.

"Overseeing Mr. Feinberg." 2011. *Times Picayune* March 17.

Page, Jeremy. 2010. "Sexual Revolution as Indian Supreme Court Sanctions Co-Habitation." *The Times* March 25.

Parrott, Matthew. 2007. "Is Compulsory Court-Annexed Medical Malpractice Arbitration Constitutional?" *Fordham Law Review* 75: 2686–2735.

Peterson, Melody. 2000. "Settlement Is Approved in Diet Drug Cases." *New York Times*, August 29.

Picou, Stephen J., Duane A. Gill and Maurie J. Cohen (eds.) 1997. *The ExxonValdez Disaster: Readings on a Modern Social Problem*. Dubuque, IA: Kendall-Hunt.

Porter, Rebecca. 2004. "New Jersey Bar Disavows Court-Annexed Arbitration." *Trial* 40 (4): 82.

Prasad, Gireesh Chandra. 2007. "Dow Offers to Clean Up Bhopal Gas Tragedy Mess." *Economic Times*, September 6.

Price, Richard. 1996. "Californians Vote on Limiting Lawsuits." *USA Today*, March 26.

Reuters. 1992. "Compensation for Bhopal Set." June 22.

———. 2004. "Bhopal Victims Struggle to Survive." December 22.

Rhode, Deborah. 2004. "Frivolous Litigation and Civil Justice Reform: Miscasting the Problem, Recasting the Solution." *Duke Law Journal* 54: 446–483.

Robinson, Glen O. 1986. "The Medical Malpractice Crisis: A Retrospective." *Law and Contemporary Problems* 49: 173–180.

Sarat, Austin, and William Felstiner. 1986. "Law and Strategy in the Divorce Lawyer's Office." *Law and Society Review* 20: 93–134.

———. 1988. "Law and Social Relations: Vocabularies of Motive in Lawyer/Client Interaction." *Law and Society Review* 22: 737–770.

Schulhofer, Stephen. 1986. "The Future of the Adversary System." *Justice Quarterly* 3: 83–94.

Schwartz, John. 2010. "For Kenneth Feinberg, More Delicate Diplomacy." *New York Times*. July 16.

Selvin, Molly, and Patricia Ebener. 1984. *Managing the Unmanageable: A History of Civil Delay in the Los Angeles Superior Court*. Santa Monica, Calif.: RAND Corporation, Institute for Civil Justice.

Shapiro, Martin. 1981. "On the Regrettable Decline of Law French: Or Shapiro Jette la Brickbat." *Yale Law Journal* 90: 1198.

Shapoo, Rubina Khan. 2010. "Supreme Court Reopens Bhopal Tragedy Case." NDTV August 31. www.ndtv.com

Sharma, Amol. 2011. "In India, the Supreme Court Takes a More Activist Role." *Wall Street Journal* May 16.

Stevens, William. 1984. "U.S. Lawyers Are Arriving to Prepare Big Damage Suits." *New York Times*, December 12.

Stewart, Larry. 1994. "Damage Caps Add to Pain and Suffering." *Insight on the News*, November 7, p. 20.

Szali, George. 1998. "Case Not Changing Awards." *Business Insurance*, October 12, p. 7.

Tinari, Frank, Kevin Cahill, and Elias Grivoyannis. 2006 "Did the 9/11 Victim Compensation Fund Accurately Assess Economic Losses?" *Topics in Economic Analysis & Policy* 6: Issue 1, Article 2.

The True Stella Awards. 2011. http://www.stellaawards.com/ accessed July 28, 2011.

Wagner, Robert. 2005. "Robert Wagner Hosts the Litigation Explosion…." *Entrepreneur*, August 1.

Will, George. 2007. "Market a Gold Mine for Predatory Lawyers." *New Orleans Times-Picayune*, November 19.

Williams, Frank. 2007. "Reinventing the Courts: The Frontiers of Judicial Activism in the State Courts." *Campbell Law Review* 29: 591–735.

Yates, Jeff, Holley Tankersley, and Paul Brace. 2010. "Assessing the Impact of State Judicial Structures on Citizen Litigiousness." *Political Research Quarterly* 63: 796–810.

Yngvesson, Barbara, and Lynn Mather. 1983. "Courts, Moots, and the Disputing Process." In *Empirical Theories About Courts*, edited by Keith Boyum and Lynn Mather. New York: Longman.

FOR FURTHER READING

Baker, Tom. 2005. *The Medical Malpractice Myth*. Chicago: University of Chicago Press.

Barnes, Jeb. 2007. "Rethinking the Landscape of Tort Reform: Legislative Inertia and Court-Based Tort Reform." *The Justice System Journal* 28: 157–181.

Black, Bernard, Charles Silver, David Hyman, and William Sage. 2005. "Stability, Not Crisis: Medical Malpractice Claim Outcomes in Texas, 1988–2002." *Journal of Empirical Legal Studies* 2: 207–259.

Bogus, Carl. 2001. *Why Lawsuits are Good for America: Disciplined Democracy, Big Business, and the Common Law*. New York: New York University Press.

Burke, Thomas. 2002. *Lawyers, Lawsuits, and Legal Rights: The Battle Over Litigation in American Society*. Berkeley: University of California Press.

Chamallas, Martha, and Jennifer Wiggins. 2010. *The Measure of Injury: Race, Gender, and Tort Law*. New York: New York University Press.

Daniels, Stephen, and Joanne Martin. 2004. "The Strange Success of the Mass Tort Class Action." *Emory Law Journal* 53: 1225.

Edwards, Linda, J. Stanley Edwards and Patricia Wells. *Tort Law*, 4th Ed. Delmar Cengage 2009.

Grisham, John. 2003. *The King of Torts*. New York: Doubleday.

Hans, Valerie. 2000. *Business on Trial: The Civil Jury and Corporate Responsibility*. New Haven, Conn.: Yale University Press.

Harel-Shalev, Ayelet. 2010. *The Challenge of Sustaining Democracy in Deeply Divided Societies: Citizenship, Rights, and Ethnic Conflicts in India and Israel*. Lanham, Md: Lexington Books.

Hensler, Deborah, Nicholas Page, Bonita Dombey-Moore, Beth Giddens, Jennifer Gross, and Erik Moller. 2000. *Class Action Dilemmas: Pursuing Public Goals for*

Private Gain. Santa Monica, Calif.: RAND Corporation, Institute for Civil Justice.

Kagan, Robert. 2006. "How Much Do Conservative Tort Tales Matter?" *Law and Social Inquiry* 31: 711–737.

Koenig, Thomas, and Michael Rustad. 2003. *In Defense of Tort Law*. New York: New York University Press.

Kritzer, Herbert. 2004. "American Adversarialism." *Law and Society Review* 38: 349–383.

Mayer, Bernard. 2000. *The Dynamics of Conflict Resolution: A Practitioner's Guide*. San Francisco: Jossey-Bass.

McCann, Michael, and William Haltom. 2006. "On Analyzing Legal Culture: A Reply to Kagan." *Law and Social Inquiry* 31: 739–756.

Moog, Robert. 2002. "Judicial Activism in the Cause of Judicial Independence: The Indian Supreme Court in the 1990s." *Judicature* 85: 268–277.

Page, Jeremy. 2010. "Sexual Revolution as Indian Supreme Court Sanctions Co-Habitation." *The Times* March 25.

Pariky, Sara, and Bryant Garth. 2005. "Philip Corboy and the Construction of the Plaintiff's Personal Injury Bar." *Law and Social Inquiry* 30: 269.

Sen, Ronojoy. 2010. *Articles of Faith: Religion, Secularism, and the Indian Supreme Court*. New York: Oxford University Press.

Shapoo, Rubina Khan. 2010. "Supreme Court Reopens Bhopal Tragedy Case." NDTV August 31. www.ndtv.com

White, G. Edward. 1985. *Tort Law in America: An Intellectual History*. New York: Oxford University Press.

TRIAL COURTS: HOW CIVIL CASES END

The modern façade of the Harris County Family Law Center in Houston, Texas, reflects a modern reality—family law cases such as divorce, child custody, and child support represent a growing part of a court's docket.

David Neubauer

Marisa Rodriguez once spent her time playing with her three children and painting landscapes in oils. But now the 39-year-old woman was confined to a wheelchair and able to provide only halting replies to her lawyer's questions. When asked if she wanted to return to her once-happy life, she could barely respond, "Yes, sure. But I can't. I tried, but I can't," referring to the horrendous automobile accident that left her with permanent brain damage (Gregor 2001e).

Marisa Rodriguez's emotional testimony came during one of the nation's most closely watched civil trials. Most tort trials focus on the responsibility of individuals—whether the other driver caused the accident by driving too fast or drinking too much. But this one focused squarely on corporate responsibility—did Ford Motor Company and/or Firestone Tire Company knowingly conceal design defects, resulting in thousands of accidents and hundreds of deaths? In hundreds of previous lawsuits, the two corporate giants had settled out of court. Now for the first time, however, a jury was seemingly to decide the issue of responsibility. Firestone had decided to try a risky defense—blame the horrendous accident on fundamental design defects by Ford.

Marisa Rodriguez's lawsuit illustrates that civil cases are now just as likely as their criminal counterparts to generate public attention and public controversy. *Rodriguez v. Firestone* (2001) also illustrates that civil lawsuits involve the processing of private disputes in a public courthouse. Chapter 10 emphasized that many civil disputes never make it to court; rather, they are resolved before the filing of a lawsuit. This chapter focuses on the corollary: The vast majority of civil cases filed are never tried; rather, they are resolved by negotiations leading to out-of-court settlements. In many respects, litigation is both a last resort and a worst resort, one that people usually try to avoid. Yet the possibility of litigation does affect how problems are handled outside court. Simply put, this chapter focuses on bargaining in the shadow of the law.

It begins by examining civil procedure, paying particular attention to how lawyers use the tools of litigation and the types of decisions that judges are called on to make. Attention then shifts to the dominant reality of the civil trial process—settlements, where civil justice is better characterized by routine administration than by adversarial adjudication. Often, the judge's principal task is to formally ratify agreements that have been reached out of court. To illustrate how bargaining occurs in the shadow of the law, this chapter explores torts, small claims, and divorce cases in some depth. How the civil trial courts dispense justice is an increasingly important topic. The last part of the chapter, therefore, examines one contemporary controversy surrounding the civil justice system: economic imbalances that affect winners and losers.

The substantive theme of this chapter emphasizes the breadth of civil cases in the United States. Debating Law, Courts, and Politics: The Billion Dollar Blame Game explores who will be responsible for paying claims associated with the Deepwater Horizon oil spill. Case Close-Up: *Rodriguez v. Firestone* (2001) focuses on big-dollar personal injury lawsuits—in this case, the battle between Ford Motor Company and Bridgestone Tire over who was responsible for Ford Explorers rolling over. Courts in Comparative Perspective: The State of Israel focuses on Israel, because Israel's procedures for handling civil lawsuits differ greatly from ours. Finally, Law and Popular Culture: *Kramer vs. Kramer* uses the movie to explore the emotional aspects of divorce.

CIVIL PROCEDURE

Civil procedure governs how noncriminal lawsuits are handled by lawyers, judges, witnesses, and litigants. Procedures are the tools of litigation that govern how to start lawsuits, how to run them, and how to finish them. The rules of civil procedure are strikingly different from those governing criminal prosecutions. For one thing, civil procedures are much more extensive, because they cover a much broader range of legal matters. Just as important, rules of civil procedure do not have a constitutional base. The extensive due process guarantees that protect those accused of violating a criminal statute are not applicable in civil proceedings. Civil litigants, for example, are not covered by the Fifth Amendment's protection against self-incrimination, which means that plaintiffs and defendants alike can be compelled to make statements before trial and can be forced to testify during trial. The contrasts between criminal and civil procedure are most apparent during trial (discussed in Chapter 12). Although the prosecution must prove the defendant guilty beyond a reasonable doubt, the plaintiff in a civil case may win on the basis of a **preponderance of evidence**, a lesser burden of proof.

English Practices

United States civil practices developed as a reaction to the formality and complexity of English procedural law, which encouraged lawyers to include every possible allegation, regardless of the likelihood that the evidence would support it. The result of such overpleading was "frightful expense, endless delay and an enormous loss of motion" (Wright 1983, 284). Although the English system was wonderfully scientific, it was also slow, expensive, and unworkable. Indeed, the dismal lore of English pleading was so rigid that one technical mistake could determine the outcome of a lawsuit (Friedman 1985). Thus, many cases were lost not on their merits but because of procedural mistakes made by the lawyers. In *Bleak House* ([1852] 1964, 109–110), Charles Dickens uses the fictional case of *Jarndyce v. Jarndyce* to highlight the rigidity and formalism of English civil procedure:

> The lawyers have twisted it into such a state of bedevilment that the original merits of the case have long disappeared from the face of the earth. It's about a will and the trusts under a will—or it was once. It's about nothing but costs now. We are always appearing, and disappearing, and swearing, and interrogating, and filing, and cross-filing, and arguing, and sealing, and motioning, and referring, and reporting, and revolving about the Lord Chancellor and all of his satellites, and equitably waltzing ourselves off to dusty death, about costs. That's the great question. All the rest, by some extraordinary means, has melted away.

For reasons like those, English civil procedure was often not suited to the needs of a newly emerging nation.

American Adaptations

Civil procedure in the early days of the republic was never as tortuous as English practice. By the middle of the nineteenth century, however, civil procedure had become so technical and detailed that it merited reform. New York took the lead, passing a complete Code of Civil Procedure in 1848. Pushed by David Dudley Field, a member of the drafting committee, the new rules came to be known as the "Field Code" and were soon adopted elsewhere, particularly in western states such as California (Friedman 1985). The pleading requirements included in those statutes are commonly referred to as "code pleading" and are still used in a handful of states.

Modern U.S. civil procedure began in 1938 with the adoption of the Federal Rules of Civil Procedure. Their purpose was to create a uniform procedure that was flexible, simple, and efficient (Wright 1983). The new rules established national uniformity in procedure for federal civil cases. Before that time, federal courts followed the procedures of the states in which they sat. The most significant feature of the federal rules was the creation of **notice pleading**, which places little stock in

TABLE 11.1 Steps of Civil Procedure	Law on the Books	Law in Action
Complaint	First paper filed stating who is being sued and why.	Under notice pleading, lawyers have only to provide bare details of the lawsuit.
Service	Process of officially bringing the complaint to the defendant.	On rare occasions, there are complaints that the papers were never delivered.
Answer	Defendant's response to allegations made by the plaintiff in the latter's complaint.	Answers are often short denials of the plaintiff's contentions.
Discovery	Process by which parties to a lawsuit exchange information about the case.	The more money involved, the more extensive the amount of discovery.
Motions	Requests that the judge make a ruling.	Motions range from procedural to dispositive.
Pretrial conference	The judge may require lawyers for all parties to meet.	The judge typically uses the pretrial conference to explore the possibility of settlement.
Settlement	Agreement about the disposition of a lawsuit reached by the parties.	Negotiations vary in intensity and type.
Trial	Fact-finding process using the adversarial process.	Trials without juries are often best described as hearings.
Enforcing judgment	Collecting money owed by the defendant.	In small-claims cases and child custody disputes, enforcing judgments are often at issue.

technicalities. Rather, the sole concern is whether the plaintiff reveals enough information that the defendant can respond and understand why he or she is being sued (Wright 1983). As a result, modern legal pleadings may be changed freely as more becomes known about the case. The facts of the case are determined by discovery, and the issues are narrowed by a pretrial conference (See Table 11.1).

The Federal Rules of Civil Procedure are relatively short, numbering only eighty-six; however, they have been the subject of considerable judicial interpretation, which is published in the *Federal Rules Decisions* and now runs to more than 100 volumes. These rules have had a major impact on state procedures. Roughly 35 states have adapted the federal rules for local use, and the remainder have revised their code pleadings to at least partially reflect the innovations of the federal rules.

STEPS IN A CIVIL LAWSUIT

The fundamental purpose of **civil procedure** is the just and efficient resolution of disputes. To achieve those goals, the rules of civil procedure are based on the guiding premise of due process of law: A person is entitled to (1) a notice that he or she is being sued and (2) an opportunity to respond to the matter. Beyond those basics, though, civil procedure can be highly technical. Because the situations that arise during a lawsuit can be diverse and complex, so is civil procedure. Its specific laws and rules are found in statutes, rules of court, and precedent.

The principal steps of a civil lawsuit consist of the complaint, service, the answer, discovery, motions, the pretrial conference, the trial, and enforcing judgment.

Although there are differences among jurisdictions, those eight steps are fairly typical of civil procedure in U.S. trial courts. To simplify the presentation, the following discussion largely assumes that there are only two parties to the case: a single plaintiff and a single defendant.

Complaint

A civil case begins when the **plaintiff** files a complaint with the trial court that will hear the case. The clerk of court stamps the complaint, indicating the time and the date it was filed, places it in a file folder, and assigns it a case number. The **complaint** notifies the defendant that he or she is being sued and for what reason.

The complaint begins by stating why the court has jurisdiction to hear the case. A complaint filed in state court, for example, would specify that the actions occurred in a given county of the state, and, therefore, that the court named has jurisdiction.

Second, the complaint provides a short statement of the facts that gave rise to the action. Thus, under notice pleading, it is sufficient to allege that, on the date stated and at a specific place, the defendant drove his automobile into the plaintiff while the latter was crossing the street, and, as a result, the plaintiff suffered certain specified injuries.

Third, the complaint states a cause of action, which is a legal theory about why the plaintiff is entitled to recovery. If an injury resulted from the automobile accident, for example, the complaint would state that the plaintiff is proceeding under tort law.

Fourth, the complaint specifies a **remedy** it wishes the court to provide. A tort action requests monetary damages. Usually, the amount of money requested is substantially larger than the case's realistic value. The plaintiff's attorney wants to make sure the requested damages are sufficient to cover the plaintiff's losses. Inflated damage estimates also establish a bargaining range around which lawyers later negotiate a settlement.

Service

After the complaint has been filed, the next step is to formally notify the **defendant**. This process is referred to as **service** and typically involves a **summons**, which is a notice informing the person that a lawsuit has been filed and telling him or her to appear in court at a certain time and place. Typically, the summons must be delivered personally to the individual, but, in some circumstances, it is sufficient to deliver the summons to the defendant's home. If the defendant is a business or some other organization, the summons may be served on any person authorized to receive service of process, usually the law firm that regularly represents the organization. In many states, the local sheriff delivers the summons; in other states, private process servers are used. After the summons has been served, the process server files an affidavit with the court indicating proof of service.

Usually, service presents no problems. However, some defendants have gone to elaborate lengths to avoid being served. Howard Hughes and financier Robert Vesco, for example, hid out for years attempting to avoid the process server. Conversely, some defendants are never notified. That abuse gave rise to the phrase "sewer service," meaning that dishonest process servers "drop them down the sewer" and later swear to a successful legal completion of service (Caplovitz 1974).

Answer

After being served with a copy of the complaint, the defendant has the opportunity to respond. The defendant's written account, termed the **answer**, is filed with the clerk of court and placed in the case file. Rules of procedure require that an answer be filed within a short period of time (20 days in federal court), but some courts are lax in enforcing that time frame. It is extremely important, however, that the defendant file an answer, because failure to respond is tantamount to an admission of liability. If the defendant does not file an answer, the plaintiff can file a motion for a **default judgment**, which, if granted, will provide the plaintiff a legal victory without a hearing on the merits of the case.

In responding to the complaint, the defendant has several options. The most common response is a denial. During the early stages of a lawsuit, attorneys are often reluctant to admit anything of importance and respond to the complaint by simply denying the important allegations. As a result, most answers are short and uninformative.

Beyond denying that the defendant is liable, the answer may assert an affirmative defense, which sets out new facts and arguments that might win for the defendant, even if everything stated in the complaint is true. For example, if the plaintiff is suing to enforce a contract, the affirmative defense might allege that the contract is null and void because the defendant entered into the contractual relationship under duress or was induced by the plaintiff's fraud. Once such issues are raised, the defendant has the additional burden of proving an affirmative defense.

Yet a third option in drafting the answer is to raise a **counterclaim**—that is, a claim made by the defendant to the effect that not only does the defendant not owe the plaintiff any money but also the plaintiff owes the defendant money. Those allegations may be based on the same facts presented in the plaintiff's complaint, or they may set forth an entirely different set of facts. Because a counterclaim involves the defendant suing the plaintiff, it starts a new lawsuit, and the plaintiff is now required to file an answer.

Taken together, the complaint and the answer are referred to as the **pleadings**. Under notice pleading, the complaint and the answer can be amended during the course of the lawsuit as new information becomes available. Once the complaint and the answer have been filed, the case is said to be at issue, which means other steps in the process may proceed.

Discovery

Discovery involves the formal and informal exchange of information between the two sides in a lawsuit. According to law professor Charles Alan Wright (1983), the inclusion of broad and flexible discovery provisions was the most significant innovation introduced by the Federal Rules of Civil Procedure. These rules rest on a basic philosophy that, before trial, every party is entitled to the disclosure of all relevant information in the possession of any person, unless the information is privileged. That philosophy runs directly counter to English practice, which provided the parties relatively few means for learning before trial what evidence other parties had developed. As a result, common-law trials were largely a game of blindman's bluff, carried out in the dark, with each party trying to "ambush" or surprise the other by introducing unanticipated evidence (*Hickman v. Taylor* 1947; *United States v. Procter & Gamble Co.* 1958). By including pretrial discovery, the framers of the rules of civil procedure rejected the sporting theory of justice. Now victory is intended to go to the party entitled to it, rather than to the side that best uses its wits (Wright 1983). The modern system is intended to equip both sides to understand fully the case before trial. Reformers hoped that this full knowledge would promote settlement in a higher percentage of cases, improve the fairness of those settlements, and also make the trial (if there was one) more orderly and less likely to be marred by surprises (Brazil and Weber 1987).

Privileged Information   The major limitation on information subject to discovery involves **privileged information**. The doctrine of privileged information reflects the judgment of courts and legislatures that certain relationships have a special status, and, therefore, their private communications should be kept confidential. The privileged relationship that has the greatest effect on litigation is that between attorney and client. Policy makers have decided that it is important for clients to feel that they can talk freely to their lawyer. If lawyers could be forced to disclose everything their clients told them, clients would be forced to decide what things to tell their lawyers and what things to keep to themselves. The effect of such a system would be to force clients to act as their own lawyers. Thus, the lawyer-client relationship is considered privileged, which means that a court cannot force a lawyer to divulge any communication with the client or any work product developed in representing the client.

Similarly, state and federal courts recognize privileges in other kinds of relationships, including husband-wife, doctor-patient, clergy-penitent, and journalist-source. Unlike the attorney-client privilege, however, most of these privileged communications are considered "qualified" rather than absolute, which means that, in some limited circumstances, a judge may force a party to disclose information that was communicated in confidence (Brazil and Weber 1987).

Tools of Discovery   Lawyers may use three principal tools of discovery to seek information from the opponent before trial: the deposition, the production of documents, and the interrogatory. The most commonly used tool is the **deposition**, which is the sworn testimony of a witness taken out of court. Typically, a person is given a notice of deposition and voluntarily appears. If the person refuses to appear, however, the court can issue a **subpoena** to compel his or her attendance. As with all subpoenas, failure to comply can be punished by a finding of **contempt of court**, which may range from a fine to imprisonment. During the taking of the deposition, a court reporter makes a verbatim transcript of the proceedings. Attorneys for all parties attend and are allowed to ask questions. Depositions provide both parties with the witnesses' statements, and if the case goes to trial, the depositions may be used as evidence.

A second tool of discovery involves the production of documents. A litigant is generally entitled to the production of all relevant documents in the possession or control of an adversary. In a tort action, for example, the defendant has the right to inspect the medical records of the plaintiff. The production of documents largely proceeds informally; the lawyers for both parties voluntarily work out a time and place for the inspection or exchange of information (Brazil and Weber 1987). If a party does not voluntarily disclose documents, however, the judge may issue a **subpoena duces tecum**, which is a court order requiring an individual to appear in court to produce specified documents pertinent to the case. In the modern era, this extends to e-mails and other electronic communications that often shed an unflattering light on the issue at hand.

The third tool of discovery is the **interrogatory**, which consists of written questions sent from one side in a lawsuit to another. Lawyers use interrogatories to get written answers to factual questions (for example, the names of witnesses or the location of important documents) or to seek an explanation of the other side's legal contentions (for example, the facts on which an opponent bases a claim).

Motions

A **motion** is a request that a judge make a ruling. The diversity of civil procedure is reflected in the variety of motions that may arise during a case. Some motions concern procedural matters relating to the conduct of the case. Disagreements over whether certain information is subject to discovery provide an example. Others are related to substantive issues. In some cases, there is a need to clarify the law applicable to the case. One party, for example, may file a motion requesting that the judge determine whether the plaintiff's or the defendant's theory of law governs the case.

The judge's ruling on motions affects cases in different ways. Some rulings provide guidance on future legal events in the case, but others are **dispositive** motions with a final judgment entered in the case. Thus, motions that are dispositive of a case mean victory for one party (and defeat for the other) without a trial. The press often reports a successful motion to dismiss as "the judge threw the case out of court," but the underlying rationale is often more complicated.

One type of dispositive motion already discussed (under "Answer") is a default judgment. Another is a motion for **summary judgment**, by which one side says, in effect, "Even assuming everything my opponent says is so, I should still win the case on the law." A motion for summary judgment is intended to weed out meritless cases before trial and is granted only if there are no major disputes over facts and there is clear and controlling law. For example, the parties may agree about how an automobile accident occurred but disagree about whether the defendant's insurance policy covers the situation in question. The judge can decide the issue without a trial by considering the agreed-on facts and reading the insurance policy. If the motion for summary judgment is granted, one side wins and there is no trial.

Data collected as part of the Civil Litigation Research Project (CLRP) shed considerable light on how motions affect the civil litigation process. Table 11.2 shows that one out of four cases was disposed by motion: Some were dismissed for a technical reason (typically the dispute was now moot); others were dismissed for cause (improper pleadings or lack of jurisdiction); still others were terminated by a default judgment or a motion for summary judgment. Most important, Table 11.2 underscores the fact that only a handful of civil cases (7 percent) are disposed by adjudication.

TABLE 11.2	How Civil Cases Are Terminated	
Resolution		**Percentage**
Tried or arbitrated		7
Includes jury trial, bench trial, and arbitration (Pennsylvania state courts)		
Disposed by motion		27
Includes dismissed for technical reasons, dismissed for cause, default judgment for plaintiff, and summary judgment		
Settled		63
Includes withdrawn, voluntary dismissal, stipulation, consent judgment, and divorce decree		
Other		5

Source: Adapted from Herbert Kritzer, "Adjudication to Settlement: Shading in the Gray," *Judicature* 70 (1986): 163. Reprinted by permission. This table is based on a random sample of 1,648 cases drawn from seven state and five federal district courts. The percentages do not add up to 100 because some cases had multiple parties.

Pretrial Conference

Like discovery, the pretrial conference plays an important part in the overall scheme of simplified pleadings introduced by the Federal Rules of Civil Procedure. Under the rules of notice pleading, complaints and answers can be limited to simple statements because the issues can be defined at the pretrial conference. Rule 16 provides that the pretrial conference can consider such matters as the clarification and simplification of issues, amendments to the pleadings, and issues of fact and law that will be tried. In federal court, and in many state courts as well, the judge may require the lawyers for all parties to attend. In practice, pretrial conferences are used for a variety of purposes, including attempting to reach an early settlement, managing the case, and preparing the case for an immediate trial (Neubauer 1975).

Enforcing Judgments

The court's official decision in a lawsuit is called a **judgment**, a court order, or a decree. An entry of a judgment for the plaintiff, however, does not necessarily mean the plaintiff will actually secure the objectives of the action. These documents are of value to the plaintiff only to the extent the defendant complies with them. The arduous process of litigation may prove to be only a preliminary step to the equally protracted travail of collecting the award. If the defendant does not voluntarily comply with the judgment, then the plaintiff must take further steps.

Some procedures for enforcing the judgment are administrative. If the case involves personal property or real estate, the plaintiff-creditor can present a copy of the judgment to the sheriff, who issues a writ to seize the items in question. But, if the defendant refuses to pay monetary damages, the plaintiff must often start separate legal proceedings to enforce the judgment. The plaintiff may seek a court order placing a lien on the defendant's property until the judgment is paid or seizing financial assets such as bank accounts. Another possibility is to garnish the defendant's paycheck and, thus, receive a small amount of money over time.

Some debtor-defendants are judgment proof; that is, they have no cash, property, or bank accounts to seize. In turn, defendants have gone to great lengths to hide their assets in an effort to avoid paying a judgment. As we shall see, some plaintiffs in small-claims court win a judgment but never collect a dime. Similarly, enforcing judgments is a major problem in divorce actions.

NEGOTIATIONS, SETTLEMENTS, AND DISPOSITIONS

Settlements are the bread and butter of the U.S. civil courts, outnumbering trials by a ratio of more than ten to one. In the U.S. district courts, for example, approximately 4 percent of civil cases are disposed by a trial—roughly 10,000 in a year (Administrative Office 2008). The data for state courts, although less reliable, point in the same direction: Depending on the state, anywhere from 1 to 4 percent of civil cases are tried each year (Schauffler, LaFountain, Strickland, and Raftery 2006). In short, voluntary settlements rather than contested trials are the predominant way that lawsuits reach disposition. In turn, some are concerned that too few cases go to trial; the issue of the vanishing jury will be discussed in Chapter 12.

Through **negotiations**, the lawyers for the opposing sides are able to arrive at a final disposition of the lawsuit, termed a **settlement**. After the defendant has satisfied the terms of the settlement (paid the money agreed on or turned over the disputed property, for example), the plaintiff voluntarily dismisses the case. Settlements benefit the litigants; the parties control the outcome of the case and are spared the costs of trial. Settlements also benefit the judicial system; trial court dockets are reduced, and, because a settlement is considered a final disposition of a case, there will be no appeal.

Whereas negotiations of civil cases largely occur in private, they proceed on the basis of public standards. Law and the legal system specify who may be sued, how an individual may be sued, who is liable, and what consequences follow from not observing these public dictates. Within these sometimes-broad parameters, litigants attempt to resolve private disputes. If these private negotiations prove unsuccessful, however, the judicial process establishes a mechanism for reaching a disposition—a public trial conducted in a public courthouse. For those reasons, Robert Mnookin and Lewis Kornhauser's seminal article (1979) argues that the resolution of private disputes is best viewed as bargaining in the shadow of the law (compare Jacob 1992).

Expectations of settlement permeate the entire civil justice process. Many litigants file civil lawsuits only as a bargaining strategy; they have no intention of bringing the case to trial. Moreover, lawyers often use civil procedure as part of an overall settlement strategy. Discovery, for example, is more often employed to elicit information helpful in negotiating a favorable settlement than to prepare the case for trial. Similarly, pretrial motions are often argued in an effort to achieve a tactical advantage during negotiations. Negotiations occur during all phases of the proceedings.

Some settlements are reached even before the defendant files the answer. Many are hammered out about the time of the pretrial conference. A few settlements, though, are not reached until the day of the trial (Provine 1987). Although a vast majority of civil cases are disposed of by settlement, there are some important differences in the intensity and the types of negotiations.

Intensity of Negotiations

How much haggling occurs during negotiations? Popular images suggest a very intense, lengthy negotiating process, with lawyers spending considerable time heatedly debating numerous offers and counteroffers before finally reaching a settlement. Such marketplace-style bargaining appears to be atypical in ordinary civil cases, however. The Civil Litigation Research Project asked lawyers to describe the nature of the negotiations in their cases (Kritzer 1991). Their responses indicate that there are relatively few exchanges of offers and counteroffers: For example, 41 percent of the cases involved no more than two offers and counteroffers. Bargaining intensity was highest in tort actions, but negotiations in divorce cases were best characterized as consisting of a single offer followed by a single counteroffer.

Lawyers were next asked to estimate how much time they devoted to negotiations. The responses indicate that only a moderate amount of time was spent on this activity. Lawyers spent a median of thirty hours per case, but only three hours (10 percent) were devoted to settlement discussions. Thus, negotiating a settlement does not constitute a dominant part of the activities of lawyers engaged in civil litigation. The number of hours spent negotiating a settlement, however, increases as the stakes escalate. In cases seeking less than $5,000, lawyers spent only 2 hours in negotiations; in cases requesting more than $50,000, the attorneys devoted an average of 10.5 hours to discussions aimed at settlement (Kritzer 1991).

Negotiations among the responsible parties is also important. Think of it as a case within a case, where lawyers for clients are trying to shift responsibility to other parties. (See Debating Law, Courts, and Politics: The Billion Dollar Blame Game.)

Types of Negotiations

What do lawyers try to gain during negotiations? Popular images suggest lawyers working to gain every last dollar due their client. Such marketplace bargaining appears to be limited to certain types of civil cases, however. According to Kritzer (1985), lawyers proceed on the basis of one of three goals: best, appropriate, or ritualistic results.

Best Result Negotiations   In best result negotiations, lawyers focus on obtaining the best possible settlement for their clients under the circumstances. This goal represents the traditional, utility-maximizing image of the negotiation process. Through initial offers and patterns of concessions, the plaintiff seeks to maximize the dollar value of the final settlement, whereas the defendant strives to minimize the amount to be paid. Cases involving considerable sums of money are most likely to involve bargaining to achieve the best result.

Appropriate Result Negotiations   Alternatively, lawyers may negotiate to obtain the appropriate result, given the alleged facts of the case, resources of the party, and options available. In pursuing that goal, lawyers may or may not adopt an adversarial stance. Rather, the process is largely shaped by the seeking of information. This model also has an analogue in the criminal arena. As stressed in Chapter 8, the guilt of the defendant is not under serious dispute in many cases, and, therefore, plea bargaining typically focuses on arriving at an appropriate penalty on the basis of the so-called going rate. Likewise, in civil cases, the basic question of liability is not in

DEBATING LAW, COURTS, AND POLITICS

■ The Billion Dollar Blame Game Trial

Soon after the explosion on the Deepwater Horizon oil rig BP announced that they would pay "all legitimate claims." The popular press quickly seized on the word legitimate and wondered if the world's second largest oil company was trying to weasel out of some of its responsibility. The business press, however, soon began to raise a more probing question about which companies would actually have to pay for the mishap. Although BP was most immediately identified with the Deepwater Horizon oil platform, the reality is that a number of different companies, all giants in their fields, were working on the rig at the time of the explosion. Given that billions of dollars are at risk, it is not surprisingly they soon became engaged in a high stakes game of finger pointing. Some have called it the billion dollar blame game.

Under the Oil Pollution Act, the owner of the well is the "responsible party" in the event of an oil spill. The Macondo well in the Gulf of Mexico was owned by BP (65 percent), Anadarko Petroleum Corporation (25 percent) and MOEX Offshore (10 percent). The terms of the companies' joint operating agreement specify that their legal liability corresponds to their share of ownership (Schwartz July 23, 2010). But the minor partners refused to pay BP's initial bills, claiming BP was negligent in managing the well. In testimony before the U.S. Senate's Homeland Security Committee, Anadarko Petroleum Corp. and MOEX Offshore said their role as minority investors prevented them from making any decisions about the Macondo well or its drilling operations. "The operations of the Macondo well were conducted with BP controlling all operating decisions," testified Anadarko chief executive James T. Hackett in prepared remarks (Tennille 2010).

The dispute between the joint owners of the well is distinct from their legal relationship to the contractors conducting the actual drilling. Transoceanic (a Swiss firm) was the owner of the Deepwater Horizon and hired by BP to drill for oil for a fee of over $500,000 per day. BP's lawsuit contends that Transocean was at fault and their lawyers are sure to echo the findings of the Coast Guard investigation which concluded that improper maintenance, insufficient staff training, and badly designed safety systems on the part of Transocean lead to the accident (Gold and Gonzalez 2011). In a counter suit, Transocean is suing BP for the replacement cost of the rig, arguing that BP's negligence caused the explosion.

Another contractor with liability exposure is Halliburton, which was responsible for placing the drilling mud in the well. According to the National Oil Spill Commission, Halliburton knew that the cement it used to seal the bottom of the well was unstable (Hammer October 29, 2010). Halliburton's response is that BP was intent on speeding up the process (to save money) and ignored their advice, including ordering them off the rig just hours before it exploded.

Another major defendant is Cameron International, the manufacturer of the blow out preventer. The initial findings from the forensic examination of this giant piece of equipment (Chapter 8) indicated that the powerful jaws had indeed tried to shear the drilling pipe but were unsuccessful because a joint of the pipe, not the pipe itself, was in position. Whether Cameron is able to escape civil liability remains to be seen.

The first phase of the consolidated oil spill litigation will center on corporate liability and is scheduled to start in February, 2012, which would prove to be a speedy trial date given the complexity of the litigation. Indeed the stakes are so high, and the number of parties so numerous, that during pretrial hearings the U.S. District Court has been forced to use two courtrooms to accommodate everyone. As discussed in Chapter 4, the Judicial Panel on Multidistrict Litigation chose U.S. District Judge Carl Barbier of New Orleans to preside over the litigation.

The billion dollar blame game trial will lack the gripping public appeal of a highly charged murder trial but it will have broad political ramifications. Trial testimony will become part of the nation's ongoing debate over energy policy. Environmentalists are sure to focus on testimony that they will claim calls for limiting off shore drilling. Representatives of the oil and natural gas industry, on the other hand, are likely to stress that safety issues have been corrected and the government needs to fully back drilling. In turn the results of the trial will impact other branches of government. Administrative agencies like the Coast Guard and Bureau of Ocean Energy Management have already held hearings and details that emerge during trial will shape regulatory policy. Likewise Congress has already held a series of hearings and what emerges from the courthouse will most certainly affect the course of future legislation.

dispute in a large proportion of cases. Rather, the lawyers negotiate the amount of money to be paid the injured party. Thus, discussions concerning damages, although consisting of a series of offers and counteroffers, actually involve an exchange of information needed to arrive at a settlement within the context of the going rate.

Ritualistic Negotiations   Finally, negotiations between lawyers in civil cases may be ritualistic, whereby the parties go through the motions of negotiations but there is neither a series of offers and counteroffers nor an exchange of facts and information that would be associated with an effort to arrive at an appropriate result. This image suggests that lawyers go through the motions of negotiations simply because it is "the way things are done." This third image also has an analogue in criminal cases. In misdemeanor courts, there is little discussion surrounding guilt or sentence. In the misdemeanor court studied by Douglas Maynard (1984), the average plea-bargaining session lasts ten minutes or less. Short negotiations also occur in civil cases; the settlement may be so immediately obvious that the parties need only engage in the ritual of bargaining before disposing of the case. The Civil Litigation Research Project found that ritualistic negotiations characterized a full 25 percent of the cases studied (Kritzer 1985).

DYNAMICS OF TRIAL COURT DISPOSITIONS: THREE CASE STUDIES

Dispositions of civil cases in the trial courts vary greatly, depending on the substance of the claim raised. Antitrust cases, for example, march to a very different drummer than do libel actions. The broad sweep of civil law makes it impossible to capture all those differences. The following in-depth examination of torts, small claims, and divorce, however, illustrates some central features of how bargaining occurs in the shadow of the law. These three case studies were selected for several interrelated reasons. First, they represent the most typical civil disputes decided by courts (Chapter 4). Second, they reflect variations in bargaining intensity and differences in types of negotiations. Finally, they highlight contrasts in the adjudicatory process (Chapter 7).

SETTLING TORT CASES

In a typical year, approximately one million tort cases are filed in state courts (Schauffler, LaFountain, Strickland, and Raftery 2006; Ostrom and Kauder 1995). A handful of these lawsuits (see Case Close-Up: *Rodriguez v. Firestone* 2001) attract considerable public attention because of the large sums of money involved (Kakalik and Pace 1986). But million-dollar jury verdicts are the exception; most tort cases are settled for relatively small sums of money.

Tort law is fluid, changing as society's values shift. Today, new torts are being recognized where no basis for a lawsuit had previously existed. Because U.S. tort law is based largely on precedents rather than on statutes, it is difficult to generalize about the status of tort law in all jurisdictions. Nonetheless, certain important changes have occurred in

CASE CLOSE-UP

■ *Rodriguez v. Firestone* (2001)

Dr. Joel Rodriguez, his wife, Marisa, and two family members were returning from a family vacation in Monterrey, Mexico, when the right rear tire of their 1998 Ford Explorer flew apart, causing the vehicle to swerve into the opposite lane before flipping over in a ditch. All four were injured, Marisa the most seriously; as the Explorer flipped over, the roof collapsed, hitting her in the head. After eight weeks in a coma, she regained consciousness, but the head trauma was severe and irreversible—her IQ was now estimated to be 73, or that of a young child.

The Rodriguez lawsuit was one of approximately one thousand filed involving the sudden shredding of a rear tire (usually the left) on a Ford Explorer. These accidents had resulted in about 250 deaths and hundreds more injured. Firestone had previously settled more than 150 cases out of court for undisclosed sums. The Rodriguez lawsuit was the first to go to trial in what some analysts categorized as a risky strategy. The defendant (Firestone) sought to shift the blame for these often horrendous accidents from defective tire manufacturing by Firestone to faulty automobile design by Ford.

Lawyers for the Rodriguez family laid the blame for the blowout on the tire company, claiming that Firestone management knew that their tires were defective but failed to take responsibility. The plaintiff began its case by calling a string of expert witnesses who testified about the disproportionately large number of damage claims filed against Bridgestone/Firestone since the mid-1990s. To buttress their case further, plaintiff's lawyers summoned a former Firestone executive, who testified that he and his co-workers had been tipped off to problems involving Firestone tires as early as 1997 (Gregor 2001a). Another expert testified that, to prevent tires from shredding, Firestone used a ninety-cent overlay on tires shipped abroad but not on those sold domestically (Gregor 2001d). Having hammered home issues of corporate greed and failure to take responsibility, the plaintiff closed by highlighting the extreme nature of the injuries suffered by Marisa. Dr. Rodriguez testified how he met his wife at a church function at the age of ten and how the sparkle in her eyes had all but disappeared. The accident had forever changed the relationships she had with her children.

Lawyers for Firestone (owned by the Japanese firm Bridgestone) countered that the accident was due to "fundamental design defects in the Ford Explorer" (Gregor 2001a). During cross-examination of plaintiff's witnesses, they suggested that lower-than-recommended tire pressures might have caused the accident. Their most important witness was Firestone chief John Lampe, who repeatedly denied his company tried to hide defects in their tires. According to his testimony, less than a tenth of a percent of the three million Wilderness AT tires sold as standard equipment on Ford Explorers had warranty problems (Pinkerton 2001). Defense also suggested that tread separation could not have caused the car to roll over. A tire expert testified that the right rear tire on the Rodriguez Explorer was probably damaged by a baseball-sized object 1,000 to 2,000 miles before the accident (Gregor 2001b).

Corporate greed was the theme of the plaintiff's closing arguments. "This is your opportunity to communicate with these people"—suggesting that the only thing that corporate America understood was money. The defense reiterated its claims that the design of the Ford Explorer, not the manufacturing of the tire, was at fault. But, in an effort to soften any potential damage award, the defense suggested that if the jurors decided to award the Rodriguez family monetary damages, fair compensation would be about $6.35 million (considerably less than the $1 billion the plaintiff asked for) (Oppel 2001b). The defense also sought to put a human face on its case by appealing to jurors to remember the 42,000 company employees who personally built the tires.

The stream of lawsuits against both Firestone Tire Company and Ford Motor Company had a number of negative consequences. The business relationship between the two companies, dating back almost 100 years, was ruptured. The CEO of Ford was eventually dismissed, partly for the negative publicity over this and other lawsuits. Both companies paid tens of millions of dollars in damage settlements. Firestone agreed to pay $41.5 million (and perhaps $10 million more) to avoid lawsuits from states (Miller 2001). Firestone was forced to recall more than 6.5 million tires, and Ford replaced an additional 13 million tires. Perhaps the most damaging of all was the bad publicity for both companies. Indeed, many analysts at the time wondered whether Firestone would be able to survive.

(continued)

In 2007, Ford Motor Company settled the last of the cases, a class action lawsuit applying to about one million people in California, Connecticut, Illinois, and Texas. Owners of Ford Broncos purchased between 1990 and 2000 are eligible for $500 vouchers to buy new Explorers or $300 to purchase other Ford or Lincoln products. In the words of Ford spokeswoman Kristen Kindley, "This does settle them all" (Thompson 2007).

---

virtually all jurisdictions in the past several decades (Litan, Swire, and Winston 1988). Here are some of the most important ways in which liability has been expanded:

- Manufacturers' liability for defective products has increased.
- Standards of negligence have been extended to a wide class of service providers not previously accustomed to being sued (for example, day care centers, amusement park operators, and not-for-profit organizations such as hospitals).
- The concept of contributory negligence has been relaxed (a plaintiff who was found negligent could not recover damages).
- Standards that plaintiffs must satisfy in proving the defendant caused their injuries have been relaxed.

This expansion of liability is at the center of the debate over the litigation explosion (discussed in Chapter 10). To critics, these changes have produced an unprecedented growth in the number of liability lawsuits in recent years. (See Courts in Comparative Perspective: The State of Israel.) Most tort cases, however, are not based on emerging theories of liability but, rather, involve an early-twentieth-century technological development—the automobile. In a typical year, for example, 4.2 million people are injured in motor vehicle accidents. That number is quite high, but the rate of injuries and fatalities (per thousand miles traveled) has declined in recent years (Ostrom, Kauder, and LaFountain 2003).

Most tort claims never become court cases. Using the well-defined rules, most injured parties are able to settle their claims against the defendant's insurance company through negotiations with claims adjusters (Ross 1970). Thus, the filing of a tort case reflects the parties' inability to achieve an early settlement. It shows that the injured party views the matter as important but does not necessarily mean a trial is anticipated. Filing, therefore, indicates that negotiations will continue but in the public forum of the courthouse. At the same time, filing produces an important shift in who is negotiating. With the plaintiff represented by a lawyer, insurance companies would be at a considerable disadvantage in court if they were to continue to use claims adjusters. Thus, after a case is filed, defendants use lawyers to represent their interests in court.

Tort cases represent parties in real conflict, and, therefore, court procedures reflect **procedural adjudication**. Tort cases, for example, typically involve some pretrial activity such as discovery and pretrial motions. And, as the stakes in the case increase, so does the amount of pretrial activity (Krystek 1994). Lawyers view the steps of civil procedure as key ingredients in the dynamics of the negotiation process. For example, lawyers use discovery procedures to learn about the content of the other party's case in hopes of improving their bargaining position. Lawyers may also use pretrial procedures for tactical reasons. Defense lawyers, in particular, are often portrayed as using pretrial procedures to delay the case and wear down the opposition. Delaying settlement works to the advantage of the insurance companies; by postponing paying money on the claim, the defendant can use the money for other purposes. Just as important, lengthy delays may pressure plaintiffs into settling for less. Consider, for example, a plaintiff who did not have many financial resources before the accident and who now finds himself or

COURTS IN COMPARATIVE PERSPECTIVE

■ The State of Israel

The wedding guests were gyrating to the disco beat when the dance floor suddenly collapsed, plunging hundreds of dancers into an abyss of concrete and dust. In the United States, the structural failure of the Versailles banquet hall would have resulted in numerous civil lawsuits. But the Israeli legal system is a mixture of English common law, British Mandate regulations, and (in personal matters) Jewish, Christian, and Muslim legal systems (Cohen 2002). As a result, the legal response in Israel was very different—almost immediately, the police arrested four people involved in the design and construction of the building and charged them with criminal negligence (Winfield 2001). Eventually, three of them were charged with manslaughter for creating the cheap and quick construction method that led to the death of 23 and the injury of almost 400 people in Israel's worst civilian disaster.

Israel, one of the United States' closest allies, declared its independence in 1948 from England and then fought a war with its Arab neighbors to preserve its existence. The Israelis defeated the Arabs in a series of wars without ending the deep tensions between the two sides. New violence broke out in September 2000. A fragile peace reached in the spring of 2005 soon gave way to new rounds of violence in the West Bank, the Gaza Strip, and Lebanon.

Israel is home to 7.5 million people (80 percent of whom are Jewish) in a geographic area slightly smaller than New Jersey. The government is a hybrid presidential-parliamentary democracy. The legislature is a unicameral parliament known as the Knesset, whose 120 members are elected by popular vote to serve four-year terms. The head of government is the prime minister, who is elected directly by the voters and also serves in the Knesset (Edelman 2000).

Israel has no formal constitution, but some of the functions of a constitution are filled by the Declaration of Establishment (1948), the Basic Laws of the Parliament (Knesset), and the Israeli citizenship law. The Israeli Supreme Court, whose justices are appointed for life by the president, has exercised an American-style power of judicial review, and, as in the United States, their decisions have played a role in the nation's internal and increasingly bitter culture war. Within that conflict, some Israelis argue that Israel should be an ultra-Orthodox nation; others argue for a more liberal relation between church and state. Amid these battles, the Israeli Supreme Court enjoys tremendous respect among the citizens. In recent years, the court has overturned a number of the legal and political privileges long enjoyed by the nation's ultra-Orthodox minority. Those decisions have enraged some of the prominent rabbis, who have gone so far as to declare the justices "wanton evildoers" and the chief justice the "enemy of Judaism."

The Israeli Supreme Court's reputation for independence is often tested by the continuing strife with the Palestinians. Based on international law, the court has tried to strike some sort of balance between governmental powers and human rights. For example, the court ruled that the nation's powerful military could deport two Palestinians who had not been convicted of any crimes but that this policy could not be used wholesale—the deportees must pose a genuine security threat (Greenberg 2002). More recently, they ordered the dismantling of an illegal West Bank settlement ("Supreme Court Orders..." 2011).

Human rights groups and Palestinians living in Israel, however, have demanded that the court be more forceful in protecting the property and the lives of innocent people. To critics, the Israeli legal system is engaged in a double standard of justice, with Palestinians unable to secure some of the basic protections routinely granted Jews.

Aharon Barak, the retired chief justice of the Israeli Supreme Court, stresses the importance of judges protecting the constitution and democracy. In *The Judge in a Democracy* (2006), he argues that judges are accountable not to politicians or public opinion but to "the internal morality of democracy." But some in Israel argue that the court has become a law unto itself, improperly extending its powers over other branches of government. To Daniel Friedmann, Israel's minister of justice and a long-time law professor, unelected judges are waging an antidemocratic revolution. This debate in many ways echoes the struggle in the United States between conservative and liberal legal theories. Indeed, key conservative legal theorists in the United States have attacked Barak's viewpoints. Robert Bork, who was not confirmed for a vacancy on the U.S. Supreme Court (Chapter 15), complains that Barak's ideas are "a textbook for judicial activists," and Richard Posner, a senior federal appellate judge, calls Barak "a legal buccaneer" (Kershner 2007a).

herself out of work. To a plaintiff in that situation, the initial settlement offer is likely to be very attractive: Not only does it represent what appears to be a lot of money, but also the money will be available immediately. Thus, the longer the case drags on, the more willing the plaintiff is to settle, even if the lawyer counsels that an even larger sum will be forthcoming if the plaintiff holds out a little longer.

Negotiations in tort cases are conducted by lawyers who specialize in such matters. Plaintiffs are typically represented by solo practitioners, who are often noted for their flamboyant behavior. Defendants are typically represented by lawyers working for large law firms, who are noted for their conservative manner. These two hemispheres of legal practice (Chapter 5), however, have something in common: They know what financial settlements are customary in tort cases. Working within those parameters, the lawyer's goal is to achieve the best result possible for his or her client. Negotiations center on two issues—liability and damages—that the lawyers may compromise on. For example, if the plaintiff perceives that the claim of legal liability is somewhat weak, he or she will be willing to settle for less in damages. The type of negotiation, however, varies with the stakes of the case. Thus, in cases involving less than $25,000, lawyers often engage in settlements aimed at achieving appropriate results (Kritzer 1985). When the stakes are low, lawyers direct efforts to arrive quickly at a customary settlement for that type of injury rather than trying to gain (or lose) a few additional dollars.

During negotiations and pretrial proceedings, the lawyers often give every indication that the case will go to trial, but such behavior largely reflects posturing. The lawyers expect to work out a settlement, and they do. Indeed, in a typical year, only 3 percent of non–domestic relations civil cases are disposed of by trial (2 percent by jury trial and 1 percent by a bench trial) (Bureau of Justice Statistics 2007). Trial dispositions are the exception, but their numbers are still sizable. Each year in the nation's 75 largest counties, almost 12,000 civil jury trials are conducted, and personal injury cases account for the overwhelming majority (Cohen 2004).

The possibility of a jury trial illustrates how bargaining occurs in the shadow of the law. Jury verdicts set the benchmarks for negotiating settlements. As specialists in injury law, both sides are well aware of the awards in past jury trials. A study of medical malpractice suits found that settlements prior to trial are strongly influenced by past jury awards. Moreover, the judgments were strongly related to factors such as the plaintiff's economic loss and the legal standards dealing with compensable damages (Danzon and Lillard 1982). Settlements averaged 75 percent of past awards in similar cases. Settlements are typically less than potential jury verdicts because trials represent risks for both sides. From the plaintiff's perspective, a jury may find the defendant not liable and, therefore, award no damages. From the insurance company's perspective, a jury may be unduly sympathetic and award the injured party more in damages than is customary. For both sides, a trial represents substantial costs, and those potential expenses are taken into consideration during bargaining. In short, a negotiated settlement allows each side to hedge its bets: The plaintiff guarantees a financial settlement by accepting less than a jury might award; the defendant protects against a potentially "outrageous" jury verdict by paying more than he or she would prefer. There is an old saying among lawyers and judges that a settlement is one that neither side likes but both can live with.

Securing and enforcing judgments in tort cases presents no particular problems. Defendants are typically large insurance companies with considerable assets, and they are in the business of paying claims. The only problem for the plaintiff is one of delay;

by appealing (Chapter 13), the insurance company can postpone paying the trial court judgment. At times, defendants use appeals to foster new settlement efforts; if the plaintiff will agree to accept a cash settlement that is less than the jury award, the defendant will pay immediately and drop the appeal.

Negotiating Small Claims

Small-claims cases constitute the largest category of civil cases. The specifics of dollar limits, court jurisdiction, and court procedure vary, but basic similarities in the issues and in the people coming to small-claims courts are apparent (Goerdt 1993). The largest number of cases involve debt collection, primarily nonpayment for goods purchased or services rendered. Another major category involves landlord-tenant disputes, mostly claims by landlords against tenants concerning past-due rent, evictions, and property damage. A smaller number of cases involve alleged property damage, largely stemming from automobile accidents.

Because the claims are small, these cases are the least likely to attract public attention. But, because they are so numerous, they are the most likely to involve ordinary citizens directly. Moreover, these courts are vital to businesses small and large that rely on small-claims courts as a relatively expeditious and inexpensive means to collect money owed (Atkinson 2004). Unlike torts and divorce, small claims are litigated on substantive standards that have not undergone major changes in recent years.

Small-claims cases involve mostly **routine administration**. A significant number of defendants never appear in court, resulting in a default judgment for the plaintiff (McEwen and Maiman 1984). Suits seeking money owed on credit and past-due rents are particularly likely to end this way. Clearly, these cases provide an inflated estimate of judicial workload. Although these cases require work on the part of the clerk, they require little judicial time.

Efforts to reach a settlement in small-claims court are best characterized as ritualistic negotiations. Resolution hearings seldom exceed the thirty minutes allotted them. These short negotiations reflect the nature of the claims being made. Disputes in small-claims courts vary along a dimension of admitted liability: That is, defendants admit no liability, partial liability, or full liability (Vidmar 1984). Thus, many cases are only partially contested (for example, when a former tenant insists that he owes only one month's rent, not two as the landlord claims), and many settlements are reached on the basis of splitting the difference (Sarat 1976).

Although the proportion is fairly small, some small-claims cases go to trial. Ordinarily, the judge conducts the hearing without a jury and the procedures are informal, lasting only a few minutes. The parties are given a brief opportunity to present their case, the judge may ask a question or two, and the so-called trial is over. Indeed, an observer of 200 cases in a Los Angeles small-claims court reported that the average trial in a contested case took only 8.9 minutes, with a range from 1 minute to 21 minutes (Yngvesson and Hennessey 1975). Thus, trials in small-claims court are better characterized as **decisional adjudication** than as the adversarial contests found in major trial courts. In essence, the judge in small-claims court is expected to seek substantive justice (McFadgen 1972) amid the welter of conflicting claims.

A study in Florida reports that cases going to trial typically involved individuals as plaintiffs and were, therefore, more complicated and less routine than those disposed of by default or settlement (Purdum 1981). Thus, whereas a claim may be small in monetary terms, the dispute and the issues underlying the dispute may be very complex, particularly if the individuals have a long history of not getting along (Yngvesson and Hennessey 1975). The flavor of these proceedings is captured in television shows such as *Judge Judy* (discussed in Chapter 6). A defendant who admits partial liability, for example, often offers a different version of what transpired to support his or her contention that less money is owed than the plaintiff is seeking, and the judge must quickly sort out these versions of past transactions (Vidmar 1984). In cases that are adjudicated like that, the outcome is more likely to be a winner-take-all than a compromise verdict (Sarat 1976).

Securing and enforcing judgments is a particular problem in small-claims cases. A study in Maine found that, in more than half the cases decided by adjudication, the defendant did not pay the plaintiff the money owed (McEwen and Maiman 1984). Similar patterns of nonpayment of judgments emerge in other studies of small-claims courts (Vidmar 1984; Hollingsworth, Feldman, and Clark 1973). Thus, some plaintiffs win the battle in small-claims court only to lose the war because the defendant is unable or unwilling to pay the money owed. Frustrations on the collection issue were angrily recorded by victorious plaintiffs in the Boston small-claims court. Typical is a 29-year-old teacher, Mrs. H., who is reported to have said "she would never go to small claims court again because of the inefficient collection procedure. She had won her case against a towing company driver, who had damaged her car, but because the driver quit the company and the company had changed its name and address, she was unable to collect" (National Institute for Consumer Justice 1972). To Mrs. H. and countless other victorious small-claims plaintiffs like her, the process of collecting from the debtor proves to be a frustrating experience.

BARGAINING DIVORCE CASES

After small claims, family law cases occupy the largest share of the U.S. civil court docket. Each year, more than 1.3 million couples legally dissolve their marriages (Schauffler, LaFountain, Strickland, and Raftery 2006). A significant number of those divorces involve minor children; indeed, half of all children will live with a single parent some time during their childhood (Bumpass and Lu 2000). The result for the judiciary is a large caseload devoted to these matters. Domestic relations cases (divorce, child custody, paternity, adoption, and child support, among other matters) constitute one-third of the civil docket of the trial courts of general jurisdiction.

In some ways, the administrative burden on the judiciary is even greater than the statistics suggest, because many of these matters involve relitigation. For example, after the judge has ordered the husband to pay child support, it is not unusual for both parties to appear in court a year or more later to adjust the amount of money owed. Indeed, repeated trips to the courthouse may occur through the years to change the terms of the divorce decree or to attempt to get the other party to comply. The movie *Kramer vs. Kramer* captures the emotional dynamics as divorcing parents battle over the custody of their child. (See Law and Popular Culture: *Kramer vs. Kramer*.)

L A W   A N D   P O P U L A R   C U L T U R E

◼ Kramer vs. Kramer (1979)

"If I understand it correctly, what means the most here is what's best for our son, what's best for Billy," says an anguished Ted Kramer during a child custody court hearing in the film *Kramer vs. Kramer*. Widely regarded as a classic, *Kramer vs. Kramer* won five Academy Awards, including Best Picture. Michael Asimov, noted UCLA law professor and film critic, describes it as "an outstanding and definitive film that treats all the elements of the divorce process seriously and which pointed the way for divorce-related films of the present" (Asimov 2000).

Kramer vs. Kramer tells the story of the Kramers: Ted (played by Dustin Hoffman), Joanna (played by Meryl Streep), and their son, Billy (played by Justin Henry). The film begins with Joanna, tired of being a housewife and upset with having put her career on hold to take care of Billy, walking away. Ted, caught up in his career and rarely around to serve as a father, is caught by surprise when Joanna leaves. He learns to be a single parent and develops a loving bond with Billy. After eighteen months, Joanna reappears and demands full custody of Billy. Ted, determined to retain the custody of Billy granted him during the earlier divorce proceedings, refuses. They go to family court.

In an unusual role reversal for child custody hearings of that day, Ted asks to retain custody despite a strong presumption favoring maternal custody. Maternal custody was preferable under the "tender years doctrine"—which dominated American family law for more than a century (Asimov 2000): A child was assumed to be better off with his or her mother, unless the father could convincingly demonstrate otherwise. On the stand, Ted openly challenges that assumption, saying, "I'd like to know what law is it that says that a woman is a better parent simply by virtue of her sex." Despite the lack of any evidence that Ted has been a bad parent or that Billy would be better off with his mother, the judge rules in favor of Joanna—granting her full custody and child support. Ted is devastated, and Billy is clearly confused and upset. The film ends when Joanna, in a last-minute change of heart, decides not to take Billy away from Ted.

The film generally receives high marks for its depiction of the devastating toll that divorce and child custody disputes take on everyone involved. As in most real child custody disputes, the lawyers for both sides "play rough," their aim to destroy the credibility of Ted and Joanna as responsible parents. Billy suffers as his parents fight over who should have custody. The lack of consideration of Billy's views leads Michael Asimov to find fault with the fictitious judge, writing, "In the real world, Judge Atkins would never have decided the custody issue cold. He would consider reports of a social worker or other professional on Billy's family situation. He might have gently interviewed Billy, asking him questions about his daily life with his dad" (Asimov 2000). Despite those shortcomings, the film provides a glimpse into the devastating and painful aspects of family court proceedings.

In an interview recorded for the DVD release of the film, Dustin Hoffman recalls a discussion he had with the woman who portrayed the court stenographer in the film. She was not an actress but an actual court stenographer who had worked in family court. He asked her, "So is this what you do, do you do divorces?" to which she replied, "I did them for years, but I burnt out, I couldn't do it anymore, it was just too painful, I really love what I'm doing now." Hoffman asked her, "What?" and she said, "Homicides." Family court judges tell a similar story. It is not uncommon for jurisdictions to rotate judges on short intervals through family court to lessen the emotional burden of dealing with family court proceedings every day for long stretches of time.

Another interesting dimension to the film's success has been its social impact. Avery Corman—author of the book the film is based on—describes it this way: "I think that *Kramer vs. Kramer* had an impact on the culture. I know I've had family court judges tell me that they used the material as the basis of making decisions in court." Regardless of whether the film has been used as family law precedent, there is little doubt that every judge and lawyer involved in divorce and child custody proceedings today has probably seen the film and analyzed it just as you will.

Not everyone is a fan of the film's portrayal of divorce and child custody. Some view the film's dramatization of the Kramers' situation as reflecting dominant cultural stereotypes popular in the media of the day. Susan Douglas (1995) sees the film this way: "The selfish bitch wife up and left the cutest, most lovable boy in America to 'find herself' while her previously neglectful husband turned into the Albert Schweitzer of dads. The movie never let us see how devoted she had been as a mom—and virtually a single mom, at that—for all those years Dad lived at the office, nor did we see what had provoked her to take the dramatic action she did."

Since 1965, revolutionary changes have occurred in family law (Jacob 1988). Through most of the twentieth century, for example, a divorce was granted only on the basis of fault—that is, one party had engaged in marital misbehavior, adultery, or extreme cruelty, for example. The necessity of blaming one party and of fabricating ugly events to justify the divorce often generated further unnecessary conflicts in already-troubled personal relationships. No longer: All states have adopted the **no-fault divorce** system, whereby marriages may be dissolved on the basis of irreconcilable differences (Marvell 1989).

Legal standards relating to custody have changed as well. Historically, the assumption that the mother was the better guardian for the children when a family broke apart went unquestioned. Today, the law makes no such assumptions. The law in most jurisdictions is gender neutral; fathers are now presumed to be equally qualified to take care of their children. Moreover, in a growing number of states, the law no longer considers sole custody to be the norm. Rather than award custody exclusively to one parent, the courts may grant legal custody of the children to both parents. Equally dramatic changes have occurred regarding property. Historically, property went to the person holding title, which typically meant the husband ended up with most of the assets and the wife received few. Now most states view marriage as a partnership, and judges are called on to divide the property fairly. Acrimonious disputes over "fair" distribution of assets are very likely to become public when the rich and famous divorce.

In *Silent Revolution: The Transformation of Divorce Law in the United States* (1988), the political scientist Herbert Jacob argues that these radical changes in the legal rules governing family life were driven by major contrasts between law on the books and law in action. Reformers argued that the rigor of the written law cultivated corruption in divorce courts because judges were presented with fraudulent divorce petitions.

> Lenient court interpretations of the evidence supporting divorce petitions had made divorce available to those willing to bend the truth, although the truth often needed to be twisted beyond all recognition in order to satisfy statutory requirement for proof of adultery. Consequently, the proof was often manufactured. (Jacob 1988, 33)

Dramatic changes in family law reflected alterations in the U.S. social, economic, and cultural context. Women's increased participation in the workforce, demands for equal rights for women, the growing number of couples living together, and the development of the birth control pill are some of the factors that have contributed to altering the social conditions of marriage as well as societal expectations about that legal relationship. Amid this societal change, political scientist Jocelyn Crowley (2003) argues in *The Politics of Child Support in America* that four sets of interest groups—social workers, conservatives, women's groups, and fathers' rights groups—shape child support policy.

Robert Mnookin and Lewis Kornhauser (1979) see the primary function of contemporary divorce law as providing a framework within which divorcing couples can determine their postdissolution rights and responsibilities. That does not mean that law and the legal system are unimportant. Rather, to divorcing spouses and their children, family law is inescapably relevant; the law affects who may divorce, when a divorce may occur, how a divorce must be procured, and often the consequences of divorce. In negotiating divorce cases, lawyers bargain in the shadow of the law. If considerable money or property is involved, the lawyers may engage in best results bargaining, in which they seek the maximum settlement for their client. But mainly divorce cases use negotiations to achieve an appropriate result. Discussions of how much child support the husband should contribute are conducted within the context of how much money he earns, how much the woman earns, and rules of thumb concerning how much is appropriate. States have adopted child support guideline models (http://www.supportguidelines.com). Similarly, questions of child custody typically center on arriving at a formula that gives both parents some role. By focusing on appropriate results, lawyers strive to reduce the acrimony between their clients. That shifts attention away from the insoluble issues of who did what to whom, considering instead what needs to be done to secure a divorce.

Divorce is a unique area of the law, because going to court to settle the dispute is mandatory. A couple cannot legally end their marriage without first receiving a judge's signature on a divorce decree. However, judges treat uncontested divorces very differently from ones in which the spouses have been unable to agree. In the vast majority of cases, the spouses have arrived at a settlement. When there is agreement on the issues, the court's role is largely one of **routine administration**. Although the judge briefly scrutinizes the papers to ensure that all is proper, he or she is unlikely to intervene in the terms of the settlement. In Connecticut, the average duration of the single brief hearing in an uncontested dissolution was four minutes (Cavanagh and Rhode 1976). Only a small percentage of divorces—"probably less than 10 percent"—involve disputes that are contested in court (Mnookin and Kornhauser 1979). Contested divorces force the judge to decide matters such as which spouse will live in the family home, the nature and scope of visitation rights, and which parent will have custody of the children. There are few legal standards that a judge can rely on in deciding questions such as those. Rather, he or she must engage in **diagnostic adjudication**. For instance, the judge must carefully weigh what is in the best interests of the children in deciding whether the father or the mother will be granted custody.

Enforcing judgments in divorce cases is a major problem. One or both parents sometimes refuse to abide by court orders specifying custody and visitation rights; indeed, "child stealing" to circumvent court orders is on the rise. Deadbeat dads—fathers who refuse to make court-ordered child support payments—have also become the subject of considerable media attention. Figures released by the Bureau of the Census (Grall 2000) report that of the 7.2 million single parents (85 percent of whom are women) who had some type of legally binding child support order, one-third received no payments whatsoever, and an additional one-fourth collected only partial payments. Traditionally, ex-wives had to institute a separate lawsuit to force their ex-husbands to comply. But legislatures are increasingly providing additional methods, including withholding money from tax return refunds and mandating the suspension of driving licenses for spouses who refuse to obey court orders. Moreover, civil collection methods are increasingly being supplemented with criminal sanctions. Thus, deadbeat fathers face jail terms if they do not contribute to the support of their children. In turn, public agencies are increasingly being called on to enforce these private civil judgments. Deadbeat dads cross all social and economic strata of society, but by and large problems of nonpayment or partial payment of court-ordered child support are problems of economics; fathers either are unemployed or earn so little in their employment that they cannot realistically comply with court-mandated levels. Indeed, African-American and never-married women fare significantly worse than their white and once-married counterparts, primarily because of social and economic factors unrelated to the court-ordered level of child support (Beller and Graham 1993).

WINNERS AND LOSERS

Defining politics as "the authoritative allocation of values" (Chapter 1) emphasizes how deeply the civil trial courts are enmeshed in the political process. The decisions reached in these public forums allocate gains and losses for private parties, ranging from money a defendant must pay the plaintiff to custody of the children after a marriage is legally dissolved.

In assessing who gets what from the civil trial courts, analysts have voiced considerable concern about which types of litigants benefit the most. Marc Galanter's (1974) provocative essay "Why the 'Haves' Come Out Ahead ..." (discussed in Chapter 7) has drawn considerable attention (Wheeler et al. 1987; Galanter 1975). What remains unclear is whether repeat players have an advantage because of their expertise and resources or because of the law on which they base their claims. An analysis of three types of cases illustrates how difficult it is to draw any firm conclusions.

Tort cases typically pit a one-shotter (the injured party) against a repeat player (an insurance company). Galanter's prediction that the defendants will come out ahead in this apparently unequal contest is not necessarily consistent with the available data, however. Studies find that people who suffer injuries in automobile accidents usually recover something for their injuries. However, people with relatively minor losses do much better than those with more serious losses (Ross 1970). Because very few cases involve serious injuries, it appears that any differences between repeat players and one-shotters is at best marginal. In essence, the contingency fee system for paying for lawyers largely neutralizes the perceived advantages held by insurance companies that have ready access to high-priced lawyers (Chapter 5).

The economic consequences of divorce can also be partially understood in terms of Galanter's distinction between haves and have-nots. After divorce, men generally end up in a better economic position than do women (Weitzman 1985; Weitzman and Dixon 1979). This is true for several interrelated reasons. For one, women are awarded custody of children 85 percent of the time (Grall 2000; Seltzer 1990). Court awards of child support do not offset the increased responsibilities that custodial mothers assume (MacCoby and Mnookin 1992), a financial problem compounded by deadbeat dads who pay either no child support or less than what has been ordered by the court. Ex-husbands are also in a better position to earn money than are their former wives, especially if the wife left the workforce during the marriage. Thus, without substantial reallocations of economic resources from husband to wife (which courts rarely grant), the average woman is worse off after divorce than her former husband, especially if she has children in her custody (Kitson and Morgan 1990).

Small-claims procedures were originally established to help the ordinary person get a day in court, but they are most often used by businesses to collect overdue bills. For example, a study of a small-claims court in Tallahassee, Florida, reports that the majority of plaintiffs (83 percent) are hospitals, physicians, utilities, department stores, collection agencies, or landlords, whereas the majority of defendants (80 percent) are individuals (Purdum 1981). In short, the overwhelming majority of small-claims cases pit repeat players (businesses or organizations) against one-shotters (individuals). Plaintiffs win the vast majority of these cases (Ruhnka, Weller, and Martin 1978; Sarat 1976). Not only are plaintiffs likely to win in small-claims courts, but also many of these victories occur because a substantial number of defendants never even appear in court. To some critics, these patterns of winners and losers in small-claims court demonstrate the advantages of "haves" in the litigation process. Perhaps individuals lose because they are intimidated by the prospect of opposing large organizations in court and, therefore, default despite possible legal defenses (Yngvesson and Hennessey 1975). But not all scholars agree with that interpretation. Others believe that plaintiffs win because the defendant's legal liability for the claim is clear and unequivocal, and the defendants lose because they cannot or will not pay what they owe. In a comparison of contested cases with default judgments, the majority of default cases reflect clear and unequivocal liability. Credit card and utility companies, for example, are likely to have signed statements of financial obligations on the part of the defendants. Moreover, collection agencies are hesitant, on economic grounds, to pursue claims where the defendant's liability is not clear-cut (Vidmar 1984).

The effects of legal representation on case outcomes in small-claims courts provide the strongest evidence of economic imbalances in the litigation process. A study in New York City reports that inequality in legal representation works uniformly to the advantage of the party with legal counsel. Particularly when cases are adjudicated, repeat players benefit from legal representation (Sarat 1976). Similarly, in Tallahassee, defendants represented by attorneys are much more likely to win than those who represent themselves (Purdum 1981). For example, litigants who did not have an attorney present were informed that they should bring witnesses and relevant papers to court, but some defendants lost because they brought only damage estimates. Interviews revealed that many litigants do not think of a damage estimator or a mechanic as a witness; they considered a witness to be a person who has observed the event in dispute (Purdum 1981).

Conclusion

For four days, the Rodriguez family nervously milled about the federal courtroom in McAllen, Texas, awaiting the verdict of the nine-member jury (Gregor 2001c). Privately, lawyers for Ford probably also contemplated how the potential verdict might affect settlements in the hundreds of similar lawsuits pending across the nation. The jury sent out two notes to the judge, but they provided little indication of what the jury was thinking—one note simply requested a chalkboard on which to write. To dampen media attention, the judge issued a gag order prohibiting the lawyers from talking about the case.

During the fourth day of jury deliberations, plaintiff and defendant reached an out-of-court settlement, reportedly for $7.5 million (Oppel 2001a). Was the settlement excessive? Perhaps. But consider that Marisa Rodriguez—who turned forty during the trial—will require constant medical care and faces virtually no chance of resuming a normal life. Her family suffers as well.

The *Firestone* case at least partially burnished the tarnished image of trial lawyers. For it was their efforts to pin down the problem that eventually led to public attention and concern. The lawyers were paid handsomely for their efforts, but most Americans agreed that the lawsuits were proper responses to what appeared to be a fundamental breakdown in quality control.

Of the millions of civil cases filed and settled every year, only a few such as the one against Firestone Tire Company will come to dominate the headlines. These unusual cases exemplify the increasing impact of civil litigation on U.S. society. Tort cases are associated with all sorts of social problems, including undeserving plaintiffs, greedy lawyers, out-of-touch judges, and runaway juries. They are blamed for all manner of social ills, including high insurance payments and doctors who abandon certain high-risk specialties. Small-claims cases likewise affect the lives of ordinary citizens in very direct ways—individuals are ordered to pay money, and businesses large and small are often frustrated when they are unable to collect. Finally, of course, divorce and its accompanying issues and problems immediately affect the lives of more than a million men and women every year, to say nothing of an even greater number of children. In many respects, however, litigation is both a last resort and a worst resort, one that people usually try to avoid. At the same time, the possibility of litigation affects the ways in which problems are handled outside court.

CRITICAL THINKING QUESTIONS

1. How does the case of *Rodriguez v. Firestone* (2001) relate to the litigation explosion argument discussed in Chapter 10? What features would conservative interest groups emphasize? What features would trial lawyers emphasize?

2. Who are the winners and the losers in civil litigation? Does Galanter's concept of haves and have-nots help us understand winners and losers in civil justice litigation, or would it be better to analyze winners and losers in terms of interest groups?

3. How does the bargaining in typical divorce cases differ from bargaining in divorce cases featured in the media? In what ways is *Kramer vs. Kramer* typical of the process? In what ways does this movie depict an atypical process?

Search Terms

child support	divorce	small claims
deadbeat dads	no-fault divorce	tort reform

Useful URLs

http://divorcesource.com
> Divorce Source offers a variety of information from starting a divorce to stopping a divorce. Of particular interest are the links to divorce laws in each of the states at http://www.divorcesource.com/info/divorcelaws/states.shtml.

http://www.nationalchildsupport.com
> National Child Support is a commercial website that offers to help collect child support payments.

http://www.childrensjustice.org
> The Center for Children's Justice is dedicated to protecting and preserving the rights of children to equal access to both parents after divorce or separation through radical legal change.

REFERENCES

Administrative Office of the U.S. Courts. 2008. *2007 Annual Report of the Director: Judicial Business of the United States Courts*. Washington, D.C.: U.S. Government Printing Office. Available online at http://www.uscourts.gov/judbus2007/contents.html.

Asimov, Michael. 2000. "Divorce in the Movies: From the Hays Code to Kramer vs. Kramer." *Legal Studies Forum* 24: 221.

Atkinson, William. 2004. "Small Claims Courts: A Secret Collection Weapon?" *Collection and Credit Risk* 9 (October): 36.

Barak, Aharon. 2006. *The Judge in a Democracy*. Princeton, N.J.: Princeton University Press.

Beller, Andrea, and John Graham. 1993. *Small Change: The Economics of Child Support*. New Haven, Conn.: Yale University Press.

Brazil, Wayne, and Gregory Weber. 1987. "Discovery." In *Encyclopedia of the American Judicial System*, edited by Robert Janosik, pp. 810–864. New York: Scribner's.

Bumpass, Larry, and Hsien-Hen Lu. 2000. "Co-Habitation: How the Families of U.S. Children Are Changing." *Focus* 21: 5–8.

Bureau of Justice Statistics. 2007. "Civil Justice Statistics." Washington, D.C.: U.S. Department of Justice. Available online at http://www.ojp.usdoj.gov/bjs/civil.htm. Retrieved December 7, 2007.

Caplovitz, David. 1974. *Consumers in Trouble: A Study of Debtors in Default*. New York: Free Press.

Cavanagh, Ralph, and Deborah Rhode. 1976. "The Unauthorized Practice of Law and Pro Se Divorce: An Empirical Analysis." *Yale Law Journal* 86: 126–157.

Cohen, Nili. 2002. "Israeli Law as Mixed System: Between Common Law and Continental Law." *Global Jurist Topics*, January 8.

Cohen, Thomas. 2004. *Tort Trials and Verdicts in Large Counties*. Washington, D.C.: U.S. Department of Justice, Bureau of Justice Statistics.

Crowley, Jocelyn. 2003. *The Politics of Child Support in America*. New York: Cambridge University Press.

Danzon, Patricia, and Lee Lillard. 1982. *The Resolution of Medical Malpractice Claims: Modeling the Bargaining Process*. Santa Monica, Calif.: RAND Corporation.

Dickens, Charles. [1852] 1964. *Bleak House*. New York: New American Library.

Douglas, Susan J. 1995. *Where the Girls Are: Growing Up Female with the Mass Media*. New York: Three Rivers Press.

Edelman, Martin. 2000. "The New Israeli Constitution." *Middle Eastern Studies* 36: 1.

Friedman, Lawrence. 1985. *A History of American Law*. 2d ed. New York: Simon & Schuster.

Galanter, Marc. 1974. "Why the 'Haves' Come Out Ahead: Speculations on the Limits of Legal Change." *Law and Society Review* 9: 97–125.

———. 1975. "Afterword: Explaining Litigation." *Law and Society Review* 9: 347–368.

Goerdt, John. 1993. "The People's Court: A Summary of Findings and Policy Implications from a Study of 12 Urban Small Claims Courts." *State Court Journal* 17: 38–43.

Gold, Russell, and Angel Gonzalez. 2011. "Spill Report Faults Transocean Rig." *Wall Street Journal*. April 23.

Grall, Timothy. 2000. *Child Support for Custodial Mothers and Fathers*. Washington, D.C.: U.S. Department of Commerce, U.S. Census Bureau.

Greenberg, Joel. 2002. "Court Says Israel Can Expel 2 of Militant's Kin to Gaza." *New York Times*, September 4, p. A9.

Gregor, Alison. 2001a. "Exec Says Failures of Tires Known." *San Antonio Express-News*, August 16.

———. 2001b. "Expert Says Tire Took Hit in Advance." *San Antonio Express-News*, August 21.

———. 2001c. "Family Waits for Verdict in Firestone Lawsuit." *San Antonio Express-News*, August 23.

———. 2001d. "90-Cent Tire Repair Bypassed U.S." *San Antonio Express-News*, August 17.

———. 2001e. "Rollover Victim Testifies; Bridgestone/Firestone Boss Takes Stand in Defense." *San Antonio Express-News*, August 18.

Hammer, David. 2010. "Investigator says Well's Cement was Faulty." *Times-Picayune* October 29.

Hollingsworth, Earl, William Feldman, and David Clark. 1973. "The Ohio Small Claims Court: An Empirical Study." *University of Cincinnati Law Review* 42: 497–515.

Jacob, Herbert. 1988. *Silent Revolution: The Transformation of Divorce Law in the United States*. Chicago: University of Chicago Press.

———. 1992. "The Elusive Shadow of the Law." *Law and Society Review* 26: 565–590.

Kakalik, James, and Nicholas Pace. 1986. *Costs and Compensation Paid in Tort Litigation*. Santa Monica, Calif.: RAND Corporation.

Kershner, Isabel. 2007. "Friends Clash Reflects Battle Over Israeli Court." *New York Times*, November 22.

Kitson, Gay, and Leslie Morgan. 1990. "The Multiple Consequences of Divorce: A Decade Review." *Journal of Marriage and Family* 52: 913–924.

Kritzer, Herbert. 1985. "The Form of Negotiation in Ordinary Litigation." Madison: University of Wisconsin, Institute for Legal Studies Working Papers.

———. 1991. *Let's Make a Deal: Understanding the Negotiation Process in Ordinary Litigation*. Madison: University of Wisconsin Press.

Krystek, Dennis. 1994. "Discovery vs. Delay in Civil District Court." *Louisiana Bar Journal* 42: 255–261.

Litan, Robert, Peter Swire, and Clifford Winston. 1988. "The U.S. Liability System: Background and Trends." In *Liability: Perspectives and Policy*, edited by Robert Litan and Clifford Winston. Washington, D.C.: Brookings.

MacCoby, Eleanor, and Robert Mnookin. 1992. *Dividing the Child: Social and Legal Dilemmas of Custody*. Cambridge, Mass.: Harvard University Press.

Marvell, Thomas. 1989. "Divorce Rates and the Fault Requirement." *Law and Society Review* 23: 543–567.

Maynard, Douglas. 1984. "The Structure of Discourse in Misdemeanor Plea Bargaining." *Law and Society Review* 18: 75–104.

McEwen, Craig, and Richard Maiman. 1984. "Mediation in Small Claims Court: Achieving Compliance Through Consent." *Law and Society Review* 18: 11–50.

McFadgen, Terrance. 1972. "Dispute Resolution in the Small Claims Context: Adjudication, Arbitration or Conciliation?" LL.M. dissertation, Harvard University.

Miller, Karin. 2001. "Bridgestone/Firestone to Pay at Least $41.5 Million to Head Off Lawsuits by States." Associated Press, November 8.

Mnookin, Robert, and Lewis Kornhauser. 1979. "Bargaining in the Shadow of the Law: The Case of Divorce." *Yale Law Journal* 88: 950–997.

National Institute for Consumer Justice. 1972. *Staff Studies on Small Claims Courts*. Boston: National Institute for Consumer Justice.

Neubauer, David. 1975. "Case Management in Three Federal District Courts: An Organizational Perspective." Paper presented at the Conference on the Application of Organizational Theory to Trial Courts, Center for Advanced Study in the Behavioral Sciences, Palo Alto, California, August.

Oppel, Richard. 2001a. "Bridgestone Agrees to Pay $7.5 Million in Explorer Crash." *New York Times*, August 25, p. C1.

———. 2001b. "Texas Jurors Deliberate in First Tire Lawsuit Since Recall." *New York Times*, August 22, p. C1.

Ostrom, Brian, and Neal Kauder. 1995. *Examining the Work of State Courts*, 1993. Williamsburg, Va.: National Center for State Courts.

Ostrom, Brian, Neal B. Kauder, and Robert C. LaFountain. 2003. *Examining the Work of State Courts, 2002*. Williamsburg, Va.: National Center for State Courts.

Pinkerton, James. 2001. "Firestone Chief Defends Company's Actions on Stand." *Houston Chronicle*, August 18.

Provine, D. Marie. 1987. "Managing Negotiated Justice: Settlement Procedures in the Courts." *Justice System Journal* 12: 91.

Purdum, Elizabeth. 1981. "Examining the Claims of a Small Claims Court: A Florida Case Study." *Judicature* 65: 25–37.

Ross, H. Laurence. 1970. *Settled Out of Court: The Social Process of Insurance Claims Adjustments*. Chicago: Aldine.

Ruhnka, John, Steven Weller, and John Martin. 1978. *Small Claims Courts: A National Examination*. Williamsburg, Va.: National Center for State Courts.

Sarat, Austin. 1976. "Alternatives in Dispute Processing: Litigation in a Small Claims Court." *Law and Society Review* 10: 339–375.

Schauffler, Richard, Robert LaFountain, Shauna Strickland, and William Raftery. 2006. *Examining the Work of State Courts, 2005*. Williamsburg, Va.: National Center for State Courts.

Schwartz, John. 2010. "BP's Partners in Well Try to Distance Themselves" *New York Times*. July 23.

Seltzer, Judith. 1990. "Legal and Physical Custody Arrangements in Recent Divorces." *Social Science Quarterly* 7: 250–266.

"Supreme Court Orders Demolition of West Bank Settlement." 2011. *Los Angeles Times* August 2.

Sullum, Jacob. 1998. *For Your Own Good: The Anti-Smoking Crusade and the Tyranny of Public Health*. New York: Free Press.

Tennille, Tracy. 2010 "Investors in Gulf Oil Well Distance Themselves From Spill." *Wall Street Journal* July 22.

Thompson, Don. 2007. "Ford Agrees to Settle Rollover Lawsuits." *New Orleans Times-Picayune*, November 29.

Vidmar, Neil. 1984. "The Small Claims Court: A Reconceptualization of Disputes and an Empirical Investigation." *Law and Society Review* 18: 515–550.

Weitzman, Lenore. 1985. *The Divorce Revolution: The Unexpected Social and Economic Consequences for Women and Children in America*. New York: Free Press.

Weitzman, Lenore, and Ruth Dixon. 1979. "Child Custody Awards: Legal Standards and Empirical Patterns for Child Custody, Support and Visitation After Divorce." *University of California, Davis Law Review* 12: 471–521.

Wheeler, Stanton, Bliss Cartwright, Robert Kagan, and Lawrence Friedman. 1987. "Do the 'Haves' Come Out Ahead? Winning and Losing in State Supreme Courts, 1870–1970." *Law and Society Review* 21: 403–446.

Winfield, Nicole. 2001. "Jerusalem Death Toll Expected to Rise." *New Orleans Times-Picayune*, May 26.

Wright, Charles Alan. 1983. *Law of Federal Courts*. 4th ed. St. Paul, Minn.: West.

Yngvesson, Barbara, and Patricia Hennessey. 1975. "Small Claims, Complex Disputes: A Review of the Small Claims Literature." *Law and Society Review* 9: 219–274.

FOR FURTHER READING

Baker, Tom. 2005. *The Medical Malpractice Myth*. Chicago: University of Chicago Press.

Bornstein, Brian, Richard Wiener, Robert Schoop, and Steven Willborn (eds.). 2008. *Civil Juries and Civil Justice: Psychological and Legal Perspectives*. New York: Springer.

Cahn, Naomi, and June Carbone. 2010. *Red Families v. Blue Families: Legal Polarization and the Creation of Culture*. New York: Oxford University Press.

Crowley, Jocelyn. 2003. *The Politics of Child Support in America*. New York: Cambridge University Press.

Edelman, Martin. 1994. *Courts, Politics, and Culture in Israel*. Charlottesville: University of Virginia Press.

Hans, Valerie. 2000. *Business on Trial*. New Haven: Yale University Press.

Jacob, Herbert. 1988. *Silent Revolution: The Transformation of Divorce Law in the United States*. Chicago: University of Chicago Press.

McClurg, Andrew, Adam Koyuncu, and Luis Eduardo Sprovieri. 2007. *Practical Global Tort Litigation: United States, Germany, and Argentina*. Durham, N.C.: Carolina Academic Press.

Overland, Sean. 2009. *The Juror Factor: Race and Gender in America's Civil Courts*. El Paso: LFB Scholarly Publishing.

Wolfson, Mark. 2001. *The Fight Against Big Tobacco*. Hawthorne, N.Y.: Aldine de Gruyter.

TRIALS AND JURIES

Although the right to trial by jury is a fundamental constitutional right, some citizens find jury duty to be a frustrating experience. At least in Houston, Texas, signs minimize frustration in trying to find the courthouse.

David Neubauer

"Why Isn't Sam Sheppard in Jail?" screamed the headline of a front-page editorial in a prominent Cleveland newspaper. For weeks, vivid headlines like that one made it clear that the press thought the police were not pressing hard enough in arresting Dr. Samuel Sheppard—a socially prominent physician—for the brutal murder of his wife. Live radio coverage of the coroner's inquest contributed to the intense media scrutiny: For six hours, Dr. Sheppard was questioned (without counsel) about his activities that night. During trial, jurors were allowed to read the daily press coverage of the trial. After conviction, Sheppard served 12 years in prison before the Supreme Court reversed his conviction, likening the trial to a "Roman holiday" (*Sheppard v. Maxwell* 1966). In holding that prejudicial pretrial publicity denied Sheppard the right to a fair and impartial trial, the Court set off a long and often-heated battle over where freedom of the press ends and the right to a fair trial begins.

Trials attract more attention than any other step of the judicial process. The national media provide detailed accounts of the trials of defendants such as Sam Sheppard and Casey Anthony. The local media offer extensive coverage of the trials of local notables, brazen murderers, and the like. Books, movies, and television use courtroom encounters to entertain. The importance of trials, however, extends far beyond the considerable public attention lavished on them. They are central to the entire scheme of Anglo-American law. Trials provide the ultimate forum for vindicating the innocence of the accused or confirming the liability of the defendant. For that reason, the right to be tried by a jury of one's peers is guaranteed in several places in the Constitution.

Given the marked public interest in trials, as well as their centrality to U.S. law, we would expect trials to be the prime ingredient in the trial court process. But trials are relatively rare events; most cases filed in court, whether criminal or civil, are settled through negotiations (Chapters 9 and 11). In a very fundamental sense, then, a trial represents a deviant case. But, at the same time, the few cases that are tried have a major impact on the operations of the entire judicial process, providing benchmarks that guide negotiations.

This chapter examines the history and the function of trials, jury selection, how prosecutors and plaintiffs approach trial, defense strategies during trial, and how jurors reach a decision. This chapter also discusses prejudicial pretrial publicity in criminal cases and considers the amount of discretion that jurors should exercise.

History and Function

Trial juries are also called **petit juries** to differentiate them from grand juries. Although judges decide questions of law that arise during trial, jurors are the judges of the facts of the case. Thus, they are responsible for returning a verdict of guilty or innocent, liable or not liable.

The tradition of using lay citizens as impartial finders of fact developed as part of a long struggle against centralized power in Britain and later in those countries that inherited the British traditions of justice. This role was first formalized in the Magna Carta of 1215 (see Exhibit 12.1), when English noblemen forced the king to recognize limits on the power of the Crown:

> No Freeman shall be taken or imprisoned, or be disseized of his Freehold, or Liberties, or free Customs, or be outlawed, or exiled or otherwise destroyed, nor will we pass upon him nor condemn him but by lawful Judgment of his peers or by Law of the Land.

In the centuries after the signing of the Magna Carta, the jury's role changed greatly. Initially, the right to be tried by a jury of one's peers applied only to noblemen (freemen), but later it was extended to average citizens. Likewise, early English juries were composed of witnesses; later, juries became impartial bodies selected from citizens who knew nothing of the events in question.

The American colonists considered the jury trial a fundamental right, and they specifically guaranteed this protection in their charters. The pivotal role that the right

EXHIBIT 12.1		Key Developments Concerning the Right to Trial by Jury
Magna Carta	1215	English noblemen have the right to a trial by a jury of their peers.
U.S. Constitution, Article III, Section 2	1789	The trial of all crimes shall be by jury and shall be held in the state where the crime was allegedly committed.
Sixth Amendment	1791	"In all criminal prosecutions, the accused shall enjoy the right to a speedy and public trial, by an impartial jury."
Seventh Amendment	1791	The right to a trial by a jury is preserved in civil suits under common law.
Griffin v. California	1965	The privilege against self-incrimination prohibits the prosecutor from commenting on the defendant's failure to testify during trial.
Sheppard v. Maxwell	1966	The defendant was denied a fair trial because of prejudicial pretrial publicity.
Duncan v. Louisiana	1968	The due process clause of the Fourteenth Amendment incorporates the Sixth Amendment's right to a jury trial.
Baldwin v. New York	1970	Defendants accused of petty offenses do not have the right to be tried by a jury of their peers.
Williams v. Florida	1970	State juries are not required by the U.S. Constitution to consist of twelve members.
Johnson v. Louisiana	1972	Federal criminal juries must be unanimous.
Apodaca v. Oregon	1972	There is no federal requirement that state juries must be unanimous.
Taylor v. Louisiana	1975	Women cannot be excluded from juries.
Ballew v. Georgia	1978	Six is the minimum number for a jury.
Burch v. Louisiana	1979	Six-member criminal juries must be unanimous.
Chandler v. Florida	1981	The right to a fair trial is not violated by electronic media and still photographic coverage of public judicial proceedings.
Batson v. Kentucky	1986	If a prosecutor uses peremptory challenges to exclude potential jurors solely on account of their race, the prosecutor must explain his or her actions.
Daubert v. Merrell Dow	1993	The trial judge must ensure that any and all scientific evidence is not only relevant but also reliable.
J.E.B. Petitioner v. Alabama	1994	Lawyers may not exclude potential jurors from a trial because of their gender.
United States v. Scheffer	1998	Doubts about the accuracy of lie detector tests justifies banning their use in court.
Kumho Tire v. Carmichael	1999	Daubert standards for scientific testimony apply to nonscientific testimony as well.
Apprendi v. New Jersey	2000	Any fact that increases the penalty for a crime beyond the prescribed statutory maximum must be submitted to a jury.
Portuondo v. Agard	2000	Prosecutors can tell jurors that the defendant's presence during trial helps them tailor their testimony to fit the evidence.
Ring v. Arizona	2002	It is unconstitutional to have a judge, rather than a jury, decide the critical sentencing issues in death penalty cases.
Blakely v. Washington	2004	Under the Sixth Amendment, juries, not judges, have the power to make a finding of guilt beyond a reasonable doubt for facts used in state sentencing guidelines.
Snyder v. Louisiana	2008	Murder conviction in a death penalty case was overturned because the judge sat idly by as prosecutors dismissed all the blacks in the jury pool.

to trial by jury plays in U.S. law is underscored by the fact that it is mentioned three times in the U.S. Constitution:

- Article III, Section 2, provides that "the trial of all crimes, except cases of impeachment, shall be by jury; and such trial shall be held in the State where the said crimes shall have been committed." This section not only guarantees the right to a trial by jury to persons accused of a crime but also specifies that such trials shall be held near the place of the offense. This prevents the government from harassing defendants by trying them far from home.
- The Sixth Amendment guarantees that "in all criminal prosecutions, the accused shall enjoy the right to a speedy and public trial, by an impartial jury." The requirement of a public trial prohibits secret trials, a device commonly used by dictators to silence their opponents. The specification of an impartial jury goes to the heart of current U.S. practices.
- The Seventh Amendment provides that "in suits at common law, where the value in controversy shall exceed twenty dollars, the right to trial by jury shall be preserved, and no fact tried by a jury, shall be otherwise re-examined in any Court of the United States, than according to the rules of the common law." This provision is a historical testament to the fact that the framers of the Constitution greatly distrusted the judges of the day.

Throughout most of U.S. history, these broad constitutional provisions had little applicability to trials in state courts. As part of the Warren Court revolution in criminal justice, however, the Supreme Court ruled that the jury provisions of the Sixth Amendment applied to state as well as federal courts (*Duncan v. Louisiana* 1968). The jury's primary purpose is to protect citizens against arbitrary governmental actions by providing the accused a "safeguard against the corrupt or overzealous prosecutor and against the compliant, biased, or eccentric judge" (*Williams v. Florida* 1970). Having incorporated the Sixth Amendment into the due process clause of the Fourteenth Amendment, the Court proceeded to consider the scope of the right to a jury trial, the size of the jury, and unanimous versus non-unanimous verdicts. In a somewhat confusing line of decisions, the Court has differentiated between juries in civil and criminal cases and between juries in state and federal courts. (See Courts in Comparative Perspective: Russia.)

Scope of the Right to a Trial by Jury

Although juries are considered "fundamental to the American scheme of justice" (*Duncan v. Louisiana* 1968), not all litigants are entitled to a trial by jury. Youths prosecuted as juvenile offenders have no right to have their cases heard by a jury. Similarly, adult offenders charged with **petty offenses** enjoy no constitutional right to be tried by a jury of their peers. The Sixth Amendment covers only adult criminals charged with serious offenses, and "no offense can be deemed 'petty' for the purposes of the right to trial by jury where imprisonment for more than six months is authorized" (*Baldwin v. New York* 1970). As a result, drunk drivers in five states—Louisiana, Mississippi, Nevada, New Jersey, and New Mexico—have no right to a jury trial if they face a jail term of six months or less (*Blanton v. City of North Las Vegas* 1989). Some state constitutions, however, guarantee a jury trial to a wider group of offenders.

COURTS IN COMPARATIVE PERSPECTIVE

■ Russia

What if the Casey Anthony trial had been held in Russia? The procedures and perhaps the outcome would have been different. For example, whereas in the United States Anthony could not be forced to testify during her criminal trial, in Russia she would have been obligated to take the stand. This, along with other differences in the systems, highlights not only unique features of American justice but also a rapidly changing Russian justice system in the post-Soviet era.

The fall of the Russian Empire at the end of World War I led to the seizure of power by the communists and the formation of the Union of Soviet Socialist Republics (USSR). The brutal rule of Josef Stalin (1924–1953) strengthened Russian dominance of the Soviet Union at a cost of tens of millions of lives. The Soviet economy and society stagnated in the following decades until General Secretary Mikhail Gorbachev (1985–1991) introduced *glasnost* (openness) and *perestroika* (restructuring) in an attempt to modernize the nation, but his initiatives inadvertently released forces that, by December 1991, splintered the USSR into 15 independent republics. Since then, Russia has struggled to build a democratic political system and market economy to replace the strict social, political, and economic controls of the communist period (Central Intelligence Agency 2011).

Today, Russia has a federated type of government. The capital is Moscow, and there are over fifty administrative divisions throughout this large country of 139,000,000 people. At the apex of the judicial branch is the Constitutional Court. Judges for all courts are appointed for life by the Federation Council on the recommendation of the president. The Court enjoys the reputation of being the most independent judicial institution in Russia (Trochev 2008).

After the collapse of the USSR, Russia reintroduced jury trials, which had been used from 1864 to 1917 (Thaman 1999). During the Soviet era, jury trials (called "people's forums") were used to try petty crimes (with the primary purpose of showing the miscreant that deviation from the communist model was not acceptable). Today, juries hear the most serious criminal cases in every part of Russia except Chechnya (Bowring 2009).

The use of jury trials is meant to correct widespread abuses in the Soviet justice system, but Russian courts are understaffed and judges are underqualified. Moreover, judges still see themselves as governmental bureaucrats who respond to the real power in the Russian justice system—the prosecutors. In short, the Russian legal system has yet to emerge as a truly independent branch of government ("Path to Reform …" 2001).

Opinion varies on the impact of juries (Kislov 1998). To some, jurors are overreacting to years of authoritarian rule—jurors choose not to believe the police and acquit guilty defendants way too often (Kolesnikov 2006). Others counter that Russian jurors are not "softhearted old uncles" and highlight numerous trial convictions for rape and murder, noting that only once did the presiding judge disagree with a jury's guilty verdict (Rudnev 1995).

Discussions of Russian justice in the post-Soviet era invariably turn to the interrelated phenomena of corruption and organized crime. Some old party bosses, for example, used their connections to create new banks with public money. In the absence of bank regulations, those institutions became cash laundromats with enormous sums of untraceable money. In an environment like this, legitimate and illegitimate businesspeople alike need protection, which is what Russian-speaking organized crime has provided on a large scale (O'Rourke 2000).

The trial of oil billionaire Mikhail Khodorkovsky focused international attention on the Russian legal system. To some, he was prosecuted because he and his colleagues had committed criminal fraud and large-scale tax evasion in the rough-and-tumble world of Russian business. But, to others, he was prosecuted because he was a political opponent of Russian president Vladimir Putin (White 2005). Thus, to some observers, this was a show trial too closely resembling the show trials of the Soviet era (Chazan 2005). Khodorkovsky was sentenced to nine years in prison. Nearing the end of his term, Khodorkovsky was tried again and sentenced to an unusually harsh term of 14 years (Chance 2011). Suggesting that the legal process has little meaning in Russia, a U.S. diplomat described the trial as "lipstick on a political pig" (Parfitt 2010).

The outcome of this trial demolished the creditability of Russian President Dmitry Medvedev's pledge to end the misuse of the law in his country (Matthews 2011; Nikiforov 1995). Indeed, opponents of the Russian regime, including Garry Kasparov, a former world chess champion, have been detained by the Russian police before important elections (Belton and Buckley 2007).

Nor are all civil litigants entitled to a trial by jury. The Seventh Amendment covers only civil cases that would have gone to a jury under English practice in 1791 (*United States v. Wonson* 1812). Moreover, because the Seventh Amendment has never been incorporated (that is, applied to states), each state has established its own rules on which types of civil disputes warrant a jury trial. As a result, equity proceedings (injunctions) and family matters (divorce and child custody) are rarely heard by juries. Likewise, some civil cases are viewed as too complex to be decided by juries (Drazan 1989). In protracted antitrust violations, for instance, judges are considered better suited to the task of sorting out evidence presented over a months-long trial (*Matsushita Electric Industrial Co. v. Zenith Radio Corp.* 1980).

Jury Size

During the fourteenth century, the size of English juries became fixed at 12, and, by the time of the American Revolution, that number was universally accepted in the colonies. To the Supreme Court, however, the number twelve was a "historical accident, wholly without significance except to mystics," and, therefore, not a constitutional requirement (*Williams v. Florida* 1970). As a result, in federal courts, criminal defendants are entitled to a twelve-person jury. In state courts in noncapital criminal cases, however, a six-person jury is large enough to promote group deliberations and provide a fair possibility of obtaining a representative cross section of the community. In *Ballew v. Georgia* (1978), the defendant's misdemeanor conviction by a five-member jury was reversed because "the purpose and functioning of the jury in a criminal trial is seriously impaired, and to a constitutional degree, by a reduction in size to below six members."

Thirty-three states specifically authorize juries of fewer than 12 in criminal cases but often only in misdemeanor cases. In federal courts, defendants are entitled to a 12-person jury unless the parties agree in writing to a small jury. However, both state and federal courts are allowed to use 6-person juries in civil trials (*Colegrove v. Battin* 1973).

There is a good deal of debate over whether small juries provide litigants with a fair trial (Landsman 2005; McCord 2005; Saks 1996). The debate stems from the fact that social science has produced inconsistent findings on the differences in the conduct of deliberations between 6- and 12-person juries. Some studies have found very few differences (Roper 1979; Pabst 1973), while others have reported significant differences (Saks and Marti 1997; Hastie, Penrod and Pennington 1983). A recent review of the empirical literature on juries (Smith and Saks 2008) reports that:

- racial, ethnic, religious, and sexual minorities are represented in a smaller percentage of 6-person as compared to 12-person juries
- larger juries deliberate longer than smaller juries
- talking time is more evenly divided among members of smaller juries, allowing for less domination by a strong voice or two compared to larger juries
- members of larger juries more accurately recall evidence both during deliberation and in individual recall afterwards
- jurors report more satisfaction in the deliberation process with 12-person juries than smaller ones

In light of these findings, it is not surprising to learn hung juries—juries unable to reach a unanimous verdict—occur more frequently with 12-person juries than 6-person juries (Hannaford-Agor, Hans, Mott, and Munsterman 2002; Kalven and Zeisel 1966).

Unanimity

The requirement that a jury reach a unanimous decision became a firm rule in England during the fourteenth century. An agreement by all jurors was perceived as an indication that their conclusion was correct and, therefore, legitimized the verdict in the eyes of the entire community. Those assumptions were shaken, however, by a pair of Burger Court decisions. Although the Court held that verdicts in federal criminal trials must be unanimous, they also upheld guilty findings by votes of 9–3 and 10–2 in state proceedings (*Johnson v. Louisiana* 1972; *Apodaca v. Oregon* 1972). In 1979, the Court applied a different arithmetic to smaller juries, requiring six-member juries to be unanimous (*Burch v. Louisiana* 1979). Those interpretations of the U.S. Constitution have had relatively little effect, however, because most state constitutions specifically require unanimity in criminal trials. Indeed, only two states—Louisiana and Oregon—permit non-unanimous criminal verdicts in felony trials.

Non-unanimous verdicts serve as a hedge against one or two jurors who refuse to go along with the conclusion of their colleagues no matter what the evidence. To their supporters, these verdicts are justified because they reduce deliberation time and eliminate the expensive, time-consuming process of conducting a second trial. Opponents counter that proof beyond a reasonable doubt has not been shown if only some of the jurors vote to convict. Those concerns receive some empirical support (Zeisel 1982). A carefully controlled experiment compared unanimous with non-unanimous juries and found that non-unanimous juries tend to hang less often, deliberate less thoroughly, and result in less satisfied jurors (Hastie, Penrod, and Pennington 1984).

The deliberation process appears to differ significantly depending on whether a unanimous or majority verdict is permitted.

> When juries were not required to be unanimous, they tended to be more verdict driven. That is, they were more likely to take the first formal ballot during the first ten minutes of deliberation and to vote often until they produced a verdict. In contrast, juries that heard the same case but were required to reach a unanimous verdict tended to delay their first vote and discussed the evidence more thoroughly (Diamond, Rose and Murphy 2006, 208).

Overall, evidence-driven juries rated their deliberations as more serious and thorough.

JURY SELECTION

Before the first word of testimony is spoken, trials pass through the critical stage of jury selection. Juries are chosen in a process that combines random selection with deliberate choice. Whether the three stages of jury selection—compiling a master list, drawing the venire, and conducting the voir dire—actually produce fair and impartial juries has been the subject of much concern. Many lawyers believe that trials are won or lost on the basis of which jurors are selected.

Master Jury List

The first step in jury selection is the compilation of a **master jury list**, which must reflect a representative cross section of the community in which the lawsuit arose.

This legal standard emerged in response to ample evidence that state and federal jury selection was systematically biased (Munsterman and Munsterman 1986). In most of the South, for example, African-American citizens were never allowed to serve on juries. In a series of cases, the Court ruled that African Americans (*Strauder v. West Virginia* 1980), Mexican Americans (*Castenada v. Partida* 1977), and women (*Taylor v. Louisiana* 1975) cannot be systematically excluded from petit juries solely on the basis of race, ethnicity, or gender. That does not mean that every jury must include African Americans or Mexican Americans if they exist in the community—but such groups may not be denied the opportunity to be equally chosen for jury service.

Voter registration lists are the most frequently used source for assembling names for the master jury list, because they are readily available, frequently updated, and collected according to the political districts that correspond to a court's geographical jurisdiction. Basing the master jury list on voter registration, however, tends to exclude the poor, the young, racial minorities, and the less educated (Kairys, Kadane, and Lehorsky 1977). Because of those limitations, many courts use additional sources, such as city or telephone directories, utility customer lists, or driver's license lists. The use of multiple sources achieves a better representation of a cross section of the community on jury panels (Munsterman and Munsterman 1986).

Venire

The second step in jury selection is the drawing of the **venire** (or jury pool). Periodically, clerks of court randomly draw names from the master jury list and then send the persons chosen a questionnaire requesting information on their eligibility to serve as jurors. State standards on these matters vary tremendously but generally involve four areas: People are excused from jury duty if they are not U.S. citizens, if they fail to meet a minimum local residency requirement, if they are unable to understand English, or if they have been previously convicted of a felony. Individuals will also be excused on the basis of **statutory exemptions** (passed by legislatures) granted doctors, lawyers, educators, ministers, and various other occupational groups. Finally, others are excused because jury duty would result in undue hardship.

Although serving on a jury is a right and a privilege of citizenship, many people consider it a nuisance. Indeed, in some jurisdictions, 60 percent of all people whose names are pulled from the master jury list return their questionnaires asking to be excused. The responses of court officials to those requests play a major role in determining the makeup of juries. In some areas, all requests are automatically granted on the assumption that any person who does not want to serve will not be a good juror (Van Dyke 1977). But, in other areas, only a few requests involving extreme hardship are granted. Citizens who are not excused from jury duty eventually receive a summons, ordering them to appear at the courthouse on a given date. The clerk's office randomly selects a number of potential jurors from the venire and directs them to a specific courtroom. It is from this venire that a trial jury is selected.

Voir Dire

The final step in jury selection is the **voir dire** ("to speak the truth"), which involves the preliminary examination of a prospective juror to determine his or her ability to judge the case fairly and impartially. Typically, judges also select several alternate jurors, who serve if one of the regular jurors withdraws during the trial.

Although the venire is sworn under oath to answer truthfully, they do not always do so. Sometimes potential jurors refuse to admit to facts or thoughts they find embarrassing to share, such as prior criminal victimization (Hannaford 2001).

The manner in which the voir dire is conducted varies tremendously. In some jurisdictions, the judge alone conducts the voir dire, whereas, in other jurisdictions, attorneys participate in some or all of the questioning. The scope of the questioning also varies. The pretrial examination of jurors may be restricted to relatively narrow issues, such as their knowledge of the case, or may contain more expansive questions about their attitudes, general experiences, and preconceptions of the case (Hans 1986). The length of time also varies. In some courts, jury selection is accomplished in less than two hours; in others, voir dire is a time-consuming process, and jury selection for even a routine case can take two or three days. Moreover, major cases have been known to require six weeks or more before the jury is seated.

During voir dire, the litigants may excuse a potential juror in one of two ways. On the basis of a **challenge for cause**, the person in question will be removed only if the trial judge agrees that the prospective juror has some deep-seated bias that would interfere with a fair trial. Although there are no limits to the number of challenges for cause, few are made and even fewer are sustained (Simon and Marshall 1972). Each party may also exercise a limited number of **peremptory challenges**, excusing prospective jurors without giving a reason. On the basis of hunch, insight, whim, or prejudice, the trial attorneys determine who will sit on the jury for that case.

Lawyers have tremendous freedom in exercising peremptory challenges, but they may not use them to exclude potential jurors solely on the basis of race (*Batson v. Kentucky* 1986) or gender (*J.E.B. Petitioner v. Alabama* 1994). Citing *Batson*, the Supreme Court has ordered new trials for several death row inmates because of racial bias during jury selection (*Miller-El v. Dretke* 2005; *Johnson v. California* 2005; *Snyder v. Louisiana* 2008). Nonetheless, some groups argue that racial discrimination in jury selection remains (Equal Justice Initiative 2010).

In practice, attorneys use the voir dire for more than just trying to choose a fair and impartial jury. One primary function is to educate citizens about the role of jurors. Attorneys and judges make frequent requests for the juror's assurance that he or she can set aside past experiences and biases to judge the case fairly and objectively. But, most important, the voir dire provides the lawyers the opportunity to attempt to influence jurors' attitudes and perhaps their later vote. Particularly in criminal cases, defense attorneys view the voir dire as necessary to ensure that potential jurors will presume the defendant is indeed innocent until proven guilty. Many lawyers, therefore, view the voir dire as the final safeguard against jurors' unstated biases or prejudices, ensuring a fair and dispassionate jury. But some critics fear that attorneys seek to select jurors prejudiced to their side. After all, a defendant is entitled to an unbiased jury but not to a jury biased in his or her favor.

Jury Consultants

In recent decades, jury selection has taken a scientific turn. Rather than relying on personal hunch, attorneys in a few highly publicized cases have employed social scientists to aid them in a more intelligent, systematic use of the voir dire. Using public opinion polls and focus groups, jury consultants help lawyers formulate questions to use in jury selection to uncover hidden biases harbored by potential jurors and to develop a profile of jurors who are most and least favorable to each side. The O. J. Simpson defense team enlisted the services of a prominent Pasadena-based trial consultant, Dr. Jo-Ellan Dimitrius, to assist in the selection of the most favorable jury possible for the former football star.

Trial consultants are hired more often by defense attorneys than by prosecutors. In reality, the consultant is deselecting jurors who are likely to be adverse to the client (Gollner 1995). This practice of packing the jury is not new; however, the profession of jury consultant is. Attorneys have always attempted to bias the jury in their favor, but now they are beginning to employ outsiders who specialize in the areas of psychology and body language. The role of jury consultants is at the heart of the movie *Runaway Jury*. (See Law and Popular Culture: *Runaway Jury*.) Perhaps the most valuable aid social science consultants can offer is to help attorneys develop trial presentations that are clear and convincing (Diamond 1990).

Jury Duty

Every year, thousands of Americans are called to serve as jurors. Jury duty is currently the only time that citizens are required to perform a direct service for their government. Nonetheless, getting out of jury duty is a national pastime. "Everybody likes jury duty—just not this week," concludes Patricia Refo, a Phoenix lawyer who chaired the American Jury Project for the American Bar Association ("Getting Out of Jury Duty …" 2007).

Some jurors experience great frustration with the process. They are made to wait endless hours in barren courthouse rooms; minimal compensation often makes for a hardship, because not all employers pay for the time lost from work; and some jurors are apprehensive about courts in general and criminal courthouses in particular.

In spite of those hardships, most citizens express an overall satisfaction with jury duty. Of 3,000 jurors surveyed, almost 90 percent stated that they were favorably impressed with jury duty and did not consider it an onerous obligation (Pabst 1973). Just as important, there is every indication that jurors take their jobs seriously. Studies suggest that jury duty can be stressful; for a handful of jurors, the trial continues long after the verdict (Hafemeister and Ventis 1992).

Considerable attention has been devoted to reducing the inconvenience of jury duty. Courts in all states use a call-in system; jurors dial a number to learn whether their attendance is needed on a particular day. An increasing number of courts are also reducing the number of days a person remains in the jury pool. Traditionally, jurors were asked to serve for a full month. Although only a few jurors were needed for a particular day, the entire pool had to be present in the courthouse every working day. A new approach is the one-day/one-trial jury system, wherein jurors are required to serve either for one day or for the duration of one trial and are then exempt from jury duty for a year or more. One-day/one-trial jury systems are successful in meeting their goals of creating more favorable juror attitudes, providing a more representative cross section of the community, saving money, and increasing the public's exposure to the courts (Kasunic 1983).

LAW AND POPULAR CULTURE

■ *Runaway Jury* (2003)

"Trials are too important to be left up to juries," stresses jury consultant Rankin Fitch (Gene Hackman). He exudes great confidence that he can deliver the jury verdict for his corporate clients. In court, he says, "Somebody always loses. Just not me." But is his confidence misplaced?

Set in pre-Katrina New Orleans, *Runaway Jury* is the story of a mysterious man, Nick Easter (John Cusak), who gets himself on the jury of a landmark case against a gun manufacturer. His motives are part swindle and part revenge. The case involves a suit filed by the widow of a man killed in an office shooting against the manufacturer of the weapon that was used. The woman claims that the manufacturer knew that the store that sold it was not obeying the laws governing firearms sales.

Runaway Jury, based on the John Grisham novel of the same name, highlights the involvement of courts in major public policy issues (see Chapter 7). In the novel, the issue is tobacco-related deaths. (See Debating Law, Courts, and Politics: Who Should Be Held Responsible for Tobacco-Related Deaths? in Chapter 11.) In the movie, the issue is gun-related deaths. (See Debating Law, Courts, and Politics: Should Gun Manufacturers Be Sued? in Chapter 7.)

Runaway Jury dramatizes the importance of trials as balancing wheels. Lawyers for both parties present their case in ways to appeal to popular standards of justice. The plaintiff stresses that the husband was the victim of a mass slaying, "gunned down in the prime of his life." The defense stresses the lawful use of guns in hunting and stresses the Second Amendment's right to bear arms.

Runaway Jury provides glimpses of contrasting types of lawyers (discussed in Chapter 5). Dustin Hoffman plays the role of a classic plaintiff lawyer motivated primarily by the prospect of a large jury award. By contrast, the defense attorney works for a large law firm that regularly represents corporate interests and frames the issues in terms of the client's bottom line on the financial statement.

Runaway Jury offers contrasting images of jury consultants. The plaintiff's lawyer shows disdain for jury consultants, hiring one only after he agrees to a lower-than-normal fee. The defense lawyer, on the other hand, is, in essence, ruled by the jury consultant. And, most certainly, the defendants are under the impression that the consultant can buy the verdict they want. But, in the end, one is not sure if the jury consultant provides anything more than stereotypes. At one point, for example, Rankin opines, "I hate Baptists almost as much as I hate environmentalists."

As we have stressed throughout this book, popular culture often distorts legal realities to fit the plot line. But few works of fiction go as far as *Runaway Jury*. The jury selection process is intended to result in a fair and impartial jury; the movie proceeds as if none of those steps even exist, suggesting that prospective jurors can talk their way onto a jury.

After watching *Runaway Jury*, be prepared to discuss the following questions:

1. In what ways does the movie distort the jury selection process? In what ways does it represent the realities of jury selection?
2. Describe three positive and three negative attributes of the jury system portrayed in *Runaway Jury*.
3. What images of legal ethics does this movie project? Are plaintiffs' lawyers any more or less likely to engage in unethical conduct than lawyers who work for large firms?
4. What themes in this movie would advocates of tort reform stress? What themes in this movie would opponents of tort reform emphasize?

THE MOVING PARTY PRESENTS ITS CASE

Once the jury has been selected and sworn in, the trial begins with a brief **opening statement** to the jury. Lawyers for each side explain the version of the facts that best supports their side of the case, how those facts will be proved, and how they think the law applies to the case.

The Burden of Proof

After the opening statements, the moving party (the prosecutor in a criminal case and the plaintiff in a civil matter) presents its case in chief, which is the main evidence offered to support its position. The moving party has the **burden of proof**, which is the duty of affirmatively proving the facts in dispute in the case. If the burden of proof is not met, the judge can grant the defense motion for acquittal before the defense even presents its case. In civil cases, the burden of proof is the **preponderance of evidence**, which is evidence that is of greater weight or is more convincing than the evidence offered in opposition. In criminal cases, however, the state must meet a more demanding standard. One of the most fundamental protections recognized in the U.S. criminal justice process is the right to be presumed innocent.

A defendant is cloaked with the legal shield of innocence. The state has the burden of proving the defendant guilty of the alleged crime; the defendant is not required to prove himself or herself innocent. Thus, the prosecution is required to prove the defendant guilty **beyond a reasonable doubt**, which is a legal yardstick measuring the sufficiency of the evidence. This burden of proof does not require the state to establish absolute certainty by eliminating all doubt—just reasonable doubt.

Rules of Evidence

Evidence refers to all types of information presented at trial. **Real evidence** includes objects of any kind—guns, documents, and business records, for example. The bulk of the evidence during trial consists of **testimony**, statements by witnesses.

Evidence is also classified as direct or circumstantial. **Direct evidence** refers to the proof of a fact without the need for other facts leading up to it. **Circumstantial evidence** is evidence that indirectly proves a main fact in question. For example, testimony that the person was seen walking in the rain is direct evidence the person walked in the rain, but testimony that the person was seen indoors with wet clothing is circumstantial evidence the person walked in the rain. Contrary to popular belief, the law considers circumstantial evidence as reliable as direct evidence, and defendants can be and have been convicted on circumstantial evidence alone.

During trial, the examination of each witness called to testify is conducted according to the following three steps. The first step, **direct examination**, consists of questioning by the attorney for the party who calls the witness. The objective is to establish the facts or the claim of that party. Attorneys generally may not ask their own witnesses **leading questions**, that is, questions that suggest the answer. For instance, if the attorney asks, "You've never seen this gun before, have you?" the witness is almost told to say "no." The second step, **cross-examination**, involves questioning by the opposing counsel. Cross-examination offers the opportunity to attack the credibility of the opponent's witness and his or her testimony and is limited to matters covered on direct examination. Leading questions are permissible, however (whereas they are not in direct examination), because they promote the purpose of cross-examination. The third step, **redirect examination**, involves questioning by the attorney who conducted the direct examination. Redirect examination is generally used to "rehabilitate" the witness following cross-examination, that is, to recapture his or her lost credibility. The subject matter is usually limited to matters covered during cross-examination.

The admission of proof at trial is governed by the rules of evidence. A trial is an adversary proceeding in which the rules of evidence resemble the rules of a game and the judge acts as an impartial umpire. These rules of evidence have developed primarily out of appellate court decisions rather than from legislative enactments. Although they may seem to be fixed and rigid, they are not. Like all other legal principles, rules of evidence are general propositions that must be applied to specific instances. During such applications, judges use a balancing test, carefully weighing whether the trial would be fairer with or without the piece of evidence in question.

The purpose of the adversary process is to get at the truth; the primary purpose of rules of evidence is to help achieve that end. For instance, a judge who feels the jury would give certain evidence undue weight or would be greatly prejudiced by that evidence would not allow it to be presented. Some rules of evidence, however, have purposes other than truthfulness. Because the law seeks to protect the secrecy of communications (legally called "privileged communications") between doctor and patient, lawyer and client, and husband and wife, such communications are normally not admissible in open court. Similarly, under the exclusionary rule, illegally seized evidence is inadmissible (even if trustworthy), because the law seeks to discourage such activities. Most major rules of evidence, however, are directed at achieving the truth. The principles governing the admissibility of evidence may be briefly summarized under the headings of trustworthiness and relevance.

Trustworthiness   This is the basic criterion for admissibility of evidence. The objective of the evidentiary system is to ensure that only the most reliable and credible facts, statements, or testimony are presented to the fact finder. The best evidence rule illustrates this point. Ordinarily, only the original of a document or object is admissible because a copy may have been altered. Similarly, a judge may rule that a person of unsound mind or a very young child is not a competent witness because he or she may not understand what was seen or heard. The mere fact that evidence is legally ruled to be admissible does not, of course, mean the jury must believe it. A wife's alibi for her husband may be competent evidence, but the jury may choose not to believe her.

Hearsay is secondhand evidence. It is testimony a witness provides that is not based on personal knowledge but is a repetition of what another person has said. An example is someone's testimony that "my brother Bob told me he saw Jones enter the store that evening." The general rule is that hearsay evidence is not admissible, because it is impossible to test its truthfulness: There is no way to cross-examine to find the truth of the matter. The rules for whether hearsay may be used are among the more complex in the law. Among the numerous exceptions are dying declarations.

Relevance   To be admissible, evidence must also be **relevant** to the case; there must be a valid reason for introducing the statement, object, or testimony. Evidence not related to an issue at trial is termed **immaterial** or **irrelevant**. If, for example, a defendant is accused of murder, the issue is whether he or she killed the deceased. Evidence about the defendant's intention to commit the offense and his or her ability to commit the offense are all relevant. But evidence about the defendant's character—prior convictions or a reputation for dishonesty, for instance—is normally inadmissible, because it is not material to the issue of whether the defendant committed the crime. If, however, the defendant testifies, such evidence is admissible during rebuttal to impeach (cast doubt on) his or her credibility.

EXPERT WITNESSES

Normally, witnesses may testify only about facts of which they have personal knowledge. A special class of witnesses—**expert witnesses**—possesses special knowledge or expertise. They are allowed to testify at trial not only about facts (as ordinary witnesses do) but also about the professional conclusions they draw from those facts. Fingerprint experts, chemists, and ballistics experts are examples of expert witnesses who often appear in criminal trials. Doctors, psychologists, and economists are examples of expert witnesses who often appear in civil trials. A heated debate over the use and misuse of expert witnesses questions whether some experts shape their testimony to fit the needs of the client who is paying them.

The opinions of properly qualified experts, however, are not admissible unless they meet other standards for admissibility. Separating science from pseudoscience is never an easy task. For much of the twentieth century, the "general acceptance" test was the dominant standard for determining the admissibility of novel scientific evidence at trial. This test was defined as follows:

> Just when a scientific principle or discovery crosses the line between the experimental and demonstrable stages is difficult to define. Somewhere in this twilight zone the evidential forces of the principle must be recognized, and while courts will go a long way in admitting expert testimony deduced from a well-recognized scientific principle or discovery, the thing from which the deduction is made must be sufficiently established to have gained general acceptance in the particular field in which it belongs (*Frye v. United States* 1923).

In the modern era, some courts rejected the "general acceptance" prong of the *Frye* test, holding that this nose-counting approach was no longer adequate in the face of rapid developments in science. Following that trend, the Supreme Court rejected the *Frye* standard, arguing that it had been replaced by the Federal Rules of Evidence. The Court assigned federal judges an active role in screening scientific evidence. "The trial judge must ensure that any and all scientific testimony or evidence is not only relevant but reliable" (*Daubert v. Merrell Dow Pharmaceuticals Co.* 1993). Later the Court extended Daubert to include nonscientific evidence as well (*Kumbo Tire v. Carmichael* 1999).

Scientific Evidence in the Age of Daubert

Scientific evidence, such as blood, firearms, and fingerprints, is now routinely admitted into evidence if it meets the traditional yardsticks of the rules of evidence—trustworthiness and relevance. When the technologies for gathering and measuring those forms of evidence first emerged, however, their use as evidence was far from routine. Moreover, not all evidence based on "science" is necessarily admissible. Polygraph examinations and testimony gained from hypnosis are generally not admissible as evidence.

Even under Daubert, just when a scientific principle or discovery crosses the line between the experimental and reliably demonstrable stages is difficult to define. *Daubert* has particular applicability in civil cases, where critics argue that "junk science" (unreliable findings by persons with questionable credentials) is producing too many civil lawsuits. *Daubert* has resulted in trial judges ruling that juries should not hear certain types of scientific evidence. Daubert's impact on forensic science in criminal cases, however, has been surprisingly less dramatic (Fisher 2008; Neufeld 2005). Indeed forensic scientific evidence either caused or contributed to wrongful convictions in roughly 57 percent of the Innocence Project's DNA exoneration cases (Garrett 2008).

The use of DNA (deoxyribonucleic acid) as evidence has sparked considerable debate. Initially, judges and lawyers debated whether such evidence was admissible, but those legal battles have now been resolved. One dimension of the contemporary debates focuses on the reliability of crime labs. In a basic sense, crime labs have become a victim of their own success, with requests for scientific tests growing faster than their budgets. Today, crime labs are processing more cases than ever before, but their expanded capacity has not been able to meet the increased demand (Nelson 2010). Increasingly, convicts and their representatives are demanding that old cases be reopened so that DNA tests (not available at the time of the original trial) can be performed. These requests are most often identified with the issue of innocents on death row (see Chapter 13). Moreover, in recent years, some crime labs have been identified as having conducted substandard tests, which has resulted in the overturning of some criminal convictions. Allegations like these prompted the Supreme Court to rule that crime laboratory reports may not be used against a criminal defendants at trial unless the analyst responsible for creating them gives testimony and subjects himself or herself to cross-examination (*Melendez-Diaz v. Massachusetts* 2009).

Objections to the Admission of Evidence

During trial, attorneys must be continuously alert, ready to make timely objections to the admission of evidence. After a question is asked but before the witness answers, attorneys may object. The court then rules on the objection and permits the evidence to be admitted or not. The judge may rule immediately or may request the lawyers to argue the legal point out of the hearing of the jury (termed a sidebar conference).

Occasionally, inadmissible evidence is heard by the jury. When that occurs and the attorney objects, the judge instructs the jury to disregard the evidence. Even with such a cautionary warning, however, jurors may still be influenced by that evidence. If the erroneous evidence is deemed so prejudicial that a warning to disregard is not sufficient, the judge may declare a **mistrial**.

THE DEFENSE PRESENTS ITS CASE

Although a trial is generally expected to be a battle along the lines of "You did it," "No, I didn't," such a view greatly oversimplifies the tactical decisions involved. In deciding on trial strategy, attorneys must carefully consider their opponent's strengths and weaknesses and how the jury is likely to react. The defense must also consider whether the trial should be before a jury or before the judge only (a **bench trial**). In some situations, the defendant alone has the option of waiving the right to trial by jury, but, in others, the opposition must also agree. Most trials, however, are jury trials. Within those constraints, the defense attorney can construct a case along one of two broad lines: burden of proof or denial (see Table 12.1).

TABLE 12.1	**Steps of the Process**	
	Law on the Books	**Law in Action**
Trial	The adversarial process of deciding a case through the presentation of evidence and arguments about the evidence.	Only a handful of felonies and even fewer misdemeanors are decided by trial.
Bench trial	Trial before a judge without a jury.	Defense prefers when the issues are either highly technical or very emotional.
Jury trial	A group of average citizens selected by law and sworn in to look at certain facts and determine the truth.	Introduces public standards of justice into the decision-making process.
Jury selection	Process of selecting a fair and impartial jury.	Each side seeks to select jurors who are biased in its favor.
Master jury list	Potential jurors are selected by chance from a list of potential jurors. List should reflect a representative cross section of the community.	Selecting only from registered voters means that the poor, the young, and minorities are less likely to be called.
Venire	A group of citizens from which jury members are chosen (jury pool).	Judges vary in their willingness to excuse potential jurors because of hardship.
Voir dire	The process by which prospective jurors are questioned to determine whether there is cause to excuse them from the jury.	Lawyers use questioning to predispose jurors in their favor.
Peremptory challenge	Each side may exclude a set number of jurors without stating a reason.	Both sides use peremptory challenges to select a jury favorable to their side.
Challenge for cause	A judge may dismiss a potential juror if the person cannot be fair and objective.	Rarely granted.
Opening statements	Lawyers discuss what the evidence will show.	Lawyers use to lead the jury to a favorable verdict.
Prosecutor's case in chief	The main evidence offered to prove the defendant guilty beyond a reasonable doubt.	Defense suggests that the prosecution has not met its burden of proof.
Witness	A person who makes a statement under oath about the event(s) in question.	Through cross-examination, defense undermines the credibility of the witness.
Expert witness	A person possessing special knowledge or experience who is allowed to testify not only about facts but also about conclusions he or she has drawn.	Some expert witnesses testify only for one side or the other because their conclusions are predictable.
Defense's case in chief	Evidence that defense may present. Because the defendant is innocent until proven guilty, the defense is not required to present evidence.	Defense may rest without calling witnesses, but jurors expect to hear reasons why they shouldn't convict.
Witness	The defendant may waive his or her privilege against self-incrimination and testify.	Defense attorneys are reluctant to call the defendant to the stand, particularly if there is a prior conviction.
Rebuttal	Evidence that refutes or contradicts evidence given by the opposing party.	Prosecutor will call witnesses to undermine a defendant's alibi.
Closing arguments	After all the evidence has been presented, each side sums up the evidence and attempts to convince the jury why its side should win.	Many trial attorneys believe that a good closing argument will win the case. Attempts to convince the jury why its side should win.

(continued)

TABLE 12.1	Steps of the Process (Continued)	
	Law on the Books	**Law in Action**
Prosecution	Because the prosecution bears the burden of proof, the prosecutor goes first and last.	The district attorney goes first and provides an orderly summary of the evidence.
Defense	Closing argument of the defense highlights the evidence leading to a not-guilty verdict.	Typically stresses that the prosecutor has failed to prove the defendant guilty beyond a reasonable doubt.
Prosecution	Rebuts defense allegations.	Impassioned statement, calling upon jurors to do their duty and convict the guilty.
Jury instructions	Explanations by the judge informing the jury of the law applicable to the case.	Legal language difficult for average citizens to follow.
Jury deliberations	Jurors are repeatedly instructed not to talk about the case. Jurors deliberate in private. Jurors select a foreperson and discuss the case. Jurors may request further instructions from the judge. Jurors take an oath to follow the law as instructed by the judge.	Jurors routinely talk with other jurors about the case. Higher-status individuals participate more. The first vote is usually decisive. Such requests produce great anxiety among lawyers. Some juries introduce popular law into the decision-making process.
Verdict	Decision that the defendant is either guilty or not guilty (acquittal).	Juries convict three out of four times. Jury verdicts often reflect a compromise.
Hung jury	Jury is unable to reach a verdict.	Defense attorneys consider a hung jury an important victory.
Post-verdict motions	Motions filed by the defense after conviction and before sentencing.	Judge must accept a verdict of not guilty.
Motion in arrest of judgment	Defense argues that the jury could not have reasonably convicted the defendant based on the evidence presented.	Trial judges are very reluctant to second-guess jury verdicts and almost never grant this motion.
Motion for a new trial	Defense argues that the trial judge made mistakes and that therefore a new trial should be held.	On very rare occasions, trial judges admit that an error occurred and set aside a jury verdict of guilty.

Because the moving party bears the burden of proof, the defense does not have to call any witnesses or introduce any evidence. Thus, one defense strategy is to force the prosecutor or the plaintiff to prove the case. The key to such a strategy is the skillful use of cross-examination. In criminal cases, the defense attorney can try to undermine the state's case and create in the jurors' minds a reasonable doubt about whether the defendant committed the crime. Similarly, in civil cases, the defense attorney can try to undermine the plaintiff's case and create in the jurors' minds doubt that a preponderance of evidence shows the defendant to be liable. But many experienced attorneys believe the burden-of-proof defense is actually weak. To gain an acquittal or a finding of no liability, the defense must give the jurors something to "hang their hats on"— that is, the defense attorney must consider ways to deny the allegations.

In a criminal case, the most straightforward way of denying the state's charges is to call the defendant to the stand. The Fifth Amendment protects a defendant from being compelled "in any criminal case to be a witness against himself." If the defendant chooses not to testify, no comment or inference can be drawn from that fact.

The prosecutor cannot argue before the jury that "if he is innocent, why doesn't he take the stand and say so?" (*Griffin v. California* 1965). But, that legal protection aside, jurors are curious about the defendant's version of what happened. They expect the defendant to argue his or her innocence, and in the secrecy of the jury room, jurors often ponder why the defendant refused to testify. In considering whether to call the defendant to the stand, the defense attorney must assess whether the story is believable. If it is not, the jury will probably dismiss it, doing more harm to the defendant's case than if he or she had not testified at all. Moreover, a defendant who testifies in his or her own behalf is subject to cross-examination like any other witness. Once the defendant chooses to testify, the prosecutor can bring out all the facts surrounding the event testified to. Just as important, once the defendant has taken the stand, the state can impeach the defendant's credibility by introducing into evidence any prior felony convictions. The defense attorney must make the difficult decision whether to arouse the jurors' suspicions by not letting the accused testify or let the defendant testify and be subjected to possibly damaging cross-examination. "Damned if they do, damned if they don't" is the conclusion of a research project that interviewed jurors in capital murder trials. In general, jurors wanted the defendants to testify during trial and were confused when they didn't. But when defendants chose to testify, jurors concluded that they were lying and showed no remorse (Antonio and Arone 2005).

In a civil case, the defense can construct a denial defense around the evidence and witnesses available. In a tort case, for example, the defense may call eyewitnesses who saw the accident differently from those summoned by the plaintiff. In a suit for manufacturing defective merchandise, the defense may call company officials to testify about how carefully the product was designed and manufactured and suggest that the real problem is that the plaintiff did not use the product in the manner intended. In tort actions requesting large sums of money, however, the central question is often the amount of damages rather than liability. In such situations, the defense may call expert witnesses to suggest that the plaintiff's injuries are much less extensive than suggested by the other side and that the amount of money requested is way out of proportion to any injuries that might have been suffered.

REBUTTAL

After the defense rests its case, the moving party may call **rebuttal** witnesses. For example, the prosecutor may call a rebuttal witness to show that the defendant's alibi witness could not have observed what she said she did because she was somewhere else at the time. Or the prosecutor may present evidence to show that the previous witnesses have dishonorable reputations. The rules of evidence regarding rebuttal witnesses are complex. In general, evidence may be presented in rebuttal that could not have been used during the prosecution's case in chief. For example, if the defendant has taken the stand, the prosecution may legitimately inform the jury of the previous convictions of the defendant in an attempt to impeach his or her credibility.

Closing Arguments

When both sides have rested (that is, completed the introduction of evidence), each party has the opportunity to make a **closing argument** to the jury. Like opening statements, closing arguments do not constitute evidence. Closing arguments allow each side to sum up the facts and indicate why it believes the jury should return a verdict in its favor. The moving party goes first, carefully summarizing the facts of the case and tying together into a coherent pattern what appeared during the trial to be isolated or unimportant matters. Next, the defense attorney highlights favorable evidence, criticizes the witnesses for the other side, and indicates why they should not be believed. Because the moving party bears the burden of proof, it is allowed the final closing argument, which is often used to rebut assertions made by the defense during its closing statements.

Closing arguments to the jury call for lawyers to muster all the art and craft, skill and guile of their profession. Closing arguments are often the most dramatic parts of the trial. There is a fine line, however, between persuasiveness and unnecessary emotionalism. Jury verdicts in criminal cases have been reversed on appeal because the prosecutor interjected prejudicial statements into the closing argument.

Jury Instructions

Although the jury is the sole judge of the facts of the case, the judge alone determines the law. Therefore, after closing arguments, the court instructs the jury in the meaning of the law that is applicable to the facts of the case. These **jury instructions** include discussions of general legal principles (proof beyond a reasonable doubt or the preponderance of the evidence), as well as specific instructions concerning the law governing the current case. In criminal cases, the judge instructs the jury in the meaning of the specific criminal law the defendant is charged with violating (for example, burglary). In civil cases, the judge instructs the jury in the meaning of the specific legal standards the defendant is charged with violating (for example, negligence). Finally, the judge instructs the jury about possible verdicts in the case and provides a written form for each. In a trial for homicide, for instance, the jury is instructed that, under state law, the jury either may find the defendant guilty of murder in the first degree, murder in the second degree, or manslaughter, or may acquit on all charges.

The judge and the attorneys prepare the jury instructions during the charging conference. Each side drafts suggested instructions, and the judge chooses the ones that seem most appropriate. If the judge rejects a given instruction, the lawyer may enter an objection on the record, thus preserving the issue for later appeal. Jury instructions are written out, signed by the judge, and then read to the jury.

Jury instructions represent a formal, detailed lecture on the law. Because faulty jury instructions are a principal basis for appellate court reversal, judges are careful in their wordings. As a result, these instructions contain extensive amounts of legal jargon not readily understood by nonlawyers (Steele and Thornburg 1991). As a result, juror comprehension of jury instructions is pitifully low (Ogloff and Rose 2007). Some have made efforts to increase jurors' understandings of these vital matters (Ellwork, Sales, and Alfini 1982; Severance and Loftus 1982). One experiment found that clarifying the meaning of the judge's jury instructions did increase understanding but that jurors still did not have an accurate knowledge of the law. The jury instructions stressed that a defendant is presumed innocent until proven guilty by the evidence beyond any reasonable doubt; yet, after hearing and reading the modern instructions on this matter, only 50 percent of the jurors understood that the defendant did not have to present any evidence of innocence (Strawn and Buchanan 1976).

THE JURY DECIDES

How juries decide has long fascinated lawyers and laypeople alike. There is a great deal of curiosity about what goes on behind the guarded jury room door. During trial, jurors are passive spectators who are not allowed to ask questions and are typically prohibited from taking notes. After the judge reads the instructions to the jury, however, the lawyers, the judge, and the litigants must wait passively, often in tense anticipation, for the jury to reach a verdict. The only hint of what is occurring during jury deliberations occurs on the rare occasions when the jurors request further instructions from the judge about the applicable law or ask to have portions of the testimony that was given in open court reread to them.

If the jury becomes *deadlocked* (they cannot reach a verdict), the trial ends with a **hung jury**. The moving party then has the option of trying the defendant again. Despite recent concerns, the rate of hung juries is low and has been stable for years (Hannaford, Hans, and Munsterman 1999). Nationwide, juries are unable to reach a decision only 6 percent of the time (National Center for State Courts 2003).

What Motivates a Jury?

Because jury deliberations are secret, research on what factors motivate a decision must be conducted indirectly. Much of what is known about how juries decide is based either on observing mock juries or on asking jurors to recall what occurred in the jury room. Researchers at the University of Chicago Law School conducted the major studies on jury deliberation. They found that rates of participation varied with social status: Men talked more than women, better-educated jurors participated more frequently, and persons with high-status occupations were more likely to be chosen as foreperson (Simon 1967; Strodtbeck, James, and Hawkins 1957). Discussions among the jurors mostly concern opinions about the trial and personal reminiscences; far less discussion of the testimony or the judge's instructions to the jury occurs (James 1958).

Juries typically reach a verdict after short deliberations. Interviews of jurors in more than 200 criminal cases revealed that juries usually take a vote as soon as they retire to chambers. In 30 percent of the cases, only one vote was necessary to reach a unanimous verdict. In 90 percent of the rest of the cases, the majority on the first ballot eventually won out (Broeder 1959). Most important, a lone juror rarely produced a hung jury. The psychological pressures associated with small-group discussions are so great that a single juror can buck predominant sentiment only if he or she can find at least one ally. Thus, jury deliberations "do not so much decide the case as bring about a consensus" (Kalven and Zeisel 1966, 488). If the jury does become deadlocked and cannot reach a verdict, the trial ends with a hung jury. The moving party then has the option of trying the case again.

But what of jury bias? Do different groups of jurors decide differently? Most research suggests that modern juries in the United States appear to perform remarkably well on the whole, deciding cases primarily on the basis of legal factors rather than extra-legal ones (Garvey et al. 2004; Ford 1986; Mills and Bohannon 1980). Even in trials involving emotional issues like sexual assault, evidence is the primary factor in decision making. Jurors were influenced by extralegal factors, but these effects were largely limited to weak cases in which the state presented little hard evidence (Reskin and Visher 1986). This is not to say that racism, sexism (including gender stereotypes), homophobia, and the like do not enter into juror decision making; they do. However, the effects of these biases appear to be minimal because they are significantly moderated by legal factors—especially the strength of the evidence (Diamond 2006; Mitchell et al. 2005; Garvey et al. 2004).

The Verdict

After the foreperson announces the **verdict**, either party may request that the jury be polled individually, with each juror voicing his or her vote in open court.

Jury verdicts dramatically determine winners and losers in the judicial process. Given that the vast majority of cases have been disposed of by a negotiated settlement, one might expect that the defendant's chances of winning are roughly 50–50. But, in reality, they are not. In criminal trials, juries convict two-thirds of the time (Roper and Flango 1983). Reliable data on how often juries find civil defendants liable is much harder to come by but points in the same direction. Examination of jury verdicts in 43 counties found the success rates for plaintiffs clustered within the 55 to 65 percent range (Roper and Martin 1986).

Do juries view cases differently than do judges? In a classic study, Harry Kalven and Hans Zeisel (1966) attempted to answer that question by comparing verdicts reached by juries with the decisions judges would have made in more than 3,500 criminal trials. Overall, they found that judges and juries agreed three out of four times, which suggests that the evidence is the primary factor shaping the jury's verdict. Subsequent studies have replicated these findings (Eisenberg et al. 2004). Judges and juries disagreed 22 percent of the time, however, with the juries voting acquittal when the judges would have convicted. But disagreements between judge and jury are tied to the seriousness of the offense. Juries convicted felons at a much higher rate than did judges, but judges convicted nonfelons at a much higher rate than did juries (Levine 1983; Roper and Flango 1983). Other factors are also involved including whether the defendant takes the stand in his or her own defense and whether the defense presents its own witnesses in an effort to disprove the state's case (Givelber and Farrell 2008).

When juries acquit in high-profile cases such as the prosecution of Michael Jackson, there are usually calls for jury reform. But isolated jury decisions should not cloud the central fact that over the years conviction rates have been remarkably consistent. Although there are some differences between states in conviction rates in felony prosecutions, within states conviction rates have remained remarkably consistent for several decades (Vidmar et al. 1997).

Prejudicial Pretrial Publicity

One of the basic rights of a defendant accused of violating the criminal law is to be tried by an impartial jury that has not been influenced by **prejudicial pretrial publicity**. (See Case Close-Up: *Sheppard v. Maxwell* 1966.) Pretrial publicity does bias juries. In a classic research study, one set of "jurors" was provided with prejudicial news coverage of a case and a control group was provided with nonprejudicial information. After listening to an identical trial involving a case where the defendant's guilt was greatly in doubt, 78 percent of the prejudiced jurors voted to convict, compared with only 55 percent of the nonprejudiced jurors (Padawer-Singer and Barton 1975). These results have been replicated many times such that is now widely accepted that even modest pretrial publicity can prejudice potential jurors against a defendant (Studebaker and Penrod 2007; Moran and Cutler 1991).

Historically very few criminal trials involved prejudicial pretrial publicity; news reports seldom extend beyond police blotter coverage (Frasca 1988). But with the advent of 24-hour cable news channels and the ease of information access through the Internet, pretrial public affects more cases today than ever before. Extensive pretrial publicity greatly strains the jury selection process. Voir dire is geared to ferreting out ordinary instances of unfairness or prejudice, not to correcting the possibility of a systematic pattern of bias. If, for example, an attorney excuses all jurors who have heard or read something about the case at hand, he or she runs the risk of selecting a jury solely from the least attentive, least literate members of the general public. If, on the other hand, an attorney accepts jurors who assert they will judge the case solely on the basis of testimony in open court, he or she cannot be certain that the juror—no matter how well intentioned—can hear the case with a truly open mind.

In trying to reconcile the conflicting principles of the First and Sixth Amendments, trial courts employ singly or in combination three techniques—limited gag orders, change of venue, and sequestering of the jury. Each of these methods, however, is a partial one and suffers from admitted drawbacks.

Limited Gag Orders

In notorious cases in which it seems likely that selecting a jury will be difficult, judges routinely issue a limited **gag order** forbidding those involved in the case—police, prosecutor, defense attorney, and defendant—from talking to the press, with violations punishable as contempt of court. Given that these people know the most about the case, the net effect is to dry up news leaks. Enforcing limited gag orders, however, is somewhat problematic, because reporters refuse to disclose their sources of information.

Change of Venue

The local area where a case may be tried is referred to as **venue**. If the court is convinced a case has received such extensive local publicity that picking an impartial jury is impossible, the trial may be shifted to another part of the state. Defense attorneys face a difficult tactical decision in deciding whether to request a **change of venue**.

CASE CLOSE-UP

■ *Sheppard v. Maxwell* (1966)

Prejudicial Pretrial Publicity

On July 4, 1954, Marilyn Sheppard—the pregnant wife of Dr. Samuel Sheppard—was bludgeoned to death in the upstairs bedroom of the couple's home in a fashionable Cleveland suburb. The case produced some of the most sensational press coverage the country had witnessed.

It was not the crime of the century, but it was certainly the crime of the decade. Sheppard told the police that he was asleep on a sofa when he was awakened by the screams of his wife. Rushing upstairs, he grappled with the intruder, only to be struck unconscious by a blow to the head. Sheppard was taken to his family's medical clinic, where he was treated by his brother, also a doctor. From the outset, officials focused suspicion on Sheppard. They interrogated him while he was still at the clinic and continued for several weeks.

The official investigation was prodded by extensive media coverage, which was critical of how the police handled the case. Day after day, vivid headlines called for the arrest of Dr. Sheppard and implied that the police were going easy because he and his family were so socially prominent. To add fuel to the fire, the paper published a front-page editorial headlined "Why Don't Police Quiz Top Suspect?" claiming somebody "was getting away with murder." At the coroner's inquest, Sheppard's attorney was present but not allowed to participate. On live radio, Sheppard was questioned for six hours about his activities the night of the murder and his lovers before that night. Six weeks after the murder, Sheppard was indicted.

The case came to trial two weeks before a general election, in which the judge was seeking re-election and the prosecutor was running for municipal court judge. The names and addresses of potential jurors were published in the paper, resulting in their receiving letters and phone calls concerning the trial. The courtroom was so packed that reporters were allowed to sit behind the defense table, meaning that Sheppard could not converse privately with his lawyer. Indeed, the din was so great that the judge installed a loudspeaker in a vain effort to allow the spectators to hear the witnesses. A radio station carried a daily broadcast from the courtroom. Every day,

newspapers printed trial testimony verbatim; no effort was made to prevent the jury from reading those accounts, even when evidence was ruled inadmissible. Not surprisingly, after a nine-week trial in which jurors were free to return home every night, Sheppard was convicted of second-degree murder.

Sheppard spent twelve years in prison. A string of appeals and habeas corpus petitions were denied. Eventually, the family hired a young Boston lawyer, F. Lee Bailey, who would go on to become one of the most famous and controversial lawyers in the United States. (Indeed, Bailey figured prominently in a trial that later received extensive media coverage—the murder trial of former football star and TV commentator O. J. Simpson.) Bailey persuaded the high court to hear the case and won a stunning victory. Justice Clark likened the trial to a "Roman holiday," holding that prejudicial pretrial publicity denied Sheppard the right to a fair and impartial trial (*Sheppard v. Maxwell* 1966).

Finding that pretrial publicity can be prejudicial is a far easier task than deciding how to control it. The essential problem is that two key protections of the Bill of Rights are on a collision course. The Sixth Amendment guarantees defendants the right to a trial before an impartial jury; decisions about guilt or innocence must be based on what jurors hear during the trial, not what they have heard or read outside the courtroom. At the same time, the First Amendment protects freedom of the press; what reporters print, say on radio, or broadcast on television is not subject to prior censorship. Without the First Amendment, there would be no problem; courts could simply forbid the press from reporting anything but the bare essentials of a crime. Although that is the practice in England, such prior restraints are not allowed in the United States (*Times-Picayune v. Schulingkamp* 1975). To Justice Clark, the answer to this dilemma lay in controlling the flow of information. In his words, "The carnival atmosphere at trial could easily have been avoided since the courtroom and courthouse premises are subject to the control of the court." But five decades later, trial courts still struggle to strike a balance between freedom of the press and the rights of criminal defendants.

They must weigh the effects of prejudicial publicity against the problem of having a trial in a more rural and conservative area whose citizens are hostile to big-city defendants, particularly if they are racial minorities. Prosecutors generally oppose such moves, because they believe the chance of conviction is greater in the local community. To justify their position, prosecutors cite the expenses of moving witnesses, documents, and staff to a distant city for a long trial.

Sequestering the Jury

A prime defect in the trial of Dr. Sheppard was the failure to shield the jury from press coverage of the ongoing trial. Indeed, jurors even read detailed newspaper stories of the trial, which included inadmissible evidence. To remedy that problem, it is now common in trials involving extensive media coverage to **sequester** the jury. The jurors live in a hotel, and their activities are carefully monitored. Sequestering, however, affects the types of jurors who are willing to serve in cases that may last a month or more. The jury selected may represent only those citizens who are willing to be separated for long periods from friends, family, and relatives, who can afford to take off from work, who are unemployed, or who look forward to a spartan existence.

TRIALS AS BALANCING WHEELS

Trials exert a major influence on the operation of the entire criminal court process. This process resembles a balance. A balance wheel regulates or stabilizes the motion of a mechanism. Although only a handful of cases go to trial, the possibility of trial operates as a balancing wheel on all other cases. And this notion of balance is closely linked to American notions of democracy.

Juries are among the most democratic of U.S. institutions. To law professor Robert Burns (1999, 9), the democratized jury trial is "one of the greatest achievements of our public culture." Instead of the trained legal experts used in most other countries, ordinary citizens are impaneled to weigh evidence and render verdicts. The use of juries represents a deep commitment to the role of laypeople in the administration of justice. The views and actions of judges and lawyers are constrained by a group of average citizens who are amateurs in the ways of the law (Van Dyke 1977). "The direct and raw character of jury democracy makes it our most honored mirror, reflecting both the good and the bad that ordinary people are capable of when called upon to do justice" (Abramson 1994, 250). For those reasons, judges, lawyers, and law professors have expressed reservations about this intrusion through the years. Jerome Frank (1949, 132) offered one of the most trenchant criticisms: "Now I submit that the jury is the worst possible enemy of this ideal of the 'supremacy of law.' For 'jury-made law' is, par excellence, capricious and arbitrary, yielding the maximum in the way of lack of uniformity, of unknowability...." This tension between the law of the amateur jury and the law of the legal professionals provides a dynamic quality to the U.S. judiciary that is absent in most other nations of the world.

Basically, juries resolve disputes that lawyers and litigants are unable to settle themselves. The existence of the jury system, therefore, serves notice to all potential litigants that failure to resolve conflict will result in its ultimate resolution by others. This threat of a jury trial clearly shapes how lawyers negotiate settlements in civil cases and how they plea-bargain in criminal cases. Although only a handful of cases go to trial, those few cases exert a major influence on the operation of the entire court process.

A routine part of the negotiation process of civil lawsuits (Chapter 11) is an assessment of the way juries have decided certain kinds of cases. Not only is much information about jury verdicts passed by word of mouth among lawyers, but also special services, such as the national Jury Verdicts Research, report who wins, who loses, and the amount of damage awards (Levine 1992). Thus, jury trials must be measured not only by their impact on specific cases but also by how those decisions affect similar cases in the future. The importance of juries as democratic institutions explains why there is an active concern over vanishing juries (See Debating Law, Courts, and Politics: Are Juries Vanishing?).

Popular Standards of Justice

Juries introduce the community's conscience and commonsense judgments into judicial decisions. The University of Chicago jury project found that popular standards of justice are by far the major reason for disagreement between judge and jury. The result is jury legislation, a jury's deliberate modification of the law to make it conform to community views of what the law ought to be (Kalven and Zeisel 1966). Over the years, federal jury conviction rates have been increasing across all types of cases. But there is some historical evidence that rural juries, for example, appear to be dubious about laws that restrict hunting privileges, and, for many years, southern juries (as well as some northern ones) have questioned federal laws proscribing racial discrimination. So federal defendants accused of those crimes have a good chance of finding friendly juries ready to come to their rescue (Levine 1983). Similarly, state juries are less likely to convict if they perceive that the potential sentence is too severe (as when a defendant who is charged with drunken driving but who caused no damage or injury stands to lose his or her driver's license for a long time). Jury verdicts thus establish boundaries on what actions the local community believes should (or should not) be punished.

In recent years, the importance of juries' introducing popular standards into the justice system has been associated with the concept of **jury nullification**—the right of juries to nullify or refuse to apply law in criminal cases despite facts that leave no reasonable doubt that the law was violated. Some advocates of jury nullification base their ideas on a perceived need to reduce government intrusion into citizens' lives; others are motivated by concern over racial injustice (Brooks 2004; Brown 1997; Butler 1995). Judges are quick to denounce jury nullification because they feel that the rule of law is undermined. But others counter that juries have been refusing to follow the law for centuries, and they have every right to send a message by not following a law they find, for whatever reason, to be flawed. Contemporary discussions focus on whether juries should be told they have the right to disregard the judge's jury instructions and substitute their own views and, if so, what the effects of doing so may be (Diamond 2007; Dunn 2007; Horowitz et al. 2006; Galiber et al. 1993).

DEBATING LAW, COURTS, AND POLITICS

■ Are Juries Vanishing?

For all the public attention devoted to trials, some law professors and judges are concerned that jury trials are disappearing. In one recent year, for example, federal courts conducted 3,600 civil jury trials, down from 5,800 in 1962 (Liptak 2007). This does not appear to be an enormous drop until one considers that the volume of cases quintupled during that same time frame (Galanter 2004).

Statistics like these lead U.S. District Judge William Young (2006) to equate vanishing juries to vanishing trials and in the end a vanishing constitution. Robert Burns (2009) takes the argument a step further and writes about *The Death of the American Trial*. To Burns, a former trial attorney and now law professor, the American trial is one of our greatest cultural achievements and has earned the admiration of most people including lawyers, judges, jurors, and social scientists. American trials (unlike those in other common law countries) have always stood at the exact point of defining tensions within our public culture. The decline, if not the death, of this system would have a number of negative consequences including the loss of a forum that has traditionally been the place where the rigidity, and sometimes the harshness, of the written law has been softened. Moreover, citizens would no longer be able to effectively tell their own story publicly in a forum of power.

This trend is nothing new, however. Ninety years ago, Raymond Moley (1928) published an influential article titled "The Vanishing Jury." In many ways, the notion of the disappearing jury reflects important practices discussed earlier; lawyers and litigants prefer to settle cases on their own terms, not those of an unknown lay jury. Thus, the vast majority of criminal cases end in a voluntary plea of guilty

(Chapter 9). Likewise, an even higher percentage of civil cases end with out-of-court settlements (Chapter 11). To these long-term factors, several more modern ones exist as well. Current thinking stresses efficient use of judicial resources, including allowing judges to enter a summary judgment if there are no disputes over facts in civil cases.

If Burns offers a lament for a dying trial system, others celebrate a vibrant jury system that shows healthy adaptation to a changing society. At the national level, trials receive extensive media coverage when the crimes are shocking and/or the defendant is a person with some social standing. At the local level, trials of local notables or sensational crimes are sure to receive morning headlines in the newspaper and lead the nightly TV news. All this public attention to real trials is fanned by fictional trials that at times are pulled from yesterday's headlines. And if the trial system is dying, as Burns and a few others argue, why do business interest groups spend so many dollars denouncing the major practitioners of the trial–plaintiffs lawyers (Chapter 10). Moreover arguments about vanishing juries and a dying trial system directly contradicts what others are saying. To many, the cure for what ails the American legal system is not more adversariness (as represented by trials) but less adversariness (as represented by ADR).

In the episodic debate over whether juries are vanishing or merely adapting it is worth remembers that while fewer cases are decided by a jury trial every year, juries nonetheless remain very important to the American legal system. Indeed, 90 percent of all jury trials in the world take place in the United States.

Uncertainty

Jury trials also affect the legal system by introducing uncertainty into the process. During a trial, the legal professionals are at the mercy of the witnesses, whose behavior is somewhat unpredictable: What a witness says and how he or she says it often means the difference between conviction and acquittal (Eisenstein and Jacob 1977). The presence of juries adds another layer of unpredictability to the process. Stories about irrational jurors form part of the folklore of any courthouse. Here are two examples:

- During jury deliberations in a drug case, two women announced that "only God can judge" and hung the jury by refusing to vote.

• After an acquittal in a burglary case, a juror put her arm around the defendant and said, "Bob, we were sure happy to find you not guilty, but don't do it again" (Neubauer 1974, 228).

Legal professionals resent such intrusions into their otherwise ordered world; they seek to reduce such uncertainties by developing norms of cooperation. Viewed in that light, negotiating settlements serves to buffer the system against a great deal of the uncertainty that results when lay citizens are involved in deciding important legal matters.

CONCLUSION

After twelve years in prison, Sheppard was retried in 1966. The prosecution put on essentially the same case, but they now faced one of the top defense attorneys in the nation. F. Lee Bailey who tore into the prosecutor's witnesses and, in closing argument, likened the prosecution's case to "ten pounds of hogwash in a five-pound bag." After deliberating for less than twelve hours, the jury returned a verdict of not guilty. But for Sam Sheppard liberty proved short lived. He died in 1970, probably sent to an early grave by journalistic excess.

In many ways, highly publicized jury trials for defendants—whether well known like Sam Sheppard and Casey Anthony or hardly known at all—are the high point of the judicial process. Indeed, along with Lady Justice, jury trials stand as the primary symbol of justice. In turn, many Supreme Court decisions emphasize the importance of adversarial procedures at trial. Yet the realities of trial present two contradictory perspectives: Full-fledged trials are relatively rare, yet trials are an important dimension of the court process. Every year, a million jurors serve in civil and criminal cases. Although only a relative smattering of cases are ever tried, the possibility of trial shapes the entire process. Thus, long after trials have declined to minimal importance in other Western nations, the institution of the trial jury remains a vital part of the U.S. judicial process. Nowhere is this more apparent than in criminal justice. Given the availability of counsel, any defendant, no matter how poor and no matter how inflamed the public is about the crime allegedly committed, can require the state to prove its case.

CRITICAL THINKING QUESTIONS

1. What if the United States did not have the right to trial by jury? How would the court system be different? Would the courts be more or less respected in the public eye?

2. Why are some jury verdicts popular with the public but others are not? To what extent do differences of opinion over the fairness of a jury verdict reinforce notions that equate justice with winning (Chapter 2)?

3. Examine several trials that have occurred over the last several months (either nationwide or in your own community). Do those trials suggest that justice would be better served if jury nullification were explained to the jury as a possible basis for their decision?

Search Terms

DNA testing   jury   jury nullification

Useful URLs

http://www.aafs.org
  The American Academy of Forensic Sciences is a professional society dedicated to the application of science to the law.

http://www.jri-inc.com
  The Jury Research Institute provides trial consulting services.

http://www.ajs.org/jc
  The National Jury Center of the American Judicature Society

REFERENCES

Abramson, Jeffrey. 1994. *We, the Jury: The Jury System and the Ideal of Democracy.* New York: Basic Books.

Antonio, Michael, and Nicole Arone. 2005. "Damned If They Do, Damned If They Don't: Jurors' Reaction to Defendant Testimony or Silence During a Capital Trial." *Judicature* 89: 60–66.

Beiser, Edward. 1975. "Six-Member Juries in the Federal Courts." *Judicature* 58: 424–436.

Belton, Catherine, and Neil Buckley. 2007. *Financial Times,* November 26.

Bowring, Bill. 2009. "Alexei Trochev: Judging Russia: Constitutional Court in Russian Politics (1990-2006)." *Journal of Law and Society* 36: 282–287.

Broeder, D. W. 1959. "The University of Chicago Jury Project." *Nebraska Law Review* 38: 744–760.

Brooks, Thom. 2004. "A Defense of Jury Nullification." *Res Publica* 10: 401–423.

Burns, Robert. 1999. *A Theory of the Trial.* Princeton: Princeton University Press.

———. 2009. *The Death of the American Trial.* Chicago: University of Chicago Press.

Butler, Paul. 1995. "Black Jurors: Right to Acquit?" *Harper's Magazine* 29: 11.

Central Intelligence Agency. 2008. *The World Factbook.* Available online at https://www.cia.gov/library/publications/the-world-factbook/geos/rs.html. Retrieved September 28, 2008.

Chance, Matthew. 2011. "Khodorkovsky Gets 14-Year Prison Term." CNN January 7.

Chazan, Guy. 2005. "Russia's Courts Go on Trial." *Wall Street Journal,* May 23.

Diamond, Shari. 1990. "Scientific Jury Selection: What Social Scientists Know and Do Not Know." *Judicature* 73: 178–183.

Diamond, Shari Seidman. 2007. "Dispensing with Deception, Curing with Care." *Judicature* 91: 20–25.

Diamond, Shari Seidman. 2006. "Beyond Fantasy and Nightmare: A Portrait of the Jury." *Buffalo Law Review* 54: 717–763.

Diamond, Shari Seidman, Mary R. Rose, and Beth Murphy. 2006. "Revisiting the Unanimity Requirement: The Behavior of the Non-Unanimous Civil Jury, 100." *Northwestern University Law Review* 100: 201–230.

Diamond, Shari, Mary Rose and Beth Murphy. 2006. "Revisiting the Unanimity Requirement: The Behavior of the Non-Unanimous Civil Jury." *Northwestern University Law Review* 100: 201–230.

Drazan, Dan. 1989. "The Case for Special Juries in Toxic Tort Litigation." *Judicature* 72: 292–298.

Dunn, B. Michael. 2007. "'Must Find the Defendant Guilty' Jury Instructions Violate the Sixth Amendment." *Judicature* 91: 12–19.

Eisenberg, Theodore, Paula Hannaford-Agor, Valarie Hans, Nicole Mott, G. Thomas Munsterman, Stewart Schwab, and Martin Wells. 2004. "Judge-Jury Agreement in Criminal Cases: A Partial Replication of Kalven and Zeisel's *The American Jury.*" *Journal of Empirical Legal Studies* 2: 171–207.

Eisenstein, James, and Herbert Jacob. 1977. *Felony Justice: An Organizational Analysis of Criminal Courts*. Boston: Little, Brown.

Ellwork, Amiram, Bruce Sales, and James Alfini. 1982. *Making Jury Instructions Understandable*. Charlottesville, Va.: Michie.

Equal Justice Initiative. 2010. "Race and Jury Selection". http://www.eji.org/eji/raceandpoverty/juryselection viewed February 21, 2011.

Fisher, Jim. 2008. *Forensics Under Fire: Are Bad Science and Dueling Experts Corrupting Criminal Justice?* New Brunswick, NJ: Rutgers University Press.

Ford, Marilyn. 1986. "The Role of Extralegal Factors in Jury Verdicts." *Justice System Journal* 11: 16–39.

Frank, Jerome. 1949. *Courts on Trial: Myth and Reality in American Justice*. New York: Princeton University Press.

Frasca, Ralph. 1988. "Estimating the Occurrence of Trials Prejudiced by Press Coverage." *Judicature* 72: 162–169.

Galanter, Marc. 2004. "The Vanishing Trial: An Examination of Trials and Related Matters in Federal and State Courts." *Journal of Empirical Legal Studies* 1: 459.

Galiber, Joseph, Barry Latzer, Mark Dwyer, Jack Litman, H. Richard Uviller, and G. Roger McDonald. 1993. "Law, Justice, and Jury Nullification: A Debate." *Criminal Law Bulletin*: 29: 40–69.

Garrett, Brandon L. 2008. "Judging Innocence." *Columbia Law Review* 108: 55–142.

Garvey, Stephen P., Paula Hannaford-Agor, Valerie P. Hans, Nicole L. Mott, G. Thomas Munsterman, and Martin T. Wells. 2004. "Juror First Votes in Criminal Trials in Four Major Metropolitan Jurisdictions." *Journal of Empirical Legal Studies* 1: 371–398.

"Getting Out of Jury Duty Is a National Pastime." 2007. CNN, July 30.

Givelber, Daniel, and Amy Farrell. 2008. "Judges and Juries: The Defense Case and Differences in Acquittal Rates." *Law and Social Inquiry* 33: 31–52.

Gollner, Philipp. 1995. "Consulting by Peering Into Minds of Jurors." *New York Times*, January 7, p. A25.

Hafemeister, Thomas, and W. Larry Ventis. 1992. "Juror Stress: What Burden Have We Placed on Our Juries?" *State Court Journal* 16: 35–46.

Hannaford, Paula. 2001. "Safeguarding Juror Privacy: A New Framework for Court Policies and Procedures." *Judicature* 85:18–25.

Hannaford-Agor, Paula, Valerie Hans, Nicole Mott, and G. Thomas Munsterman. 2002. *Are Hung Juries a Problem?* Washington: The National Center for State Courts.

Hans, Valerie. 1986. "The Conduct of Voir Dire: A Psychological Analysis." *Justice System Journal* 11: 40–59.

Hastie, Reid, Steven Penrod, and Nancy Pennington. 1984. *Inside the Jury*. Cambridge, Mass.: Harvard University Press.

Horowitz, Irwin A. and Kenneth S. Bordens. 2002. "The Effects of Jury Size, Evidence Complexity, and Note Taking on Jury Process and Performance in a Civil Trial." *Journal of Applied Psychology* 87: 121–130.

Horowitz, Irwin A., Norbert L. Kerr, Ernest S. Park, and Christine Gockel. 2006. "Chaos in The Courtroom Reconsidered: Emotional Bias and Juror Nullification." *Law and Human Behavior* 30: 163–181.

James, Rita. 1958. "Status and Competence of Jurors." *American Journal of Sociology* 69: 563–570.

Kairys, David, Joseph Kadane, and John Lehorsky. 1977. "Jury Representativeness: A Mandate for Multiple Source Lists." *California Law Review* 65: 776–827.

Kalven, Harry, and Hans Zeisel. 1966. *The American Jury*. Boston: Little, Brown.

Kasunic, David. 1983. "One Day/One Trial: A Major Improvement in the Jury System." *Judicature* 67: 78–86.

Kislov, Aleksandra. 1998. "Juries on Trial." *World Press Review* 46: 45.

Kolesnikov, Andrei. 2006. "Is Russia Ready for Jury Trials?" Available online at cnn.com. Retrieved October 23, 2007.

Landsman, Stephen. 2005 "In Defense of the Jury of 12 and the Unanimous Decision Rule." *Judicature* 88: 301–305.

Levine, James. 1983. "Using Jury Verdict Forecasts in Criminal Defense Strategy." *Judicature* 66: 448–461.

———. 1992. *Juries and Politics*. Pacific Grove, Calif.: Brooks/Cole.

Liptak, Adam. 2007. "Cases Keep Flowing In, but the Jury Pool Is Idle." *New York Times*, April 30.

Matthews, Owen. 2011. "Legal Nihilism Continues in Russia." *Newsweek* January 10–17, p. 5.

McCord, David. 2005. "Juries Should Not Be Required to Have 12 Members or to Render Unanimous Verdicts." *Judicature* 88: 301–305.

Mitchell, Tara L., Ryann M. Haw, Jeffrey E. Pfeifer, and Christian A. Meissner. 2005. "Racial Bias in Mock Juror Decision-Making: A Meta-Analytic Review of Defendant Treatment." *Law and Human Behavior* 29: 621–637.

Moley, Raymond. 1928. "The Vanishing Jury." *Southern California Law Review* 2: 97.

Moran, Gary, and Brian Cutler. 1991. "The Prejudicial Impact of Pretrial Publicity." *Journal of Applied Social Psychology* 21: 345–367.

Munsterman, G. Thomas, and Janice Munsterman. 1986. "The Search for Jury Representativeness." *Justice System Journal* 11: 59–78.

Nelson, Mark. 2010. *Making Sense of DNA Backlogs— Myths vs. Reality*. Washington, DC: National Institute of Justice.

Neubauer, David. 1974. *Criminal Justice in Middle America*. Morristown, N.J.: General Learning Press.

Neufeld, Peter J. 2005. "The (Near) Irrelevance of *Daubert* to Criminal Justice and Some Suggestions for Reform." *American Journal of Public Health* 95: S107–S113.

Nikiforov, Ilya. 1995. "Russia." *The World Factbook of Criminal Justice Systems: Russia*. Washington, D.C.: U.S. Department of Justice, Bureau of Justice Statistics. Available online at http://www.ojp.usdog.gov/bjs.

O'Rourke, P. J. 2000. "The Godfather Decade." *Foreign Policy* (November): 74.

Ogloff, James and V. Gordon Rose. 2007. "The Comprehension of Jury Instructions." In Neil Brewer and Kipling Williams. *Psychology and Law: An Empirical Perspective*. New York: The Guildford Press.

Pabst, William. 1973. "What Do Six-Member Juries Really Save?" *Judicature* 57: 6.

Padawer-Singer, Alice, and Allen Barton. 1975. "The Impact of Pretrial Publicity on Jurors' Verdicts." In *The Jury System in America: A Critical Overview*, edited by Rita James Simon. Newbury Park, Calif.: Sage.

Parfitt, Tom (27 December 2010). "WikiLeaks: Rule of Law in Mikhail Khodorkovsky Trial Merely 'Gloss.'" London: The Guardian.

"Path to Reform, The—or Another Dead End?" 2001. *The Economist*, June 2, p. 1.

Reskin, Barbara, and Christine Visher. 1986. "The Impacts of Evidence and Extralegal Factors in Jurors' Decisions." *Law and Society Review* 20: 423–439.

Roper, Robert. 1979. "Jury Size: Impact on Verdict's Correctness." *American Politics Quarterly* 7: 438–452.

———. 1980. "Jury Size and Verdict Consistency: 'A Line Has to Be Drawn Somewhere'?" *Law and Society Review* 14: 972–995.

———. 1986. "A Typology of Jury Research and Discussion of the Structural Correlates of Jury Decisionmaking." *Justice System Journal* 11: 5.

Roper, Robert, and Victor Flango. 1983. "Trials Before Judge and Juries." *Justice System Journal* 8: 186–198.

Roper, Robert, and Joanne Martin. 1986. "Jury Verdicts and the 'Crisis' in Civil Justice: Some Findings from an Empirical Study." *Justice System Journal* 13: 321.

Rudnev, Valery. 1995. "Jurors Are Not 'Softhearted Old Uncles.'" *Current Digest of the Post-Soviet Press* 47 (12): 11.

Saks, Michael. 1996. "The Smaller the Jury, the Greater the Unpredictability." *Judicature* 79: 263–265.

Severance, Lawrence, and Elizabeth Loftus. 1982. "Improving the Ability of Jurors to Comprehend and Apply Criminal Jury Instructions." *Law and Society Review* 17: 153–198.

Simon, Rita James. 1967. *The Jury and the Defense of Insanity*. Boston: Little, Brown.

Simon, Rita James, and Prentice Marshall. 1972. "The Jury System." In *The Rights of the Accused in Law and Action*, edited by Stuart Nagel. Newbury Park, Calif.: Sage.

Smith, Alisa, and Michael J. Saks. "The Case for Overturning *Williams v. Florida* and The Six-Person Jury: History, Law, and Empirical Evidence." *Florida Law Review* 60 (2008): 441–470.

Steele, Walter, and Elizabeth Thornburg. 1991. "Jury Instructions: A Persistent Failure to Communicate." *Judicature* 74: 249–254.

Strawn, David, and Raymond Buchanan. 1976. "Jury Confusion: A Threat to Justice." *Judicature* 59: 478–483.

Strodtbeck, F., Rita James, and C. Hawkins. 1957. "Social Status in Jury Deliberations." *American Sociological Review* 22: 713–719.

Studebaker, Christina, and Steven Penrod. 2007. "Pretrial Publicity and Its Influence on Juror Decision Making." In Neil Brewer and Kipling Williams. *Psychology and Law: An Empirical Perspective*. New York: The Guilford Press.

Thaman, Stephen C. 1999. "Europe's New Jury System: The Cases of Spain and Russia." *Law and Contemporary Problems* 62: 233–259.

Trochev, Alexei. 2008. *Judging Russia: Constitutional Court in Russian Politics (1990-2006)*. Cambridge: Cambridge University Press.

Van Dyke, Jon. 1977. *Jury Selection Procedures: Our Uncertain Commitment to Representative Panels*. Cambridge, Mass.: Ballinger.

Vidmar, Neil, Sara Sun Beale, Mary Rose, and Laura Donnelly. 1997. "Should We Rush to Reform the Criminal Jury?" *Judicature* 80: 286–290.

White, Gregory. 2005. "Khodorkovsky Gets 9-Year Sentence." *Wall Street Journal*, June 1.

Young, William. 2006. "Vanishing Trials, Vanishing Juries, Vanishing Constitution." *Suffolk University Law Review* 40: 67.

Zeisel, Hans. 1982. "The Verdict of Five Out of Six Civil Jurors: Constitutional Problems." *American Bar Foundation Research Journal* (Winter): 141–156.

Zeisel, Hans, and Shari Diamond. 1974. "Convincing Empirical Evidence on the Six Member Jury." *University of Chicago Law Review* 41: 281–295.

FOR FURTHER READING

American Jury Project. 2005. *Principles for Juries and Jury Trials*. Chicago: American Bar Association.

Antonio, Michael E. 2006. "'I Didn't Know It'd Be So Hard': Jurors' Emotional Reactions to Serving on a Capital Trial." *Judicature* 89: 282–288.

Baird, Vanessa, and Debra Javeline. 2007. "The Persuasive Power of Russian Courts." *Political Research Quarterly* 60: 429–442.

Clarke, George. 2008. *Justice and Science: Trials and Triumphs of DNA Evidence*. Rutgers University Press.

Cornwell, Erin York. 2010. "Opening and Closing the Jury Door: A Sociohistorical Consideration of the 1955 Chicago Jury Project Scandal." *Justice System Journal* 31:49–72.

Dann, Michael, Valerie Hans, and David Kaye. 2007. "Can Jury Trial Innovations Improve Juror Understanding of DNA Evidence?" *Judicature* 90: 152–156.

Feigenson, Neal. 2000. *Legal Blame: How Jurors Think and Talk About Accidents*. Washington, D.C.: American Psychological Association.

Foglesong, Todd, and Peter Solomon. 2001. *Crime, Criminal Justice, and Criminology in Post-Soviet Ukraine*. Washington, D.C.: U.S. Department of Justice, National Institute of Justice, Office of Justice Programs.

Jonakait, Randolph. 2004. *The American Jury System*. New Haven, Conn.: Yale University Press.

Levine, James, and Steven Zeidman. 2005. "The Miracle of Jury Reform in New York." *Judicature* 88: 178–184.

Lucci, Eugene A. 2005. "The Case for Allowing Jurors to Submit Written Questions." *Judicature* 89: 16–19.

Neff, James. 2002. *The Wrong Man: The Final Verdict on the Dr. Sam Sheppard Case*. New York: Random House.

Oldham, James. 2006. *Trial by Jury: The Seventh Amendment and Anglo-American Special Juries*. New York: New York University Press.

Pole, J.R. 2010. *Contract and Consent: Representation and the Jury in Anglo-American Legal History*. Charlottesville, VA: University of Virginia Press.

Solomon, Peter, and Todd Foglesong. 2000. *Courts and Transition in Russia: The Challenge of Judicial Reform*. Boulder, Colo.: Westview Press.

Vidmar, Neil, James Coleman, Jr., and Theresa Newman. 2010. "Rethinking Reliance on Eyewitness Confidence." *Judicature* 94: 16–19.

"Vanishing Trial, The." 2004. (special issue) *Empirical Legal Studies* 1: 459–984.

THE APPELLATE PROCESS

Built in the classical style, the Tenth Circuit Court of Appeals in Denver, Colorado, was once a post office and home to the Pony Express. Today, courts of appeals like this one are the principal policy makers in the federal courts.

David Neubauer

Betty Anne Waters never doubted her brother's innocence. The high school dropout went back to school and worked her way through law school to work for his release. After nearly twenty years, her efforts paid off when she found a box of evidence sitting in the basement of the courthouse with Kenneth Waters's name on it. DNA tests showed that he was not the murderer, and he was released from prison. Kenneth Waters died shortly after being released from prison in 2001 and the film *Conviction* starring Hillary Swank tells his story.

The freeing of Kenneth Waters and other innocents on death row illustrates the important role appellate courts perform in the U.S. judicial system. Some cases involve correcting errors; others involve policy making. Although the American public now routinely think of the U.S. Supreme Court as an important policy-making institution (whose decisions are either roundly cheered or venomously denounced, depending on one's point of view), other appellate courts—both state and federal—are also important decision makers in U.S. government.

This chapter examines the appellate court process in the states and in the U.S. courts of appeals, first by discussing the nature of the appellate process and appellate court procedure. Attention then turns to the appellate courts' examination of litigants' cases, procedural attempts to respond to growing caseloads, and substantive efforts to reduce the volume of appellate filings. The explosive growth in appellate court caseloads will be explored, along with the resulting adoption of expedited processing techniques. Although many appellate court cases are of interest only to the immediate parties, some have much broader implications. Thus, the policy-making role of state supreme courts will be examined. Finally, the chapter discusses how multijudge appellate courts make decisions, focusing on concepts that political scientists have used to identify factors (other than legal criteria) that affect judicial discretion.

This chapter has two substantive themes. One is the contentious issue of gay marriage. We will examine the impact of a state supreme court opinion finding a basis for gay marriage in that state and also focus on Canada, where the courts have made similar rulings. The other theme is innocents on death row. We will examine the debate over this issue, and we will probe the movie *The Hurricane*, which presents one such case.

THE NATURE OF THE APPELLATE PROCESS

Appellate review represents the last decision point in the judicial process. **Appellate courts** subject the action of the first court to a second look, examining not a raw dispute as it is being presented but, rather, a controversy that has already been packaged and decided in a trial court proceeding. Thus, appellate courts provide a degree of detachment and the opportunity for reflection by a group of judges. In essence, the decisions of a single judge are subjected to review by a panel of judges who are removed from the heat engendered by the trial and, consequently, are in a position to take a more objective view of the questions raised. As such, appellate review lends legitimacy to the adjudicative process. By providing the loser at trial with the prospect of a second look, appellate courts hold out the possibility that the result will differ after a group of judges scrutinizes the matter.

Of the millions of cases decided each year by trial courts, only a few are ever reviewed by higher courts. But the relative handful of cases decided by appellate courts are critically important for the entire judicial process. Institutionally, appellate courts integrate a diverse judiciary marked by local control and a strong sense of independence. Thus, through opinion writing, appellate courts strive to achieve uniformity in the law of the jurisdiction. Whereas decisions of trial court judges are binding only on that judge, decisions of appellate court judges are binding on all judges within the jurisdiction.

One of the few aspects of the U.S. judicial process about which there is a consensus is that every loser in a trial court should have a right to **appeal** to a higher court. Appellate courts were created partly in the belief that several heads are better than one. Thus, appellate courts operate as multimember or collegial bodies with decisions made by a group of judges. The group may be composed of as few as three or as many as twenty-eight judges (as in the U.S. Ninth Circuit Court of Appeals). On courts of last resort, all judges typically participate in all cases. On intermediate appellate courts, on the other hand, decisions are typically made by rotating three-judge panels. In important cases, however, all judges may participate; this is termed an *en banc hearing* (Giles, Walker, and Zorn 2006; Smith 1990). To unravel the complexities of the review process, we begin by discussing the purposes and the scope of appeal.

The Purposes of Appeal

The most obvious function of appellate courts is **error** correction. During trial, judges engage in a significant amount of spur-of-the-moment decision making. As one trial judge phrased it, "We're where the action is. We often have to 'shoot from the hip' and hope you're doing the right thing. You can't ruminate forever every time you have to make a ruling. We'd be spending months on each case if we ever did that" (Carp and Stidham 1996, 292). As reviewing bodies, appellate courts oversee the work of the lower courts, ensuring that the law was correctly interpreted and applied. Thus, the error correction function of appellate review protects against arbitrary, capricious, or mistaken decisions by a trial court judge. (See Law and Popular Culture: *The Hurricane*.)

The other primary function of appellate courts is policy formulation, sometimes referred to as the "lawmaking function." Policy formulation occurs when appellate courts fill in the gaps in existing law, clarify old doctrines, offer new interpretations of current law, and, on occasion, even overrule previous decisions. It is through policy formulation that appellate courts shape the law in response to changing conditions in society. Stated another way, error correction is concerned primarily with the effect of the judicial process on the individual litigants, whereas policy formulation considers the impact of the appellate court decision on other cases.

Scope of Appellate Review

A basic principle of U.S. law is that the losing party has the right to one appeal. Nonetheless, the scope of appellate review is subject to several important limits and exceptions. Only parties who have lost in the lower court may file appeals. But prosecutors may not appeal not-guilty findings. The Fifth Amendment states: "nor shall any person be subject for the same offense to be twice put in jeopardy of life or limb." That provision protects citizens from **double jeopardy** (a second prosecution of the same person for the same crime by the same sovereign after the first trial). Double jeopardy prevents repeated harassment of an accused person and reduces the danger of convicting an innocent one. Thus, once a not-guilty verdict is returned in a criminal case, jeopardy in a legal sense has occurred, and the prosecutor cannot appeal.

LAW AND POPULAR CULTURE

■ *The Hurricane* (1999)

The Hurricane depicts the roller-coaster life of Rubin "Hurricane" Carter, who went from being the top middleweight boxing contender to serving a life sentence in prison. The hit movie offers an uplifting story of Carter's 20-year battle to be released from prison for the triple murders he contended he never committed. While in prison, Carter (played by Denzel Washington) wrote his autobiography, *The Sixteenth Round,* in which he stated he had found inner peace by withdrawal. His plight was immortalized in the Bob Dylan song "Hurricane."

Separating fact from fiction is difficult, but this much is known. Early on the morning of June 17, 1967, two African-American men walked into the Lafayette Bar in Paterson, New Jersey, and opened fire, killing the bartender and two patrons. The police quickly focused on Paterson's most famous (some would say infamous) citizen, Rubin Carter. *The Hurricane* is set against national racial unrest; the summer of 1967 was a time of continued racial tension. Only one year before, the Watts neighborhood of Los Angeles had exploded in riots when a white police officer beat an African-American cab driver. The year 1967 saw the Newark Rebellion. In the movie, racial animosity is embodied by fictional police officer Della Pesca, depicted as a corrupt racist who has been persecuting Rubin Carter for years. The movie portrays the cops framing Carter by using as key witnesses two men who were burglarizing a nearby factory. According to the movie, the two were promised freedom if they testified against Carter.

The movie has been criticized for seriously distorting reality. Selwyn Raab (1999), who covered the trial for the *New York Times*, writes that the movie "presents a false vision of the legal battles." Filmmakers, of course, have always taken dramatic license, simplifying history, creating fictional characters, and rearranging events for narrative purposes. But, even by filmmakers' standards, *The Hurricane* stretches the truth more than most. One contortion involves who worked to free Carter. The movie depicts a secretive Canadian commune that befriended Carter and worked to free him (obviously suggesting that the legal system was conspiring to keep

him falsely in prison). In reality, all the evidence about constitutional violations, prosecutorial misconduct, and manipulated witnesses was uncovered by defense lawyers (often working without a fee).

In addition, the movie confusingly compresses the two trials into one brief courtroom sentencing scene. In fact, during the first trial, the two white burglars placed Carter and his accomplice at the scene of the crime. A decade later, that conviction was overturned in state court because the prosecution had failed to disclose that the two witnesses had been promised dismissals of their burglary charges if they testified. Carter was tried and convicted a second time. This time the prosecution argued that Carter murdered the white tavern owner in retaliation for an earlier murder of an African-American bar owner. Almost another decade passed before a federal judge ruled that the prosecution had "fatally infected the trial" by arguing, without proof, a motive of racial onus.

Although he was released from prison in 1985, Rubin "Hurricane" Carter is still fighting to clear his name. In a recent book, *The Eye of the Hurricane* (Carter and Klonsky 2011) he concedes guilt to a host of regrettable crimes, including assaults and robberies but not murders, because of anger in growing up in a segregated world.

As you watch this movie, ask yourself the following questions:

1. How has the law regarding the rights of criminal defendants changed since Carter's original trial in 1967? On the basis of the movie, would these changes have affected the outcome of the original trial?

2. What if Carter had sought to review his conviction after the passage of the Anti-Terrorism and Effective Death Penalty Act of 1996? Would Carter have won his freedom or remained in prison?

The official website for *The Hurricane* can be found at http://www.the-hurricane.com.

Appeals are also discretionary; that is, the losing party is not required to seek appellate court review. The lone exception involves capital punishment cases: When a jury imposes a sentence of death, the case must be appealed regardless of the defendant's wishes. Typically, this automatic review is heard directly by the state supreme court, thus bypassing any intermediate courts of appeals. Capital punishment cases aside, appeal is discretionary in all civil and criminal cases.

There are also limits on when cases may be appealed. Typically, the losing party may appeal only from a final judgment of the lower court. In that context, a judgment is considered final when it ends the action in the court in which it was brought and nothing more is to be decided. For example, after a jury finds the defendant guilty and the judge imposes sentence, the work of the trial court is complete. In very limited situations, however, litigants may appeal **interlocutory** (nonfinal) orders. Prosecutors, for example, may file an interlocutory appeal on certain pretrial rulings that substantially hinder the state's ability to proceed to trial (suppression of evidence, for example).

Appeals are also restricted to questions of law; findings of fact are not appealable (except in one or two states). Because appellate courts have not been directly exposed to the evidence, they are reluctant to second-guess findings of fact made by lower tribunals. Thus, appellate courts hear no new testimony and consider no new evidence. Rather, they focus on how decisions were made in the trial court, basing their review on the appellate court record. Questions of law that are commonly raised on appeal include defects in jury selection, improper admission of evidence during the trial, and erroneous statements of the law in the judge's instructions to the jury. In criminal appeals, the appellant may also claim violations of constitutional rights such as illegal search and seizure or improper questioning of the defendant by the police.

Appeals are also confined to issues properly raised in the trial court. Recall from Chapter 12 that, during trial, attorneys must make timely objections to the judge's rulings on points of law. When an attorney makes such an objection and the trial judge overrules it, their disagreement over that point of law has been preserved in the trial record for appeal.

Finally, the right to appeal is limited to a single appeal, within which all appealable issues must be raised. Intermediate courts of appeals hear appeals from U.S. district courts and most appeals from state courts of general jurisdiction (Chapter 4). In the less populous states that do not have intermediate appellate bodies, the initial appeal is filed with the court of last resort (see Table 13.1). These courts have **mandatory jurisdiction**; that is, they must hear all properly filed appeals. After the first reviewing body has reached a decision, however, the right to one appeal has been exhausted. The party losing the appeal may request that a higher court review the case again, but such appeals are discretionary; the higher court does not have to hear the appeal. The U.S. Supreme Court and most state supreme courts largely have **discretionary jurisdiction**; that is, they can pick and choose the cases they will hear. Most appeals are decided by intermediate courts of appeals and are never heard by state or national supreme courts.

TABLE 13.1	State Appellate Court Structures		
Court of Last Resort Only	**Court of Last Resort and One Intermediate Appellate Court**	**One Court of Last Resort and Two Intermediate Appellate Courts**	**Two Courts of Last Resort and One Intermediate Appellate Court**
Delaware	Alaska	Alabama	Oklahoma[a]
District of Columbia	Arizona	New York	Texas
Maine	Arkansas	Pennsylvania	
Montana	California	Tennessee	
Nevada	Colorado		
New Hampshire	Connecticut		
Rhode Island	Florida		
South Dakota	Georgia		
Vermont	Hawaii[a]		
West Virginia	Idaho[a]		
Wyoming	Illinois		
	Indiana		
	Iowa[a]		
	Kansas		
	Kentucky		
	Louisiana		
	Maryland		
	Massachusetts		
	Michigan		
	Minnesota		
	Mississippi		
	Missouri		
	Nebraska		
	New Jersey		
	New Mexico		
	North Carolina		
	North Dakota[a]		
	Ohio		
	Oregon		
	South Carolina[a]		
	Utah		
	Virginia		
	Washington		
	Wisconsin		

[a]Court of last resort assigns cases to intermediate appellate court.
Source: Data from David Rottman, Carol Flango, Melissa Cantrell, Randall Hansen, and Neil LaFountain, *State Court Organization 1998* (Williamsburg, Va.: National Center for State Courts, 2000). Used with permission.

APPELLATE COURT PROCEDURES

The details of appellate court procedures vary among the nation's 51 legal systems. Nonetheless, each judicial system employs the same language (see Table 13.2) and generally follows these six steps (Meador 1974).

Launching the Appeal   An appeal does not follow automatically from an adverse trial court judgment. Rather, the **appellant** (the losing party in the lower court) must take affirmative action to set an appeal in motion. The first step consists of filing a notice of appeal. Rules of appellate procedure fix a precise time—usually 30 or 60 days—within which this short written statement must be filed.

Preparing and Transmitting the Record   The appellate court record consists of the materials that go forward to the appellate court. Many of those items (for example, papers and exhibits) are already in the case file. A major item not in the clerk's office is the transcript of the testimony given at the trial. To include that in the record, the court reporter prepares a typewritten copy and files it with the court.

TABLE 13.2	Steps of Criminal Procedure: Appeal and Postconviction Remedies	
	Law on the Books	**Law in Action**
Appeal	Legal challenge to a decision by a lower court.	Virtually certain if the defendant is convicted at trial.
Mandatory	Appellate court must hear the case.	Many appeals are "routine," which means they have little likelihood of succeeding.
Discretionary	Appellate court may accept or reject.	Appellate courts hear a very small percentage of discretionary appeal cases.
Notice of appeal	Written statement notifying the court that the defendant plans to appeal.	Standards for indigent defenders mandate that an appeal must be filed.
Appellate court record	The transcript of the trial, along with relevant court documents.	Some appellate courts prefer a focused record of contested matters, whereas others want the entire record.
Briefing the case	Written statement submitted by the attorney arguing a case in court.	Defense lawyers make numerous arguments in hopes that one will be successful.
Oral argument	Lawyers for both sides argue their cases before appellate court justices, who have the opportunity to question lawyers.	Judges often complain that they learn little during oral argument. To expedite decision making, some courts limit oral argument to select cases.
Written opinion	Reasons given by appellate courts for the results they have reached.	Only appellate court opinions are considered precedent.
Disposition		
Affirmed	Appellate court decision that agrees with the lower-court decision.	Seven out of eight criminal appeals are affirmed.
Remanded	Case is sent back to the lower court for a hearing on a specific issue.	Often, an indication that the appellate court is troubled by the judge's action but doesn't wish to reverse.
Reversed	The lower-court decision is set aside, and further proceedings may be held.	Defendants are very often remanded and reconvicted following retrial.

Typically, the transcript contains the entire trial proceedings, although some reviewing bodies will request only the portions of the lower-court proceedings that are at issue.

Writing and Filing Briefs   A **brief** is a written argument that sets forth the party's view of the facts of the case, the issues raised on appeal, and the precedents supporting the party's position. First to be filed is the appellant's brief, which lists alleged errors on questions of law that were made at trial. Next, the winning party in the lower court (termed the **appellee** or the **respondent**) files a brief setting forth arguments supporting the decision of the lower court. The appellant then has the option of filing a reply brief.

Oral Argument   The lawyers for both parties are allotted a limited time to argue their side of the case before the appellate court panel. The appellant's argument, for example, briefly discusses the facts of the case, traces its history through the lower courts, and presents legal arguments for considering the lower court's decision to be erroneous. **Oral argument** provides the opportunity for face-to-face contact between judges and lawyers, during which judges typically ask questions about particular issues in the case.

Writing the Opinion   After the case has been argued, the court recesses to engage in group deliberations. Decisions are made in private conference; one judge in the majority is assigned to write the **opinion**, which summarizes the facts of the case and discusses the legal issues raised on appeal. If the case is an easy one, the opinion may be short, perhaps no more than a page or two. But if the legal issues are complex, the court's opinion may run into dozens of pages. Some cases involve such a number of conflicting legal issues that the judges do not agree among themselves on the correct answer. Judges who disagree with the majority often write **dissenting opinions** explaining why they believe their fellow judges reached the wrong conclusions.

Disposing of the Case   The court's opinion ends with a disposition of the case. The appellate court may **affirm** (uphold) the lower-court judgment, the court may **modify** the lower-court ruling by changing it in part but not totally reversing it, or the court may **reverse** (set aside) the previous decision with no further court action required. A disposition of reversed and remanded means the decision of the lower court is overturned and the case is sent back to the lower court for further procedures, which may range from holding a hearing to conducting a new trial. Finally, the appeals court may **remand** the case to the lower court with instructions for further proceedings.

Appellate courts modify, reverse, remand, or reverse and remand only if they find error, a mistake made by a judge in the procedures used at trial or in the legal rulings during the trial. If the error is substantial, it is called **reversible error** by the higher court. If it is trivial, it is called **harmless error** (Traynor 1970). Thus, the appellate court may find error but affirm the lower court, anyway.

THE BUSINESS OF THE APPELLATE COURTS

A diverse array of matters are brought to appellate courts for review. A handful have never been heard by trial courts. Appeals from some administrative agencies go directly to appellate courts (Sheehan 1993). The U.S. courts of appeals, for example, hear appeals from federal administrative agencies such as the National Labor Relations Board (NLRB), the Immigration and Naturalization Service (INS), and the Occupational Safety and Health Administration (OSHA). Similarly, state supreme courts possess **original jurisdiction** over a small number of matters, such as disciplining errant judges and disbarring lawyers. Those exceptions aside, the cases heard by appellate courts involve their **appellate jurisdiction** (the review of cases already decided by a trial court). The business of appellate courts differs in important ways, however, from the cases heard in the trial courts.

The bulk of trial court filings are never appealed, because the parties reach a mutually agreeable, voluntary settlement. Moreover, not all cases that are appeal eligible (that is, the judgment is contested in the lower court) are actually appealed. As a result, only a very small percentage of state trial court cases are reviewed by higher courts. In short, appellate court cases are unrepresentative of trial court cases. Appellate court cases, for example, consist principally of cases that were decided by trial. The uneven flow of cases from trial courts to reviewing bodies is best explored by examining civil and criminal appeals.

Civil Appeals

Who appeals and why is an important topic in discussions of the politics of legal mobilization (Zemans 1983). Appeals are discretionary, and some losing parties choose not to pursue the case further. Like decisions to file cases in the trial court, decisions to appeal are based on many factors, but three factors seem to be especially important.

First, decisions to appeal are influenced by how much litigants have lost in the lower court; high-stakes cases are appealed at a higher rate than those involving lesser dollar amounts. Insurance companies, for example, are almost certain to appeal a million-dollar jury award but are less likely to seek appellate court review when the jury awards only $1,000 in damages. Thus, appellate court cases are unrepresentative of trial court filings because large dollar amounts are more likely to be involved.

Second, decisions to appeal are related to the likelihood of success. According to one survey, the most important factor in deciding whether to appeal adverse outcomes in U.S. district courts was the lawyers' perceptions of the likelihood of success (Rathjen 1978). Although the odds of winning on appeal are less than 50–50, the types of cases vary. Thus, the lawyers' gatekeeping role is particularly important in shaping the business of appellate courts; lawyers are most likely to recommend an appeal when they perceive they have a good chance of winning.

Third, decisions to appeal are affected by financial considerations. Appeals are expensive. The appellant must pay a filing fee, compensate a lawyer, bear the expense of preparing the trial court transcript, and pay for printing the brief. Those costs can be extensive—even a simple case can run into thousands of dollars—and clearly deter some litigants from appealing. On the other hand, financial factors encourage some types of appeals. Some say it is cheaper to pursue legal policy change through the courts than through legislation. Moreover, appealing a large trial court award may be part of a strategic attempt to negotiate a postdecision settlement that is less than the lower court's verdict.

Despite those obstacles, a substantial number of civil appeals are filed each year, and the numbers are increasing. In the U.S. courts of appeals, the federal government is the prime consumer as both appellant and appellee. The business of the courts of appeals, once dominated by private economic disputes, now emphasizes cases involving governmental activity. Indeed, in half of these matters, the U.S. government is a direct party.

The mix of cases heard by state appellate bodies differs from that heard by their federal counterparts. Torts, family law, estates, real property, and contracts take center stage. Here, private parties (both individuals and businesses) are the prime consumers, and governmental bodies appear less frequently.

Data from the federal courts indicate that civil appellants are more successful than those appealing criminal convictions. In a typical year, only 6 percent of federal criminal appeals are reversed, compared with 12 percent for all appeals (Scalia 2001).

Outcomes of civil appeals have been investigated in terms of Galanter's (1974) distinction between "haves and have-nots" (Chapter 7). A study of 16 state supreme courts from 1870 to 1970 found a general pattern that the "haves" come out ahead (Wheeler et al. 1987). Similarly, the relative advantage of parties with superior litigation resources was modest (Wheeler et al. 1987). Also, research on three of the federal courts of appeals concluded that the parties with superior litigation resources fared better than their weaker opponents (Songer and Sheehan 1992).

Criminal Appeals

For decades, most defendants found guilty by judge or jury did not file an appeal, because they could not afford the expense of hiring a lawyer. That pattern changed significantly in the early 1960s. A series of Warren Court decisions, based on the Equal Protection Clause of the Fourteenth Amendment, held that economically impoverished defendants cannot be barred from effective appellate review. Indigent defendants, therefore, are entitled to a free trial court transcript (*Griffin v. Illinois* 1956) and a court-appointed lawyer (*Douglas v. California* 1963). (Indigents, however, are not normally provided free legal service to pursue discretionary appeals.) As a result of those rulings, it is now rare for a convicted defendant not to appeal a trial verdict of guilty. Indeed, indigent defendants have everything to gain and nothing to lose by filing an appeal. For example, if the appeal is successful but the defendant is reconvicted following a new trial, the sentencing judge cannot increase the sentence out of vindictiveness (*North Carolina v. Pearce* 1969; *Texas v. McCullough* 1986).

Besides being enlarged by changes in constitutional standards, the scope of criminal appeals has been affected by a major statutory innovation—sentencing guidelines (Chapter 9)—whose adoption expanded the right to appeal: In many jurisdictions, appellants are no longer limited to contesting their guilt or innocence but may independently challenge the severity of the sentence (Williams 1992, 1995a). Changes in constitutional and statutory standards have resulted in an exponential increase in the number of criminal appeals filed. Whereas criminal appeals composed only 10–15 percent of total appeals before 1963, today they constitute about half of total appellate volume.

Criminal appeals exhibit four key features: First, criminal appeals are relatively homogeneous; by and large, they are drawn from a fairly narrow stratum of the most serious criminal convictions in the trial courts (Davies 1982). For example, more than half the criminal appeals filed in five appellate courts stem from convictions for crimes of violence (homicides and armed robberies, primarily). And, as one would expect from discussions of plea bargaining, these appeals cases typically involve substantial sentences (Chapper and Hanson 1990).

Second, criminal appeals are routine; they seldom raise meritorious issues (that is, they do not raise new or important points of law) (Wold and Caldeira 1980). Current standards for effective assistance of counsel force lawyers to appeal, no matter how slight the odds of appellate court reversal. As a result, a significant number of criminal appeals lack substantial merit. According to one intermediate appellate court judge, "If 90 percent of this stuff were in the United States Post Office, it would be classified as junk mail" (Wold 1978).

Third, criminal appeals are rarely successful; appellate courts often find no reversible error in the trial court proceedings. Thus, the vast majority of criminal appeals affirm the conviction. Roughly speaking, defendants win on appeal only one out of eight times. Further, a closer look indicates that some appellate court reversals produce only minor victories for some criminal defendants. For example, some "reversals" produce a modification but do not otherwise disturb the conviction (Neubauer 1992). Moreover, if the appellate court reverses and remands the case to the lower court for a new trial, half of the defendants are convicted a second time (Roper and Melone 1981). Thus, although the public perceives that many criminals are freed on technicalities, in reality, appellate court reversals are relatively rare. Moreover, private attorneys are no more successful on appeal than court-appointed attorneys (Williams 1995b).

Fourth, the handful of criminal defendants who are successful on appeal are likely to involve the least serious offenses and offenders. In Louisiana, appellants convicted of nonviolent offenses in which a relatively light sentence was imposed are the most likely to win on appeal. Conversely, appellants convicted of violent crimes and sentenced to long prison terms are least likely to gain a reversal. A close reading of the opinions showed that, in serious cases, the judges strained to find a way not to reverse even if error was present (Neubauer 1992, 1991).

CASELOADS AND EXPEDITED PROCESSING TECHNIQUES

After World War II, the judiciary experienced an appellate caseload explosion. Appeals filed in the U.S. courts of appeals skyrocketed, increasing by 705 percent from 1961 to 1983. The state courts exhibited a similar pattern. The number of appeals doubled every decade (Marvell 1989). And considerable evidence shows not only an increase in quantifiable indicators but also a qualitative shift: Appellate cases today are more complex than those filed decades ago (Cohen 2002). Today state appellate courts process nearly 300,000 cases a year (National Center for State Courts 2011). The appellate caseload explosion has prompted fundamental changes in the way appellate courts hear and decide cases. The initial response has been to increase resources available to the appellate courts, and that has been followed by efforts to improve efficiency.

Increasing Resources

For a court of last resort facing a rising and unmanageable caseload, the most drastic relief is the creation of an intermediate court of appeals (Leflar 1976). That approach was adopted for the federal judiciary with the passage of the Court of Appeals Act of 1891 (Chapter 3). Similar responses occurred at the state level. Today, only states with small populations have not created intermediate courts of appeal.

The creation of additional judgeships is another obvious structural response to caseload growth. Thus, during the nineteenth century, most states added two or more judgeships to their state supreme courts. More recently, the size of intermediate appellate courts has increased dramatically, expanding from 184 in 1956 to roughly 1,000 today. The high cost of judgeships makes legislative bodies reluctant to adopt that response, however (Marvell 1989).

Providing judges with additional staff is another response to rising caseloads. Turn-of-the-century appellate judges typically worked alone, but, today, they are assisted by **law clerks**, who are often called "elbow clerks" because they work for individual judges. In addition, many states employ **staff attorneys** who work for the entire court (Douglas 1985). Law clerks and staff attorneys supply information to the judges by analyzing the lawyers' arguments and researching the appellate record and relevant case law. Staff attorneys usually work on cases before the oral argument stage, and their memoranda and draft opinions are circulated to all judges hearing the appeal. Law clerks, on the other hand, often begin work on a case after arguments, and their work products are seldom seen by other judges (Crump 1986).

Logical as it might first appear, increasing resources is not necessarily the solution to the problems of appellate caseload explosion. As capacity increases, so does demand (Flango and Blair 1980). In short, those responses do not provide long-term solutions.

Improving Efficiency

Given the inherent limits of trying to cope with the pressing problem of appellate caseload explosion by increasing resources, appellate courts have engaged in a fundamental re-evaluation of the appellate process in an effort to make more efficient use of existing resources. The guiding premise is that all appellate cases are not the same. At one end of the continuum are cases that are universally considered significant. Judges on the Rhode Island Supreme Court (Beiser 1973) and the U.S. courts of appeals (Howard 1977) estimate that 10 percent of their cases contain the potential for "law-making." At the other end of the continuum are cases that everyone agrees raise no new or important issues. (As discussed previously, most criminal appeals are routine.) These cases are referred to by a variety of terms: routine, easy, hopeless, frivolous, nonmeritorious, or repetitious (Davies 1981; Wold and Caldeira 1980). Expedited processing techniques concentrate the scarce commodity of judicial time on the appeals that raise truly meritorious issues.

Elimination of oral argument is one type of truncated procedure. A number of judges view oral arguments as not particularly helpful in deciding routine cases. Thus, some courts have eliminated oral argument altogether in straightforward cases.

Summary affirmations are another type of truncated appellate court procedure. Opinion preparation consumes more of the appellate judge's time than any other activity, and, for that reason, the opinion-writing process is a prime candidate for increasing the efficiency of appellate courts (Neubauer 1985). In a summary judgment, the court affirms the decision of the lower court without providing a written opinion and often without granting oral argument (Green and Keyes 1986).

Unpublished opinions are a third type of truncated appellate court procedure. The litigants are given written reasons for the decision reached, but the opinion is not published and, therefore, may not be cited as precedent. Unpublished opinions save considerable judicial time, because unpublished opinions need not be as polished as published opinions. Moreover, unpublished opinions reduce the proliferation of case law that judges and lawyers must research (Braun 2000).

The rehearing settlement conference is another much-discussed innovation designed to reduce judges' workloads and to expand their available time. Opposing counsel meets with a judge or a staff attorney mainly for the purpose of settling a case before the court considers the appeal. The conferences are said to foster settlement because a respected and competent mediator can find middle ground between parties who may be reluctant to initiate settlement discussions on their own for fear of damaging their bargaining position.

In recent years, considerable public attention has shifted toward another way of dealing with appellate caseload explosion—limiting multiple appeals by prisoners.

Postconviction Remedies

After the appellate process has been exhausted, state as well as federal prisoners may challenge their convictions in state and federal courts on certain limited grounds. These postconviction remedies are termed **collateral attacks** because they are attempts to avoid the effects of a court decision by bringing a different court proceeding. **Postconviction remedies** differ from appeals in several important ways. First, they may be filed only by those actually in prison. Second, they may raise only constitutional defects, not technical ones. Third, they may be somewhat broader than appeals. Whereas appeals are limited to objections made by the defense during the trial, postconviction petitions can bring up issues not raised during trial and assert constitutional protections that have developed since the original trial. Finally, postconviction remedies are unlimited in number: A prisoner can file numerous petitions at all levels of the court system.

Habeas Corpus Relief

Postconviction remedies are collectively referred to as "habeas corpus relief." **Habeas corpus** (Latin for "you have the body") is a judicial order to someone holding a person to bring that person immediately before the court and is protected by Article I of the U.S. Constitution. The writ of habeas corpus has been described as the "great writ" because it prevents the government from jailing citizens without ever filing charges. Many totalitarian regimes have no such protections; even some Western democracies allow the police to detain a person suspected of a crime for up to a year without formally accusing the person of any wrongdoing.

Supreme Court Expansions and Contractions

Originally, habeas corpus was regarded as an extraordinary means for determining the legality of detention before trial. But the great writ of liberty has undergone considerable transformation in recent decades (Freedman 2003). In 1963, the Warren Court greatly expanded the application of habeas corpus, making it much easier for state prisoners to seek judicial relief in federal courts (*Fay v. Noia* 1963; *Townsend v. Sain* 1963; *Sanders v. United States* 1963). Those decisions opened the floodgate for federal review. The annual number of habeas corpus petitions jumped from 2,000 in 1960 to more than 68,000 in 1996 (Administrative Office 2002). Whether the actual workload of the federal courts increased as rapidly as the number of petitions is an open question. Most decisions are made on the basis of written records; more time-consuming evidentiary hearings are relatively rare. How often prisoners actually win depends on the time period being considered. In 1970, more than 12,000 petitions were granted—an indication that state courts were slowly adopting the new procedural requirements of the Warren Court revolution in criminal justice. By the 1980s, however, prisoners were rarely successful; fewer than 2 percent gained release (Flango 1994).

Warren Court decisions expanding habeas corpus relief were steadily cut back by the Burger Court, which ruled that if state courts provide a fair hearing, federal courts cannot consider Fourth Amendment search-and-seizure questions in habeas corpus proceedings (*Stone v. Powell* 1976). The Rehnquist Court likewise repeatedly tightened restrictions on prisoner petitions, often stressing the finality of state court proceedings (*Butler v. McKeller* 1990; *Saffle v. Parks* 1990; *Keeney v. Tamayo-Reyes* 1992).

Congress Restricts Federal Habeas Corpus

For more than two decades, Congress considered proposed changes in habeas corpus proceedings (Smith 1995). That inconclusive debate was shattered by the Oklahoma City bombing in 1995. Victims were anxious to channel their grief into tangible reform, and one avenue was habeas corpus reform (Gest 1996). Thus, as the 1996 elections loomed, Congress passed the Antiterrorism and Effective Death Penalty Act. In terms of habeas corpus, the act does the following:

- It creates one-year deadlines for filing habeas petitions.
- It limits successive petitions.
- It restricts the review of state prisoner petitions if the claim was adjudicated on the merits in state courts.
- It requires a "certificate of appealability" before a habeas petition may be appealed to a federal court of appeals.

Moving with unusual speed, the Supreme Court agreed to hear a challenge to the new law within two months of passage. During a rare June hearing, the justices expressed skepticism about Congress curtailing the power of the Supreme Court. In the end, a unanimous court held that the law was constitutional (*Felker v. Turpin* 1996).

On the surface, the debate over closing federal courthouses to state prisoners seems to be an argument over the number of cases filed. Prisoner petitions are typically portrayed as frivolous matters. Even though prisoners rarely win (2.8 percent), only 30 percent were dismissed by the courts as frivolous (Fradella 1999). In reality, it is a debate over the fate of death row inmates. Writs of habeas corpus play a particularly important role in capital punishment cases. After exhausting appellate remedies, defendants engage in lengthy challenges to the sentence of death by filing

DEBATING LAW, COURTS, AND POLITICS

■ Innocents on Death Row?

Kenneth Waters could not have murdered Katharina Brow in 1980 because he was in court that morning answering a charge of assaulting a police officer. But authorities were unable to verify his alibi. The jury then convicted Waters of first-degree murder and armed robbery largely on the testimony of two of his ex-girlfriends, who testified that Waters had bragged about the murders and even sold some of the victim's jewelry. Waters steadfastly denied his guilt, and his sister took up his cause. She discovered a box of evidence labeled with her brother's name sitting in the courthouse basement. The box contained the knife used in the murder and pieces of clothing with blood samples still on them. She then enlisted the help of the Innocence Project, which had DNA testing done on the newly discovered evidence. Kenneth Waters was not a match. The prosecutor eventually agreed not to contest a motion for a new trial (Associated Press 2001). The case has been made into a movie titled *Conviction* (2010) staring two-time Oscar winning actress Hilary Swank.

In *Actual Innocence*, Barry Scheck, Peter Neufeld, and Jim Dwyer (2000) cite cases such as that of Kenneth Waters to argue that many convicts are wrongly on death row. According to their most recent estimates, 273 death row inmates have been exonerated (Innocence Project 2011). Similarly, an influential article, "A Broken System: Error Rates in Capital Cases, …" examines 5,760 capital verdicts imposed between 1973 and 1995 (Liebman, Fagan, and West 2000a). The authors report that 68 percent of all verdicts fully reviewed were found to be so seriously flawed that they had to be scrapped and retried. And, where retrials were known, only 18 percent resulted in the reimposition of the death penalty (Liebman, Fagan, and West 2000b). Studies such as those lead liberals to argue that "for every seven people executed in this country since 1976, when the Supreme Court reinstated capital punishment, an eighth person—completely innocent—has been condemned to die and later exonerated" (American Civil Liberties Union 2000).

But not all are convinced that the capital appeals process is broken. Barry Latzer and James Cauthen (2000) argue that the statistical conclusions cited previously are flawed. They distinguish between two types of errors: conviction errors and sentencing errors. Their analysis shows that conviction errors constitute only a small

percentage of appellate court reversals in capital cases. It is sentencing errors, then, that dominate reversals—and this is to be expected, because capital cases receive much closer scrutiny than noncapital appeals. Overall, conservatives argue that the process is working—the few wrong trial court verdicts are indeed identified and corrected on appeal.

In recent years, the debate over innocents on death row has focused on DNA testing. To be sure, some who have been freed from death row or life imprisonment were later found to be innocent because of witnesses who lied at trial. But some have been freed after reexamination of trial evidence using advanced DNA testing techniques that were not available during the original trial. Barry Scheck, for one, argues that all convicts on death row should legally be entitled to have the original evidence retested. In *House v. Bell* (2006) the Supreme Court recognized for the first time the use of DNA evidence in postconviction review of death penalty cases and has extended this overview in some habeas corpus proceedings (*Skinner v. Switzer* 2011). Conservatives quickly counter that calls for retesting are yet another delaying tactic for defendants who were convicted on the basis of overwhelming physical and testimonial evidence.

To date, there has been no conclusive proof that an innocent person has been executed since the death penalty was reinstated in 1976. But that possibility exists, and attention has recently focused on Ruben Cantu, who was convicted of capital murder in San Antonio, Texas, in 1985, largely on the testimony of an eyewitness. Cantu protested his innocence but was executed in 1992. Now the crime's lone witness has recanted and a co-defendant said police pressured him to name Cantu (Olsen 2005). Conclusive evidence that Cantu, or another person, was executed but innocent will likely greatly alter the debate over the death penalty.

What do you think? Does the number of innocent persons released from death row or life imprisonment indicate that the capital appeals process is broken, or that it is actually working as it should? Do you think that all convicts on death row should have the right to have physical evidence retested using more advanced DNA techniques, or should such requests be granted only upon a strong showing that the suspect might indeed be innocent?

multiple writs of habeas corpus in various state and federal courts. The result is a very lengthy review process. Former Chief Justice William Rehnquist criticized his colleagues for providing capital offenders with "numerous procedural protections unheard of for other crimes" and "for allowing endlessly drawn out legal proceedings." Others counter that the death penalty is qualitatively different from other types of sanctions, so multiple scrutiny of such cases is more than justified.

Supporters of the old system stress the need not to short-circuit justice. The argument for keeping the federal courthouse doors open is forcefully stated by former Supreme Court Justice John Paul Stevens, who notes that federal habeas proceedings reveal deficiencies in 60 to 70 percent of the capital cases (*Murray v. Giarratano* 1989). Supporters also argue not only that there should be no rush to judgment but also that death row inmates should have access to legal assistance but often don't. The vast majority of postconviction cases are **pro se**; that is, the prisoner is appearing on his or her own behalf. Recall from Chapter 5 that the Court has held there is no right to counsel after the first appeal has been exhausted. Many death row defendants, for example, must rely on overworked volunteer attorneys.

The long-standing controversy over closing federal courthouse doors to state prisoners has largely been ended, only to be replaced by a different debate: Now attention focuses on innocents on death row. (See Debating Law, Courts, and Politics: Innocents on Death Row?)

DECISION MAKING ON APPELLATE COURTS

Earlier in this chapter, we emphasized the importance of appeals courts. In both reviewing lower-court decisions and making policy, they enjoy some freedoms not available to trial court judges—but they also face unique challenges. First, their decisions may be reviewable. For example, a state court of last resort decision that involves a constitutional challenge is reviewable by the U.S. Supreme Court, and, obviously, decisions of the U.S. circuit courts of appeals are reviewable by the U.S. Supreme Court. Thus, although most appellate court decisions are the final word and will not be reviewed, some are reviewed, and that leads to the possibility that appeals court judges will consider whether their decisions might be rebuffed and overturned on a subsequent appeal. Second, appellate courts are multijudge bodies; therefore, consensus and agreement are important in ways that trial judges do not have to worry about. A judge who has a preferred outcome in a case cannot achieve that outcome without the agreement and cooperation of at least one other judge. Those features of appellate courts mean that it is useful to consider how political scientists have tried to study decision making in appellate courts.

For over 60 years, political scientists have tried to identify variables that structure the exercise of judicial discretion. In *The Roosevelt Court: A Study of Judicial Politics and Values*, C. Herman Pritchett (1948) proposed that, in some cases, judicial discretion is limited by clear law or guiding precedent. But, in other cases, the law is unclear or contradictory, thus leaving the justices considerable discretion. How do we know that? The presence of a dissenting opinion provides the most obvious indicator that legitimate alternatives were open to the judges: After reading the same record, hearing identical oral arguments, and researching the same law, the appellate judges still reached different conclusions. The presence of dissents leads political scientists to doubt the power of *stare decisis* and other legal doctrines to account for some judicial decision making. Rather, formal dissents are clear indications that judges seriously disagree on how to decide a case. Unanimous decisions, too, can mask significant internal disagreements that judges choose to paper over for a variety of reasons (Epstein, Segal, and Spaeth 2001; Songer 1982).

Following Pritchett's pioneering work, political scientists became interested in analyzing the votes (rather than the opinions) appellate court judges cast in nonunanimous decisions. Dissenting opinions are a regular feature of appellate courts. Conflict is clearly a prominent feature of Supreme Court decision making; since World War II, roughly 60 percent of cases decided by written opinion have involved dissent. Likewise, dissent on the U.S. courts of appeals has occurred approximately 10 percent of the time in recent years (Teets-Farris 2002; Goldman and Lamb 1986).

Disagreement also occurs on state courts of last resort (Brace and Hall 1990). On average, 18 percent of state supreme court decisions involve dissents; for some courts, it is as high as 40 percent (Glick and Pruet 1986). On appellate courts with mandatory jurisdiction, the rate of dissent is relatively low. Confronted with a number of straightforward cases, judges often find there is only one way to decide the matter. But where appellate courts enjoy a discretionary jurisdiction, rates of dissent are higher (Glick and Pruet 1986; Hall 1985; Canon and Jaros 1970).

Explaining Decision Making on Appellate Courts Today

Pritchett's pioneering work led to a variety of ways to study decision making on appellate courts, but today political scientists generally consider four broad categories of explanations in trying to understand judicial behavior: legal, attitudinal, institutional, and strategic.

Legal Factors

The legal model asserts that appellate judges make decisions based primarily on the facts of the case before them, the meaning of legal statutes involved, and the controlling legal precedent (*stare decisis*) (Segal and Spaeth 2002). Scholars find that the law does matter. But, as we have stressed throughout this book, the law at times is contradictory or fails to provide one definitive way to solve a contemporary problem. As we just discussed, scholars point to dissent among appellate court judges as proof that the legal model has limits in helping us understand judicial decision making.

Attitudinal Dimensions

The attitudinal model argues that judges are similar to other policy makers and that they see their votes in cases as a way to express their views on politics and society. In the attitudinal model, the explanatory factors that help us understand why judges do what they do are related primarily to judges' ideologies and values (attitudes and beliefs) (Segal and Spaeth 2002, 1993).

Institutional Differences

There are also some institutional differences that are worth considering. As mentioned repeatedly, appellate groups work as multijudge panels. Social scientists are well aware that groups have dynamics that do not exist when a single judge acting in isolation decides a case. For example, a policy-oriented judge acting by herself can always obtain her most preferred outcome, but when the most preferred outcome can be obtained only by getting one or more other judges to go along, the dynamic is different. Other institutional rules that are unique to multijudge courts may also matter in understanding judicial decision making.

Strategic Considerations

Another way of thinking about judges on appellate courts is to view them as strategic actors. Like the attitudinal approach, the strategic approach assumes that judges act on their attitudes but that they are less like legal robots (doing whatever their attitudes predicate) and more like smart policy makers acting strategically to get their most preferred outcome in this or a subsequent case (Epstein and Knight 1998).

In appellate courts, decisions are made by a group rather than by an individual. As members of collegial bodies, appellate court judges interact to produce a group product. Studies of appellate court judges find that consensus is encouraged and dissensus is discouraged (Glick 1971; Ulmer 1971).

Together, these four explanations provide us with a range of factors that can help us understand judicial decisions. The next section considers what we know about state supreme courts. That is followed by an examination of the U.S. courts of appeals.

STATE SUPREME COURTS

State courts of last resort decide about 25,000 cases each year. By and large, the decisions reached are the final word. Most litigants do not appeal, and those who do find that the U.S. Supreme Court is unlikely to grant review. The great majority of the decisions of the state courts of last resort involve error correction; although of utmost importance to the individual litigants, such decisions have little impact beyond the immediate parties. But, increasingly, state supreme courts are playing a prominent role in governmental policy making (Glick 1991).

The policy-making role of state supreme courts first came to widespread prominence during the Warren Court era. Although, in theory, federal law is supreme over conflicting state law, in practice, state supreme courts did not always follow the authoritative pronouncements of the nation's highest court. Noncompliance was most pronounced in race relations cases, with southern state supreme courts often aiding and abetting their states' overwhelming resistance to desegregation (Tarr and Porter

1988). Noncompliance also occurred in areas as diverse as police interrogations, search and seizure, and church-state relations (Johnson and Canon 1984).

The increasing policy-making role of state supreme courts explains why interest groups are now more likely to litigate in these judicial arenas (Epstein 1994). This is particularly the case in the area of tort reform, where advocates on both sides are increasingly willing to spend large sums in an attempt to get their candidate(s) elected. Campaign spending has resulted in greater electoral competition (Bonneau 2007). Thus, recent campaigns for positions on state supreme courts in Illinois, Ohio, Pennsylvania, Michigan, and Texas have become multimillion-dollar political battles. In short, judicial campaigns that were once low key have now become highly visible (Chapter 6).

Because state supreme court decisions are so important, political scientists have begun a serious effort to better understand how and why judges decide cases the way they do. Researchers have examined the influence of legal, attitudinal, institutional, and strategic factors on appellate judges on state supreme courts.

Legal Factors and State Supreme Courts

Legal factors are important in assessing decision making on state supreme courts. State constitutional law varies from state to state. State constitutions differ from their national counterpart in important ways. Whereas the Founding Fathers were intent on creating a framework for government, drafters of state documents have typically been more concerned with restricting the power of state governments (Tarr 1998). Thus, details that state constitutions put into the basic document itself the U.S. Constitution leaves to Congress. For those reasons, state constitutions tend to be longer and more specific than their federal counterpart; the average state constitution is more than three times as long. (Alabama has the longest constitution, with more than 172,000 words.) The restrictive nature of many state constitutions, coupled with the detailed nature of their provisions, is a major source of litigation. The more extensive the substantive and procedural limitations imposed, the greater is the opportunity for a litigant to oppose governmental policy on state constitutional grounds and, thus, the greater is the likelihood of participation by the state supreme court in determining the ultimate policy in that state (Tarr and Porter 1988).

The substance of the limitations that state constitutions impose is also important in determining the policy-making roles of state supreme courts. This can be seen most clearly by focusing on state bills of rights (Cauthen 2000). Some state bills of rights afford relatively narrow protection, entailing little more than a reiteration of the constitutional guarantees of the federal Bill of Rights. Others, however, offer more detailed and extensive protections. For example, seventeen state constitutions contain ERAs (equal rights amendments); ten expressly protect privacy rights; and several others guarantee, in some form, a right to environmental quality. Construing documents that reflect such lively topical issues virtually requires state supreme courts to engage in broad policy making (Tarr and Porter 1988). Likewise, the tremendous expansion of statutory law in the twentieth century heavily involved state supreme courts in the task of statutory interpretation.

Historically, the performance of state supreme courts was often lackluster. Starting in the early 1970s, however, a number of state courts of last resort gradually reawakened to their legitimate authority to construe provisions of their state constitutions independently of the U.S. Supreme Court's interpretation of analogous rights in the federal Constitution. The phrase **new judicial federalism** refers to the movement in state supreme courts to reinvigorate state constitutions as sources of individual rights over and above the rights granted by the federal Constitution. This movement occurred partially as a response to the growing conservatism of the U.S. Supreme Court (Galie 1987). Just as important, though, new judicial federalism reflects the growing understanding that the federal Constitution establishes minimum guarantees of individual rights rather than maximum protections (Abrahamson and Gutmann 1987; Emmert and Traut 1992). In some instances, for example, state supreme courts have interpreted state bill of rights provisions regarding criminal procedures more expansively than the equivalent sections of the U.S. Bill of Rights. Researchers have identified hundreds of state supreme court decisions that interpret state charters to be more rights generous than their federal counterpart (Fino 1987). In that regard, decisions recognizing the right of same-sex marriage have proven to be extremely controversial. (See Case Close-Up: *Goodridge v. Department of Public Health* 2003.)

The image of the new judicial federalism is that of a wholly liberal legal movement, but empirical research suggests a more complex pattern. An examination of all fifty state supreme courts' criminal procedure decisions based on state constitutional law decided from the late 1960s to the end of 1989 found a "hidden conservatism." Two-thirds of the criminal rulings endorsed—not repudiated—the conservative holdings of the U.S. Supreme Court (Latzer 1991). Moreover, federal law continues to predominate. State supreme courts rely on federal law for almost four of every five decisions (Esler 1994).

Attitudinal Dimensions of Voting

Do judges' social backgrounds affect the way they decide certain cases? That question has generated considerable research, some of which has produced conflicting results. Some evidence suggests, for example, that certain personal factors—such as religion, gender, age, race, pre-judicial career, and the level of prestige of law school education—are related to judicial behavior. However, only political party affiliation seems to have any significant and consistent capacity to explain and predict the outcomes of judicial decisions. In 1961 and 1962, Stuart Nagel conducted one of the first and most widely cited social background studies. He found that political party affiliation was associated with the decisional propensities of state supreme court justices. Democratic judges were more liberal than Republican judges, voting more often for the defendant in criminal cases, for the employee or union in labor-management cases, for the economic underdog in a wide variety of economic cases, and for the injured party in personal injury cases. National as well as state-specific studies have confirmed the importance of party identification (Gryski and Main 1986).

In a classic study of the Michigan Supreme Court, Glendon Schubert (1959) demonstrated the existence of liberal and conservative blocs on a variety of issues, such as workers' compensation cases and contributory negligence matters. Another early study found that the policy preferences of the Pennsylvania Supreme Court justices were important determinants of voting (Fair 1967). More recent research points in the same direction for supreme courts in Illinois (Bradley and Ulmer 1980) and Ohio (Tarr and Porter 1988).

CASE CLOSE-UP

■ *Goodridge v. Department of Public Health* (2003)

Same-Sex Marriages

On November 18, 2003, the Massachusetts Supreme Judicial Court (SJC) handed down the most important victory to date in the campaign to recognize same-sex marriages (*Goodridge v. Department of Public Health* 2003). The legal question was simple, but the politics were extremely complicated. The legal question was whether the Massachusetts Constitution required the state to recognize same-sex unions. Advocates of gay marriage argued that the state constitution requires equal protection of gays and lesbians and their right to marriage, and opponents argued that Massachusetts could legally deny same-sex couples the rights of marriage.

In resolving the legal question, the court ruled that "the Massachusetts Constitution affirms the dignity and equality of all individuals. It forbids the creation of second-class citizens. In reaching our conclusion we have given full deference to the arguments made by the Commonwealth. But it has failed to identify any constitutionally adequate reason for denying civil marriage to same-sex couples." In so doing, it wrote that the "Massachusetts Constitution is, if anything, more protective of individual liberty and equality than the Federal Constitution." Recognizing that although it had resolved the legal question the political question remained very much up in the air, the court remanded the case and then stayed its own judgment for 180 days to allow the Massachusetts legislature to act.

The gloves were off. Opponents of gay marriage quickly moved to do everything possible to prevent Massachusetts from recognizing gay marriage. In addition to efforts at the state level, President Bush entered the fray when he made reference to protecting the sanctity of marriage in his State of the Union Address. And gay marriage would spark many heated exchanges during the 2004 presidential race between President Bush and Senator John Kerry, who is from Massachusetts (and who supported civil unions but not marriage). In an effort to respond to the concerns of the court, the Massachusetts State Senate crafted a law that would recognize "same sex unions" with the legal protections afforded marriage. When they asked the SJC for an advisory opinion, however, the court (in February 2004) once again reiterated its view that marriage meant marriage and that same-sex couples should be afforded the full rights, privileges, and

responsibilities and recognition associated with traditional marriage.

Governor Mitt Romney (R) rejected the SJC's interpretation and called on states to protect marriage between a man and a woman. In legislative proceedings that stretched over several years, the Massachusetts legislature failed to pass a constitutional amendment that would ban same-sex marriage. In the meantime, the SJC ruling took effect, and, on May 17, 2004, Massachusetts became the first state to legally recognize same-sex marriage.

On the first day approximately 1,000 couples sought marriage licenses and by its first anniversary more than 6,000 same-sex couples had said their marriage vows. On the one-year anniversary of the first same-sex marriages, a *Boston Globe* survey showed that slightly more than a majority of residents (56 percent) approved of same-sex marriages. Over time, it appears that the legal question and the political one, too, may have been resolved in Massachusetts (Greenberger 2005). But the same cannot be said across the nation where the issue has spawned political action and inaction at virtually every level of government.

In the United States, as in Canada (see Courts in Comparative Perspective: Canada), federalism results in contradictory policies about gay marriages. At the local level, mayors in San Francisco, California, and New Paltz, New York, briefly granted marriage licenses to same-sex couples making a request. At the state level, legislatures in a few states (often under prodding by the judiciary) have created legal unions that, while not called marriages, are explicitly defined as offering all the rights and responsibilities of marriage under state law to same-sex couples. Other state legislatures like those in California and New York have legalized same sex marriages. And the Iowa supreme court did the same.

But gay marriage has sparked major political opposition. Twenty-six states have passed constitutional amendments explicitly barring the recognition of same-sex marriage. In addition, most states have statutes restricting marriage to two persons of the opposite sex. Legislatures in some states have failed to take any action and voters in states like Maine have specifically rejected such proposals. Clearly, the decisions of a handful of state supreme courts have impacted both law and politics across the nation.

From the perspective of a book on law, courts, and politics in the United States, an important question is,

(continued)

Why are battles over same-sex marriages being fought primarily in state, as opposed to federal, courts? The answer is that, in the area of discrimination based on sexual orientation, the U.S. Supreme Court has had little to say and what it has said is somewhat contradictory. *Bowers v. Hardwick* (1986) upheld Georgia's antisodomy law, refusing to recognize a right to privacy in that area. More recently, however, the Court upheld equal protection claims, striking down by a 6–3 vote a Colorado referendum that prohibited local governments from passing laws protecting "homosexual, lesbian or bisexual orientation, conduct, practices or relationships" (*Romer v. Evans* 1966). And, during the 2002 term, the Court reversed *Bowers*, holding in *Lawrence v. Texas* that due process protections made unconstitutional a Texas law that restricted homosexual sodomy. The Court's opinion in *Lawrence* raised questions about the few remaining states that had legislation outlawing homosexual sex. To make matters even more complicated, in 1996, Congress passed and President Clinton signed into law the Defense of Marriage Act (DOMA), which defines, for federal purposes, marriage as a union between a man and a woman. Thus, with all the confusing signals about the protections for same-sex marriage at the federal level, activists turned their attention to state judicial systems and with the *Goodridge* decision in Massachusetts scored a major victory.

But results of the challenges in the states have been mixed. Since the *Goodridge* decision, high courts in New Jersey, New York, and Washington have all turned back efforts to allow same-sex marriage. Yet the California Supreme Court in a 5–4 decision on May 15, 2008, became the second state (after Massachusetts) to overturn a ban on same-sex marriage, allowing gays and lesbians in the largest state in the union to marry legally. The California Supreme Court declared marriage a basic civil right and cited the importance of equal protection. The first same-sex marriages in California were conducted on June 16, 2008. But voters later passed Proposition 8 which banned such unions. Later the U.S. District Court struck down Proposition 8 and the government refused to appeal, meaning there is no way for the Supreme Court to rule.

The debate is not over with opponents of the decision saying they will use the electoral process to pass a constitutional amendment banning gay marriage. In a sign of changing times and a shifting partisan landscape, and in contrast to former Massachusetts Republican Governor Mitt Romney, the Republican governor of California, Arnold Schwarzenegger, said he accepted the decision of the California Supreme Court and would not support a constitutional amendment to reverse it.

Since interest in judicial attitudes began, scholars have struggled to find a way to measure and analyze those attitudes. Traditionally, votes in previous cases and party identification have been used as surrogates for judicial attitudes. More recently, Brace, Langer, and Hall (2000) developed a measure of state supreme court judicial preferences that is more sensitive to the complexity of the state judicial environment. They show that this new measure is statistically related to decision making in state supreme courts. Similarly, Langer and Wilhelm (2005) report major differences in the ideology of state supreme court chief justices. These differences are related to both the state political environment and the method of selection—popularly elected chief justices are more liberal.

Of course, some types of cases leave little room for judges' policy preferences to have an impact. Many appellate cases have seemingly obvious results. But it is also true that the few cases in which ideology is relevant tend to be the most important ones, because the court's decision affects people other than the immediate parties. Thus, they are particularly important to study in the context of law and politics.

Institutional Differences Among State Supreme Courts

Whereas one may describe the typical federal court, there is no typical state supreme court. Rather, the legal and political contexts in which these courts operate differ substantially. That has led scholars to consider how some of those differences in the way

COURTS IN COMPARATIVE PERSPECTIVE

■ Canada

Gay Marriage Rights

The government is obliged to recognize the right of gays and lesbians to marry people of their own gender, decided a panel of the Ontario Superior Court. The 3–0 ruling came in response to a lawsuit filed by a lesbian couple and a gay couple who had been married in a Toronto church but whose marriage ceremonies the provincial government had refused to register as legally binding (Krauss 2002). The national government, making its displeasure known, pledged to appeal to the Canadian Supreme Court. The decision of the Ontario Superior Court in many ways paralleled the holding of the Massachusetts Supreme Judicial Council in *Goodridge v. Department of Public Health* (2003).

Canada and the United States share the longest unfortified border in the world. Economically and technologically, Canada has developed in parallel with the United States, but the governmental systems of the two nations differ. Canada became a self-governing dominion within the British Empire in 1867. It has a parliamentary democracy. Canada is a confederation with power shared between the national government (based in Ottawa) and its ten provinces and three territories. Thus, like the United States, Canada has a dual court system.

The legal systems of the two nations share many characteristics. Both have their roots in English common law. Each contains a state (or province, as it is called in Canada) with a civil law heritage stemming from French influence. Both are also federated nations with separate state and national courts. The national-level courts are headed by the Supreme Court of Canada with nine justices. The provincial courts are named variously court of appeal, court of Queen's Bench, superior court, supreme court, and court of justice.

But the legal systems of the two nations also differ in important ways. One is judicial selection—Canada has no tradition of political selection of judges (Johnson and Songer 2009). The judges of the Supreme Court of Canada are instead appointed by the prime minister through the governor general. Moreover, provincial judges are appointed by the national government. The apolitical nature of Canadian judicial selection is the reason that Canadian courts have not historically been involved in policy making (Miller 1998). Thus, through the years, the judiciary has played an important, but largely invisible, role in the Canadian political system (Baar 1991).

After the passage of the Canadian Charter of Rights and Freedoms in 1982, however, Canadian courts became more actively involved in policy making (Miller 1998). Indeed, the nation has experienced a "Rights Revolution." (Petter 2010). Criminal procedure has changed greatly in ways roughly comparable to the changes made by the Warren Court in the United States. Similarly, the Supreme Court of Canada has an equal rights agenda that makes ending gender discrimination a key priority (Epp 1998).

The increased prominence of Canadian courts in politics is supported and encouraged by interest groups. The two most frequent intervenors are the Women's Legal Education and Action Fund and the Canadian Civil Liberties Association. Unions and associations representing native groups, on the other hand, get a chillier reception from the court (Brodie 2002). The interest groups fall into five overlapping categories: (1) language rights groups, who counter language separatism; (2) civil libertarians, who oppose censorship and state support for religious schools; (3) equality seekers, who stress rights for women, gays, and the disabled; (4) social engineers, who seek to ameliorate economic inequities; and (5) postmaterialists, who are based in the knowledge industry (Morton and Knopf 2000). But, as in the United States, use of the courts by liberal interest groups has begotten the rise of conservative interest groups. Thus, over the last two decades, religiously conservative advocacy groups have pursued their political interests through litigation (Hoover and den Dulk 2004).

In Canada, as in the United States, federalism results in contradictory policies about gay marriages. Whereas an Ontario court upheld them, the courts in another province—British Columbia—rejected such claims, and Quebec passed legislation recognizing such unions. Overall, courts in eight of Canada's ten provinces and one of three territories held that marriage laws were unconstitutionally heterosexist—and redefined marriage as "the voluntary union for life of two persons to the exclusion of others."

Two years after the original court of appeal decision, the Canadian government upheld the Supreme Court decision. In 2005, Parliament passed the Civil Marriage Act, thus making Canada the fourth country in the world—after the Netherlands, Belgium, and Spain—to officially recognize same-sex marriages and to provide the mechanism by which same-sex partners can be legally married.

the state supreme courts process and decide cases might influence case outcomes. Whereas, on the U.S. Supreme Court, the most senior justice in the majority decides who will write the opinion (Chapter 15), in state supreme courts, the opinion may be assigned randomly or on a rotational basis. There is also significant variation to the order in which the justices of a court discuss cases and cast votes (Hall 1990).

Another important difference centers on the control state supreme courts exercise over their dockets. In states that have not established intermediate courts of appeals, the responsibility for appellate review falls directly on the state supreme court. In such circumstances, the state's highest court finds itself relegated to dealing with a succession of relatively minor disputes, devoting its energies to error correction rather than to more time-consuming efforts to shape state law. By contrast, in the states that have created intermediate courts of appeals, the lower appellate courts are primarily concerned with error correction. That leaves the state's highest court free to devote more attention to cases that raise important policy questions (Tarr and Porter 1988).

Discretionary review at the highest level transforms the nature of the judicial process. The high court is no longer merely reacting to disputes brought to it by adversaries; it is selecting those disputes in which it chooses to participate. In sum, the architecture of the system tells the judges of the top court to be creative (Carrington, Meador, and Rosenberg 1976).

Strategic Considerations in Voting on State Supreme Courts

In a series of articles over the past twenty years, political scientists Melinda Hall and Paul Brace have worked to incorporate aspects of the legal, attitudinal, and institutional models of judicial decision making into our understanding of state supreme court decisions. Their research convincingly shows that these models are useful in predicting appellate court decision making at levels other than the U.S. Supreme Court. For example, Hall found that institutional forces such as prior representational service, single-member districts, and whether the vote was near the beginning or the end of a term help explain the votes of supreme court justices in death penalty cases (1992). And Brace and Hall (1993) found that judicial attitudes in addition to the institutional factors are important in those same death penalty cases. Later, Brace and Hall (1997) would find that justices' attitudes reflect those of their constituencies (states) and that those views are moderated by institutional factors. Other parts of their work strongly suggest that state supreme court justices also act strategically. Thus, it can fairly be asserted that the various models of judicial decision making do help us understand how and why state supreme court justices reach the decisions they do.

U.S. COURTS OF APPEALS

Judges on U.S. appeals courts, and their decisions, have recently become the focus of considerable research by political scientists (Hettinger, Lindquist, and Martinek 2006). In the vast majority of cases, a review by a U.S. court of appeals will be the final word. So those decisions obviously matter to the parties involved. But the decisions also set the contours of law and policy for all the district courts in the circuit and provide guidance should other circuit judges choose to adopt their legal reasoning. Thus, appeals courts are a critical part of the federal judiciary but have been studied less frequently than the Supreme Court because research understandably started with the most important legal institution and is now working its way into the appeals courts and state courts of last resort. Appellate court justices are nominated by the president and confirmed by the Senate (see Chapter 6). Researchers are using the legal, attitudinal, institutional, and strategic models to try to understand their behavior.

Legal Factors and Courts of Appeals

U.S. courts of appeals decide over 60,000 cases a year. Many of those appeals are straightforward and generate unanimous decisions. But others clearly present the judges with opportunities to exercise discretion. Every year, a large number of cases are decided by three-judge panels in which at least one judge dissents, and a smaller number are reviewed en banc after an initial decision by a three-judge panel. Decision making on appeals courts has been understood mostly in legal terms. That is primarily because appeals court judges have an obligation to apply precedent as established by the Supreme Court when it is appropriate for the case at hand (Songer, Segal, and Cameron 1994). For example, Benesh (2002) finds support for the legal model with clear evidence that precedent is important in appellate court decision making. Thus, the legal model has proved useful in understanding appellate court decision making, but attitudes are clearly important, too.

Attitudinal Dimensions of Voting on Courts of Appeals

Sheldon Goldman (1966) was one of the first to conclude that Republican judges tended to be more conservative than their Democratic colleagues. The importance of the appointing president's party affiliation continues today. Republican and Democratic presidents differ greatly in policy goals, the procedures they employ in making their selections, and the backgrounds of the judges they actually appoint (Chapter 6). Those differences appear to be systematically related to the behavior of the judges they appoint. Research has shown a convincing relationship between the views of the appointing president and the appellate court judges he appoints (Songer, Sheehan, and Haire 2000; Songer and Davis 1990). Overall, judges appointed by Democratic presidents have rendered a greater percentage of liberal decisions than jurists selected by GOP presidents. Evidence also suggests that judges' votes are more predictable at the beginning and end of their careers (Kaheny, Haire, and Benesh 2008).

Although evidence for partisan influence on judicial behavior is convincing, it by no means suggests that Democrats always take the liberal position on all issues or that Republicans always opt for the conservative side. Rather, the research points to tendencies in close cases. Overall, partisan differences show only a modest ability to predict appellate court decision making.

Institutional Differences Among Courts of Appeals

Unlike the Supreme Court, where there are just nine justices who always meet in the same location, the thirteen circuit courts of appeals are scattered across the country and the justices serve on rotating three-judge panels. Research shows that these circuits differ in their ideological environment, which is probably a function of both the justices on the court and the political culture of the region (Songer, Sheehan, and Haire 2000). Thus, one can think of the political setting of a court as an institutional constraint operating to determine the contours of acceptable policy making.

Another important variation is the fact that the composition of the three-judge panels is constantly changing. Thus, which judges constitute the panels and whether the judges follow precedent established by the rest of the circuit—sometimes referred to as "horizontal stare decisis"—is clearly an interesting application of the study of institutional factors that can determine appellate judicial behavior (Lee 2005).

Strategic Considerations on Courts of Appeals

Research on the U.S. courts of appeals continues to become more sophisticated and rigorous. In a groundbreaking book, Songer, Sheehan, and Haire (2000) offer a careful examination of U.S. courts of appeals judges using the U.S. Courts of Appeals Database. Their empirical analysis finds that the rate of reversal of lower-court decisions by appeals courts has stayed relatively constant over the years, that partisanship continues to affect judicial voting, and that regional differences across the circuits may be less important than previously believed. This book coincided with a great deal of research that has given us a much better understanding of decision making on U.S. appeals courts. The research employs various components of the legal, attitudinal, strategic, and institutional models of decision making. For example, research has focused on the determinants of whether an en banc hearing is granted (George 1999; Solimine 1988), whether appeals courts judges write separately (Hettinger, Lindquist, and Martinek 2003), how frequently and why judges dissent (Teets-Farris 2002), and whether there is presidential or home-state influence on appeals court decisions (Songer and Ginn 2002). The evidence from these studies generally supports the conclusion that judges on the courts of appeals do engage in policy making and that the attitudinal, strategic, and institutional models help us understand judicial behavior. Two studies, in particular, help us see that point.

In a wide-ranging analysis of dissenting behavior on the U.S. courts of appeals, Hettinger, Lindquist, and Martinek (2004) compare the attitudinal and strategic models as to how well they help us explain dissenting behavior by appeals court judges. From the pioneering work of Pritchett (1948) forward, dissents (one judge's disagreements with the decisions of the majority) have been a major focus of appellate court studies because they are unique to appellate judicial bodies. The authors conclude that "ideological disagreement between a judge and the majority opinion writer [as the attitudinal model would predict] is a more persuasive explanation of the decision to dissent than a strategic account in which a judge conditions a dissent on whether circuit court intervention would obtain the judge's preferred outcome [as the strategic model would predict]" (123). This study is useful because it emphasizes the importance in contrasting and comparing multiple explanations for appellate judicial behavior. Although the authors conclude that when it comes to dissenting behavior they believe attitudes (ideology) are more important, they recognize that in explaining other behavior the strategic model might be more powerful.

Likewise, Sarah Benesh (2002) tries to integrate some of the explanations by applying a principal-agent theory to understand judicial decision making on the courts of appeals. Principal-agent models assume that judges are motivated by attitudes but recognize that they are constrained by the fact that they are supposed to apply precedent established by the Supreme Court. In addition, Benesh argues that appellate court judges would prefer to see their views put into law and, thus, would act strategically to minimize the likelihood that their decisions would be reversed on appeal. Principal-agent theory argues that "one party, the principal, enters into a contractual relationship with another, the agent, in the expectation that the agent will subsequently choose actions that produce outcomes desired by the principal" (7). In this study, the principal is the U.S. Supreme Court, and the agent is the U.S. courts of appeals. Benesh finds support for the legal model with clear evidence that precedent is important in appellate court decision making but also finds evidence for the attitudinal and strategic models. In the end, the principal-agent theory, though not perfect, works to help understand appellate court judges as acting on attitudes, as cognizant of the situation around them, and as constrained by the law as it has been articulated by the U.S. Supreme Court.

Our understanding of U.S. courts of appeals voting has come a long way since the publication of Howard's (1981) *Courts of Appeals in the Federal Judicial System: A Study of the Second, Fifth, and District of Columbia Circuits.* Today's research is informed by theories of judicial behavior that include legal, attitudinal, institutional, and strategic explanations and is increasingly empirical and sophisticated.

CONCLUSION

The freeing of Kenneth Waters from a life sentence for a murder he didn't commit is the ultimate "feel-good story"—perhaps even exceeding the more dramatized case of Rubin "Hurricane" Carter, who, some still think, was indeed a murderer. But not all who proclaim their innocence are indeed innocent. Consider Ricky McGinn, who steadfastly claimed that he hadn't raped and murdered his 12-year-old stepdaughter. His death sentence was stayed while a forensic lab ran a more sophisticated DNA test than had been available during the first trial. The new tests, however, confirmed the original findings—and a month later, McGinn was executed (McGraw 2000).

The conflicting stories of Kenneth Waters and Ricky McGinn fuel the nation's ongoing debate over the death penalty and also highlight differences of opinion about the role of appellate court review in the nation's justice system. To some, the documentation of more than 100 innocents on death row (or serving life sentences) for murders they did not commit underscores why the doors to the federal courthouse should remain open. To supporters of greater access to appellate review, notions of fundamental fairness demand that prisoners have easy access to more powerful forensic tests unavailable when they were first convicted. Others, however, believe the system is fundamentally sound and that use of the death penalty is slow and deliberate, resulting in only those who deserve the punishment receiving the sentence.

The increase in criminal prosecutions in trial courts is one reason that appellate court caseloads have increased dramatically in recent years. The explosive growth of appeals not only reflects the greater willingness of litigants to ask reviewing bodies to correct errors but also represents the greater role appellate courts play in policy making. For decades, decisions of the U.S. courts of appeals have established new governmental policy in a variety of areas. More recently, state supreme courts have also emerged as important policy makers. Under the rubric of new judicial federalism, state supreme courts are often interpreting their own state constitutions in ways that provide greater protections than those in the U.S. Constitution. In deciding appeals, appellate court judges are influenced by political as well as legal factors. Significant research suggests that legal, attitudinal, institutional, and strategic factors are important in explaining judicial discretion.

CRITICAL THINKING QUESTIONS

1. In the public's mind, appellate review drags on endlessly and results in a lack of finality in the process. Do you think that this is a significant problem or that it is merely one of appearance?

2. In what ways are appellate cases unrepresentative of cases filed in the trial courts?

3. In recent years, why have interest groups been giving increasing importance to state and federal appellate courts?

Search Terms

Anti-Terrorism and Effective   habeas corpus
    Death Penalty Act

Useful URLs

http://www.law.cornell.edu/topics/appellate_procedure.html
    Cornell's Legal Information Institute provides an excellent overview of appellate procedure.

http://www.sado.org
    The State Appellate Defender Organization (Michigan) provides information about appeal.

REFERENCES

Abrahamson, Shirley, and Diane Gutmann. 1987. "The New Federalism: State Constitutions." *Judicature* 71: 88–109.

Administrative Office of the United States Courts. 2002. *Judicial Business of the United States Courts*. Washington, D.C.: U.S. Government Printing Office.

American Civil Liberties Union. 2000. "Act Now to Stop the Execution of the Innocent." Available online at http://www.aclu.org/death-penalty/.

Associated Press. 2001. "DNA Frees Man After 19 Years in Prison." March 15.

Baar, Carl. 1991. "Judicial Activism in Canada." In *Judicial Activism in Comparative Perspective*, edited by Kenneth M. Holland. New York: St. Martin's Press.

Beiser, Edward. 1973. "The Rhode Island Supreme Court: A Well-Integrated Political System." *Law and Society Review* 8: 167–186.

Benesh, Sara C. 2002. *The U.S. Courts of Appeals and the Law of Confessions: Perspectives on the Hierarchy of Justice*. New York: LFB Scholarly Publishing.

Bonneau, Chris. 2007. "The Effects of Campaign Spending in State Supreme Court Elections." *Political Research Quarterly* 60: 489–499.

Brace, Paul, and Melinda Hall. 1990. "Neo-Institutionalism and Dissent in State Supreme Courts." *Journal of Politics* 52: 54–70.

———. 1993. "Integrated Models of Judicial Dissent." *Journal of Politics* 55: 914–935.

———. 1997. "The Interplay of Preferences, Case Facts, Context, and Rules in the Politics of Judicial Choice." *Journal of Politics* 59: 1206–1231.

Brace, Paul, Laura Langer, and Melinda Gann Hall. 2000. "Measuring the Preferences of State Supreme Court Justices." *Journal of Politics* 62: 387–413.

Bradley, Robert, and S. Sidney Ulmer. 1980. "An Examination of Voting Behavior in the Supreme Court of Illinois: 1971–1975." *Southern Illinois University Law Journal*: 245–262.

Braun, Jerome. 2000. "Eighth Circuit Decision Intensifies Debate Over Publication and Citation of Appellate Opinions." *Judicature* 84: 90–95.

Brodie, Ian. 2002. *Friends of the Court: Privileging of Interest Group Litigants in Canada*. Albany: State University of New York Press.

Canon, Bradley, and Dean Jaros. 1970. "External Variables, Institutional Structure and Dissent on State Supreme Courts." *Polity* 4: 185–200.

Carp, Robert, and Ronald Stidham. 1996. *Judicial Process in America*. 3rd ed. Washington, D.C.: CQ Press.

Carter, Rubin "Hurricane" and Ken Klonsky. 2011. *The Eye of the Hurricane*. Chicago: Lawrence Hill Books.

Carrington, Paul, Daniel Meador, and Maurice Rosenberg. 1976. *Justice on Appeal*. St. Paul, Minn.: West.

Cauthen, James. 2000. "Judicial Innovation Under State Constitutions: An Internal Determinants Investigation." *American Review of Politics* 21: 19–42.

Chapper, Joy, and Roger Hanson. 1990. "Understanding Reversible Error in Criminal Appeals." *State Court Journal* 14: 16–24.

Cohen, Jonathan. 2002. *Inside Appellate Courts: The Impact of Court Organization on Judicial Decision Making in the United States Courts of Appeals*. Ann Arbor: University of Michigan Press.

Conviction. (2010). http://www.imdb.com/title/tt1244754/

Crump, David. 1986. "Law Clerks: Their Roles and Relationships with Their Judges." *Judicature* 69: 236–240.

Davies, Thomas. 1981. "Gresham's Law Revisited: Expedited Processing Techniques and the Allocation of Appellate Procedures." *Justice System Journal* 6: 372–404.

———. 1982. "Affirmed: A Study of Criminal Appeals and Decision-Making Norms in a California Court of Appeal." *American Bar Foundation Research Journal*: 7: 543–648.

Douglas, Charles. 1985. "Innovative Appellate Court Processing: New Hampshire's Experience with Summary Affirmance." *Judicature* 69: 147.

Emmert, Craig, and Carol Ann Traut. 1992. "State Supreme Courts, State Constitutions, and Judicial Policymaking." *Justice System Journal* 16: 37–48.

Epp, Charles. 1998. *The Rights Revolution: Lawyers, Activists, and Supreme Courts in Comparative Perspective*. Chicago: University of Chicago Press.

Epstein, Lee. 1994. "Exploring the Participation of Organized Interests in State Court Litigation." *Political Research Quarterly* 47: 335–351.

Epstein, Lee, and Jack Knight. 1998. *The Choices Justices Make*. Washington, D.C.: CQ Press.

Epstein, Lee, Jeffrey A. Segal, and Harold J. Spaeth. 2001. "The Norm of Consensus on the U.S. Supreme Court." *American Journal of Political Science* 45: 362–377.

Esler, Michael. 1994. "State Supreme Court Commitment to State Law." *Judicature* 78: 25–32.

Fair, Daryl. 1967. "An Experimental Application of Scalogram Analysis to State Supreme Court Decisions." *Wisconsin Law Review* 1967: 449–459.

Fino, Susan. 1987. *The Role of State Supreme Courts in the New Judicial Federalism*. Westport, Conn.: Greenwood Press.

Flango, Victor. 1994. *Habeas Corpus in State and Federal Courts*. Williamsburg, Va.: National Center for State Courts.

Flango, Victor, and Nora Blair. 1980. "Creating an Intermediate Appellate Court: Does It Reduce the Caseload of a State's Highest Court?" *Judicature* 64: 75–78.

Fradella, Henry. 1999. "In Search of Meritorious Claims: A Study of the Processing of Prisoner Civil Rights Cases in a Federal District Court." *Justice System Journal* 21: 23–55.

Freedman, Eric M. 2003. *Habeas Corpus: Rethinking the Great Writ of Liberty*. New York: New York University Press.

Galanter, Marc. 1974. "Why the Haves Come Out Ahead: Speculations on the Limits of Social Change." *Law and Society Review* 9: 95–160.

Galie, Peter. 1987. "State Supreme Courts, Judicial Federalism and the Other Constitutions." *Judicature* 71: 100–110.

George, Tracey E. 1999. "The Dynamics and Determinants of the Decision to Grant En Banc Review." *Washington Law Review* 74: 213–274.

Gest, Ted. 1996. "The Law That Grief Built." *U.S. News & World Report*, April 29, p. 58.

Giles, Michael, Thomas Walker, and Christopher Zorn. 2006. "Setting a Judicial Agenda: The Decision to Grant En Banc Review in the U.S. Courts of Appeals." *Journal of Politics* 68: 852–866.

Glick, Henry. 1971. *Supreme Courts in State Politics*. New York: Basic Books.

———. 1991. "Policy Making and State Supreme Courts." In *The American Courts: A Critical Assessment*, edited by John Gates and Charles Johnson. Washington, D.C.: CQ Press.

Glick, Henry, and George Pruet. 1986. "Dissent in State Supreme Courts: Patterns and Correlates of Conflict." In *Judicial Conflict and Consensus: Behavioral Studies of American Appellate Courts*, edited by Sheldon Goldman and Charles Lamb. Lexington: University of Kentucky Press.

Goldman, Sheldon. 1966. "Voting Behavior on the United States Courts of Appeals, 1961–1964." *American Political Science Review* 60: 374–383.

Goldman, Sheldon, and Charles Lamb, eds. 1986. *Judicial Conflict and Consensus: Behavioral Studies of American Appellate Courts*. Lexington: University of Kentucky Press.

Green, Dale, and Michael Keyes. 1986. "Motion on the Merits: An Effective Response to Appellate Congestion and Delay." *Judicature* 70: 168–170.

Greenberger, Scott. 2005. "One Year Later, Nation Divided on Gay Marriage." *Boston Globe*, May 15.

Gryski, Gerard, and Eleanor Main. 1986. "Social Backgrounds as Predictors of Votes on State Courts of Last Resort: The Case of Sex Discrimination." *Western Political Quarterly* 39: 528–537.

Hall, Melinda. 1985. "Docket Control as an Influence on Judicial Voting." *Justice System Journal* 10: 243–255.

———. 1990. "Opinion Assignment Procedures and Conference Practices in State Supreme Courts." *Judicature* 73: 209–214.

———. 1992. "Electoral Politics and Strategic Voting in State Supreme Courts." *Journal of Politics* 54: 427–446.

Hettinger, Virginia A., Stefanie Lindquist, and Wendy L. Martinek. 2003. "Acclimation Effects and Separate Opinion Writing in the U.S. Courts of Appeals." *Social Science Quarterly* 84: 792–810.

———. 2004. "Comparing Attitudinal and Strategic Accounts of Dissenting Behavior on the U.S. Courts of Appeals." *American Journal of Political Science* 48(1): 123–137.

———. 2006. *Judging on a Collegial Court: Influences on Appellate Decision Making*. Charlottesville: University of Virginia Press.

Hoover, Dennis, and Kevin den Dulk. 2004. "Christian Conservatives Go to Court: Religion and Legal Mobilization in the United States and Canada." *International Political Science Review* 25(1): 9–34.

Howard, J. Woodford. 1977. "Role Perceptions and Behavior on Three U.S. Courts of Appeals." *Journal of Politics* 39: 916–938.

———. 1981. *Courts of Appeals in the Federal Judicial System: A Study of the Second, Fifth, and District of Columbia Circuits*. Princeton, N.J.: Princeton University Press.

Hume, Robert. 2009. "Courting Multiple Audiences: The Strategic Selection of Legal Groundings by Judges on the U.S. Courts of Appeals." *The Justice System Journal* 30:14–33.

Innocence Project. 2011. "Know the Cases." *www.innocenceproject.org* retrieved August 29, 2011.

Johnson, Charles, and Bradley Canon. 1984. *Judicial Policies: Implementation and Impact*. Washington, D.C.: CQ Press.

Johnson, Suan, and Donald Songer. 2009. "Judge Gender and the Voting Behavior of Justices of Two North American Supreme Courts." *The Justice System Journal* 30: 265–278.

Kaheny, E. B., Haire, S. B. and Benesh, S. C. (2008), "Change over Tenure: Voting, Variance, and Decision

Making on the U.S. Courts of Appeals." *American Journal of Political Science*, 52: 490–503.

Krauss, Clifford. 2002. "Court Rules That Ontario Must Recognize Same-Sex Marriages." *New York Times*, July 13.

Langer, Laura, and Teena Wilhelm. 2005. "The Ideology of State Supreme Court Chief Justices." *Judicature* 89: 78–86.

Latzer, Barry. 1991. "The Hidden Conservatism of the State Court 'Revolution.'" *Judicature* 74: 190–197.

Latzer, Barry, and James Cauthen. 2000. "Capital Appeals Revisited." *Judicature* 84: 64–71.

Lee, Emery G., III. 2005. "Precedent Direction and Compliance: Horizontal Stare Decisis on the U.S. Court of Appeals for the Sixth Circuit." *Seton Hall Circuit Review* 1: 5–25.

Leflar, Robert. 1976. *Internal Operating Procedures of Appellate Courts*. Chicago: American Bar Association.

Liebman, James, Jeffrey Fagan, and Valerie West. 2000a. "A Broken System: Error Rates in Capital Cases, 1973–1999." *Texas Law Review* 73: 1862.

———. 2000b. "Death Matters: A Reply to Professors Latzer and Cauthen." *Judicature* 84: 72–77.

Marvell, Thomas. 1989. "State Appellate Court Responses to Caseload Growth." *Judicature* 72: 282–291.

McGraw, Dan. 2000. "Texan's Test Says Guilty." *U.S. News & World Report*, July 24, p. 26.

Meador, Daniel. 1974. *Appellate Courts: Staff and Process in the Crisis of Volume*. St. Paul, Minn.: West.

Miller, Mark. 1998. "Judicial Activism in Canada and the United States." *Judicature* 81: 262–265.

Morton, F. L., and Rainer Knopf. 2000. *The Charter Revolution and the Court Party*. Peterborough, Ont.: Broadview Press.

Nagel, Stuart. 1961. "Political Party Affiliation and Judges' Decisions." *American Political Science Review* 55: 843–850.

———. 1962. "Ethnic Affiliations and Judicial Propensities." *Journal of Politics* 24: 92.

National Center for State Courts. 2011. "Appellate Caseloads" available online at http://www.ncsconline.org/d_research/csp/2008_files/Appellate.pdf.

Neubauer, David. 1985. "Published Opinions Versus Summary Affirmations: Criminal Appeals in Louisiana." *Justice System Journal* 10: 173–189.

———. 1991. "Winners and Losers: Disposition of Criminal Appeals Through the Louisiana Supreme Court." *Justice Quarterly* 8: 85–106.

———. 1992. "A Polychotomous Measure of Appellate Court Outcomes: The Case of Criminal Appeals." *Justice System Journal* 16: 75–87.

Olsen, Lise. 2005. "The Cantu Case: Death and Doubt." *Houston Chronicle*, November 20.

Petter, Andrew. 2010. *The Politics of the Charter: The Illusive Promise of Constitutional Rights*. Toronto: The University of Toronto Press.

Pritchett, C. Herman. 1948. *The Roosevelt Court: A Study of Judicial Politics and Values, 1937–1947*. New York: Macmillan.

Raab, Selwyn. 1999. "Separating Truth from Fiction in 'The Hurricane.'" *New York Times*, December 28.

Rathjen, Gregory. 1978. "Lawyers and the Appellate Choice: An Analysis of Factors Affecting the Decision to Appeal." *American Politics Quarterly* 6: 387–405.

Roper, Robert, and Albert Melone. 1981. "Does Procedural Due Process Make a Difference? A Study of Second Trials." *Judicature* 65: 136–141.

Scalia, John. 2001. *Federal Criminal Appeals, 1999 with Trends 1985-99*. Washington, D.C.: U.S. Department of Justice, Bureau of Justice Statistics. Available online at http://www.ojp.usdoj.gov/bjs/pub/pdf/fca99.pdf.

Scheck, Barry, Peter Neufeld, and Jim Dwyer. 2000. *Actual Innocence: Five Days to Execution and Other Dispatches from the Wrongfully Convicted*. New York: Doubleday.

Schubert, Glendon. 1959. *Quantitative Analysis of Judicial Behavior*. New York: Free Press.

Segal, Jeffrey A., and Harold J. Spaeth. 1993. *The Supreme Court and the Attitudinal Model*. New York: Cambridge University Press.

———. 2002. *The Supreme Court and the Attitudinal Model Revisited*. Cambridge, U.K.: Cambridge University Press.

Sheehan, Reginald. 1993. "Federal Agencies and the Supreme Court: An Analysis of Litigation Outcomes, 1953–1988." *American Politics Quarterly* 20: 478–500.

Smith, Christopher. 1990. "Polarization and Change in the Federal Courts: En Banc Decisions in the U.S. Courts of Appeals." *Judicature* 74: 133–137.

———. 1995. "Federal Habeas Corpus Reform: The State's Perspective." *Justice System Journal* 18: 1–11.

Solimine, Michael E. 1988. "Ideology and En Banc Review." *North Carolina Law Review* 67: 29–76.

Songer, Donald. 1982. "Consensual and Nonconsensual Decisions in Unanimous Opinions of the United States Courts of Appeals." *American Journal of Political Science* 26: 225–239.

Songer, Donald, and Reginald Sheehan. 1992. "Who Wins on Appeal? Upperdogs and Underdogs in the United States Courts of Appeals." *American Journal of Political Science* 36: 235–258.

Songer, Donald, Reginald Sheehan, and Susan B. Haire. 2000. *Continuity and Change on the United States Courts of Appeals*. Ann Arbor: University of Michigan Press.

Songer, Donald R., and Sue Davis. 1990. "The Impact of Party and Region on Voting Decisions in the United States Courts of Appeals, 1955–1986." *Western Political Quarterly* 43: 317–328.

Songer, Donald R., and Martha Humphries Ginn. 2002. "Assessing the Impact of Presidential and Home State Influences on Judicial Decisionmaking in the United States Courts of Appeals." *Political Research Quarterly* 55(2): 299–328.

Songer, Donald R., Jeffrey A. Segal, and Charles M. Cameron. 1994. "The Hierarchy of Justice: Testing a Principal-Agent Model of Supreme Court–Circuit Court Interactions." *American Journal of Political Science* 38: 673–696.

Tarr, G. Alan. 1998. *Understanding State Constitutions*. Princeton, N.J.: Princeton University Press.

Tarr, G. Alan, and Mary Cornelia Porter. 1988. *State Supreme Courts in State and Nation*. New Haven, Conn.: Yale University Press.

Teets-Farris, Monica. 2002. "Why Judges 'Respectfully Dissent': An Analysis of Dissent on the U.S. Courts of Appeals." Unpublished Ph.D. dissertation, Department of Political Science, University of New Orleans.

Traynor, Roger. 1970. *The Riddle of Harmless Error*. Columbus: Ohio State University Press.

Ulmer, S. Sidney. 1971. *Courts as Small and Not So Small Groups*. New York: General Learning Press.

Wheeler, Stanton, Bliss Cartwright, Robert Kagan, and Lawrence Friedman. 1987. "Do the 'Haves' Come Out Ahead? Winning and Losing in State Supreme Courts, 1870–1970." *Law and Society Review* 21: 403–445.

Williams, Jimmy. 1992. "Sentencing Guidelines and the Changing Composition of Criminal Appeals: A Preliminary Analysis." *Judicature* 76: 94–97.

———. 1995a. "Controlling the Judge's Discretion in Sentencing: Appellate Review of Departures Made in Sentencing Guidelines Cases." *Justice System Journal* 17: 229–240.

———. 1995b. "Type of Counsel and the Outcome of Criminal Appeals: A Research Note." *American Journal of Criminal Justice* 19: 277–285.

Wold, John. 1978. "Going Through the Motions: The Monotony of Appellate Court Decision-Making." *Judicature* 62: 58–65.

Wold, John, and Gregory Caldeira. 1980. "Perceptions of 'Routine' Decision-Making in Five California Courts of Appeal." *Polity* 13: 334–347.

Zemans, Frances. 1983. "Legal Mobilization: The Neglected Role of the Law in the Political System." *American Political Science Review* 77: 690–703.

For Further Reading

American Political Science Association. 2006. "Symposium—The Politics of Canada." *PS: Political Science and Politics* 39: 813–848.

Banks, Christopher P. 1999. *Judicial Politics in the D.C. Circuit Court*. Baltimore: Johns Hopkins University Press.

Barclay, Scott. 1999. *An Appealing Act: Why People Appeal in Civil Cases*. Evanston, Ill.: Northwestern University Press.

Barclay, Scott, Mary Bernstein, and Ann-Maria Marshall (eds.). 2009. *Queer Mobilizations: LGBT Activists Confront the Law*. New York: New York University Press.

Baum, Lawrence. 2006. *Judges and Their Audiences: A Perspective on Judicial Behavior*. Princeton, N.J.: Princeton University Press.

Belbot, Barbara, and Craig Hemmens. 2010. *The Legal Rights of the Convicted*. El Paso: LFB Scholarly Publishing.

Bosworth, Matthew. 2001. *Courts as Catalysts: State Supreme Courts and Public School Finance Equity*. Albany: State University of New York Press.

Burnett, Cathleen. 2002. *Justice Denied: Clemency Appeals in Death Penalty Cases*. Boston: Northeastern University Press.

Cain, Patricia. 2000. *Rainbow Rights: The Role of Lawyers and Courts in the Lesbian and Gay Civil Rights Movement*. Boulder, Colo.: Westview Press.

Clarke, George. 2007. *Justice and Science: Trials and Triumphs of DNA Evidence*. Rutgers University Press.

Clarkson, Stephen, and Stepan Wood. *A Perilous Imbalance: The Globalization of Canadian Law and Governance*. Vancouver: University of British Columbia.

Eskridge, William. 2002. *Equality Practice: Civil Unions and the Future of Gay Rights*. New York: Routledge.

Flemming, Roy. 2004. *Tournament of Appeals: Granting Judicial Review in Canada*. Vancouver: University of British Columbia Press.

Giles, Michael W., Virginia A. Hettinger, Christopher Zorn, and Todd Peppers. 2007. "The Etiology of the Occurrence of En Banc Review in the U.S. Court of Appeals." *American Journal of Political Science* 51(3): 449–463.

Goldberg-Hiller, Jonathan. 2002. *The Limits to Union: Same-Sex Marriage and the Politics of Civil Rights*. Ann Arbor: University of Michigan Press.

Gould, Jon. 2007. *The Innocence Commission: Preventing Wrongful Convictions and Restoring the Criminal Justice System*. New York: New York University Press.

Hall, Melinda. 2007. "Voting in State Supreme Court Elections: Competition and Context as Democratic Incentives." *Journal of Politics* 69: 1147.

Holmes, Lisa, and Jolly Emery. 2006. "Court Diversification: Staffing State Courts of Last Resort Through Interim Appointment." *Justice System Journal* 27: 1–46.

Huff, C. Ronald and Martin Killias (eds.). *Wrongful Conviction: International Perspectives on Miscarriages of Justice*. Philadelphia: Temple University Press.

Klein, David, and Gregory Mitchel (eds.). 2010. *The Psychology of Judicial Decision Making*. New York: Oxford University Press.

Langer, Laura. 2002. *Judicial Review in State Supreme Courts: A Comparative Study*. Albany: State University of New York Press.

Lopeman, Charles. 1999. *The Activist Advocate: Policy Making in State Supreme Courts*. Westport, Conn.: Praeger.

Metz, Tamara. 2010. *Untying the Know: Marriage, the State, and the Case for their Divorce*. Princeton: Princeton University Press.

Miller, Banks. 2010. "Describing the State Solicitors General." *Judicature* 93: 238–246.

Murdoch, Joyce, and Deb Price. 2001. *Courting Justice: Gay Men and Lesbians v. The Supreme Court*. New York: Basic Books.

Perino, Michael. 2006. "Law, Ideology, and Strategy in Judicial Decision Making: Evidence from Securities Fraud Actions." *Journal of Empirical Legal Studies* 3: 497–524.

Pinello, Daniel. 2003. *Gay Rights and American Law*. New York: Cambridge University Press.

Proveda, Tony. 2001. "Estimating Wrongful Convictions." *Justice Quarterly* 18: 689.

Vladmir, Kogan. 2010. "Lessons from Recent State Constitutional Conventions." *California Journal of Politics and Policy* Vol. 2: Article 3.

Westerland, C., Segal, J. A., Epstein, L., Cameron, C. M. and Comparato, S. (2010), "Strategic Defiance and Compliance in the U.S. Courts of Appeals." *American Journal of Political Science*, 54: 891–905.

Williams, Robert. 2009. *The Law of American State Constitutions*. New York: Oxford University Press.

Zalman, Marvin, Brad Smith, and Angie Kiger. 2008. "Officials' Estimates of the Incidence of 'Actual Innocence' Convictions. *Justice Quarterly* 25: 72–100.

THE SUPREME COURT: DECIDING WHAT TO DECIDE

Stephen Meinhold

Despite its role as a co-equal branch of government, the Supreme Court did not have its own building until 1935. After oral argument, lawyers often hold press conferences on these steps predicting victory in their case.

Jane Roe was a pregnant, homeless, 21-year-old Dallas waitress. Because an 1856 Texas law made abortion illegal, Jane Roe confronted the option either of traveling to another state to obtain a safe, but expensive, abortion or of seeking an illegal and potentially life-threatening back-alley procedure. An adoption lawyer introduced her to two young female lawyers who were looking for plaintiffs to challenge state laws restricting abortion. Thus, on March 3, 1970, Jane Roe was listed as the lead plaintiff in a class action lawsuit filed in U.S. District Court for the Northern District of Texas. Named as defendant was Henry Wade, the district attorney of Dallas County, Texas. Three years later, the Supreme Court ruled in Jane Roe's favor. Surprisingly, the initial reaction to *Roe v. Wade* was muted; former president Lyndon Johnson had died the day before, thus banishing to the back pages comments about the Court's expansion of the right to privacy to include a woman's right to an abortion. But, over the

414

years, the controversy has increased, focusing unprecedented attention on the nation's highest court.

Since deciding *Roe v. Wade* in 1973, the justices of the Supreme Court have been faced with dozens of opportunities to decide abortion-related issues. Most of the time, they have refused to decide the cases, but thirty-three times the Court has said "yes" (most recently in *Gonzales v. Carhart* 2007), thereby intentionally putting itself in the maelstrom of this contentious social, political, and legal issue. *Roe v. Wade* (1973) did not end either the legal or the political battle over abortion. Why do the justices decide to hear cases such as *Roe*? Why would the justices regularly vote to hear cases that deal with one of the most contentious issues—abortion—ever decided by the Court? Especially when fewer than 100 cases in any year are given the full attention of the Court? The answer to those questions is found in the unique position of the Supreme Court in our society, the ideological preferences of the justices, and the legal activities of interest groups and plaintiffs in the lower courts.

This chapter begins by discussing the Supreme Court's jurisdiction and the types of petitions litigants must file if they wish one last review of their case. Through doctrines of access, the Supreme Court decides what types of cases the federal courts will or will not hear, thus effectively limiting some disputes that litigants might wish decided but the Court chooses to ignore. Next, attention shifts to the lawyers and litigants who mobilize the law by seeking Supreme Court review. The Court's procedures and the criteria employed receive considerable attention. Finally, the chapter explores the types of cases on the Court's docket and examines tensions between the Court and Congress over which branch of government should choose what types of cases the Supreme Court should decide. (See Courts in Comparative Perspective: The International Court of Justice.)

JURISDICTION OF THE SUPREME COURT

Which cases the Supreme Court can hear—whether federal or state—is specified, ever so briefly, in the Constitution and further fleshed out by federal statutes and decisions of the Court itself. As discussed in Chapter 3, debates over the jurisdiction of the federal judiciary are as old as the nation itself, and this long-standing controversy continues.

Original Jurisdiction

A very small fraction of the cases decided by the Supreme Court arise under its original jurisdiction. Article III of the Constitution specifies that the Court has **original jurisdiction** in all cases affecting ambassadors, other public ministers, and consuls, and cases in which a state is a party. Original jurisdiction cases typically involve suits between two or more states concerning matters such as ownership of offshore oil deposits, territorial disputes caused by shifting river boundaries, and controversies over water rights when a river flows through or between two or more states (Zimmerman 2006). Original jurisdiction cases go directly to the Supreme Court without first being considered by a lower court; in essence, the nation's highest

COURTS IN COMPARATIVE PERSPECTIVE

■ The International Court of Justice

The sight of Slobodan Milosevic standing before a court of law answering charges of war crimes was something many thought they would never see. The Yugoslav leader was blamed for starting four Balkan wars and was charged with crimes against humanity for the 1999 expulsion of hundreds of thousands of Kosovo Albanians from their homes as well as the massacre of civilians in villages such as Racak and Bela Crkva. He was the first former head of state delivered by a government to face an international war crimes court.

The specifics of Milosevic's alleged crimes aside, his prosecution raises two important questions: Who should decide who tries international criminals? And should a permanent world criminal court be created? Past efforts at establishing international tribunals have largely been ad hoc. The International Criminal Tribunal for the Former Yugoslavia was established by Resolution 827 of the United Nations (UN) Security Council in May 1993. Based in The Hague, Netherlands, it was the first international body convened for the prosecution of war crimes since the Nuremberg and Tokyo trials held in the aftermath of World War II. Currently, the tribunal has 919 employees representing 76 different nationalities, and its 2010–11 budget was $302 million. The tribunal may not try suspects in absentia, and it may not impose the death penalty. The maximum sentence is life imprisonment. To date, 161 people have been indicted; 115 of these proceedings have concluded: 56 people were sentenced, 10 were acquitted, 13 were referred to national jurisdiction, and 36 had their indictments withdrawn or are deceased. An additional 46 proceedings are ongoing, with 21 of those currently at trial. Two individuals indicted for war crimes remain at large. The longest sentence was that of forty years given to Goran Jelisic, a Bosnian Serb prison camp guard.

The creation of this tribunal reflects a broader trend of international justice. The oldest and most far reaching of these bodies is the International Court of Justice, also based in The Hague, Netherlands. It is the principal judicial organ of the UN and superseded the Permanent Court of International Justice established after World War I. The court consists of 15 judges, chosen by the UN General Assembly and the Security Council. No two judges may be from the same country. All members of the UN are automatically members of the court. The court's jurisdiction is limited to deciding disputes arising over interpretations of treaties, questions of international law, and breaches of international obligation.

Several factors limit the effectiveness of the International Court of Justice. Chief among them is the lack of enforcement power. If a member nation fails to comply with a judgment of the court, an appeal for assistance may be made to the Security Council. Moreover, the United States excludes all its own domestic matters from the court's jurisdiction and reserves the right to decide what constitutes domestic matters. Thus, the United States has refused to accept decisions of the World Court and, in any event, could block enforcement by casting a veto in the Security Council.

After the creation of the International Criminal Tribunal for the Former Yugoslavia, the next logical step was the establishment of an International Criminal Court to prosecute serious violations of humanitarian law. On July 1, 2002, the International Criminal Court (ICC) was established pursuant to the Rome Statute, a treaty signed by 106 states that participated in the United Nations Diplomatic Conference of Plenipotentiaries on the Establishment of an International Criminal Court. In 2000, President Clinton signed that treaty on behalf of the United States, but it has never been ratified by the U.S. Senate, and George Bush continues to signal his opposition to the court. In an unusual move, President Bush, in 2002, notified the UN that the United States was officially withdrawing its name from the treaty. Conservative Republicans are vehemently opposed to such a body, fearing loss of U.S. sovereignty and the possibility that military personnel would be prosecuted, making it very unlikely the Senate will ratify the document. In 2011, the Obama administration supported a UN resolution authorizing the ICC to investigate Libyan President Gadhafi, and some have wondered whether that signals a softening in the U.S. opposition to the ICC, but Senate confirmation of the treaty appears highly unlikely.

As for Slobodan Milosevic, he defiantly denied the right of the International Court to try him. He angrily shouted at the judges during court proceedings and even refused to read some of the documents handed to him in court. His trial dragged on for four years before he died in prison. In comparison, another recent high-profile state

(continued)

leader accused of war crimes—Saddam Hussein—was tried by a court created by his own nation, not an international tribunal. He was convicted of war crimes against humanity, sentenced to death, and hanged on December 30, 2006. Courts of International Justice seldom penetrate popular culture but after World War II the movie *Judgment at Nuremberg* (1961) dramatized the trial of the leaders of the NAZI government in Germany. More recently the movie *Blood Diamond* (2006) has offered an insight into African civil wars (See Law and Popular Culture: War Crimes, Supermodels, and Blood Diamonds).

---

tribunal sits as a trial court from which there is no appeal. Those cases are a very minor part of the work of the Court, typically representing only 1 percent or less of the workload. In an earlier era, the justices sat as a trial court listening at length to the presentation of evidence and the arguments of lawyers, but no longer. Now the Court appoints a **special master**, who makes recommendations.

Appellate Jurisdiction

The vast majority of cases that come to the Supreme Court arise under its **appellate jurisdiction**, which Congress defines and can alter at any time. Since the passage of the Judiciary Act of 1925, the Supreme Court has functioned, for all intents and purposes, as a court of discretionary jurisdiction. The Court has not been expected to take on the function of primarily correcting errors committed by other courts. Rather, the intent of the 1925 act was that, after a decision in a trial court and after at least one review in federal or state appellate court, further appeal to the Supreme Court should be permitted only if the case presents important issues of federal law (Brennan 1983). In the words of Justice John Paul Stevens (1982, 180), "It is far better to allow the state supreme courts and federal courts of appeal to have the final say on almost all litigation than to embark on the hopeless task of attempting to correct every judicial error that can be found." Against that historical understanding, many litigants petition for Supreme Court review, but only a handful are successful. Appellate jurisdiction cases come to the Supreme Court by three methods: appeal, certiorari, and certification.

Appeal   Appeals review lower-court decisions that have declared a state or federal law unconstitutional. Until 1988, **appeals** could be filed from adverse decisions in U.S. courts of appeals, U.S. district courts, three-judge district courts, or state supreme courts (the source of most appeals). According to the statutes, the Supreme Court has an obligation to decide appeals, but, in practice, the Court treats them in approximately the same discretionary manner as the writ of certiorari. Nonetheless, according to Justice William Brennan (1983, 232):

> Cases on appeal consume a disproportionate amount of the limited time available for oral argument. That's because time and again a justice who would conscientiously deny review of an issue presented on certiorari cannot conscientiously say that when presented on appeal the issue is insubstantial. Policy considerations that give rise to the distinction between review by appeal and review by writ of certiorari have long since lost their force, and abandonment of our appellate jurisdiction (leaving a writ of certiorari as the only means of obtaining Supreme Court review) is simply recognition of reality.

LAW AND POPULAR CULTURE

■ War Crimes, Supermodels, and Blood Diamonds

An international supermodel is attending a dinner hosted by one of the most recognized world leaders of the twentieth century. Later in the evening she is awakened and presented with a small bag of diamonds as a gift from the president of a country who is alleged to have committed war crimes by exchanging arms for diamonds with revolutionary forces responsible for killing and maiming tens of thousands of innocent civilians. This sounds like the plot from a popular fiction novel or a James Bond movie, but unfortunately the story is real and the characters are familiar. The dinner was hosted by Nelson Mandela, former president of South Africa; and Charles Taylor, the former president of Liberia who is currently standing trial on crimes against humanity, was in attendance. And Naomi Campbell, the international supermodel, was also present.

Had the gift been any other precious gemstone it might have gone unnoticed and Ms. Campbell would never have appeared in a war crimes tribunal, as she did on August 5, 2010 when she testified about the events of that night. The diamonds are alleged to be "blood diamonds"—which is a term used to describe diamonds that are mined in a war zone and used to support a revolutionary insurgency. In this trial prosecutors for the Special Court for Sierra Leone were alleging in a criminal tribunal that former president of Liberia, Charles Taylor, during his regime, had routinely traded guns to the Revolutionary United Front (RUF) in Sierra Leone in exchange for diamonds. The arms were used by the RUF to kill and maim tens of thousands of innocent civilians.

The Special Court for Sierra Leone was established by the government of Sierra Leone and the United Nations on August 14, 2000 and is located in the Hague Netherlands. It is funded with voluntary donations from countries around the world and its purpose is to investigate alleged violations of humanitarian law committed in Sierra Leone since 1996. The Court has issued 13 indictments with the most famous one being against former Liberia President, Charles Taylor. Mr. Taylor was arrested in 2006 and has been imprisoned during the trial of more than three years. Mr. Taylor is

the first African leader to face an International Criminal Court and his case demonstrates how the global community uses the courtroom to try and bring rogue leaders to justice. But Ms. Campbell's testimony about "blood diamonds" also drew attention to another legal approach used by the international community to affect public policy—international cooperation and agreements.

In 2000 the United Nations Security Council began taking actions that eventually led to the Kimberly Process Certification Scheme, which is an agreement between governments, nonprofit organizations and diamond producers to ensure that diamonds sold on the market were legally exported. In 2001 both outgoing president Bill Clinton and incoming president George Bush used Executive Orders to ban the importation of diamonds from Liberia into the United States.

The events surrounding the Sierra Leone civil war and the use of "blood diamonds" to fuel the war crimes are fictionalized in the film *Blood Diamond* (2006) starring Leonardo DiCaprio and Djimon Hounsou who plays Solomon Vandy. In a moving final scene Hounsou gives an address about the impact of blood diamonds on his country and family to a conference being held in Kimberly, South Africa intended to represent the real events surrounding the United Nations efforts to establish the Kimberly Process. His speech receives a standing ovation.

Charles Taylor's trial is over and he remains in prison awaiting the verdict. Meanwhile most observers believe the Kimberly Process Certification Scheme has worked to reduce the trade in illegal "blood diamonds."

Discussion Questions

1. What is the potential impact of international criminal tribunals being voluntarily funded by nations around the world?

2. What challenges do prosecutors face in mounting cases against world leaders accused of war crimes?

3. Discuss how both the international trial and international agreements were aimed at trying to end the root criminal behavior of war atrocities.

Those views have been unanimously shared by the justices, and, after two decades of lobbying, Congress narrowed the Court's mandatory appeal jurisdiction in 1988 to include only the small number of cases decided by three-judge district courts (see Chapter 3).

Certiorari   If a case does not fall under the limited criteria of appeal, the losing party in the lower court has no statutory right to appeal. But discretionary review by the writ of certiorari may be sought. From the Latin, **certiorari** means "to make sure." Thus, a request for certiorari (or "cert" for short) is like an appeal, but one that the high court is not required by law to accept for decision. It is literally a writ from the higher court asking the lower court for the record of the case. Most cases reviewed by the Supreme Court come via the writ of certiorari, and, of those, most come from the U.S. courts of appeals.

Certification   Although most cases come to the Court as appeals or writs of certiorari, Congress also provides that appellate courts (not the losing party) may submit a writ of certification requesting the justices to clarify or "make certain" a point of federal law. **Certification** is rarely used, and it is rarer still for the Court to decide important cases in this way.

DOCTRINES OF ACCESS

The broad provisions of Article III of the Constitution outlining the jurisdiction of the Supreme Court and the slightly more detailed congressional legislation specifying appellate jurisdiction are, at best, only imperfect guides to understanding how the Court decides to decide. The Court's own interpretations of Article III and its rulings on congressional legislation play a major role in shaping what types of cases the Supreme Court will hear.

The cases that the judiciary may decide are governed by **doctrines of access**. Although courts are passive and reactive governmental institutions, they are not required to hear all disputes brought to them. Before deciding a case's substantive issues (termed a decision "on the merits"), a judge must be satisfied that a number of prerequisites have been met. These procedural and substantive requirements function as gatekeeping devices, allowing access to the judiciary to some types of cases (and litigants) but denying access to other types of cases (and litigants). These restrictions have been developed primarily by the courts themselves and, therefore, represent self-imposed limits on judicial power. For that reason, doctrines of access are also referred to as "rules of judicial self-restraint," because they reflect the concern of the judiciary that some disputes are best handled elsewhere (*United States v. Butler* 1936). Viewed from that perspective, doctrines of access lie at the heart of defining the powers of the three separate branches of government.

Questions concerning doctrines of access rarely arise in the average suit, in which one private party sues another private party. In suits for breaching a contract or causing a tort, these matters are self-evident. Rather, these questions are more likely to arise in policy lawsuits, particularly public policy cases concerning the environment, reapportionment, abortion, civil rights, and affirmative action. Hence, rules governing access primarily concern the federal courts. The Supreme Court justices play a major role in crafting doctrines of access (Taggart and DeZee 1985). Indeed, these issues are the basis of a substantial number of the Court's formally decided cases (Rathjen and Spaeth 1979).

The Court has considerable discretion over which public matters will be adjudicated and which will not (Orren 1976). The justices may simply decide that they do not want to decide certain issues. For that reason, doctrines of access change, depending on which justices interpret them. The Warren Court, seeing the judiciary as an instrument for correcting or preventing injustices, expanded the scope of litigants who could bring suit in federal court. More recently, the Burger and Rehnquist Courts, articulating a more restrictive role of the judiciary, limited and narrowed the range of litigants who could sue. For example, during the Burger Court, denials of access almost always allowed conservative decisions in the lower courts to stand. Moreover, justices often voted for or against granting access, depending on the ideological result of the lower-court decision (Cameron, Segal, and Songer 2000). It is too early to tell, but the Roberts Court appears to be continuing the recent traditions of limiting access to the nation's highest court.

Doctrines of access are closely tied to the justices on the Court at a particular time, thus leading Adamany (1991) to conclude that they are used largely to achieve policy results. Indeed, from the perspective of the formal law, they have been characterized as "inconsistent, contradictory, even chaotic, and enshrouded by mysteries analogous to those of theology" (Harris 1983, 360). The legal dimensions of doctrines of access can best be discussed under the headings of justiciability, standing, ripeness and mootness, and political questions.

Justiciability

A **justiciable** (pronounced jus-*tish*-able) case is defined as a case that is proper to be decided by a court. That rather bare-bones definition is usually fleshed out with additional requirements that the court must have standards on which to make a decision and that the court must also possess a remedy to correct the problem. Cases that fail to meet those standards are said to be nonjusticiable.

One component of the concept of justiciability is the prohibition against an **advisory opinion**, which is a formal decision by a court about a question of law submitted by the legislature or by an executive officer but not actually presented to the court in a concrete lawsuit. For the federal courts, this prohibition dates to 1793, when President Washington addressed the Supreme Court, asking the justices to define his constitutional authority to decide certain questions relating to the U.S. policy of neutrality with respect to the ongoing war in Europe. Chief Justice John Jay responded that the Court would not and could not provide legal advice, because its role was confined to deciding cases that arose in the course of bona fide litigation. More than a century later, that position was reaffirmed in *Muskrat v. United States* (1911). The rationale is that the courts cannot accept advisory opinions because they present hypothetical situations that lack the liveliness found in actual disputes. Most states follow the federal lead in prohibiting advisory opinions, although a handful allow the state supreme court to issue advisory opinions if requested by the governor or the attorney general.

Standing

Standing is the legal analogue to the question "Who are you to complain?" and refers to a person's right to bring or join a lawsuit. Although the concept of standing is among the most amorphous in the entire domain of public law, three basic components provide some degree of specificity.

The first element of standing is the requirement that the case involve an actual dispute and not merely a theoretical one. Article III of the Constitution limits federal judicial power to cases and controversies. That simple phrase has been interpreted by the Supreme Court to require that the controversy be "definite and concrete." "It must be a real and substantial controversy" (*Aetna Life Insurance Co. v. Haworth* 1937). The case-or-controversy doctrine states a fundamental principle of the adversary system: Courts will hear only concrete disputes and not abstract issues.

A second element of standing to sue incorporates the requirement of adversity. The courts require that the parties in the lawsuit have something to lose and, therefore, will argue and present issues with an intensity and vigor not found in a disinterested litigant who has no personal stake in the case outcome. Today, the requirement of adversity rules out friendly lawsuits, but that was not always true. In 1936, for example, a company president sued his own company to prevent its compliance with a major New Deal statute, and the Court held the law to be unconstitutional (*Carter v. Carter Coal Company* 1936). Under contemporary standards, that case would be denied standing to sue because it was a "friendly" suit lacking true adversity.

The final element of standing is the requirement that the legal injury suffered by the plaintiff be direct. The litigant must have a substantial and immediate interest in the litigation. Stated another way, one may not bring a lawsuit solely on behalf of a third party (except in the case of a legal guardian or next of kin). Thus, a neighbor cannot sue for an injury suffered by another neighbor, and a doctor cannot sue for a legal injury suffered by a patient. But a parent can file suit on behalf of a minor child, a surviving spouse can assert a legal injury suffered by the deceased, and a group can sue on behalf of its members.

Taxpayer Lawsuits   One of the most vexing problem areas concerning standing to sue centers on suits brought by citizens against the government. An individual brings a **taxpayer lawsuit** to challenge the spending of public money for a particular purpose. In 1923, the Supreme Court held that a taxpayer's stake in how public money is spent is so minute and uncertain that it did not satisfy the requirement of standing to sue. The Court eased that limitation somewhat in 1968 (*Flast v. Cohen* 1968). By 1982, however, as the Supreme Court and the country had grown more conservative, taxpayer lawsuits were once again relegated to the "dubious"—if not prohibited—category (*Valley Forge Christian College v. Americans United for Separation of Church and State* 1982).

Class Actions   Standing requirements are particularly important considerations in group use of the courts. In particular, there are four prerequisites in **class action** lawsuits:

- There must be so many people in the class (group) that it would be impractical to name them all as individual parties.
- The class must be clearly recognizable by virtue of its well-defined interest that raises the same questions of law and fact.

- The representative parties' claims must be typical of the class's claims.
- The representative parties must fairly and adequately protect the interests of the class.

If all four requirements are met, the court will certify that the class may maintain the lawsuit.

The Supreme Court, however, has erected some important barriers to those activities, holding that, in order to meet requirements of standing to sue, the members of the class must have suffered a specific harm rather than have an abstract "public interest." For example, in *Sierra Club v. Morton* (1972), the Court held that purely ideological interests in the environment are not enough to establish standing to challenge governmental action that a litigant believes will be environmentally harmful. Whereas the Warren Court tended to expand the grounds on which interest groups could file class actions, the Burger, Rehnquist, and, most recently, Roberts Courts have tended to slow down or even roll back concepts of standing, particularly for class actions.

Ripeness and Mootness

Under the ripeness doctrine, a case must have matured from a theoretical dispute to a live one. Thus, a case is said to be **ripe** for adjudication if the legal issues involved have evolved to the point that a clear decision can be reached. An example of how courts apply the ripeness doctrine is the litigation contesting Connecticut's law prohibiting the sale of birth control devices and also the dissemination of information about birth control. To clear away legal obstacles to the opening of a birth control clinic in New Haven, the law was challenged, but the Court dismissed the case on the grounds that the law had never been enforced (*Poe v. Ullman* 1961). After the clinic opened anyway, its president was arrested and convicted of a misdemeanor. This new case reached the Court in *Griswold v. Connecticut* (1965). The issue could no longer be dismissed for lack of ripeness, and the Court overturned the Connecticut law as a violation of the newly discovered constitutional right to privacy.

A legal cousin of the concept of ripeness is the doctrine of **exhaustion of remedies**. A plaintiff lacks standing to sue if he or she has not exhausted all other available remedies before coming to court. The underlying principle is that courts should be the last resort in resolving disputes. A failure to exhaust all administrative remedies will result in dismissal of the court case because it is not ripe for adjudication.

If ripeness involves a plaintiff filing a premature claim, mootness represents the opposite situation—a plaintiff being too late to seek relief from the courts. Simply stated, courts do not decide dead issues. The passage of time or a change in circumstances may make an issue **moot**. Mootness standards are, however, flexible, as the two following cases illustrate.

By the time her challenge to Texas's abortion law reached the high court, Jane Roe was no longer pregnant. Because there was no active controversy, the case appeared to be moot. But the Supreme Court elected to hear the case, noting that few, if any, cases of pregnancy, abortion, or childbirth would ever be reviewed by appellate courts before the end of the biological period of gestation. Based on pressing concerns of public policy, the Court carved out an exception to the mootness doctrine. (See Case Close-Up: *Roe v. Wade* 1973.)

CASE CLOSE-UP

■ *Roe v. Wade* (1973)

Abortion Rights

Over a pizza in a small Dallas restaurant, Jane Roe poured out her troubled history to the two women she had just met. She was unemployed, was virtually homeless, and already had a five-year-old daughter living with someone else. During the summer, she had worked selling tickets in a traveling carnival when she was raped. The doctor who diagnosed her pregnancy curtly told her she could travel to other states such as California or Colorado, where abortions were legal and safe (but neglected to say that abortions were also cumbersome and expensive). Also left unsaid was the common knowledge that a quick trip to Mexico could easily procure a cheap, but potentially life-threatening, back-alley abortion.

As she told her story, Jane Roe (the female version of John Doe) decided that she trusted Sarah Weddington and Linda Coffee. That trust was of critical importance, because the two were young lawyers who were searching for a plaintiff who was willing to challenge Texas's abortion law. Jane Roe explained that she was very angry when she learned she could not get an abortion and would be forced to bear a child whom she did not want and could not care for. Sarah Weddington was also angry, but for different reasons. Her anger stemmed not from personal experience with an unwanted pregnancy and potential risks of illegal abortion but from an ideological commitment—she wanted to change the law to improve the plight of women. Sarah Weddington (who would become lead counsel) was one of a new breed—women were just beginning to graduate from law school in appreciable numbers. Indeed, Weddington was the first woman hired by Fort Worth as an assistant city attorney (Faux 1989). Although there was no chance that a lawsuit would directly benefit Jane Roe, Roe agreed to serve as plaintiff in a test case (Chapter 7).

Because the lawsuit challenged the constitutionality of a state law, it was heard by a three-judge panel of the U.S. District Court for the Northern District of Texas, located in Dallas. One of the judges was Sarah Hughes, a Lyndon Johnson appointee and one of the few female judges on the federal bench at the time. The three-judge panel declared the Texas law unconstitutional but refused to issue an injunction prohibiting its enforcement (*Roe v. Wade*, 314 F. Supp. 1217 [N.D. Tex., 1970]). That "mixed" holding left neither side satisfied, and, therefore, both sides appealed to the U.S. Supreme Court. (To preserve standing, Jane Roe carried the baby to term and gave the infant up for adoption immediately after birth.)

On May 3, 1971, the Court noted probable jurisdiction and preparations began for oral argument. But, by the time the Court heard oral argument on December 13, 1971, the Court consisted of only seven justices. In September 1971, a gravely ill Justice Hugo Black had resigned. A few days later, Justice John Harlan likewise resigned because of declining health. President Nixon's nominations of Lewis Powell and William Rehnquist to fill those vacancies had been confirmed by the Senate in early December, but swearing in was not scheduled until after Christmas.

Chief Justice Warren Burger opened the Court's oral argument session with the traditional announcement: "We will hear arguments in No. 18, *Roe against Wade*." Sarah Weddington began her allotted thirty minutes by reviewing the lower-court decisions but was interrupted by the chief justice, who asked whether a previous decision had decided the matter. "No," she replied and went on to detail that, for poor women like Jane Roe for whom abortions were not necessary to save their lives, Texas law offered no real choice; they faced either unwanted childbirth or medically unsafe self-abortions. At that point, White interrupted to comment, "So far on the merits, you've told us about the important impact of the law, and you make a very eloquent policy argument against it." But he added that the Court could not simply be involved with matters of policy and wanted to know the constitutional basis of her argument (Craig and O'Brien 1993).

Jay Floyd, the assistant attorney general of Texas, next strode to the lectern and argued that this controversy was not one for the courts. Arguments about freedom of choice were misleading, he continued, but one of the justices interrupted with a statement, "Maybe she makes her choice when she decides to live in Texas." In the same vein, Justice Thurgood Marshall demanded to know, "What is Texas' interest in the statute?" (Craig and O'Brien 1993).

(continued)

Following oral argument, the Court met in conference; the discussions were inconclusive and the actual vote in dispute. A few days later, the chief justice assigned Blackmun to write the opinion, but Douglas strongly objected, stating that Burger had voted in the minority and, therefore, as the most senior justice in the majority, he (Douglas) was entitled to assign. Douglas then defused the controversy by noting that he chose to assign Blackmun. The task proved daunting. In May, Blackmun circulated a draft that met with little enthusiasm. Troubled that such a major decision might be decided by a shorthanded court, the Court (in a highly unusual move) set *Roe v. Wade* (1973) for reargument in the fall (Craig and O'Brien 1993).

Roe v. Wade (1973) was reargued on October 10, 1972, and discussed in conference on October 12, 1972. The tentative vote was 6–3 to rule the abortion laws unconstitutional. Blackmun's opinion, which had been in preparation for almost a year, was circulated, and each of the justices in the presumed majority offered suggestions, most of which Blackmun incorporated into his draft opinion. At the Court's conference on January 12, 1973, Burger unexpectedly announced he was joining the majority (Barnum 1993).

On January 22, 1973, Justice Blackmun delivered the opinion of the Court. The first part dealt with matters of justiciability and standing. Because Jane Roe had already given birth to the child, the case was theoretically moot; the Court observed, however, that pregnancy would rarely outlast the litigation process. Therefore, the law should not be so rigid and should support a finding of "nonmootness."

The heart of the opinion struck down state abortion laws because they denied women the constitutional right to privacy. In support, Blackmun cited *Griswold v. Connecticut* (1965), which declared that, although the phrase *right to privacy* is not found in the Constitution, its spirit pervades the document. Blackmun's opinion clearly reflects a compromise, because he wrote that, whatever the source, "this right … is broad enough to encompass a woman's decision whether or not to terminate her pregnancy." But this right was a qualified one. The state's "important interests in safeguarding health, maintaining medical standards, and protecting life" were "sufficiently compelling" to justify government regulation. The opinion established a controversial "trimester analysis" that barred any regulation of abortion during the first three months of pregnancy; allowed limited restrictions to protect the woman's health and safety during the second three months; and permitted the government to ban abortion only during the final trimester—when the fetus was thought capable of living on its own.

In dissent, Justice Byron White (a Kennedy appointee) said the decision allowed for abortion to satisfy "the convenience, whim, or caprice of the putative mother." And, in a separate dissent, Rehnquist (a recent Nixon appointee) said the ruling "partakes more of judicial legislation than it does of a determination of the intent of the drafters of the Fourteenth Amendment."

Challenges to abortion laws and the *Roe* decision itself have repeatedly returned to the Supreme Court. In 1989, the Court, by a 5–4 vote, gave the states greater authority for limiting abortions (*Webster v. Reproductive Health Services* 1989). In 1992, the Court barely reaffirmed the centerpiece of *Roe*. Chief Justice Rehnquist and Byron White, who had dissented in *Roe*, were joined by two Reagan appointees—Scalia and Thomas—in voting to overturn *Roe*. But a majority, including three nominees of Republican presidents opposed to abortion—O'Connor, Kennedy, and Souter—reaffirmed the concept of the right to privacy, stressing the importance of precedent and the need to preserve the integrity of the Court. At the same time, the joint opinion (joined by Blackmun and Stevens) upheld state restrictions, including parental consent for minors, a 24-hour waiting period, and notification of husbands (*Planned Parenthood of Southeastern Pennsylvania v. Casey* 1992).

In a controversial decision, the Court issued an opinion on what is often referred to as "partial birth" abortion. In *Stenberg v. Carhart* (2000), the Court declared (5–4) unconstitutional a Nebraska law making the practice illegal on the grounds that it placed an undue burden on women and because it did not provide an exception for the health of the mother. However, in 2003, the Congress passed and President Bush signed into law the Federal Abortion Ban, which placed limitations on access to certain medical procedures. Interest groups immediately filed lawsuits. The lower court ruled the federal law unconstitutional; but, in 2007, the Supreme Court in *Gonzales v. Carhart* reversed the lower-court decision and upheld the law. The court's 5–4 decision argued that the law did not place an undue burden on women, while the dissent of Justice Ginsburg argued that the law violated the privacy rights of women. The decision demonstrated that President Bush's appointees, Chief Justice Roberts and Samuel Alito, will likely adopt a conservative position on the issue of abortion.

In essence, the high court is as profoundly divided over abortion as the American people are. The Court's views mirror public opinion polls indicating that most Americans favor abortion rights but oppose making abortion easy to obtain.

(continued)

Whereas *Brown v. Board of Education* (1954) reflected the concerted efforts of an interest group, *Roe v. Wade* (1973) began as a case involving two lawyers who were vitally interested in women's issues. But, over the years, abortion has attracted attention from a variety of interest groups. *Webster* (1989), for example, attracted an unprecedented number of amicus curiae briefs: A total of 78 were filed: 46 on behalf of the appellants (pro-life) and 32 for the appellees (pro-choice). Altogether, more than 400 organizations signed on as co-sponsors, and thousands of individuals joined in one form or another. Both sides directed their arguments to garnering the vote of Justice Sandra Day O'Connor, who was perceived as the pivotal vote in a likely 4–1–4 voting alignment. There is little doubt that the amicus briefs had an impact, shaping the opinions. O'Connor's concurring opinion, for example, cited the appellees' briefs three times and, on several occasions, referred to the briefs containing medical and scientific information (Behuniak-Long 1991). Amicus briefs were numerous in *Gonzales v. Carhart* (2007), and the case, along with a companion case, was supported by NARAL Pro-Choice America and Planned Parenthood.

Beyond efforts in the courts to overturn *Roe*, there have been many attempts by legislatures to dismantle the decision. Numerous constitutional amendments to overturn *Roe* have been proposed, but none has passed Congress. Legislation has narrowed the impact, however, by refusing to require public financing of abortions for poor women and restricting certain medical procedures. And the Court has upheld many laws that make abortions more difficult to obtain.

The Court, conversely, was not willing to make an exception to mootness in a case involving an adult bookstore. City News & Novelty, Inc., challenged the policy of Waukesha, Wisconsin, that required sellers of sexually explicit material to obtain and annually renew a license. The city denied the permit, and City News mounted a long-running legal battle to secure its permit. Probably because of its extensive legal expenses, City News eventually closed its business, at which point the U.S. Supreme Court declared the case moot, perhaps finding a convenient way not to decide this controversial matter (*City News & Novelty, Inc. v. City of Waukesha* 2001).

Political Questions

The most interesting—and also the most ambiguous—component of doctrines of access concerns **political questions**, under which the justices refuse to decide questions they think should properly be decided by other branches of government. The political questions doctrine has little to do with whether politics or controversy is involved in a case. Rather, it is closer to the notion of separation of powers, which emphasizes that each branch of government has its own arena, wherein that branch is the most appropriate decision maker.

The inherent flexibility of the political questions doctrine is underscored by its uneven history. The term was first mentioned in 1803 by Chief Justice John Marshall in *Marbury v. Madison* (1803), but the Court made no attempt to elaborate on its meaning until 1849. In a case arising from the Dorr Rebellion, the Court held that what constitutes a republican form of government under Article IV of the Constitution was a "political question" best left to Congress and the president to decide (*Luther v. Borden* 1849).

Over the course of its history, the Court has considered a variety of issues to be political questions, including ratification of constitutional amendments, federal policies regarding aliens, and many practices of political parties. Because the justices have considerable discretion in identifying such questions, no clear-cut definition exists that will allow the rapid identification of a political question. Indeed, definitions of political questions have proved to be contradictory and do not necessarily square with the Court's practices (Peltason 1955).

Clearly, what constitutes a political question depends on the perceptions of the justices who are sitting at the time the case comes into the federal judicial system. "Political questions are those which judges choose not to decide and a question becomes political by the judge's refusal to decide it" (Peltason 1955, 10). Thus, the political questions doctrine has been called a carefully crafted cop-out or an escape hatch. In essence, a court identifies a political question when the judges sense they lack capacity to resolve the issue before them (Bickel 1962).

Whatever the rule was before 1960, the political questions doctrine has been narrowed since then. Following the reasoning in *Baker v. Carr* (1962), the Warren Court drastically reduced the content of the political questions doctrine in other areas (Wasby 1993). It is still applicable, however, in matters relating to foreign affairs or national defense. The validity of treaties under international law and the recognition of foreign governments are still considered political questions, meaning that the Court will not interfere with decisions reached by the executive branch (Franck 1992). The federal courts also used the political questions doctrine as the basis for refusing to decide the validity of the Vietnam War.

MOBILIZING THE LAW TO REACH THE SUPREME COURT

Cases do not arrive at the Supreme Court's doorstep "like abandoned orphans in the night" (Cortner 1975, vi). Rather, working within the jurisdictional powers of the Supreme Court, litigants, lawyers, and interest groups often engage in major efforts to have their cases decided by the nation's highest judicial body. Along the way, some litigants have become celebrities (Irons 1988). But, mainly, litigants, either individuals or organizations, contribute their names to the lawsuit. Taking a case to the Supreme Court requires most litigants to obtain financial support; only corporations, the government, and some wealthy individuals can afford the lengthy process of litigation and appeals on their own. Thus, the actions of lawyers, interest groups, and the solicitor general primarily determine which cases the Court will be asked to hear.

Lawyers

For most lawyers, arguing a case before the Supreme Court is a once-in-a-lifetime opportunity: Having tried the case in the lower court, they doggedly pursue their clients' interests all the way to the top. Other lawyers who argue before the Supreme Court, however, are retained just for that purpose—other lawyers try the case in the lower court and argue the initial appeals but, when the decision is made to appeal to the Supreme Court, lawyers particularly knowledgeable in Supreme Court practice are hired. Former law clerks to the justices are twice as likely to later serve as counsel or amicus as are lawyers with similar education who have not clerked (O'Connor and Hermann 1995).

In *The Supreme Court Bar: Legal Elites in the Washington Community*, Kevin McGuire (1993) explores which lawyers argue before the nation's highest court, finding two distinct groups. One group consists of a social network of notable lawyers who practice before the Court, strongly anchored in Washington, D.C. These lawyers have a good many common ties, including graduating from an elite law school, being former law clerks to the justices and/or alumni of the solicitor general's office, and practicing in leading law firms in Washington. They are primarily counsel to business interests. Although these lawyers practice most often in Washington, D.C., other members of the elite Supreme Court bar can be found in Chicago and New York. Beyond this inner circle of regular Supreme Court practitioners is the second group: a larger outer circle of relatively inexperienced litigators. These lawyers do not practice in D.C. and often appear in noncommercial cases. Thus, this group handles the problems of individuals arguing civil liberties and criminal cases. In many ways, the contrasting groups of lawyers who appear before the Supreme Court reflect the two hemispheres of legal practice (discussed in Chapter 5). Moreover, there is evidence that, as repeat players, the Supreme Court bar enjoys more success in winning their cases than lawyers who are less experienced (McGuire 1995).

Interest Groups

Interest groups regularly bring cases to court to facilitate the development of legal doctrines useful to their cause (Epstein 1985). Besides directly sponsoring cases, interest groups may also participate in Supreme Court litigation by filing **amicus curiae** ("friend of the court") briefs in cases in which they are not direct parties. Initially, friend of the court briefs were used to provide the court with neutral information about the case at hand, but, today, amicus briefs (often shortened to plural *amici*) are used to advocate a particular position (Krislov 1963). A longitudinal study of interest groups' participation as amici curiae revealed that they participated in 53 percent of the noncommercial cases decided by the Supreme Court between 1970 and 1980 (O'Connor and Epstein 1984). Who are these groups? The Supreme Court is remarkably accessible to a wide array of organized interests. Participation is not restricted to corporations, governments, or public or private law firms. More than 40 percent of the amicus briefs were filed by citizen or advocacy groups; business, trade, or professional associations; and unions. Thus, the groups filing amicus briefs reflect not only groups with narrow interests but also general-membership organizations (Caldeira and Wright 1990a). Indeed, social scientists have become increasingly involved in the submission of amicus curiae briefs to the courts (Roesch et al. 1991).

The legal arguments contained in amicus briefs may parallel those offered by the direct parties but more often adopt a different perspective, stressing positions the principal litigants do not wish to emphasize. Thus, amicus briefs present the Court with a range of viewpoints about the legal question presented in the case. For that reason, they appear to be important to the Supreme Court's decision-making process. Indeed, one study found that amici were directly mentioned in 18 percent of the opinions written by the justices, a statistic that probably underestimates how important the briefs are (O'Connor and Epstein 1983).

How successful have interest groups been in achieving their objectives? Through the years, liberal interest groups have enjoyed a high rate of success in court. The National Association for the Advancement of Colored People (NAACP) Legal Defense Fund has used the courts with far greater continued success than any other organization, gaining victories in lawsuits involving school desegregation, the death penalty, and employment discrimination. It is too early to tell if conservative interest groups will

LAW AND POPULAR CULTURE

■ *The Cider House Rules* (1999)

"All I said was, I don't wanna perform abortions. I have no argument with you performing them," says Homer Wells (Tobey Maguire) to Dr. Wilbur Larch (Michael Caine) when asked whether he wants to perform an abortion. *The Cider House Rules* is the Academy Award–winning adaptation of John Irving's best-selling novel of the same name. The central character in the film—Homer Wells—is an orphan who develops a bond with Dr. Larch, the orphanage doctor. Larch teaches Homer everything he knows, including how to perform abortions.

Dr. Larch views a woman's right to abortion as her choice and preferable to unwanted childbirth or unsafe attempts to terminate a pregnancy. But his efforts to change Wells's views are rebuffed. At one point he asks Homer, "You know how to help these women. How can you not feel obligated to help them when they can't get help anywhere else?" Homer replies, "One: It's illegal. Two: I didn't ask how to do it. You just showed me." Not long after this exchange, Homer leaves the orphanage to explore the world, only to find that he cannot escape his past.

Homer takes a job as an apple picker at an orchard where cider is made. He soon learns that his male supervisor is sleeping with his own daughter Rose (Erykah Badu), and Rose is now pregnant. His reluctance to perform abortions at the orphanage is soon replaced by a tempered willingness to help this victim of incest. When Rose decides to have an abortion, Homer performs it himself.

The Cider House Rules confronts the complex issue of abortion head on and presents many of the dimensions to this important policy debate. These are the same issues the Court faced in *Roe v. Wade* (1973) and has continued to face ever since. John Irving does not deny that abortion and a woman's right to choose are at the center of the film. He is a noted supporter of Planned Parenthood and says that he was affected by something his grandfather, an obstetrician and professor of obstetrics, wrote: "As for abortion, Grandfather was wise to observe that 'as long as there are unwanted pregnancies, women will attempt to rid themselves of them'" (Irving 1999).

Regardless of your view on abortion, the film captures much of the debate around this contentious issue remarkably well. Among the issues it examines are (1) the legal availability of abortion and the consequences if it were made illegal (the specter of unsafe abortions), (2) what to do with the children of unwanted pregnancies (orphanages), and (3) the availability of abortion providers (at first, Homer is reluctant to employ the medical procedure he knows how to perform). Indeed, David Bruce, an online film reviewer, wrote that *The Cider House Rules* provides "every university class on ethics, law, religion, and civics a noteworthy story to discuss and ponder" (2000).

Chapter 1 argued that courts are important policy makers. In no area of law is that more evident than in abortion. When the Supreme Court hears cases dealing with abortion and women's reproductive rights, the themes appearing in *The Cider House Rules* are on trial. Who should decide the availability of abortion: Doctors like Larch—without regard for society's expectation or the law? Or legislatures—such as the Texas legislature, which passed the law restricting abortion that ultimately led to *Roe v. Wade*? Or courts—as the Supreme Court did in deciding *Roe* and the thirty-one cases thereafter, clarifying that decision? Or society as a whole—perhaps allowing a majority or even a plurality to decide the issue for everyone? *The Cider House Rules* lays bare the difficulty of solving this issue to everyone's satisfaction.

After watching this movie, be prepared to answer the following questions:

1. How does *The Cider House Rules* portray the rule of law?
2. Do films such as this contribute to or detract from a debate by society about contentious issues?
3. Are the courts the right institution to settle issues such as abortion? Why or why not?
4. In what way is Homer's concern about performing abortions similar to or different from pharmacists' refusal to fill prescriptions for the contraceptive known as the "morning-after pill"?

enjoy similar long-term success. Older groups are more successful in litigation, but only a few were in existence before 1970. Lee Epstein (1985, 156) concludes, "Many of the newer groups, including the National Chamber Litigation Center and the conservative public interest law firms, wish to sponsor more cases and to otherwise increase their litigation activities. Doing so would increase their proficiency in litigation and allow them to attain repeat-player status, but their ability to achieve such goals depends upon their ability to attract adequate funding." Assuming that such resources will be available, conservative interest group litigation will become an increasingly important phenomenon. Overall, scholars have focused on successful litigation campaigns. Examining losers indicates that the conventional wisdom concerning the efficacy of group use of the courts may be misplaced (Epstein and Rowland 1991). (See Law and Popular Culture: *The Cider House Rules*.)

The Solicitor General

The **solicitor general** is the chief litigator for the executive branch and an important player in determining which cases the U.S. Supreme Court decides to hear (Black and Owens 2011; Pacelle 2003). He or she is appointed by the president and is the third-ranking official in the Department of Justice but also has an office on the first floor of the Supreme Court building. Usage of these dual offices underscores the job's special role: The solicitor general's principal task is to represent the executive branch in the Supreme Court. At the same time, the justices depend on the solicitor general to look beyond the government's narrow interest. Because of the solicitor general's "dual responsibility" to the judicial and executive branches, the officeholder is sometimes called the "tenth justice," an informal title that underlines the special relationship with the Supreme Court (Caplan 1988).

The office of the solicitor general functions like a small, elite, very influential law firm whose client is the U.S. government. The staff consists of fewer than two dozen of the most able attorneys found anywhere. Indeed, four former solicitors general—William Howard Taft, Robert Jackson, Thurgood Marshall, and the most recent justice—Elena Kagan—were later appointed to the Supreme Court; another—Robert Bork—was nominated but not confirmed; and a number of others have been appointed to the U.S. courts of appeals. The solicitor general's most visible responsibility is to represent the United States in litigation before the Supreme Court. As such, the office argues all government cases before the nation's highest tribunal. But the influence of the office extends farther.

Roughly half of the work of the solicitor general's office involves coordinating and controlling appeals by the federal government. With few exceptions, all governmental agencies must first receive authorization from the solicitor general to appeal an adverse lower-court ruling to the courts of appeals or to the Supreme Court. Without that control, the Supreme Court would receive a variety of views on the same issue from different governmental agencies. The office requests Supreme Court review only in cases with a high degree of policy significance and in which the government has a reasonable legal argument. During the 1998 term, the solicitor general filed twenty-one petitions requesting that the Court review adverse lower-court decisions involving the government, whereas lawyers for losing parties in cases involving the government filed 2,682 petitions (Baum 2001). Thus, the solicitor general rejects many cases from governmental agencies because they are not viewed as "cert. worthy"

(Puro 1981). This winnowing of cases that will be appealed to the Supreme Court becomes very important because (as will be shown in Chapter 15) the solicitor general is very successful in those cases pushed forward by that office (Salokar 1992).

The influence of the solicitor general at the Court goes beyond helping the justices set their docket. The Court also turns to the solicitor general for help on legal problems that appear especially vexing. Two or three dozen times a year, the justices invite the office to submit briefs in cases in which the government is not a party. In essence, the justices treat the office as a counselor to the Court, advising it about the meaning of federal statutes and of the Constitution (Caplan 1988).

Another of the solicitor general's principal functions is to decide when the government will appear as an amicus curiae to urge executive branch policies on the courts in cases in which the federal government is not a direct party (Segal 1990, 1988). By Supreme Court rule, the solicitor general can file a "friend of the court" brief without the permission of the parties to the suit, and the solicitor general is the only amicus regularly given time to argue a case before the Court. Those discretionary opportunities allow maximum flexibility for the solicitor general to advocate the policy positions of the president before the Supreme Court. When the solicitor general chooses to enter an amicus brief, the position argued is consistent with the preferences of the president (Meinhold and Shull 1998; Salokar 1992). Furthermore, recent evidence finds that the solicitor general is frequently successful when he files as an amicus and that success is enhanced when the justices are ideologically close to the president (Bailey, Kamoie, and Maltzman 2005; Deen, Ignagni, and Meernik 2003). Thus, the solicitor general not only provides legal views on cases but also offers the justices political signals about how the administration would prefer that a case be resolved.

Because of the staff's long-term stability, the solicitor general is a classic instance of a repeat player with all the advantages attendant on that status (Caldeira and Wright 1988). In addition, because of careful selection of cases, expertise in procedure, and consistency in legal argument, the office of solicitor general enjoys tremendous credibility with the justices (McGuire 1998; Puro 1981). For those reasons, the solicitor general has a very high rate of success in petitioning the Supreme Court and in winning cases argued on their merits. The Solicitor General wins nearly two thirds of all the cases where they participate (Epstein, Segal, Spaeth, and Walker 2007).

The solicitor general's unique position as attorney for the government and trusted source of legal reasoning for the Supreme Court emphasizes the reality of law and politics. The legal decisions reached by the solicitor general about whether to appeal a case and what position to take are influenced in part by his desire to maintain credibility with the Court but nevertheless still parallel the policy positions and preferences of the president. Thus, the solicitor general represents a unique conduit for the president—chosen by popular election—to influence the agenda and decisions of a nonelected judiciary.

CASE SELECTION

Every year, the Supreme Court is besieged by requests from thousands of disgruntled litigants asking to have the decisions against them reviewed (and reversed). Most are disappointed. Over the course of a full term, some 8,000 litigants think that their cases should be heard by the Court, but the justices agree with fewer than 100. Those numbers underscore the fact that the Court cannot give careful attention to that many cases, so the justices choose a very small percentage of the total for full review on the merits and deny the remainder.

The process begins with appeals and writs of certiorari being considered by the justices individually. Historically, the justices read only a small portion of the petitions and supporting materials, choosing instead to delegate much of the work of identifying meritorious petitions to their law clerks. For almost 40 years the justices have combined resources to create a certiorari pool. Under this arrangement, certiorari petitions are randomly assigned to one of the combined clerks from the participating justices' offices; the law clerk then prepares a 2- to 25-page memo that is circulated to all participating justices. Some of the justices then have one of their own clerks review the pool memo (Baum 2001). Eight justices currently participate in the pool; only Justice Alito's chambers reviews every petition. Although the clerks make recommendations about which cases should be granted review, the justices sometimes ignore their recommendations. Nevertheless, critics of the cert pool point to research that shows the strong likelihood that a petition's final outcome will be determined by a law clerk rather than a judge (Peppers 2006; Ward and Weiden 2006). However, given that the vast majority of all cases reviewed by the clerks would likely be rejected anyway, it is doubtful that many important cases are overlooked because a clerk failed to recommend granting certiorari.

The Rule of Four

After individual review, the Court conducts a collective review of all the requests. At a weekly conference, the justices discuss and vote on the petitions. In the earliest years of certiorari review, the justices discussed every petition during conference. But caseload pressures no longer allow that luxury. Before each weekly conference, the chief justice circulates a discuss list containing the cases deemed worthy of conference time. All other requests are automatically denied, unless a justice specifically requests that a case be put on the conference agenda (Cooper and Ball 1996; Perry 1991; Caldeira and Wright 1990b).

By custom, the Supreme Court will not agree to hear a case unless at least four of the Court's nine justices vote to review the lower-court ruling. This procedure is commonly referred to as the **rule of four**. A denial of certiorari leaves the ruling of the lower court undisturbed and formally means only that the Court has decided not to decide the case (Brenner 1993). Thus, a denial of review does not mean that the Court agrees with the outcome of the case in the lower court and, therefore, carries no significance as a legal precedent. As Justice Felix Frankfurter explained, "It simply means that fewer than four members of the Court deemed it desirable to review a decision of the lower court as a matter 'of sound judicial discretion'" (*State v. Baltimore Radio Show* 1950). Such statements about the nonmeaning of certiorari denials are not accepted by many Court observers, however. And some infer consideration of the merits when the Court consistently leaves undisturbed lower-court decisions seemingly at variance with past Court rulings. Lawyers sometimes cite certiorari denials in their briefs to suggest that a legal issue is not settled (Wasby 1993). In particular, the media are notorious for reporting denials of certiorari as if the Court were agreeing

---

| **EXHIBIT 14.1** | **Rule 10: Considerations Governing Review on Certiorari** |

1. A review on writ of certiorari is not a matter of right, but of judicial discretion, and will be granted only when there are special and important reasons therefor. The following, while neither controlling nor fully measuring the Court's discretion, indicate the character of reasons that will be considered.

    a. When a United States court of appeals has rendered a decision in conflict with the decision of another United States court of appeals on the same matter; or has decided a federal question in a way in conflict with a state court of last resort; or has so far departed from the accepted and usual court or judicial proceedings, or so far sanctioned such a departure by a lower court, as to call for an exercise of this Court's power of supervision.

    b. When a state court of last resort has decided a federal question in a way in conflict with the decision of another state court of last resort or of a United States court of appeals.

    c. When a state court or United States court of appeals has an important question of federal law which has not been, but should be, settled by this Court, or has decided a federal question in a way in conflict with applicable decisions of this Court.

Source: U.S. Supreme Court Rule 10, effective January 1, 1990.

with (affirming) the lower-court decision (Slotnick and Segal 1998). An important feature of the initial review process is that the law clerks and the justices have considerable discretion in determining which of the cases will be decided by the Court.

Screening Criteria

Why do the justices grant a select few litigants the right to be heard on the merits but deny most such requests? In trying to answer that important question, scholars face two principal difficulties. First, the Court provides only general guidance on its handling of petitions for review. Rule 10 (shown in Exhibit 14.1) states the technical criteria for acceptance of a case, but this official statement of the legal factors the Court considers in deciding whether to grant certiorari only establishes a starting point for the justices. Working within the broad framework of Rule 10, the Court grants review only if the case involves a substantial **federal question**. A large proportion of petitions do not meet those standards, resulting in the dismissal of many cases "for want of a substantial federal question." But the Court only rarely gives any reasons for granting or denying. Thus, no body of case law exists on what constitutes a "substantial federal question." A second difficulty is that the Court rarely publicly announces certiorari votes. Thus, scholars are forced to work indirectly by statistically comparing cases granted certiorari with those denied. Fortunately, some justices leave behind very detailed notes on conference votes that can be used by scholars to reconstruct the behind-the-scenes dynamics of the Court.

One of the earliest attempts to explain the exercise of the Supreme Court's discretion to grant certiorari was developed by Joseph Tanenhaus and his associates (1963). Their cue theory hypothesizes that the Supreme Court justices are concerned with reducing their workload and therefore "employ cues as a means of separating those petitions worthy of scrutiny from those that may be discarded without further study" (p. 123). More specifically, cue theory proposes that certiorari is more likely to be granted when one or more cues are present. Cue theory says that the justices tend to accept cases they think are important. But these cues are effective only to the extent that they select the issues the justices consider salient. Given that the cues are, in fact, surrogates for salient issues, they must be constantly updated (Teger and Kosinski 1980). Researchers have proposed a number of theoretical explanations for the behavior of appellate courts in case selection. Current research identifies five criteria the Supreme Court appears to use in selecting cases for review: the federal government as petitioner, conflicting interpretations of the law, ideological preferences of the justices, amicus curiae activity, and the presence of certain issue areas.

Federal Government as Petitioner When the federal government petitions for a hearing, the Supreme Court is significantly more likely to grant certiorari (Caldeira and Wright 1988; Ulmer 1984; Tanenhaus et al. 1963). Descriptive data drive this point home. In recent years, 50–70 percent of the solicitor general's certiorari requests have been granted. Other petitioners were successful less than 5 percent of the time (Baum 2001; Salokar 1992). These empirical findings dovetail with the earlier discussion about the care the solicitor general demonstrates in screening agency requests for certiorari, eliminating those that are not a good vehicle for Supreme Court litigation and picking those with a higher degree of policy significance. However, the reason for that success is somewhat elusive. The solicitor general is clearly the ultimate "repeat player" (Galanter 1974), functioning with a skilled team of lawyers who are in a unique position to influence the Court. Yet, some have suggested that the difference between the solicitor general and most of the other legal elites who appear before the Supreme Court is really one of degree and not kind (McGuire 1998). Thus, it is not legal experience but something else—perhaps institutional deference—that explains the tremendous advantage the solicitor general enjoys in getting on the Court's docket.

Conflict Over the Law The Supreme Court is also more likely to grant certiorari in cases involving conflicting interpretations of the law (Tanenhaus et al. 1963). One indicator of conflict in the law is a reversal of the trial court by the appellate court. Another is a dissenting opinion written by an appellate court judge. A third is contrasting interpretations of the same law reached by different circuits of the U.S. courts of appeals. Those factors—reversal, dissent, and conflicting circuit court interpretations—signal ferment in the lower courts and suggest issues worthy of a closer look. All other factors being equal, the Supreme Court has shown a greater willingness to grant a hearing. Law clerk after law clerk interviewed by H. W. Perry (1991) said that "first you look for" conflict in the law. The appearance of conflict is apparently so important that when Ulmer (1984) randomly sampled all paid cases on the Court's docket for a thirty-year period (1947–1976), he found that lawyers often padded or puffed claims of a conflict. Furthermore, although many cases in which conflict is present are not heard, the presence of conflict is one of the most important variables predicting whether the Court will grant certiorari (Black and Owens 2009; Caldeira and Wright 1988) and suggests that legal concerns and policy are important in determining what cases get heard.

The Justices' Ideological Preferences   Studies consistently find that case selection decisions are related to the ideological preferences of the justices. In essence, disagreements over case selection reflect "the first battleground on the merits" (Linzer 1979). Justices are more likely to vote to hear cases in which the lower-court decision ran contrary to their basic liberal or conservative stance. Liberals, for instance, are more inclined to hear cases brought by criminal defendants than are conservatives (Ulmer 1972). In economic cases, the liberal Warren Court granted certiorari more frequently to petitions that involved conservative lower-court decisions. Conversely, the more conservative Burger Court consistently accepted more petitions involving liberal lower-court decisions than those involving conservative lower-court decisions (Armstrong and Johnson 1982).

Justices can also use their positions and current cases to send signals to interest groups and other policy leaders that they would like to decide cases in a particular area. In a recent study, Baird (2007) shows that justices' policy preferences do have an impact on the Court's agenda and that there is a lag period of a few years between when the Court sends the signal and when the "policy entrepreneurs" respond.

However, justices must also consider the ideological positions of their colleagues on the Court. Recent research shows that justices act strategically—in that they are more likely to vote to hear cases in which they think the ultimate decision of the Court will reflect their own ideological preferences (Caldeira, Wright, and Zorn 1999). However, justices planning to vote to "affirm" have a lot to lose if the are acting strategically and miscalculate the final outcome in the case (Benesh, Brenner, and Spaeth 2002). In contrast, it is common for justices to exercise a "defensive denial" of certiorari by voting not to hear a case when they think the final decision on the merits would be contrary to their preferred outcome (Boucher and Segal 1995; Perry 1991; Krol and Brenner 1990).

Acting ideologically and strategically makes the Court more prone to reverse the cases it hears. A lower-court decision consistent with the policy preferences of the Court is best left undisturbed. During the Court's 2010 term, 57 cases (70%) were reversed. The impact of ideology is clearly important in deciding what to decide.

Amicus Curiae Activity   The Supreme Court is also more likely to vote to hear a case on the merits if the case involves amicus curiae activity. Although political science has a long and rich tradition of studying interest group activity before the Court in "friend of the court" briefs on decisions on the merits, only recently have researchers systematically investigated the effects of amicus briefs on the decision to decide. Caldeira and Wright (1988) argue that powerful interests are unlikely to stand by passively as the Supreme Court legitimizes literally hundreds of decisions in the lower courts each year and calls many others into question. Rather, interest groups will attempt to influence the Court's agenda by filing amicus curiae briefs in support of granting certiorari. But that activity must be selective. Interest groups rationally file only if the lower-court decision is unfavorable to their position. Moreover, such activity involves a nontrivial expense. Thus, even interest groups with a large budget for litigation cannot and do not file amicus curiae briefs with reckless abandon. The data support that position. The presence of amicus curiae briefs significantly increases the chances that the justices will bind a case over for full treatment. More specifically, 36 percent of cases in which one or more amici were filed were granted certiorari, compared with only 5 percent of the cases without amici.

Overall, Caldeira and Wright (1988) suggest that the justices attempt to select cases for full review with the greatest potential social, economic, or political significance consistent with their own ideological predispositions. The potential significance of Supreme Court decision making is proportional to the demand for adjudication among the interested parties, and the filing of amicus briefs in support of (or in opposition to) granting certiorari provides the justices significant information about the demand for adjudication in that area.

Issue Areas   Finally, some studies suggest that the Court is more likely to grant certiorari in certain types of issue areas than in others. One cue that Tanenhaus and his colleagues (1963) found to be important in the granting of certiorari was the presence of civil liberties issues. To the list of important cues, Provine (1980) has added labor disputes, criminal cases, and federalism. Subsequent research found that the relationships discovered by Tanenhaus continued to exist in later terms of the Court (Armstrong and Johnson 1982; Teger and Kosinski 1980). Alas, researchers have been maddeningly inconsistent about which types of cases might interest the Court more and how to define the various categories. Thus, not all studies are in agreement. Ulmer (1984) found no empirical evidence that civil liberties issues act as cues, a negative conclusion shared by Caldeira and Wright (1988).

THE COURT'S DOCKET

The Court formally begins its term on the first Monday in October and recesses in early summer. Officially, the Court's term is identified by calendar year, dated from the opening session. Thus the 2011 term began on October 3, 2011, and includes all cases decided before the summer of 2012. Informally, scholars refer to Court eras according to the chief justice—the Warren Court (1953–1969), the Burger Court (1969–1986), the Rehnquist Court (1986–2005), and now the Roberts Court (which began in 2005).

The Number of Cases

Over 8,000 cases are filed with the Supreme Court during a typical year (Table 14.1). Very few cases involve original jurisdiction (typically just one or two every year). During the 2010 term, less than one-quarter of the filings were paid cases, which require the payment of a $300 filing fee and the printing of 40 copies of each brief. These financial obstacles to seeking Supreme Court review are relaxed for indigents, who are not required to pay a filing fee and are asked to submit only the original and ten copies of their petition. **In forma pauperis** ("in the manner of a pauper") petitions come primarily from prison inmates and, typically, lack the polished prose and sophisticated legal analysis characteristic of paid cases. Yet these petitions are not categorically frivolous and unimportant (Watson 2006). The Court docketed nearly 7,000 unpaid cases during the 2010 term. These unpaid cases seldom raise new and significant constitutional issues and, therefore, are much less likely to be granted certiorari. During the 2010 term, only 12 in forma pauperis cases were granted full review, compared with 71 paid cases.

TABLE 14.1	Statistical Profile of the U.S. Supreme Court Workload, 2009 Term
Kinds of Cases	**Number of Cases Filed**
Paid cases	1,566
In forma pauperis cases	6,519
Total	8,085
Disposition of Cases	**Number of Cases**
Denied, dismissed, or withdrawn	7,917
Summarily decided	91
Granted review	77

Source: Data from "The Statistics," *Harvard Law Review* 124: 411 (2010).

Although less than one-half percent of the in forma pauperis petitions were granted review, some of the Supreme Court's most important decisions have resulted from those filings. This book has highlighted two such groundbreaking decisions: *Gideon v. Wainwright* (1963), which established the constitutional right to court-appointed counsel (Chapter 5); and *Miranda v. Arizona* (1966), which imposed constitutional limits on police interrogations (Chapter 8).

The Supreme Court can take one of three actions on a petition for hearing. It can deny the petition altogether, leaving the lower-court decision standing. That is the fate of nearly 99 percent of all requests for review. Alternatively, the Court can accept the case and decide it summarily without oral argument and without a full written opinion (Wasby et al. 1992), often with the use of a **per curiam decision**—a short, unsigned memorandum opinion briefly setting forth the issues, the applicable law, and the Court's decision. Finally, the Court can accept the case for oral argument and decide the matter by a full, signed opinion.

The Kinds of Cases

The Court's discretionary jurisdiction to decide what to decide entails more than merely selecting a manageable number of cases for oral argument and written opinion. The Court also sets its own substantive agenda, functioning much like a roving commission responding to social and political forces (O'Brien 2000). In written opinions, the justices structure litigation patterns by setting forth legal doctrines that indicate what kinds of claims have a good chance of winning and what types of issues are no longer welcome (Baird 2004; Goldstein and Stech 1995). Landmark decisions are particularly important tools that justices utilize to encourage the filing of certain types of cases. Many of the Case Close-Ups in this book clearly fall into this category, including *McCreary v. ACLU* (2005), which indicated a willingness on the part of the nation's highest court to consider the role of religion in American life (Chapter 2); *Brown v. Board of Education* (1954), which put the issue of race on the nation's (and the Court's) agenda (Chapter 7); and *Roe v. Wade* (1973), which ushered in subsequent lawsuits concerning not only reproductive freedom but also the right to privacy (this chapter).

Richard Pacelle (1991) provides a detailed examination of those factors in his book *The Transformation of the Supreme Court's Agenda*, which explores major changes over a fifty-six-year period in the kinds of cases the Supreme Court decides. During the 1930s and 1940s, the Court heard numerous lawsuits dealing with economic, federalism, and regulatory issues. Today, however, those issues have been replaced by due process, substantive rights, civil liberties, and equality issues. Overall, these changes reflect a shift from a jurisprudence of "property" to a jurisprudence of "status" (Grossman and Wells 1988). In particular, the Court now hears a number of cases dealing with criminal justice, a subject matter largely absent from the docket before the 1960s.

Although the Court is most associated with decisions interpreting the Constitution, that image is only partially accurate. Each year, less than half the Court's docket consists of constitutional cases. The majority involve the interpretation of federal statutes and administrative rules. In recent years, for example, the Court has decided cases stemming from the Environmental Protection Act, Clean Water Act, Illegal Immigration Reform and Responsibility Act, National Labor Relations Act, Controlled Substances Act, Freedom of Information Act, Americans with Disabilities Act, and Securities Exchange Act.

Caseload Growth

With so many cases filed each year, it is easy to forget that, in the early years of the country, the Supreme Court had little to do. Not a single case was filed during the Court's first two terms, and only five were filed in 1793. As a result, the first chief justice, John Jay, spent much of his tenure abroad on diplomatic assignments and resigned in 1795 to assume a position he considered much more important: governor of New York. The Court did not begin to emerge as a significant branch of the government until John Marshall became chief justice. Despite the growing importance of its decisions, however, the Court still received relatively few requests for review. Over a 100-year period, annual changes were relatively erratic: During some decades (the 1920s and the 1940s, in particular), increases in caseload were dramatic, but, during others, caseload growth was gradual (McLauchlan 1980). Thus, it was not until World War II that the Court received more than 1,000 filings per year. Beginning in the 1950s, however, filings have increased dramatically, as Figure 14.1 illustrates.

A closer look shows that the increasing caseload of the Supreme Court is directly tied to a dramatic surge in petitions filed by prisoners. Until the mid-1980s, in forma pauperis petitions constituted less than half the cases filed; today, they contribute 75 percent. By contrast, paid cases have remained remarkably stable over the last decade, fluctuating slightly with no apparent trend. Thus, the same political and social forces that have filled U.S. prisons to overflowing (Chapter 9) are also clogging the docket of the U.S. Supreme Court.

An Overburdened Supreme Court, Not?

At one time, concerns about the ability of the Supreme Court to handle rapidly rising caseloads were frequently voiced and calls for reform were made. In the late

FIGURE **14.1**
Cases Filed in the U.S. Supreme Court Since 1950

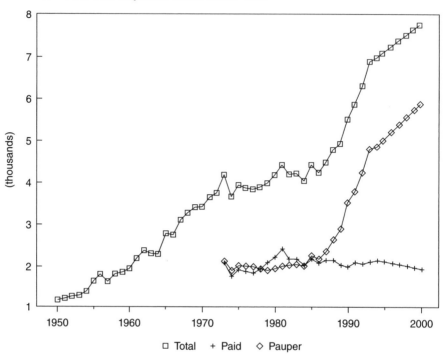

Source: Data from Gerhard Casper and Richard Posner, *The Workload of the Supreme Court* (Chicago: American Bar Foundation, 1976), p.3; "Statistical Recap of Supreme Court's Workload During Last Three Terms," *United States Law Week*, vols. 44–65; "The Statistics," *Harvard Law Review* 115, no. 1 (November 2001), pp. 539–550.

nineteenth century, mounting backlogs led to the creation of the U.S. courts of appeals. And, in the early twentieth century, growing caseloads resulted in the passage of the Judiciary Act of 1925. Although jurisdictional reforms occasionally bring relief, Supreme Court dockets have invariably continued upward (Jucewicz and Baum 1990; Stewart and Heck 1987).

Occasionally, the chief justice has complained, as did Chief Justice Warren Burger when he referred to the "overburdened" Supreme Court. In his first State of the Federal Judiciary Message, he declared that "we cannot keep up with the volume of work" brought before the Court (Burger 1971, 859). The perceived problem is that receiving (and thereby having to review) too many cases undermines the Court's capacity to do its job effectively. Thus, to some observers, the Court—because of **caseload** growth— is unable to give careful consideration to the cases decided by opinion and to bring about uniformity and consistency in the law. According to then–Chief Justice William Rehnquist, "Today we decline to review cases involving important questions of federal law not previously decided by our Court, cases which the Court would have unquestionably heard and decided as little as 30 years ago. [W]e are simply unable to take and decide many cases which raise important and undecided issues under the Constitution and the statutes of the United States" ("Chief Justice" 1987, 1). Of

DEBATING LAW, COURTS, AND POLITICS

■ Should Congress or the Court Decide Who Decides?

When a state passes a law that requires a woman to get permission from the biological father of her baby before getting an abortion, should the Supreme Court be required to consider the constitutionality of the law? Currently, the Court does not have to, and some people think that is bad. Over time, Congress has required the Supreme Court to hear fewer and fewer appeals from lower-court decisions. Those changes culminated in 1988, when the Supreme Court's appellate jurisdiction became almost entirely discretionary. That means that the Court has the complete power to pick and choose which cases it will hear. The Constitution grants Congress, not the Court, the power to determine its appellate jurisdiction. When Congress passed the Judiciary Act of 1925, nearly 80 percent of the Court's docket consisted of cases Congress had mandated that the Court hear (O'Brien 2000). Today, however, less than 1 percent of the cases heard by the Court in a typical year are mandatory. For all intents and purposes, Congress has given to the Court the very important power to decide for itself who will get a hearing before the Supreme Court. Congress has given the Court more power over its docket several times, but rarely have they taken that power away.

Only once has Congress successfully passed legislation limiting (as opposed to expanding) the Court's discretionary jurisdiction. After the Civil War, Congress took away the Court's power to hear appeals in habeas corpus cases (Baum 2001). And several times since then, Congress has considered legislation to remove from the Court's discretion controversial cases such as legislative reapportionment, school busing, school prayer, and abortion. But none of those efforts has passed. Even though the Constitution's grant of power over the types of cases the Court hears was given to Congress, they have mostly handed it over to the Court. To some critics, this is problematic, because they fear the possibility of an unchecked Supreme Court that uses illegitimate criteria to decide which cases to hear, thereby restricting access from individuals and groups the Court deems unworthy of consideration.

Changing the Court's discretionary jurisdiction is not the only means by which Congress can try to influence what the Court decides to decide. Congress sets the

Court's budget and confirms justices. It can also impeach justices, enact legislation directly affecting the Court's decisions, and pass constitutional amendments. Throughout the history of the Court, however, only a handful of proposals have been advanced to reduce its budget, and no justices have ever been impeached. Each year, the Court makes a number of statutory decisions, and, on occasion, Congress rejects the Court's interpretation of those statutes. Hausegger and Baum (1998) find that only 5 percent of the Court's statutory decisions made between 1978 and 1989 were overturned by Congress. Even fewer of the Court's constitutional decisions are overturned by congressional acts. Recently, Congress reacted to the Court's decision in *Reno v. American Civil Liberties Union* (1997), overturning sections of an act to protect children from pornography on the Internet by passing another law that tried to avoid the problems the Court noted in its decision. But the Court again found the law unconstitutional.

The final and perhaps most dramatic avenue available to Congress is passing a constitutional amendment that overturns a Court decision. Baum (2001) points out that, during the 106th Congress, amendments were introduced that would overturn Supreme Court decisions dealing with congressional term limits, campaign spending, prayer in school, flag desecration, and abortion. However, since the Constitution was ratified in 1789, there have only been five occasions where Congress has successfully passed an amendment that reacted to a Supreme Court decision (and one of those was not ratified by the states).

It appears the question posed in the title of this debate is irrelevant. Regardless of who you think should decide which cases the Supreme Court gets to hear, one thing is clear—the Court has asserted its power to determine its docket, and Congress has acquiesced. As one observer notes, it "is striking how little use Congress actually made of its enormous powers over the Court during the twentieth century" (Baum 2001, 248).

What do you think? Should Congress or the Court decide which cases will get a hearing in the highest court in the land? Has Congress given up too much of its power to control the Supreme Court's docket?

particular concern is that the growing caseload prevents the Court from resolving some important intercircuit conflicts (Hellman 1995).

Discussions about workload have persisted because, in the face of increasing requests for review, the Court is hearing a smaller and smaller percentage of those cases. Whereas in the 1960s and 1970s the Court would routinely hear and decide more than 100 cases a year, today the number is closer to 80. To some, that reflects not an overburdened Supreme Court but one that is not working hard enough. Political science professor Beverly Cook (1994) finds that the Court selects cases that are of significance to different constituencies. In essence, the justices engage in a selective response to external social and political pressures—a theme highlighted in many places in this book. Today, the battles over caseloads typically reflect not procedural but substantive concerns. (See Debating Law, Courts, and Politics: Should Congress or the Court Decide Who Decides?)

Conclusion

For years, Norma McCorvey (known to most people only by the legal pseudonym of Jane Roe) was the pro-choice poster child. By agreeing to challenge Texas's antiabortion law, she set in motion legal and political discussions that continue unabated more than a quarter of a century later. Starting about 1984, she began to acknowledge she was Jane Roe and also admitted that she fabricated the story of a rape to make people more sympathetic to her plight. In 1991, she decided to put herself on the front lines, taking a job at a Dallas abortion clinic. In 1994, she wrote a book titled *I Am Roe*, chronicling, among other matters, being a lesbian, having abused drugs and alcohol, being raped as a teenager, and spending years in reform school in Texas. Then, in 1995, she apparently reversed course. She joined Operation Rescue, a conservative religious organization strongly opposed to abortion. Sarah Weddington now says that if she had it to do over again, she wouldn't use McCorvey as the plaintiff (Waldman and Carroll 1995). Norma McCorvey was merely a Roe of convenience. Like many of the immediate parties profiled in our Case Close-Ups, McCorvey merely lent her name to a broader movement and then disappeared—to be remembered only in legal footnotes and textbooks.

Thirty years after *Roe v. Wade*, rulings on abortion continue to play a prominent role on the Supreme Court's docket. In deciding the most recent case—*Gonzales v. Carhart* (2007)—the justices undoubtedly knew that it was not the last time they would have to face this thorny issue. In *Gonzales*, decided 5–4, the Court upheld the Federal Abortion Ban, reversing the lower court and restricting certain forms of medical procedures in the second trimester of a pregnancy. The decisions of the justices (at least four) to hear the case illustrate the continuing pressure on the Court to decide important legal, social, and political questions.

The Court enjoys virtually complete discretion in deciding what to decide. In exercising that important authority, the Court does not seek to correct every injustice that may have occurred in the lower courts but, rather, confines itself to deciding a select group of important cases. Out of the thousands of requests for review, the

Court selects fewer than 100 for full consideration. Most of those cases involve issues over which the lower courts have reached conflicting results. All are tough cases, and good arguments can be made on both sides. This power to decide what to decide enables the Court to set its own agenda, determining which issues will be the subject of Court output. How the Court disposes of that agenda is the subject of Chapter 15.

CRITICAL THINKING QUESTIONS

1. In defining jurisdiction, justices and commentators have often expressed concern that the Court is the only major branch of government whose leaders are not directly elected by the people. Would the jurisdiction of the Court be different if the justices were popularly elected? Might the jurisdiction be more expansive in some areas but more restrictive in others?

2. Popular rhetoric often stresses a simple formula—liberals want to expand the jurisdiction of the Court, and conservatives want to restrict it. But political and legal reality is more complicated. In what areas might liberals wish to restrict the Court's jurisdiction? In what areas might conservatives wish to expand the Court's jurisdiction? How might these assessments change across time?

3. Public discussions of the Court stress procedural concerns, such as excessive caseloads and lengthy delay in deciding cases. To what extent do those voicing those concerns really have a substantive agenda? Why do critics of some Court decisions choose to stress procedural matters rather than substantive disagreements?

Search Terms

abortion
abortion rights debate

Roe v. Wade
U.S. Supreme Court

Useful URLs

http://www.supremecourtus.gov
    The official website of the Supreme Court of the United States contains information on the current docket.

http://www.supremecourthistory.org
    The Supreme Court Historical Society is dedicated to the collection and preservation of the history of the Supreme Court of the United States. The site features a digital library of articles and books and legal and constitutional history.

http://www.usdoj.gov/osg
    This is the official website of the Office of the United States Solicitor General.

http://www.lexsite.com/services/network/scba/history.shtml
    The Supreme Court Bar Association involves lawyers who regularly practice before the Court.

REFERENCES

Adamany, David. 1991. "Judicial Policy Making: The Supreme Court." In *The American Courts: A Critical Assessment*, edited by John Gates and Charles Johnson. Washington, D.C.: CQ Press.

Armstrong, Virginia, and Charles Johnson. 1982. "Certiorari Decisions by the Warren and Burger Courts: Is Cue Theory Time Bound?" *Polity* 15: 141–150.

Bailey, Michael A., Brian Kamoie, and Forrest Maltzman. 2005. "Signals from the Tenth Justice: The Political Role of the Solicitor General in Supreme Court Decision Making." *American Journal of Political Science* 49 (1): 72–85.

Baird, Vanessa A. 2004. "The Effect of Politically Salient Decisions on the U.S. Supreme Court's Agenda." *Journal of Politics* 66(3): 755–772.

———. 2007. *Answering the Call of the Court: How Justices and Litigants Set the Supreme Court Agenda*. Charlottesville: University of Virginia Press.

Barnum, David. 1993. *The Supreme Court and American Democracy*. New York: St. Martin's Press.

Baum, Lawrence. 2001. *The Supreme Court*. 7th ed. Washington, D.C.: CQ Press.

Behuniak-Long, Susan. 1991. "Friendly Fire: Amici Curiae and *Webster v. Reproductive Health Services*." *Judicature* 74: 261–270.

Benesh, Sara C., Sarul Brenner and Harold Spaeth. 2002. "Aggressive Grants by Affirm-Minded Justices." *American Politics Research* 30(3):219–34.

Bickel, Alexander. 1962. *The Least Dangerous Branch*. Indianapolis: Bobbs-Merrill.

Black, Ryan C. and Ryan J. Owens. 2009. "Agenda Setting in the Supreme Court: The Collision of Policy and Jurisprudence." *The Journal of Politics* 71:1062–1075.

Black, Ryan C. and Ryan J. Owens. 2011. "Solicitor General Influence and Agenda Setting on the U.S. Supreme Court." *Political Research Quarterly* Online only.

Boucher, Robert, and Jeffrey Segal. 1995. "Supreme Court Justices as Strategic Decision Makers: Aggressive Grants and Defensive Denials on the Vinson Court." *Journal of Politics* 57: 824–837.

Brennan, William. 1983. "Some Thoughts on the Supreme Court's Workload." *Judicature* 66: 230.

Brenner, Saul. 1993. "Access to the United States Supreme Court: The Rule of Four or the Rule of Five?" *Southeastern Political Review* 21: 841–853.

Bruce, David. 2000. Review of *The Cider House Rules*. Available online at www.hollywoodjesus.com/cider_house.htm. Retrieved May 2003.

Burger, Warren. 1971. "The State of the Judiciary—1971." *American Bar Association Journal* 57: 855–859.

Caldeira, Gregory, and John Wright. 1988. "Organized Interests and Agenda Setting in the U.S. Supreme Court." *American Political Science Review* 82: 1109–1127.

———. 1990a. "Amici Curiae Before the Supreme Court: Who Participates, When, and How Much?" *Journal of Politics* 52: 782–806.

———. 1990b. "The Discuss List: Agenda Building in the Supreme Court." *Law and Society Review* 24: 807–836.

Caldeira, Gregory A., John R. Wright, and Christopher Zorn. 1999. "Strategic Voting and Gate-keeping in the Supreme Court." *Journal of Law, Economics, and Organization* 15(3): 549–572.

Cameron, Charles M., Jeffrey A. Segal, and Donald Songer. 2000. "Strategic Auditing in a Political Hierarchy: An Informational Model of the Supreme Court's Certiorari Decisions." *American Political Science Review* 94 (1): 101–116.

Caplan, Lincoln. 1988. *The Tenth Justice: The Solicitor General and the Rule of Law*. New York: Vintage Books.

"Chief Justice Urges National Appeals Court, Repeal of Court's Mandatory Jurisdiction." 1987. *The Third Branch* 19: 1.

Cook, Beverly. 1994. "A Critique of the Supreme Court's 1982 Agenda: Alternatives to the NYU Legal Model." *Justice System Journal* 17: 135–151.

Cooper, Philip, and Howard Ball. 1996. *The United States Supreme Court: From the Inside Out*. Upper Saddle River, N.J.: Prentice Hall.

Cortner, Richard. 1975. *The Supreme Court and Civil Liberties Policy*. Palo Alto, Calif.: Mayfield.

Craig, Barbara Hinkson, and David O'Brien. 1993. *Abortion and American Politics*. Chatham, N.J.: Chatham House.

Deen, Rebecca E., Joseph Ignagni, and James Meernik. 2003. "The Solicitor General as Amicus 1953–2000: How Influential?" *Judicature* 87(2): 60–71.

Epstein, Lee. 1985. *Conservatives in Court*. Knoxville: University of Tennessee Press.

Epstein, Lee, and C. K. Rowland. 1991. "Debunking the Myth of Interest Group Invincibility in the Courts." *American Political Science Review* 85: 205–217.

Epstein, Lee, Jeffrey A. Segal, Harold J. Spaeth and Thomas G. Walker. 2007. *The Supreme Court Compendium: Data, Decisions, and Developments*. 4th ed. Washington, DC: CQ Press.

Faux, Marian. 1989. *Roe v. Wade: Marking the 20th Anniversary of the Landmark Supreme Court Decision That Made Abortion Legal*. New York: Penguin.

Franck, Thomas. 1992. *Political Questions/Judicial Answers: Does the Rule of Law Apply to Foreign Affairs?* Princeton, N.J.: Princeton University Press.

Galanter, Marc. 1974. "Why the 'Haves' Come Out Ahead: Speculations on the Limits of Legal Change." *Law and Society Review* 9: 97–125.

Goldstein, Leslie, and Diana Stech. 1995. "Explaining Transformations in Supreme Court Policy." *Judicature* 79: 80–85.

Grossman, Joel, and Richard Wells. 1988. *Constitutional Law and Judicial Policy Making*. 3d ed. New York: Longman.

Harris, Richard. 1983. "Judicial Action: Justiciability." In *The Guide to American Law: Everyone's Legal Encyclopedia*, Vol. 6. St. Paul, Minn.: West.

Hausegger, Lori, and Lawrence Baum. 1998. "Behind the Scenes: The Supreme Court and Congress in Statutory Interpretation." In *Great Theatre: The American Congress in Action*, edited by Herbert F. Weisberg and Samuel C. Patterson. New York: Cambridge University Press.

Hellman, Arthur. 1995. "By Precedent Unbound: The Nature and Extent of Unresolved Intercircuit Conflicts." *University of Pittsburgh Law Review* 56: 720–724.

Irons, Peter. 1988. *The Courage of Their Convictions: Sixteen Americans Who Fought Their Way to the Supreme Court*. New York: Free Press.

Irving, John. 1999. Available online at http://www.plannedparenthood.org/About/PRESSRELEASES/121699cider_author.html.

Jucewicz, Joseph, and Lawrence Baum. 1990. "Workload Influences on Supreme Court Case Acceptance Rates, 1975–1984." *Western Political Quarterly* 43: 123–135.

Krislov, Samuel. 1963. "The Amicus Curiae Brief: From Friendship to Advocacy." *Yale Law Journal* 72: 694–721.

Krol, John, and Saul Brenner. 1990. "Strategies in Certiorari Voting in the United States Supreme Court: A

Reevaluation." *Western Political Quarterly* 43: 335–342.

Linzer, P. 1979. "The Meaning of Certiorari Denials." *Columbia Law Review* 79: 1227–1305.

McGuire, Kevin. 1993. *The Supreme Court Bar: Legal Elites in the Washington Community*. Charlottesville: University of Virginia Press.

———. 1995. "Repeat Players in the Supreme Court: The Role of Experienced Lawyers in Litigation Success." *Journal of Politics* 57: 187–196.

———. 1998. "Explaining Executive Success in the U.S. Supreme Court." *Political Research Quarterly* 51: 505–526.

McLauchlan, William. 1980. "An Exploratory Analysis of the Supreme Court's Caseload from 1880–1976." *Judicature* 64: 32.

Meinhold, Stephen S., and Steven A. Shull. 1998. "Policy Congruence Between the President and the Solicitor General." *Political Research Quarterly* 51: 527–537.

O'Brien, David. 2000. *Storm Center: The Supreme Court in American Politics*. 5th ed. New York: Norton.

O'Connor, Karen, and Lee Epstein. 1983. "Court Rules and Workload: A Case Study of Rules Governing Amicus Curiae Participation." *Justice System Journal* 8: 35–45.

———. 1984. "The Role of Interest Groups in Supreme Court Policy Formation." In *Public Policy Formation*, edited by Robert Eyestone. Greenwich, Conn.: JAI Press.

O'Connor, Karen, and John Hermann. 1995. "The Clerk Connection: Appearances Before the Supreme Court by Former Law Clerks." *Judicature* 78: 247–249.

Orren, Karen. 1976. "Standing to Sue: Interest Group Conflict in the Federal Courts." *American Political Science Review* 70: 723–741.

Pacelle, Richard. 1991. *The Transformation of the Supreme Court's Agenda: From the New Deal to the Reagan Administration*. Boulder, Colo.: Westview.

———. 2003. *Between Law & Politics: The Solicitor General and the Structuring of Race, Gender, and Reproductive Rights Litigation*. College Station: Texas A&M University.

Peltason, Jack. 1955. *Federal Courts in the Political Process*. New York: Random House.

Perry, H. W. 1991. *Deciding to Decide: Agenda Setting in the United States Supreme Court*. Cambridge, Mass.: Harvard University Press.

Provine, Doris Marie. 1980. *Case Selection in the United States Supreme Court*. Chicago: University of Chicago Press.

Puro, Steven. 1981. "The United States as Amicus Curiae." In *Courts, Law and Judicial Processes*, edited by S. Sidney Ulmer. New York: Free Press.

Rathjen, Gregory, and Harold Spaeth. 1979. "Access to the Federal Courts: An Analysis of Burger Court Policy Making." *American Journal of Political Science* 23: 360–382.

Roesch, Ronald, Stephen Golding, Valerie Hans, and N. Dickon Reppucci. 1991. "Social Science and the Courts: The Role of Amicus Curiae Briefs." *Law and Human Behavior* 15: 1–11.

Salokar, Rebecca Mae. 1992. *The Solicitor General: The Politics of Law*. Philadelphia: Temple University Press.

Segal, Jeffrey. 1988. "Amicus Curiae Briefs by the Solicitor General During the Warren and Burger Courts: A Research Note." *Western Political Quarterly* 41: 135–144.

———. 1990. "Supreme Court Support for the Solicitor General: The Effect of Presidential Appointments." *Western Political Quarterly* 43: 137–152.

Slotnick, Elliot, and Jennifer A. Segal. 1998. *Television News and the Supreme Court: All the News That's Fit to Air?* New York: Cambridge University Press.

"Statistics, The." 2007. *Harvard Law Review* 121: 436–449.

Stevens, John Paul. 1982. "Some Thoughts on Judicial Restraint." *Judicature* 66: 177–183.

Stewart, Joseph, and Edward Heck. 1987. "Caseloads and Controversies: A Different Perspective on the 'Overburdened' U.S. Supreme Court." *Justice System Journal* 12: 370.

Taggart, William, and Matthew DeZee. 1985. "A Note on Substantive Access Doctrines in the United States Supreme Court: A Comparative Analysis of the Warren and Burger Courts." *Western Political Quarterly* 38: 84–93.

Tanenhaus, Joseph, Marvin Schick, Matthew Muraskin, and Daniel Rosen. 1963. "The Supreme Court's Jurisdiction: Cue Theory." In *Judicial Decision-Making*, edited by Glendon Schubert. New York: Free Press.

Teger, Stuart, and Douglas Kosinski. 1980. "The Cue Theory of Supreme Court Certiorari Jurisdiction: A Reconsideration." *Journal of Politics* 42: 834–846.

Ulmer, S. Sidney. 1972. "Supreme Court Justices as Strict and Not-So-Strict Constructionists: Some Implications." *Law and Society Review* 8: 13–32.

———. 1984. "The Supreme Court's Certiorari Decisions: Conflict as a Predictive Variable." *American Political Science Review* 78: 901–911.

Waldman, Steven, and Ginny Carroll. 1995. "Roe v. Roe." *Newsweek*, August 21, pp. 22–24.

Wasby, Stephen. 1993. *The Supreme Court in the Federal Judicial System*. 4th ed. Chicago: Nelson-Hall.

Wasby, Stephen, Steven Peterson, James Schubert, and Glendon Schubert. 1992. "The Per Curiam Opinion: Its Nature and Functions." *Judicature* 76: 29–38.

Watson, Wendy. 2006. "The U.S. Supreme Court's *In Forma Pauperis* Docket: A Descriptive Analysis." *The Justice System Journal* 27: 47–60.

Zimmerman, Joseph. 2006. *Interstate Disputes: The Supreme Court's Original Jurisdiction*. Albany: State University of New York Press.

FOR FURTHER READING

Armatta, Judith. 2010. *Twilight of Impunity: The War Crimes of Slobodan Milosevic*. Durham: Duke University Press.

Brenner, Saul, and Joseph Whitmeyer. 2009. *Strategy on the United States Supreme Court*. New York: Cambridge University Press.

Carruba, Clifford J. 2005. "Courts and Compliance in International Regulatory Regimes." *Journal of Politics* 67(3): 669–689.

Epstein, Lee. 1985. *Conservatives in Court*. Knoxville: University of Tennessee Press.

Irons, Peter. 1988. *The Courage of Their Convictions: Sixteen Americans Who Fought Their Way to the Supreme Court*. New York: Free Press.

Johnson, Timothy, and Jerry Goldman (eds.). 2009. *A Good Quarrel: America's Top Legal Reporters Share Stories from Inside the Supreme Court*. Ann Arbor: University of Michigan Press.

Jost, Kenneth. 2007. *The Supreme Court A to Z: A Ready Reference Encyclopedia*, 4th edition. Washington, D.C.: CQ Press.

Kelley, Judith. 2007. "Who Keeps International Commitments and Why? The International Criminal Court and Bilateral Nonsurrender Agreements." *American Political Science Review* 101(3): 573–589.

Meernik, James, Kimi Lynn King, and Geoffrey Dancy. 2005. "Judicial Decision Making and International Tribunals: Assessing the Impact of Individual, National, and International Factors." *Social Science Quarterly* 86 (3): 683–703.

Meernik, James, and Christopher Farris. 2006. "International Criminal Defense: Background on Judicial Decision Making at the International Criminal Tribunal for Rwanda." *Judicature* 89: 326–333.

Moghalu, Kingsley Chiedu. 2008. *Global Justice: The Politics of War Crimes Trials*. Stanford, Calif.: Stanford University Press.

Nicholson, Chris and Paul M. Collins, Jr. 2008. "The Solicitor General's Amicus Curiae Strategies in the Supreme Court." *American Politics Research* 36:382–415.

Pacelle, Richard. 1991. *The Transformation of the Supreme Court's Agenda: From the New Deal to the Reagan Administration*. Boulder, Colo.: Westview.

———. 2006. "Amicus Curiae or Amicus Presidentis?: Reexamining the Role of Solicitor General in Filing Amici." *Judicature* 89: 317–325.

Patton, Dana. 2007. "The Supreme Court and Morality Policy Adoption in the American States." *Political Research Quarterly* 60: 468–488.

Peppers, Tood C. 2006. *Courtiers of the Marble Palace: The Rise and Influence of the Supreme Court Law Clerk*. Stanford: Stanford University Press.

Powell, Emilia Justyna, and Sara McLaughlin Mitchell. 2007. "The International Court of Justice and the World's Three Legal Systems." *Journal of Politics* 69 (2): 397–415.

Romano, Cesare. 2012. *The Sword and the Scales: The United States and International Courts and Tribunals*. Cambridge: Cambridge University Press.

Schwartz, Bernard. 1995. *A History of the Supreme Court*. New York: Oxford.

Terris, Daniel Ceasare Romano, and Leigh Swigart. 2008. *The International Judge: An Introduction to the Men and Women who Decide the World's Cases*. Boston: Brandeis University Press.

Ward, Artemus and David L. Weiden. 2006. *100 Years of Law Clerks at the United States Supreme Court*. New York: New York University Press.

THE SUPREME COURT: THE JUSTICES AND THEIR DECISIONS

Picture of current Supreme Court justices.

Steve Petteway, Collection of the Supreme Court of the United States.

"I know it when I see it," Justice Potter Stewart once famously said of pornography (*Jacobellis v. Ohio* 1964). And, if you haven't noticed, it's easy to see *it* when you're surfing the Internet. "I was on my way to the White House when I encountered the topless women," is how political columnist Leonard Pitts Jr. (1998) describes how he found pornography on the Internet. Mistyping three letters led not to the official website of the president's house but to a site promising access to "young teens, hot lesbians, and hard-core nymphomaniacs" for only $19.95 a month. (Mistyping the letters today no longer takes the Internet surfer to the porn site.) Congress and the president have sought to end such practices with legislation intended to protect adults and children from online pornography; but it has not been without legal controversy.

Congress and the president first entered the arena of pornography on the Internet with the 1996 Communications Decency Act and later the Child Online Protection Act (1998), each passed by Congress and signed into law by President Bill Clinton. The Supreme Court got involved on June 26, 1997, ruling (7–2) that portions of the

Communications Decency Act of 1996 (see Case Close-Up: *Reno v. American Civil Liberties Union* 1997) were unconstitutional on First Amendment grounds. Advocates of the legislation were outraged. Senator Dan Coats (R-Ind.) said about the Court's decision, "A judicial elite is undermining democratic attempts to address pressing social problems" (CNN 1997). The next year, Congress revised the previous law and attempted once again to limit, in particular, children's access to pornography on the Internet by passing the Child Online Protection Act (COPA). The Supreme Court again declared the law unconstitutional, this time in *Ashcroft v. American Civil Liberties Union* (2004), finding that the law in its effort to protect children prohibited otherwise constitutionally protected speech. Meanwhile, the Congress had crafted the PROTECT (Prosecutorial Remedies and Other Tools to End the Exploitation of Children Today) Act of 2003, which was aimed at a broad array of protections for children, including a prohibition on pornography aimed at children and virtual or computer-generated child pornography. The legislation was signed into law by President George W. Bush.

In May 2008, after 20 years of trying to place restrictions on child pornography on the Web, the Supreme Court finally sided with Congress and the president. In *United States v. Williams* (2008), the justices considered whether the PROTECT Act was unconstitutionally overbroad, limiting more free speech than was necessary to accomplish the goal of protecting children. Justice Scalia, writing for a seven-person majority and upholding the law, noted that the First Amendment does not protect individual efforts to traffic or purport to traffic in child pornography (whether the children are real, virtual, or purely fictional). Two justices, Souter and Ginsburg, issued a dissenting opinion, arguing that the statute remained overbroad and that they did not believe the restriction on the First Amendment was warranted.

Efforts to curtail, limit, or otherwise control pornography on the Internet are not going away. Pornography opponents, free-speech advocates, legislators, and interest groups are all involved in fighting the battle over how the First Amendment will be applied to the Internet. The Supreme Court's role in this controversy is to figure out how to balance all those perspectives.

The U.S. Supreme Court has been called the most mysterious, most remote, and least understood branch of U.S. government. The justices are among the most anonymous leaders in American life, rarely speaking to reporters and never allowing cameras in the courtroom. In other ways, however, the Court is less secretive about what it does than any other governmental institution. Through written opinions, which average more than 4,000 pages each year, the justices explain the reasons for their actions. This written product is closely scrutinized by judges, lawyers, law professors, political scientists, and, at times, even lay citizens. Through those decisions, the justices affect more people than any other nine individuals in the nation.

This chapter focuses on the Court as a legal and political institution—first by examining the political nature of the process of selecting the justices. After dissecting the decision-making process step by step, it considers the critical importance of the justices' policy preferences. The last part of the chapter examines the contemporary debate over the Supreme Court by surveying recent controversial decisions and the varying voting alignments (from the Warren Court through the Roberts Court) and investigating why Supreme Court decisions are not necessarily the final word.

SELECTING THE JUSTICES

In declaring "[t]he most important appointments a President makes are those to the Supreme Court of the United States," President Richard Nixon (1971, 24) echoed the sentiments of every modern-day chief executive. Appointing a Supreme Court justice provides the president with the opportunity to leave an enduring mark on the U.S. legal system and most probably to extend his influence well beyond his own term of office.

Even though nominations to the Court are important to the president, the nation's highest elected official has no control over the frequency or the timing of that valuable political opportunity. A vacancy occurs when a sitting justice dies or steps down from the Court, meaning that a president's opportunity to nominate a justice is essentially a random and irregular event (Atkinson 1999; Squire 1988; King 1987). Franklin Roosevelt had no vacancies to fill during his first term, but had five in his second. However, four justices left the Court in Richard Nixon's first three years in office, providing him the opportunity to fulfill his campaign promise of appointing strict constructionists to the Court. Jimmy Carter never had the chance to make a single nomination during his four-year tenure. Bill Clinton was the first Democrat in 26 years to fill a vacancy on the Court, nominating two justices to the nation's highest court. George W. Bush had no vacancies to fill for the first five years of his term, but in rapid succession he saw his nominee John Roberts confirmed as the seventeenth chief justice and then Samuel Alito confirmed for the seat being vacated by retiring justice Sandra Day O'Connor. President Obama has already left his mark on the Supreme Court by appointing two women, Sonia Sotomayor and Elena Kagan. With his two appointments there are now five justice appointed by Republican presidents and four by Democratic presidents. Table 15.1 shows the current composition of the Supreme Court.

TABLE 15.1	Supreme Court Justices in Order of Seniority					
Name	Year of Birth	Home State	Religion	Year of Appointment	Appointed By	Senate Vote
John Roberts	1955	Indiana	Catholic	2005	George W. Bush	78–22
Antonin Scalia	1936	New York	Catholic	1986	Reagan	98–0
Anthony Kennedy	1936	California	Catholic	1988	Reagan	97–0
Clarence Thomas	1948	Georgia	Catholic	1991	George H. W. Bush	52–48
Ruth Bader Ginsburg	1933	New York	Jewish	1993	Clinton	96–3
Stephen Breyer	1938	Massachusetts	Jewish	1994	Clinton	87–9
Samuel A. Alito Jr.	1950	New Jersey	Catholic	2006	George W. Bush	58–42
Sonia Sotomayor	1954	New York	Catholic	2009	Obama	68–31
Elena Kagan	1960	Massachusetts	Jewish	2010	Obama	63–37

The Nomination Process

The formal process of appointing a justice to serve on the Supreme Court is guided by the same constitutional provisions that govern the selection of other Article III judges: The president nominates, the Senate confirms, and the justice serves during good behavior (Chapter 6). Thus, for all practical purposes, Supreme Court justices enjoy lifetime positions; none has ever been removed from office.

The informal process of appointing a justice to the Court, however, is strikingly different from that used to select lower-court judges. Presidents give Supreme Court nominations a degree of personal attention that is matched only by the scrutiny devoted to cabinet appointments and the president's closest advisers. At the same time, however, presidents increasingly find that their choices are scrutinized by a greater array of official and unofficial participants in the selection process. But not all presidents use the same process. David Yalof (1999) points out that presidents vary in their development of criteria to be used in selecting a nominee and the level of responsibility for the process they delegate. Complicating the president's selection is the fact that a wide range of liberal and conservative interest groups now actively lobby for the confirmation or the defeat of presidential nominees. The recent partisan confirmations of Elena Kagan (63–37), Sonya Sotomayor (68–31) and Samuel Alito (58–42), the nomination and subsequent withdrawal of Harriet Miers by George W. Bush, the appointment controversy around Clarence Thomas (52–48), and the failed nomination of Robert Bork are examples of that conflict (Comiskey 2004; Overby et al. 1992; Bronner 1989). Such competition sets the stage for the intersection of law, courts, and politics in determining who will sit on the nation's highest legal institution.

The Criteria for Nomination

What types of people do presidents choose to fill a Supreme Court vacancy? The most influential selection criteria include objective merit, personal and political friendship, policy preferences, and symbolic representation. Obviously, more than one of those factors is present in most of the nominations, and, as will be shown, these considerations vary from president to president and from vacancy to vacancy as well (Abraham 2007).

Merit In selecting judges for the lower federal courts, presidents seek nominees who are qualified, but other criteria, such as political support and senatorial courtesy, are also important. Nominations to the Supreme Court reverse that equation. For the Supreme Court, merit plays a critical role. Presidents first seek nominees who have strong legal credentials and whose ethical behavior is unquestioned. Indeed, "the great majority of justices had already achieved eminence by the time they were selected for the Court"—in judicial, legal, or public careers (Scigliano 1971, 107). Although not all nominees have been topflight lawyers, in only a few instances have the ethics or the credentials of a nominee been seriously questioned (Baum 2001).

Nominees whose qualifications to serve on the Supreme Court are not immediately obvious run the distinct risk of not being confirmed at all. That was most certainly the case with President Bush's 2005 nomination of his longtime friend and lawyer Harriet Miers. Even though she had a distinguished career as a corporate lawyer in Dallas and later as chief White House counsel, her qualifications were questioned by a wide variety of groups and people. In the end, President Bush withdrew her nomination. Neither of President Barack Obama's nominees (Sotomayor or Kagan) faced serious questions about their qualifications.

An indicator of the importance of judicial qualifications is the fact that, on the Court today, all the nine justices have previously served on the U.S. courts of appeals. It is safe to say that the path to the Court now leads through lower-court chambers.

Personal and Political Friendship   A nomination to the Supreme Court is one of the most important rewards that presidents can bestow on their political supporters. It should come as no surprise, therefore, to learn that presidents have frequently awarded those prizes on the basis of personal and political friendship. Indeed, historically half of the justices were personal friends of the appointing president (Scigliano 1971), but this is less so today. Not only do such persons appear to be deserving but also the president can have considerable confidence in the nominee's ideological "correctness." More broadly, 90 percent of all nominees have come from the president's party and most have been active in party politics (Baum 2001). Deviations from this norm are rare: William Brennan, for example, was a registered (but inactive) Democrat before being picked by Republican Dwight Eisenhower.

Earlier presidents all selected primarily personal acquaintances for vacancies on the high court, but recent presidents have exhibited a different pattern. Clinton is reported to have seriously considered several political allies but, in the end, demurred to two experienced jurists—Stephen Breyer and Ruth Bader Ginsburg. The lone recent exception appears to be George W. Bush's troubled choice of Harriet Miers. Bush was not friendly with either John Roberts or Samuel Alito before nominating them to the high court nor was Obama friends with Sotomayor or Kagan—although he had previously appointed Kagan to serve as the U.S. Solicitor General. This pattern suggests a shift away from personal and political factors and toward other nomination criteria, such as the policy preferences of the nominee.

Policy Preferences   Modern presidents have sought nominees who share their policy preferences regarding the role of the Supreme Court in U.S. political life and the interpretation of the Constitution (Watson and Stookey 1995). Most certainly, President Reagan's nominees to the high court reflected his conservative principles. His four nominees—Sandra Day O'Connor, Antonin Scalia, Anthony Kennedy, and William Rehnquist (elevating him from associate justice to chief justice)—were chosen because they were known conservatives. President Clinton's selections to the Court reflected his middle-of-the-road stance. His two nominees—Ruth Bader Ginsburg and Stephen Breyer—were known as moderate, middle-of-the-road jurists (Goldman et al. 2003). More so than any previous president, George W. Bush made conservatism the defining and dominant criterion for selection to the Court. For example, in announcing the nomination of John Roberts to fill a vacancy on the Court, the president stressed code phrases that his conservative supporters clearly wanted to hear: "He will strictly apply the Constitution and laws, and not legislate from the bench" (quoted in Neubauer and Meinhold 2006). The nomination and confirmation of the conservative Samuel Alito to replace the more moderate Sandra Day O'Connor has resulted in an increased awareness of the policy preferences of the nominees. Both of Barack Obama's nominees have consistently voted in a liberal direction and have voted the same way in 94% of the cases in which they participated.

Although presidents seek to nominate judges who reflect their policy preferences, they have not always been successful. Historical accounts abound with tales of presidents who were disappointed by their appointees' voting records. For instance, President Dwight Eisenhower (1965) considered his Supreme Court nomination of Earl Warren to be the biggest mistake he made as president (Kahn 1992; Warren 1977). Conversely, Democrat John Kennedy was responsible for nominating the conservative Byron White to the bench. To avoid such ideological surprises, chief executives increasingly prefer to appoint individuals with prior judicial experience, arguing that former judges provide a decision-making record that can serve as a guide to their subsequent behavior (Gates and Cohen 1988).

Anecdotal evidence aside, how successful are presidents in appointing like-minded justices to the Court? The evidence suggests they mostly are successful. Justices do reflect the political preferences of their appointing presidents, at least in some issue areas and for a short time after their appointment (Gates and Cohen 1988; Heck and Shull 1982). In a study of the voting behavior of Supreme Court justices from 1937 to 1994, Segal, Timpone, and Howard (2000) conclude, "Presidents appear to be reasonably successful in their appointments in the short run, but justices on average appear to deviate over time away from the presidents who appointed them." Such deviation is probably due, in part, to the fact that the issues confronting the Court change and often differ from those most salient to the president at the time the nominee was selected a decade or more ago. It also matters how many justices the president gets to appoint, as found by Lindquist, Yalof, and Clark (2000), who conclude that a president's influence is greatest when he gets more than one appointment and when those appointees vote cohesively. There is then a powerful opportunity for this judicial bloc to advance the president's interest, as happened with the Reagan and Nixon appointees. Clinton's does nominees (Ginsburg and Breyer) vote together 85 percent of the time; Bush's appointees (Roberts and Alito), 96 percent of the time—the highest of any two judge pair; and Obama's nominees (Sotomayor and Kagan) 94 percent—the second highest percentage.

Symbolic Representation   Symbolic representation also often plays a major role in influencing a president's choice to fill a vacancy on the Supreme Court, a candidate's geographic background, religious preference, race, ethnicity, or gender may make a potential nominee especially attractive. Indeed, when a president nominates a member of the opposing political party to the Supreme Court, it is often a symbolic gesture (Marshall 1993). In turn, by nominating a person with the "correct" symbolic background, presidents hope to gain voter support while rewarding loyal political followers.

Throughout the nineteenth century, geography was a prime consideration in efforts to engage in symbolic representation. Presidents sought to win political support through the appointment of justices from each of the expanding nation's rival sections. Geography was a less important factor in the twentieth century, but, occasionally, it played a role. During the 1968 campaign, Nixon promised to appoint a southerner to the Court, and, after two unsuccessful attempts (Clement Haynsworth and G. Harold Carswell), he succeeded with the confirmation of Lewis Powell.

Religious preference has also been a factor in some appointments. Through the years, the high court has been overwhelmingly Protestant in its makeup, but the period from 1894 until 1949 exhibited a tradition of a so-called Catholic seat. That tradition was revived in 1957 amid some controversy when Eisenhower appointed William Brennan. Today, however, the controversy over a Catholic seat seems a reflection of an earlier era; the nomination of five Roman Catholic jurists—Scalia, Kennedy, Thomas, Roberts, and Alito—by Republican presidents, and Obama's recent nomination of Sotomayor has hardly attracted attention.

Much more controversial than any of the Catholic appointees to the Court was the nomination of Louis Brandeis, the first Jewish justice, by President Woodrow Wilson in 1916. Conservatives bitterly fought his nomination because of his social and economic views (often accompanied by an underlying element of anti-Semitism). Indeed, when Brandeis took his seat on the Court, Justice James McReynolds did not speak to him for three years and once refused to sit next to him for a Court picture-taking session. Herbert Hoover's nomination of Benjamin Cardozo in 1932 thus established a so-called Jewish seat on the Supreme Court, which continued until 1969. When Abe Fortas resigned, President Nixon broke the tradition of a Jewish seat by choosing Harry Blackmun, a Protestant. Thus, no Jewish justice sat on the nation's highest court for a quarter of a century until Ruth Bader Ginsburg became the 107th justice of the Court. With Obama's appointment of Kagan there are now three Jews on the Court, six Catholics (Ginsburg, Breyer and Kagan) and no protestant—the first time in decades the Court does not have a protestant. Protestants have dominated the Court including times when all of the justices were protestant (Scheb, Sharma, and Glennon 2010).

In the modern era, geography and religion have been reduced to minor factors in selecting Supreme Court nominees. Today, race and gender have become more important factors in presidents' use of Supreme Court nominations to pursue political support (Perry 1991). In 1967, Thurgood Marshall became the first African American to serve on the Court. When he retired, President George H. W. Bush nominated another African American, Clarence Thomas, to continue the tradition.

The selection of Sandra Day O'Connor in 1981 brought the first woman to the Court. For his first nomination to the high court, President Clinton also chose a woman—Ruth Bader Ginsburg. The two women reflect different backgrounds, however. Although gender shaped O'Connor's choice of a public, as opposed to a private, career, her voting and opinion-writing behavior provides scant evidence of a distinctly feminine perspective (Davis 1993). Ginsburg, on the other hand, was in the forefront of the women's movement, serving as director of the American Civil Liberties Union's Women's Rights Project and arguing six important gender-based discrimination cases before the Supreme Court.

Future presidents will face considerable political pressure to maintain African-American, female and Latino representation on the Court, and to increase its diversity even more. Indeed, George W. Bush was criticized by some, including his wife, for choosing a male to replace Justice Sandra Day O'Connor when she stepped down. After Roberts had been nominated for O'Connor's seat, Chief Justice Rehnquist passed away. President Bush switched Roberts's nomination to the position of chief justice and tapped a woman for the vacancy, only to be forced to withdraw her nomination. The travail of Harriet Miers illustrates how tricky selections motivated by symbolic representation can be.

Interest Groups

Interest groups now take an active part in the Supreme Court nomination process (Bell 2002). In the past, interest groups were concerned primarily with the cases the Supreme Court heard and trying to influence those outcomes. Today, however, interest groups see nominations to the Court as a way to influence the outcome of future cases and to raise money and energize their supporters. Their role has become so public that some senators object to the pressure they are trying to exert on the process. During the confirmation hearings for Chief Justice Roberts, Patrick Leahy (D-Vt.) said, "These outside lobbying groups, whether on the right or the left, have become, for me anyway, basically irrelevant." Others would argue that his statement could not be further from the truth. During the John Roberts confirmation hearings, interest groups from both the left and the right mobilized to either support or oppose his nomination (Neubauer and Meinhold 2006). So far, though, the evidence suggests that interest groups have been more effective in blocking a nomination than they have been in influencing who is chosen by the president.

One group in particular has historically had more influence than others—the American Bar Association (ABA). Before the Bush administration, the president would send the ABA Standing Committee on the Federal Judiciary the name of the nominee in advance of the public announcement, and the committee would rank the nominee as "well qualified, qualified, or not qualified." Some presidents have paid greater attention to those rankings than have others, but the ABA was presumed to have some influence on the process. In 2001, President Bush announced that he would no longer send the names to the ABA committee in advance of the public announcement—effectively treating the ABA the same as any other interest group. President Obama restored the ABA's formal role in the process, but In many ways the ABA has now been eclipsed by more partisan groups (Caldeira and Wright 1998), offering further evidence that nominations are as political as they are legal.

SENATE CONFIRMATION

The president is also constrained by the requirement that the Senate confirm the choice. Moraski and Shipan (1999) contend that "presidents act strategically to choose the best nominee they can, given the constraints they face." Such constraints include a potentially hostile Judiciary Committee and Senate. Whatever the calculus used by a particular president, important external influences and competing institutional agendas must be considered: all the more reason to study who presidents choose and who they almost choose.

After the president has made a selection, the name is sent to the Senate Judiciary Committee, which questions the nominee on a wide range of issues, including constitutional philosophy (Guliuzza, Reagan, and Barrett 1994). That questioning, however, typically reveals little of the nominees' legal or political philosophies (Comiskey 1993). During controversial nominations, the hearings rate as high drama in the media and are considered a significant part of the confirmation process. Conversely, the hearings in noncontroversial nominations are often theatrics, a mere formality. Nonetheless, even in noncontroversial nominations where approval seems certain, senators can use the hearings to influence the next nomination even before it is made (Watson and Stookey 1995). For example, in questioning Supreme Court nominee John Roberts, senators appeared to focus not on Roberts but instead on the nominee whom Bush would eventually select to fill the O'Connor vacancy (namely, Samuel Alito).

After holding hearings, the Judiciary Committee makes a recommendation to the full Senate, and a date for the confirmation vote is set. Most nominations sail smoothly through the confirmation process, usually in less than two months from submission to the final vote (Wasby 1993). Indeed, recent confirmation votes tend to be lopsided, with only three successful nominees receiving less than a two-thirds margin. Controversial nominations, however, may take longer, with the fate of some genuinely in doubt (Segal 1987). Shipan and Shannon (2003) find that the confirmation happens faster when nominees have judicial experience or are sitting senators and when there is less ideological disagreement between the president and the Senate. When the executive and the legislative branches of government are controlled by the same political party, it makes sense that the president will have a greater chance of getting his nominees confirmed.

The confirmation process was overtly political throughout the nineteenth century. The Senate rejected or tabled Supreme Court nominations for virtually every conceivable reason, including the nominee's political views, opposition to the incumbent president, a desire to hold the vacancy for the incoming president, interest group pressures, and "on occasion even the nominee's failure to meet minimum professional standards" (Monaghan 1988, 1202). Before 1900, one-quarter of the nominees to the Supreme Court failed to win confirmation. From 1900 to 1967, though, presidents fared considerably better, with only one nomination failing to win confirmation. Since 1968, the pendulum has swung back. To be sure, thirteen nominees won Senate confirmation during this period, but several proved controversial. William Rehnquist's nomination to be associate justice in 1972 and his subsequent elevation to the post of chief justice in 1986 both generated significant opposition, as did President George H. W. Bush's choice of Clarence Thomas and George W. Bush's nomination of Samuel Alito.

Most pointedly, the seven unsuccessful nominations since 1968 (Table 15.2) reflect two primary factors: First, a nominee's policy preferences are a major source of Senate opposition, although, typically, mere disagreement with the views of the nominee is not enough to cause rejection. The second key factor is the competence or the ethical standards of the nominee. The nominations of Abe Fortas, Clement Haynsworth, G. Harold Carswell, Douglas Ginsburg, and Harriet Miers floundered amid charges of lack of ethics and/or lack of competence. Johnson and Roberts (2004) demonstrate that presidents can enhance the chances of success for their nominees or at least reduce the likelihood of a hostile Senate by using their political capital and going public to offer their support. Of the seven unsuccessful presidential efforts in recent years, the defeat of Robert Bork has attracted the most widespread interest. (See Debating Law, Courts, and Politics: The Rejection of Robert Bork.)

	TABLE 15.2	Unsuccessful Twentieth-Century Supreme Court Nominations			

Nominee	President	Year	Outcome	Discussion
John Parker	Hoover	1930	Rejected 39–41	Parker, a prominent North Carolina Republican and a judge on the Fourth Circuit Court of Appeals, was opposed by the American Federation of Labor, who read his opinions as indicating a hostility to labor. The NAACP also opposed the nomination. Parker might still have won, except for several progressive Republicans who would have voted against anyone Hoover nominated.
Abe Fortas	Lyndon Johnson	1968	Withdrawn after vote to end cloture rejected 47–48	After Fortas had served for three years as associate justice, Johnson tried to elevate his longtime friend to the post of chief justice. Johnson's unpopularity over the Vietnam War, coupled with charges of ethical impropriety against Fortas, led the Senate to refuse to confirm. In 1969, Fortas resigned amid threat of impeachment for his financial dealings with a convicted felon.
Homer Thornberry	Lyndon Johnson	1968	Moot after rejection of Fortas	A longtime Texas friend, Thornberry was caught up in the backlash against an unpopular president who would soon leave office.
Clement Haynsworth	Nixon	1970	Rejected 45–55	Haynsworth, of the Fourth Circuit, was Nixon's initial choice to fulfill his election promise of appointing a southerner to the Supreme Court. Opposed by labor and civil rights groups, he was rejected because of questions about professional ethics involving the ownership of stock in companies connected to cases before his court.
G. Harold Carswell	Nixon	1970	Rejected 47–52	Carswell was Nixon's second attempt to complete his southern strategy. Also opposed by labor and civil rights groups, he was defeated after publicity surrounding a 1948 campaign speech that supported white supremacists and segregation.
Robert Bork	Reagan	1987	Rejected 42–58	Moderate southern Democrats voted against Bork for being too ideologically extreme.
Douglas Ginsburg	Reagan	1987	Withdrawn before official nomination	After the rejection of Bork, the White House announced the pending nomination of Ginsburg, but nine days later withdrew it amid reports he smoked marijuana while a Harvard Law School professor.
Harriet Miers	George W. Bush	2005	Withdrawn after nomination	Withdrawn amid skepticism about her legal credentials and complaints from conservatives that she might not be conservative enough.

D E B A T I N G   L A W,   C O U R T S,   A N D   P O L I T I C S

■ The Rejection of Robert Bork

The controversy over President Reagan's nomination of Robert Bork for a seat on the Supreme Court stemmed partially from several political situations. First, the 1986 election had produced a Democratic majority in the Senate (54–46). Second, Reagan's power had waned. He was a lame duck who had suffered prestige and credibility gaps because of the Iran-Contra hearings and other political setbacks. Third, the ideological balance of the Court seemed to be at stake (Ruckman 1993). Retiring Justice Powell had been on the winning side of more 5–4 decisions than any other justice. Replacing him with a conservative would provide a fifth conservative justice, thus altering the balance of voting power on the Court—something liberals preferred to avoid. Those factors in combination suggested the potential for defeating the nomination (Stookey and Watson 1988).

The political situation interplayed with the controversy over the nominee himself. Unlike Fortas, Carswell, or Haynsworth, Bork was an academician with nearly impeccable ethical and intellectual credentials that normally would have provoked little excitement. Instead, the hearings were stirred by emotions about legal concepts. Robert Bork was noted for his intellectual passion, as represented in a career of provocative conservative writings. Opponents portrayed Bork's ideology as an ardent, almost reactionary, conservatism.

Civil rights groups found Bork insensitive to the rights of racial minorities, and women's groups feared that Bork's confirmation would result in undoing past gains for women's rights (Stookey and Watson 1988). For those reasons, the Bork nomination produced an unprecedented level of interest group activity. Numerous liberal groups held press conferences, sent mailings, organized rallies, and took out newspaper advertisements in a successful effort to defeat the nomination. Simultaneously, many conservative organizations engaged in similar activities, sponsoring television ads, starting letter-writing campaigns, and urging telephone calls in an attempt to win on the Senate floor.

In the end, Bork and the Reagan administration were unable to persuade moderate southern Democrats, who saw him as an extremist with opinions that were out of step with the times. Thus, unlike the defeats of Haynsworth and Carswell, the vote rejecting Bork was largely along party lines.

After a brief misstep (the abortive choice of Douglas Ginsburg), the White House nominated another conservative, Anthony Kennedy, who had strong backing among Republican senators, and he was quickly approved amid minimal controversy.

The defeat of Robert Bork for a seat on the Supreme Court continues to divide scholars and commentators. Social activists on both the left and the right portray the fight over Bork as the defining moment in the ongoing controversy over the political and ideological balance of power on the federal bench. The conservative version is set forth in *Ninth Justice: The Fight for Bork* (McGuigan and Weyrich 1990) and *The Judges War* (McGuigan and O'Connell 1987), written by major lobbyists for Bork. Conservatives see the origins of the judges' war in the presidency of Jimmy Carter, whom they accuse of using political litmus tests in selecting federal judge nominees (although Carter did not get an opportunity to select a Supreme Court justice). Thus, opposing President Reagan's well-qualified nominees on philosophical grounds unfairly changed the rules of the game and served as yet another example of how the U.S. establishment is out to sabotage their conservative revolution. A strikingly different version of the Bork defeat is set forth in *People Rising* (Pertschuk and Schaetzel 1989), written by leaders of the anti-Bork coalition. They detail how difficult it was to mobilize opposition to Bork, stressing internal debates and disagreements among a wide array of groups that expressed misgivings over Bork's philosophy. The authors stress that they learned how to mount a campaign against a justice from the successful efforts of conservatives in California to unseat Chief Justice Rose Bird of the California Supreme Court.

Debate over whether Bork received fair treatment continues. The two sides disagree over past practices of the Senate Judiciary Committee and proper standards for the opposition party to defeat a presidential nominee. In *The Selling of Supreme Court Nominees*, John Maltese (1995) argues that politics has always been at the heart of the Supreme Court selection process. According to his theory, the first "Borking" of a presidential appointee

(continued)

came in 1795 with the defeat of John Rutledge's nomination as chief justice. What is different about today's appointment process, he argues, is not its politicization but the range of players involved and the political techniques they use.

Defeat elevated Robert Bork to national prominence. His views, once expressed only in law reviews, gained a national audience with the publication in 1989 of his book *The Tempting of America*, which set forth his conservative views of law.

Senate confirmation votes reflect many of the same political considerations that influence presidents in their initial selection. Policy preferences of presidents and senators are of primary importance. When a strong president nominates a highly qualified, ideologically moderate candidate, the nominee passes the Senate in a lopsided, consensual vote. Because presidents have often chosen to nominate that type of candidate, consensual Senate votes have been fairly common. When presidents nominate a less well qualified, ideologically extreme candidate (especially when the president is in a weak political position), then a conflictual vote is likely. Appointments that are ideologically distant from the president also take more time to confirm (Shipan and Shannon 2003). Surprisingly, presidents have nominated quite a few candidates of that description through the years, and, therefore, conflictual votes occur periodically (Segal, Cameron, and Cover 1992; Cameron, Cover, and Segal 1990).

The bruising battle over Bork left political scars that have been slow to heal. Subsequent presidents appeared to avoid controversial nominations. Perhaps typical is the quick confirmation of David Souter. When Justice William Brennan, 84, resigned from the Supreme Court citing "advancing age and medical condition," President George H. W. Bush hoped to place a conservative on the Court without a bloody confirmation fight. Acting quickly, the president nominated David Souter, 50, a lifelong bachelor and Rhodes scholar. The selection was viewed as a surprise because, despite more than 20 years in public life, Souter's judicial philosophy was largely a blank slate. Liberals were fearful and conservatives apprehensive. In particular, pro-choice groups feared that he might be the fifth vote needed to overturn *Roe v. Wade* (1973). Conservatives, on the other hand, were concerned that Souter might not be conservative enough and, therefore, might *not* provide the needed fifth vote to anchor a conservative Court. During three days of nationally televised confirmation hearings, Souter discussed his general judicial philosophy but refused to state his views on specific cases and issues. During the confirmation hearings, Souter appeared neither highly political nor threatening. By an overwhelming margin (90–9), the U.S. Senate confirmed David Souter to be the 105th justice of the Supreme Court.

President Clinton likewise avoided controversy, choosing to tap those who would not be controversial over those who were likely to provoke a fight with conservative Senate Republicans. Stephen Breyer, for example, was noted for being a moderate pragmatist and a legal technician during his thirteen years on the federal appellate bench (O'Brien 2003).

Nominations can be particularly contentious if the nominee holds ideological views different from those held by the retiring justice. The nomination of John Roberts is a case in point. Originally, he was nominated to fill the seat being vacated by Sandra Day O'Connor—widely regarded as the most centrist justice on the Court.

His selection became much less contentious when it was shifted to replace the recently deceased William Rehnquist. Now one conservative was replacing another conservative, which did not affect the balance of power on the Court. The nomination of Samuel Alito involved a deeper political struggle because he was viewed as much more conservative than O'Connor and, therefore, more likely to shift the Court in a more conservative direction.

President Obama made headlines with his first nominee Sonya Sotomayor who, after being confirmed, became the Court's first Latino justice. Obama's second pick Elena Kagan resulted in three women on the Court for the first time ever. The confirmation votes for both Sotomayor and Kagan fell basically along partisan lines with Democratic senators supporting their nominations and Republicans in opposition which has led some observers to conclude that we have now officially entered a period of partisan votes on Supreme Court nominations.

THE DECISION-MAKING PROCESS

Whenever a new justice is appointed to the Supreme Court, observers speculate about the impact the newcomer may have on the Court. At the same time, analysts recognize that new justices, like anyone assuming a new position, must undergo an adjustment period before becoming completely assimilated into the Court. This adjustment period has been called the "freshman effect." A majority of the justices undergo a period of transition, but some experience this effect more than others (Hurwitz and Stefko 2004; Bowen and Scheb 1993; Hagle 1993). New justices have historically authored fewer majority opinions and asked fewer questions during oral argument.

One aspect of the freshman effect is adapting to the ebb and flow of the Court's docket. As Justice Brennan once noted, "Such factors as workload, unfamiliarity with … procedures and the unique nature of constitutional decision-making tend to create difficulties for any neophyte justice" (quoted in Heck 1979, 710). The rules and procedures by which the Court conducts its business are easily mastered. What takes longer is assimilating the informal norms that give life and substance to the formal structure. Newly appointed justices find that the Court operates much like nine separate law firms, each with its own support staff. In essence, the justices lead separate, even isolated lives; they deal with one another only in quite formalized settings and then retreat to their own chambers.

Briefing

After the Court accepts a case for review, the lawyers for both parties prepare written **briefs** setting forth the arguments and precedents for their side of the case. Each side also has the opportunity to file reply briefs. Interest groups and the government often file amicus curiae briefs as well, each offering a position on how the controversy should be settled. In the briefs, the lawyers muster evidence to support their interpretations of constitutional provisions and statutory language, particularly discussing relevant Supreme Court decisions. Although Supreme Court rules limit briefs to a maximum of fifty pages (and thirty pages for amici), the justices and their law clerks are nonetheless inundated with reading material. Examples of highly regarded Supreme Court briefs can be found in a series called *Landmark Cases and Briefs*, available in many libraries and more recently on the Web at sites such as http://www.findlaw.com.

Oral Argument

The time allowed for **oral argument** is strictly limited. Except in cases of extraordinary public importance, each side is allotted thirty minutes, which the attorneys for the parties may, if they wish, share with counsel for interest groups who have filed amici.

The lawyers come prepared with arguments they wish to present, but rarely do they get very far before they are forced to respond to questions from the justices. Justices Scalia, Souter, and Ginsburg are known to pepper lawyers with questions: During one hour-long argument, this trio asked more than fifty questions, a practice that some observers consider disruptive of the proper functioning of oral argument (Mauro 1993). According to Justice Scalia, he asks the lawyers tough questions because he wants to give each attorney his or her best shot at overcoming what is, in his mind, the major obstacle to deciding the case in favor of that side (Adler 1987). Thus, the justices, more so than the attorneys, actually control the direction of oral argument. Responding to such queries is tricky business, because the lawyers are arguing not to a collective court but to nine individual justices, each of whom has his or her own thought process. Attorneys are acutely aware of the justices' voting patterns and seek to plug their arguments into those patterns in an effort to assemble a coalition of five justices in their favor. In turn, the justices use oral argument to help them reach a final decision. As Chief Justice Rehnquist (1987, 277) wrote, oral argument is the only time before conference "when all of the judges are expected to sit on the bench and concentrate on one particular case." Johnson, Wahlbeck, and Spriggs (2006) have shown that the quality of legal arguments presented varies and that the better the legal argument the more likely it is that party will be victorious. At times, justices use questions much like a post office to send messages to another justice; part of oral argument, therefore, reflects the justices arguing with one another through the lawyers (Johnson 2004). Oral arguments are not televised or broadcast simultaneously, but the transcripts and audiorecordings are later released by the Court to the media. The transcripts are widely available, and many audiorecordings are available on the Web at http://www.oyez.org.

Conference

Two or three days after oral argument, the justices assemble in private—behind closed doors—to discuss the cases recently argued and to take a tentative vote. Only the justices attend the conferences, which are not open to the public or to other Court personnel. The chief justice presides, opening the discussion by reviewing the facts of the case, stating the decision of the lower court, outlining his (or her) understanding of the applicable case law, and stating how he (or she) thinks the case should be decided

(Rehnquist 1987). Next, the associate justices present their views in order of seniority (determined by years of service on the Court, not biological age). Because their colleagues have already voiced similar positions, the more junior justices generally speak quite briefly. "The truth is that there simply are not nine different points of view in even the most complex and difficult case, and all of us feel impelled to a greater or lesser degree to try to reach some consensus that can be embodied in a written opinion that will command the support of at least a majority of the members of the Court" (Rehnquist 1987, 290). When the discussion ends, the chief justice tallies the votes in what is called the "original vote on the merits." In an earlier era, discussion and voting were separate, with voting conducted in reverse order of seniority. Today, however, the justices discuss and then vote.

Discussions in conference are less freewheeling than they once were. Largely because of the press of cases, the justices no longer have time to reach agreement and compromise on opinions for the Court. On the basis of a reading of the briefs, the lawyers' presentations during oral argument, and discussions with their clerks, the justices have developed strong opinions about the case before conference. Moreover, the justices evaluate cases "on the basis of their own, frequently strong, attitudes about policy" (Baum 1995, 117). Conferences, therefore, serve only to discover consensus (O'Brien 2003). According to Chief Justice Rehnquist (1987, 295), "This is not to say that minds are never changed in conference; they certainly are. But it is very much the exception and not the rule...." Thus, it is through opinion writing, rather than the face-to-face discussions during conference, that the justices communicate and negotiate.

Opinion Assignment

Soon after the original vote in conference, the chief justice, if in the majority, assigns one of the justices to write the majority opinion explaining the results reached. If the chief justice is in the minority, then the most senior associate justice in the winning coalition makes the assignment. The opinion assigner can assign the opinion to any justice in the winning coalition, including himself or herself. The justice who writes the majority opinion has substantial control over its content and, as a consequence, can strongly influence the future development of the law on the subject (Bonneau et al. 2007). It is not surprising, therefore, that opinion assignment has been a frequent area of interest for Supreme Court scholars (Brenner and Palmer 1988). Four factors emerge as the most important considerations.

Workload   Equality of workload is an important, unwritten rule of the Supreme Court (Spaeth 1984). As Chief Justice Warren explained after his retirement, "I do believe that if [assigning opinions] wasn't done ... with fairness, it could well lead to gross disruption in the Court.... During all the years I was there ... I did try very hard to see that we had an equal workload...." (Lewis 1969). That each justice does receive an equal share (that is, one-ninth) of the Court's opinions to write is borne out by a comprehensive study of 6,275 opinion assignments from the beginning of the Taft Court in 1921 to the 1973 term of the Burger Court. Elliot Slotnick (1979) found that, since World War II, the chief justices have tended to assign to each justice approximately the same number of majority opinions. Similarly, Chief Justice

Burger's assignment practices indicated a record of equality unmatched by any of his predecessors (Spaeth 1984). Likewise, Chief Justice Rehnquist attempted to achieve an equal distribution of opinions (Davis 1990; Rehnquist 1987). Roberts has continued this trend during his tenure. In the 2010-11 term, justices authored between 7 (Alito, Breyer, Kagan, and Sotomayor) and 11 (Kennedy) opinions.

Ideology   Selection of a justice in the ideological middle is another important factor in assigning the writing of the majority opinion. Any justice is free to change his or her vote at any time before the public announcement of the decision. Thus, the other members of the majority opinion coalition are not powerless, especially when the vote is close (that is, 5–4). The author of the Court's opinion, therefore, is not a free agent; typically, he or she must also satisfy the views of at least four other justices. In cases with a minimum winning coalition, the justice closest to the dissenters may be selected, because he or she is viewed as the person most capable of writing an opinion that will maintain the initial coalition (Rhode and Spaeth 1976; Rhode 1972). Others, however, have found that this strategy may not work as well as previously believed (Brenner and Spaeth 1988).

Specialization   Issue specialization is another factor influencing opinion assignment. Justice Blackmun's selection by Chief Justice Burger to write the Court's 1973 abortion decision was made, in part, because of his medical law expertise. (He had previously served as chief counsel for the Mayo Clinic in Rochester, Minnesota.) Assigning the majority opinion on the basis of issue specialization was a commonplace occurrence on the Warren Court. Chief Justice Warren, for example, wrote a disproportionate number of opinions on reapportionment and voting rights, Black on racial discrimination matters, and Brennan on cases dealing with censorship and obscenity. Just as important, Warren tended to select as issue specialists justices who had the same ideological views as he did, or similar ones (Brenner 1984). Chief Justice Burger likewise used issue specialization as a criterion in assigning opinions (Brenner and Spaeth 1986).

Self-Assignment   Self-assignment is a final consideration in choosing a justice to speak for the Court. Since Marshall, there has been a tradition on the Court of the chief justice assigning himself the task of writing decisions in important cases. Slotnick's data (1979) bear out that proposition: Chief justices self-assigned 25 percent of important cases, a figure matched by Warren Burger (Spaeth 1984) and, more recently, by William Rehnquist (Davis 1990). Thus, it appears far from a statistical accident that Warren assigned himself to write the Court's opinion desegregating public schools (*Brown v. Board of Education* 1954) and that Burger also assigned himself the task of writing the first important school desegregation case of his tenure (*Swann v. Charlotte-Mecklenburg* 1971).

Opinion Writing

Writing opinions is the justices' most difficult and time-consuming task. Opinion writing—especially majority opinion writing—provides justices with the most obvious opportunity to influence the direction of the law. Maltzman, Spriggs, and Wahlbeck (2000) show that justices act strategically as they prepare their majority opinions so that they will attract sufficient justices to determine the outcome of the case (at least four others) and the future of law in a particular area. The justice assigned to write for the Court typically begins by giving the law clerk a summary of the conference discussion, a description of the result reached by the majority during conference, and views on how a written opinion can best be prepared expressing that reasoning (Rehnquist 1987). Law clerks' views are presumed to reflect those of the justices who chose them (Brenner 1992). Over the years, law clerks have taken on more responsibility in opinion writing, but their role has been important since they were first made available to the justices back in 1886. Justices vary tremendously in their delegation of responsibility for writing opinions to their law clerks. Wahlbeck, Spriggs, and Sigelman (2002) find the "fingerprints" of law clerks in the opinions of both Thurgood Marshall and Lewis F. Powell Jr. but note that "Powell's clerks displayed less autonomy than Marshall's." The increasing role of the law clerk points to the future importance of Supreme Court scholars knowing and revealing more about these individuals and their policy preferences.

When the law clerk's rough draft is ready, the justice revises and edits; only after the justice is satisfied with the draft opinion is it circulated to the other justices for their reactions. If a justice agrees with the draft opinion, he or she writes a letter expressing a desire to join the opinion. If a justice agrees with the essential points of the opinion but wishes changes to be made in it before joining, he or she sends a letter to that effect. At other times, however, justices urge major substantive alterations before they will agree to have their names attached to the opinion. Justice Brennan, for example, sent a twenty-one-page list of revisions on Earl Warren's initial draft of *Miranda v. Arizona* (1966) (O'Brien 2003). Factors such as the size of the winning majority coalition, their ideological heterogeneity, their positions taken, the author's workload, and the complexity of the case have all been shown to affect the willingness of the author to accommodate others (Wahlbeck, Spriggs, and Maltzman 1998; Rehnquist 1987).

During opinion writing, the justices exchange ideas and suggest changes in approach and emphasis. Those exchanges can and do change justices' votes. As Justice Jackson once announced from the bench, "I myself have changed my opinion after reading the opinions of the members of the Court. And I am as stubborn as most. But I sometimes wind up not voting the way I voted in conference because the reasons of the majority didn't satisfy me" (Westin 1958, 123). These group interactions account for what J. Woodford Howard (1968) has called the "fluidity of judicial choice" (Maltzman and Wahlbeck 1996; Dorff and Brenner 1992; Brenner 1980). One analysis of the period 1946–1975 found that justices changed their votes about 7 percent of the time (Dorff and Brenner 1992). Maltzman and Wahlbeck (1996) suggest three reasons justices might change their votes between the conference and the final resolution of the case: (1) their initial view may not be firmly held, (2) changes have occurred in the winning coalition during opinion-drafting exchanges, and (3) there are unrelated institutional considerations (for example, desire to assign the majority opinion, loyalty to the institution, or avoidance of being in the minority). Compromise is inevitable but never easy. Multiple drafts are not unheard of. In one case, Brennan circulated ten printed drafts before one was approved as the Court's opinion. Moreover, on some occasions, the direction of the decision itself may change, which necessitates reassignment of the majority opinion (Brenner 1986). But the justices stress that votes are not interchangeable: Bargaining—as in "I'll vote for you on the abortion case if you'll vote with me on the capital punishment decision"—does not occur.

Opinion writing reflects not only fluidity of judicial choice but also issue fluidity. In roughly half of the full-opinion cases, there is a divergence between the questions presented by the parties and the questions ultimately decided by the justices. On some occasions, the final opinion provides an authoritative answer to questions that have not been asked and, on other occasions, disregards issues that the parties have presented (McGuire and Palmer 1995). Issue fluidity reflects the fact that the justices search for cases that permit them to expand their preferences and that present opportunities to accommodate conflicting approaches to deciding the outcome.

Announcement of Opinion

By a self-imposed rule, the Court decides every case argued that term, although, on rare occasions, cases have been held over to the next term, sometimes for reargument. When the opinion is ready, it is announced from the bench, and copies are made available to the public. And, to add a modern wrinkle, the Court now makes its decisions instantly available on the Internet. Particularly toward the end of the term, the Court hands down a flurry of decisions, sometimes as many as six a day.

Like all appellate court decisions, those of the Supreme Court operate at two levels: results and reasons. First, the result settles the dispute between the immediate parties by announcing the Court's decision on how to resolve the controversy. This announcement is always found in the last few lines of the opinion. Second, the opinion explains the reasons the Court reached the decision it did. Through such reasons, the justices develop the law, providing directions for how the lower courts should decide similar cases in the future. But the reasons do not always command the support of five or more justices. In an **opinion of the Court**, a majority of the justices agree not only on the result but also on the legal reasons for that outcome. At times, however, no single opinion is joined by five or more justices. In that event, the opinion is known as the **plurality opinion** of "Justice" and whatever justices join with him or her. A plurality opinion, although decisive for the parties, is usually not regarded as having strong precedential value. The Court's first death penalty decision (*Furman v. Georgia* 1972) is a case in point. Some decisions include **concurring opinions**, whereby a justice agrees with the results reached by the majority but disagrees with the reasoning used to reach that conclusion. Concurring opinions argue that the Court went too far or didn't go far enough or that the law would have been better served by proceeding on a totally different legal theory.

Finally, of course, justices may disagree with the Court's decision and write a **dissenting opinion**. If nothing else, dissents serve to keep the majority honest. They point out the weaknesses of the decision and, even if the decision is not later reversed, may dissuade future courts from extending the argument made in the case.

The Justices' Policy Preferences

The Supreme Court is characterized by division rather than consensus, with unanimous opinions rare and getting rarer. But it wasn't always this way. From John Marshall's appointment as chief justice in 1801 to the end of the Charles Evans Hughes era in 1941, the Court exhibited relatively stable, cohesive behavior (Haynie 1992). Through turbulent periods of war, rebellion, economic depression, and political cleavage, the high court maintained the "norm of consensus." But that "norm" masked serious disagreement about how cases should be decided. Even during the early "consensual" eras, when public disagreement was rare, privately the justices disagreed about many legal issues (Epstein, Segal, and Spaeth 2001). The pattern of consensus radically changed in the early 1940s (Walker, Epstein, and Dixon 1988). The Court's most recent term (2010–2011) continued the trend of frequent dissents, with nearly as many dissenting opinions (47) as majority opinions (75) (SCOTUSblog.com). Moreover, fifteen of the seventy-five cases (20 percent) were decided 5–4, meaning that a change in a single vote would have altered the outcome (SCOTUSblog.com).

Skyrocketing rates of dissent "radically changed the way scholars viewed the judiciary. Before 1941, traditional legal approaches provided satisfactory explanations for a Supreme Court whose institutional practices led to consensus decisions with relatively low levels of expressed disagreement" (Walker, Epstein, and Dixon 1988, 362). But some researchers felt that focusing exclusively on stability and change in constitutional doctrine using the tools of legal and historical analysis was too limiting (Epstein, Walker, and Dixon 1989).

C. Herman Pritchett was the first to recognize the scholarly implications of the Court's abandonment of a norm of consensus (Chapter 13). As he argued, "It is precisely because the Court's institutional ethos has become so weak that we must examine the thinking of the individual justices" (1954, 22). That rethinking propelled the field of public law into the era of judicial behavior, a theoretical perspective that continues to dominate scholarly perceptions of the U.S. legal system. The central question is: Why do justices vote the way they do? Most of the cases coming to the Court present the justices "with an effective choice situation which gave them the perceived freedom to decide the case in a manner consistent with their policy values" (Goldman 1969, 219–220). This view is commonly referred to as the "attitudinal model" (Segal and Spaeth 1989).

Political scientists have come to consider it axiomatic that justices decide cases on the basis of policy preferences. Before nomination, justices have developed firm ideas about many of the issues they will be called on to decide. Their attitudes are further refined while serving on the Court, when justices confront actual cases presenting specific dimensions of those issues. Their policy preferences mold how justices approach cases and structure choices among alternative policies. Thus, like policy makers in the legislative and executive branches of government, Supreme Court justices "make decisions largely in terms of their personal attitudes toward policy" (Baum 1995). A common technique used by scholars to analyze the ideological divisions on the Court is bloc analysis.

Bloc Analysis

Bloc analysis is one way of examining the ideological divisions on the Court. Table 15.3 shows the percentage of cases in which pairs of justices supported the same opinion during the 2010 term. Clearly, some groups of justices vote together much more often than other groups. The justices who most often voted together were Chief Justice Roberts and Justice Alito (96 percent); Justice Sotomayor and Justice Kagan, the two newest members of the Court and both appointed by President Obama (94 percent); followed closely by Justices Ginsburg and Kagan (91 percent) and Justice Roberts and Scalia (90 percent). High levels of agreement are found on both the conservative *and* the liberal wings of the Court. It is also use to look at the justice pairs that frequently disagree with each other. The most frequent disagreements occurred between Justice Ginsburg and her colleague Justice Alito, who agreed on the outcome in just 29% of the cases—only 12 times in the entire year. In her first term on the Court, Justice Kagan disagreed with her new colleagues (Roberts, Scalia, Kennedy, Thomas, and Alito) in about 50 percent of the cases the court heard.

Another way to examine bloc voting is to look at coalitions. Because 5–4 decisions are so important, scholars often consider which groups of five justices make up the majority in those decisions. During the 2010 term there were 16 cases decided by a 5–4 vote. Roberts, Scalia, Kennedy, Thomas, and Alito (the five most conservative members of the Court) voted together in ten of those cases (SCOTUSblog.com). Kennedy was also in four more 5–4 decisions but in those cases he voted with the liberal members of the Court—Ginsburg, Breyer, Sotomayor, and Kagan. The appearance of Kennedy in 14 of the 16 (88%) of the 5–4 decisions makes him a central figure in the Court's modern jurisprudence. Indeed during the past five terms Kennedy's participation with the other Conservative members to form a 5 member majority has increased from 45 percent in 2005 to 63 percent in 2010.

TABLE 15.3	Percentage of Agreement in Votes Between U.S. Supreme Court Justices, 2010 Term								
	JR	**AS**	**AK**	**CT**	**RG**	**SB**	**SA**	**SS**	**EK**
Roberts (JR)		90	90	89	65	72	96	71	69
Scalia (AS)	90		83	86	65	65	86	67	70
Kennedy (AK)	90	83		86	66	74	88	73	72
Thomas (CT)	89	86	86		65	70	89	68	66
Ginsburg (RG)	65	65	66	65		85	63	85	91
Breyer (SB)	72	65	74	70	85		69	87	87
Alito (SA)	96	86	88	89	63	69		72	68
Sotomayor (SS)	71	67	73	68	85	87	72		94
Kagan (EK)	69	70	72	66	91	87	68	94	

Note: The numbers are percentages of cases in which a pair of justices agreed on an opinion. Both unanimous and nonunanimous cases are included.
Source: Data from SCOTUSblog.com. Available online at http://www.scotusblog.com.

Those patterns, and the lack of patterns, suggest two principal qualifications of bloc analysis. First, the justices do not always vote together in predictable ways. Cases that cut across usual policy preferences are most likely to produce atypical voting patterns. (See Law and Popular Culture: *The People vs. Larry Flynt.*) Second, just because justices cast similar votes, it does not signify that the justices consulted one another or even tried to exert influence on one another. Thus, voting agreements seem to reflect justices who hold similar policy preferences and, for that reason, come to cast identical votes.

The Attitudinal Model

As we noted in Chapter 13, the attitudinal model is the prevailing method of studying the votes of Supreme Court justices. It assumes that justices' votes are a function of their policy preferences (Segal and Spaeth 2002, 1992). The model is remarkably elegant. Justices are policy makers, and they vote the way they do because they are interested in seeing their policy views made into law. About the only challenge in the attitudinal model is how to measure the ideology of the justices (Segal and Cover 1989). Once we can agree that Scalia is politically conservative (and agree on how to measure Scalia's ideology), it is easy to predict that he will vote in a conservative direction in cases before the Court. Study after study has reaffirmed the value of the attitudinal model. But it cannot be the entire explanation for Supreme Court voting. Some of the votes that are consistent with the ideology of the justice may have been cast for a different reason (for example, commitment to precedent), and some votes are not consistent with the attitudinal model (for example, a liberal vote cast by Scalia). To fill out the explanation, we look to the strategic and legal models.

The Strategic Model

The strategic model assumes that justices are policy makers who act strategically to achieve their most preferred outcome (Epstein and Knight 1998). That sometimes means that they cast votes that appear to be contrary to the attitudinal model but that are designed to further their goals. Consider the following scenario: Acting solely on attitudes, Justice A ends up with his or her least preferred outcome (say, a reversal of a lower-court decision he or she agrees with). However, by being willing to moderate his or her views, Justice A may be able to put together a coalition of judges to achieve his or her second most preferred outcome (say, a reversal of the lower-court decision but on narrow legal grounds). Or maybe it is in Justice A's best interest to vote against his or her stated attitudes because the case is important to Justice B and Justice B may be inclined to vote with him or her on a subsequent case about which Justice A feels more strongly than he or she does about the current one before the Court.

The strategic model is very intuitive because it appears to describe much of the behavior we witness on the Court (Maltzman, Spriggs, and Wahlbeck 2000), but it

LAW AND POPULAR CULTURE

■ *The People vs. Larry Flynt* (1996)

"If the First Amendment will protect a scumbag like me, it will protect all of you." Those words from Larry Flynt (portrayed by Woody Harrelson) perhaps best summarize both popular reactions to pornography and the difficulty the Supreme Court has in applying the First Amendment to this emotional area. Flynt is referring to the Supreme Court case *Hustler Magazine v. Falwell* (1988), which considered whether the First Amendment protects speech aimed at public officials that is offensive and causes emotional distress. The case involved a parody of an ad campaign for Campari (an alcoholic beverage) implying that evangelist Jerry Falwell and his mother had been involved in an incestuous relationship. Larry Flynt published the parody in his *Hustler* magazine. Two aspects to the film are noteworthy: One is the treatment of the Supreme Court and its institutional dynamics; the second is the expectation by Flynt and his lawyers that he will not win.

According to the website of film critic and law professor Rob Waring, director Milos Forman and producer Oliver Stone went to great lengths to recreate the interior of the Supreme Court and to hire actors who were similar in appearance and dialect to the justices on the Court when Flynt's case was heard. Such efforts are unusual in Hollywood and are particularly interesting in this situation, because one can listen to the actual oral argument on the Internet (http://www.oyez.org) and compare it with the dramatized version in the film. Your own experience at the Court or pictures of the Court can be compared with the stylized version presented by Forman and Stone.

Another reason this film is interesting is the expectation by Flynt and his lawyer, Alan Isaacman (played by Edward Norton), that the Court will not look favorably upon Flynt or his cause. Isaacman even shows some reluctance to appeal the case to the Supreme Court for fear of the way his client will behave—Flynt had become notorious for his outrageous courtroom conduct. But the Court ruled 8–0 in his favor.

This chapter's discussion of judicial decision making might have led to a different prediction. The Court in 1988 was ideologically divided and becoming more and more conservative in its decision making after the addition of justices nominated by President Ronald Reagan. Indeed, Larry Flynt himself even said in an interview with Larry King when the film opened, "I knew they didn't like me." If one considered ideology or party affiliation alone, a unanimous decision in favor of *Hustler* would appear very unlikely. Thus, this film—and this case—present an opportunity to consider the complexity of predicting Supreme Court justices' votes. The experience is made all the more interesting because of the ability to view the film version of the events, listen to the oral argument, and read the decision.

Regardless of one's opinions of Larry Flynt and *Hustler*, the film does represent a rare example of Hollywood treating a real Supreme Court case in an unorthodox manner, providing both visual images of the Court's chambers and footage of a re-enacted oral argument that affords us the opportunity to contrast the film version with what really happened.

After watching this movie, be prepared to discuss the following questions:

1. How realistic is the film in depicting the Supreme Court? After viewing the Supreme Court scenes in the film and listening to the actual oral argument in the case of *Hustler Magazine v. Falwell* (1988), discuss the level of realism in the film.

2. Consider the justices on the Court at the time of the case, their political ideology and party identification, and the issues presented in the case. On the basis of that information, predict how each justice would vote. Why was the outcome in the case different from what you predicted?

3. In what ways does *The People vs. Larry Flynt* characterize the Supreme Court differently than the other court proceedings shown in the film?

To learn more about the film, visit these websites:

http://medialibel.org/cases-conflicts
http://www.usfca.edu/pj/articles/larry_flynt.htm

also adds substantial complexity to efforts to explain Supreme Court voting. Critics charge the additional complexity is unnecessary because Supreme Court justices are relatively unconstrained and can vote as they wish with few consequences. Thus, the additional complexity and difficulty of assessing the strategic model empirically make it inferior to the elegant power of the attitudinal model. Nevertheless, the strategic model is gaining attention and is proving useful for explaining Supreme Court behavior, especially in the areas of coalition building and voting to grant certiorari (see Chapter 14).

The Legal Model

Many law professors and political scientists start with the legal model in their efforts to explain the behavior of Supreme Court justices. The legal model asserts that justices' decisions are the product of the legal statutes involved in the case, their meaning and precedent. Political scientists for the most part long ago abandoned a simple application of the legal model, recognizing that there was too much disagreement among the justices about the meaning of the law, precedent, and so on, to make this a useful explanatory or predictive model. The abandonment may be premature, though, because scholars have begun to reconsider the importance of the legal and political context of cases (Gillman and Clayton 1999).

In a more nuanced effort to describe the effects of legal factors on Supreme Court voting, Richards and Kritzer (2002) argue that there is support for "jurisprudential regimes," which are defined as "a key precedent, or a set of related precedents, that structures the way in which the Supreme Court justices evaluate key elements of cases in arriving at decisions in a particular legal arena" (308). They have found evidence for the "jurisprudential regime" model in cases dealing with free expression and the Establishment Clause.

The purpose of our brief discussion of each of the prevailing paradigms used to explain Supreme Court justice voting is to encourage the reader to consider the sophisticated methods political scientists employ in their work and to offer directions for further analysis. Each of the models has passionate supporters and vocal detractors, but the common element is that they all contribute to an improved understanding of the politics of the Court.

FROM WARREN TO ROBERTS

Scholars and journalists frequently refer to the Court by the name of the chief justice who leads it. Although the chief justice is just one of nine votes, the position does carry significant opportunity to shape the Court and its decisions. The chief justice assigns the opinion if he is in the majority, which happened nearly 80 percent of the time between 1953 and 1990 (Maltzman and Wahlbeck 1996). He also begins the discussion in conference and is responsible for the administrative functioning of the Court. There have been just seventeen chief justices in the Court's history; the most recent four are Warren, Burger, Rehnquist, and Roberts.

The Warren Court

Although it is now almost 40 years since Chief Justice Earl Warren stepped down, the **Warren Court** (1953–1969) continues to command our attention because, in the areas of civil liberties and civil rights, it remains the benchmark against which subsequent periods of the Supreme Court will be measured. The Warren Court revolutionized constitutional law and U.S. society as well, handing minorities victories they had not been able to obtain from reluctant legislatures and disinclined chief executives.

The Warren Court first captured national attention with its highly controversial 1954 decision in *Brown v. Board of Education* that invalidated racial segregation and struck down the legal doctrine of "separate but equal" (Chapter 7). Moreover, the Court first confronted the difficult problem of defining obscenity and considerably narrowed the grounds for prosecution of obscene material (*Roth v. United States* 1957). But the Court's liberal heritage did not firmly emerge until President Kennedy's appointment of Justice Arthur Goldberg in 1962 (Baum 1995). In 1962, the Warren Court began the reapportionment revolution in *Baker v. Carr* (1962), eventually holding that legislative districts must be drawn on the basis of population—"one man, one vote" (*Reynolds v. Sims* 1964). Another controversial decision banned prayers in public schools (*Engel v. Vitale* 1962). But what produced the greatest controversy was the adoption of a series of broad rules protecting criminal defendants, including the right to counsel (*Gideon v. Wainwright* 1963) (Chapter 5), the exclusionary rule (*Mapp v. Ohio* 1961), and limits on police interrogations (*Miranda v. Arizona* 1966) (Chapter 8). The Warren Court put the issues of civil liberties and civil rights on its docket and eventually on the nation's agenda as well. The number of civil liberties cases heard increased every term, as did the number of civil liberties cases decided in a liberal direction (Segal and Spaeth 1989). It was no surprise when Richard Nixon, in his 1968 presidential campaign, made the Warren Court decisions on criminal procedure a major issue and indirectly suggested that the Court had gone too far, too fast in civil rights.

The Burger Court

With his four appointments, Nixon achieved remarkable success in influencing the Court. After Burger, Blackmun, Powell, and Rehnquist took the bench, support for civil liberties quickly began to diminish, dropping from 80 percent in 1968 to only 34 percent in 1985 (Segal and Spaeth 1989). The undercutting of and withdrawal from Warren Court decisions was most apparent in criminal cases. *Miranda* was weakened but not overturned. Similarly, despite clamor by conservatives, *Mapp* was not overruled, although the Court began creating "good faith" exceptions to the exclusionary rule (see Chapter 8). Although support for civil liberties did decline, the Burger Court did not cut back on Warren Court criminal procedure rulings as much as some had expected.

On balance, the **Burger Court** (1969–1986) was more conservative than its predecessor, but there was no constitutional counterrevolution, only modest adjustments. In establishment-of-religion disputes, for example, the Court moved from a separationist to an accommodationist posture. Nonetheless, state aid to elementary and secondary religious schools was struck down (*Lemon v. Kurtzman* 1971), and the posting of the Ten Commandments in classrooms was prohibited (*Stone v. Graham* 1980). Just as important, the Burger Court began to tackle new sets of issues not previously treated. In gender discrimination, women were not given the same amount of legal protection as had been given to racial minorities, but the tone of opinions was moderate to liberal, not conservative (Wasby 1993). Similarly, in the burning area of reverse discrimination, racial quotas were rejected, but some forms of affirmative action were upheld (*Board of Regents v. Bakke* 1978). During the early years of the Burger Court, the death penalty was struck down but later reinstated (Chapter 9). And, in one of the most controversial decisions ever issued, the Burger Court struck down a variety of requirements that interfered with a woman's right to obtain an abortion (*Roe v. Wade* 1973) (Chapter 14).

Amid that diversity, it is hard to capture the essence of the Burger Court. Indeed, the Burger Court is probably best characterized by the headline "Burger Court Leaves an Unclear Legacy," because the Court was marked by pragmatism and compromise, and, therefore, its tricky track record was harder to categorize than pundits predicted (Wasby 1993, 17). In reality, the Burger Court in the 1980s was dominated by a four-judge center bloc—Blackmun, Powell, Stevens, and White—that needed only one additional vote to carry the day. Powell was the most centrist of the centrist justices on most other matters and, for that reason, was often called on to craft the majority opinion when the Court was split 5–4. Thus, the late Burger Court was dominated by a middle group of justices composed primarily of Republicans.

The Rehnquist Court

The **Rehnquist Court** (1986–2005) officially began when William Rehnquist was elevated from associate justice to chief justice. To replace Rehnquist, Ronald Reagan chose Antonin Scalia, known for his conservative intellectual firepower. Some date the beginning of the Rehnquist Court with the 1988 appointment of Anthony Kennedy, who has provided a conservative vote far more dependably than did his predecessor Lewis Powell. And, as the number of liberals on the Court has been depleted by advancing age, the ranks of the conservatives have swollen. David Souter was tapped by President George H. W. Bush to take the seat occupied by William Brennan, and Clarence Thomas replaced Thurgood Marshall, thus removing two of the most recognized liberals from the Warren Court. Despite the Reagan and Bush appointments, the shift to the right has not been as rapid and consistent as some hoped and others feared.

During Rehnquist's tenure as associate justice and, later, chief justice, he watched the Court move toward him ideologically. A firm voting bloc of five conservative justices included Scalia, Thomas, Kennedy, O'Connor, and Rehnquist. However, it was apparent that the conservatives did not always agree among themselves. O'Connor's deference to legislatures, for example, was at times at odds with Scalia's bold libertarian brand of conservatism. As a result, the conservative Rehnquist Court was not consistently conservative, and voting alliances could not be neatly divided into liberal and conservative camps. On the solid right were the three consistently conservative judges—Rehnquist, Scalia, and Thomas. In the middle were two cautious judges who often held the balance of power—Kennedy and O'Connor. That left Stevens, Breyer, Souter, and Ginsburg to hold down the more liberal wing of the Court. It was that rough alignment that accounts for the fact that decisions were often made by slim margins, with the moderates on the Court making prediction difficult. Thus, the two centrist conservatives—O'Connor and Kennedy—often controlled the direction of the Court in cases dealing with posting the Ten Commandments in public places (Chapter 2), affirmative action, and raising the minimum age for execution to eighteen (Chapter 8).

The conservative drift overseen by Rehnquist can be summarized this way: "His 30 years have coincided with a national political turn toward the right and have produced a clear break from a time when the Court was an engine of social change" (Biskupic 2002). When the Rehnquist era ended, he was known as a congenial and well-liked chief justice who presided over a Court that was "characterized by its zeal to curb federal power and to leave the problems of society—its poor, weak and disadvantaged—to the states" (Biskupic 2002).

The Roberts Court

The **Roberts Court** (2005–) began on the first Monday in October 2005, when John Roberts officially assumed his duties as the nation's seventeenth chief justice. In selecting Roberts, President George W. Bush clearly stated his desire to place his conservative imprint on the Supreme Court (Neubauer and Meinhold 2006). And the fact that Roberts was relatively young, 50 at age of appointment, suggests that he might have a truly long-term impact on the Court.

Roberts came to the Court with impeccable legal credentials. He showed his mastery of complex constitutional issues during the Senate Judiciary Committee hearings, setting a high bar for future nominees. But, beyond his legal credentials, which made it difficult for many senators to vote against him, Roberts came to the Court with a reputation for being a conservative in the Rehnquist mold. Indeed, Roberts had earlier clerked for Rehnquist.

So far the Roberts Court is shaping up to be as conservative as his supporter had hoped, a solid voting bloc of four conservative justices—joined reliably by Kennedy has lead to many conservative outcomes. But the story is still being written. Obama's two appointments—Sotomayor and Kagan—have just settled into their new roles and are reliably part of a four justice liberal coalition. If Obama is re-elected and one of the conservative members of the courts retires you can expect a major confirmation battle as the ideological balance of the court will be up for grabs in a way that it has not been for many years.

IMPACT AND IMPLEMENTATION

The Supreme Court affects U.S. political life in fundamental and often controversial ways. As the discussion of the Supreme Court from Warren to Roberts illustrates, few areas of U.S. law and politics remain untouched by its decisions. But what goes on after the Court renders a decision? Impact and implementation are far from automatic. Consider, for example, the Court's decision protecting pornography on the Internet. (See Case Close-Up: *Reno v. American Civil Liberties Union* 1997.)

CASE CLOSE-UP

■ *Reno v. American Civil Liberties Union* (1997)

Pornography on the Internet

On February 1, 1996, Congress passed the Communications Decency Act of 1996 (CDA), and President Clinton quickly signed the bill into law. Almost as quickly, the American Civil Liberties Union and other interest groups filed a lawsuit seeking to declare the law unconstitutional. From the beginning, the case was destined for the Supreme Court because it had all the elements of a landmark case: First Amendment issues, the emergence of a new technology (the Internet), pornography, civil liberties, and congressional action. Thus, the stage was set from the day the bill became law for an eventual Supreme Court battle that would become *Reno v. American Civil Liberties Union* (1997).

The two provisions that led to the controversy in this case are referred to by the Court as "indecent transmission" and "patently offensive display." The first one criminalizes the "knowing transmission of obscene or indecent messages to any recipient under 18 years of age." The second provision "prohibits the knowing sending or displaying of patently offensive messages in a manner that is available to a person under 18 years of age." The Court ruled 7–2 that those provisions violated the First Amendment to the Constitution. Justice Stevens, the author of the majority opinion, wrote for the Court: "We are persuaded that the CDA lacks the precision that the First Amendment requires when a statute regulates the content of the speech. To deny minors access to potentially harmful speech, the CDA effectively suppresses a large amount of speech that adults have a constitutional right to receive and to address to one another." He concluded, "The interest in encouraging freedom of expression in a democratic society outweighs any theoretical but unproven benefit of censorship."

The reactions were swift. President Clinton issued a statement the day of the decision, saying, "We can and must develop a solution for the Internet that is as powerful for the computer as the V-chip will be for television, and that protects children in ways that are consistent with America's free-speech values…. With the right technology and ratings systems … we can help ensure that our children don't end up in the red-light districts of cyberspace" (Broder 1997). Members of Congress got in on the action, too. Senator Dan Coats (R-Ind.) said the decision showed that "a judicial elite is

undermining democratic attempts to address pressing social problems. The Supreme Court is purposely disarming the Congress in the most important conflicts of our time" (Broder 1997). The ACLU and other free-speech proponents were thrilled with the decision and spoke approvingly of the Court's handling of First Amendment rights and the Internet.

For many Supreme Court cases and controversies, that would have been the end of the story, but not for this one. Congress was determined to regulate online pornography aimed at children. The Court would not get the last word—or would they? As a direct response to the Court decision, Congress passed the Child Online Protection Act (COPA) in 1998. President Clinton signed this law, too. And it has become clear in public opinion polls about Internet issues that child protection from pornography is important to parents. This law (COPA) "narrowed the scope of the original CDA by targeting commercial materials on the Internet that are deemed harmful to minors" (Schwartz 1998). As one assistant to Representative Michael Oxley (R-Ohio) put it, "We read the Supreme Court decision (on the original CDA) closely and rewrote (the proposed legislation) to apply the principles of pornography law to the Web." But opponents of the bill, such as Barry Steinhardt of the Electronic Frontier Foundation, counter that "at first glance … they appear relatively benign in that they are supposedly limited to commercial pornographers who market their sites to minors, but when you look beneath that veneer, you quickly discover that they apply to any Web site that has a commercial component and material that some community could consider harmful to minors" (Schwartz 1998). Once again, the American Civil Liberties Union and others filed a lawsuit. This time, in *Ashcroft v. American Civil Liberties Union* (2004), the Court held that the CDA likely violated the First Amendment. Congress had already reacted by passing the PROTECT Act in 2003. This time, however, the key elements of the law would be upheld in *United States v. Williams* (2008), with Scalia reasoning that child pornography, of any kind, and its trafficking whether real or alleged is not protected by the First Amendment.

But pornography on the Internet continues to flourish, and the political debate about how to curtail or stop it continues. Congress passes a law, the Court declares it

(continued)

unconstitutional on First Amendment grounds, the legislative and executive branches, along with the public, react negatively, they revise the law and pass it again, and then the Court finds once again that the First Amendment has been violated. This issue is interesting because it brings to bear all the forces described in this book—including political, economic, social, and legal. Parents have a stake in protecting their children, government has a stake in limiting obscene speech, businesses have an economic stake in promoting the Internet,

interest groups have a stake in both more and less pornography on the Internet, the legislative and executive branches have an interest in passing and implementing laws that are popular with the public, the courts have an interest in protecting the Constitution. Everyone has an interest and a perspective, and, somehow, the Court has to balance those competing demands. These cases illustrate the complexity of Supreme Court decision making and the difficulty of balancing the intersection of law, courts, and politics.

Reactions and Responses

Reactions to Supreme Court decisions vary from strong support to loud condemnation. To be sure, some rulings attract little interest beyond the legal community. But, as the Court has increasingly decided disputes with widespread public policy ramifications, reactions from an array of lawyers and law professors, elected officials, and interest groups have become a common media staple. In turn, an occasional decision strikes a deep nerve in the body politic, prompting public outrage. Decisions about public displays of the Ten Commandments and striking down state laws prohibiting homosexual conduct elicit strong emotional reactions.

At times, implementation is almost complete and immediate. In the years following *Roe v. Wade* (1973), for example, several million women ended their pregnancies with legal abortions. By contrast, the events following *Brown v. Board of Education* in 1954 demonstrate that the implementation of other rulings may be prolonged. It was not until 1970 that the vast majority of southern school systems were truly integrated. The Court's 1963 decision in *Abington v. Schempp*, declaring prayers in public schools unconstitutional, is an example of a decision that has been implemented in varying degrees across the nation.

Those reactions and responses illustrate that Supreme Court decisions are rarely the final word in disputes that have public policy ramifications. Rather, rulings of the nation's highest court interact with those of other governmental agencies and lower courts. A major body of political science literature explores why judicial policies often experience implementation setbacks (Canon and Johnson 1998).

Political Institutions

Impact and implementation of Supreme Court decisions are affected first and foremost by how the core institutions of the legal system change the law. More than any other public agency, Congress tends to be the focal point of public reaction to judicial policies. What Congress can do in response to a Court decision depends, in large part, on the nature of that decision. If the decision involves a statutory interpretation, Congress can attempt to "reverse" the Court by rewriting the statute and thereby changing the meaning given by the judiciary. For example, in 1984, the Supreme Court ruled that, when an institution receives federal aid, only the program or activity that actually got the aid, not the entire institution, is covered by four federal civil rights laws (*Grove*

City College v. Bell 1984). In 1988, Congress passed a new law specifying that the entire institution would be affected. Congress, however, does not often reverse statutory interpretations. Between 1954 and 1990, the Supreme Court declared a total of 562 state and federal laws and 7 executive orders unconstitutional. But Congress was successful in passing remedial legislation only 7 percent of the time (Meernik and Ignagni 1997). Factors related to a successful response by Congress include the involvement of the executive branch, interest groups, and public opinion (Meernik and Ignagni 1997; Eskridge 1991).

If the decision involves an interpretation of the U.S. Constitution, however, it is considerably more difficult for Congress to reverse the Court. Amending the Constitution is a difficult and complicated task, requiring a two-thirds vote in both houses of Congress and ratification by three-quarters of the states (Vile 1991). Only four Supreme Court decisions have been overruled by constitutional amendments in U.S. history. The most recent was the Twenty-Sixth Amendment, passed in 1971, which lowered the voting age to eighteen. In *Oregon v. Mitchell* (1970), the Court had lowered the voting age to eighteen in federal, but not state, elections. That decision was widely viewed as both unwise and unworkable. The situation was resolved by the Twenty-Sixth Amendment, which granted 18-year-olds the right to vote in all levels of elections. However, the amendment route can be used only when there is considerable agreement that the policy inherent in the Court's decision ought to be altered. And even then, it's far from a sure thing. In a very unpopular decision, the Court ruled a Texas statute that banned flag burning unconstitutional (*Texas v. Johnson* 1989). Congress moved to pass a constitutional amendment, but even with significant public support, it was difficult to mobilize enough votes to pass the proposed amendment. Nonetheless, elected officials are fond of recommending this approach in issue areas such as religion, abortion, and same-sex marriages (Stumpf 1965). Similar unsuccessful activity occurs in every Congress (Baum 2001).

Congress can also respond to Supreme Court decisions by engaging in general retaliation. At times, Congress has refused to appropriate sufficient funds for the Court's operation. At other times, Congress has been more pointed. Article III prohibits Congress from reducing judges' salaries and was intended to prevent fiscal punishment for unpopular decisions. In an inflationary era, however, the failure to increase salaries is tantamount to a reduction in salary. In 1964, Congress raised the salaries of all federal judges except those on the Supreme Court by $7,000; the justices received only a $4,500 raise. During the debate, several representatives made it clear that dissatisfaction with the Supreme Court's reapportionment decisions motivated their actions (Canon and Johnson 1998).

Interpreters of Law

Impact and implementation of Supreme Court decisions are also affected by how those rulings are interpreted by judges and lawyers. Important policy announcements almost always require interpretation by someone other than the policy maker (Canon and Johnson 1998). Some Court decisions are ambiguous because the issue is complex or the subject matter is difficult to resolve in a judicial opinion. Sometimes, the judges may even be vague intentionally—to potentially give other members of the legal system greater discretion (Staton and Vanberg 2008). In obscenity cases, for example, it has proved difficult to fashion a precise definition of prohibited material. Justice Potter Stewart once remarked that he could not define hard-core pornography but he "knew it when he saw it" (*Jacobellis v. Ohio* 1964). Court decrees may also be unclear because the justices are sharply divided in their reasoning. Court opinions, after all, are often the product of the writing justice, who crafts a compromise document that will garner five votes. The result can be opinions that are ambiguous because they contain a lot of conflicting language.

Part of the interpreting population consists of lawyers who hold elected public office—attorneys general and district attorneys—and who represent public agencies, such as school boards and local governments. Their interpretations are the first link in the chain of events that gives a judicial decision its impact. Others look to the interpreting population for guidance on the meaning of the decision and possible responses. Although not official, their legal advice shapes how their clients respond.

Judges are also a critical part of the interpreting population. Bradley Canon and Charles Johnson (1998) suggest that a judge's response reflects his or her overall enthusiasm for the higher court's policy. Most reactions fall within "the zone of indifference," which means the judge has a neutral reaction to the policy. At other times, the judge is very enthusiastic about the policy and will interpret it broadly, pushing its logic to the limit and praising it in the opinion. On the other side of the zone of indifference are the judges who refuse to accept a higher-court policy. They have three basic options: defiance, avoidance, and limitation of the policy's application. Defiance means that the judge simply does not apply the policy in cases coming before the court. Desegregation brought out considerable trial court defiance by many state and some federal district court judges. The effects of such defiance can be overcome only by a long and often expensive appellate court process. But, overall, defiance is relatively rare. A more common response is avoidance. Judges can avoid interpreting and applying an unacceptable higher-court policy by disposing of the case on procedural or technical grounds, thus obviating the need to consider the Supreme Court ruling on its merits. Finally, a lower-court judge who does not accept a higher court's decision can limit its application. A common technique is distinguishing the precedent. By stressing certain facts in the case, the lower-court judge may find a way to hold that the offensive Supreme Court decision is not applicable to the case at hand.

Consumers of Law

Impact and implementation of Supreme Court decisions are also affected by the users of the legal system. Canon and Johnson (1998) call one set of users the "implementing population." In many of the controversial Supreme Court rulings, implementation is a group effort by bureaucratic organizations. Police departments, for example, were openly hostile to *Miranda*, but after considerable initial resistance, many eventually adopted interrogation practices that met Supreme Court mandates and accommodated the needs of law enforcement officers (Milner 1971).

Also found in the outer ring of the legal system are interest groups to whom a favorable Court decision is a valuable resource because it declares the law in favor of one side and against the other. Stuart Scheingold (1974) suggests that judicial decisions create rights that are best understood as political resources and, therefore, are best viewed as the beginning (and not the end) of a political process.

Ultimately, a Court decision merely serves as another tool for persuading others to behave as certain interests want. Thus, Supreme Court rulings frequently motivate proponents and opponents to take political action. The clearest example involves *Roe v. Wade* (1973). Antiabortion groups, flying the banner of pro-life, mobilized to lobby for restrictive state and federal legislation. More quietly, pro-abortion groups, calling themselves pro-choice, supported *Roe*. But, in the aftermath of *Planned Parenthood of Southeastern Pennsylvania v. Casey* (1992), pro-choice groups have become much more politically visible and active in lobbying to protect the political resources they had won earlier in the Supreme Court.

One way that interest groups affect impact and implementation is by sponsoring follow-up litigation. Given that Court decisions are often somewhat vague, cases are filed to test the limits. Another common technique is to expand the scope of the conflict. Losers in the judicial arena are often quick to turn to the legislature for redress, pressuring elected representatives to pass corrective legislation in their favor. Conversely, winning groups seek to protect their hard-fought court victories.

Political, Social, and Economic Forces

Political, social, and economic forces also affect the impact and implementation of Supreme Court decisions. The role of the outer ring of the legal system is best examined in relation to public opinion. As Peter Finley Dunne's (1949) turn-of-the century barroom philosopher, Mr. Dooley, cynically remarked, "The Supreme Court follows the election returns." More eloquently, Justice Felix Frankfurter wrote, "The Court's authority—possessed of neither the purse nor the sword—ultimately rests on sustained public confidence in its moral sanction" (*Baker v. Carr* 1962). Indeed, much evidence points to the fact that the Court strives mightily to improve and maintain its positive public image—including, among other things, refusing to televise its oral arguments (Perry 1999). And its actions appear to have worked. No other American political institution enjoys such a high level of public goodwill (Caldeira and Gibson 1992; Gibson and Caldeira 1992). This reservoir of public support is sometimes referred to as "legitimacy" or "diffuse support." It is argued that the Court's legitimacy gives it the latitude to hand down unpopular decisions and still achieve compliance.

Supreme Court decisions rarely arouse public interest (Caldeira 1991). When they do, however, it has been shown that people's reactions to those decisions may influence their views of the Court (Franklin and Kosaki 1989; Grosskopf and Mondak 1998; Hoekstra 2000; Hoekstra and Segal 1996; Mondak 1991, 1992). Public perceptions of *Bush v. Gore* (2000) were heavily charged with political ideology: The decision was applauded by Republicans and rejected by Democrats (Kritzer 2001). However, despite being the most widely publicized case ever, it does not appear to have resulted in any deleterious consequences for the Court's public support and, therefore, its legitimacy (Gibson, Caldeira, and Spence 2003; Kritzer 2001). Is *Bush v. Gore* (2000) an anomaly? Does the public ever change its views of the Court? And, if so, do such changes get translated into Supreme Court decisions? (See Courts in Comparative Perspective: Japan.)

There is little disagreement about the contention that public opinion affects the Supreme Court—but how? One line of thinking is that voters express their preferences by electing presidents who then appoint justices to the Court, thereby bringing

COURTS IN COMPARATIVE PERSPECTIVE

■ Japan

Article 9 of the Japanese constitution (imposed by General Douglas MacArthur in 1947) explicitly banned all military forces in Japan. But, by 1955, conservative politicians, eager to reassert national independence, decreed that Article 9 applied only to offensive forces. When the creation of the Japanese defensive forces was challenged in court, Judge Shigeo Fukushima (a member of the leftist Young Jurists League) decided that Article 9 meant what it said and declared the new military unconstitutional. His decision was reversed on appeal, and he was subsequently reassigned to a minor provincial court, his once-promising judicial career over (Ramseyer and Rasmusen 2000).

Japan is a major world economic power; politically, it is a staunch ally of the United States. Its 127 million people occupy a geographical area slightly smaller than California. It is one of the most homogeneous countries in the world, with 99 percent of its people being native Japanese.

Modern Japan emerged after devastating defeat during World War II with heavy damage to the economy and high loss of life. Although the emperor retains his throne as a symbol of national unity, actual power rests in networks of powerful politicians, bureaucrats, and business executives. The legislative branch, known as the Diet, includes the House of Representatives and the House of Councilors. The executive branch consists of the prime minister and a cabinet appointed by the prime minister.

The Japanese legal system is based on Buddhist ethical principles, a U.S.-style constitution imposed after World War II, a continental-style civil law, and a German-inspired criminal code. But, in sharp contrast to the situation in the United States, lawyers are a rare breed—only 700 pass the bar in a given year. Moreover, the nation has very few judges. People who wish to become judges major in law as undergraduates and then apply to the Legal Research and Training Institute (LRTI), the only national law school in the nation (Dammer and Albanese 2011). The pass rate averages

about 3 percent a year. LRTI graduates become lawyers, and every year some 70 to 130 lawyers become judges. They are selected and promoted by the Supreme Court Secretariat—the body that effectively ended Judge Fukushima's judicial career.

The judicial branch is headed by the Supreme Court, whose members are appointed by the cabinet. The highest court consists of 15 judges, typically five of whom were practicing lawyers, five were lower-court judges, and five were bureaucrats. Although the court has the power of judicial review, it has rarely used that power. Indeed, it has held legislation unconstitutional only about half a dozen times in its entire history (Ramseyer and Rasmusen 2001). Several factors explain why the Japanese Supreme Court, unlike other such bodies around the world, has failed to become a major political actor in its nation (Ledbetter 2001).

For one, the short tenure of justices does not allow them to carve out a policy-making role. Justices are typically appointed in their early sixties, and, given that they must retire by the age of seventy, they serve only short terms.

Another factor is the limited role of law in Japanese society. The culture emphasizes private reconciliation of disputes rather than public confrontation. Thus, few lawsuits are filed; when they are filed, they take years to resolve, thus further weakening the independent role of courts in the nation.

But perhaps most important, Japan is not a nation that values independence. The political style tends toward consensus building. For most of the postwar era, the nation's politics have been controlled by the Liberal Democratic Party (LDP), which is conservative and business oriented. Governmental bureaucracies are very powerful. Thus, in the long run, the judges of Japan reflect the dominant political forces—conservative and largely faceless bureaucrats. Such a system allows little room for wayward judges, such as Fukushima, whose political views are out of step.

the Court into line with the political climate of the day—albeit with some delay (Norpoth and Segal 1994). Another line of thinking posits that the effect is direct, that the Court responds directly and independently to the public mood (Mishler and Sheehan 1993, 1994). Both sides make convincing arguments, and it is entirely possible that both sides are right. That is, as the political, economic, and social forces converge, sometimes it is the appointment power that translates the public will into Supreme Court policy direction; at other times, it is a more immediate and direct transference of the public's desires. In high-profile, highly salient cases—such as those dealing with abortion, religion, same-sex marriages, and the death penalty—we find it hard to believe that the Court does not take a more nuanced look at the landscape of public opinion before reaching its decisions. But even in cases where public sentiment is likely to be nonexistent scholars have recently found an impact of public opinion on the Court's decisions (Casillas, Enns, and Wohlfrath 2011). Thus, the evidence for both sides may be correct—the public influence is both direct and indirect. And recent evidence suggests that, when the Court deviates too far from the ideological norm of the public, its support erodes (Durr, Martin, and Wolbrecht 2000).

Overall, legislatures, bureaucracies, lawyers, judges, interest groups, and the public are all interested parties in Supreme Court litigation. The Court is pressured by each of those actors but, in the end, possesses a legitimacy that allows it to make decisions that will inevitably upset a number of interests. That legitimacy allows the Court to move freely in matters of major social consequence and still achieve compliance with its decisions.

CONCLUSION

United States v. Williams (2008) is just one in a long line of cases in which the Supreme Court has had to decide how to balance the First Amendment protections of freedom of speech with the role of government in protecting people. It illustrates the complexity of the issues the Court faces and the unique role it plays in our government and society. Regulation of access to pornography on the Internet by children is popular with the public, legislators, and presidents, and the Court currently contains a majority of ideologically conservative justices. Yet, it took nearly 20 years before the Court would uphold a law that was aimed at limiting child pornography on the Internet.

Analyzing this case, along with its predecessor *Reno v. American Civil Liberties Union* (1997), where the Court struck down a similar effort by Congress, will challenge you to use the understanding of institutional and individual behavior gained in this chapter to separate the broad trends from the anomalous outliers. Does *Reno v. American Civil Liberties Union* (1997) or *United States v. Williams* (2008) reflect the expected direction and the way the current Court will handle issues relating to pornography and the Internet?

In addition to these controversial decisions, this chapter also examined the more mundane workings of the Court: the process by which its members are chosen, its organization and decision-making apparatus, and the influence of the most recent chief justices. Lower-court methods of implementing and of defying Supreme Court decisions were discussed, as were various analyses of justices' voting habits. Rigorous analysis notwithstanding, Supreme Court decisions remain unpredictable, largely because of the fluid and interrelated forces—political, social, economic, and individual—that affect them. That unpredictability is perhaps the most telling characteristic of our nation's highest court. Students of the complexities of the law and of the Supreme Court that applies it gain a unique perspective on these powerful—yet ultimately human—institutions.

CRITICAL THINKING QUESTIONS

1. If President Obama gets the opportunity to appoint a third justice to the Supreme Court it will likely be a replacement for a reliable conservative vote. Will this change the decision criteria Obama uses to select a nominee? How will this change the debate around the appointment in the public and the United States Senate?

2. Amid great public applause, Congress and the president have sought to ban pornography in the United States, most recently by outlawing Internet smut. But the Supreme Court has often stymied those efforts. Why have justices appointed by Republican presidents not voted the way their appointing president would have liked? Does this incongruence between the appointing president and judicial behavior suggest that democracy is working, or not?

3. In selecting a person to fill a vacancy on the U.S. Supreme Court, how do Democratic presidents differ from Republican presidents? In particular, how do they differ in regard to the type of person they seek and also the nature of the interest groups they consult? Despite those differences, in what ways are Republican and Democratic presidents' nominees and strategies similar?

4. Why do legislators continue to propose constitutional amendments to overturn *Roe v. Wade* (1973), even though *Roe* has been the law of the land for over thirty years?

Search Terms

justices of the Supreme Court   U.S. Supreme Court

Useful URLs

http://www.supremecourtus.gov
   The official website of the U.S. Supreme Court.

http://supct.law.cornell.edu/supct/justices/fullcourt.html
   The Legal Information Institute provides biographies of the justices and allows you to track their rulings.

http://www.findlaw.com/casecode/supreme.html
   U.S. Supreme Court opinions.

http://www.law.cornell.edu/rules/supct
   Rules of the United States Supreme Court.

http://www.oyez.org
   The Oyez Project website contains a multimedia database with abstracts of key constitutional cases, digital audio of oral arguments, and more.

REFERENCES

Abraham, Henry. 2007. *Justices, Presidents, and Senators: A History of the U.S. Supreme Court Appointments from Washington to Bush II*, 5th edition. New York: Rowman & Littlefield.

Adler, Stephen. 1987. "Scalia's Court." *The American Lawyer* (March): 18.

Atkinson, David. 1999. *Leaving the Bench*. Lawrence: University Press of Kansas.

Baum, Lawrence. 1995. *The Supreme Court*. 3d ed. Washington, D.C.: CQ Press.

———. 2001. *The Supreme Court*. 7th ed. Washington, D.C.: CQ Press.

Bell, Lauren Cohen. 2002. *Warring Factions: Interest Groups, Money, and the New Politics of Senate Confirmation*. Columbus: Ohio State University Press.

Biskupic, Joan. 2002. "Rehnquist." *USA Today*, June 28, p. A4.

Bonneau, Chris W., Thomas H. Hammond, Forrest Maltzman, and Paul J. Wahlbeck. 2007. "Agenda Control, the Median Justice, and the Majority Opinion on the U.S. Supreme Court." *American Journal of Political Science* 51(4): 890–905.

Bork, Robert. 1989. *The Tempting of America: The Political Seduction of the Law*. New York: Free Press.

Bowen, Terry, and John Scheb. 1993. "Freshman Opinion Writing on the U.S. Supreme Court, 1921–1991." *Judicature* 76: 239–243.

Brenner, Saul. 1980. "Fluidity on the United States Supreme Court: A Reexamination." *American Journal of Political Science* 24: 526–535.

———. 1984. "Issue Specialization as a Variable in Opinion Assignment on the U.S. Supreme Court." *Journal of Politics* 46: 1217–1225.

———. 1986. "Reassigning the Majority Opinion on the United States Supreme Court." *Justice System Journal* 11: 186–195.

———. 1992. "The Memos of Supreme Court Law Clerk William Rehnquist: Conservative Tracts, or Mirrors of His Justice's Mind?" *Judicature* 76: 77–81.

Brenner, Saul, and Jan Palmer. 1988. "The Time Taken to Write Opinions as a Determinant of Opinion Assignments." *Judicature* 72: 179–185.

Brenner, Saul, and Harold Spaeth. 1986. "Issue Specialization in Majority Opinion Assignment on the Burger Court." *Western Political Quarterly* 39: 520–527.

———. 1988. "Majority Opinion Assignments and the Maintenance of the Original Coalition on the Warren Court." *American Journal of Political Science* 32: 72–81.

Broder, John M. 1997. "Clinton Readies New Approach on Smut." *New York Times*, February 9, p. 21.

Bronner, Ethan. 1989. *Battle for Justice: How the Bork Nomination Shook America*. New York: Norton.

Caldeira, Gregory. 1991. "Courts and Public Opinion." In *The American Courts: A Critical Assessment*, edited by John Gates and Charles Johnson. Washington, D.C.: CQ Press.

Caldeira, Gregory, and James Gibson. 1992. "The Etiology of Public Support for the Supreme Court." *American Journal of Political Science* 36: 635–664.

Caldeira, Gregory A., and John R. Wright. 1998. "Lobbying for Justice: Organized Interests, Supreme Court Nomination, and the United States Senate." *American Journal of Political Science* 42(2): 499–535.

Cameron, Charles, Albert Cover, and Jeffrey Segal. 1990. "Senate Voting on Supreme Court Nominees: A Neoinstitutional Model." *American Political Science Review* 84: 525–534.

Canon, Bradley, and Charles Johnson. 1998. *Judicial Policies: Implementation and Impact*. Washington, D.C.: CQ Press.

Casillas, C. J., Enns, P. K. and Wohlfarth, P. C. (2011), "How Public Opinion Constrains the U.S. Supreme Court." *American Journal of Political Science*, 55: 74–88.

CNN. 1997. "Reaction Mixed to Court's Internet Ruling." Available online at http://CNN.com/US/9706/26/web.smut. Retrieved May 2003.

Comiskey, Michael. 1993. "Can the Senate Examine the Constitutional Philosophies of Supreme Court Nominees?" *PS: Political Science and Politics* 26: 495–500.

———. 2004. *Seeking Justices: The Judging of Supreme Court Nominees*. Lawrence: University Press of Kansas.

Davis, Sue. 1990. "Power on the Court: Chief Justice Rehnquist's Opinion Assignments." *Judicature* 74: 66–72.

———. 1993. "The Voice of Sandra Day O'Connor." *Judicature* 77: 134–143.

Dammer, Harry, and Jay Albanese. 2011. *Comparative Criminal Justice Systems*, 4th edition. Belmont: Cengage.

Dorff, Robert, and Saul Brenner. 1992. "Conformity Voting on the United States Supreme Court." *Journal of Politics* 54: 762–775.

Dunne, Peter Finley. 1949. *Mr. Dooley at His Best*. New York: Archon.

Durr, Robert H., Andrew D. Martin, and Christina Wolbrecht. 2000. "Ideological Divergence and Public Support for the Supreme Court." *American Journal of Political Science* 44: 768–776.

Eisenhower, Dwight D. 1965. *The White House Years: Mandate for Change, 1953–1956*. New York: New American Library.

Epstein, Lee, and Jack Knight. 1998. *The Choices Justices Make*. Washington, D.C.: CQ Press.

Epstein, Lee, Jeffrey A. Segal, and Harold J. Spaeth. 2001. "The Norm of Consensus on the U.S. Supreme Court." *American Journal of Political Science* 45: 362–377.

Epstein, Lee, Thomas Walker, and William Dixon. 1989. "The Supreme Court and Criminal Justice Disputes: A Neo-Institutional Perspective." *American Journal of Political Science* 33: 825.

Eskridge, William N., Jr. 1991. "Overriding Supreme Court Statutory Interpretation Decisions." *Yale Law Journal* 101.

Franklin, Charles, and Liane Kosaki. 1989. "Republican Schoolmaster: The U.S. Supreme Court, Public Opinion, and Abortion." *American Political Science Review* 83: 751–772.

Gates, John, and Jeffrey Cohen. 1988. "Presidents, Supreme Court Justices, and Racial Equality Cases: 1954–1984." *Political Behavior* 10: 22–36.

Gibson, James, and Gregory Caldeira. 1992. "Blacks and the United States Supreme Court: Models of Diffuse Support." *Journal of Politics* 54: 1120–1145.

Gibson, James L., Gregory A. Caldeira, and Lester Kenyatta Spence. 2003. "The Supreme Court and the U.S. Presidential Election of 2000: Wounds, Self-Inflicted or Otherwise?" *British Journal of Political Science* 33: 535–556.

Gillman, Howard, and Cornell W. Clayton, eds. 1999. *The Supreme Court in American Politics: New Institutionalist Interpretations*. Lawrence: University Press of Kansas.

Goldman, Sheldon. 1969. "Backgrounds, Attitudes and the Voting Behavior of Judges: A Comment on Joel Grossman's Social Backgrounds and Judicial Decisions." *Journal of Politics* 31: 214.

Goldman, Sheldon, Elliot Slotnick, Gerard Gryski, Gary Zuk, and Sara W. Schiavoni. 2003. "Bush Remaking the Judiciary: Like Father Like Son?" *Judicature* 86: 282–309.

Grosskopf, Anke, and Jeffrey J. Mondak. 1998. "Do Attitudes Toward Specific Supreme Court Decisions Matter? The Impact of *Webster* and *Texas v. Johnson* on Public Confidence in the Supreme Court." *Political Research Quarterly* 51: 633–640.

Guliuzza, Frank, Daniel Reagan, and David Barrett. 1994. "The Senate Judiciary Committee and Supreme Court Nominees: Measuring the Dynamics of Confirmation Criteria." *Journal of Politics* 56: 773–787.

Hagle, Timothy. 1993. "'Freshman Effects' for Supreme Court Justices." *American Journal of Political Science* 37: 1142–1157.

Haynie, Stacia. 1992. "Leadership and Consensus on the U.S. Supreme Court." *Journal of Politics* 54: 1158–1169.

Heck, Edward. 1979. "The Socialization of a Freshman Justice: The Early Years of Justice Brennan." *Pacific Law Journal* 10: 707–728.

Heck, Edward, and Steven Shull. 1982. "Policy Preferences of Justices and Presidents." *Law and Policy Quarterly* 4: 327.

Hoekstra, Valerie J. 2000. "The Supreme Court and Local Public Opinion." *American Political Science Review* 94: 89–100.

Hoekstra, Valerie J., and Jeffrey A. Segal. 1996. "The Shepherding of Local Public Opinion: The Supreme Court and Lamb's Chapel." *Journal of Politics* 58: 1079–1102.

Howard, J. Woodford. 1968. "On the Fluidity of Judicial Choice." *American Political Science Review* 62: 43–56.

Hurwitz, Mark S., and Joseph V. Stefko. 2004. "Acclimation and Attitudes: 'Newcomer' Justices and Precedent Conformance on the Supreme Court." *Political Research Quarterly* 57(1): 121–129.

Johnson, Scott, and Christopher Smith. 1992. "David Souter's First Term on the Supreme Court: The Impact of a New Justice." *Judicature* 75: 238–243.

Johnson, Timothy R. 2004. *Oral Arguments and Decision Making on the United States Supreme Court*. Albany: State University of New York Press.

Johnson, Timothy R., and Jason M. Roberts. 2004. "Presidential Capital and the Supreme Court Confirmation Process." *Journal of Politics* 66(3): 663–683.

Johnson, Timothy R., Paul J. Wahlbeck, and James F. Spriggs II. 2006. "The Influence of Oral Arguments on the U.S. Supreme Court." *American Political Science Review* 100(1): 99–113.

Kahn, Michael. 1992. "Shattering the Myth About President Eisenhower's Supreme Court Appointments." *Presidential Studies Quarterly* 22: 47–56.

King, Gary. 1987. "Presidential Appointments to the Supreme Court: Adding Systematic Explanation to Probabilistic Description." *American Politics Quarterly* 15: 373.

Kritzer, Herbert M. 2001. "The Impact of *Bush v. Gore* on Public Perceptions and Knowledge of the Supreme Court." *Judicature* 85: 36.

Ledbetter, James. 2001. Personal correspondence.

Lewis, Anthony. 1969. "A Talk with Warren on Crime, the Court, the Country." *New York Times Magazine*, March 16, pp. 64–65.

Lindquist, Stefanie A., David A. Yalof, and John A. Clark. 2000. "The Impact of Presidential Appointments to the U.S. Supreme Court: Cohesive and Divisive Voting Within Presidential Blocs." *Political Research Quarterly* 53(4): 794–814.

Maltese, John. 1995. *The Selling of Supreme Court Nominees*. Baltimore: Johns Hopkins University Press.

Maltzman, Forrest, James F. Spriggs II, and Paul J. Wahlbeck. 2000. *Crafting Law on the Supreme Court: The Collegial Game*. Cambridge, U.K.: Cambridge University Press.

Maltzman, Forrest, and Paul J. Wahlbeck. 1996. "Strategic Policy Considerations and Voting Fluidity on the Burger Court." *American Political Science Review* 90: 581–592.

Marshall, Thomas. 1993. "Symbolic Versus Policy Representation on the U.S. Supreme Court." *Journal of Politics* 55: 140–150.

Mauro, Tony. 1993. "Yakety-Yak Justices Talk Back." *USA Today*, October 7, p. A2.

McGuigan, Patrick, and Jeffrey O'Connell. 1987. *The Judges War*. Washington, D.C.: Free Congress Research and Education Foundation.

McGuigan, Patrick, and Dawn Weyrich. 1990. *Ninth Justice: The Fight for Bork*. Lanham, Md.: University Press of America.

McGuire, Kevin, and Barbara Palmer. 1995. "Issue Fluidity on the U.S. Supreme Court." *American Political Science Review* 89: 691–702.

Meernik, James, and Joseph Ignagni. 1997. "Judicial Review and Coordinate Construction of the Constitution." *American Journal of Political Science* 41: 447–467.

Melone, Albert. 1990. "Revisiting the Freshman Effect Hypothesis: The First Two Terms of Justice Anthony Kennedy." *Judicature* 74: 6–13.

Milner, Neal. 1971. *The Court and Local Law Enforcement*. Newbury Park, Calif.: Sage.

Mishler, William, and Reginald Sheehan. 1993. "The Supreme Court as a Countermajoritarian Institution? The Impact of Public Opinion on Supreme Court Decisions." *American Political Science Review* 87: 87–101.

———. 1994. "Response." *American Political Science Review* 88: 716–724.

Monaghan, Henry. 1988. "The Confirmation Process: Law or Politics?" *Harvard Law Review* 101: 1202.

Mondak, Jeffrey. 1991. "Substantive and Procedural Aspects of Supreme Court Decisions as Determinants of Institutional Approval." *American Politics Quarterly* 19: 174–188.

———. 1992. "Institutional Legitimacy, Policy Legitimacy, and the Supreme Court." *American Politics Quarterly* 20: 457–477.

Moraski, Bryon T., and Charles R. Shipan. 1999. "The Politics of Supreme Court Nominations: A Theory of Institutional Constraints and Choices." *American Journal of Political Science* 43: 1069–1095.

Neubauer, David, and Stephen Meinhold. 2006. *Battle Supreme: The Confirmation of John Roberts and the Future of the Supreme Court*. Belmont, Calif.: Wadsworth.

Nixon, Richard. 1971. "Transcript of President's Announcements." *New York Times*, October 22, p. 24.

Norpoth, Helmut, and Jeffrey Segal. 1994. "Popular Influence on Supreme Court Decisions." *American Political Science Review* 88: 711–716.

O'Brien, David. 2003. *Storm Center: The Supreme Court in American Politics*. 6th ed. New York: Norton.

Overby, L. Marvin, Beth Henschen, Julie Strauss, and Michael Walsh. 1992. "Courting Constituents? An Analysis of the Senate Confirmation Vote on Justice Clarence Thomas." *American Political Science Review* 86: 997–1006.

Perry, Barbara. 1991. *A "Representative" Supreme Court? The Impact of Race, Religion and Gender on Appointments*. New York: Greenwood Press.

———. 1999. *The Priestly Tribe: The Supreme Court's Image in the American Mind*. Westport, Conn.: Praeger.

Pertschuk, Michael, and Wendy Schaetzel. 1989. *The People Rising: The Campaign Against the Bork Nomination*. New York: Thunder's Mouth.

Pitts, Leonard, Jr., 1998. "Tripping Through the Cyberporn Maze." *New Orleans Times-Picayune*, October 15.

Pritchett, C. Herman. 1954. *Civil Liberties and the Vinson Court*. Chicago: University of Chicago Press.

Ramseyer, J. Mark, and Eric Rasmusen. 2000. "Skewed Incentives: Paying for Politics as Japanese Judge." *Judicature* 83: 190.

———. 2001. "Why Are Japanese Judges So Conservative in Politically Charged Cases?" *American Political Science Review* 95: 331.

Rehnquist, William. 1987. *The Supreme Court: How It Was, How It Is*. New York: Morrow. © 1987 by William H. Rehnquist. By permission of Chief Justice William H. Rehnquist.

Rhode, David W. 1972. "Policy Goals, Strategic Choice, and Majority Opinion Assignments in the U.S. Supreme Court." *American Journal of Political Science* 16: 652–682.

Rhode, David W., and Harold Spaeth. 1976. *Supreme Court Decision Making*. San Francisco: Freeman.

Richards, Mark J., and Herbert M. Kritzer. 2002. "Jurisprudential Regimes in Supreme Court Decision Making." *American Political Science Review* 96(2): 305–320.

Ruckman, P. S. 1993. "The Supreme Court, Critical Nominations, and the Senate Confirmation Process." *Journal of Politics* 55: 793–805.

Scheb, John, Hemant Kmar Sharma, and Colin Glennon. 2010. "A Supreme Court with Protestants: Does It Matter?" *Judicature* 94:12–15.

Scheingold, Stuart. 1974. *The Politics of Rights: Lawyers, Public Policy and Political Change*. New Haven, Conn.: Yale University Press.

Schwartz, John. 1998. "Bill Limiting Web Site Access Passes; House Seeks to Recast Anti-Smut Communications Decency Act." *Washington Post*, February 2, p. 4.

Scigliano, Robert. 1971. *The Supreme Court and the Presidency*. New York: Free Press.

Segal, Jeffrey. 1987. "Senate Confirmation of Supreme Court Justices: Partisan and Institutional Politics." *Journal of Politics* 49: 998–1015.

Segal, Jeffrey, Charles Cameron, and Albert Cover. 1992. "A Spatial Model of Roll Call Voting: Senators, Constituents, Presidents, and Interest Groups in Supreme Court Confirmations." *American Journal of Political Science* 36: 96–121.

Segal, Jeffrey, and Albert Cover. 1989. "Ideological Values and the Votes of U.S. Supreme Court Justices." *American Political Science Review* 83: 557–565.

Segal, Jeffrey, and Harold J. Spaeth. 1989. "Decisional Trends on the Warren and Burger Courts: Results

from the Supreme Court Data Base Project." *Judicature* 73: 103–107.

———. 1992. *The Supreme Court and the Attitudinal Model*. New York: Cambridge University Press.

———. 2002. *The Supreme Court and the Attitudinal Model Revisited*. Cambridge, U.K.: Cambridge University Press.

Segal, Jeffrey, Richard Timpone, and Robert Howard. 2000. "Buyer Beware? Presidential Influence Through Supreme Court Appointments." *Political Research Quarterly* 53: 557–573.

Shipan, Charles R., and Megan L. Shannon. 2003. "Delaying Justice(s): A Duration Analysis of Supreme Court Confirmations." *American Journal of Political Science* 47(4): 654–668.

Slotnick, Elliot. 1979. "Who Speaks for the Court? Majority Opinion Assignment from Taft to Burger." *American Journal of Political Science* 23: 60–77.

Spaeth, Harold. 1984. "Distributive Justice: Majority Opinion Assignments in the Burger Court." *Judicature* 67: 299–304.

Squire, Peverill. 1988. "Politics and Personal Factors in Retirement from the United States Supreme Court." *Political Behavior* 10: 180–190.

Staton, Jeffrey K., and Georg Vanberg. 2008. "The Value of Vagueness: Delegation, Defiance, and Judicial Opinions." *American Journal of Political Science* 52(3): 504–519.

Stookey, John, and George Watson. 1988. "The Bork Hearing: Rocks and Roles." *Judicature* 71: 194.

Stumpf, Harry. 1965. "Congressional Response to Supreme Court Rulings: The Interaction of Law and Politics." *Journal of Public Law* 14: 377–395.

Vile, John. 1991. "Proposals to Amend the Bill of Rights: Are Fundamental Rights in Jeopardy?" *Judicature* 75: 62–67.

Wahlbeck, Paul J., James F. Spriggs II, and Forrest Maltzman. 1998. "Marshalling the Court: Bargaining and Accommodation on the United States Supreme Court." *American Journal of Political Science* 42: 294–315.

Wahlbeck, Paul J., James F. Spriggs II, and Lee Sigelman. 2002. "Ghostwriters on the Court? A Stylistic Analysis of U.S. Supreme Court Opinion Drafts." *American Politics Research* 30: 166–192.

Walker, Thomas, Lee Epstein, and William Dixon. 1988. "On the Mysterious Demise of Consensual Norms in the United States Supreme Court." *Journal of Politics* 50: 361–389.

Warren, Earl. 1977. *The Memoirs of Earl Warren*. New York: Doubleday.

Wasby, Stephen. 1993. *The Supreme Court in the Federal Judicial System*. 4th ed. Chicago: Nelson-Hall.

Watson, George, and John Stookey. 1995. *Shaping America: The Politics of Supreme Court Appointments*. New York: HarperCollins.

Westin, Alan. 1958. *The Anatomy of a Constitutional Law Case*. New York: Macmillan.

Yalof, David Alistair. 1999. *Pursuit of Justices: Presidential Politics and the Selection of Supreme Court Justices*. Chicago: University of Chicago Press.

FOR FURTHER READING

Baird, Vanessa A. 2004. "The Effect of Politically Salient Decisions on the U.S. Supreme Court's Agenda." *Journal of Politics* 66(3): 755–772.

Barnhart, Bill, and Gene Schlickman. 2010. *John Paul Stevens: An Independent Life*. DeKalb, Ill. Northern Illinois University Press.

Breyer, Stephen. 2005. *Active Liberty: Interpreting our Democratic Constitution*. New York: Alfred Knopf.

Burns, James McGregor. 2010. *Packing the Court: The Rise of Judicial Power and the Coming Crisis of the Supreme Court*. New York: Penguin Books.

Eisgruber, Christopher. 2007. *The Next Justice: Repairing the Supreme Court Appointment Process*. Princeton: Princeton University Press.

Epstein, Lee, Rene Lindstadt, Jeffrey A. Segal, and Chad Westerland. 2006. "The Changing Dynamics of Senate Voting on Supreme Court Nominees." *Journal of Politics* 68(2): 296–307.

Epstein, Lee and Jeffrey Segal. 2007. *Advice and Consent: The Politics of Judicial Appointments*. New York: Oxford University Presss.

Flynt, Larry, and Kenneth Ross. 1997. *Unseemly Man*. Los Angeles: Newstar.

Irons, Peter. 2000. *A People's History of the Supreme Court*. New York: Penguin.

Johnson, Timothy R., and Jason M. Roberts. 2004. "Presidential Capital and the Supreme Court Confirmation Process." *Journal of Politics* 66(3): 663–683.

Krehbiel, K. (2007), "Supreme Court Appointments as a Move-the-Median Game." *American Journal of Political Science*, 51: 231–240.

Maltz, Earl. 2000. *The Chief Justiceship of Warren Burger, 1969–1986*. Columbia: University of South Carolina Press.

Merida, Kevin, and Michael Fletcher. 2008. *Supreme Discomfort: The Divided Soul of Clarence Thomas*. New York: Broadway Books.

Murphy, Walter. 1964. *Elements of Judicial Strategy*. Chicago: University of Chicago Press.

Powe, Lucas. 2000. *The Warren Court and American Politics*. Cambridge, Mass.: Harvard University Press.

Rhode, David, and Kenneth A. Shepsle. 2007. "Advising and Consenting in the 60-Vote Senate: Strategic Appointments to the Supreme Court." *Journal of Politics* 69(3): 664–677.

Schubert, Glendon. 1959. *Quantitative Analysis of Judicial Behavior*. Glencoe, Ill.: Free Press.

———. 1965. *The Judicial Mind*. Evanston, Ill.: Northwestern University Press.

Segal, Jeffrey, Lee Epstein, Charles Cameron, and Harold Spaeth. 1995. "Ideological Values and the Votes of U.S. Supreme Court Justices Revisited." *Journal of Politics* 57: 812–823.

Segal, Jeffrey, and Harold Spaeth. 1992. *The Supreme Court and the Attitudinal Model*. New York: Cambridge University Press.

Simon, James. 1995. *The Center Holds: The Power Struggle Inside the Rehnquist Court*. New York: Simon & Schuster.

Slotnick, Elliot, and Jennifer Segal. 1998. *Television News and the Supreme Court: All the News That's Fit to Air?* New York: Cambridge University Press.

Songer, Donald R., and Reginald S. Sheehan. 1990. "Supreme Court Impact on Compliance and Outcomes: *Miranda* and New York in the United States Courts of Appeals." *Western Political Quarterly* 43: 297–316.

Stevens, John Paul. 2011. *Five Chiefs: A Supreme Court Memoir*. Boston: Little, Brown.

Thomas, Clarence. 2008. *My Grandfather's Son: A Memoir*. New York: Harper.

Williams, Juan. 1998. *Thurgood Marshall: American Revolutionary*. New York: Times Books.

Woodward, Bob, and Scott Armstrong. 1979. *The Brethren: Inside the Supreme Court*. New York: Simon & Schuster.

Glossary

Access: Supreme Court doctrines that govern who may sue and the powers of courts to provide redress.

Acquittal: Decision of the trial jury or judge that the defendant is not guilty.

Adjournment: Delay in trial ordered by the judge, usually at the request of one of the lawyers.

Adjudicate: To judge. An adjudication is the formal giving or recording of a judgment for one side in a lawsuit.

Administrative law: Law that governs the duties and proper running of an administrative agency.

Administrative regulations: Rules and regulations adopted by administrative agencies that have the force of law.

Admiralty and maritime law: Law derived from the general maritime law of nations, modified by Congress. Applicable not only on the high seas but also on all navigable waterways in the United States.

Adversary system: Proceeding in which the opposing sides have the opportunity to present their evidence and arguments.

Advisory opinion: Judicial ruling in the absence of an actual case or controversy; a ruling in a hypothetical case without bona fide litigants.

Affadavit: Sworn, written declaration.

Affirm: In an appellate court, to reach a decision that agrees with that reached by the lower court.

Alimony: Court-ordered support payments from one spouse to the other following the dissolution of a marriage.

Alternative dispute resolution (ADR): Less adversarial means of settling disputes that may not involve a court.

American Bar Association (ABA): Largest voluntary organization of lawyers in the country.

American Judicature Society: Court reform organization that historically stressed court unification and merit selection of judges.

Amicus curiae: Latin phrase for "friend of the court." A person or group who has no right to appear in a lawsuit but is allowed to introduce argument, authority, or evidence to ensure that the court receives all relevant information.

Analytical jurisprudence: School of jurisprudence that attempts to systematize the law utilizing tools of logic.

Anglo-American law: *See* Common law.

Answer: Defendant's response to allegations made by the plaintiff in the latter's complaint. When the answer is filed, the case is said to be "at issue."

Appeal: Legal challenge to a decision by a lower court. In the U.S. Supreme Court, certain cases are designated appeals under federal law; formally, these cases must be heard by the Court.

Appellant: The party, usually the losing one, that seeks to overturn the decision of a lower court by appealing to a higher court.

Appellate court: Court that hears appeals on points of law from trial courts.

Appellate jurisdiction: Authority of a court to hear, determine, and render judgment in an action on appeal from an inferior court.

Appellee: Party, usually the winning one, against whom a case is appealed. Also called the *respondent*.

Arbitration: Submission of a dispute to a neutral party for resolution under an agreement by the parties to be bound by the decision.

Arraignment: Stage of the criminal process in which the defendant is formally informed of the charges and is allowed to enter a plea.

Arrest: Physical taking into custody of a suspected law violator.

Assault: Violent attempt or threat to hurt another.

Assigned counsel system: Arrangement whereby attorneys are provided for people accused of a crime who are unable to hire their own lawyers. The judge assigns a member of the bar to provide counsel to a particular defendant.

Attainder: *See* Bill of attainder.

Attrition: Process by which criminal justice officials screen out some cases and advance others to the next level of decision making.

Bail: Security (money or bail bond) given as a guarantee that a released prisoner will appear at trial.

Bail bondsman: Businessperson who obtains release on bail for persons held in custody by pledging to pay a sum of money if the defendant fails to appear in court as required.

Bailiff: Minor officer of a court usually serving as an usher or a messenger.

Baker v. Carr: U.S. Supreme Court ruling (1962) that legislative apportionment could be challenged and reviewed by federal courts.

Bankruptcy: Legal procedure under federal law by which a person is relieved of all debts after placing all property under the court's authority. An organization may be reorganized or terminated by the court to pay off creditors.

Bar: Community of attorneys permitted to practice law in a particular jurisdiction or court.

Barrister: Segment of the English legal profession that argues cases in the major trial courts.

Battery: Unlawful use of violence upon another. Battery always includes assault.

Bench: Reference to the court or to the judges composing the court.

Bench trial: Trial conducted without a jury in which the judge serves as the trier of fact.

Bench warrant: Order issued by the court itself, or from the bench, for the arrest of a person; it is not based (as is an arrest warrant) on a probable cause showing that a person has committed a crime, but only on the person's failure to appear in court as directed.

Beyond a reasonable doubt: Burden of proof required by law to convict a defendant in a criminal case.

Bifurcated trial: In criminal proceedings, a special two-part trial proceeding in which the issue of guilt is tried in the first step, and, if a conviction results, the appropriate sentence or applicable sentencing statute is determined in the second step.

Bill of attainder: Legislative act declaring a person guilty of a crime and passing sentence without benefit of trial.

Bill of Rights: First ten amendments to the Constitution, which provide numerous protections to citizens against government action.

Bond: *See* Bail.

Booking: Process of photographing, fingerprinting, and recording a suspect's identifying data subsequent to arrest.

Bound over: If, at the preliminary hearing, the judge believes that sufficient probable cause exists to hold a criminal defendant, the accused is said to be bound over for trial. Also called a *bind over*.

Brief: Written statement submitted by the attorney arguing a case in court. It consists of a statement of the facts of the case, presents legal arguments in support of the moving party, and cites applicable law.

Brown v. Board of Education: Historic 1954 Supreme Court decision that declared separate public schools for African-American and white students to be inherently unequal.

Burden of proof: Need to prove the fact(s) in dispute.

Burger Court: U.S. Supreme Court under the leadership of Chief Justice Warren Burger, 1969–1986.

Burglary: Unlawful entry of any fixed structure, vehicle, or vessel, with or without force, with intent to commit a felony or larceny.

Calendar: List of cases to be heard in court on a specific date, containing the title of the case, the lawyers involved, and the case number.

Canon law: System of church law.

Capias: Bench warrant.

Capital crime: Any crime punishable by death.

Capital punishment: Use of the death penalty (that is, execution) as the punishment for the commission of a particular crime.

Case: General term for an action, cause, suit, or controversy, at law or equity.

Casebook: Law textbook containing leading edited judicial opinions on a particular legal subject.

Case law: Law that develops through the interpretation of statutes, constitutions, and other forms of written law.

Caseload: Number of cases requiring judicial action at a certain time, or the number of cases acted upon in a given court during a given time period.

Case method: Teaching device using case law and the Socratic method to educate students in law school.

Cause: Case, lawsuit, litigation, or action—civil or criminal.

Caveat emptor: Latin phrase meaning "let the buyer beware." A common-law doctrine that purchasers of goods must inspect them to avoid being cheated by merchants.

Certification: Rarely used method of appealing to the U.S. Supreme Court by which the lower court formally identifies questions of law for decision. Also, the process by which a federal court sometimes refers a question about state law to a state court and delays deciding the case until the question is answered.

Certiorari, writ of: Writ issued by the U.S. Supreme Court, at its discretion, to order a lower court to prepare the record of a case and send it to the Court for review. Most cases come to the Court as petitions for writs of certiorari.

Challenge for cause: Method for removing a potential juror because of specific reasons, such as bias or prejudgment. Can be granted only by the judge.

Chambers: Private office of a judge.

Chancery, Court of: Old English court dealing with equity matters. Most U.S. state governments have merged chancery and law courts into one.

Change of venue: *See* Venue.

Charge: In criminal justice, an allegation that one or more specified person(s) committed a specific offense.

Charge bargaining: A type of plea bargaining in which, in return for a guilty plea, the prosecutor allows the defendant to plead guilty to a less serious charge than the one originally filed.

Charge to the jury: *See* Jury instructions.

Charging document: Information, indictment, or complaint that states the formal criminal charge against one or more named defendant(s).

Circumstantial evidence: Indirect method of proving the material facts of the case. Testimony that is not

based on the witness's personal observation of the material events.

Civil law: Law governing private parties; other than criminal law.

Civil procedure: Method and means of enforcing civil law.

Class action: Lawsuit brought by one person or group on behalf of all persons in similar situations.

Clearance rate: Percentage of crimes known to the police that they believe they have solved through an arrest.

Clerk of court: Elected or appointed court officer responsible for maintaining the written records of the court and for supervising or performing the clerical tasks necessary to conduct judicial business.

Closing argument: Statement made by an attorney at the end of the presentation of evidence to summarize the case for the jury.

Code: Compilation of laws arranged by chapters.

Collateral attacks: Attempts by state and federal prisoners to avoid the effects of a court decision by bringing a different court proceeding.

Common law: Law developed in England by judges who made legal decisions in the absence of written law. Such decisions served as precedents and became "common" to all of England. Common law is judge made, uses precedent, and is uncodified.

Compensatory damages: Money awarded to a person for actual harm suffered.

Complaint: In civil law, the first paper filed in a lawsuit. In criminal law, a charge signed by the victim that a person named has committed a specified offense.

Concurring opinion: Opinion by a member of an appellate court that agrees with the result reached by the court but disagrees with or departs from the court's rationale for the decision.

Consent decree: Court-sanctioned agreement settling a legal dispute and entered into by the consent of the parties.

Constitution: Fundamental rules that determine how those who govern are selected, the procedures by which they operate, and the limits to their powers.

Constitutional Convention: Convention in Philadelphia in 1787 that framed the Constitution of the United States.

Constitutional courts: Federal courts created by Congress under its power under Article III of the Constitution to create courts inferior to the Supreme Court.

Constitutional law: Law that consists of court decisions that interpret and expand the meaning of a written constitution.

Contempt of court: Failure or refusal to obey a court order. May be punished by a fine or imprisonment.

Contingency fee: Fee arrangement in some civil cases in which the attorney receives a percentage of any award won by the plaintiff, typically one-third.

Continuance: Delay in trial granted by the judge at the request of either attorney in a case.

Contract: An agreement, usually written, that affects the legal relationships between two or more parties.

Conviction: Final judgment or sentence that the defendant is guilty as charged.

Corporal punishment: Punishment applied to the body, such as whipping or branding.

Count: Each separate offense of which a person is accused in an indictment or an information.

Count bargaining: A type of plea bargaining in which the defendant pleads guilty to some, but not all, of the counts contained in the charging document, which reduces the potential sentence.

Counterclaim: Claim made by a defendant in a civil lawsuit that, in effect, sues the plaintiff.

Court: Place where judges work.

Court decision: Determination by a court that settles a controversy.

Court of last resort: Court from which there is no appeal.

Court of record: Court whose proceedings are permanently recorded, thereby providing a record for a higher court to review.

Court-packing plan: Famous attempt by President Franklin Roosevelt in 1937 to secure congressional approval of legislation permitting the president to nominate a new Supreme Court justice for every sitting justice on the Court who, upon reaching seventy years of age, did not retire. Congress rejected Roosevelt's proposal.

Court reporter: Person present during judicial proceedings who records all testimony and other oral statements made during the proceedings.

Courtroom work group: Regular participants in the day-to-day activities of a particular courtroom. Members (judge, prosecutor, and defense attorney) interact on the basis of shared norms.

Court unification: A simplified state trial court structure, with rule-making centered in the supreme court, system governance authority vested in the chief justice of the supreme court, and state funding of the judicial system with a statewide judicial system budget.

Crime: Any violation of the criminal law.

Criminal justice wedding cake: Model of the criminal justice process in which criminal cases form a four-tiered hierarchy with a few celebrated cases at the top and each descending layer increasing in size as its importance in the eyes of officials and the public diminishes.

Criminal law: Laws passed by government that define and prohibit antisocial behavior.

Cross-examination: At trial, the questions of one attorney put to a witness called by the opposing attorney.

Cruel and unusual punishment: Punishment, by the government, that is prohibited by the Eighth Amendment to the Constitution.

Culpability: Blameworthiness or responsibility in whole or in part for the commission of a crime. Guilty parties are said to be culpable.

Damages: Sum of money awarded by a court as compensation to a person who has suffered loss or injury to his person, property, or rights through the unlawful act, failure to act, or negligence of another.

Decisional adjudication: Court hearing that focuses on the quick resolution of uncomplicated legal and factual issues.

Declaratory judgment: Judicial pronouncement declaring the legal rights of the parties involved in an actual case or controversy, but not ordering a specific action.

De facto: In fact; in reality.

Default judgment: Judgment awarded to the plaintiff because the defendant has failed to answer the complaint.

Defendant: Person against whom a lawsuit or prosecution is brought.

De jure: As a result of law; as a result of official action.

Delinquent: Person found to have violated the criminal law, but whose age prevents defining him or her as a criminal.

De novo: "Anew"; a second time.

Deposition: Process of obtaining a witness's sworn testimony out of court.

Determinate sentencing: Term of imprisonment, imposed by a judge, that has a specific number of years.

Diagnostic adjudication: Court hearing largely devoted to determining the cause of a problem and devising the proper treatment to eliminate it or to mitigate its most damaging effects.

Dicta: *See* Obiter dictum.

Directed verdict: Order from a judge to the jury ordering the latter to decide the case in favor of one of the parties for failure of the other party to prove its case.

Direct evidence: Evidence derived from one or more of the five senses.

Direct examination: At trial, the questions asked of a witness by the attorney who called the witness to the stand.

Disbar: To take away a lawyer's right to practice law.

Discovery: Pretrial procedure in which parties to a lawsuit ask for and receive information—such as testimony, records, or other evidence—from each other.

Discretionary choice: Lawful ability of an agent of government to exercise choice in making a decision.

Discretionary jurisdiction: Jurisdiction that a court may accept or reject in particular cases. The U.S. Supreme Court has discretionary jurisdiction over most cases that come to it.

Dismissal: Order disposing of a case without a trial.

Dispositive: Settling a matter finally and definitively.

Dissenting opinion: Opinion written by a judge of an appellate court that states the reasons for disagreeing with the majority decision.

Diversity of citizenship: Specific type of federal lawsuit between citizens of two different states in which the amount in controversy exceeds $50,000.

Divisions: In federal courts, places where U.S. district courts conduct business within the district.

Divorce: Dissolution of the marital relationship through judicial action.

Docket: Listing of cases to be heard by a court.

Doctrines of access: Rules and procedures established by the judiciary that affect access to the courts.

Domestic relations: Relating to the home. The laws of divorce, custody, support, adoption, and so forth.

Double jeopardy: Fifth Amendment prohibition against a second prosecution after a first trial for the same offense.

Dual court system: Court system consisting of a separate judicial structure for each state in addition to a national structure. Each case is tried in a court of the same jurisdiction as that of the law or laws involved.

Due process of law: Right guaranteed in the Fifth, Sixth, and Fourteenth Amendments of the U.S. Constitution and generally understood to mean the due course of legal proceedings according to the rules and forms that have been established for the protection of private rights.

En banc: Situation in which all members of an appellate court participate in the disposition of a case.

Engel v. Vitale: U.S. Supreme Court decision (1962) stating that public school officials may not require pupils to recite a state-composed prayer at the beginning of each school day.

Enjoin: To issue an injunction.

Equal Protection Clause: Clause in the Fourteenth Amendment that forbids any state to deny to any person within its jurisdiction the equal protection of the laws. This is the major constitutional restraint on the power of government to discriminate against persons because of race, national origin, or sex.

Equal Rights Amendment (ERA): Constitutional amendment proposed by Congress in 1972, designed to guarantee women equality of rights under the law. The amendment fell three states short of ratification.

Equity: Branch of law that provides for remedies other than damages and is, therefore, more flexible than common law.

Error: Mistake made by a judge in the procedures used at trial or in legal rulings during the trial that allows one side in a lawsuit to ask a higher court to review the case.

Error, writ of: Method of appeal by which an appellate court orders a lower court to send up a case for review of alleged mistakes made by the lower court. Used in some states but not in federal court.

Evidence: All types of information presented at a trial or other hearing.

Exclusionary rule: Judiciary-created rule holding that evidence obtained through violations of the constitutional rights of the criminal defendant must be excluded from the trial.

Exhaustion of remedies: Doctrine that requires persons aggrieved to avail themselves of all administrative remedies before seeking judicial relief.

Ex parte hearing: Judicial hearing with only one party present.

Expert witness: One qualified to speak authoritatively and give testimony on technical matters because of his or her special training or skill.

Ex post facto law: Law passed after the commission of an act, making the act (which was legal when it was committed) illegal.

Extradition: Legal process whereby an alleged criminal offender is surrendered by officials of one state to officials of the state in which the crime is alleged to have been committed.

Fact pleading: English system of civil procedures that required a high degree of specificity in the facts stated in the complaint. Used in one or two states.

Federalism: Political system in which governmental powers are divided between a central government and state governments.

Federal question: Case that contains a major issue involving the U.S. Constitution or U.S. laws or treaties.

Felony: The more serious of the two basic types of criminal behavior; usually bears a possible penalty of one year or more in prison.

Field Code of Civil Procedure: Code of civil procedure adopted in New York in 1848, named after David Dudley Field, and used with modifications in several states.

Fine: Sum of money to be paid to the state by a convicted person as punishment for an offense.

Furman v. Georgia: U.S. Supreme Court ruling (1972) that statutes leaving arbitrary and discriminatory discretion to juries in imposing the death sentence are in violation of the Eighth Amendment.

Gag order: Judge's order that lawyers and witnesses not discuss the trial with outsiders.

Garnishment: Process whereby money owed to one person as a result of a court judgment may be withheld from the wages of another person (who is known as the "garnishee").

Geographical jurisdiction: Physical area over which courts can hear and decide disputes.

Geography of justice: Significant variations in the sentencing patterns of judges within the same political jurisdiction.

Gideon v. Wainwright: U.S. Supreme Court ruling (1963) that an indigent defendant charged in a state court with any noncapital felony has the right to counsel under the due process clause of the Fourteenth Amendment.

Good time: Reduction of the time served in prison as a reward for not violating prison rules.

Grand jury: Group of citizens who decide if persons accused of crimes should be indicted (true bill) or not (no true bill).

Gregg v. Georgia: U.S. Supreme Court ruling (1976) that (1) the death penalty is not, in itself, cruel and unusual punishment and (2) a two-part proceeding—one for the determination of innocence or guilt and the other for determining the sentence—is constitutional and meets the objections noted in *Furman v. Georgia*.

Gubernatorial appointment: Method of judicial selection in which the governor appoints a person to a judicial vacancy; does not involve an election.

Guilty: Word used by a defendant in entering a plea or by a jury in returning a verdict, indicating that the defendant is legally responsible as charged for a crime.

Habeas corpus: Latin phrase meaning "you have the body." A writ inquiring of an official who has custody of a person whether that person is imprisoned or detained lawfully.

Harmless error: Error made during a trial that an appellate court believes is insufficient for reversing a judgment.

Hearsay: Out-of-court assertion or statement, made by someone other than the testifying witness, that is offered to prove the truth of the matter stated. Hearsay evidence is excluded from trials unless it falls within one of the recognized exceptions.

Hierarchical jurisdiction: Refers to differences in the functions of courts and involves original as opposed to appellate jurisdiction.

Holding: In a majority opinion, the rule of law necessary to decide the case. That rule is binding in future cases.

Homicide: The killing of one human being by another.

Hung jury: Jury that is unable to reach a verdict.

Illegal search and seizure: Act in violation of the Fourth Amendment of the U.S. Constitution.

Immaterial: Evidence that neither proves nor disproves the issue of a trial.

Immunity: Grant of exemption from prosecution in return for evidence or testimony.

Impaneling: Selection and swearing in of a jury.

Impeach: To question the truthfulness of a witness's testimony.

Impeachment: Official accusation against a public official brought by a legislative body seeking his or her removal.

Imprisonment: Placing a person in a prison, jail, or similar correctional facility as punishment for committing a crime.

In camera: "In chambers"; the hearing of a case or part of a case in private (without spectators).

Incarceration: *See* Imprisonment.

Incompetent: Testimony that cannot be admitted in evidence, such as hearsay evidence.

Incorporation: Theory that the Bill of Rights has been incorporated or absorbed into the due process clause of the Fourteenth Amendment, thereby making it applicable to the states.

Incumbent: The holder of an office or a position.

Indeterminate sentence: Sentence that has both a minimum and a maximum term of imprisonment, the actual length to be determined by a parole board.

Index crimes: Specific crimes used by the Federal Bureau of Investigation in reporting the incidence of crime in the United States in the Uniform Crime Reports.

Indictment: A grand jury's formal accusation of a criminal offense made against a person.

Indigent: Person who is too poor to hire a lawyer.

Inferior courts: Trial courts of limited jurisdiction; also, any court lower in the judicial hierarchy.

In forma pauperis: Latin phrase meaning "in the manner of a pauper." In the U.S. Supreme Court, cases brought in forma pauperis by indigent persons are exempt from the Court's usual fees and from some formal requirements.

Information: Formal accusation charging someone with the commission of a crime, signed by a prosecuting attorney, that has the effect of bringing the person to trial.

Initial appearance: Appearance before a judge during which the accused is informed of the charges, given his or her constitutional rights, informed of the amount of bail, and given a date for a preliminary hearing.

Injunction: Court order directing someone to do something or refrain from doing something.

Injury: Harm. Violation of another person's legal rights. Not limited to a physical injury.

Inquisitorial system of justice: System in which the accused is considered guilty until the accused can prove himself or herself innocent.

In re: "In the matter of; concerning." The designation of judicial proceedings in which there are no adversaries.

Insanity: Lack of criminal responsibility. A defect of reason caused by a disease of the mind such that a person did not know at the time of an act that the act was wrong and/or did not know the nature and quality of the act, according to a prevailing legal doctrine.

Integrated bar: System whereby membership in a state bar association is required in order to practice law.

Inter alia: "Among other things."

Interest groups: Collection of persons who share some common interest or attitude, who interact with one another directly or indirectly, and who ordinarily make demands on other groups.

Interlocutory: Provisional; temporary; while a lawsuit is still going on.

Intermediate courts of appeal: Judicial bodies falling between the highest, or supreme, tribunal and the trial court. Created to relieve the jurisdiction's highest court from hearing a large number of cases.

Internal theories of law: Theories of jurisprudence that view law as a closed, self-sufficient body of rules that are certain, predictable, and free from the subjective views of the legal actors.

Interrogatory: Form of discovery in which written questions about a lawsuit are submitted to one party by the other party.

Irrelevant: Testimony that has no bearing on the issue of trial.

Islamic law: Legal system based on revelations to the prophet Muhammad found in the Qur'an and the Sunna.

Jail: Local, municipal, or county institution used to house those awaiting trial, those convicted of a misdemeanor, and those convicted of a felony and awaiting transfer to a prison.

JP: A low-level judge. *See also* Justice of the peace.

Judgment: Official decision of a court deciding the matter.

Judicial activism: Variously defined. A philosophy proposing that judges cannot decide cases merely by applying the literal words of the Constitution or by discerning the intention of the framers, but must and should openly recognize that judicial decision making is choosing among conflicting values. Judges should so interpret the Constitution as to keep it reflecting the current values of the American people.

Judicial conduct commission: Official body that investigates allegations of misconduct made against judges.

Judicial election: Method of judicial selection in which the voters choose judicial candidates in a partisan or nonpartisan election.

Judicial notice: Rule that a court will accept certain things as common knowledge without proof.

Judicial reformers: Individuals and groups who stress the need for change in the American judiciary.

Judicial restraint: Variously defined. A philosophy proposing that, in deciding cases, judges should declare unconstitutional only those legislative actions and executive actions that clearly violate the words of the Constitution or the intent of the framers and that constitutional changes should be left to the formal amendatory process.

Judicial review: Power of a court to declare acts of governmental bodies contrary to the Constitution null and void.

Jurisdiction: Power of a court to hear a case in question.

Jurisprudence: The study of law and legal philosophy.

Jury: Group of persons summoned and sworn to decide on facts at issue. The use of the word *jury* by itself refers to the petit (that is, trial) jury rather than the grand jury.

Jury instructions: Instructions given to the jury by the judge in which the judge outlines what the jury must find to rule for the plaintiff and what they must find to rule for the defendant.

Jury pool: Persons who have been summoned for jury duty but who have not yet been subjected to a voir dire hearing.

Justice: Fairness in treatment by the law.

Justice of the peace (JP): Low-level judge, sometimes without legal training, typically found in rural areas of some states, empowered to try petty civil and criminal cases and to conduct the preliminary stages of felony cases.

Justice of the peace courts: Historically, the name for lower courts in rural areas; have been mostly replaced by magistrates.

Justiciable: Describes controversies that are within the proper jurisdiction of a court and appropriate for judicial resolution.

Juvenile: Not yet an adult for the purposes of the criminal law.

Juvenile court: The class of courts that have, as part of their authority, original jurisdiction over matters concerning persons statutorily defined as juveniles.

Juvenile delinquency: Violation of a criminal offense by a person who is not yet an adult for the purposes of the criminal law.

Larceny: Unlawful taking or attempted taking of property other than a motor vehicle from the possession of another, by stealth, without force, and without deceit, with intent to permanently deprive the owner of the property.

Law: Body of rules enacted by public officials in a legitimate manner and backed by the force of the state.

Law clerk: Law student or lawyer employed by a judge, typically for a short period of time, who assists in legal research and writing.

Law review: Legal journal edited by law school students.

Leading question: Question that suggests the answer and, therefore, is inadmissible.

Legal: Conforming to the law; according to the law; required or permitted by law; not forbidden by law.

Legal fiction: Assumption or doctrine of law that something is true or a state of facts exists that has never taken place.

Legal mobilization: Process by which a legal system acquires its cases.

Legal realism: School of jurisprudence that stresses a pragmatic approach concerning the actual workings of the rules of law. It provides the intellectual basis for the study of law by social scientists.

Legislation: Rules of general application, enacted by a lawmaking body. Most often the term is used to refer to a statute.

Legislative courts: Judicial bodies created by the U.S. Congress under Article I (legislative article) and not Article III (judicial article).

Legislative election: Method of judicial selection in which the legislature, and not the voters, chooses judges.

Liable: Responsible for something (such as harm done to another person). Having a duty or an obligation enforceable in court by another person.

Libel: Written defamation of another person.

Litigants: Parties to a court case.

Litigation: Lawsuit or a series of lawsuits.

Lower courts: *See* Trial courts of limited jurisdiction.

Magistrate: Judicial officer having jurisdiction to try minor criminal cases and conduct preliminary examinations of persons charged with serious crimes.

Majority opinion: Opinion in a case that is subscribed to by a majority of the judges who participated in the decision. Also known as the opinion of the court.

Major trial courts: *See* Trial courts of general jurisdiction.

Malpractice: Professional misconduct or the below-standard performance of professional duties. Usually applies to suits against physicians and lawyers.

Mandamus: Latin phrase meaning "we command." An order issued by a court that directs a lower court or other authority to perform a particular act.

Mandatory jurisdiction: Jurisdiction that a court must accept. Cases falling under a court's mandatory jurisdiction must be decided officially on their merits, though a court may avoid giving them full consideration.

Manslaughter: Unlawful act of killing of a human being, characterized by the absence of premeditation or intent.

Mapp v. Ohio: U.S. Supreme Court ruling (1961) that evidence obtained in violation of the Fourth Amendment must be excluded from use in state as well as federal trials.

Marbury v. Madison: U.S. Supreme Court ruling (1803) that established the power of the Court to review acts of Congress and declare invalid those it found in conflict with the Constitution.

Master jury list: Compilation of a representative cross section of the community in which the lawsuit arose.

Mechanical jurisprudence: Belief that judges only discover the law and do not make it.

Mediation: Process whereby a neutral third party intervenes in a controversy to assist the parties in achieving a resolution. The mediator may only recommend, not impose, a settlement.

Memorandum decision: Court ruling giving only what has been decided and what should be done but without reasons for the decision.

Merit selection: Method of judicial selection involving a judicial nominating commission, selection by the governor, and typically a judicial retention election.

Minor: Person or infant who is under the age of legal competence. The age varies by area of law: under twenty-one in some states; under eighteen in others.

Miranda v. Arizona: U.S. Supreme Court decision (1966) holding that, prior to interrogation, the police must inform the suspect of his or her right to remain silent.

Miscellaneous docket: Term formerly used to refer to the listing of in forma pauperis cases to be heard by the U.S. Supreme Court.

Misdemeanor: Lesser of the two basic types of crime; usually punishable by no more than one year of imprisonment.

Missouri Bar Plan: A method of judicial selection that combines merit selection and popular control in retention elections.

Mistrial: Invalid trial.

Modify: In an appellate court, to reach a decision that disagrees in part with the result reached in the case by the lower court.

Monetary damages: Compensatory damages—payment for actual losses suffered by a plaintiff. Punitive damages—money awarded by a court to a person who has been harmed in a malicious or willful way.

Moot: Case that no longer presents a justiciable controversy because the issues involved have become dead.

Motion: Application made by one of the litigants requesting the judge to make a decision.

Municipal courts: Trial courts of limited jurisdiction created by local units of government.

Murder, first degree: Killing of another with premeditation and intent. The killing of another during the commission of a felony, even though there was no premeditation or intent, is murder in the first degree and is called a "felony murder."

Negligence: Theory of tort recovery involving a legal duty, a breach of duty, proximate cause, and injury.

Negotiate: Discuss, arrange, or bargain about a settlement or compromise between the parties of a lawsuit.

New judicial federalism: Movement in state supreme courts to reinvigorate states' constitutions as sources of individual rights over and above the rights granted by the U.S. Constitution.

No-fault divorce: Divorce in which neither party must allege or prove fault (adultery, cruelty, and so on) to dissolve the marriage; the grounds are generally incompatibility or failure of the marriage.

Nolle prosequi: Ending of a criminal case because the prosecutor decides or agrees to stop prosecuting. When this happens, the case is "nollied," "nolled," or "nol. prossed."

Nolo contendere: Latin phrase meaning "I will not contest it." A defendant's plea of "no contest" in a criminal case means that he or she does not directly admit guilt but submits to sentencing or other punishment.

Nonpartisan election: Election in which candidates who are not endorsed by political parties are presented to the voters for selection.

Normal penalties: Norms for proper sentencing based on the crime committed and the defendant's prior record.

Notice pleading: Type of civil procedure adopted in the 1938 Federal Rules of Civil Procedure that permits pleadings to be less technical than those required under fact pleading.

No true bill: The decision of a grand jury not to indict a person for a crime.

Obiter dictum (also *dictum* or *dicta*): The part of the reasoning in a judicial opinion that is not necessary to resolve the case. Dicta are not necessarily binding in future cases.

Objection: Act of taking exception to a statement or procedure during a trial.

Obscenity: Work that, taken as a whole, appeals to a prurient interest in sex by depicting sexual conduct as specifically defined by legislation or judicial interpretation in a patently offensive way and that lacks serious literary, artistic, political, or scientific value.

Opening statement: Address made by attorneys for both parties at the beginning of a trial in which they outline for the jury what they intend to prove in their case.

Opinion: Reasons given for the decision reached by an appellate court.

Opinion of the Court: Decision of the U.S. Supreme Court that has strong precedential value because a majority of the justices agree on the result and the reasons for that result.

Oral argument: Part of the appellate court decision-making process in which lawyers for both parties plead their case in person before the court.

Ordinance: Law enacted by a local governmental body for the regulation of some activity within the community.

Original intent: Doctrine that judges should interpret the Constitution in accordance with the intent of the framers.

Original jurisdiction: Jurisdiction in the first instance; commonly used to refer to trial jurisdiction (as compared with appellate jurisdiction). Appellate courts, however, have limited original jurisdiction.

Overrule: To annul an earlier decision by depriving the rule on which it was based, as well as the case itself, of all authority as precedent.

Panel: Group of appellate judges, less than the full membership of the court, assigned to review a case on appeal.

Paralegal: A professional without a law degree who does legal research and assists lawyers in drafting documents and preparing arguments. May possess a two-year associate degree or an appropriate certificate plus a four-year degree.

Pardon: Act of executive clemency that has the effect of releasing an inmate from prison and/or removing certain legal disabilities from persons convicted of crimes.

Parens patriae: Doctrine that the juvenile court treats the child as a kind and loving father. Also refers generally to the judicial exercise of protective powers over persons who are unable to care for themselves, such as children, the mentally ill, or the incompetent.

Parole: Early release from prison on the condition of good behavior.

Parole board: Administrative body whose members are chosen by the governor to review the cases of prisoners eligible for release on parole. The board has the authority to release such persons and to return them to prison for violating the conditions of parole.

Partisan election: Election in which candidates endorsed by political parties are presented to the voters for selection.

Party prosecution: The responsibilities of the parties in an adversary proceeding to define the legal issues in the case and present evidence supporting their position.

Penal code: Criminal law of a jurisdiction.

Penitentiary: *See* Prison.

Per curiam decision: An unsigned opinion of the court, often quite brief; *per curiam* is a Latin phrase meaning "by the court."

Peremptory challenge: Method used to remove a potential juror from the jury without specifying the reason for doing so.

Perjury: Deliberately testifying falsely under oath about a material fact; a criminal offense.

Personal injury: Negligence lawsuits, often involving automobile accidents.

Personal property: An individual's possessions other than land.

Petitioner: One who files a petition (such as a writ of certiorari) with a court seeking action or relief.

Petit jury: Trial jury (as distinguished from a grand jury).

Petty offense: Minor criminal offense that does not entitle the defendant to a trial by jury.

Plaintiff: Person or party who initiates a lawsuit.

Plea bargaining: Process through which a defendant pleads guilty to a criminal charge with the expectation of receiving some benefit from the state.

Pleadings: Process of making formal written statements of each side of a case.

Plea of guilty: Confession of guilt to a criminal offense in open court.

Plenary consideration: Full consideration.

Plurality opinion: On the U.S. Supreme Court, any written opinion that reflects the views of less than a majority of the justices who heard the case, but more than any other view.

Policy litigation: Future-oriented lawsuit with numerous parties, in which the plaintiff seeks changes in future behavior and the outcome affects more than the immediate litigants.

Political question: Doctrine that courts will not decide cases involving issues for which a final decision is clearly left to one of the political branches by the Constitution.

Political science: The systematic study of government and politics.

Politics: According to David Easton's definition, "the authoritative allocation of values for a society."

Postconviction remedy: Set of procedures by which a person who has been convicted of a crime can challenge in court the lawfulness of a judgment of conviction or penalty or of a correctional agency action and, thus, obtain relief in situations where this cannot be done by a direct appeal.

Precedent: Case previously decided that serves as a legal guide for the resolution of subsequent cases.

Prejudicial pretrial publicity: Prejudicial information, often inadmissible at trial, that is circulated by the news media before a trial and reduces the defendant's chances of a trial before an impartial jury.

Preliminary hearing: Pretrial hearing to determine if there is probable cause to hold the accused for the grand jury.

Preponderance of the evidence: In civil law, the standard of proof required to prevail at trial. For a plaintiff to win, he or she must show that the greater weight, or preponderance of the evidence, supports his or her version of the facts.

Presentence investigation: Report submitted by a probation department to a judge containing information about the offender upon which the judge can base his or her sentencing decision.

Preventive detention: Holding a defendant in custody pending trial in the belief that he or she is likely to commit further criminal acts or fee the jurisdiction.

Prima facie evidence: Evidence deemed by the law to be sufficient to establish a fact, if that fact cannot be disproved.

Prior record: Defendant's previous history of arrests and criminal convictions.

Prison: Correctional facility for housing adults convicted of felony offenses.

Prisoner petition: Civil lawsuit filed by a person incarcerated in prison who alleges violations of his or her rights during trial or while in prison.

Private law: The law governing conflicts among private parties (for example, contracts, property, torts, and divorce).

Privilege: Something not enjoyed by everyone. The government is not required to provide legal assistance in civil cases.

Privileged information: In evidence, communications that may be kept confidential or private.

Probable cause: Standard used to determine if a crime has been committed and if there is sufficient evidence to believe a specific individual committed it.

Probate: Proof that a written instrument is the last will and testament of a deceased person.

Probation: Punishment for a crime that allows the offender to remain in the community without incarceration but subject to certain conditions.

Pro bono publico: Latin phrase meaning "for the public good." Legal services rendered without charge.

Procedural adjudication: Court hearings that reflect the adversarial system of justice with a heavy reliance placed on formal rules of evidence and procedure.

Procedural law: Law that outlines the legal procedures to be followed in starting, conducting, and finishing a lawsuit.

Product liability: Theory of tort recovery that imposes liability on the manufacturer, seller, or distributor of dangerous products for injuries sustained by consumers and bystanders who use the product.

Property: Legal right to use or dispose of particular things or subjects.

Proprietary law schools: Private law schools run for profit.

Pro se: Litigant who represents himself or herself without counsel.

Prosecutor: Public official who represents the state in a criminal action.

Public defender: Attorney employed by the government to represent indigent defendants.

Public law: Laws governing operations of government and the government's relationships with persons (for example, constitutional law, criminal law, and administrative law).

Punitive damages: Money beyond actual damages awarded against a defendant whose conduct was so wanton, reckless, or reprehensible as to justify additional punishment.

Quash: To void or annul.

Rape: Unlawful sexual intercourse, by force or without legal or factual consent.

Ratio decidendi: Those statements in a judicial opinion that are essential to the resolution of the case and are binding precedent.

Real evidence: Objects, such as fingerprints, seen by the jury.

Real property: Ownership of land.

Reapportionment: Redrawing of legislative district lines to reflect changed conditions. Typically, in the United States, performed to reflect population shifts following each decennial census.

Reasonable doubt: State of mind of jurors when they do not feel a moral certainty about the truth of the charges and when the evidence does not exclude every other reasonable hypothesis except that the defendant is guilty as charged.

Rebuttal: Introduction of contradictory evidence.

Recall elections: Method used in some states to remove judges from office. Recall elections allow the voters to remove judges from the bench directly.

Recognizance: The releasing of an accused person from custody without requiring a property or money bond.

Record: Written or taped account of all of the acts and proceedings in an action or suit in a court of record.

Recuse: To disqualify oneself as a judge in a case because of some personal involvement or interest.

Redirect examination: Follow-up questions asked of his or her own witness by the attorney who originally called the witness to the stand.

Rehnquist Court: U.S. Supreme Court under the leadership of Chief Justice William Rehnquist, 1986–2005.

Release on recognizance (ROR): Release of an accused from jail on his or her own obligation rather than on a monetary bond.

Relevant: Applying to the issue in question; related to the issue.

Remand: To send back. When a case is remanded, it is sent back by a higher court to the court from which it came for further action.

Remedy: Vindication of a claim of right. A legal procedure by which a right is enforced or the violation of a right is prevented or compensated.

Respondent: Party in opposition to a petitioner or an appellant who answers the claims of that party.

Restitution: To restore or to make good on something. For example, to return or pay for a stolen item.

Retainer: Advance paid by a client to an attorney to engage his or her services.

Retention election: Part of merit selection in which the incumbent judge runs for re-election without an opponent.

Reverse: In an appellate court, to reach a decision that disagrees with the result reached in the case by the lower court.

Reversible error: Error made at trial serious enough to warrant a new trial.

Right: Legal ability to perform or refrain from the performance of actions or the ability to control objects in one's possession. It also entails the ability to control the actions of others.

Ripe: Case that is ready for court action because the controversy has jelled sufficiently. Courts will not decide an issue before the need to do so.

Robbery: Unlawful taking or attempted taking of property that is in the immediate possession of another, by force or the threat of force.

Roberts Court: U.S. Supreme Court under the leadership of Chief Justice John Roberts, 2005–.

Roe v. Wade: U.S. Supreme Court decision (1973) holding that the right to privacy, grounded in the Fourteenth Amendment's due process guarantee of personal liberty, encompasses and protects a woman's decision whether to bear a child.

Romano-Germanic family of laws: System of law using statute or codes in which precedent is absent as a legal concept. Created by the Romans and codified in the Code of Justinian. Most widely used system of laws in the Western world.

Routine administration: Matter that presents the court with no disputes over law or fact.

Rule of four: Tradition of the U.S. Supreme Court whereby a vote of four justices grants certiorari, and the Court agrees to hear the case.

Rules of court: Rules and regulations adopted by courts governing how lawsuits shall be conducted.

Search and seizure: Search for and taking of persons and property as evidence of a crime.

Search warrant: Written order, issued by judicial authority, directing a law enforcement officer to search for personal property and, if found, to bring it before the court.

Self-incrimination: Forcing a suspect to provide evidence against himself or herself; prohibited by the Fifth Amendment.

Senatorial courtesy: Custom in the U.S. Senate that requires the president to clear judicial appointments with the senators of the state wherein the appointment occurs when the senators are of the president's party.

Sentence: Punishment imposed on a defendant found guilty of committing a criminal act.

Sentence bargaining: A type of plea bargaining in which the defendant pleads guilty knowing the sentence that will be imposed; the sentence in the sentence bargain is less than the maximum.

Sentencing discrimination: Illegitimate influences in the sentencing process based on the characteristics of the defendant.

Sentencing disparities: Unequal sentences resulting from the sentencing process itself.

Sentencing guidelines: Attempt to reduce disparities and discrimination in sentencing by providing judges with a structure to guide their decisions.

Separation of powers: Constitutional arrangement whereby legislative, executive, and judicial powers are exercised by three separate and distinct branches of government.

Sequestered: Isolated from the community. Applies to jury members until they reach a final verdict.

Service: Process of formally delivering the complaint or a subpoena to the defendant or a witness in a civil suit.

Settlement: Agreement about the disposition of a lawsuit reached by the parties involved.

Slander: Defamation that is spoken or not preserved in permanent form.

Small-claims court: Lower-level court whose jurisdiction is limited to a specific dollar amount (for example, damages may not exceed $1,500).

Socialist law: Legal system that originated in the former Union of Soviet Socialist Republics following the Russian Revolution of 1917 and was used in the Soviet Union and its satellite nations in Eastern Europe.

Social theories of law: Theories of jurisprudence that view law as part of the larger social order rather than in moral, ethical, or logical isolation.

Sociological jurisprudence: Social theory of law, founded by Roscoe Pound, that stresses studying "law in action" rather than viewing law as a closed, self-sufficient body of rules.

Socratic method: Socrates' method of teaching, which uses the systematic questioning of another to reveal his or her hidden ignorance or to elicit a clear expression of a truth supposed to be known by all rational beings.

Solicitor: One segment of the legal profession in England. Solicitors do the routine office work dealing with clients directly and prepare cases for the barristers, who argue in the higher courts.

Solicitor general: Third-ranking official in the U.S. Department of Justice, who conducts and supervises government litigation in the Supreme Court.

Specialized federal courts: Courts authorized to hear a limited range of cases, such as taxes or patents.

Special master: Person appointed by a court to hear evidence and submit findings and recommendations based on that evidence. The Supreme Court typically uses special masters in original jurisdiction cases.

Speedy trial: Refers to the right of the defendant to have a prompt trial, as guaranteed by the Sixth Amendment of the U.S. Constitution.

Staff attorneys: Lawyers who work for all the judges of the appellate court.

Standing: Requirement that the party who files a lawsuit have a legal stake in the outcome.

Stare decisis: Latin phrase meaning "let the decision stand." The doctrine that principles of law established in earlier judicial decisions should be accepted as authoritative in similar subsequent cases.

State supreme court: General term for the highest court in a state.

Status offense: Action that would not constitute a crime if the person were an adult (for example, truancy) but can subject a youngster to the juvenile court process.

Statute: Written law enacted by a legislature.

Statutes of limitations: Statutes that prescribe the time period in which lawsuits must be filed.

Statutory exemptions: Rules adopted by legislatures exempting certain types of persons or occupations from jury duty.

Statutory rape: Carnal knowledge of a female child below the age fixed by statute. The child lacks legal capacity to consent, so the crime can be committed where no force is used.

Stay: To halt or suspend further judicial proceedings. Appellate courts sometimes issue a stay to suspend action in a lower court while the upper court considers the case.

Stipulation: Agreement reached by opposing lawyers during litigation relating to certain facts and the qualifications of expert witnesses, among other things.

Subject matter jurisdiction: Types of cases that courts have been authorized to hear and decide.

Subpoena: Order from a court directing a person to appear before the court and to give testimony about a cause of action pending before it.

Subpoena duces tecum: Order from a court directing a person to appear before the court with specified documents that the court deems relevant in a matter pending before it.

Substantive law: Law that deals with the content or substance of the law, for example, the legal grounds for divorce.

Suit: Court action of any kind in either law or equity.

Summary decision: Decision in a case that does not give it full consideration.

Summary judgment: Decision by a judge to rule in favor of one party because the opposing party failed to meet a standard of proof.

Summons: Court order directing the defendant to appear in court at a specified time and place, either in person or by filing a written answer to the plaintiff's complaint.

Taxpayer lawsuit: Lawsuit brought by a person who claims standing on the basis of his or her status as a taxpayer. Such standing is only rarely granted.

Temporary restraining order (TRO): Form of injunctive relief. An emergency remedy issued by a court to prevent any action until the court can hear arguments.

Test case: Lawsuit brought to clarify, overturn, or establish a legal principle. Usually sponsored by an interest group.

Testimony: Giving of evidence by a witness under oath.

Theft: Popular name for larceny.

Tort: Private or civil wrong in which the defendant's actions cause injury to the plaintiff or to property, and the usual remedy is money damages. Tort is not limited to personal injury.

Traditional litigation: Retrospectively oriented lawsuit with two parties, in which the plaintiff seeks relief for the past behavior of the defendant and the outcome affects the immediate litigants.

Transcript of record: Printed record prepared for review of a case by a higher court. The words *transcript* and *record on appeal* are used interchangeably by appellate courts.

Treaty: Formal agreement between or among sovereign states creating rights and obligations under international law. In the United States, all treaties must be ratified by a two-thirds vote of the Senate.

Trial: Fact-finding process using the adversarial method.

Trial court: Judicial body with primarily original jurisdiction in civil or criminal cases. Juries are used and evidence is presented.

Trial courts of general jurisdiction: Trial courts responsible for major criminal and civil cases.

Trial courts of limited jurisdiction: Lower-level state courts, such as a justice of the peace court, whose jurisdiction is limited to minor civil disputes or misdemeanors.

Trial de novo: Latin phrase meaning a trial "from the beginning." Cases appealed from the lower courts that have no transcript are heard in their entirety "from the beginning."

True bill: Bill of indictment by a grand jury.

Trustworthiness: Basic criterion for the admissibility of evidence, which seeks to ensure that only the most reliable and credible facts, statements, or testimony is presented to the fact finder.

Unauthorized practice of law: Nonlawyers doing things that only lawyers are permitted to do.

Unified court system: *See* Court unification.

Uniform Crime Reports (UCR): Annual statistical tabulation of "crimes known to the police" and "crimes cleared by arrest," published by the Federal Bureau of Investigation.

Vacate: To make void or annul. Appellate courts sometimes vacate a lower-court decision, requiring the lower court to reconsider the case.

Venire: Group of citizens from which members of the jury are chosen.

Venue: Geographic location of a trial, which is determined by constitutional or statutory provisions.

Venue, change of: Removal of a case from one jurisdiction to another. It is usually granted if the court believes that a defendant cannot receive a fair trial in the area where the crime occurred.

Verdict: Decision of a trial court.

Voir dire: French phrase meaning "to speak the truth." The process by which prospective jurors are questioned to ascertain if there is cause to remove them from the jury.

Waive: To abandon or throw away; in modern law, to abandon or surrender a claim, privilege, or right.

Warrant: Writ, issued by a court, authorizing the seizure of a certain person or a certain property.

Warren Court: U.S. Supreme Court under the leadership of Chief Justice Earl Warren, 1953–1969.

Webster v. Reproductive Services: U.S. Supreme Court decision (1989) that, for the first time, upheld significant government restrictions on abortion.

Will: Legal declaration, usually in writing, of a person's wishes as to the disposition of his or her property after death.

Witness: One who has seen, heard, or acquired knowledge about some aspect of a lawsuit.

Writ: Written court order commanding certain action(s).

Writ of certiorari: *See* Certiorari, writ of.

Writ of error: Common-law writ issued by an appellate court to review a decision of a lower court upon appellant's contention that errors were committed by the lower court.

Case Index

Subject Index

('t' indicates a table; 'f' indicates a figure)